HARDPRESS.NET
HOME OF HARD-TO-FIND BOOKS

The Congregational Review
by Unknown

THE

CONGREGATIONAL REVIEW.

DEVOTED TO

THEOLOGY AND LITERATURE.

VOLUME VII.

EDITORS:
WM. BARROWS, J. C. BODWELL, E. P. MARVIN, J. T. TUCKER,
E. CUTLER, J. E. RANKIN.

ASSOCIATE EDITORS:
GEO. F. MAGOUN, Grinnell, Iowa.   A. L. CHAPIN, Beloit, Wisconsin.
H. M. STORRS, Cincinnati, Ohio.

Sanctos ausus recludere fontes.

BOSTON:
BY THE PROPRIETORS, 13, CORNHILL.
LONDON: TRÜBNER AND CO.
1867.

BOSTON:
PRINTED BY AUG. A. KINGMAN,
50 Bromfield St.

CONTENTS OF VOLUME VII.

No. XXXV.

No. XXXVI.

No. XXXVIII.

THE

CONGREGATIONAL REVIEW.

VOL. VII.—JANUARY, 1867.—No. 35.

ARTICLE I.

THE RATIONALE OF IMPUTATION.

"WHAT's in a name?" That Imputation expresses to the minds of many good men certain fundamental truths, is evident from the tenacity with which the dogma is held. That it is an inadequate expression of those truths to the minds of many other good men, is equally evident from the pertinacity with which the dogma is rejected. Agreement in respect of the underlying truths, which are alike precious to both, both may concede, is much more important than agreement in respect of the name by which those truths may be designated. Any disagreement that issues in ill feeling and harsh language between brethren is greatly to be deprecated. It is proposed, not to renew bitterness and strife by defending or denouncing the dogma either in its technical name or in its standard forms of statement, but simply to offer a conciliatory explanation of facts and truths involved in the controversy.

It is obvious that much of the friction and fire has been occasioned by confounding things separate. To avoid this mistake, the elements of the subject should be discussed under terms of definite and uniform force. Apart from the controversy, to impute is to charge upon, ascribe to, or set to the account of,

according to the nature of the thing imputed and of the object
to which it is imputed ; and to impute good or ill to a person is
to impute what really belongs to him, or what is supposed to
belong to him, and not what is known or supposed not to belong to him, as properly his own.   In the controversy, to
impute sin or righteousness is to impute to a person what is not
strictly his own but belongs to another.   This technical sense
is not founded on the word as used in our English version of
the Scriptures, but on the word as used by theologians to express the effect of Adam's sin upon his race, the laying upon
Christ the sin of mankind, and the justification of believers on
Christ's account.   The scriptural use of the terms, " impute,"
" imputed," " imputeth," " imputing," is with the force of ascribing to one what is his own and not another's.   The eating
of the flesh of one's sacrifice was not charged upon the offerer,
but upon the eater himself.   Ahimelech entreated Saul not to
" impute " to him an offence of which he was not guilty.
Shimei besought forgiveness of David for an offence confessed ;
saying : " Let not my lord impute iniquity unto me."   David
said : " Blessed is the man unto whom the Lord imputeth not
iniquity," meaning, as is clear from the context, the man's own
iniquity.   Paul made this equivalent to " the blessedness of the
man unto whom God imputeth righteousness without works,"
explaining in the context that by "righteousness without works"
he meant justification by faith.   " For we say that faith was
reckoned to Abraham for righteousness."   Abraham's faith was
his own and not another's, even though it was wrought in him
by the Holy Spirit ; and as this was what was reckoned to him
for righteousness, the righteousness itself was his own, even
though it was the gift of God.   So much, it is conceived, will
be readily admitted by all candid examiners of the scriptural
use of the term " impute " ; and there would be an obvious
advantage in conformity to this use in all religious discourse,
unless the truths in question should be imperilled as a consequence.

The first problem which Imputation, as a dogma, is employed
to solve, is the relation of Adam to his posterity and the effect
of his sin upon them.   The advocates of imputation, employ-
ing it in its technical sense of causing one to bear the iniquity

of another, affirm that God imputes Adam's sin to his race, in accordance with a divinely established covenant with him, so that the race is punished for his sin, not as their own, nor in consequence of their own, but antecedent to their own ; and that on this theory alone can the various ills, physical, mental and moral, as well as providential, to which every child is born, be reconciled with the justice of God.   The opponents of imputation plead the sovereignty of God as entirely shielding his justice in respect of the evils to which mankind are subject on account of the sin of their fallen head, and affirm that all penal evils are visited upon the sufferers simply and wholly on account of their own sin, except in so far as they may be traced to the fall through that native depravity whereby it is certain that the first moral act of every child will be sinful.   Each of these positions undoubtedly contains important truth ; possibly, important error.   To eliminate the error, and exhibit the truth so as to invite agreement, it is necessary to distinguish sin from corruption, and punishment from evil consequences and providential inflictions.

There is an important difference between sin and corruption. The difference is so great that the latter is the consequence of the former.   The proper sphere of sin is not in the senses nor in the sensibilities, not in the appetites nor in the passions, not in the affections nor in the intellect, nor yet in all these combined, but in the will.   It must be conceded that the will of Adam before the first transgression was in a holy activity. The current of his volitions was in the direction of holiness. If he chose some things in preference to others, his choices were holy ; and they would have been holy, even if his preferences had been different, for the whole bent and energy of his will were in the line of obedience to God.   But, as all must concede, before he sinned his will was invested with the mysterious and fearful power to set itself in opposition to God.   His fall was the exercise of that power, the self-determination of his will into the line of disobedience.   From the instant of that act the whole bent and energy of his will were against God.   His will had not the power to determine itself back into its former holy activity.   In his remorse and shame and fear and subjection to the curse, and in the holiness and happiness he had lost, there were motives enough for the exercise of such power if he had it. The fact that he did not reinstate himself is proof that he did not possess the power. It is entirely illogical, and contrary to fact, that the leaping from holiness into sin demonstrates the possession of power to leap back out of sin into holiness. The fallen man still had a will, but his will had not the power to undo or reverse its sinful self-determination. The first sin was not a rise, but a fall. Holiness and sin are not on the same level. Sin, like matter, gravitates downwards. The unfallen man could not rise higher than the plane of perfect holiness. No more could the fallen man rise above the plane of entire sinfulness. The unfallen, however, could fall, but the fallen could not rise. The difference is not in the loss of his will by the fall, but in the loss of power in his will. A man has power to commit suicide, but having committed it he has not the power of self-restoration. There are lungs in his body, but no breath in his lungs. Sin is ruinous. It consists in the activity of the will against God. The law of sin is the law of death. The apostle Paul couples the two as "the law of sin and death." The whole current of the volitions of the fallen and sinful will of Adam was in the direction of unholiness. If he now chose some things in preference to others, his choices were unholy; and they would have been unholy, even had his preferences been different. In his fallen and unrenewed state he might even yield to certain requirements, as tilling the ground, discharging his obligations as a husband and father, and yet his choices in thus yielding not be holy. For there are certain commands to the unregenerate, to which disobedience would be unholy, and yet obedience itself not be holy; inasmuch as the obedience, though right in itself, may yet be rendered while the will is still set in the direction of unholiness. Thus it is seen that the sphere of sin is in the will, and that the nature of sin is active opposition of the will to God.

The consequences of sin should not be mistaken for sin itself. These are many and great and lamentable. But to apprehend them aright, attention must be directed to them, not simply as found in Adam's posterity, but also and primarily as found in Adam himself. And even in him they should be clearly distinguished from God's governmental discipline of him. The banishment from the garden, the subjection to toil and suffering, and all else that is peculiar to the curse, belong to God's governmental discipline of, or to his providential inflictions upon, his fallen subjects.   There were consequences of sin entirely distinct from the curse and antecedent to it.   They are found in the shame which evinces conscious pollution, in the sensitive fear which made even the twilight seem articulate with vindictive wrath from on high, and in the hiding among the trees, which betrayed neither penitence for their sin nor disposition to return to obedience, but repugnance to communion with God, and complete alienation of their affections from him.   The reason was less clear and comprehensive and reliable ; the understanding was darkened and sluggish and liable to false conclusions ; the affections were impure, the sensibilities were obtuse and lethargic, the appetites and passions were inordinate, and the moral sentiments generally were so impaired that henceforth the fallen man would naturally and of choice be the servant of sin.

According to the common and scriptural usage, Adam's sin was imputed to him, and his moral corruption is imputed to his sin. If the distinction and statement be substantially correct, and in the main acceptable, the way is prepared to inquire into the bearings of his sin upon his descendants.   That their whole constitution and their general condition have been affected and modified, is the common consent.   So much is confessedly the teaching of the Scriptures.   It is argued that all who arrive at the age of discretion are properly and personally sinners, and that there is in all some degree of moral corruption, and that all are subjected to the general evils involved in the curse.   The sins of each may be imputed to him and not to another, and a part of the moral corruption of each may be imputed to his sin. But how is it between the beginning of personal existence and the age of discretion ?   As to this important interval of human life, the light shed upon it in advance by the word of God, and reflected back by subsequent experience and observation, must be the authority for all assertions, and the guide and test of all induction.   In every infant there is found, or supposed to be found, such a constitution as renders it certain that the first intelligent moral act will be sinful.   This, whatever it is, is called ·by

various names, according to the requirements of consistency
with the different theories adopted; as native depravity, corruption of nature, proclivity to sin, tendency to sin, sinful nature.   But antecedent and additional to what is expressed by
such phrases, some affirm that there is such an imputation of
Adam's sin to all his posterity as makes them, even in their
infancy, liable to punishment on account of it; and that a part
of the punishment to which they are liable on account of his
sin, in distinction from their own, is really inflicted upon all in
that "inherent corruption, which in fact results from the penal
withholding of divine influences."[1]   Thus there is, on the one
side, the assertion of liability to punishment in the race on account of the sin of Adam imputed; and on the other, the assertion of liability to punishment on account of depravity either
inherited or acquired.   The truth which these positions are
designed to guard can not be self-contradictory.   That there
is here some confusion of notions, as well as looseness of expressions, must be obvious, especially in view of the distinction
already made between sin and its consequences.   And it will
facilitate the further investigation of the subject, to distinguish
clearly between punishment and things which are often confounded with it.

It is common among some denominations who do not style
themselves orthodox, to use certain important words so as to
pervert their true meaning.   In their religious discourse the
words, grace, mercy, justice, atonement, sacrifice, faith, and
punishment, are often and perhaps generally used out of their
evangelical significations.   Rationalistic writers also are fond of
using the word punishment as having merely the force of the
natural consequence of violating a law of nature.   Hence
there is all the greater importance in evangelical discourse that
the word should be used in its strict signification.   In the Gospel punishment means the infliction of the penalty of the law
upon the transgressor; that is, it is retribution for unforgiven
sin.   Punishment is inflicted for sin, and not for moral taint or
corruption.   And as mankind are on probation while in this
world, punishment is inflicted, when inflicted at all, after this

[1] Princeton Theological Essays.   First Series.   pp. 147–8.

present life is ended.   There is an incompatibility in the punishment and pardon of the same individual. He who is punished was never pardoned, and he who is pardoned will never be punished.   It is therefore incongruous, and injurious to the cause of truth, to speak of punishment as having been inflicted in any degree upon " the man unto whom the Lord imputeth not iniquity."   Not to impute iniquity was understood by the inspired writers as a negative form of expression for the forgiveness of iniquity ; hence it is contended that imputation is the opposite of remission.   But the difficulty is that every recipient of forgiveness has first been made the victim of punishment, at least in some degree ; since imputation is so far forth equivalent to punishment, so that he whose own sin is covered has already been punished for the sin of Adam.   For according to authority : "When Adam's sin is said to be imputed to his posterity, it is intended that his sin is laid to their charge and they are punished for it."[1]   Plainly such use of the word punishment must lead to much misapprehension and perplexity ; and unless a manifest equivalent, and more, can be gained by it, it ought to be abandoned.   Moreover the possibility of salvation by grace was declared before the curse upon man was pronounced ; God's governmental judgments and providential discipline in this world, therefore, should not be designated as punishment. The destruction of the antediluvians from the earth was not strictly punishment, but only a hastening of death as the appointed condition to punishment.   And discipline is administered to the pardoned as well as to the unpardoned : " For whom the Lord loveth he chasteneth, and scourgeth every son whom he receiveth."

The organic relations of the first progenitor and his progeny may now be treated with less ambiguity.   It is a familiar form of expression, and accepted as truthful, that they are bone of his bone and flesh of his flesh.   If this be true of the physical constitution, it is analogous to that which is true of the mental, moral, and spiritual ; so that they are mind of his mind, heart of his heart, and will of his will.   As they are his offspring, they are in his image and partakers of all that essentially belonged to his nature as a man and as a sinner.   What was the

[1] Princeton Essays. First Series. p. 136.

essential nature of his will? That its moral nature was holy before his fall and sinful afterwards, no evangelical mind will question. But what was its essential nature as a will? When he was created was his will in essential activity, or was it at rest until wakened into activity by the presentation of a motive? It is a principle in phoronomics that matter at rest can never put itself in motion, and that matter in motion can never put itself at rest. The principle is equally true in respect of the human will, and it is a metaphysical impossibility that Adam's will should have put itself into activity if it was in absolute rest at the instant of his creation. The very idea of will is that of willing. Adam therefore was created with will already in holy activity. His breathing was not more essential to his physical life, than his willing was to his moral life. The original nature of his will was that of a holy willing, or willing of holiness. But by his sin his will lost its holy nature and took a nature just the contrary. He was now entirely sinful in respect of this superinduced nature of his will, and he had not the power to throw this off and resume his original nature. His nature as fallen was now fixed for the whole period of his probation at least, and for the whole succession of coming generations. He was originally constituted with a holy nature, and with the mysterious power to exchange that nature for one and only one other, and in one and only one way. He exercised that power, after having been informed that the exercise of it would be at his peril. He made that exchange of natures, once and once for all. The power to make it once was lost in the very experiment. He had thrown himself, not from one position to another on the same level, but from a higher level to a lower. His nature as now constituted, that is. as sinful, was not of God's making, but of his own. Its chief characteristic was not the impaired physical and mental constitution, but the self-set opposition of the will to God. All other characteristics of his fallen and sinful nature were only secondary to that, and became transmissible only as and because that was transmissible. His offspring, therefore, are like him in all that characterized his essential nature as fallen and sinful. They are begotten, as inspiration expresses it, " in his own likeness, after his image." They are not only bone of his bone and flesh of his flesh, but will of his will and sin of his sin.   That is, their wills are individualizations of his, even as their bodies are of his body.   And as the very nature of will is willing, they come into existence with wills already and naturally set against God ; not as a punishment for his sin imputed to them, but as the legitimate and inevitable consequence of the self-induced and essential nature of his will as fallen.   Their wills are in essential activity as soon as they begin to exist as persons.   From the start of personal existence their wills are moving in the direction of unholiness, even as his was moving in the direction of holiness.   Let it be granted that all choices are made in view of motives ; it can not be denied that Adam, mature at the instant of his creation, could either make a motive or be affected by one presented by God.   But a choice is the preference of one thing to another ; the will therefore must be already in motion, or choice is impossible.   There must be already a current, or neither of two or more channels open to it will be filled by it.   And let it be granted that, in the case of Adam's posterity, there is a period or interval between the beginning of personal existence and the first intelligent or self-conscious choice ; may it not be true, and is it not true, that the will, during that interval, is nevertheless unconsciously and with all its might set in the direction contrary to holiness ? Let the immediate foundation upon which a stone is said, in common parlance, to rest, be removed, and the stone will instantaneously fall ; but it would not and could not fall, were it not already in absolute motion by the whole force of its gravity.   Just so the first specific and self-conscious choice made by every child of Adam would not certainly be sinful, unless his will were already in absolute motion against God and holiness by the whole force of that sinful bent and determination which it received in becoming an individualization of the fallen parent will.   It is sometimes admitted by those who contend that all holiness and sin consist in exercises, that such exercises may begin much earlier than is commonly supposed ; and that those who die previously to all self-conscious moral exercises are saved in some way by Christ.   In other words, they admit that grace in some degree is necessary to the salvation of infants, because of their inherent tendency to actual specific sins.   But this tendency is often spoken of as if it belonged, not to the will, but to the natural affections, appetites, passions, or sensibilities ; or to some inherited taint of the soul, some corruption of the moral nature, in distinction from the will.   If now, in the absence of specific exercises, a general exercise of the will, from the very beginning of personal existence, has been rationally accounted for, why may not technical "imputation" and technical "exercises" be waived for the sake of agreement that, by the divinely constituted laws of human nature, the descendants of Adam are really sinful from their earliest personal existence by reason of the essential bent and motion of their wills in the direction of unholiness, and that all other taint or corruption, included in the notion of inherent depravity, is either in consequence of such personal sinfulness, or else was legitimately inherited along with the sinful bent of their individual wills?   In this way, it is not necessary to regard inherent corruption as a punishment, nor to assume the imputation of Adam's sin to his posterity to account for that corruption ; for there can be not even an apparent conflict between the justice of God and the law which he has established, whereby, in the whole realm of created things, like is propagated by its like. In this way, too, there is no occasion to speak of any real tendency to sin except in the will itself, or to deny to the infant a real moral character and that a sinful one.   While the sinful will of every child is a direct consequence of the first man's sin, yet no one is punished while on probation, and no one is ultimately punished for any sin but his own.

The next inquiry is in respect of the asserted and denied imputation of the sins of mankind to Christ.   It is contended that, just as Adam's sin was imputed to his posterity so as to make them liable to punishment without regard to any sinfulness of their own, and so that they are in fact punished to some extent at least for his sin, even so the sins of mankind were imputed to Christ, not as his own indeed, but so as to make him liable to punishment for them, and so that he bore punishment for them in his vicarious sufferings and death.   It is contended, on the other hand, that Christ bore the penalty of sin only in a figurative sense, and that the assertion of his punishment is by implication the assertion of his guilt, and derogatory to the justice of God.   Both of these positions are intended to cover the same precious truth of atonement for sin by the sufferings and death of Christ.   Their respective defenders part at the threshold on imputation, and then mutually recede by confounding penalty and punishment, or by misunderstanding one another in the use of these terms.

Now there is the same objection to technical imputation in regard to the relation of Christ to the sins of the world, as in regard to the relation of Adam's posterity to his sin ; it is not the common and scriptural use of the term, nor is it necessary to a consistent and scriptural representation of the condition of the race as affected by the fall.   And there is an important distinction between penalty and punishment which might have prevented much of the embarrassment attending the discussion of this part of the subject.   These terms, in common discourse, are often used interchangeably, and in the main perhaps with perfect propriety ; and each term is used to express the different notions which in this discussion ought to be kept distinct, just as the term " promise " is used to express the inducement offered and the reward bestowed.   In strictness of speech, penalty is the threat or menace which is affixed to the law to deter the subjects from transgressing it ; punishment is the execution and experience of that threat or menace for transgression itself.   There may be a penalty before transgression, as in the law of Paradise ; bnt there can be no punishment until after transgression.   Thus penalty does not necessarily imply that guilt has already been contracted, while punishment involves guilt actually incurred.   In the State, an innocent man may be convicted of murder, and suffer the infliction of the penalty for that crime ; and because he is believed to be guilty, he is said to be punished, while in himself he is not punished, because he is innocent ; but his endurance of the penalty is no satisfaction to the State for the crime of the real murderer, in case the real murderer is afterwards found ; and his death is divested at once of its ignominy, while the murderer himself is punished. In war, a hostage is sometimes put to death, and yet he himself is regarded as neither guilty nor punished, while in his death the belligerent to whom he belongs is regarded as both guilty and punished ; the hostage himself endures penalty but not punishment. So in the divine administration respecting the death of Christ for the ungodly, accuracy in the use of these terms is essential to both exactness of statement and agreement therein. In what sense, then, did Christ bear the sins of mankind? Did God charge their sins upon him as his own? The advocates of imputation do not assert this, and they shrink from the thought as instinctively as their opponents. Both, however, accept, and mean to accept in the fullest legitimate import, the inspired declaration: " He was wounded for our transgressions"; "Who his own self bare our sins in his own body on the tree"; " While we were yet sinners, Christ died for us." Now the person who was the subject of such vicarious sufferings and death, was " He who, being in the form of God, thought it not robbery to be equal with God, but made himself of no reputation, and took upon him the form of a servant, and was made in the likeness of men." He was the eternal Son of God, yet was, by the power of the Holy Ghost, " made of a woman," so as to be " the son of David, the son of Abraham." He was not God and man, but God-man; not a human person in union with a divine nature, but a divine person in union with a human nature. In his proper person, his generic and essential nature was the same as his divine paternity, will of his will, and holiness of his holiness; yet by the force of his human maternity he was " made like unto his brethren," in respect of all those infirmities which were consequences of sin, and inheritable apart from a sinful will. As simply divine, he could not be tempted, but as divine-human, he could be, and was, tempted, in all points like as we are, yet without sin. He could be the subject of providential discipline, therefore, but there was no susceptibility to punishment. He could endure the penalty of sin, but punished he could not be. He suffered, however, not as an innocent man convicted on evidence and believed to be guilty, nor as a hostage overpowered by the enemy; but as a voluntary and self-substituted sacrifice to God for the sin of the world, instrumentally slain by men who, but for his self-surrender, had no power over his life. Possibly the Jews believed him guilty of blasphemy; but they did not and could not believe him guilty of the charges upon which they demanded his death at the hands of the Roman procurator.   "He was numbered with the transgressors," in that he suffered guiltless the penalty of crimes for which his murderers deserved to be punished; and his endurance of the penalty of their sins was the visible symbol of his internal endurance of the immeasurably greater penalty of "the iniquity of us all."   His sufferings were finite in respect of time, because of his human nature; but infinite in respect of value, because of the infinite glories of his divine person who endured them in that human nature.   The sin of the world was not charged upon him, nor was he punished for it: yet he bore the penalty of the sin of the world, not merely in a figurative, but even in a literal sense.   The Father was not angry with him; for he had already declared, "This is my beloved Son, in whom I am well pleased."   The declaration of prophecy that "The Lord hath laid on him the iniquity of us all," must be interpreted consistently with the declaration of Christ that "Therefore doth my Father love me, because I lay down my life, that I might take it again."   The will of Christ was never so at variance as not at the same time to be one with the will of the Father.   It was the Father's will that the Son should die for the ungodly, yet in such a sense that the Son acquiesced in that will perfectly and made it his own.   For this purpose the Father gave or sent the Son, and for this purpose the Son came.   There was no schism in the Godhead; the Trinity was perfect Unity.   Christ offered his life freely in sacrifice; not by constraint from the Father, nor by a helpless succumbing to his enemies.   For he said: "No man taketh it from me, but I lay it down of myself.   I have power to lay it down, and I have power to take it again.   This commandment have I received of my Father." It were as true that the Son was angry with himself, as that the Father was angry with the Son.   The agony and the crimson were not symbols of Christ's repentance of the world's sin laid to his charge, but proofs of his supernatural power to appreciate perfectly the heinousness of the world's sin, and to realize to his own person as God-man the unutterable burden and terribleness of the penalty.   God hates sin with infinite hatred, and yet in view of the penalty, had compassion toward the sinner; but he could not make his compassion available, except the penalty deserved by the sinner should be borne by a sinless

and adequate substitute.   Hence the Son, himself the sovereign law-giver, as well as the creator of his subjects, in
obedience to the Father, assumed " the likeness of sinful flesh,"
and took the place of the law-breaker under the penalty of the
law, and thus removed the otherwise irrepressible conflict between the immanent divine impulse to punish, and the voluntary
divine impulse to pardon, so that God " might be just, and the
justifier of him which believeth in Jesus."

Christ offered himself as a vicarious sacrifice, however, not
for the consequences of sin, but for sin itself ; not for any so-
called depravity or corruption or proclivity or disease that may
inhere in human nature aside from the will, but primarily for
that self-determination of the will from the direction of holiness
and God into the direction of unholiness and Satan, by the first
man, whereby a sinful bent and movement are entailed upon
the individual wills of all his posterity, and secondarily for all
the specific sins of Adam and his race, that grow out of that
generic sinful determination of the will.   For mankind needed
no atonement for any disordered state of the sensibilities, or for
any intellectual weakness, or for any physical infirmity, but
only for the generically guilty movement of the will, and the
specifically guilty volitions or choices into which that movement develops and by which it is manifested.   That Christ
" took our infirmities, and bare our sicknesses," is explained by
Matthew as referring to his miracles of exorcising and of healing.   There was nothing piacular in the various ills he endured
from his birth to his entrance into Gethsemane the very evening
before his death : these were only incidentally necessary in his
preparation to expiate the guilt of the world by his blood. " In
all things it behooved him to be made like unto his brethren ;
that he might be a merciful and faithful High Priest in things
pertaining to God, to make reconciliation [Greek, τὸ ἱλάσκεσθαι,
expiation] for the sins of the people."

It remains to inquire for the truth involved in the assertion
and denial of the imputation of the righteousness of Christ to
believers.   One position is, that, as mankind are punished for
Adam's sin, and Christ was punished for the sins of mankind,
so the righteousness of Christ in the endurance of that punishment is made over as a free gift to as many as believe on him.

The other position is, that Christ by his vicarious sufferings sat-isfied, not the distributive, but merely the general justice of God, so as to make it merely consistent to pardon the penitent, although their guilt is permanent.   Practically and experiment-ally, justification by faith is the same, whatever theory may be adopted to explain it.   But theoretically both these positions are deficient.   Logically the former is exposed to the objection, that as the sin of all mankind was imputed to Christ, so the right-eousness of Christ should be imputed to all mankind ; the lat-ter is exposed to the objection that, since the distributive justice of God is not satisfied even in the case of the forgiven, then their guilt is permanent, and pardon leaves the character of God liable to reproach, and their own character under the im-possibility of holiness, so that the employment of the redeemed in heaven ought to be confession and supplication instead of ex-clusive praise.   The inadequateness of each position is owing largely to the peculiar fundamental notion of what the atone-ment is, as related to the justice of God.   On the one side, the sufferings of Christ are viewed as such a mere equivalent for the ill-desert of Adam as to admit of the salvation of some, or all deceased infants, and of a general probation and offer of grace to all who live to years of intelligent moral action, and such a further equivalent for the sins of a portion of the race, as to admit of the salvation of that portion.   On the other side, the sufferings of Christ are regarded not as an equivalent, but less than an equivalent, to the ill-desert of the saved, and perhaps even of one of the saved, who have " sinned after the similitude of Adam's transgression."   Would it not be more in harmony with the Scriptures to say, that the sufferings and death of Christ were on account of the infinite excellence and glories of his person as the God-man, not only an equivalent, but immeasurably more than an equivalent, to the ill-desert of all mankind, however far down the coming ages the succession of generations may run, so that, in perfect accordance with the divine justice, whether general or distributive, or both, while God is not obligated to save any of any class, yet some, or all who died in infancy may be saved, and all who repent and be-lieve will be saved, and all the impenitent and unbelieving might be saved, and still all who finally neglect so great salvation

must be condemned to a " sorer punishment " than mere legal
ill-desert demands ?   And would not such a statement represent
God as a merciful sovereign in the atonement, and a merciful
sovereign in salvation and punishment, and relieve the mind of
embarrassment in respect of the justice of the ways of God
with mankind ?   In this view, the justice of God is satisfied in
the general so far as the granting of probation and the offer of
grace, and satisfied in particular as to every one of the saved,
and yet dissatisfied to an intenser degree with every one who
ultimately treats the offer of grace with contempt.

The atonement is a basis upon which the sinner is both permitted and obligated to enter into a treaty of reconciliation with
God.   If the sinner accepts the atonement, the faith by which
he accepts it is reckoned to him for righteousness for Christ's
sake.   His faith is not Christ's righteousness, and Christ's
righteousness is not his faith ; but his own faith is reckoned to
him as his righteousness.   And his righteousness is at first
merely seminal ; on the part of God, negatively, judicial abso-
lution, and positively, regeneration.   The resultant of his faith
as instrumental, and of the Holy Spirit's regenerating power as
efficient, is the restorative principle, or the seminal beginning,
of a personal righteousness which is to be developed, "through
sanctification of the Spirit, and belief of the truth,"—through
a gradual purging and sloughing of the consequences of sin,
and assimilation of the spirit and life of Christ, " unto a perfect man, unto the measure of the stature of the fulness of
Christ."   The expiation of his sin and guilt was the work of
Christ ; the purification from the consequences of his sin, from
"the old man, which is corrupt according to the deceitful lusts,"
is the work of the Holy Spirit.   By his faith he appropriates
first the atoning efficacy of the blood of Christ, and then the
sanctifying efficacy of the influence exerted by the Holy
Spirit, and thus approximates, in personal righteousness,
towards the standard written : " Be ye holy ; for I am holy."
In the process of sanctification, believers in Christ, in proportion to their faith, " are members of his body, of his flesh, and
of his bones" ; and the current of the will also is stemmed and
held and set backward and upward towards the level of that
state of holiness from which it originally burst forth into its

downward course, until, in the blessed consummation of the work of grace, it shall flow again and for ever confluent with the will of God.

It may be objected, however, as it sometimes is, that if a sinful nature is transmissible, a holy nature should be transmissible also. Had Adam remained holy, his holy nature would indeed have been transmitted to his offspring. But he fell by sin, and thus took upon himself a sinful nature, and henceforth holiness was impossible for him except by the gracious gift of regeneration by the Holy Spirit. Inspiration is silent as to whether he was thus graciously renewed. But let it be granted that he was regenerated, even before he " begat a son in his own likeness, after his image," his essential nature as a fallen sinful man was still the same as before his renewal. The fall was a complete exchange of entire holiness for entire sinfulness ; regeneration is only a change from entire sinfulness into some degree of holiness. As regeneration is not a complete change of the generic nature of the will, so as to make the natural movement holy, but only the introduction of a germ of holiness by the Holy Spirit, so that the will, as thus empowered by the Holy Spirit, henceforth makes holy choices, even the regenerate can not with safety be left to themselves, since without the continuous presence and aid of the Spirit they would still continue to sin. Hence they are admonished in the Scriptures not to grieve the Spirit, but to walk after the Spirit, and to mind the things of the Spirit. As they were born of the Spirit when they received the seminal principle of holiness, so that seminal principle of holiness must be developed, if at all, by the indwelling and life-giving and sanctifying Spirit. " If any man have not the Spirit of Christ, he is none of his." As regenerate, every Christian may say with the apostle : " I am crucified with Christ ; nevertheless, I live ; yet not I, but Christ liveth in me ; and the life which I now live in the flesh, I live by the faith of the Son of God, who loved me, and gave himself for me." The regenerate live, not by the power of their own wills to be holy, but by faith in Christ, which is wrought in them and kept alive and operative by his indwelling Spirit. The moment they forsake the Spirit, or are forsaken by the Spirit, they begin again to sin. Examples are given in the

Scriptures of regenerated men who afterward sinned.   All Christians sin more or less, and all but deluded fanatics acknowledge it.   Christ's law of church discipline implies the need of it because even the best are liable to sin.   John says : " If we say that we have no sin, we deceive ourselves and the truth is not in us."   And Paul says : " With the mind I myself serve the law of God ; but with the flesh the law of sin."   But how do these declarations consist with another by John ? " Whosoever is born of God doth not commit sin ; for his seed remaineth in him ; and he can not sin, because he is born of God." Plainly this is said in reference to the sanctification of believers, and their abiding in Christ, and his Spirit abiding in them.   In proportion as they have been made righteous by regeneration and partial sanctification, and live in the Spirit, they do not and can not sin ; and when they shall have become complete in Christ, then this declaration will be true of them practically, as it is now theoretically, to the fullest extent.   But until that consummation, this passage of John must be interpreted by that of Paul : " Now if I do that I would not, it is no more I that do it, but sin that dwelleth in me."   Calvin's remark of David, that " when all religion seemed to be extinct in him, a live coal was hid under the ashes," is applicable to every sinning believer.   If anything more is needed to establish the position, that the generic nature of the will is not changed in regeneration, two passages more should be enough.   One is that of Christ in his reply to the doubting Nicodemus : " That which is born of the flesh, is flesh ; and that which is born of the Spirit, is spirit," where the distinction seems to be clear and emphatic.   And the other, which is of Paul, confirms this application of it : " For I delight in the law of God, after the inward man ; but I see another law in my members warring against the law of my mind, and bringing me into captivity to the law of sin which is in my members."   In his " members " he certainly includes his will, if indeed he does not have special reference to it ; for he says : " To will is present with me ; but how to perform that which is good, I find not."   And this he ascribes to " a law, that when I would do good, evil is present with me."   Grace, then, is not transmissible, and the children of the regenerate need to be born again in order to enter into the kingdom of God.   Yet the diminution of sin in the regenerate may so far forth mitigate the consequences of sin, both in themselves and in their offspring, though it does not change the sinful bent of their wills ; and this fact may be one of the principles upon which the Abrahamic covenant was founded.   But grace operates on men, not as a race, but as individuals.   Each individual must be renewed for himself. And the fact that the Holy Spirit in renewing and sanctifying any person, thus isolates him, as it were, from the whole race beside, as the wind blowing where it listeth may select a single leaf of the forest, may be one reason why the completely sanctified after the resurrection, " neither marry, nor are given in marriage ; but are as the angels which are in heaven." Nicodemus could readily understand the natural birth, but he could not understand the supernatural.   Christ assured him, however, that to be born of the Spirit was an entirely different thing from being born of the flesh.   Grace was not to be confounded with nature.

The discussion may be summed up as follows : There is a universal native depravity which is neither a punishment of Adam's sin, nor sinless and yet leading to sin, but really sinful, and imputable to every one as his own, and for which he needs an atonement in order to salvation.   For to assume inherent corruption apart from the will, and technical imputation to account for it, is to necessitate another assumption to account for imputation itself, and so on ad infinitum, since no covenant founded upon justice, can make that just which is intrinsically unjust ; and to assume a sinless depravity, by which a will at rest is certain to be put in motion, is to assume that which is metaphysically impossible, and to exclude those who die in infancy from grace and heaven.   There is also an atonement which is neither an exact equivalent to any particular amount of ill-desert, nor a mere satisfaction of the general justice of God, but incomparably more than an equivalent for the ill-desert of the race, and therefore satisfying general justice for all, and distributive justice for all that shall be saved, and at the same time enhancing the demands of justice upon all that finally reject it.   There is moreover a righteousness for believers, which is neither the imputation of that which belongs to another, nor a mere compact whereby they may be treated as holy without the displacement of sinfulness by holiness, but which is a free gift freely appropriated in its seminal principle, organic in its growth, transforming in its effects, and as a personal attribute ultimately exclusive of guilt. And furthermore there is no occasion for sarcastic flings about repenting of another's sin, or feeling complacency for native innocence and escape from the unsatisfied demands of justice.

ARTICLE II.

PERCIVAL'S LIFE AND LETTERS.

The Life and Letters of James Gates Percival. By JULIUS H. WARD. Boston : Ticknor & Fields. 1866.

MORE than thirty years ago, a tall, thin, bent, sharp-visaged man, wrapped in a scrimped and faded camlet cloak, with pantaloons so short as to disclose a long stretch of yarn stocking between them and shoes ever innocent of polish, the whole surmounted by a shabby fur cap, might have been seen flitting through the streets of New Haven more like the restless ghost of some old resuscitated pilgrim, than a real denizen of that shadowy town. He seemed neither knowing nor known among the living generation. Curious traditions were afloat among us collegians about this uncanny recluse, as that he kept bachelor's hall in a dingy solitude somewhere up Broadway, in the midst of a great library of outlandish books with which he held most familiar communion ; that he was an unbeliever of almost everything which other people supposed to be true ; and whether he was to be pitied as a moon-stricken unfortunate, or abhorred as an atheist, was a question not easily to be resolved by many a good Christian who heard so many strange rumors and stories about the poet Percival.

He was indeed a solitary and inexplicable man, as the wierd picture of him fronting the title-page of Mr. Ward's beautiful volume might more than intimate. One can scarcely conceive

of a human being more totally unfitted by constitutional eccen-
tricities for the business of a world like this.   Even for the
gentler services of society, his temperament opposed an almost
insuperable barrier.   Some persons are so nervously organized,
that just to point a finger at them makes them shudder and
start.   Percival throughout, in spirit as well as in body,
was a bundle of such nerves.   He would make you think of a
dry leaf holding on tremulously to its bough in the November
winds.   Without his seeking your commiseration, you could
not withhold it from him.   He carried the impress of habitual
suffering, in his unconscious and ordinary moods ; nor could
the companionship of the few with whom he was freest, do
much to lift him into happier regions.   There was a dash of
madness in his nature.   No one was more aware of it than
himself, as is evident from the lines he wrote of his own mental
discordance.

> " There is a middle place between the strong
> And vigorous mind a Newton had,
> And the wild ravings of insanity,
> Where . . . .
> . . . . will is weak and judgment void of power.
> Such was the place I had."

Of the life thus inauspiciously provided for, this book is the
laborious and faithful record.   Its author, or as he modestly
styles himself, its editor, is a young Episcopal clergyman of
much literary ability and critical taste, who finds time, amid
an assiduous discharge of pastoral duties, to contribute largely
to our choice periodical belles lettres.   We think that this is
his first published volume.   Its materials have been in a process of collection for several years.   The biographer, in fact,
began his work while an undergraduate in the venerable university of which Percival was also an alumnus.   Putting himself in correspondence with the poet's surviving friends, and
rummaging old chests, attics, and memories for facts and reminiscences, with a genuine antiquarian zest, Mr. Ward has got
together a rich store of information which probably exhausts
his subject so far as any important matter is involved.   After
the narrative was about ready for the press, a file of valuable
letters was discovered, as we happen to know, in a Western

State, which the author forthwith proceeded to incorporate with his memoir, at the cost of re-writing a large section of his manuscript. Such thorough working, in these rapid and superficial days, deserves commendatory mention. It properly enhances our valuation of a book, as it invites our confidence in its guidance. The story is largely told by the letters of the poet and his correspondents. An appendix of some of Percival's prose papers and other excerpts, is furnished. We must not omit to note the completeness of the page in side and top helps to the contents of the book. The giving of the age of its subject on every leaf, is a convenience which never should be neglected in a biography, as we have had occasion to say before this. These marginal clues, and the index at the end, make this volume a model for imitation, in its way.

The son of a respectable physician in a Connecticut country town, Percival began life in the midst of the quiet and beautiful rural scenery for which he afterward showed a passionate love, and the description of which lends to his poetry some of its richest charms. A boy of delicate organization and tremulous temperament, he was amiable and excitable; a born idealist, yet keenly observant of natural objects and incidents; fond of books, and remarkably apt at learning, yet with a sharp relish for outdoor pursuits and enjoyments, but preferring their solitary quest to the company of the lads of the village. At the age of fifteen, in 1810, he was ready to enter college, where he at once drew attention to his fine scholarship and most unique habits. Behind no one in his class in the severer studies, he was already smitten with the poetic *furore*, some rather crude indulgence of which in public exposed him to annoying ridicule from his thoughtless associates. With a year's interruption in his course, he was graduated, in due time, with the high regard of his college mates, as a brilliant and sound scholar, and with distinguished marks of honor from the heads of the institution; with not a few misgivings, however, as is very apparent, concerning the orbit which so eccentric a luminary would be likely to describe.

Looking around for a profession, that of medicine fixed his choice, from early association rather than from any special taste. With characteristic facility he mastered the elements of this science, and passed his examinations with a success which was unparalleled in the annals of the New Haven school. Admirable as was his medical education, no one could have been less adapted to the details of the calling. A malignant fever broke out within the circle of his new practice, of which five of his patients died, which so wrought upon his feelings that he refused further cases. A few years after, he made another attempt in his native town, among his father's old patrons, but "one man criticised his bill so sharply that Percival in disgust destroyed all the rest of them," and again abandoned the business. In later life, his friends procured him a commission as assistant surgeon to the army, which he held for a brief period. If he drew any blood from the defenders of his country, there is no record of the fact. His doctorate was of no use to him beyond the reputation which it helped to give him as a man of science.

His sensitiveness was an incurable disease which made him the helpless victim of an habitual depression of spirits, dashed with a lurking suspicion of people with whom he came in contact; while, now and then, these morbid humors would give place to gushes of high exhilaration. His constitutional malady was doubtless aggravated by the loss of his father in early boyhood, which threw him into the hands of well-intentioned, but not sufficiently appreciative instructors. His moods were fitful beyond all calculation. Disappointed in an early love affair, and otherwise harrassed, his mind was unhinged to the verge of self-destruction. Sad as this was, one can hardly read without a smile his attempts to batter his skull in pieces against the orchard trees, and to dash out his brains by beating his head with "a large cobble-stone." This failing, he made a more serious affair of it, though fortunately without success, with opium. Through life, it was rare that a female could catch his eye in conversation, except by the most furtive glance, though often he would talk to them at great length, in this downcast way. He would not walk near the mouth of an iron furnace in blast, lest the horrid glare should overcome his power of resistance, and make a victim of him. Music acted upon him like a spell. At times he abandoned himself to it with an almost absurd passion. He studied it scientifically and practically, carrying his accordion under his old cloak to his friends' rooms, and when the fit was on him, running his accompaniments to their singing into the small hours of the morning.   When first he began discoursing sweet sounds on this instrument, people heard its unearthly strains stealing about their ears the whole of one livelong night.   His sensibility was so delicate that, without uttering an audible note, or producing one from an instrument, he could enjoy all the harmony of a musical performance, listening to its sounds where no sound was, with exquisite pleasure, his lips moving as if in regular vocalization.   Once he walked to Niagara, and when the noise of many waters gathered strength as he approached the cataract, his walk quickened to an "Indian trot," and he arrived at last upon a full run, at the very top of his powers of locomotion.   His emotions were excessive.   In his own words : "his agony was the rack of hell; his joy the thrill of heaven." To himself, this was scarcely an exaggeration.   This temperament deterred him from attempting a domestic, or even an intimately social life.   He preferred to live by himself so exclusively that it was almost as difficult to get access to his study, as anciently to penetrate the temple of Bona Dea.   His door was always kept fastened, and, with rare exceptions, visitors had to accept his entertainment in the outside passage-way. Yet, says a friend :

" Percival was not a misanthrope.   During an acquaintance of twenty five years, I never knew him to do an act or utter a word which could countenance this opinion.   He indulged in no bitter remarks, cherished no hatred of individuals, affected no scorn of his race ; on the contrary, he held large views concerning the noble destinies of mankind, and expressed deep interest in its advancement toward greater intelligence and virtue."   p. 388.

We have no difficulty in believing this.   It is a mistake to construe a reluctance freely to mingle in society, into a personal aversion to men, or an indifference to their welfare.   Yet a secluded life is not the best ; it breeds unwholesome and semi-barbarous habits, both mental and physical.   Though Percival never essentially changed his practice in this respect, it is pleasant to find that as he grew older, he gradually came into a more easy intercourse with others, much to his own evident increase of enjoyment, and always to their very high gratification.

The careful observer will not fail to find, in this peculiar man, what Henry Taylor says, with a nice penetration, is essential to the true poetic spirit : "The poet . . . ought to have something of the woman in his nature ; . . . because the poet should be *hic et hæc homo*—the representative of human nature at large, and not of one sex only."[1]   There was, in fact, a large infusion of the feminine element in Percival's constitution. The fineness of his physical organization, the etherial look of his eye and of his whole expression, were exact types of the delicacy of his feelings, the shrinking of his soul from all coarseness and lowness of sentiment and aim.   He had all of a woman's quickness of perception ; and much the same habit of reaching conclusions more through the intuitional than the ratiocinative faculties.   But to infer from this an effeminateness in his writings, would be a very groundless conclusion.

Not much incident diversifies the progress of this story, yet its power deepens upon you to the end, like that of some ancient drama, in which human forces are struggling at great disadvantage against natural agencies and the invincible fates. Your interest in it is not unlike that which the weary hand to hand contest of poor Gilliatt, in the Toilers of the Sea, with the storms of the British Channel, excites.   Our poet, on his own isolated, wave-washed rock, had much the same wasting time of it, with about an equal compensation.   His mature life divided itself into two general departments of labor—first, as a literary, and next as a scientific scholar.   Up to about thirty five years of age, he was mostly engrossed with publishing successive volumes of poetry, and in various efforts in periodical editorship.   His first volume—a "dingy, rough and ragged" duodecimo, was issued when he was twenty five years old.   In those days of his poetic creations, he composed with great rappidity, throwing off pages of elaborate and finished verse with a feverish impetuosity, more like that of the old Welsh bards than as mortals now generally are supposed to weave their tuneful measures.   While in College, he read to a comrade "seventeen stanzas of nine lines each," written before the eleven o'clock recitation, one morning.   He spent but little care on revision and correction, perhaps to the detriment of his poetic

[1] Notes from Life, in Six Essays. p. 152. London.

fame. His critics vainly called his attention to this point, censuring what often seemed a plethora of verbal and imaginative opulence in his productions, an embarrassment of riches. That he did not heed them could not be set down to indolence; for, in his philological studies, he would spend an entire day in examining the roots and branches of a single and not very important word. He poured the unstinted affluence of his soul into his versification, with this complete *abandon*, on principle. It was a part of his theory of the art poetical. He says:

"I do not like that poetry which bears the marks of the file and burnisher. I like to see it in the full ebullition of feeling and fancy, foaming up with the spirit of life, and glowing with the rainbows of a glad inspiration. When there is a quick swell of passion, and an ever coming and going of beauty, as the light of the soul glances over it, I could not have the heart to press it down to its solid quintessence. . . . I like to see something savage and luxuriant in works of imagination, throwing itself out like the wild vines of the forest, rambling and climbing over the branches, and twining themselves into a mass of windings." p. 242.

His genius was tropical. Church's "Heart of the Andes" would have mirrored to him his own efflorescent nature. In close accord with this demand for the sumptuous garniture of the Muse, was his ideal of her spirit. He loved "the rich fancy, the deep feeling, the strong passion, and the vivid imagery of the early school of the days of Elizabeth": and was quite willing to overlook "their negligence, and occasional coarseness," their sins against rhetoric and probability, "for the deep and rich vein that shines through them." He was no believer in Wordsworth's theory of making poetry of the trivial and commonplace objects and incidents of the day, much as he appreciated the occasional power of that great master. "Poetry should be a sacred thing, not to be thrown away on the dull and low realities of life." He did not paint after the Pre-raphaelites, either in subjects or handling. He sought, in nature, the most faultless images of the grand and the lovely, the purest types of beauty in form, color, grouping; and in human nature, whatever was best and noblest in purpose, passion, sentiment, action; these lines and lineaments of the nearest to finite perfection, the poet should, in his view, gather up and embody in his works, giving to "its forms the expression of angels, and throwing over its pictures the hues of immortality." This only should satisfy his aspiration—"the perfect vision of all-embracing truth, the vital feeling of all-blessing good, and the living conception of all-gracing beauty." The only extravagance which he sees in poetry is, "to clothe feeble conceptions in mighty language,"—a remark applicable as well to prose composition. Percival escaped this fault generally ; his grand embroideries are not hung on unsubstantial nothings. But his reluctance to use the file should not be a precedent to young writers or older. It sometimes betrayed him into a weak line, as this :

> " Ye Clouds ! who are the ornament of heaven :"

which is tame beside Byron's

> " Ye Stars ! which are the poetry of heaven."

Literature which lives beyond its own century is not ordinarily of the extemporaneous kind. The "fatal facility" is the very *phthisis pulmonalis* of our bills of literary mortality.

Percival's poems are the most complete realization of the rich and ornate style of poetry, of anything produced by our authors. His descriptions of external nature are unrivalled for their truthfulness and splendid coloring. From childhood he had studied the life and laws of the animate and inanimate things around him, with a closeness and intelligence which nothing could escape. With not less than even Ruskin's exact acquaintance with the visible universe, and affection for it, he knew and loved tree, shrub, wave, cloud, everything which lent grandeur and gracefulness to earth and sky, even to the mosses and the lichens reflecting in their russet tints, from lofty and lowly rock-walls, "the sunsets of a thousand years." He never tires of these objects. He revels among them in the very spirit of the old Greek worship of material beauty. He would have been as much at home as any of them, among the river and forest and mountain gods of the days, when

> " Celestials left their skies
>   To mingle with thy race, Deucalion ;
>   And Pyrrha's daughters saw, in shepherd guise,
>   Amid Thessalian vales, Latona's son."[1]

[1] Schiller's Poems and Ballads : "The Gods of Greece." p. 297.

His poetry shines with the light of this external splendor. And there is no end to the illustrations thus supplied to his discoursing of the workings of the human mind and heart. Nothing can be happier than his power thus to throw light into the actings of the soul, from these outer realms of truth. It is wonderful how limpid and cheerful his poetry habitually is, considering his own melancholic tendencies. In early life he wrote one poem, "The Suicide, "which was literally as black as Erebus. The whole atra-biliousness of his spirit was poured through its stanzas, with terrible surge. But, excepting this, there is very little in his pages which would reveal his peculiar characteristics. In the apt words of one of his reviewers: "Here is no indulgence of moroseness, gloom or misanthropy, but the poet seems determined that, for himself and his readers, nature shall be arrayed in her most gorgeous attire, and language yield her finest intonations." It reminds one of Hawthorne's exquisite talk about the fragrance and the delicacy of the beds of water lilies shooting up their pure petals out of the dark ooze of Concord river. He does not adventure very far into the whirl and conflict of the stronger passions; seldom allows himself to be drawn into the grapple of the greater questions which vex the speculative poets and philosophers. This may have lessened his hold on the sympathies of his generation; for men are held more firmly and swayed more strongly through their ethical nature, than through their æsthetic taste or imaginative alertness. The greatest poets must show themselves akin to the greatest of all, in something of that wondrous insight into the mysteries of the human soul, and that earnest, tender, impassioned entering into the struggles of universal humanity, which makes Hamlet and King Lear absolute over all thoughtful minds, unlearned as well as learned. Percival certainly was not unfamiliar with these subjects. His every day life was passed under the shadow of these dim, overhanging realities of the spiritual world. If his avoidance of them, so uniformly, has deprived him of the first rank as a poet of power, no one can challenge his right to that position as the poet of beauty.

His published volumes availed him little as a means of support. His newspaper editing was even less remunerative.

His poems, thoughadmired by the public, found a very limited sale. His employers in the periodical line failed, or otherwise came short of their promises. "I have been most scurvily treated by the proprietors of the Herald," he writes to one of his friends. But it must be admitted that he also was fickle in his adherence to business contracts, to a very annoying degree. He knew nothing about business, and seemed to have little sense of the binding obligation of a bargain to work for others, if he found the employment irksome, or the compensation inadequate. There was no intentional dishonesty about this to his consciousness, but a lack of moral perception. Book publishers soon became his mortal aversion, for he thought that they were leagued to pilfer him. His disgust at authorship bursts out amusingly. "I know of no more contemptible being than an author who writes for money. . . . . If I must labor for subsistence, I will not labor with my pen, particularly when I am paid at a meaner rate than a shoeblack." It even turns into a disgust for books themselves.

" Some are mad after books ; they study their health out and find it trash. Two or three clear turns of the eye will tell them as much as an age of mere reading ; and half of written knowledge is very good to keep children out of mischief—most of the rest ought to be burnt up. I have added to the mountain of books, and the myriad of authors. But I sometimes think I had better be annihilated, books and all, than be the means of making fools gape, and girls cry, as perhaps I may." p. 97.

Yet, a few pages further on, he is carrying a pocket full of these very abhorred books to a young lady who had somewhat smitten him with her charms, to read her selections. The sequel proved that her fancy for them was even less than his own. His rising reputation was no equivalent to him for the abject poverty of his circumstances. While hard at work daily, even into the late hours of night, his income was not over seventy dollars annually for several years. He was never free of pecuniary embarrassments. When he had some better prospects, he once endorsed a tailor's bill of one hundred dollars for a brother, for which he was at length arrested by a Connecticut sheriff. Had his personal habits not been as inexpensive and frugal almost as an American Indian's, he must have died, as

Otway did, of sheer starvation. If his hardships were no greater than those of many of our literary men of good habits, "the more's the pity." His genius and its pecuniary unprofitableness to him, may furnish another section to the long story of the "Vanity and the Glory of Literature."

But no degree of penury could starve out from his soul the literary enthusiasm which was a part of his essential life. He craved knowledge as the sea draws into it the rivers. His pleasure in study was a mighty passion. His powers of mental abstraction and of protracted labor were amazing. Once, having a poem to prepare for some public occasion, he sat down at his desk in the evening, when, as he related it, "he was suddenly aroused by what seemed to him a large conflagration illuminating the apartment. He started to the window, and found the morning breaking in the east. He had written all night." He read with a like avidity, and with an intuitive comprehension of his author, hardly cutting the leaves of books as exacting even as Greek tragedies, so his biographer tells us. "He read faster than another could count the lines upon the page," and seemed to know what to skip as worthless (a blessed art) as well as what to take into his never full receptacle. His memory was as tenacious as his eye was rapid. He wrote out a geological report of several hundred printed octavo pages, for the legislature of Connecticut, without referring to his field notes, making copious citation of localities and facts which had occupied his investigations during several years. His knowledge became a proverb. It was as nearly encyclopædic as any one man's is likely to be. So early as his examination for a medical diploma, the learned faculty for several hours tried vainly to exhaust his acquaintance with that science. His linguistic learning "was almost equal to that of Cardinal Mezzofanti." Besides being a thorough classic, he was familiar with every European tongue except the Turkish, and had carried his studies into several of the Asiatic languages. He accustomed himself to original composition in foreign dialects. When Ole Bull came to New Haven, Percival addressed him an ode of welcome, in Danish, which was printed in the city papers. He told his friend, Professor Shepard, that "he had versified in thirteen languages," and "he had imitated all the

Greek and German metres" : a marked departure—this devotion to foreign tongues—from his favorite, Schiller's method, who read these as little as possible, lest it should impair his perception of the purity and strength of his own ; and, though he was acquainted with the English, preferred, for this reason, to read even Shakespeare in German.[1] The teeming fertility of our poet's mind crops out in his familiar letters. At one time he had projected this list of literary adventures : "four tragedies, two epics, two moral poems, and a plan of a series of poetical tales." Several of these, however, went no further than their titles.

One might suspect that much of this mass of erudition must have been very superficial, were not the proof abundant that whatever he undertook as a matter of serious study, he habitually prosecuted with most conscientious diligence. His scholarly fidelity was worthy of all praise. While yet a young man, he undertook to bring out a new and annotated edition of the English translation of Malte Brun's Geography. Very soon he found that the translation was so incorrect that its publication would be a disgrace to American letters. Although his contract did not contemplate any such additional task, and his stipulated compensation was quite too small to justify it, he immediately set to work to amend the translation almost to the extent of a new version of the text. His wages had been calculated at eight dollars a day. But so much extra work did he volunteer, for the sake of fulness and correctness, that his eight dollars dwindled to but fifty cents a day. His connection with Webster's lexicographal labors is well known. He was engaged to carry the large dictionary through the press. At first, his responsibility was little more than mechanical. But his superior learning began directly to detect errors, and sometimes blunders, in the copy as well as the proof. He could not endure this unfaithfulness to sound scholarship. The result was, that his duties were extended to the author's manuscript, which was passed under his inspection before it went to press. The entire history of this curious partnership in editing, but a glimpse at which is here given, would make a notable chapter in the curiosities, not to say, quarrels, of authorship.

[1] Henry Taylor's Notes from Life. p. 184 ; note.

Several times, Percival would have utterly broken off his connection with the work, through the vexation in which it involved him; but it could not go on without him. He toiled like a veritable literary navvy at the drudgery, from morning to night, and almost from night to morning. It tires one just to read of his plodding through those great pages. He must have keenly sympathized with Charles Lamb's quaint saying, as many others surely have: "All things read raw to me in manuscript." He was too learned for his business. He would strike against some etymological, or other query, and keep the printers waiting for copy or revise for days, while he persisted in ferreting out the object of his search. This was a too expensive way of dictionary-making for all concerned, himself included; yet he once said, that it was the most pleasant work he ever did. His ideal of perfection exhausted every body's patience but his own.

Entrusted with the geological survey of Connecticut, he set about the work in the same exhaustive way. The appropriations for this enterprise contemplated the term of two or three years as sufficient for its completion. But so minutely did Percival conduct his inquiries, that five years were consumed before the final report was made, and then the geologist had to be coerced by a legislative act to bring his labors to a conclusion. On foot and horseback, he struck across the State on parallels so near together, that he actually had been personally "in contact with every one of the four thousand six hundred square miles in the State," carefully comparing over eight thousand specimens, and many more dips and bearings. His last labor was a similar examination of the State of Wisconsin, in the midst of which he died, at the age of sixty one. Says a brother scientist, Professor Shepard, "He felt that he could live on bread and water, or even give up these if necessary; but he could not violate his convictions of what was true and right. He was a perfect martyr to his literary and scientific conscientiousness." p. 413.

Percival had the vague reputation of being an infidel. He seldom attended religious service in any church. Some of his poems, the earlier particularly, express unchristian sentiments. But these he justified on the ground "that a poet should not be held responsible for either logical or illogical inferences against him, drawn from his wayward or transient fancies, and that he could use poetically unchristian or pagan mythology without subjecting himself to the charge of adopting either." His scepticism was not of the sneering or scoffing schools. It doubtless did include many doctrines which are dear to the majority of believers as vital truths of redemption. He did not call in question the grand realities of God and providence and immortality. When an undergraduate, he listened with interest to the finished and earnest discourses of Fitch and Taylor. He even spoke of the revivals of his day with respect, as usefully affecting not a few persons. Once he went so far as to correspond with an Episcopal professor in Trinity College, Hartford, respecting taking orders under that church. In 1827, a Boston friend sent him Channing's sermon on "Unitarian Christianity most favorable to piety," which he read with much approbation. But afterwards, in 1835, "he regarded the rational theology as anti-poetic in influence, and of very doubtful efficacy in working upon the masses." His extensive and exceedingly choice library was rich in theological literature, every remarkable addition to which he eagerly sought for. But he probably had no very connected and harmonious system of opinions in this department of knowledge, though acquainted with the speculative schools. He reverenced goodness and purity, and all spiritual excellence with a childlike sincerity, and was himself as unblemished as a little child. What were his views of Jesus Christ, beyond a profound admiration of his human nobleness and virtues, this volume gives us no means of knowing. It is affecting to be told that, smitten with fatal sickness among strangers quickly changed into most hearty friends, in Wisconsin, "he expressed no fears of the future. Occasionally we saw him on his knees, engaged in prayer. Two or three weeks before he died, he would frequently exclaim, 'My God! my God!' evidently relying on a Supreme power." It is not easy to judge of the inward state of such a self-communing man.

Our notes are not yet exhausted, and we must still do a little more toward setting our subject in as distinct a light as practicable. While afield on his scientific surveys, he was often taken by the boys, and even farmers, for an escaped inmate of some lunatic asylum.   He was very taciturn, and if he at all observed the strange movements of the people who would keep watch upon him, he seldom would make any explanations. Now and then, however, he would try a practical conclusion with them.   One day a farmer beset him with a peremptory demand to know what he was doing.   Percival tried to hurry away, but his questioner followed him up, insisting, that, as a servant employed by the State and paid in part by *his* taxes, Percival should satisfy his inquisitiveness.   "I'll tell you what we'll do," said the Doctor to his assistant; "We can't stop, but we'll refund.   Your portion of the geological tax" (to the farmer)"—let me see—it must be about two cents.   We prefer handing you this to encountering a further delay."   At times, his adventures were almost romantic.   On this same geological tour, he one evening asked for food and lodging at the door of a ladies' seminary.   His shabbiness was nearly a bar to his reception, but urging his weariness, his request was granted.   In the course of the evening, conversation was started, and the Principal found her mendicant guest familiar with many topics. They came at length to poetry, and the lady expressed her high admiration of Percival; "when, checking herself," as she noticed a startled look in her auditor, "she asked: ' Do you know Percival?' 'Have you read his poetry?'   To which the stranger replied, in his gentle, lisping tone, 'I—am—Mr. Percival, and I sometimes write poetry.'"   At another time, announcing his name at a rural cottage door, a small lad stepped out upon the floor and declaimed one of his poems, learned as a school exercise, quite overjoyed to have found his admired author.   In Wisconsin, the poet was surprised to find that his poetical fame had preceded him, and had prepared the way for some of the sweetest ministrations of friendship which soothed his closing and his dying days.

His conversational powers were unique and prodigious.   He would talk on in a low, soft monotone by the hour, if not interrupted.   He preferred standing, and without moving his position, leaning on a mantel-piece, would not cease his monologue till after midnight.   Once, a lady, where he was one of a small circle of friends, asked him a question about the hickory, and he directly set off on a dissertation on hickory trees, which was only suspended by the break-up of the party at two o'clock of the morning. At a street corner he has been known to hold a friend in such a talk till midnight, and sometimes in severely cold weather, when he had not tasted food for twelve hours. Verily, one would be justified in dodging such an unconscionable talker, behind almost any sort of cover. The common requirements of human comfort, and even existence, seemed to him a matter of blessed ignorance. Many never understood him; but many did gradually learn to comprehend and value him, in spite of all his oddness. He knew it, and it gave a serener tone to his evening of life. His death brought out many tributes of honor and love—*laudato a laudatis*. Dear friends, as well as delighted admirers of his genius, were proud to hang their garlands upon his sepulchre.

This volume fills a place in American biography which has stood long enough empty. Its work will not need to be done over again, and, on the whole, could not well be done better. We miss the always pleasant attraction of literary reference, and criticism of contemporary writers, which gives so much charm to the correspondence of Southey and Niebuhr. There is almost nothing of this in Percival's letters, beyond a few disparaging allusions to Cooper, Willis, and the like; and this, of course, his editor could not mend. A page or two devoted to a comparison of Goethe and Schiller shows what he could have done. His unceasing recountings of his buisness difficulties and straitened finances grow wearisome at times, and might have been abridged, where it is merely a repetition of the same story to different persons. The plan adopted of using so much the reminiscences of Percival's acquaintances, necessitates, moreover, the going forwards and backwards over the same ground more than is always pleasant. But, on this mode of procedure, that is unavoidable; and the inconvenience is, in a measure, counterbalanced by the greater variety thus communicated to the narrative. The book has instructed and delighted us. It has given us a psychological study of much value, and has deepened our sympathy with humanity in its erratic and, at first sight, repellant manifestations.

ARTICLE III.

THE NAME AND THE NUMBER OF THE BEAST.[1]

῏Ωδε ἡ σοφία ἐστίν· ὁ ἔχων τὸν νοῦν ψηφισάτω τὸν ἀριθμὸν τοῦ θηρίου·
ἀριθμὸς γὰρ ἀνθρώπου ἐστὶ, καὶ ὁ ἀριθμὸς αὐτοῦ χξϛ´.

"Here is wisdom. Let him that hath understanding count the number
of the beast; for it is the number of a man; and his number is six hundred three score and six."—*Rev.* xiii. 18.

THE method which has been usually taken to determine the
name of the Beast from the number here given, can hardly be
satisfactory to any one who studies the word of God consider-
ately and reverently, and who regards this book as the revelation of Jesus Christ to his servant John, given for the comfort
and support of Christians amid the fires of persecution in his
day. The method takes this text as a mere riddle; deals with
it in a way for which there is no parallel in the Bible, and no
sound principle in sacred hermeneutics; and with a result that
settles nothing about it. Who can believe that the wisdom and
understanding here so emphatically appealed to are simply the
guesswork of a Sibylline oracle; or that " the victory over the
name," Rev. xv. 21, is merely the success of those who have
solved the riddle? Besides, the problem of the name, so presented and treated, is manifestly an indeterminate one, admitting of many different solutions, all legitimately wrought out,
as in point of fact, many have been; as may be seen in the commentaries. Hengstenberg gives a different sort of solution, from
Ezra ii. 13; but one which seems to be equally fanciful, con-
jectural and indecisive.

Another solution is here proposed, wrought out in the legitimate method of finding the appropriate data for it in the language and usages of the times in which the Apocalypse was

[1] This interpretation of a passage, so vexing to critics and occasioning so many
theories, is offered as a new and possibly satisfactory exegesis. The author of this
Article does not propose the view as originally his own. It was suggested to him
by an eminent scholar, whose name, if given, would at once command respect and
critical attention for the interpretation proposed. EDITORS.

written, and the purpose for which it was written. The purpose was, to comfort the people of God, and to encourage Christians to be faithful to Christ even unto death, amid the flames of the persecution which was then raging against the church in the Roman Empire.

In the style of the ancient prophets, the persecuting power is depicted in this chapter by two beasts seen in vision, bloody monsters ; the first symbolical of the Roman pagan power on the throne of the Cæsars, and the second with lamb-like horns, yet speaking as a dragon, personating the devilish worldly wisdom then so prevalent in the philosophy, jurisprudence, and pagan priestcraft of that time. Both beasts being in mutual coöperation were but the earthly organs of the great dragon, the prime mover of the whole. It would seem that the readers of the Revelation in St. John's day, could not misunderstand the import of the vision of these beasts to be other than the then pagan persecuting power, actuated by the cunning and malice of the devil.

If they apply to any other and later persecuting power, as the papacy, it is because of the common lineage and likeness of all Antichrists. But the primary application was undoubtedly to the pagan power then persecuting the church. Of what use could it be, for the purpose of the revelation, to reveal to the church of that day the papacy of mediæval and modern times ?

Now among the crafty and bloody expedients of the second beast, this was one : to cause all men to "receive a mark in their hand, or in their forehead," so as to be publicly known as liege vassals and worshippers of the first beast. And whosoever would not receive the mark was to be outlawed and persecuted to death. Such is the figurative representation.

The figurative form was no doubt taken from the practice among the Romans, of branding their slaves with some mark, or letter, or letters, particularly such as had run away from their master, or had committed some crime. The brand was intended, not so much to mark the ownership of the slave, as to be a punishment or disgrace put upon him. A slave who had been branded was called stigmatias, or stigmaticus ; that is, one punctured, inscribed, lettered, with some mark or

letters burned into the right hand or forehead.   Such slaves
were stigmatized, held in contempt.

Here, then, we have a clew to the import of the mark, the
name, the number of the name, which all were required to receive
in their right hand, or in their forehead, who would escape the
persecuting power of the beast.   The whole representation is
figurative, and of course to be interpreted metaphorically, not
literally.   But the real mark intended, whatever it was, was
the test which Christians were required voluntarily to undergo
in those times.

Let us now inquire, what were the discriminating tests and
conduct which the persecuting authorities of that day required
of Christians.   History tells us.   In general, those who were
known to be Christians, or suspected, or informed against, as
such, were dragged before the tribunal, and required, as a mark
of contempt and renunciation of Christ and his cause, to pay
religious homage to the image of the emperor, and with their
own hands to offer sacrifices to the pagan gods.   Persuasions,
intimidations, tortures and death were made use of to compel
them to do this.   But the faithful and true of Christ's disciples
refused, and suffered accordingly.   Many failed to withstand
the severe test ; and, overcome by their fears, submitted and
received the mark, the brand of apostasy from Christ, and of
vassalage to the beast.   The former were the martyrs who
gained the victory in the contest over the beast, his mark, and
name, and the number of his name ; the latter were vanquished
by the beast, by his mark, and name, and the number of his
name ; that is to say, vanquished by the expedients and power
of the beast signified and set forth by the mark, the name, and
the number of the name.

But what was that which was signified by the mark, the
name, and the number, three forms of expression apparently
synonymous and epexigetical of each other ?

Here it should be premised that the name may not necessarily
be a single word, or a personal designation or patronymic.   It
may be composed of several words like the names given in
Hosea i. 6 and 9.   " Call her name Lo-ruhamah.".   Septuagint ; οὐκ ἠλετημηένη.   " Call his name Lo-ammi."   Septuagint ;
οὐ λαός μου.   It is likely this was such, as the style of the an-

cient prophets is everywhere adopted by St. John in the Revelation.   It is, however, evidently some allegorical mark, name,
and number, descriptive of the beast and of the apostates who
received it.

Another thing should have been premised, namely, that usually
it was, and must have been, only the initial letters of the names
that were, or could be, branded literally in the hand or in the
forehead of the stigmatized slaves.   Hence here, in the three
Greek numeral letters, we have the initials of the name or inscription referred to.

What three Greek words, then, do we find that will fulfill
all these conditions of the problem?   These will: Χριστοῦ ξυλοῦ
στίγμα; meaning the mark, brand, stigma, of the cross of
Christ.   Or, if we adopt the various reading of some of the
ancient copies which had an iota for the middle letter, it will
mean the stigma of Christ Jesus, making the number expressed
by the letters six hundred and sixteen.   Both readings are substantially the same in import.   Or, otherwise grammatically
rendered, it may mean, one stigmatized or branded with the cross
of Christ; the reproach of the crucified Galilean.   The name
is at once allegorical and descriptive of the antichristian beast,
and of those who worshipped his image and bowed their necks
to his yoke.   The reproach of the cross, meekly and joyfully
borne by the faithful and true, was indeed an honor in God's
esteem, and for having it the martyrs are glorified.   But the
reproach of the cross accepted as the mark of the beast, is
another thing, which forfeited the crown of victory and glory;
and it is manifestly the latter which is presented in the text as a
significant and solemn warning against apostasy amid the fires
of persecution.   So understood, how forcible and effective it
must have been in St. John's day and afterwards.

" Here then is wisdom."   Not so much to find out the meaning of the figurative representation, as to ponder upon it, and
to be governed by its admonitions in the fiery trial.   As to the
the number, " it is the number of a man," such as is common
among men, having nothing Sibylline or enigmatic in it.   The
three numeral letters could not be seen or thought of, as inscribed on the forehead, without noticing that they constituted

the number six hundred and sixty six ; and tbc mention of this serves to imprint them on the memory.

Finally, in the light of this interpretation, how significant and forcible is the passage in Rev. xv. 2. In vision St. John saw the place of the heavenly glory, " as it were a sea of glass mingled with fire," all resplendent with the reflected glory of the Sun of heaven. And he saw " them that had gotten the victory over the beast, and over his image, and over his mark and over the number of his name, stand on the sea of glass having the harps of God." In the conflict with the persecuting beast they came off' conquerors over every crafty and cruel expedient to compel them to abjure Christ as their Lord and their God. Therefore are they before the throne of God, crowned as victors.

ARTICLE IV.

THE RESURRECTION OF CHRIST.

ONE of the foundation facts of the Gospel is the Resurrection of Jesus Christ. Upon it the Apostle makes to rest the truth of the entire Gospel, the utility of preaching and the value of Christian faith. " If Christ be not risen, then is our preaching vain, and your faith is also vain ; ye are yet in your sins." 1 Cor. xv. 14 and 17. It is God's testimony to the fact of Christ's Messiahship, Rom. i. 4, Acts ii. 24, 32, 36, and hence to the truths which he taught, and to the sufficiency and accept-ableness of his atoning work. Rom. iv. 25. Moreover it stands as voucher for the resurrection of the dead, 1 Cor. v. 16, 1 Cor. xvi. 26, and for the fact of a general judgment. Acts xvii. 31.

It can not be amiss then to pass in review the evidences that our Lord did actually rise from the dead. In doing this, refer-ence will be freely made to the Gospel narratives and to the statements of Apostles, but only as historic authority. Of the credibility of this authority, however, it is scarcely neces-sary to state, that it is, to say the least, second to no possible human testimony.   In proof of this, witness the simplicity of their character, their unflinching fidelity in recording their own faults and their Master's censures, the great change wrought in their own views by the occurrence to which they testify, and their subsequent self-denying and heroic devotedness, in the face of privation, peril and death, to the work of heralding the Gospel of a risen Saviour.

A first fact, very important to be established, is that our Lord was really dead when he was supposed to be.

Many a man has been resuscitated after life seemed to be extinct.   Did Christ die for our sins, or did he only seem to die?   Was he raised again for our justification, or only resuscitated from faintness or a swoon?   Such is the practical point involved here.

We note, then, that those who had procured his condemnation and crucifixion, sought, and would be satisfied with nothing less than his death.   This, and this alone, as they supposed, would silence his reproofs, and put an end to his pretensions.   Hence they would look well to the evidence that he was verily dead.

His persecutors were prepared to use extra means to hasten his death.   That their religious scruples might not suffer from his remaining upon the cross on the passover Sabbath, they asked of Pilate that his legs might be broken ; and this request was granted.   Soldiers came where he hung, charged with this business, and they actually broke the legs of those crucified with him, and desisted in his case only because they saw that he was already dead.   John xix. 32, 33.

When he expired it was in full view of friends and foes.   The multitude had not yet all retired from the spot.   There were present still careless saunterers and bitter enemies and loving disciples and a band of soldiers with a centurion in command detailed to watch him.   Each saw from the standpoint of his own peculiar interest in the event the usual signs of death ; and all were alike convinced that what some desired and others dreaded to see, and still others officially watched for, had occurred.

It excited wonder that he should die so soon, and its effect could not but be to increase the thoroughness of the examination. Pilate himself shared this surprise, and would not be satisfied of the fact till he was assured of it officially. He called the centurion whom he had appointed to watch the cross, and inquired of him if Jesus were already dead ; and not until he received that officer's answer, would the governor allow the body to be taken down and buried.

In ascertaining the fact, the soldiers had taken measures to put it beyond the possibility of doubt. One of them thrust a spear into his side, and so deeply that if any vitality remained, it would certainly have appeared. John xix. 34.

Even if life had not been extinct, this wound would have been mortal. It was a thrust upward in the region and in the direction of the heart. The spear used was unquestionably narrow and tapering, not widening to the breadth of a man's hand within six or eight inches from its point. Yet the wound was large enough to admit the hand ; else why should Thomas, who was probably a spectator at the time, have afterwards spoken with singular fitness and precision of putting his " finger " in the print of the nails, and thrusting his " hand " into his side." John xx. 25.

Moreover, it scarcely admits of a doubt, that the weapon actually reached the heart, piercing both the surrounding membrane, and the organ itself. " There came out water and blood." John xix. 34. The water was probably the serous liquor which fills the membrane, and lubricates the organ for its constant action ; the blood, who can doubt, flowed directly, and ere it was yet cold, from the central organ of circulation, from the heart itself.[1]

On such evidence the centurion was able to certify Pilate officially that the body on the cross was really lifeless, and thereupon the governor hesitated not to give it in charge to the friends who begged for it. Mark xv. 44, 45.

It is difficult to conceive how stronger evidence, that Jesus did die then and there, could have been furnished. So, then, it was from the dead that he was raised, if raised at all.

---

[1] A different explanation supposes that the " water and blood " represent the thin and thicker elements into which the blood is separated by the collapse of the veins as death crowds the circulation towards the larger vessels. Either supposition would indicate the actual occurrence of death.

A second point of importance is the fact that great pains were taken to prevent any imposition which might be attempted by the friends of Jesus in regard to his resurrection.

So intent were they on putting down forever the influence and pretensions of this hated man, that they set themselves to guard every point. Hence, when some of them remembered a prediction of his that he would rise from the dead, they took measures to prevent the farce of a pretended fulfilment.

He had been buried by his friends. But the next day, " the chief priests and Pharisees came together unto Pilate saying : " Sir, we remember that deceiver said, while he was yet alive, ' after three days I will rise again.' Command, therefore, that the sepulchre be made sure until the third day, lest his disciples come by night and steal him away, and say unto the people, He is risen from the dead ; so that the last error shall be worse than the first." Matt. xxvii. 62–64. They little thought that in this they were, under God, preparing the most conclusive proof of his resurrection, should it actually occur. Pilate gave the matter into their own hand with a charge to do the work effectually. " Ye have a watch : go your way, make it as sure as ye can." Matt. xxvii. 65.

Let it be borne in mind here that our Lord was buried in a " new tomb hewn out of a rock," Matt. xxvii. 60, so that there was no egress except in one direction, and if the door was properly closed and guarded, there could be no removing the body by stealth. Moreover he was buried alone, Matt. xxvii. 60, so that if the event against which they were so watchful should occur, there could be no question as to the identity of the person raised.

Now what did these men do in pursuance of their special desire, and in accordance with Pilate's strict charges ? They first made the stone, which the disciples had rolled to the door of the sepulchre, fast in its place, Matt. xxvii. 66, probably with masonry. Then they " sealed " it very carefully, most likely impressing upon the green mortar Pilate's official seal, signifying that the tomb was closed by his order, and that no man could break it open with impunity. This done it would seem to be enough. But the governor's orders were to make it as sure as they could, and their own inclination was nothing behind his injunction.   Accordingly they added a guard of armed men.   Matt. xxvii. 66.   It afterwards appears probable that these were Pilate's own soldiers.   In the judgment of enemies then these precautions were quite sufficient.

We come now to examine the direct proof that Christ did rise from the dead.

According to the narrative, the guard is overawed, the seal broken, and stone removed by divine interposition.   " There was a great earthquake ; for the angel of the Lord descended from heaven and came and rolled back the stone from the door, and sat upon it.   His countenance was like lightning, and his raiment white as snow.   And for fear of him the keepers did shake and become as dead men."

This is the account which the soldiers themselves, as they came into the city, first gave of the matter.   True they afterwards told another story about it, which we shall refer to in its place.

This fact, however, is patent to all.   The body is missing from the tomb on the morning of the third day.   Friends are astonished at it, not knowing what to think ; enemies are perplexed and alarmed, and set themselves to devise some new means of preventing the very belief which they had taken so much pains already to forestall.

It is important to observe that the witnesses were not expecting the event, to the fact of which they testify.   It is said that " the wish is father to the thought," and that when men are intensely excited, and are expecting apparitions and ghosts, they are easily deceived, and fancy that they see what they expect, whether it be a matter of desire or dread.   Such was evidently not the case here.   For though our Lord had repeatedly told them that he would rise from the dead, his predictions were sealed words to them.   They did not comprehend him. Accordingly when the first visitors came to the tomb, it was not to greet the living, but to embalm the dead.   They came with " sweet spices " that they might " anoint him."   Mark xvi. 1. Not knowing what had happened at the tomb, three women, Mary Magdalene, Mary the mother of Jesus, and Salome, were saying among themselves as they approached : " Who shall roll us away the stone from the door of the sepulchre?" Mark xvi. 3. Others came also, but probably not in the same company. They seemed to have known nothing about the sealing of the stone, much less the presence of an armed guard of Roman soldiers. By this time, however, the guard had fled, and some of them soon after entered the city, and in close conversation with the chief priests, told them the startling facts in the case. Math. xxviii. 11. When the women reached the spot and looked, they saw that the stone was rolled away, and that the body was gone. Luke xxiv. 2, 3. The first impulse of Mary Magdalene was to run to the city and inform Peter and John, John xx. 2, who seem to have lodged apart from the other disciples. She unburdened her heart in the words: "They have taken away the Lord out of the sepulchre, and we know not where they have laid him." Peter and John ran instantly to the sepulchre, John xx. 3, 4, leaving Mary to follow them as best she could. Meantime the other women, who had tarried at the sepulchre and entered it after she had left, saw an angel in the tomb, Matt. xxviii. 5, 6, who announced that Jesus had risen from the dead and bid them "Come, see the place where the Lord lay." He also charged them to "go quickly and tell his disciples," and to arrange for a meeting in Galilee.

Some of these women fled in terror and said nothing to any one. Mark xvi. 8. Others, Matt. xxviii. 9, in compliance with the direction of the angels, immediately set out to find the nine whom Mary Magdalene had not sought. Soon after they left, Peter and John reached the sepulchre, John outrunning Peter, and looking in, but not entering till Peter came up, when both went in together. John xx. 3—6, and 8. They saw that the body was missing; that the grave-clothes were folded and laid by in the exactest order, John xx. 7; showing clearly, on the one hand, that the grave had not been rifled: not for valuables, for these articles were of more value than a corpse; not for the corpse itself, for they who steal dead bodies do not stay to fold and arrange what they leave behind; and showing, on the other hand, that friends had not taken the body away, for they would have taken the grave-clothes also.

From these circumstances, the germ of a belief seems to have sprung up in the mind of John, John xx. 8, that Jesus

was really risen from the dead, but the two departed, the angel
who had just before been seen by the women not appearing to
them.   They had scarcely left, however, when Mary Magdalene, who by this time had returned and was lingering in tears
near the sepulchre, stooped down to take another view of the
place where her Lord had lain.   As she gazed, two angels,
John xx. 12, appeared to her, as one had to the other women,
and addressed her, saying : " Woman, why weepest thou?"
Her answer, in nearly the same words that she had spoken to
Peter and John, showed that she had not yet a suspicion that
the Lord had really risen : " She saith unto them, because they
have taken away the Lord, and I know not where they have
laid him."   Having said this, she turned around, and Jesus
stood before her, John xx. 14, and also inquired :   Woman,
why weepest thou?"   She did not know him, but supposed
him to be the keeper of the garden in which the tomb was situated, and still intent upon finding the body that she might embalm it, she said : " Sir, if thou have borne him hence, tell me
where thou hast laid him, and I will take him away."   Upon
this the supposed gardener called her by name and enabled her
to know him, speaking as the risen Jesus ; yet he suffered her
not to touch him, but bade her go and tell the disciples.   Thus
was Mary Magdalene the first mortal who saw the risen Saviour.
Mark xvi. 9.

Nearly at the same time, yet afterwards, he appears to the
other women, who on seeing the angels, had at once left the
sepulchre to tell, as they were bidden, the other disciples that he
was alive.   As they went, Jesus met them, saying, " All hail."
And they came and held him by the feet and worshipped
him.   Matt. xxviii. 9.   They receive from the Lord himself a
repetition of the command which the angels had given to bear
the glad news to the sorrowing disciples.

These two appearances to different women, and in different
places occurred early in the morning.   Later in the day he is
seen by Peter, 1 Cor. xv. 5, Luke xxiv. 34, and still later,
towards evening, by two individuals, as they walked sorrowfully to a neighboring village about seven miles distant, where
he ate bread with them, having first blessed and broken it after
his usual manner.   Then he vanished out of their sight, and

the two disciples, contrary to their first intention, rose up the same hour and returned to Jerusalem, that they might tell the brethren what had convinced them that Jesus was indeed risen. Mark xvi. 12, 13, Luke xxiv. 13–35. On returning, they found eight others of the disciples assembled. Judas had hung himself; Thomas was not present. The doors were closed when these two disciples narrated what had happened in the way, and how Jesus was known to them in breaking of bread. It was evening. Matthew says it was also meal time. Jesus appeared again standing in the midst of them and saying : " Peace be unto you." And when they were terrified and oppressed, supposing they had seen a spirit, he upbraided them for their unbelief, saying : " Behold my hands and my feet that it is I myself. A spirit hath not flesh and bones as ye see me have." Then, in order to convince them, he showed them his hands and his feet. And still failing, he resorted to the same method that had served to satisfy the two disciples at Emmaus ; for " when they believed not for joy, he called for food, and receiving a broiled fish and a honey comb, he ate before them. Then were the disciples glad when they saw the Lord."

These five appearances occurred each in a different place, and under different circumstances, but all in the vicinity of Jerusalem, and on the very day of his resurrection.

It is important also to notice that they found the disciples who are the witnesses in the case, not only not expecting the resurrection, but exceedingly incredulous. The statement of the women respecting the vision of angels, astonished them ; and when they added that they had seen the Lord, " their words seemed to them as idle tales, and they believed them not." The appearances were not to those who were at the time in a trance, but to men walking, talking and eating. The recognition was not instantaneous, as might have been anticipated, if it were an optical illusion merely, incident to an excited state of mind, but a gradual yielding to the force of evidence. Mary Magdalene supposed him to be a gardener, and only recognized her Lord when he called her familiarly by name. The two on the road to Emmaus entered into conversation with a stranger, for their eyes were holden that they should not know him. They believed only when he broke bread, as he formerly had done, and ate before them, and having opened their eyes to know him, vanished out of their sight. The ten, gathered at evening, were ready to believe that a spirit stood before them and conversed with them, and not until they had handled and found him verily flesh and bones, and not a spirit, not until he had eaten in their sight, would they believe. So far from being at first helped by the predictions which the Scriptures contained, or which Christ had himself uttered, to a belief that he could rise from the dead, they did not even recall them, much less understand the events, and the exposition of the risen Saviour himself assisted them to it.

We mark, then, well, this plain fact: As much greater as is the reluctance to believe on the part of these disciples, so much greater the evidence of the facts which overcame it; and so much more conclusive the testimony of those who are convinced by it.

The value of a sceptic's testimony will appear still further in the case of unbelieving Thomas. It was fortunate, if we may so speak, that Thomas was not present when our Lord first met his disciples in assembly. There are to be other appearances, and Thomas shall be present, and his most determined unbelief shall be overcome.

When the other disciples said to him : " We have seen the Lord," he distinctly announced his intention to reject all testimony, and accept nothing but the evidence of his own senses : " Except I shall see in his hands the print of the nails, and put my finger into the print of the nails, and thrust my hand into his side I will not believe." At the end of a week, on the next Lord's day evening, the disciples were again assembled, and this time Thomas was with them. Again the Lord is visibly present. He came as before, when the doors were shut, evincing his indifference to barriers or bolts. Standing in the midst he said : " Peace be unto you." And now he addresses himself to overcome the incredulousness of Thomas, granting him the very evidence that he asked for : " Reach hither thy finger and behold my hands, and reach hither thy hands and thrust it into my side, and be not faithless but believing." It is enough for even Thomas, as his exclamation, " My Lord and my God ! " fully evinces.

Our Lord's next appearance seems to have been on the shore of a lake in Galilee. Seven of the disciples were gathered together. They had spent the night, not in dreamy sleep, when illusions are apt to occur, but in a toilsome and fruitless effort to catch fish. In the morning a stranger stands on the shore. They are within speaking distance. He addresses them familiarly, asking if they have any meat. Being answered in the negative, he tells them to "cast the net on the right side of the ship," assuring them that they shall have success. And now they are not able to draw it for the multitude of the fishes.

Once before this, three of these same men had met with a similar experience. When Peter and the sons of Zebedee, then partners in business, were first called to the discipleship, they had been fishing all night in vain. Jesus, who had been addressing the multitude from one of their boats, directed them to let down their nets for a draught. It was done; and the nets were broken with success, and two boats filled with fish to the point of sinking. Who can doubt that the present marvel recalled, and was intended to recall the former, and with it the words then uttered: "Henceforth ye shall catch men." John instantly recognized the stranger. Peter immediately girt his fisher's coat about him and jumped into the sea to go to his risen Master. The others hastened to the shore dragging the net full of large fishes, "a hundred and fifty and three." Fire and cooked fish and bread, also, are upon the shore. Jesus bids them "come and dine," presiding in his usual manner at the meal. The disciples, by this time somewhat accustomed to the visits of their Master, dared not ask him for his name, "knowing that it was the Lord." This was the third time that he showed himself to his disciples collectively.

After this he is seen on a mountain in Galilee, by the eleven doubtless, and five hundred other brethren at once. They saw and worshipped, but the ever faithful doubt, sure to put credulity out of the question, was even then present with some, who not having had the repeated proofs with which the chosen witnesses had already been favored, scarcely dared to trust the evidence of their own senses.

Still again the Lord is seen by James, probably at Jerusalem; then by all the apostles. Dr. Robinson remarks that "this was apparently an appointed meeting; the same which Luke speaks of as occurring in Jerusalem immediately before the ascension." It was of course our Lord's last interview with his disciples. Thence he led them out as far as Bethany, gave them their commission to preach the Gospel to every creature, and lifting up his hand blessed them, and was parted from them, a cloud receiving him out of their sight. Even then he left an angel behind him to explain to them the significance of his manner of departure, and to remind them of their immediate duty. "Ye men of Galilee, why stand ye gazing up into heaven? This same Jesus whom ye have seen taken up from you into heaven, shall so come in like manner as ye have seen him go into heaven." They will see him no more. Their duty henceforth is to comply with his already uttered commands.

Last of all the risen Saviour is seen by Paul also, as "of one born out of due time."

Here then are eleven distinct manifestations of the Lord as risen from the dead. The first ten were to those who had been best acquainted with him before his death, and who were therefore able to testify directly to his identity. The last is of the nature of inspired testimony, and depends for its value, in part, at least, on the accompanying signs wrought by the apostle.

Of the ten, nothing is wanting that could add the least credibility to evidence. Had there been but one appearance, though thousands had witnessed it; had he appeared only on the first day after his resurrection, though never so many times; had he appeared only in one particular manner, or appealed to only one class of evidences in proof of his identity; had he appeared to only one class of persons, as to the woman in the bewilderment of sorrow-stricken affection; or to the eleven disciples stunned by a sudden disappointment; or had these been so far assured by the predictions as to have seized the merest allusion to satisfy a credulous desire; had the witnesses been otherwise than extremely distrustful, and ready to believe in a ghost rather than a real resurrection; had there been no Thomas determined not to believe till his own finger should press the place where the nail had entered, and his own hand follow the spear; had the witnesses all been miraculously furnished, so as to have continued on the earth but a day, as was the fact with the angels, the case would have been different, and the evidence less conclusive. But as it was, the manifestations being in diverse manners, during a period considerably extended, and to such a variety of persons whom he satisfied by such varied tests, and of whom large numbers remained many years on the earth to confirm the testimony of the apostles, nothing is left to be desired.

We are at liberty therefore, to sum up the evidence by combining the assertions made by Luke and Peter and Paul respecting it. Says the first : " He shewed himself alive after his passion by many infallible proofs, being seen of them forty days, and speaking of the things pertaining to the kingdom of God." Acts i. 3. Says the second : " Him God raised up . . . and showed him openly . . . . unto witnesses chosen before of God, even to us who did eat and drink with him after he rose from the dead." Acts x. 40, 41. Of the five hundred brethren who saw him at one time, Paul affirms, twenty years after : " The greater part remain unto this present, but some are fallen asleep." 1 Cor. xv. 6.

Besides this direct and overwhelmingly conclusive proof, there are two branches of corroborative evidence. The first is the substantial confession of enemies contained in the expedient resorted to by the chief priests, to hide the facts as first stated by the soldiers.

They bribed these men of the guard to say : "His disciples came by night and stole him away while we slept." Matt. xxviii. 12, 13. The statement carried its falsehood on the face of it. In the first place, it was death for a Roman soldier to sleep while on guard ; and it is incredible that every one of a large guard should be so reckless of consequences as to fall asleep all together ; or if they did, that none of them should have been awakened by the noise necessarily incident to a removal of the body from a tomb closed with a " very great" stone, and sealed. It is equally incredible that the few frightened and defenceless disciples of Christ should have attempted to elude the guard, or dared in its presence to break the governor's seal. In the second place, supposing that they did all fall asleep, their testimony is manifestly good for nothing as to what occurred while they were asleep. They were competent to say that the tomb was open and the body gone, when they awoke; but were no more able to assert that it was stolen, than that it was raised from the dead.   But desperate measures require desperate means, and it is no wonder that the chief priests having resolved upon so absurd a story and one attended with so much personal danger to the soldiers, should offer a large sum of money, and strong assurances also that if this should come to the governor's ears he should be " persuaded " and they secured.   Matt. xxviii. 11–15.

The other corroborative evidence is a divine voucher for the witnesses.   We refer to the miracles and signs which everywhere followed their testimony; from the tongues of fire on the day of Pentecost to the healing power which accompanied Peter's shadow as it fell upon the sick by the wayside, from the impotent man leaping and walking in the temple, to the healing virtue of the apostle's handkerchiefs carried by the friends of the suffering and laid upon them.

Let it be noted that the apostles always referred the miracles wrought by them to the power of the Lord Jesus as raised from the dead.   Acts ii. 32, 33.   Acts iii. 15, 16.   Acts iv. 10.

The miracle, then, had a double force as pertaining to our subject.   First, as accrediting the veracity of the apostles.   It testified that they were honest men, acting in no feigned character, but reporting what they verily believed.   Secondly, as attesting independently the facts which they state.   When therefore Peter and John disclaim all power to heal the impotent man, and declare boldly that it was done through him "whom God hath raised from the dead, whereof we are witnesses," the soundness of the man before the multitude is indisputable evidence that God endorsed both the witnesses and their testimony.   And the force of this endorsement the enemies of the Gospel felt and acknowledged, though unwillingly, when they said : "What shall we do to these men? for that a notable miracle hath been done by them is manifest to all them that dwell in Jerusalem and we can not deny it."   Acts iv. 16.

ARTICLE V.

THE LOGICAL CONNECTIONS OF SABELLIANISM.

HAVING made a statement of Sabellianism in a former article, it is proper now to consider some of the connections of the doctrine as it stands related more or less to other forms of error. Its special aim, in the first instance, consists in the view taken of the Trinity, but it has affiliation with other views equally unscriptural, and unites in the support of conclusions drawn from false schemes of doctrine on other topics than the Trinity, which are by no means of secondary importance.

As the first instance in point, the notion of evil and of the origin of sin, which Sabellianism accepts, claims attention. It has been shown that one great objection to the admission that Christ had a human soul was because that, in the view of the Sabellian, this admission was equivalent to assuming that Christ had a sinful nature. Had the doctrine of man's sinfulness as first created been accepted, this objection would have been obviated; for to have declared that Christ had a human soul such as it was before the fall of man, such as it was while yet in the state of innocence, would have been to assume Christ's complete human nature, so as to maintain, at the same time, his sinlessness. But, instead of accepting this doctrine of the commencement of sin, the Sabellian followed the Manichæan notion, assuming that instead of being created in a state of innocence, man was really by nature a sinning soul from the first. The race began its career in alliance with such evil, both of nature and circumstance, as made sin necessary. The Manichæan doctrine of original evil was like that of the Persian dualism, in holding that good and evil were two principles existing from eternity; but differed also from it, in holding to the personality of both these principles. The Persian held these principles as personified in Ormuzd the good being, and Ahriman the evil one; but the Manichæan held strictly only to the personality of the good being, thus adopting the Buddhistic view. The opposition of good and evil was not that of two personal beings in array against each other; but it was the opposition of spirit

against matter. On the one side there is God from whom
nothing but good can proceed ; on the other side, matter, darkness, and discord composing the essence of original evil. The
conflict is between God as a spirit, and matter as being the
essence of evil. That which resists God is the "blind force of
nature." This "blind force," is the Manichæan devil. As
matter existed from eternity, it followed that God had the resistance of its dark forces to contend with from the first.
When he made man, giving him a complex nature of body and
soul, a compound of matter and spirit, it involved the necessity of his becoming a sinner through the evil of matter in his
composition. Such being the nature of man by creation, the
problem with God was to subdue these blind forces of evil evolving sin in man, through discipline ; to emancipate the soul of
man from this bondage to evil, thence to be free and pure forever. The spirit of man through this discipline of conflict with
evil and suffering, will at length be set free from evil in man's
nature as allied with matter, and nothing will be left of matter
but a "dead residuum," which is finally annihilated. The evil
incident in matter will slough off from the living spirit, so that
the spiritual in man, being set free from matter, will be saved.
This course of discipline may be extended after death. There
may still be attached to the soul in its disembodied state such
physical tendencies derived from its contact with matter as will
render further discipline necessary. That discipline may be
attended with future suffering, but in the end the soul will be
set free from all these physical tendencies, and rise to purity
and peace. Thus in the Manichæan notion of evil there is no
future punishment ; but at most only future discipline, in order
to effect the complete spiritual deliverance of man.

Nor according to this notion of evil, can the resurrection of
the body be allowed ; for, in the body lies the main force of
evil in man, evolving acts of sin. By death the soul is separated from this mass of physical corruption, set free from its
taint ; and hence to allow a resurrection of the body and its
union again with the soul, would be to unite the soul again to
corruption. The body therefore must be left to death and annihilation. Or if by any supposition the soul should become
so involved with the forces of evil in matter as not to be set

free from them, then both soul and body must go to annihilation. Such a possibility however is foreign to the general drift of the theory.

The views of the Manichæan in respect to Christ do not concern us here, for this discussion requires a notice of only so much of these views as was held in common with those of the Sabellian. The Sabellian, in his theory of the Trinity, adopted the Manichæan notion of sin, as appears in the opposition of Athanasius to Apollinaris. As already noticed, the Sabellian denied that Christ had a human soul, because, according to Manichæism, this would have been equivalent to the assertion that Christ was a sinner. Also the Sabellian agreed with the Manichæan in representing that the human nature, or what appeared to be the human nature of Christ, as well as his personality, ceased after the crucifixion, and that he was reäbsorbed in the person of God. Also, as the Manichæan, the Sabellian was careful not to allow the existence of a personal devil; careful to disallow or be silent upon the resurrection of the body, and the doctrine of future punishment. In short, Sabellianism and Manichæism have a logical agreement in respect to the existence of evil, a personal devil, the resurrection of the body, and future punishment.

If we examine the modern developments of Sabellianism, we shall find that it still holds this connection with Manichæism as to evil and the origin of sin. For illustration, it is so generally conceded that Dr. Bushnell holds the Sabellian notion of the Trinity, as not to require discussion in this connection. If any reference were necessary, his treatment of what he calls " an Instrumental Trinity," would seem to be sufficient. Accordingly in his discussion of " Nature and the Supernatural," he in effect endorses the Manichæan theory of sin. This is seen in the declaration that Satan is not a person, but only a " name that generalizes bad persons or spirits with their bad thoughts and characters." Instead of a personal being, Satan is only a name significant of the aggregate of all evil thoughts and practices as they occur in the lives of God's moral creatures. The devil, according to this view, has only a poetical existence. He is only that " bad possibility" which " environs" God from the beginning ; which " bad possibility" answers to the Manichæan notion of the " kingdom of darkness." This " bad possibility" answers to the Manichæan " eternity of matter." Satan is the " bad possibility" eternally existing prior to the world's creation, emerging at the creation into the " bad actuality," which it is the problem of Jehovah's government to master. At best, neither according to the ancient Manichæan, nor according to Dr. Bushnell, is Satan a creature in any sense directly from the creative power of God, but on the contrary is a development or evolution from matter through some convulsion.

Dr. Bushnell has the same idea of man as first created, as the Manichæan. He says that " the plan of God, in the creation and training of powers, was to bring them on so as to finally vanquish the bad possibility or necessity that environed him before the worlds were made." And again, " evil is a hell of oppositions, riots, usurpations, in itself ; and bears a front of organization only as against good." That is, evil has no positive existence, no personal leadership, but is simply an aggregate, or organization of tendencies against good for which the word Satan is a convenient epithet.

Again, the necessity of sin in man, as the result of his having been created with a physical nature, and thus allied with evil forces from the first, finds a response in the seventh chapter of "Nature and the Supernatural," under the title of "Anticipative Consequences." The spirit of this chapter is that everything was so foreordained as to man's nature and relations, that upon man's creation he must begin life as a sinner. And yet the author complains of the mere naturalist, as for instance Mr. Parker, for insisting that sin is the result of "discordant causes" in human nature alone, and claims that upon this supposition, mankind can not be blamed for sin, for in that case God has put the evils into man out of which actual sin must grow. Yet upon the statement of Dr. Bushnell, it is equally difficult to blame man for being a sinner. According to him evil existed in the world before man was brought into it. When created, he was created into a "realm of deformity and discord." "Prey, death, deformed objects, and hideous monsters were in the world long before the arrival of man." Sin was already organic in the world. The very atmosphere was pestilent and contagious of sin, or of causes that must result in sin. Into this organism of circumstance man is introduced and environed, and by necessary consequence becomes a sinner. How then is he to be blamed? It is not claimed by this that upon the whole Dr. Bushnell and Mr. Parker are alike in their views, for this would be a gross act of injustice to the former. It is important, however, to note the point of logical connections between these men, who upon other points are so at variance.

Dr. Bushnell believes in a personal God, and consequently in the supernatural; while Mr. Parker, though not always consistent with himself, believes in the absolute, accepting in the main the positive philosophy of Comte, according to which God is not a person, but an abstract force of law, and accordingly there is no such thing as the supernatural. There is only nature. There being only nature, Mr. Parker is consistent in assuming that sin is the result of "discordant causes" in human nature; consistent also in not blaming men for it, and because he believes it altogether for the best that man should begin his career thus, and by progress rise to something better. He declares himself everywhere an optimist. No blame is to be attached to God or man for sin, sin being for the best as existing at the initiation of progress.

Dr. Bushnell believing in a personal God and the supernatural, instead of finding all the "discordant causes" of sin in human nature, finds them as well outside of human nature, in the prearrangement of things, in the organic condition of this world into which man was created, and of which he became a part. Nor logically according to this theory is any fault to be found with God or man on account of sin, for it is for the best that human progress should begin under these conditions. Mr. Parker readily admitted what he called the "great capacity for ugliness in nature," and it has been well said that the reason why he could not accept this "ugliness" as marks of divine premeditation, and call them "anticipative consequences," was because he did not believe in the supernatural, as he did not believe in a personal God.

The advocate of naturalism, and the advocate of the supernatural, agree as to the necessity of sin as evolved from evil causes, and upon the whole as the best order of discipline that could have been devised, so that in the final result all will be for the best; all of these considerations being according to the Manichæan view of sin.

It is true that Mr. Parker in some sort apparently rejects Manichæism, especially in the way of ascribing less importance to sin as guilt; and yet substantially he accepts that view in so far as he can without admitting the personality of God, and supernatural agency; believes that all men will be saved finally, even from the "grossest and worst sin"; that all which man suffers must be for the "good of the sufferer"; that in suffering progress is made toward purity and peace; so that if there is suffering hereafter, Mr. Parker does not call that future punishment, but "future progress."

The Sabellian maintains more or less this view of suffering, and hence to such degree as the doctrine is received, and has influence, doubt is entertained as to the resurrection, silence maintained on the subject of future punishment, while the plain inference from the handling of other topics is, that there is no faith held in either of these doctrines. Some say that their minds are unsettled in relation to them, or that they doubt them, or deny their truth.

Again, both the naturalist and supernaturalist put great stress upon the fatherhood of God. They assume that his love for his creatures is so tender that he would not allow them to suffer if he could help it. He allows it more from the lack of power to prevent it, than because he judges it wise to ordain it. The infinite benevolence of God is maintained by assuming the Manichæan theory of sin, according to which he was so "environed" with evil from eternity, his hands so tied by the "kingdom of darkness," that he was compelled to permit sin and the suffering consequent to man, as the best thing that could be done. God himself suffers infinite grief, that his creature man should have to pass through such an ordeal of pain.

Owing to the stress put upon this view of the divine benevolence, the early Sabellian was called in the West, a Patripassian. We have a modern presentation of this view in a book written by the Rev. Charles Beecher, under the title of "Redeemer and Redeemed." Mr. Beecher believes that "Jesus was God become man," according to the Sabellian doctrine. It follows that God himself suffers on account of sin. Because "holiness is pleasant to him, sin is unpleasant." Sin gives "real pain" to God. From the whole drift of the chapter on "Divine Sorrow," one would suppose that God were really made miserable by man's sin, and nearly bereft of the attribute of infinite blessedness; because "his blessedness was mixed with endurance;" "a cup of felicity mingled with drops of bitterness," "a blessedness largely of anticipation qualified by present sorrow."

Just so, Mr. Parker, the naturalist, is a Patripassian in all but admitting the personality of God. God is "infinite love only." He is "only Father"; the "infinite tenderness" of love, the "infinite sympathizer." There are some things which resemble an admission of something like divine personality. He disliked being called a pantheist, but as it would seem, the dislike was owing more to the prejudice which was likely to be arrayed against him under that title than from any sincere objection to pantheism. On one occasion he apparently opposed the statement that "God was only an idea formed in the mind of the individual, projected into ideas of omnipresence" and of other attributes; but concluded his remarks by giving the impression that after all nothing positive could be affirmed as to the divine person.

On another occasion he writes to a friend: "I am no pantheist, and never was;" and then writes in his journal: "God is the soul of man, and gives us all the life we live. Reason is not personal, but is a great plane, which cuts the center of all souls, the larger the soul, the greater portion of the one and indivisible God is intercepted thereby. The life of God is in my soul; it is in vain that you tell me of a God out of me. All nature is his dress, stars spangle his robe, and light is but his garment." Nature, then, as material and as force, is the personality of God. It would be difficult for Comte to give a more vivid expression of pantheism. God is an abstract law or idea, while man, star, and light, which he wears as a garment, compose his personality. Mr. Parker's Patripassianism is the exquisite sentimentalism with which he endows his abstraction of God, calling him the "All-Father"; while the Patripassianism of the Sabellian is the endowment of God as a person with this same exquisite sentimentalism.   In either case the kingly attributes of God are set aside.   There is no longer sovereignty, justice, or the love of law and order.   God does not appear to any purpose as the author of a moral government, as the dispenser of law to moral beings, and holding them accountable for their conduct.   There is something in these views very soothing to the sinful heart, which can not bear to think of God as a being of holiness and justice, who hates iniquity, and is angry with the wicked every day.   It is pleasant for the guilty to be told that God, instead of the righteous Father, is only the weak father who feels badly when his children do wrong, such a father as Eli, who uses no authority to restrain his children, however wickedly they may do.   In so far as these opinions of God remove the dread accountability for guilt, and set aside the solemn duty of immediate repentance, they meet the approbation of the sinner who desires nothing so much as free license without fear of the consequences of guilt. This fact alone is sufficient to show that these views are false. It suggests an ancient description of the way in which the wicked took courage to go on in his evil way.   " He hath said in his heart God hath forgotten : he hideth his face : he will never see it.   The Lord shall not see, neither shall the God of Jacob regard it."   God may weep over sin as long as he pleases, and feel as badly about it as he chooses, the guilty are never moved by it so long as there is no sword of justice behind the tears to take vengeance on the incorrigible.   If there is only such a God, he is of no more account than the ancient jester who mimicked knighthood in the castles of nobility ; who, instead of a sword of steel, was permitted to wear a wooden sword, " a dagger of lath."   Such an idea of God is a jest.

The ostensible reason, however, for insisting on this sentimentalism in the "All-Father," is not the satisfaction which it gives the sinner.   This undoubtedly is the main incentive to the argument, but to make a show of it would betray its weakness. Ostensibly, therefore, the argument is urged to show that God is so loving that he could not be the author of sin.   But this may be shown by taking a different view of sin than the Manichæan.   Look at man created in the image of God as a free moral agent ; innocent, but with freedom of will to choose either good or evil. He is placed under a moral government exactly adapted to his nature, the laws of which are plain to his understanding, and their force binding on his conscience. Let the beginning of his sin date with his first disobedience, with no antecedent cause of sin in matter, force or circumstance capable of compelling it into actuality. If it come, let it come by man's freedom of election. If man makes this election and falls into sin, let it appear that the circumstances were such as were calculated above all others possible to conceive the best adapted to have secured his steadfastness in holiness; so that prior to his fall the idea of obtaining, or maintaining, holiness through suffering and conflict, was inconceivable as a necessity. In the mind of God it might be certain that man thus created would become a sinner, in view of which the consequences of sin might be consistently anticipated in the light of certainty. Here let the distinction be clearly drawn between certainty and necessity. God knew that man would certainly sin; and knew at the same time that it was not necessary that he should sin. He knew that man would certainly fall from his primal innocence; but did not secure that fall by any necessity, directly or indirectly, immediately or mediately. In this view both God and man are put in a higher plane of being. God is perfect in all his attributes, the creator of all, independent of all, and the source of moral government, both in its inception as lawmaker, and in its enforcement as the executor of law. Man, too, is elevated above the control of any prearranged mechanism of forces, and stands out as a free, intelligent, moral being. God is not the Indian Brahma slumbering and sleeping in the ages, while the evil evolutions proceed, with no power to thwart them in his best waking moments; nor a God bound in Manichæan fetters, the chief evidence of his love being found in his sighs and tears over the sin and suffering which he is compelled to permit. On the contrary, God's love never appears so great as when it is seen in the offer of mercy to man, as a sinner by his own act of disobedience, being a free agent under a moral government. Here the love of God is an act of free grace. The offer of salvation through Christ is not made as the remedy for the blunder of having permitted sin; nor as a compensation to balance the necessity of sin; nor as an element in a course of discipline by suffering and conflict with evil, in which man is conceived of as in sin by creation; thence, by progress to be taken up out of sin. In either of these schemes the love of God appears only as a part of the necessary order of things. It comes in as a make-weight to adjust the balance of the system. The work of Christ, founded upon such a love, comes as a thing in course. It is no more a work of love than it is a work of justice, or reason, or determination.

The work is especially one of love, only when considered as the evidence of love to those who do not merit it; when it appears that God so loved the world that he gave his Son for its salvation, as a free act; when he was under no obligation to do it, no necessity requiring it either as a matter of justice, or as a balance in the order of creation. The love of God is infinite only when it is sovereign love, offering conditions of pardon to the sinner who has ruined himself by his own act; when at the same time, if this manifestation of love had been withheld, God's throne would have been forever guiltless, and his benevolence without the possibility of impeachment. The great love of God appears in this, that in the exhibition of it, he goes infinitely beyond all that could be required of him. It is a love infinitely above the low plane of the pantheist's exquisite sentimentalism, notwithstanding his railing at it as " horrid Calvinism," or the " heathenism of New England orthodoxy." The railing, however, is to be considered not an evidence that the divine benevolence is not set forth most completely by this orthodoxy; but that the persistent rebel against God's government does not like to be reconstructed under God's plan of salvation, however great the exhibition of his love in that plan. The same is true in a degree, where under the lead of the Sabellian, God's sovereignty, independence, power, and justice are held in the background, under the false plea of their harshness; while the sentimental Patripassianism is put in the foreground as though it were certain sinners would never repent and give their hearts to God while appearing as a governing God; as though rebels against God would accept of any plan of reconstruction that should imply his right and power to put down rebellion, and punish traitors.

In showing the logical connection of Sabellianism with other unscriptural schemes of doctrine, reference has been made to the philosophy of Comte. The two have the natural relation of theology to philosophy. The one is germane to the other. They are each of them old errors. There is nothing new or progressive in them except that which pertains to freshness of statement or rhetoric. Comte may boast of progress and of leading the race forward ; but instead of progress in philosophy, he restates Buddhism ; instead of leading the race forward he thrusts it back thirty centuries ; instead of new discovery he commits a plagiarism on the dead remains of East Indian speculation.

There is nothing new either in the boasted discoveries of the theology in alliance with this philosophy. It carries the present back eighteen centuries, when under the lead of reason in defiance of revelation and in the rejection of faith, men undertake to engraft the Gospel of Christ upon heathen philosophy, with the intention of receiving as truth no more of the teachings of Scripture than may be brought into this relation with heathenism. This theology goes hand in hand with its cognate philosophy of pantheism in all but the last step.

Denying the personality of Christ in the Godhead, it denies his personality as a man in assuming that he had no human soul, and declares that at length all that appeared personal in him is reabsorbed in God, the necessary inference being that the body of the Christian is lost as well as that of his Saviour ; and that by his union with the Saviour he also is reabsorbed in the Father, so that there is but one person, God.

The heaven of the positive philosophy lies but one step beyond in the road of absorbing personality, which is, that God himself as a person is absorbed in the absolute ! Then hallelujah to Chaos and old Night ! only that there is left no voice to sing, either created or uncreate.

Very likely the theology in question is not carried out with logical consistency, in many instances, for that would sink it entirely in the pantheistic philosophy. It may be held with tenacity only in some of its more plausible points, in pursuance with which the Gospel may be preached with somewhat of effect. But the preaching can never be so effective as that based upon a pure biblical theology, while at best it involves consequences in the long run disastrous to the church of Christ. The pantheists are right in asserting that consistency requires the boldest advocates of this theology to come thoroughly over into their philosophy. When Christ is defined as but "the moral power of God," addressing itself to men, the abstraction must be conceded as a long advance in that direction.

Both the theology and the philosophy agree in making humanity their watchword, the drift of it being to bring God down to the low plane of human capacity, and to elevate man into the high plane of Deity, especially in all that relates to moral law and accountability. The relation of the theology and the philosophy is illustrated by the coming in of the tide. There is often much in the theology that looks like true veneration of God, as the billows on the surface roll high, as if mounting up toward heaven; but the philosophy is the fatal undertow that carries all back again into the abyss. There is too little of God; too much of man. The human increases on the side of the philosophy, in the definition given to "character." The theologian says "Christ is the moral power of God," addressing itself to the redemption of man. The philosopher says the same thing, only with more emphasis, when he asserts that "the soul of God is poured into the world through the thoughts of men." This constitutes the moral element in man, as the basis of character. Character, therefore, in all men, is divine. Hence in the article on "Character" in the April number of the *North American Review*, it was said that "Voltaire was an apostle of Christian ideas, only the names were hostile to him." He was like "the man in the Gospel who said, no, and went." Voltaire of course must come out right in the end. It is impossible that it should be otherwise in that worship of humanity which needs no personal God or revelation. The tendency of these views is seen in the writings of Sue, George Sand, Dumas, with all that style of literature, in this country or abroad, which represents the vilest and most abandoned of the race as pursuing only a course of development which comes out right at last. The course may be a hard one, fraught with much evil and suffering; but according to the Manichæan notion of evil, this course at length runs free of evil as any could. These are the developments of the divine in man, the way in which the soul of God is poured into the world through the thoughts of men. Accordingly, instead of the condemnation of the literature just referred to, there should be thankfulness for the Gospels according to Voltaire, Dumas, George Sand, and Ralph Waldo Emerson.

It is hardly necessary to say in conclusion, that the revelation of God in the Scriptures by Jesus Christ, and the Holy Spirit, one God in three Persons, involves less of absurdity, even in the light of reason, than this philosophy, or any scheme of theology in alliance with it.

ARTICLE VI.

THE LEGACY OF THE EARLY CHURCH TO FUTURE GENERATIONS.

It is our object in this article to show the great Christian ideas which the Fathers promulgated, and which have proved of so great influence on the Middle Ages, and our own civilization. These were declared before the Roman Empire fell; and if they did not arrest ruin, still alleviated the miseries of society, and laid the foundation of all that is most ennobling among modern nations. The early church should be the most glorious chapter in the history of humanity. While the work of destruction was going on in every part of the world, both by vice and violence, there was still the new work of creation proceeding with it, a precious savor of life to future ages. If there is anything sublime, it is the power of renovating ideas amid universal degeneracy. They are seeds of truth, which grow, and ripen into grand institutions. These did not become of sufficient importance to arrest the attention of historians until they were cultivated by the Germanic nations in the Middle Ages.

It could be shown that almost every thing which gives glory to Christian civilization had its origin in the early church. Few are aware what giants and heroes were those fathers and saints whom this age has been taught to despise. We are really reaping the results of those conflicts, conflicts with bigoted Jewish sects,, conflicts with the high priests of paganism, with Greek philosophers, with Gnostic Manichæan illuminati, with the symbolists, soothsayers, astrologers, magicians, which mystic superstition conjured up among degenerate people. And not merely their conflicts with the prince of the power of the air alone, but with themselves, with their own fiery passions, and tangible outward foes. They were illustrious champions and martyrs in the midst of a great Vanity Fair, in a Nebuchadnezzar fire of persecutions, an all-pervading atmosphere of lies, impurities and abominations which cried to heaven for vengeance. They solved for us and for all future generations the thousand of new questions which audacious paganism proposed in its last struggles ; they exposed the bubbles which charmed that giddy generation of -egotists ; they eliminated the falsehoods which vainglorious philosophers had inwrought with revelation ; and they attested, with dying agonies, to the truth of those mysteries which gave them consolation and hope amid the terrors of a dissolving world. They absorbed even into the sphere of Christianity all that was really valuable in the system they exploded, whether of philosophy or social life, and transmitted the same to future ages. And they set examples, of which the world will never lose sight, of patience, fortitude, courage, generosity, which will animate all martyrs to the end of time. And if, in view of their great perplexities, of circumstances which they could not control, utter degeneracy and approaching barbarism, they lent their aid to some institutions which we can not endorse, certainly when corrupted, like Manichæism and ecclesiastical denomination, let us remember that these were adapted to their times, or were called out by pressing exigencies. And further, let us bear in mind that, in giving their endorsement, they could not predict the abuse of principles abstractly good and wise, like poverty, and obedience, and chastity, and devout meditation, and solitary communion with God. In all their conduct and opinions, we see, nevertheless, a large-hearted humanity, a toleration and charity for human infirmities, and a beautiful spirit of brotherly love. If they advocated definite creeds with great vehemence and earnestness, they yet soared beyond them, and gloried in the general name they bore, until the fundamental doctrines of their religion were assailed.

For two centuries, however, they have no history out of the records of martyrdom. We know their sufferings better than any peculiar ideas which they advocated. We have testimony to their blameless lives, to their irreproachable morals, to their good citizenship, and to their Christian graces, rather than to any doctrines which stand out as especial marks for discussion or conflict, like that which agitated the councils of Nice or Ephesus. But if we were asked what was the first principle which was brought out by the history of the early church, we should say it was that of martyrdom. Certainly the first re-corded act in the history of Christianity was that memorable scene on Calvary, when the founder of our religion announced the fulfillment of the covenant, made with Adam in the garden of Eden. And as the deliverance of mankind was effected by that great sacrifice for sin, so the earliest development of Christian life was the spirit of martyrdom. The moral gran-deur with which the martyrs met reproach, isolation, persecu-tion, suffering, and death, not merely robbed the grave of its victory, but implanted a principle of inestimable power among all future heroes. Martyrdom kindled an heroic spirit; not for the conquest of nations, but for the conquest of the soul, and the resignation of all that earth can give in attestation of grand and saving truths. We have a few examples of martyrs in pagan antiquity, like Socrates and Seneca, who met death with fortitude, but not with faith, not with indestructible joy that this mortal was about to put on immortality. The Christian martyrdoms were a new development of humanity. They taught the necessity of present sacrifice for future glory, and more for the great interests of truth and virtue, with which good men had been identified. They brought life and immortality to the view of the people, who had not dared to speculate on their future condition. Their martyrs inspired a spirit into society that nothing could withstand, a practical belief that the life was more than meat, that the future was greater than the

present; and this surely is one of the grand fundamental
principles of Christianity. They incited to a spirit of fortitude
and courage under all the evils of life, and gave dignity to men
who would otherwise have been insignificant. The example
of men who rejoiced to part with their lives for the sake of
their religion became to the world the most impressive voice
which it yet heard of the insignificance of this life when compared with the life to come. "What will it profit a man to
gain the whole world and lose his own soul?" became thus one
of the most stupendous inquiries which could be impressed on
future generations, and affected all the relations of society.
Martyrdom was one solution of this mighty question which introduced a new power upon the earth, for we can not conceive of
Christianity as an all-conquering influence, except as it unfolds
a new and superior existence, in contrast with which the present
is worthless. The principle of martyrdom, setting at defiance
the present, led to unbounded charity, and the renunciation of
worldly possessions. What are they really worth? Every
martyr had the comparative worthlessness of wealth and
honor and comfort profoundly impressed upon his mind, in
view of the greatness of the infinite, and the importance of the
future.

The early martyrdoms thus brought out with immeasurable
force the principle of faith, without which life can have no object, faith in future destinies, faith in the promises of God, faith
in the power of the cross to subdue finally all forms of evil.
The sacrifice of Christ introduced into the world sentiments of
unbounded love and gratitude, that He, the most perfect type
of humanity, and the Son of God himself, should come into
this world to bear its sins upon the cross, and thus give a
heaven which could not be bought by expiatory gifts. It was
love which prompted the crucifixion of Jesus; and love produced love, and stimulated thousands to bear with patience the
evils under which they would have sunk. The martyrdoms of
the early Christians did not indeed kindle sentiments of gratitude; but they inspired courage, and led to immeasurable forms
of heroism. The timid and the shrinking woman, the down-
trodden slave, and the despised pauper, all at once became
serene, lofty, unconquerable, since they knew that though their

earthly tabernacle would be destroyed, they had a dwelling in the heavens free from all future toil and sorrow and reproach. Martyrdoms made this world nothing and heaven every thing. They proved a powerful faith in the ultimate prevalence of truth, and created an invincible moral heroism, which excited universal admiration. And they furnished models and examples to future generations, when Christians were subjected to bitter trials.

We can not but feel that martyrdom is one of the most impressive of all human examples, since it is the mark of a practical belief in God and heaven. And while we recognize it as among the most interesting among spiritual triumphs, we are persuaded that the absence of its spirit, or its decline, is usually followed by a low state of society. Epicureanism is its antagonistic principle, and is as destructive as the other is conservative. The moment men are unwilling to sacrifice themselves to a great cause, they virtually say that temporal and worldly interests are to be preferred to the spiritual and the future. The language of the Epicurean is intensely egotistic. It is : " Soul, take thine ease ; eat, drink, and be merry ;" to which God says, " Thou fool." Christianity was sent to destroy this egotism, which undermined the strength of the ancient world, and created a practical belief in the future, and a faith in truth. Without this faith, society has ever retrograded ; with it there have been continual reforms. It is an important element of progress, and a mark of dignity and moral greatness.

It is not strange that the early Christians should have been persecuted ; it would have been more extraordinary if they had not been. The new faith was offensive to all the old powers and all the leading classes of society. It shocked the prejudices and undermined the institutions and condemned the habits of both Jew and pagan. It was aggresssive, dictatorial, uncompromising, revolutionary, even while it was meek and non-resistant. It was the strangest of paradoxes ; to the Jew a stumbling-block, and to Greeks foolishness.

The Jew could not tolerate opinions which dissipated his dreams of temporal dominion, abrogated the rites and ceremonies of the temple, subverted the institutions of Moses, and declared a peasant of Galilee to be that promised Messiah who they supposed was to lead them to glory and worldly distinction.

The Greeks despised a faith which set at naught the wisdom of their cherished schools, denounced the pride of reason, and made such a small account of art and literature and elegant social culture.

The Romans were indignant at the lofty claims of Christianity, which proclaimed all the various religions which they had tolerated to be equally false and idolatrous, which denounced all forms of polytheism, and which applied the great law of love to all the forms and institutions which they had built up on injustice and inequalities.

The whole Gentile world saw itself attacked in its religions, its vices, its virtues, its laws, its customs, its symbols, its pomps, its pleasures, its wars, its superstitions, its literature, its ideas, its traditions, its glories.

Even the new virtues which were commended were repugnant to the rich, the mighty, and the noble. What more revolting and inexplicable to a proud heathen, grown rich by extortion or powerful by war than the duty of forbearance, forgiveness of injuries, indifference to wealth and fame, poverty, humility, self-abnegation? What more humiliating that the forgiveness of sins was granted, not for works of virtue, but solely in consequence of the virtues of another; that salvation was not by works, but by faith?

When then the Christians, a small and despised body of plebians, entirely unimportant and generally illiterate, attacked all that was ancient and venerable in philosophy and religion, and showed a dogged contempt for the opinion of their superiors, and assailed the very foundations of society, and, banded together, defied the wrath of man, no wonder they were treated with rudeness, bitterness, and scorn; yea, scourgings, imprisonments and death. They had provoked the issue. They had waged war upon religion and manners and social institutions, and they would have been unworthy of their high calling had they quailed or yielded. And they doubtless had great strength given them supernaturally, so that they made a great impression and gained many converts.

In proportion to their victories were their sufferings. Their first persecutors were the Jews, and the most respectable of the nation, Scribes, Pharisees, priests, rulers.

The first Christian martyr, Stephen, a deacon, defended himself with dignity, boldness and eloquence; but was not permitted to finish his defence, and was carried out beyond the city walls and stoned. Neither the sight of his sufferings, nor the touching beauty of his dying words allayed the excitement.

The death of Stephen was succeeded by a general persecution at Jerusalem in which two thousand Christians were martyred.[1] Soon after they were driven out of the city and scattered as witnesses of the truth — μαρτυρες — in all the region round about. The apostles were all victims except John. James was summarily destroyed by order of Herod; St. James the Just was thrown from the walls of the temple; St. Paul was crucified at Rome during the reign of Nero; Andrew was crucified in Achaia; Thomas suffered death in East India; Bartholomew was crucified with his head downwards; Simon Zelotes and Peter were crucified during the reign of Nero; Matthew died violently in Ethiopia; Philip was crucified in Heliopolis; Mark was dragged through the streets of Alexandria, immured in a dungeon and then burned; Jude suffered in Edessa; Luke was hanged on an olive tree in Greece.[2] Before the close of the apostolic age the Christians were torn in pieces by wild beasts, burned at the stake, crucified, beheaded. These cruelties were connived at by the Roman government; they were not directly ordered. No systematic persecution began till the reign of Nero, and in this he probably confounded Christians with Jews, without personal enmity to either, with a view of gaining popular favor by surrendering to the vengeance of the people an obnoxious class whom he traduced as authors of the conflagration which he himself had caused. Tolerant as were the professed principles of the imperial government, yet a hostile influence was perpetually at work against the Christians.

All the priests and augurs and soothsayers of paganism, were inflamed with implacable animosity; and when any calamity could not be traced to obvious and natural causes, the priests of the old religion ever had the art to make the superstitious peo-

---

[1] Southwell's Book of Martyrs.   Page 9.   [2] Schaff, Ap. Ch.   Page 387.

ple believe it was caused by the anger of the gods in consequence of the insults offered by the hated sect.   Moreover, the
Christians were supposed to be conspirators against the imperial
majesty ; and although their king was a spiritual and invisible
head rather than a temporal potentate, yet the minds of the
Romans were too practical and literal to understand the distinction.   Nor was it to be expected that the emperors, as supreme
pontiffs of the state religion, however liberal and tolerant, could
look with indifference on a movement which tended to weaken
the religion of which they were the acknowledged protectors.
The Christians never hesitated to avow their hostility to all the
gods of Rome, and used all their influence to destroy the ancient superstitions.   Peaceful and nonresistant as they were in
ordinary matters, yet they were enemies to the whole heathen
region, as much as William Lloyd Garrison and Wendell Phillips were to the institution of slavery.   And the more far-
sighted and enlightened the emperors were, the more they were
persuaded of the revolutionary tendencies of Christianity.   And
hence we see the reason why such good emperors as Trajan
and Marcus Aurelius, should have been among the most bitter
of persecutors.

It does not fall in with the design of this article to detail the
various persecutions to which the Christians were subjected
from Nero to Diocletian.   Most noble witnesses could be mentioned, who are immortal, Dyonysius the Areopagite, Ignatius,
Polycarp, Alexander bishop of Rome, Justin Martyr, Ponthi-
nus of Lyons, Blandina the slave, Leonidas the father of Origen, Perpetua and Felicitas of Carthage, Tertullius, Stephen
and Sextus of Rome, Dyonysius of Paris, Cyprian of Carthage,
Justa and Rufina of Seville, these, and others who are famous,
attested to the faith with dying agonies.   The Catholic church
enrolls in her catalogue of saints ninety illustrious martyrs, who
died in the single persecution of Diocletian.

The number who perished in the various persecutions it is
difficult to estimate.   Doubtless there are exaggerations.   One
hundred thousand are said to have perished in France alone.
In the cemetery of St. Calixtus at Rome, it is stated that one
hundred and seventy four thousand martyrs, including forty six
bishops, are buried.   It is difficult to credit a statement which

has so little direct evidence to sustain it, but the extent of the Catacombs, in which the Christians are supposed to be buried at Rome, leads us to infer that the number of martyrs must have been exceedingly numerous, when we remember that the Christians were outlawed by successive edicts, that they were exposed to all the malignity of rulers and priests, and that, in the time of Diocletian, they probably comprehended one third of the whole population, we may conclude that vast numbers were destroyed by tortures of the most revolting nature. The atrocity of these torments exceeds anything recorded in history; and the reports of them must have overwhelmed the whole empire into grief, for we can scarcely suppose that even pagans could have rejoiced in the decimation of their families and households. Never, before or since, has the church suffered so universal and terrible an affliction; and it is impossible, after the lapse of fifteen hundred years, not to be moved by the records of that final conflict with paganism, and not to feel exultation that so much courage and faith were exhibited by the followers of Christ. And the same class of sentiments is seen in the final triumph of all the martyrs, whether bishops, women, or slaves. Their last hours of victory were worthy of their stainless lives, their elevation of soul, their charity and faith. Whatever their torments, whether scourged, or lacerated, or torn by wild beasts, or exposed to insults, or burned in the fire, or pierced with the sword, or torn limb from limb, nothing was heard but exultation, as if more than mortal strength were given them, so that they might say : "O death, where is thy sting! O grave, where is thy victory!" In their anguish they mutually exhorted each other to patience, and they were full of ineffable visions of glory in store for them. It would take a large volume to contain the accounts of their endurance in their last hours of suffering. It was rare for any to apostatise, whatever their torments. And their words of victory were handed down to future ages for the comfort of all similarly placed.

Shall we seek a connection between their martyrdom and civilization? They bore witness to a religion which is the source of all true progress upon earth; they attested to its divine truth amid protracted agonies; they were illustrious examples for all ages to contemplate.

Perhaps the most powerful effect of their voluntary sacrifice was to secure credence to the mysteries of Christianity. Socrates died for his own opinions; but who was ever willing to die for the opinions of Socrates? But innumerable martyrs exulted in the privilege of dying for the doctrines of him whose sacrifice saved the world. Nor to these had death its customary terrors, since they were assured of a glorious immortality. They impressed the pagan world with a profound lesson that the future is greater than the present; that there was to be a day of rewards and punishments. Amid all the miseries and desolations of society, it was a great thing to bear witness to the reality of future happiness and misery. The hope of immortality must have been an unspeakable consolation to the miserable sufferers of the Roman Empire. It gave to them courage and patience and fortitude. It inspired them with hope and peace. Amid the ravages of disease, and the incursions of barbarians, and the dissolution of society, and the approaching eclipse of the glory of man, it was a great and holy mystery that the soul should survive these evils, and that eternal bliss should be the reward of the faithful. Nothing else could have reconciled the inhabitants of the decaying empire to slavery, war, and pillage. There was needed some powerful support to the mind under the complicated calamities of the times. This support, the death and exultation of the martyrs afforded. It was written on the souls of the suffering millions that there was a higher life, a glorious future, an exceeding great reward. It was impossible to see thousands ready to die, exulting in the privilege of martyrdom, anticipating with confidence their " crown," and not feel that immortality was a certitude, brought to light by the Gospel. And the example of the martyrs kindled all the best emotions of the soul into a hallowed glow. Their death, so serene and beautiful, filled the spectators with love and admiration. Their sufferings brought to light the greatest virtues, and diffused their spirit into the heart of all who saw their indestructible joy. Is it nothing, in such an age, to have given an impulse to the most exalted sentiments that men can cherish? The welfare of nations is based on the indestructible certitudes of love, friendship, faith, fortitude, self-sacrifice. It was not Marathon so much as Thermopylæ which imparted vitality to Grecian heroism, and made that memorable self-sacrifice one of the eternal pillars which mark national advancement. So the sufferings of the martyrs, for the sake of Christ, warmed the dissolving empire with a belief in heaven, and prepared it to encounter the most unparalleled wretchedness which our world has seen. They gave a finishing blow to Epicureanism and sceptical cynicism. So that in the calamities which soon after happened, men were buoyed with hope and trust. They may have hidden themselves in caves and deserts, they may have sought monastic retreats, they may have lost faith in man and all mundane glories, they may have consumed their lives in meditation and solitude, they may have anticipated the dissolution of all things, but they awaited in faith the coming of their Lord. Prepared for any issue or any calamity, a class of heroes arose to show the moral greatness of the passive virtues, and the triumphs of faith amid the wrecks of material grandeur. Were not such needed, at the close of the fourth century? Especially were not such bright examples needed for the ages which were to come? Polycarp and Cyprian were the precursors of the martyrs of the Middle Ages, and were of the Reformation. Early persecutions developed the spirit of martyrdom, which is the seed of the church, impressed it upon the mind of the world, and prepared the way for the moral triumphs of the Beckets and Savonarolas of remote generations. Martyrdoms were the first impressive facts in the history of the church, and the idea of dying for a faith, one of the most signal evidences of superiority over the ancient religions. It was a new idea, which had utterly escaped the old guides of mankind.

Another great idea which was promulgated by the church long before the empire fell, was that of benevolence. Charities were not one of the fruits of paganism. Men may have sold their goods and given to the poor, but we have no recerd of such deeds. Hospitals and eleemosynary institutions were nearly unknown. When a man was unfortunate, there was nothing left to him but to suffer and die. There was no help from others. All were engrossed in their schemes of pleasure or ambition, and compassion was rare. The sick and diseased died without alleviation. " The spectator who gazed upon the magnificent buildings which covered the seven hills, temples, arches, porticoes, theatres, and baths and palaces could discover no hospitals and asylums, unless perchance the temple of Æsculapius, on an island in the Tiber, where the maimed and the sick were left in solitude to struggle with the pangs of death." But the church fed the hungry, and clothed the naked, and visited the prisoner, and lodged the stranger. Charity was one of the fundamental injunctions of Christ and of the apostles. The New Testament breathes unbounded love, benevolence so extensive and universal that self was ignored. Self-denial, in doing good to others, was one of the virtues expected of every Christian. Hence the first followers of our Lord had all things in common. Property was supposed to belong to the whole church, rather than to individuals. "Go and sell all that thou hast" was literally interpreted. It devolved on the whole church to see that strangers were entertained, that the sick were nursed, that the poor were fed, that orphans were protected, that those who were in prison were visited. For these purposes contributions were taken up in all assemblies convened for public worship. Individuals also emulated the whole church, and gave away their possessions to the poor. Matrons, especially, devoted themselves to these works of charity, feeding the poor, and visiting the sick. They visited the meanest hovels and the most dismal prisons. But "what heathen," says Tertullian, "will suffer his wife to go about from one street to another to the houses of strangers? What heathen would allow her to steal away into the dungeon to kiss the chain of the martyr?" And these works of benevolence were not bestowed upon friends alone, but upon strangers; and it was this, particularly, which struck the pagans with wonder and admiration, that men of different countries, ranks, and relations of life, were bound together by an invisible cord of love. A stranger, with letters to the "brethren," was sure of a generous and hearty welcome. There were no strangers among the Christians; they were all brothers; they called each other brother and sister; they gave to each other the fraternal kiss; they knew of no distinctions; they all had an equal claim to the heritage of the church. And this generosity and benevolence extended itself to the wants of Christians in distant lands;

the churches redeemed captives taken in war, and even sold the consecrated vessels for that purpose on rare occasions, as Ambrose did at Milan. A single bishop in the third century, supported two thousand poor people. Cyprian raised at one time a sum equal to four thousand dollars in his church at Carthage, to be sent to the Manichæan bishops for the purposes of charity. Especially in times of public calamity was this spirit of benevolence manifested, and in striking contrast with the pagans.[1] When Alexandria was visited with the plague during the reign of Gallienus, the pagans deserted their friends upon the first symptoms of disease; they left them to die in the streets, without even taking the trouble to bury them when dead ; they only thought of escaping from the contagion themselves. The Christians, on the contrary, took the bodies of their brethren in their arms, waited upon them without thinking of themselves, ministered to their wants, and buried them with all possible care, even while the best people of the community, presbyters and deacons, lost their own lives by their self-sacrificing generosity.[2] And when Carthage was ravaged by a similar pestilence in the reign of Gallus, the pagans deserted the sick and the dying, and the streets were filled with dead bodies, which greatly increased the infection. No one came near them except for purposes of plunder, but Cyprian, calling his people together in the church, said : " If we do good only to our own, what do we more than publicans and heathens." Animated by his words, the members of the church divided the work between them, the rich giving money, and the poor labor, so that in a short time the bodies which filled the streets were buried.

And this principle of benevolence has never been relinquished by the church. It is one of the foundation pillars of monastic life in the Middle Ages, when monasteries and convents were blessed retreats for the miserable and unfortunate, where all strangers found a shelter and a home ; where they diffused charities upon all who sought their aid. The monastery itself was built upon charities, upon the gifts and legacies of the pious. In pagan Rome men willed away their fortunes to favorites ; they were rarely bestowed upon the poor. But Christianity

---

[1] Neander, vol. 1, Sec. 3.   [2] Euseb. 1. vii., c. 22.

inculcated every where the necessity of charities, not merely as a test of Christian hope and faith, but as one of the conditions of salvation itself.   One of the most glorious features of our modern civilization is the wide-spread system of public benevolence extended to missions, to destitute churches, to hospitals, to colleges, to alms-houses, to the support of the poor, who are not left to die unheeded as in the ancient world.   Every form of Christianity, every sect and party, has its peculiar charities ; but charities for some good object are a primal principle of the common creed.   What immeasurable blessings have been bestowed upon mankind in consequence of this law of kindness and love !   What a beautiful feature it is in the whole progress of civilization !

The early church had set a good example of patience under persecution, and practical benevolence extended into every form of social life which has been instituted in every succeeding age, and to which the healthy condition of society may in a measure be traced.

The next mission of the church was to give dignity and importance to the public preaching of the Gospel, which has never since been lost sight of, and has been no inconsiderable element of our civilization.   This was entirely new in the history of society.   The pagan priest did not exhort the people to morality, or point out their religious duties, or remind them of their future destinies, or expound the great principles of religious faith. He offered up sacrifices to the Deity, and appeared in imposing ceremonials.   He wore rich and gorgeous dresses to dazzle the senses of the people, or excite their imaginations.   It was his duty to appeal to the gods, and not to men ; to propitiate them with costly rites, to surround himself with mystery, to inspire awe, and excite superstitious feelings.   The Christian minister had a loftier sphere.   While he appealed to God in prayer, and approached his altar with becoming solemnity, it was also his duty to preach to the people, as Paul and the apostles did throughout the heathen world, in order to convert them to Christianity, and change the whole character of their lives and habits.   The presbyter, while he baptized believers and administered the symbolic bread and wine, also taught the people, explained to them the mysteries, enforced upon them the obligations, appealed to their intellects, their consciences and their hearts. He plunged fearlessly into every subject bearing upon religious life, and boldly presented it for contemplation.

" There was nothing touching in the instability of fortune, in the fragility of loveliness, in the mutability of mortal friendship, in the decay of system, in the fall of thrones and empires, which he did not present to give humiliating impressions of worldly grandeur. Nor was there any thing heroic in sacrifice, or grand in conflict, or sublime in danger, nothing in the loftiness of the soul's aspirations, nothing in the glorious promises pertaining to everlasting life, on which he did not dwell in order to stimulate his hearers to run with patience the race set before them. It was his privilege to dwell on the elder history of the world, on the beautiful simplicities of the patriarchal age, on the stern and marvellous story of the Hebrews, on the glorious visions of the prophets, on the songs of the inspired melodists, on the countless beauties of the Scriptures, on the character, teachings and mission of the Saviour. It was his to trace the spirit of the boundless and the eternal, faintly breathing in every part of the mystic circle of superstition, unquenched even amidst the most barbarous rites of savage tribes, and in all the cold and beautiful shapes of Grecian mould. The inward soul of every religious system, the philosophical spirit of all history, the deep secrets of the human heart, when grandest or most wayward, were his to search out and develop." [1]

What a grand theatre for the development of mind, for healthy instruction and commanding influence, was opened by the Christian pulpit. There was no sphere equal to it in moral dignity and force. It threw into the shade the theatre and the forum. And in times when printing was unknown, it was almost the only way by which the people could be taught. It vastly added to the power of the clergy, and gave them an influence that the old priests of paganism could never exercise. It created an entirely new power in the world, a moral power indeed, but one to which history presents no equal. The philosophers taught in their schools, they taught a few admiring pupils; but the sphere of their teachings was limited, and also the number whom they could address. The pulpit became an institution. All the Christians were required to assemble regularly for public instruction as well as worship. On every

[1] Sergeant Talford's Essays.

seventh day the people laid aside their secular duties and devoted themselves to religious improvement.   The pulpit gave
power to the Sabbath ; and what an institution is the Christian
Sabbath.   To the Sabbath and to public preaching, Christendom owes more than to all other sources of moral elevation
combined.   It is true that the Jewish synagogue furnished a
model to the church ; but the Levitical race claimed no peculiar
sanctity, and discharged no friendly office beyond the precincts
of the temple.   In the synagogue the people assembled to
pray, or to hear the Scriptures read and expounded, not to receive religious instruction.   The Jewish religion was as full of
ceremonials as the pagan, and the intellectual part of it was
confined to the lawyers, to the rabbinical hierarchy.   But the
preaching of the great doctrines of Christianity was made a
peculiarly sacred office, and given to a class of men who
avoided all secular pursuits.   The Christian priest was the recognized head of the society which he taught and controlled.
In process of time, he became a great dignitary, controlling
various interests, but his first mission was to preach, and his
first theme was the crucified Saviour.   He ascended the pulpit
every week as an authorized as well as a sacred teacher
and, in the illustration of his subjects, he was allowed great
latitude in which to roam.   It is not easy to appreciate what a
difference there was between pagan and Christian communities
from the rise of this new power, and we might also say institution, since the pulpit and the Sabbath are interlinked and associated together.   Whatever the world has gained by the Sabbath, that gain is intensified and increased vastly by public teaching.   It placed the Christian as far beyond the Jew, as the Jew
was before beyond the pagan.   It also created a sacerdotal
caste.   The people may have had the privilege of pouring out
their hearts before the brethren, and in speaking for their edification, but all the members were not fitted for the secular office
of teachers.   Christianity claims the faculties of knowledge, as
well as those of feeling.   Teaching was early felt to be a great
gift ; implying not only superior knowledge, but superior wisdom and grace.   Only a few possessed the precious charisma
to address profitably the assembled people, χάρισμα διδασκαλίας,
and those few became the appointed guides of the Christian

flocks, *ὑδασκαλοί.* Other officers of the new communities shared with them the administration, but the teacher was the highest officer, and he became gradually the presbyter, whose peculiar function it was to discourse to the people on the great themes which it was their duty to learn. And even after the presbyter became a bishop, it was his chief office to teach publicly, even as late as the fourth and fifth centuries. Leo and Gregory, the great bishops of Rome, were eloquent preachers.

Thus the church gradually claimed the great prerogative of eloquence. Eloquence was not born in the church, but it was sanctified, and set apart, and appropriated to a thousand new purposes, and especially identified with the public teaching of the people. The great mysteries, the profound doctrines, the suggestive truths, the touching histories, the practical duties of Christianity were seized and enforced by the public teacher; and eloquence appeared in the sermon. In pagan ages, eloquence was confined to the forum or the senate chamber, and was directed entirely into secular channels. It was always highly esteemed as the birthright of genius, an inspiration like poetry, rather than an art to be acquired. But it was not always the handmaid of poetry and music; it was brought down to earth for practical purposes, and employed chiefly in defending criminals, or procuring the passage of laws, or stimulating the leaders of society to important acts. The gift of tongue was reserved for rhetoricians, lawyers, politicians, philosophers, not for priests, who were intercessors with the Divine. Now Christianity adopted all the arts of eloquence, and enriched them, and applied them to a variety of new subjects. She carried away in triumph the brightest ornament of the pagan schools, and placed it in the hands of her chosen ministers. The pulpit soon began to rival the forum in the displays of a heaven-born art, which was now consecrated to far loftier purposes than those to which it had been applied. As public instruction became more and more learned, it also became more and more eloquent, for the preacher had opportunity, subject, audience, motive, all of which are required for great perfection in public speaking. He assembled a living congregation at stated intervals; he had the range of all those lofty inquiries which entrance the soul; and he had souls to save, the greatest conceivable motive to a good man who realizes the truths of the Gospel. All human enterprises and schemes become ultimately insipid to a man who has no lofty view of benefitting mankind, or his family, or his friend. We were made to do good. Take away this stimulus, and energy itself languishes and droops. There is no object in life to a seeker of pleasure or gain, when once the passion is gratified. What object of pity so melancholy as a man worn out with egotistical excitements, and incapable of being amused. But he who labors for the good of others is never ennuied. The benevolent physician, the patriotic statesman, the conscientious lawyer, the enthusiastic teacher, the dreaming author, all work and toil in weary labors, with the hope of being useful to the bodies, or the intellects, or the minds of the people. This is the great condition of happiness. There is an excitement in gambling as in pleasure, in money-making as in money-spending, but it wears out, or exhausts the noble faculties, and ends in ennui or self-reproach and bitter disappointment. It is not the condition of our nature, which was made to be useful, to seek the good of others. They are the happiest and most esteemed who have this good constantly at heart. There can be no unhappiness to a man absorbed in doing good. He may be poor and persecuted like Socrates; he may walk barefooted, and have domestic griefs, and be deprived of his comforts, but he is serene, for the soul triumphs over the body. Now what motive so grand as to save the immortal part of man. This desire filled the ancient Christian orator with a preternatural enthusiasm, as well as gave to him an unlimited power, and an imposing dignity. He was the most happy of mortals when led to the blazing fire of his persecutors, and he was the most august. The feeling that he was kindling a fire which should never be quenched, even that which was to burn up all the wicked idols of an idolatrous generation, unloosed his tongue and animated his features. The most striking examples of seraphic joy, of a sort of divine beauty playing upon the features, are among orators. In animated conversation a person ordinarily homely, like Madame de Stael, becomes beautiful and impressive. But in the pulpit, when the sacred orator is moving a congregation with the fears and hopes of another world, there is a majesty in his beauty which is nowhere else so fully seen.   There is no eloquence like that of the pulpit, when the preacher is gifted and in earnest.   Greece had her Pericles and Demosthenes, and Rome her Hortensius and Cicero.   Many other great orators we could mention.   But when Greece and Rome had an intellectual existence such as that to which our modern times furnish no parallel, in our absorbing pursuit of pleasure and gain, and amid the wealth of mechanical inventions, there were, even in those classic lands, but few orators whose names have descended to our times, while, in the church, in a degenerated period, when literature and science were nearly extinct, there were a greater number of Christian orators than what classic antiquity furnished.   Yea, in those dark and miserable ages which succeeded the fall of the Roman Empire, there were in every land remarkable pulpit orators, like those who fanned the Crusades.   There was no eloquence in the Middle Ages outside the church.   Bernard exercised a far greater moral power than Cicero in the fulness of his fame.   And in our modern times, what orators have arisen like those whom the Reformation produced, both in the Roman Catholic church, and among the numerous sects which protested against her?   What orator has Germany given birth to equal in fame to Luther?   What orator in France has reached the celebrity of Bossuet, or Bourdaloue or Massillon?   Even amid all the excitements attending the change of government, who have had the power on the people like a Lacordiaire or Monod?   In England, the great orators have been preachers, with a very few exceptions; and these men would have been still greater in the arts of public speaking had they been trained in the church. In our day, we have seen great orators in secular life, but they yield in fascination either to those who are accustomed to speak from the sacred desk, or to those whose training has been clerical, like many of our popular lecturers.   Nothing ever opened such an arena of eloquence as the preaching of the Gospel, either in the ancient, the mediæval, or the modern world, not merely from the grandeur and importance of the themes discussed, but also from the number of the speakers.   In a legislative assembly, where all are supposed to be able to address an audience, and some are expected to be eloquent, only two or three can be

heard in a day.   Only some twenty or thirty able speeches are
delivered in Congress or Parliament in a whole session; but in
England, or the United States, some thirty thousand preachers
are speaking at the same time; many of whom are far more
gifted, learned, and brilliant than any found in the great councils of the nation. Nor is this eloquence confined to the Protestant church; it exists also in the Roman Catholic in every land.
There are no more earnest and inspiring orators than in Italy
or France. Even in rude and unlettered and remote districts,
we often hear specimens of eloquence which would be wonderful in capitals.   What chance has the bar, in a large
city, compared with the pulpit, for the display of eloquence?
Probably there are more eloquent addresses delivered every
Sunday from the various pulpits of Christendom than were
pronounced by all the orators of Greece during the whole
period of her political existence.   Doubtless there are more
touching and effective appeals made to the popular heart every
Sunday in every Christian land, than are made during the
whole year beside on subjects essentially secular.   Then what
an impulse has pulpit oratory given to objects of a strictly philanthropic character.   The church has been the nurse and
mother of all schemes of benevolence since it was organized.
It is itself a great philanthropic institution, binding up the
wounds of the prisoner, relieving the distressed, and stimulating great enterprises. For all of this, the pulpit has been
called upon, and has lent its aid; so that the world has been
more indebted to the eloquence of divines than to any other
source.   Who can calculate the moral force of one hundred and
fifty thousand to two hundred thousand Christian preachers in
a world like ours, most of whom are arrayed on the side of
morality and learning. It may be said that these benefits may
more properly be considered to flow from Christianity as revealed in the Bible, that the Bible is the cause of all this
great impulse to civilization. We do not object to such an interpretation; nevertheless in specifying the influence of the church,
even before the empire fell, the creation of pulpit eloquence
should be mentioned, since this has contributed so much to the
moral elevation of Christendom. Christianity would be shorn
of half her triumphs were it not for the public preaching of her

truths.   Paganism had no public teachers who regularly taught the people, and stimulated their noblest energies.   It was a new institution, these Sabbath day exercises, and has had an inconceivable influence on the progress and condition of the race.   The power of the Gospel was indeed the main and primary cause, but the church must have the credit of appropriating what was most prized in the intellectual centres of antiquity, and giving to it a new direction.   Christian oratory is also an interesting subject to present in merely its artistical relations.   Its vast influence no one can question.

But great Christian orators did not arise until it was safe to worship God in consecrated churches.   So long as the Christians assembled in upper chambers, or retired places, we do not read of remarkable preachers, whose sermons have come down to us.   We have apologies and letters and dissertations instead. In times of persecution, it is not to be supposed that men of genius would be allowed by the goverment, or the still dominant and fashionable pagan classes, to stimulate the religious passions of the people except in secret conventicles.   We have no record of churches generally attended, and unguarded, so that all could enter, for several generations after the apostolic age, not until the reign of. Alexander Severus in the third century, and then they were of modest and unpretending form. There was not indeed much scope for oratory of any description under the emperors.   There were lawyers rather than advovocates.   The jealousy of the government was fatal to all bold and lofty flights.   Cicero would not have been permitted in the reign of Tiberius or Nero, to give vent to his passionate invectives against bad men or bad laws as in the times of the republic.   Popular eloquence is scarcely possible under any despotic government, when it is confined to secular subjects.   It is only among the clergy that it can thrive, and only by them that it can be extensively cultivated.   The highest flights of pagan oratory that remain to us are adulatory panegyrics of the emperors.   Rhetoric may have been taught as an art, but was not allowed to soar to grand themes, and was confined to trite subjects, and subtle questions, and ancient characters.   There was no emotion, no strong appeal to passions, no lofty injunction of duties.   The pagan orator found only a listless and criti-

cal audience of brother scholars, who extinguished all enthusiasm, but the Christian preacher was cheered by the earnest
looks of a breathless crowd, who hung upon his lips with trans-
porting ardor, and who even interrupted his address by warm
acclamations.

The eager listeners of Chrysostom, even in listless and volup-
tious Antioch, crowded around his pulpit in solemn earnestness
to hear him discourse, and with the authority of an ambassador
from heaven, not with tricks of rhetoric, but simply and ur-
gently on the majesty of God, on the littleness of man, on his
degeneracy and obduracy, on his natural inclination to sin, on
the power of Satan as a permitted agent of evil, on the certainty of future retribution, on the mercy, the mission and the character of Christ, on his life and death, on his glorious resurrection, on the redemption which he made for man, and on the
ineffable glories of the world to come.   These truths, so solemn
and so grand, he preached with singular boldness and earnestness, illustrating them by his vast erudition, and enlivening
them with an inexhaustible fund of metaphor and images, and
with the power of depicting the passions with dramatic skill.
He was a master of pulpit art, if sacred eloquence does not disclaim this term, the last representation of the Greek mind, but
softened and expanded by the influence of the Gospel.   For
twelve years he preached at Antioch, the oracle of all classes of
people, the friend of the rich and the protector of the poor.
And these were the years of his truest glory.   His fame as an
orator extended far and near, even to the uttermost parts of the
empire.   Senators, generals, statesmen, princes came to witness
his power, and went away to extol his genius.   He had an immense eclat, more so than any churchman of his age.   And
when to all his great gifts and graces, he added the virtues of
a humble Christian, parting with a splendid patrimony to feed
the poor and clothe the naked, utterly disdainful of riches, except as a means of doing good, living abstemiously and most
sedulously shunning the society of his idolators, indefatigable in
his labors, rebuking sin wherever it was to be found, incorrup-
tible, befriending the learned and the unfortunate, a man acquainted with grief, and isolated by his great superiority, pensive, gentle, sincere, his influence extended beyond the sphere

of pulpit eloquence. He was beloved by the people and had a great ascendency over their minds. There are few instances in that troubled age more impressive than when he shielded Antioch from the vengeance of the angry Theodosius. That turbulent and dissipated city had been disgraced by a mob which insulted the authority of the emperor, and maltreated his officers. His anger knew no bounds, and he threatened the same punishment he afterwards inflicted upon Thessalonica, and for a less offence. The people abandoned themselves to fear ; the theatres were closed ; the schools were shut ; the prisons were filled ; the citizens were scourged, and the whole city wore the appearance of grief and desolation. Chrysostom improved the occasion to preach to the people, and every day ascended his pulpit, and there gathered around him the whole city, timid and repentant. The whole city was a church. The entire day was consumed with public prayers. The anger of Theodosius was appeased, and the city was saved. It was a sublime spectacle to see this simple priest, unclothed even with episcopal functions, surrounded for weeks with the population of a great city, ready to do whatever he suggested, and looking to him as a temporal deliverer, as well as a spiritual guide.

So soon as there was freedom of public worship great orators arose who had a more complete control of the minds of their hearers than in the best days of Athens or Rome. "Whenever the oratory of the pulpit coincided with human passion, it was irresistible ; and sometimes when it encountered it, it might extort an unwilling triumph. When it appealed to faction, to ferocity, to sectarian animosity, it swept away its audience, like a torrent, to any violence or madness to which it aimed ; when to virtue, to piety, to peace, it at times subdued the most refractory, and received the homage of devout obedience." The bishop reserved this great power to himself, and in general a promising orator was elevated to the episcopal rank like Chrysostom and Augustine. And this new moral power was ever at work, so soon as Christianity was tolerated, with increasing energy in all parts of the empire. Whatever the superstition, or popular ignorance, or vices of the times, yet, from the pulpit were ever heard the tones of eloquence reminding the people of providence, of redemption, of immortality, and of retribution.

Man was perpetually taught to feel that he was an accountable and immortal being, destined to a noble existence. And not merely the more solemn and abstruse points of faith were presented, but questions bearing upon morality and social life. No part of Christian literature so vividly reflects the times as the sermons of Basil, of Chrysostom, of Augustine, and of Ambrose.

As the bishop of the early church assumed the office of public teacher, so eloquence became his highest claim on the popular mind. The most of the eminent Christian orators were bishops, even when prelatic power had reached a lofty eminence. Chrysostom, when patriarch of the East, still preached every Sunday as he did at Antioch. Gregory when pope ascended the pulpit regularly.

The eminent bishops and fathers of the church are immortal for different gifts and excellences. Though every great orator was a bishop, yet every great bishop was not an orator. Some are identified with the discipline of the church like Cyprian, some with doctrinal controversies like Athanasius, some with monastic institutions like Basil, some with prelatic authority like Ambrose, some with Christian literature like Jerome. Origen, though not a bishop, is known for his wonderful learning in the interpretation of the Scriptures, Tertullian for his views of Christian life, Augustine for his system of theology, Leo for his efforts to build up a theocratic power in Rome.

But all of these yielded to the Christian orators for immediate influence. Sacred eloquence became an art, and enforced the grand idea, still recognized, that the world was to be saved by the " foolishness of preaching." And this art and this idea have gained ground with every succeeding century, and will continue, more and more, to be one of the great powers of the world till Christianity shall complete her triumphs.

Again, who can estimate the debt which civilization, in its largest and most comprehensive sense, owes to the fathers of the early church, in the elaboration of Christian doctrine. They found the heathen world enslaved by a certain class of most degrading notions of God, of deity, of goodness, of the future, of rewards and punishments. Indeed its opinions were wrong and demoralizing in almost every pulpit pertaining to the spiritual relations of man. They met the wants of their times by seizing on the great radical principles of Christianity, which most directly opposed these demoralizing ideas, and by giving them the prominence which was needed. Moreover, in the church itself, opinions were from time to time broached, so intimately allied with pagan philosophies and oriental theogonies, that the faith of Christians was in danger of being subverted. The Scriptures were indeed recognized to contain all that is essential in Christian truth to know; but they still allowed great latitude of belief, and contradictory creeds were drawn from the same great authority. If the Bible was to be the salvation of man, or the great thesaurus of religious truth, it was necessary to systematize and generalize its great doctrines, both to oppose dangerous heathen customs and heretical opinions in the church itself. And more even than this, to set forth a standard of faith for all the ages which were to come: not an arbitrary system of dogmas, but those which the Scriptures most directly and emphatically recognized. Christian life had been set forth by the martyrs in the various forms of teaching, in the worship of God, in the exercise of those virtues and graces which Christ had enjoined, in benevolence, in charity, in faith, in prayer, in patience, in the different relations of social life, in the sacraments, in the fasts and festivals, in the occupations which might be profitably and honorably carried on. But Christianity affected thought and knowledge as well as external relations. It did not declare a rigid system of doctrines when first promulgated. This was to be developed when the necessity required it. For two centuries there were but few creeds, and these very simple and comprehensive. Speculation had not then entered the ranks, nor the pagan spirit of philosophy. There was great unity of belief, and this centred around Christ as the Redeemer and Saviour of the world. But, in process of time, Christianity was forced to contend with Judaism, with Orientalism, and with Greek speculation, as these entered into the church itself, and were more or less embraced by its members. With downright paganism there was a constant battle, but in this battle all ranks of Christians were united together. They were not distracted by any controversies whether idolatry should be or should not be tolerated. But when Gnostic principles were embraced by good men, those which, for instance, entered into monastic or ascetic life, it was necessary that some great genius should arise and expose their oriental origin, and lay down the Christian law definitely on that point. So when Manichæism, and Arianism, and other heretical opinions, were defended and embraced by the Christians themselves, the fathers who took the side of orthodoxy in the great controversies which arose, rendered important services to all subsequent generations, since never, probably, were those subtle questions pertaining to the trinity, and the human nature of Christ, and predestination and other kindred topics, discussed with so much acumen and breadth. They occupied the thoughts of the whole age, and emperors entered into the debates on theological questions with an interest exceeding that of the worldly matters which claimed their peculiar attention. It is not easy for Christians of this age, when all the great doctrines of faith are settled, to appreciate the prodigious excitement which their discussion called forth in the times of Athanasius and Augustine. The whole intellect of the age was devoted to theological inquiries. Everybody talked about them, and they were the common theme on all public occasions. If discussions of subjects which once had such universal fascination can never return again, if they are passed like Olympic games, or the discussions of Athenian schools of philosophy, or the sports of the Coliseum, or the oracles of Dodona, or the bulls of mediæval Popes, or the contests of the tournament, or the "field of the cloth of gold," they still have a historical charm, and point to the great stepping-stones of human progress. If they are really grand and important ideas, which they claimed to be, they will continue to move the most distant generations. If they are merely dialectical deductions, they are among the profoundest efforts of reason in the Christian schools of philosophy.

When Christianity was established as a life among her professors, and hence became a great power in the world, there was necessarily a great conflict of opinions arising from the Jewish and Ooriental Greek elements of culture which became united with the new faith. The religious tendencies of the old world became mixed up with the inner developments of Christian life so as to undermine the foundations of Christian faith. The Greek and Oriental mind seized upon one sided views of the truth as it was in Jesus, and attempted to harmonize this with the simple Scriptures. In the chaotic state of all opinions attending the breaking up of old systems and their conflict with the new, crude doctrines were advanced and entertained which concealed the simplicity of truth. Thus heresies arose at an early period and threatened serious consequences. Only minds of great clearness and comprehensive grasp detected the subtle, though popular errors which were gradually creeping in, and which were often advanced by men of learning and culture. Even some of the great lights of the church embraced these dangerous views, like Tertullian in his alliance with the Montanists, and Origen in his allegorical teachings. The clear sighted and practical guides of the church could not see these innovations without alarm and disquiet, and lifted up their voices against them. Controversies arose, and were carried on with a rancour and bitterness, as well as earnestness, which were a great scandal to the church. Yet what would have become of the church if the more orthodox of the fathers had not met the new danger at the outset? And it frequently happened that the rising heresies were advocated by men of great purity of character and popular eloquence. The early heretics were generally men of blameless lives, severe intellectual culture and extensive influence like Origen, Arius and Sabellius. But the greater the authorities the more imminent the danger.

We can not, of course, enter into the controversies through which the church elaborated the system of doctrines now generally received, nor describe those great men who gave such dignity to theological inquiries. Clement was raised up to combat the Gnostics, Athanasius to head off the alarming spread of Arianism, and Augustine to proclaim the efficacy of divine grace against the Pelagians. The treatises of these men and of other great lights on the trinity, on the incarnation, and on original sin had as great an influence on the thinking of the age and of succeeding ages, as the speculations of Plato, or the syllogisms of Thomas Aquinas, or the theories of Kepler, or the expositions of Bacon, or the deductions of Newton, or the dissertations of Burke, or the severe irony of Pascal. They did not create revolutions, since they did not labor to overturn, but they stimulated the human faculties, and conserved the most valued knowledge. Their definite opinions became the standard of faith among the eastern Christians, and were handed down to the Germanic barbarians. They were adopted by the Catholic church, and preserved unity of belief in ages of turbulence and superstition. One of the great recognized causes of modern civilization was the establishment of universities. In these the great questions which the fathers started and elaborated were discussed with renewed acumen. Had there been no Origen, or Tertullian, or Augustine, there would have been no Anselm, or Abelard, or Erigena. The speculations and inquiries of the Alexandrian divines controlled the thinking of Europe for one thousand years, and gave that intensely theological character to the literature of the Middle Ages, directing the genius of Dante as well as that of Bernard. Their influence on Calvin was as´marked as on Bossuet. Pagan philosophy had no charm like the great verities of the Christian faith. Augustine and Athanasius threw Plato and Aristotle into the shade. Nothing more preëminently marked the great divines which the Reformation produced, than the discussion of the questions which the fathers had systematized and taught. Nor was the interest confined to divines. Louis XIV. discussed free will and predestination with Racine and Fenelon, even as the courtiers of Louis XV. discussed probabilities and mental reservations. And in New England, at Puritan firesides, the passing stranger in the olden times, when religion was a life, entered into theological discussions with as much zest as he now would describe the fluctuations of stocks or passing vanities of crinoline and hair dyes. Nor is it one of the best signs of this material age that the interest in the great questions which tasked the intellects of our fathers is passing away. But there is a mighty permanence in great ideas, and the time, we trust, will come again when indestructible certitudes will receive more attention than either politics or fashions.

The influence of the fathers is equally seen in the music and poetry which have come down from their times. The church succeeded to an inheritance of religious lyrics unrivalled in the history of literature. The *Magnificat* and the *Nunc dimittis* were sung from the earliest Christian ages.   The streets of the Eastern cities echoed to the seductive strains of Arius and Chrysostom.   Flavian and Diodorus introduced at Antioch the antiphonal chant, which, improved by Ambrose, and still more by Gregory, became the joy of blessed saints in those turbulent ages, when singing in the choir was the amusement, as well as the duty of a large portion of religious people.   So numerous were the hymns of Ambrose, Hilary, Augustine and others, that they became the popular literature of centuries, and still form the most beautiful part of the service of the Catholic church.   Who can estimate the influence of hymns which have been sung for fifty successive generations?   What a charm is still attached to the mediæval chants?   The poetry of the early church is preserved in those sacred anthems.   They inspired the barbarians with enthusiasm, even as they had kindled the rapture of earlier Christians in the church of Milan.   The lyrical poets are immortal, and exert a wide-spread influence. The fervent stanzas of Watts, of Steele, of Wesley, of Heber, are sung from generation to generation.   The hymns of Luther are among the most valued of his various works. " From Greenland's icy mountains," that sacred lyric, shall live as long as the " Elegy in a Country Church-yard," or the " Cotter's Saturday Night," yea, shall survive the " Night Thoughts," and the " Course of Time."   There is nothing in Grecian or Roman poetry that fills the place of the psalmody of the early church.   The songs of Ambrose were his richest legacy to triumphant barbarians, consoling the monk in his dreary cell, and the peasant on his vine-clad hills, speaking the sentiment of a universal creed, and consecrating the most tender recollections.   So that Christian literature, in its varied aspects, its exegesis, its sermons, its creeds and its psalmody, if not equal in artistic merit to the classical productions of antiquity, have had an immeasurable influence on human thought and life, not in the Roman world merely, but in all subsequent ages.

But the great truths which the fathers proclaimed in reference to the moral and social relations of society are still more remarkable in their subsequent influence.

The great idea of Christian equality struck at the root of that great system of slavery which was one of the main causes of the ruin of the empire.   Christianity did not break up slavery; it might never have annihilated it under a Roman rule, but it protested against it so soon as it was clothed with secular power.   As in the sight of heaven there is no distinction of persons, so the idea of social equality gained ground as the relations of Christianity to practical life were understood.   The abolition of slavery, and the general amelioration of the other social evils of life, are all a logical sequence from the doctrine of Christian equality, that God made of one blood all the nations of the earth, that they are equally precious in his sight, and have equal claims to the happiness of heaven.   All theories of human rights radiate from, and centre around, this consoling doctrine.   That we are born free and equal may not, practically, be strictly true; but that the relations of society ought to be viewed as they are regarded in the Scriptures, which reveal the dignity of the soul and its glorious destinies, can not be questioned; so that oppression of man by man, and injustice, and unequal laws militate with one of the great fundamental revelations of God.   Impress Christian equality on the mind of man, and social equality follows as a matter of course.   The slave was recognized to be a man, a person, and not a thing.   Whenever he sat down, as he did once a week, beside his master, in the adoration of a common Lord, the ignominy of his hard condition was removed, even if his obligations to obedience were not abrogated.   As a future citizen of heaven, his importance on the earth was more and more recognized, until his fetters were gradually removed.

From the day when Christian equality was declared, the foundations of slavery were assailed, and the progress of freedom has kept pace with Christian civilization, although the apostles did not directly denounce the bondage that disgraced the ancient world.   It was something to declare the principles which, logically carried out, would ultimately subvert the evil, for no evil can stand forever which is in opposition to logical deductions from the truths of Christianity.   Moral philosophy is as much a series of logical deductions from the doctrine of loving our neighbor as ourself as that great network of theological systems which Augustine and Calvin elaborated from the majesty and sovereignty of God.   Those distinctions which Christ removed by his Gospel of universal brotherhood can never return or coexist with the progress of the truth. A vast social revolution began when the eternal destinies of the slave were announced. It will not end with the mere annihilation of slavery as an institution; it will affect the relations of the poor and the rich, the unlucky and the prosperous in every Christian country until justice and love become dominant principles. What a stride from Roman slavery to mediæval serfdom! How benignant the attitude of the church, in all ages, to the poor man! The son of a peasant becomes a priest, and rises, in the Christian hierarchy, to become a ruler of the world. There was no way for a poor peasant boy to rise in the Middle Ages, except in the church. He attracts the notice of some beneficent monk; he is educated in the cloister; he becomes a venerated brother, an abbot, perhaps a bishop or a pope. Had he remained in service to a feudal lord, he never could have risen above his original rank. The church raises him from slavery, and puts upon his brow her seal, and in his hands the thunderbolts of spiritual power, thus giving him dignity and consideration and independence. Rising, as the clergy did in the Middle Ages, in all ages, from the lower and middle classes, they became as much opposed to slavery as they were to war. It was thus in the bosom of the church that liberty was sheltered and nourished. Nor has the church ever forgotten her mission to the poor, or sympathized, as a whole, with the usurpations of kings. She may have aimed at dominion, like Hildebrand and Innocent III., but it was spiritual domination, control of the mind of the world. But she ever sympathized with oppressed classes, like Becket, even as he defied the temporal weapons of Henry II. The Jesuits even respected the dignity of the poor. Their errors were trust in machinery and unbounded ambition, but they labored in their best ages for the good of the people. And in our times, the most consistent and uncompromising foes of despotism and slavery are in the ranks of the church. The clergy have been made, it is true, occasionally, the tools of despotism, and have been absurdly conservative of their own privileges, but, on the whole, have ever lifted up their voices in defence of those who are ground down.

The elevation of woman, too, has been caused by the doctrine of the equality of the sexes which Christianity revealed; not " woman's rights " as interpreted by infidels; not the ignoring of woman's destiny of subservience to man, as declared in the garden of Eden and by St. Paul, but her glorious nature which fits her for the companionship of man.   Heathendom reduces her to slavery, dependence and vanity.   Christianity elevates her by developing her social and moral excellences, her more delicate nature, her elevation of soul, her sympathy with sorrow, her tender and gracious aid.   The elevation of woman did not come from the natural traits of Germanic barbarians, but from Christianity.   Chivalry owes its bewitching graces to the influence of Christian ideas.   Clemency and magnanimity, gentleness and sympathy, did not spring from German forests, but the teachings of the clergy.   Veneration for woman was the work of the church, not of pagan civilization or Teutonic simplicity.   Even in the latter days of the Empire woman arose immeasurably in popular estimation, and showed virtues such as Cornelia and Volumnia never blazed in.   The equality of the sexes was acknowledged by Jerome when he devoted himself to the education of Roman matrons, and received from the hand of Paula the means of support while he labored in his cell at Bethlehem.   How much more influential was Fabiola and Marcella than Aspasia or Phryne.   It was woman who converted barbaric kings, and reigned, not by personal charms, like Eastern beauties, but by the solid virtues of the heart.   Woman never occupied so proud a position in an ancient palace as in a feudal castle.   When Paula visited the East, she was welcomed by Christian bishops, and the proconsul of Palestine surrendered his own palace for her reception, not because she was high in rank, but because her virtues had gone forth to all the world, and when she died, a great number of the most noted people followed her body to the grave with sighs and sobs.   The sufferings of the female martyrs are the most pathetic exhibitions of moral greatness in the history of the early church.   And in the Middle Ages, whatever is most truly glorious or beautiful can be traced to the agency of woman.   Is a town to be spared for a revolt, or a grievous tax remitted, it is a Godiva who intercedes and prevails.   Is an imperious priest to be opposed, it is an Ethelgiva who alone dares to confront him even in the king's palace.   It is Ethelburga, not Ina, who reigns among the Saxons, not because the king is weak, but his wife is wiser than he.   A mere peasant girl, inspired with the sentiment of patriotism, delivers a whole nation, dejected and disheartened, for such was Joan of Arc.   Bertha, the slighted wife of Henry, crosses the Alps in the dead of winter, with her excommunicated lord, to remove the curse which deprived him of the allegiance of his subjects.   Anne, Countess of Warwick, dresses herself like a cook maid to elude the visits of a royal duke, and Ebba, abbess of Coldingham, cuts off her nose to render herself unattractive to the soldiers who ravage her lands. Philippa, the wife of the great Edward, intercedes for the inhabitants of Calais, and the town is spared.

The feudal woman gained respect and veneration because she had the moral qualities which Christianity developed.   If she entered with eagerness into the pleasures of the chase or the honor of the banquet, if she listened with enthusiasm to the minstrel's lay and the crusader's tale, her real glory was her purity of character and unsullied fame.   In ancient Rome men were driven to the circus and the theatre for amusement and for solace, but among the Teutonic races, when converted to Christianity, rough warriors associated with woman without seductive pleasure to disarm her.   It was not riches, nor elegance of manners, nor luxurious habits, nor exemption from stern and laborious duties which gave fascination to the Christian woman of the Middle Ages.   It was her sympathy, her fidelity, her courage, her simplicity, her virtues, her noble self-respect, which made her a helpmeet and a guide.   She was always found to intercede for the unfortunate, and willing to endure suffering.   She bound up the wounds of prisoners, and never turned the hungry from her door.   And then how lofty and beautiful her religious life.   History points with pride to the religious transports and spiritual elevation of Catharine of Siluria, of Margaret of Anjou, of Gertrude of Saxony, of Theresa of Spain, of Elizabeth of Hungary, of Isabel of France, of Edith of England.   How consecrated were the labors of woman amid feudal strife and violence.   Whence could have arisen such a general worship of the Virgin Mary had not her beatific loveliness been reflected in the lives of the women whom

Christianity had elevated? In the French language she was worshipped under the feudal title of Notre Dame, and chivalrous devotion to the female sex culminated in the reverence which belongs to the Queen of Heaven. And hence the qualities ascribed to her, of Virgo Fidelis, Mater Castissima, Consolatrix Afflictorum, were those to which all lofty women were exhorted to aspire. The elevation of woman kept pace with the extension of Christianity. Veneration for her did not arise until she showed the virtues of a Monica and a Nonna, but these virtues were the fruit of Christian ideas alone.

We might mention other ideas which have entered into our modern institutions, such as pertain to education, philanthropy, and missionary zeal. The idea of the church itself, of an esoteric band of Christians amid the temptations of the world, bound together by rules of discipline as well as communion of soul, is full of grandeur and beauty. And the unity of this church is a sublime conception, on which the whole spiritual power of the Popes rested when they attempted to rule in peace and on the principles of eternal love. However perverted the idea of the unity of the church became in the Middle Ages, still who can deny that it was the mission of the church to create a spiritual power based on the hopes and fears of a future life? The idea of a theocracy forms a prominent part of the polity of Calvin, as of Hildebrand himself. It is the basis of his legislation. He maintained it long concealed in the bosom of the primitive church, and it was gradually unfolded, though in a corrupt form, by the Popes, the worthiest of whom kept the idea of a divine government continually in view, and pursued it with a clear knowledge of its consequences. And those familiar with the lofty schemes of Leo and Gregory, will appreciate their efforts in raising up a power which should be supreme in barbarous ages, and preserve what was most to be valued of the old civilization. The autocrat of Geneva clung to the necessity of a spiritual religion, and aimed to realize that which the Middle Ages sought, and sought in vain, that the church must always remain the mother of spiritual principles, while the state should be the arm by which those principles should be enforced. Like Hildebrand, he would, if possible, have hurled the terrible weapon of excommunication. In cutting men off from the fold, he would also have cut them off from the higher privileges of society.   He may have carried his views too far, but they were founded on the idea of a church against which the gates of hell could not prevail.   Who can estimate the immeasurable influence of such an idea, which, however perverted, will ever be recognized as one of the great agencies of the world?   A church without a spiritual power, is inconceivable ; nor can it pass away, even before the material tendencies of a proud and rationalistic civilization.   It will assert its dignity when thrones and principalities shall crumble in the dust.

Such are among the chief ideas which the fathers taught, and which have entered even into the modern institutions of society, and form the peculiar glory of our civilization. When we remember this, we feel that the church has performed no mean mission, even if it did not save the Roman Empire.   The glory of warriors, of statesmen, of artists, of philosophers, of legislators, and of men of science and literature in the ancient world, still shines, and no one would dim it, or hide it from the admiration of mankind.   But the purer effulgence of the great lights of the church eclipses it all, and will shine brighter and brighter, until the seed of the woman shall bruise the serpent's head.   This is the true sun which shall dissipate the shadows of superstition and ignorance that cover so great a portion of the earth, and that shall bring society into a healthful glow of unity and love.

ARTICLE VII.

PULPIT ORATORY.

[INTRODUCTORY NOTE. The author of the following article was born in Georgia, Vt., a little town on Lake Champlain, which has furnished no less than eight ministers of the Gospel. His mother, a devotedly pious woman, died in his early life ; but she had dedicated her son to God, and in due time, he became a new creature in Christ Jesus. He fitted for college in his native town at a country academy ; entered and passed through the University of Vermont, without being affected by religious influences. He studied law and was admitted to the bar ; but there was still no change in his purpose of life. In the spring of 1858, he returned for a few weeks to St. Albans, Vt., where he had commenced his professional study, without any especial reason for doing so. But God had a reason. It was during a season of revival. Daily morning prayer-meetings were held. He attended them. On a day set apart by the church for fasting and prayer, his pastor took him by the arm and walked with him to his house. To the inquiry, "Are you not more than usually interested on the subject of religion?" he replied, "No; but I have shed more tears to-day, than before since my mother died." His pastor urged him to go home to his room, and spend several hours with his Bible and in prayer. He agreed to do so. In the evening he came to his pastor's study. He had encountered fearful opposition. All his infidel readings, in which he had largely indulged in college, came flooding in upon his memory. He asked himself, "Is there any God?" The next morning in accordance with his wishes, his pastor requested prayers for him It had been his pastor's purpose to word the request thus: "A young man motherless, dedicated to God in infancy and liberally educated, asks prayers for himself. Let us pray that he may become a minister of the Gospel." But the last sentence was accidentally omitted. On afterwards learning of this omission, Mr. Clark regarded it as entirely providential; for he, then, had never dreamed of giving up his chosen profession, and it might have given him a fatal shock, had it been suggested. In a few days, the controversy was settled. He at once decided to go to Andover Theological Seminary, where he finished his course in Aug. 1861. Having been early taught the Catechism, he naturally adopted thorough theological views. He soon received a call from the Congregational church in St. Johnsbury Centre, Vt., where, having been united in marriage to Miss Abby Fairchild of St. Albans, he labored with great fidelity and favor for about two years, when an affectionate people were called to follow him to the grave. He was decided and fearless in his opinions, direct and earnest in his style, and energetic in his delivery; a workman that needed not to be ashamed. His preaching was more and more upon heavenly things, was more and more fervent, till he passed away. He died April 25th, 1865, aged 30 years. The following article was prepared for an Associational exercise. It will illustrate the man, no less than disclose his views of preaching; and, as it will be seen, is upon a subject in respect to which he could speak understandingly.—EDS.]

IT is a question which has been much discussed among the writers on elocution, whether the bar, the senate or the pulpit furnishes the best field for the display of oratory. We do not propose to touch upon this question, but yet upon one which forms a branch of it. We ask, What characteristics does the pulpit, as distinguished from the other stand-points of the orator, give to the preacher's discourse? What is the nature of pulpit oratory, distinctively such?

This is to be found in the end which it is designed to produce; for an understanding of the end toward which it tends, and of the nature of the material upon which it works, gives the law for its method.

The end of preaching we believe to be the promotion of the glory of God through the sanctification of human souls. And the question is, therefore, what kind of preaching tends most to produce this end? Ascertain this, and we know, at once, what is the character of pulpit discourse, and may, if we will, compare it with the discourse peculiar to other departments of oratory.

By the instrumental agency of what kind of preaching are human souls to be sanctified? This is our problem. Sanctification is the end, and it is obvious that different theories as to the nature of this process will give rise to different styles of preaching. But there are some things about it which are above question.

Sanctification is a permanent state of the soul rather than a transient one. Sanctification is for eternity. Therefore that which is evanescent is, from the nature of things, excluded from the preacher's discourse. No changes will he seek to produce in his hearers, that are not abiding. Short-lived efforts form no part of his work. He has gained nothing, absolutely nothing, if the results of his discourse are only temporary. What of their effects is not endless is valueless.

It is in this characteristic of the effect that it is to produce, that pulpit oratory, as we conceive, differs most widely from the other departments of oratory. If only his auditory is wrought upon to pass a vote, if from the judge or the jury a verdict can be extorted, or where mere recreation is the end, as is so much the case with that nondescript, the modern lyceum-lecture or literary address, if the audience is entertained, though the very next day the mental states, which his eloquence produced, have vanished forever, though his hearers settle down permanently into the very opposite of these states, still the secular orator has triumphed. He has gained his end; a very different end from that which the sacred orator has to produce, only some one act. He seeks to produce not an act, but a life.

Other orators may therefore make use of that which can be of little or no use to him. They may use that which would be

a positive detriment to him.   There is a law of mental and
spiritual, as well as of physical action and reaction. Exaltation
is followed by depression.   So while the orator, whose end is
necessarily a transient one, may, for the purpose of attaining
that end, produce exaltation and excitement, he, whose end is
defeated by the subsequent inevitable depression, can not.   The
production of anything which can properly be called excitement is therefore a positive hindrance to the preacher in his
work.   Not that he is not to kindle emotion, not that he is not
to arouse feeling, but that he is not to do this except as they
will influence permanently the state of the soul.

The preacher, then, needs a correct psychology.   He needs
to know very thoroughly the laws of the human soul.   He
must understand what of the elements of it can be turned to
permanent uses, and what is only transient ; to what part of the
complex man his appeal must be addressed to produce abiding
effects.   To point out this for him is the business of mental
science, and to make himself familiar with the results of a true
mental science, is one of the essential prerequisites of his preparatory study.

Now all agree that what produces the most even flow of
right action is a deep and abiding sense of duty.   Only
awaken this sentiment and turn it upon your side, and the work
is done.   All are familiar with Mr. Webster's eloquent exposition of the omnipresence of duty, in the most celebrated of his
jury addresses.   Get this conviction inwrought into the soul,
that duty is omnipresent, and then enlighten that soul as to
what duty is, and you produce that permanent state of right
acting, which sanctification implies.   This, then, is the main
scope of the preacher's work.   Here is ample room and verge
enough for all his efforts.   He will accustom his hearers to the
words, " you ought," and to hear them in a way as if that
ended the matter.   " You ought " will be a finality.

This, no doubt, will make preaching somewhat didactic.   It
will be instructive, demonstrative of Christian duty, doctrinal,
inasmuch as it is out of Christian doctrines that Christian duties
grow ; and therefore doctrinal not for doctrine's own sake, but
for the sake of demonstrating the duty ; of laying a sure
foundation for it.   A calm, clear, but conclusive and forcible

proof of what the requirements of God are, which is but another phrase for the duty of man, must engross a great part of the preaching which results in the sanctification of men. And that, because the sentiment of duty is the most powerful and the most steady of the sentiments of the soul.

Men continue to act more patiently and more persistently, when moved by this sentiment, than when moved by any other. Awaken this in the soul, and you have launched the man out upon a current which will bear him onward. Your influence over him has not ceased with the sound of your words, but it abides. A gush of emotion, a flood of feeling soon flows away. Its effects were only transitory, but a conviction of duty is remorseless. It follows the man everywhere. It is in their calm, but serious and deep convictions of right and wrong, that you have any security for the permanent right conduct of men. It is the preaching that creates these, which forms intelligent, reliable, everyday Christians, as distinguished from those of revival seasons alone ; and these are not created by the same preaching which greatly awakens the emotions, or excites the feelings.

To illustrate : Will not a man whose object it is to secure the largest possible collection, to be taken up immediately at the close of his discourse, and another whose aim is habits of systematic liberality in giving, in his hearers, discourse in very different ways? But it is an effect most akin to the latter, that the preacher of the Gospel wishes to produce.

There is a place, a wide place for fervor and glow and emotion ; for, mere intellectual conviction is cold, and perhaps lifeless, but after all, as we conceive the nature of the material upon which the preacher works, these are not the chief things ; and he is ever to be on his guard that he does not make them such. There is a spiritual law analogous to that in accordance with which a fever is followed by a chill ; and it is worth some preachers' while to take care lest their desire to produce a present effect induce them to throw their hearers into a fever.

It may be thought, perhaps, that preaching directed to the unregenerate, forms an exception to this rule, if in the main it be sound. Regeneration being an instantaneous act, and differing thus from sanctification, which is a progressive one, the two, as to the method of proclaiming them, are not in the same category. To persuade a man to repent of sin, or accept offered mercy and salvation, you may address him as does the orator, urging an assembly to pass a vote ; you may kindle his emotion and awaken his feeling. You have the same scope for your eloquence. that any other speaker has who desires to work up his audience to a single act.

Probably impassioned discourse has a wider field in addressing the unconverted, than in preaching to those already of the household of faith ; and this, too, the more because they are less influenced by the sentiment of duty. But yet even here, the rule for the preacher is not that for the mere secular orator. For is it a merely transient effect that he is to produce ? For the sake of persuading a sinner to declare himself upon the Lord's side to-night, may the preacher arouse his fears, work upon his sympathies, awaken his feelings, excite his hopes, cut him loose from the control of his calm, deliberate reason, be satisfied with what he induces him to do to-night ?

What is regeneration ? Though instantaneous, it is the beginning of a new life ; not so much the conclusion of, as the entrance upon a new life. It is a part of, and the first part in sanctification itself ; and is, therefore, in the main, to be produced by the same kind of preaching. He who tries to produce regeneration, tries to produce a permanent effect, and therefore everything that can be called excitement, that is, which from the law of mind and spirit must be followed by reaction, must be avoided by the preacher. What this is, it is his business to know enough of mental philosophy to understand. Not all feeling or emotion is of this nature, but some is, and while such may be used by the secular, it can not be by the sacred orator.

See what kind of preaching Christ used towards the unconverted : " If any man come unto me, let him sit down first and count the cost." He wanted no impulsive, emotional choice, but a calm, deliberate, a consenting determination to be his. No gush of mere feeling would bring a man to him. And that preaching by the ministers of Christ, which secures a real, rather than an apparent success, however awakening of emotion it may be, must be such as to lead the sinner to action only after having converted the soul. It must reach and affect his most deep-seated and abiding convictions. He must be led up to a choice which carries with it the whole man, the calm, deliberate reason, as well as the awakened sympathies. If not, then the work must be done over again. The sinner must go over upon the Lord's side to stay ; and he can not do that, till his deliberate judgment, profound convictions, and determined purpose, as well as his quick feelings, go with him. The production of regeneration, no less than of sanctification, is the production of a permanent state, and must be grounded on what, from the nature of the soul, is most permanent in it, and that is not, so to speak, its heated part.

So fundamental is this principle in preaching, that we suggest by way of query, whether their different theories of the permanency of the state introduced by regeneration, is not enough alone to account for, and is not the real reason of, the difference which has been so long remarked between the revival scenes of different denominations of Christians? It is certainly the fact, that excitement of feeling and great emotional activity are most cultivated among those denominations which do not look upon regeneration as of necessity a permanent change, the regenerate of to-day being perhaps unregenerate again by the day after to-morrow ; and that revivals are looked upon with confidence, among the denominations that hold a different theory of regeneration, in proportion as they are characterized by an absence of all excitement, but by deep, though calm seriousness.

The preacher then will derive aid from the manuals of oratory, only as he understands what is the characteristic difference between his discourse and that of other public speakers. He is laboring for permanent effect alone, and he must never sacrifice his end to any more transient success. He will probably enough find that the law of his end rigidly forbids him not only from the adoption of some of the principles and methods, but also from the cultivation of some of the graces of orators of another class. The affording of a present pleasure, unless it contribute to future influence over his hearers, is an end aside from his great aim. That is future and permanent effects alone.

All ornamentation attracting the eye away from that which it adorns ; all flights of eloquence, admired for themselves alone, for their form rather than their substance, are for other orators than him. His discourse is like his spirit, serious, earnest, straight-forward, with no by-play among the graces, aiming with a single eye at the cultivation of an abiding and deep Christian sentiment among his hearers. There is warmth and glow and fervor, but the steady, hearty glow of a sea-coal fire. His mark is the conscience of the hearer, and travel through what path he will, this he must reach ; not the intellectual alone, but the moral through the intellectual, the conscience through the reason, action, because it is right. His success is not an audience hushed, with bated breath, lest they lose one of his eloquent words ; not the countenance lit up with admiration, or suffused with tears which he has bid magnetically to flow, but a church under the control of intelligent and steady Christian principle, doing, day by day, in the eyes of a gainsaying world, the works of righteousness.

That is the most successful preaching upon which the hearers most practice year after year. That preaching which makes the sharpest discrimination between right and wrong ; which insists most strongly upon the authority of the law of God ; which binds men with chains of moral conviction, and carries with it the deliberate judgment ; which deals most with principles, and so takes not a man by storm for an hour, but makes conquest of him for the remainder of his days ; too earnest to be prosy ; calm, but not dull ; aiming to produce permanent change in the moral state of men. This makes the work of the sacred very different from that of the secular orator, but gives most promise of attaining the sole end of preaching : God glorified by sanctified souls.

ARTICLE VIII.

THEOLOGY IN POLITICS: AN ANALYTICAL ILLUSTRATION.

THE political notions of a famous preacher and platform orator have already illustrated many things to thoughtful persons. A multitude of pens have pointed the moral. How powerless popular teachers and leaders are, after all, in a country where opinion is at the foundation of every thing, when they palpably go amiss, was even superficially obvious. How strong individual conviction and independent views are in a land of common schools was anew made very plain. But no less plain that a man of noble sympathies and most effective eloquence for the cause of the people and of liberty and human rights will still be admired and listened to in a republic, notwithstanding a clear variation of judgment on a vital and foremost point in public policy. If any have been accustomed to confound wit and beauty of speech and humane sentiments with all sound thinking, they have been instructed by this escapade.

Perhaps it was never clearer in any other case that logical and theological error begets uncertain political courses. The most of us have some recollection of a great outcry not long since about politics in religion. There may be need of a counter caveat against unsound theology in politics. Our brilliant Brooklyn orator having furnished large occasion for the first, now illustrates the second. All his errors of thinking and teaching, in both kinds, grow out of a lack of that theological thoroughness which he has often ridiculed and denounced, and which is sure at last to repay him who abuses and assails it; a lack also, we need not omit to say, touching one who has become public property, in his mind itself.

A sermon preached sometime before the Cleveland letter, furnishes ready specific illustrations. The text was: "Overcome evil with good." The preacher had the unchanged rebels of the South in his eye. The huge assumption is quietly made that undiscriminating leniency exhausts the meaning of "good." So in his address at the May anniversaries before the American Missionary Association, to which we listened as a bright and enjoyable speech in spirit and style, there was the same fallacy. The Gospel of forgiveness, as the only cure for the South, the old simple Gospel of God's love for sinners, was urged; forgiveness as the first and main thing, bathing rebellion in clemency, with a most marvellous omission of the requirement of repentance and heartfelt submission to law, was his burden.

In this sermon occurs the following passage, taken from the *Independent*, which contains its central fallacy:

"I know men say that forgiveness ought to be conditioned on repentance. Please tell me where you find that doctrine. Shall I find it where it says: 'If thy brother trespass against thee seven times in a day, and seven times in a day turn again to thee, saying, I repent; thou shalt forgive him? But that does not say that you shall not forgive him if he does not repent. And I ask those that attempt to justify their unforgiveness to listen. 'If thine enemy hunger, feed him.' It does not say that when your enemy is reconciled to you, when he has come to you and repented, then you are to feed him; it says that while he is yet your enemy you are to feed him. 'If he thirst, give him drink; for in so doing thou shalt heap coals of fire on his head.' This kind of conduct will strike him with a remorse so pungent that it shall burn out the dross, and leave only the pure gold of a better life.

"But let us go back to the teaching of our Saviour, which formed a part of our preliminary service. 'Ye have heard that it hath been said, Thou shalt love thy neighbor and hate thine enemy; but I say unto you, Love your enemies.' Take notice of that word. I will not construe it in the narrow sense of personal affection. Take it in the large sense of benevolent love. Interpret the command as enjoining upon you the duty of exercising benevolent dispositions, kindly, well-wishing, genial thoughts and feelings toward your enemies. 'Bless them that curse you.' Men say: 'That man is a wicked man, and has behaved hatefully to me; and still behaves hatefully to me; and I can not forgive him: I am not called to. If he will lay aside his wickedness, I will forgive him; I do not wish him any harm; but I can not forgive him so long as he persists in his present course.' Now Christ says, 'Love that man, bless him, pray for him, though he has despitefully used you, and is actually persecuting you; and you are to do it, that you may be the child of your heavenly Father, and that you may be in his likeness. You are the agent that is to work a moral change in the man; and your forgiveness, your lenity, your great-mindedness, your goodness, heaped on him, are the instruments which God has placed in your hands by which to change him. Nothing breaks a child's heart so quick as not treating him as he deserves.' "

It is not more manifest that the preacher here flies in the face of Scripture in the previous verse of Luke: " If thy brother trespass against thee rebuke him; and if he repent forgive him ;" than it is that he flies in the face of experience. Have there never been any instances of children abusing leniency, and taking advantage of forbearance? The heart of an already penitent child will be broken by not treating him as he deserves; that of an inpenitent child all the world knows, can not be counted on to yield to mere kindness and demission of justice. God says once in Scripture that his people would be melted at the recollection of his tenderness with them after they should repent, but he says also : " Because sentence against an evil work is not executed speedily, therefore the heart of the sons of men is fully set in them to do evil." And as a specimen of his own governmental regimen with an offending people, when under sore discipline, we have this with other examples : " If they shall confess their iniquity and the iniquity of their fathers, with their trespass which they trespassed against me, and that they also have walked contrary unto me ; and that I also have walked contrary unto them, and have brought them into the land of their enemies ; if then their uncircumcised hearts be humbled, and they then accept of the punishment of their iniquity : then will I remember my covenant with Jacob, and also my covenant with Isaac, and also my covenant with Abraham will I remember ; and I will remember the land." This was a holy Old Testament administration of mercy on conditions, under a covenant which could only be made good to any particular generation of the descendants of the fathers with whom the covenant was made, if they fulfilled the conditions, and it tallies with the instructions of Christ, and is a safer guide in public affairs than the hasty and mistaken generalizations of the sermon.

Let us analyze this subject of forgiveness. The word is a popular one of no very exact meaning. And, unquestionably, for God to forgive and for man to forgive are two different things, constantly confounded, with the uttermost unconscious-

ness of a distinction that is obvious at a glance. Some professed theologians even, all of whom Mr. Beecher is wont to
attack as useless refiners, lagomachists, do not seem to have
thought it out.

1. In man's forgiveness the chief thing is the softening and
surrender of exasperated personal feeling. In God's there is
nothing of this at all. Our personal feelings when excited, are
in a measure selfish. God has nothing of the kind. And
when he forgives there is no change in personal feeling whatever; while when we forgive, in almost all cases, this is the
whole of it. For we simply can not, for the most part, do
more. As to wrong, as wrong, we can not at all, save by ourselves doing wrong.

2. God's forgiveness is just the proper remission of the penalty of sin, as sin; and in this sense man has no power to forgive. The differential of the two kinds of forgiveness is two
distinct elements having nothing in common. This sense is
" governmental," not moral. And it is not only the highest,
it is the proper sense of the word. All other is derived and
diminutive, having less extent. It were well if, by way of distinction between forgive and pardon, the latter word were confined to this sense, and the former were used only for ceasing to
feel resentment. Perhaps theology will some time carry this
distinction into language; the tendency of usage is to it, and
there is foundation for it stated in Webster's Dictionary. " Forgiveness, Synonym."

"Forgiveness is Anglo Saxon, and pardon Norman French.
Forgive points to inward feeling and supposed alienated affection;
when we ask forgiveness we primarily seek the removal of anger.
Pardon looks more to outward things or consequences."

> "Exchange forgiveness with me, noble Hamlet."—*Shak.*

> "What better can we do than prostrate fall
> Before Him reverent, and there confess
> Humbly our faults, and pardon beg."— *Milton.*

3. In neither human nor divine forgiveness is the giving up
of a just judgment of sin, as wrong, properly included. This
would be moral and the culmination of wrong. Never is sin
as such, or wrong as such the subject of man's forgiveness, for
this is not the subject of wounded personal feeling at all. Re-

sentment as personal is against injury as personal. Man has no jurisdiction over sin as such; no power to remit penalty. Over wrong as such, to reverse correct moral judgments, what being in the universe has jurisdiction? Clearly distinct, in the simplest analysis, both from personal feeling on account of injury, and from the function of a governor to hold amenable to penalty for wrong done, is a just moral judgment of right and wrong on themselves. When God remits all penalty, he yet retains all his ethical estimate of the sin pardoned utterly unchanged. So does a good man when he gives up resentment or his claim to requital for wrong done him. An erring child forgiven is blamed still for his transgression by any parent who deserves the name righteous. A sinner pardoned is eternally blamed by God. For moral distinctions are so immutable as to be ineffaceable.

It is very true that many persons give up their moral judgment of iniquities when they give up their personal resentment for the wound or harm these iniquities had caused themselves; which only shows it is doubtful whether they ever had any moral judgment to be respected at all, anything more than selfish anger at harm or exhibited enmity. Just so many parents seem to suppose that when they forgive the injury of a child's act which was at once both injurious and sinful, this is all that is necessary, and never send their child to God to seek the other and real forgiveness for it as sin, which only shows they do not consider whose it is really to forgive.

4. Men are also called to pardon in a sense analogous to that in which God does, but not the same. In the family, in society, and in the state we hold offenders liable to consequences or penalties for transgression which we can remit, for cause. To certain effects upon their relations and upon public opinion, men are subject for sin, even, but not to its proper penalty. And everybody knows the difference between remission in these cases, and forgiveness as a matter of feeling. And everybody can see that while neither is real pardon, bestowed by a moral governor over wrong, which belongs only to God, the conditions on which each can be justly bestowed differ.

(*a*) Real pardon is never granted without repentance ; never goes before it, only follows. God never forgives the unconverted, those who still hate right and hate him.

(*b*) Remission of domestic, social, or state penalties, being analogous, has analogous conditions. They are like, though not the same. A son who continues an enemy to the family, a neighbor who is a pest in the community, an unchanged rebel to the state is not the proper subject of restoration. To grant it is mischievous and unrighteous. It were not only to treat him as he does not deserve, but all the obedient and loyal as they do not deserve, and righteous loyalty as it does not deserve. It could not be expected to soften his heart, but to harden theirs.

On the other hand personal ill-will to our enemies is to be given up without conditions. This is simply and only because it is wrong. It can never in any conceivable case do us or others any good. We have no right to the feeling at all. We must give it up, not in order to make enemies repent, but even if they never repent to all eternity. And the Saviour's directions, wofully misapplied in the extract from the sermon, apply only to this case, not to the other cases. If our brother trespass against us over and over again, and come every time and say, " I repent," as may be expected of a " brother," we must return love for his injury, simply because love is the sum of duty and goodness, without reference to what we believe about his sincerity in what he says, when he repeats the trespass so often, or about his obtaining forgiveness for the sin couched in his trespass, or not.

Now if anybody who sees these distinctions can draw from the requirement upon persons to give up wrong feeling the conclusion that rebels under a national government are to be restored and " reconstructed" without any sort of repentance or mollification of their ferocious disloyalty, then Mr. Beecher is right. It is enough for men who can understand a distinction well taken to state it. Popular orators are under temptation to sneer at logic and metaphysics. But it is always found that they are stronger with the world after all on the side of truth and right, than mere humanitarian rhetoric that traverses just thinking and sound policy. The sermon was simply a blunder in theology. To stand for justice, and to treat men who are incorrigible as they deserve works beneficent moral changes when indiscriminating moon-struck leniency fails.   The duties of benevolence to sinners and secessionists are always binding, and good men and patriots discharge them in all charities, but to maintain law, and distinguish disloyalty by retribution is a duty of the profoundest benevolence also.   Christian men, full of all love and nobleness have been praying these years, in the very spirit of the one hundred and forty third Psalm : " Of thy mercy cut off our enemies and destroy all them that afflict our souls !" and in the same spirit they are called to pray and act still.

In his Fort Sumter oration, which Mr. Beecher has seldom surpassed for mere eloquence, though it attracted less notice than other great oratorical efforts of his, because the papers containing it, and the public mind as well, were full of the assassination, that occurred the night after its delivery, he said :

" Let no man misread the meaning of this unfolding flag ! It says, 'Government has returned hither.' It proclaims, in the name of vindicated government, peace and protection to loyalty ; humiliation and pains to traitors.   There may be pardon, but no concession. There may be amnesty and oblivion, but no honeyed compromises. The nation to-day has peace for the peaceful, and war for the turbulent.   The only condition of submission is, not to be forgiven beforehand, as rebels, more turbulent now than on that 14th of April, a year ago, and as mistaken Union men demand, but to submit !   No cheap exhortations to forgetfulness of the past will do. God does not stretch out his hand, as he has for four dreadful years, that men may easily forget the might of his terrible acts."

And of the leaders and chief conspirators, he then said :

" A day will come when God will reveal judgment, and arraign at his bar these mighty miscreants ; and then every orphan that their bloody game has made, and every widow that sits sorrowing, and every maimed and wounded sufferer, and every bereaved heart in all the wide regions of this land, will rise up and come before the Lord to lay upon these chief culprits of modern history their awful witness.   And from a thousand battle fields shall rise up armies of airy witnesses, who, with the memory of their awful sufferings, shall confront the miscreants with shrieks of fierce accusation ; and every pale and starved prisoner shall raise his skinny hand in judgment.

Blood shall call out for vengeance, and tears shall plead for justice, and grief shall silently beckon ; and love, heart-smitten, shall wait for justice. Good men and angels shall cry out, ' How long, O Lord, how long wilt thou not avenge !' And then these guiltiest and most remorseless traitors, caught up in black clouds, full of voices of vengeance and lurid with punishment, shall be whirled aloft and plunged downward forever and ever, in an endless retribution ; while God shall say : ' Thus shall it be to all who betray their coun-try,' and all in heaven and upon the earth will say, 'Amen ' !"

To be sure, along with this was a more exuberant and roseate picture of the new era to begin with that day. The military over-throw of treason and slavery was held up as the same with the restoration of universal loyalty. " To drop the musket" was the same as " to return to allegiance." He congratulated the Presi-dent, so soon to sink in his blood, on beholding "the auspicious consummation of the national unity." He charged the banner reërected over the ruined fortress : " Tell the air that not a spot now sullies thy whiteness. A race set free ! a nation re-deemed !" " Let us pray for the quick coming of reconciliation and happiness under this common flag !" He declared the des-truction of " class-interests :" "deadly doctrines have been purg-ed away in blood !" " the industry of the Southern States is re-generated, and now rests upon a basis that never fails to bring prosperity," " the South, no longer a land of plantations, but of farms, will find no hindrance to the spread of education, schools, books and papers, churches," etc., " the leaders are swept away ;" "from the day the sword cut off the cancer, (the South) began to find her health. What then shall hinder the rebuilding of this republic? The evil spirit is cast out ; why should not this nation cease to wander among tombs cutting itself ;" all which, as description or prophecy, the most exhilar-ant optimism of Mr. Seward could hardly excel. And nothing could be worse, for the interests of truth and right and of the nation than to have the shallow and erroneous theology which is its parent universally accepted. But our object in these crit-icisms has been logical and theological rather than political. It can not be successfully maintained in reply to them, as is alleg-ed in other questions of doctrine, that the analogy from human government misleads. The analogy here seems the other way, from the divine government to the human. We can not carry it so far as to claim that there shall be reparation in behalf of traitors before forgiveness. But we may at least claim that there shall be repentance, not spiritual repentance as of the sin of rebellion in the sight of God, but of the wrong of rebellion toward the nation and toward men. We may insist on the analogy, for Mr. Beecher does also ; first claiming, with wonderful confusion of thought, that God bathes and attracts all sinners, ever so hardened as they may be, in the same element of love which he pours upon holy angels and saints, and then teaching that in the spheres of society and government we shall do likewise. We decline to believe the theology.

ARTICLE IX.

THE PRAYING, WITH THE ANOINTING, THAT SAVES THE SICK: AN EXEGESIS.

" Is any sick among you ? Let him call for the elders of the church ; and let them pray over him, anointing him with oil in the name of the Lord. And the prayer of faith shall save the sick ; and the Lord shall raise him up ; and if he have committed sins they shall be forgiven him."—*James* v. 14, 15.

ALL admit that this is a very extraordinary passage. It was probably the occasion of the Papal sacrament of extreme unction ; though that is totally different from the anointing with oil as here prescribed. Extreme unction is never administered till the sick person is supposed to be at the point of death ; so that a spiritual benefit alone can be expected from the ceremony ; which in reality serves merely as an opiate to the conscience, both of the dying and the living.

But let us see if we can throw light upon this obscure passage. We learn from ancient history, as well as from the inspired word, that pure olive oil was accounted nutritious, healthful, and medicinal. The quality and the value of that oil depended very much on the time of gathering the fruit, and on the manner of preparing it.

In order to extract the oil, the fruit was bruised in a mortar, or ground in a mill, or trodden by the feet. The beaten oil was made by bruising the fruit in a mortar. Exodus xxvii. 20, also xxix. 40 ; Levit. xxiv. 2, and Numbers xxviii. 5. And this pure oil was much used in culinary preparations. Wheat boiled in it was a common dish in Syria. Hasselquist speaks of bread baked in olive oil as peculiarly nourishing. And Faber mentions that eggs fried in olive oil are a favourite dish with Saracens and Arabians.

And it was probably on account of the common use of oil in food that the meat offerings, Levit. ii. 4 ; vi. 15 ; viii. 26 ; Num. vii. 19, were mixed with oil.

This oil was also used for anointing the body after a bath, as giving the skin a smooth and comely appearance. This, was the practise of Egyptians, Jews, Greeks and Romans. Those also who ran for the civic crown at the Olympic games anointed themselves with it to give elasticity to their limbs, that so they might win the prize and be crowned amidst the applause of their countrymen.

Besides, there is much to be said of the use of this oil for medicinal purposes among the ancients. Josephus, Ant. 17. 6 ; § 5, mentions it as among the remedies employed in the case of Herod, who was immersed in an oil-bath. Celsus, *de Medecina* 2 : 14, 17 ; and 3 : 6, 9, 19, 22 ; and 4 : 2, speaks of the use of this oil in fevers and other diseases as applied by friction. Pliny, 15 : 4, 7 ; and 23 : 3, 4, says that " olive oil is good to warm the body and fortify it against cold ; and also to cool the heat of the head ; and for many other purposes."

Oil mixed with wine was used externally and internally by the soldiers of Ælius Gallus in a time of disease. And this compares well with the use of it as made by the good Samaritan, in the case of the man who went down to Jericho and fell among thieves, Luke x. 34. The prophet Isaiah alludes to the like use of oil in medical treatment. Isaiah i. 6. And thus a fitting symbol, so to speak, if not an efficient remedy, was furnished for Christ's disciples in the miraculous cures which they were enabled to perform. Thus in Mark vi. 13, when they were sent forth by two and two, having power over unclean spirits, they " cast out many demons, and anointed with oil many that were sick and healed them."

With a similar intention it was probably enjoined by James in the passage under consideration; and, as it appears, was practised by ancient Christians in general, in the first centuries of Christianity. An instance of cure by this means is mentioned by Tertullian *ad Scap.* ch. 4. The medicinal use of oil is mentioned in the Mishna, and it shows how common was this practise in medicine by the Jews.

But says Bloomfield, in loco : " That oil is highly salutary in various disorders will not prove that it is here ordered by James as a medical means ; for, from the Gospels, Mark vi. 13, and other places, we learn that this was used by the disciples in conjunction with miraculous power. Nay, our Lord himself condescended to employ certain symbolical media, so to speak, in working miracles."

In accordance with that remark of Bloomfield, it will be perceived that in the case of the blind man, John ix. 6, Jesus made clay and anointed his eyes, saying : " Go wash in the pool of Siloam." " And he went, and washed, and came seeing." How can we suppose that there was any power in the clay ? Was it not as a mere symbol that it was employed ? So oil in this passage of James seems to be used as a mere symbol of healing. For it is said expressly, " That the prayer of faith shall save the sick" ; and that " if he have committed sins they shall be forgiven him." It was the Lord's miraculous power that raised the sick. It was done through the faith of miracles.

There is abundance of evidence in both Testaments that various miracles were wrought through certain symbolical media that could really have had no influence in producing the marvellous results ; as for instance the sounding of rams'-horns in prostrating the walls of Jericho ; the washing of Naaman, the Syrian leper, in the Jordan ; the healing of Hezekiah through the lump of figs ; and the brazen serpent, a look upon which was attended with the cure of those who had been bitten by fiery serpents. In all such cases these media were symbolically employed.

Enough has been said to prepare us to understand the use of

oil in this passage of James.   As the ancients used oil medicin-
ally, this furnished a suitable occasion for the symbolical use of
it when the elders of the church were to pray for a miraculous
cure, and accordingly Bloomfield says : "Upon the whole it involves the least difficulty to suppose that by the healing in
question is meant preternatural healing ; otherwise the strong
expressions, ἡ εὐχὴ τῆς πίστεως, κτλ., must be taken with a limitation.   And there can be little doubt, that in the next generation, the thing became a solemn religious ceremony, comprehending a symbolical rite, the use of which tended to produce
the blessing prayed for."

And Dr. Scott has this sensible remark upon the subject :
" It can not be supposed that these miraculous cures could be
performed at all times ; but there seems to have been some impression on the mind of the person who wrought the miracle and
a peculiar exercise of faith."

Bengel also, in his Gnomon of the New Testament, in re-
marking upon James v. 14, 15, says :

" What Christ had committed to the apostles, Mark vi. 13, was
afterward continued in the church even after the apostles' times ; and
this very gift, remarkably simple, conspicuous, and salutary, continued longer than any other."   See an instance in Macarius p. 272.
" And Ephraem Syrius has a remarkable testimony to the like effect.
James clearly assigns the application of this oil to the presbyters,
who were the ordinary ministers.   This was the highest faculty of
medicine in the church ; as in 1 Cor. vi., we have its highest judicial order.   O happy simplicity ! interrupted and lost, through unbelief !   For such the Latin church has its extreme unction, and the
Greek its εὐχέλαιον.   From the force of experience they assign
much less efficacy in restoring health to this mystery or sacrament,
than James does to the apostolic usage.   Whitaker very forcibly
says against Duræus : ' Let them use oil who are able by their
prayers to obtain recovery for the sick ; let those who can not do
this abstain from the empty sign.'   For the only design of that anointing originally was miraculous healing ; failing in which it is but
an empty sign."

These remarks of Bengel seem very forcible and appropriate
to the case.   Some persons will have it that if there were now
extraordinary measures of faith in the persons anointing, and

those who are anointed, an extraordinary blessing might be obtained in this age in behalf of the sick. But we are not now called on to settle that question. But let it be carefully observed by all, that the saving of the sick, and the raising him up to health can not be ascribed to the oil, but to "The prayer of faith."

ARTICLE X.

SHORT SERMONS.

"And he [the eunuch] went on his way rejoicing."—*Acts* viii. 39.

WE find here a simple, natural and instructive incident. An officer, high in rank, under Candace, the Ethiopean queen, is returning home from Jerusalem. The man is religiously inclined, and just now is in an inquiring state of mind, and so, while journeying in his private carriage, he reads the Scriptures. Philip, a devout man, and watching for opportunities to do good, is led by the Spirit and his own Christian heart, when he sees this man, to have religious conversation with him. He does not wait for an introduction, but in that easy way, common to a useful Christian, easy by use, he opens the matter of personal religion and faith in Christ. The eunuch believes in the Lord Jesus, when he is fully presented, and at once is consecrated to Christ in baptism, just as the prophet, in the passage read, had said that Christ should "sprinkle many nations." Then the eunuch "went on his way rejoicing." We have for a topic:

The Joy of the Young Christian.

I. Because he is a pardoned sinner.

His conscience has troubled him; the Bible has troubled him; and the review of his life has troubled him. Now with pardon he feels that the blood of Jesus Christ has cleansed him from all sin, and so he has peace with God. The heavy load, long carried, is lifted by the gracious One, who says: "Come unto me, all ye," etc.

II. Because he is at peace with himself.

He has known his course of impenitence to be unsafe and sinful, and yet has persisted in following it, and all the while has condemned himself for doing it. He has been constantly saying: "What I do I allow not." Now this is all ended. He is not only reconciled to God, but to himself, and so may well go on his new way rejoicing.

III. Because the Holy Spirit has ceased to strive with him. It has been the labor of the Spirit to convict him of his sins, to show him the only way of justification, and to portray before him the Judgment of the great day. All this has made the man's heart as a battle field, from which peace and comfort fled. But now having yielded all that God demanded, the battle is ended, peace is declared, and the man may well go on his way of life rejoicing.

IV. Because the terrors of the world to come are gone.

These alarming words of God have been in his ear: "Whatsoever a man soweth," etc., "Every one shall give account," etc., Except ye repent," etc. Then comes often the thought that he may be close on the other world, and that all his future of joy depends on his living till he repents; of which there is much doubt. These terrors he has in his mirth and prosperity and adversity. Very much of the time "a dreadful sound is in his ears." But now repenting and receiving Christ, all this is ended, and he may well rejoice.

V. Because he has now a joyful, noble aim and end in view.

Conversion enlarges the mind and heart of the man. His worldly, narrow, selfish ends are exchanged for the universe as a field, and for Christ as a master. His life now takes hold on eternity, and feels ennobled by his new and wide-reaching relations, embracing the world to come. He has a new thought, that "man's chief end is to glorify God and enjoy him forever," and he is very happy in it.

Inferences and Uses.

1. No place is so much of a "desert," where Philip found the eunuch, that the Christian, like Philip, can not make it a fruitful field.

2. To be studious of the Scriptures, though not understanding them, is a hopeful condition.

3. Publicly professing Christ is a joyful thing.

4. All of a life that is religious is joyful.

a. It begins in joy. "Go in peace, thy sins," etc.

b. It is continued in joy. "Shout for joy all ye that are," etc. The lack of joy in a Christian is the lack of religion.

c. The Christian life culminates in the joys of heaven. He comes home to Mount Zion with song and everlasting joy.

"Be it known unto you therefore, men and brethren, that through this man is preached unto you the forgiveness of sins; and by him all that believe are justified from all things, from which ye could not be justified by the law of Moses."—*Acts* xiii. 38, 39.

THE text is a clear statement of the doctrine of Justification, unmistakably suggestive of the following analysis.

I. Its nature and intent are judicial, meeting the demands of the divine government, and making the sinner just. Those who have been legally tried at the bar of the highest court, found guilty, and sentenced to eternal punishment, are, by its provision, "justified," made legally just, and so absolved and discharged. It is the act of the judge, announcing and putting on record the decision of the court, which both vindicates and honors the law, and unbinds the prisoner. But the transaction has this marked peculiarity that it is more than judicial, having in it the very essence of free and abounding grace. For it is not the case of discharge on the ground of the vindicated innocence of the accused, nor on the ground of his making restitution. It is the case of discharge by the substitution of a Friend who is able and willing to bear all demands, the accused having been found guilty, and utterly unable to make restitution. Justification is, therefore, " an act of God's free grace, wherein he pardoneth all our sins and accepteth us as righteous in his sight, only for the righteousness of Christ imputed to us."

II. The only ground of justification, the sole procuring cause, is the sacrificial death of Christ : " Be it known unto you that through this man is preached unto you the forgiveness of sins ; and by him, all that believe are justified." The most reasonable, holy and benevolent law runs: " The soul that sinneth it shall die." The law, being a transcript of God's character, fairly represents God's estimate of the sinner, an accursed creature. The law demanding perfect obedience constantly, it is plain that the sinner can do no more at any time than what the law requires at that time, and so can never do anything to make restitution for past transgressions. Hence the imperative need of an infinite Redeemer to take our place and make appointed and accepted satisfaction.

III. The means or process of justification is faith. "By him, all that believe are justified." The sinner, truly believing God, and casting himself upon the divine promise, finds an answering response within him, the " witness of the Spirit," that he is justified. This answers the full purpose of the declaration of acquittal by the judge in open court. It is better than a miraculous voice from the skies. All the faculties of the soul obey it. The law re-.

laxes its grasp, the conscience abandons the prosecution, and a sure
and joyful hope springs eternal in the soul.

IV. The results of justification are the "forgiveness of sins," justification "from all things," such as the law of Moses, whether
ceremonial or moral, could never effect. We are justified and saved
by grace. We are brought by the first act of faith, into a justified
state, which is permanent, bringing all its glorious consequences.
We are adopted into Christ's family, have a vital union to him,
which imparts life eternal. And how much is implied in that life
eternal with Christ and God! Oh, the goodness of God! the
happiness of the justified!

ARTICLE XI.

LITERARY NOTICES.

1. — *Sermons Preached upon Several Occasions.* By ROBERT
SOUTH, D. D. In five volumes. Vol. I. 8vo. New York:
Hurd & Houghton. 1866.

ONE need read but a few of these discourses to detect the secret
of their wide and sustained popularity, in this second century of
their life. They are full of weighty thought expressed in a vigorous, terse, and piquant style, and projected with the force of a
thorough, downright earnestness. South's mind was logical, ana-
lytical, forensic, keen in its perceptions, taking the directest line to
its objects, and bristling all over with genuine wit: in a word, escaping, by a singular felicity, the dulness of his times in serious
literature, he wrote in much the same way as the best of our
modern didactic authors, if indeed we have any that can justly
stand this comparison.

His method is intellectual, not emotional or devotional. He satisfies the understanding, but not the heart; by which we, of course,
do not mean that he always carries our convictions. He was a
practiced polemic, and a close reasoner, but he opens no fountains
of sensibility except the facetious. He moves on in measured, afflu-
ent, well-balanced, but never heavy periods; is not metaphysical;
is never sentimental or fanciful; is never mystical ;never reminds
you of Charles Auchester's transcendental description of a chande-

lier in a dusky church—"a mystery hung in circumambient nothingness." He divides his sermons minutely, but naturally, and does
not drag his "heads" about as Achilles Hector's. He sees the
vices of society with a sagacious eye, and freely assails them, with
courtiers and princes for his hearers as well as lesser folk. He is
not much given to doctrinal discussion, but the old Calvinistic formations crop out very sharply in spots. If his audience gained not
much spiritual nutriment or stimulation, they must have gathered
a large amount of clearly cut ideas about religion and morals; must
have been conscious of a fine exercise of mental discrimination;
certainly could not have slept very much under such a fusillade of
epigrammatic pyrotechnics as he was very prone to exhibit.

South was a partizan of the religious and civil establishment of
the kingdom under Charles II., under whom he wanted not occasion
for saying the most caustic things he could level at the universal
degradation around him. But this was not his only target. Born
in Cromwell's day, he had first sharpened his pen in the laudation
of the Protector, but possibly without a deeper motive than to chime
in with the then dominant side. We do not mean by this that he
was a time-server, a place-hunter, for even down to his death in
Queen Anne's reign, he could never be persuaded to take the often
offered mitre of an English bishop. But his hatred of the Puritans,
however excited, became a passion. He never spares them nor their
great chief. He hurls himself upon them with a dash which fairly
takes you captive. His wit and raillery flashes about them like the
chain-lightning around some granite mountain-peak. You know
that it did not hurt them, so there is no call for pity. If the pyro-
technist chooses thus to explode his rockets, it is a fine exhibition for
the spectators. We would commend this doughty doctor, as a
study, to such of our young enthusiasts as think that this subject is
not yet worn out. If the Puritan development of Christian civilization is still to be cannonaded, let us have a regular gunnery practice, with something harder than unbaked cakes. Pepys, the dia-
rist, a contemporary of South, and of the same church, seems to
have thought that even thus early the diversion did not pay. "The
business," says he, "of abusing the Puritans begins to grow stale,
and of no use, they being the people that at last will be found the
wisest."

But South deserves to be studied by our preachers for a loftier purpose than this. We do not recommend him as a model; yet many
of his points are admirable. For this, we are glad that the Riverside press is reproducing his works in its best style of mechanical
execution. We hope the edition will have a sufficient sale to just

ify the energetic prosecution of the plan, by the same publishers, of issuing a library of standard British divines, in the same form, under Professor Shedd's supervision, to the extent of some fifty or more volumes. Nothing in the book line could be worthier of the capital and labor of our enterprising publishers.

2. — *History of the United States, from the Discovery of the American Continent.* By GEORGE BANCROFT. Vol. IX. 8vo. Boston: Little, Brown & Co. 1866.

THE first volume of this work was issued thirty-two years ago: one more is to complete the series. It has already taken its place among the best productions of the modern school of historical authorship. It is fortunate that this national work was undertaken by one of the ablest writers on national births and growths, a careful student of political science, himself practically versed in the art of statesmanship, and trained in that particular school of it which would help him, better perhaps than any other, to hold the balances of judgment fairly among the questions which have demanded his inquiry. As a general fact, we think that his decisions and generalizations will stand the test of the study and thought of the future.

There is something sublime in the winnowing and sifting processes of the human mind, as the ages wear on. The point where this makes itself particularly felt in the present volume, is the elevation to which Washington rises above the best of his associates, in masterly forecast and strength of understanding; as he is seen also to transcend many of illustrious name among them, in moral purity and patriotic consecration. There is no effort on the historian's part to show this. It comes out irresistibly through the movement and the force of events, without the cheap appliances of wordy panegyric. We can not suppose that the author has any object to accomplish by damaging the military or civic fame of leading men of that day; but, by simply citing them as witnesses in their own case, he leaves not a few of them with less lustre glorifying their memories than he found them. If he has wrongly understood his witnesses, it has not been for lack of time to perfect his examinations, six years having elapsed since the publication of his eighth volume. Washington's task, during those darkest days of our Revolution, 1776–1778, seems almost superhuman. Brave as were most of his subordinate commanders, not more than one or two of them were really fit for the conduct of a campaign; and some of them, as Sullivan, were stupid to a degree. Washington was the subject of the most unprincipled cabals and plots, among such men as Conway, Gates, and their flatterers, in which better men, as Schuyler, Mifflin, Wayne, were sometimes compromised. Congress even hung on his shoulders like a millstone. It is amazing to see them, out of regard to a blind popular clamor, putting more trust in such a braggart as Charles Lee, than in the Commander-in-Chief. While they expected every thing of him, they hampered his authority, and most lazily provided for his wants. They were haunted with a fear that he might Cromwellize the government, if not kept in hand very tightly; yet even the Adamses were feverish for rapid military effects, praying, in their private letters, that Providence would in mercy give them a hero equal to the times! On the floor of Congress, John Adams could say: "In this house I feel myself to be the superior of General Washington" —not the first or the last time that a man has made a mistake in measuring his own girth. We have often been reminded in these pages, of the trials of President Lincoln in our late war. There were, in both these terrible conflicts, the same ambition, jealousies, and blunders of political and incompetent commanders, the same hurry to get through the struggle, the same patience demanded to guide the states safely to the end; and we are proud to add, the same substantial confidence of the masses of the people in their illustrious chiefs at the head of affairs, notwithstanding temporary appearances to the contrary. Cautious as he was compelled to be by the almost constant necessities of his situation, Washington was known to be as fearless as the rashest soldier, when personal daring and exposure were called for. The trust he inspired was deeply mingled with a heroic admiration. His name had more power over the people of this land, in the worst of those days, than Congress and all the other magnates combined, so safe is the innermost intuition of the public heart.

Mr. Bancroft's historical method and style are more than good. His powers of graphic description and characterization are finely displayed in his accounts of the crossing of the Delaware, the battles of New Jersey, and those which directly preceded the surrender of Burgoyne; and in his portraits of the Howes, Franklin, Chatham and Fox. His historical criticism is clear; his disquisitions on the growth of American institutions, the settlement of our form of government, are concise and able. We see just how the state-rights difficulty sprung out of germs which were scattered into this nation in its earliest colonizing. What at last held its home exclusively at the South, was at first, and for a long while, the common sentiment of the whole land. It is inspiriting to trace the steady development of our fundamental principles, through the reverses as well as successes of our arms, one excrescence after another sloughing off; to observe the deep grounding of our national fabric in the religious instincts of our fathers, to contemplate the utter impossibility of the task which our enemies undertook to accomplish. Not only geographical dimensions were against them, but the course of civilization as well; and we may add, the progress of the kingdom of heaven upon the earth. We rise from the perusal of this volume with a stronger faith that, out of all our present embarrassments and collisions, the same God will securely lead us, who led the men of the Revolution to peace and more than kingly empire.

If we were to make any serious stricture on Mr. Bancroft's treatment of his subject, it would be that occasionally he is tempted to become too antithetical for the severest truth, setting things in contrast too sharply for the right historical shading, an error into which Lord Macaulay has so much fallen. Our author is a man of very positive opinions, and never flinches from their as positive expression. We do not object to this under proper guards. But we would rather not have found (p. 501) so loose a person as Rousseau coupled, by any tie, with Jonathan Edwards. The " religiosity" which, Mr. Bancroft thinks, they shared largely in common, we presume means only a susceptibility to quick impression from supernatural subjects, in which many another vile soul has partaken as deeply as did the libidinous Genevese.

3. — *Superstition and Force.* Essays on the Wager of Law—the Wager of Battle—the Ordeal—Torture. By HENRY C. LEA. Large 12mo. Philadelphia: Henry C. Lea. 1866.

THESE essays are studies from the civil life of the Middle Ages. They aim to trace the attempts of that period of semi-civilization to elicit truth and adjudge justice through the methods above specified. In times when the present modes of sifting facts by careful judicial process were unknown and impossible, these shorter, more direct, but wofully superstitious and violent ways were hit upon to decide controversies. The "Wager of Law" would seem to have consisted mainly in the amount of hard swearing which could be arrayed in defence or accusation of a compromised person. These oaths were graduated to the nature of the questions at issue, and to the condition and standing of the parties, a certain number of compurgators being required to establish a point according to the grade of the subject. If the crime of perjury was thought no more of in those days than now, in high circles and in low, not much progress towards ascertaining the truth would be likely, in many cases, to be made. It is to be hoped that the fear of purgatorial pains, if nothing more, operated some check upon false swearing.

The "Wager of Battle" was the duel, in person, or by proxy, in which might stood a decidedly better chance than right, except as a guilty conscience rendered null the powers or the skill of the combatant. This is not to be confounded with the common duel, which then, as now, was the medium of repairing damaged honor, or inflicting retaliation for insult. The judicial combat was a very serious affair in theory, and a very absurd one in fact, as a great many serious frivolities still are, more especially in the ecclesiastical direction. Women and churchmen were exempted from these lists, but sometimes they waived their privilege and entered them in deadly earnest. Classes of persons and communities employed professional champions to maintain their quarrels; and by and by, almost every kind of dispute came under this arbitrament. The "Ordeal" was the submission of disputed matters to such tests as boiling water, hot iron, fire, cold water, standing in constrained and exhausting postures to test the power of endurance, swallowing the eucharistic bread, the trial of the lot and of blood, and various other ingenious devices. This had a deep hold in the popular superstition, and at one time was universally in use. If the accused person sank in deep water, he was of course guilty. If he swam ashore, he sometimes was thrown back to try it again, until he went down from exhaustion, if not from crime. The "Torture" was the culmination of persecuting, false conscientiousness and cruelty, the history of which will never be written, for language has no words in which to describe its atrocities. They are beyond the powers of human thought, though the melancholy facts of human experience.

The author has treated these topics in the temper of a patient investigator, and of a candid and charitable man. He gives the origin of these institutions, for such they were; traces their development in different nations; describes their methods of administration; discusses their growth and their decline, with the causes of their gradual disuse, and their relations to the then dominant church, and to the subsequent introduction of European jurisprudence. We can not speak too highly of the manner in which the essayist has done his work. It is not intended to be exhaustive, but to put the reader upon the right track of understanding the real philosophy and spirit of what is so foreign to our age, that we are in danger of widely mistaking its true conditions. He regards these aberrations

as not altogether the direct fruit of human malignancy : rather, to a
large extent, as the blind gropings of ignorant, bewildered men, for
a test of guilt and innocence which they needed, but knew not how
to find. We accept this construction as far as justice demands,
with gravest abatements under the last topic discussed. The book
is an excellent one to show us out of what Christian civilization
sprung, and the great price with which it has been purchased.

4. — *A History of the Gipsies :* with Specimens of the Gipsy
Language. By WALTER SIMSON. Edited with Preface, Intro-
duction, and Notes, and a Disquisition on the Past, Present, and
Future of Gypsydom. By JAMES SIMSON. 12mo. New York :
M. Doolady. London : Sampson Low, Son & Co. 1866.

WE confess to some surprise in reading this book. We had supposed that this erratic people numbered a few thousands of strolling
mendicants, a sort of half-civilized Bedouin race hanging on to the
skirts of society : but here we are told that there are some four
millions of them in Europe and America alone ; and that they are
dispersed all over the globe, from " farthest Ind" to the end of daylight, inclusive. We had regarded them as entitled to considerable
antiquity ; but we now find that they were none other than the
"mixed multitude" which accompanied the Hebrew exode under
Moses—straggling or disaffected Egyptians who went along to ventilate their discontent, or to improve their fortunes. That they
have always been called Egyptians, whence the name, Gipsy, and
have liked the pedigree, seems evident. We are not prepared to
take issue with these authors on any of the points raised by them.
Theories about the genesis of the Gipsies are very contradictory, as
any one may see by turning to the notice of them in the New American Cyclopædia. The subject in its present shape is novel, and we
freely add, very sensational.

The senior partner in the authorship of this book, was a Scotch-
man, who made it his life-long pleasure to go a Gipsy hunting, to
use his own phrase. He was a personal friend of Walter Scott,
and published some fragments on this topic in *Blackwood's Magazine*
so early as 1817. His enthusiasm was genuine, his diligence great,
his sagacity remarkable, and his discoveries rewarding. He left
these unpublished, and his editor has given them to the world with
an equal amount of his own information and speculation. What
ever may be thought of parts of these, the book is undoubtedly the
fullest and most reliable contribution which our language contains
upon the subject. If it overdoes the matter, as we suspect it does,
a large residuum of valuable knowledge will well repay its perusal.

The Gipsy dialect, which appears to be substantially the same the world over, is singularly like the language of the Hindus, thus confirming the oriental origin of this people. Their appearance in Europe synchronises with about the beginning of the fifteenth century. Then they are represented as having been mostly wanderers, living in tents, or otherwise out of doors, subject to chiefs who called themselves earls, dukes, etc., after the titles of the magnates around them. Their employment was, to a great extent, stealing, which was much the case also with most of those in that day who had skill or strength to do it. Tinkering has always been an hereditary business with them; hence, their Scottish name of Tinklers. They have also largely engrossed the profession of fortune-telling. The editor of this volume thinks that John Bunyan was one of them; possibly he was : but we take it that all tinkers have not therefore been Gipsies. At present, the better sort have mostly settled in towns, in mercantile, manufacturing and other employments. Some distinguished British lawyers, physicians and clergymen, are affirmed to have had a strong infusion of Gipsy blood in their veins. They naturally take to music and athletic arts. They are cunning, skillful, adroit, hard to be beaten at almost any game they may choose to play. We have about concluded, while reading these pages, that our Yankee nation must, in some way, have split off laterally from this strangely ubiquitous and self-sustaining tribe. Indeed, the book assures us that our country is full of this people, mixed up as they have become, by marriage, with all the European stocks during the last three centuries. This amalgamation has done much to merge them in the general current of modern education and civilization; yet they retain their language with closest tenacity, as a sort of free-mason medium of intercommunion; and while they never are willing to own their origin among outsiders, they are very proud of it among themselves.

This volume is valuable for its instruction, and exceedingly amusing anecdotically. It overruns with the humorous. But it is clumsily put together, and is badly manufactured. There are too many front and back stairs to it. It repeats itself too much, and could have been greatly condensed, particularly in its closing Disquisition. It dogmatizes too much. Its special aversion is Mr. George Borrow of Gitano memory. It also offends against the purity of English composition, as no good writers, this side the water, allow themselves to do. It habitually uses " will " and " would," for shall and should; " learns " horses to do this and that instead of teaches them; " lays off" by the roadside, when it should lie off. It shows the lack of literary practice in its authorship. Yet it will be our best authority on this topic, until some one shall fuse its materials, and other similar, into a more artistic and less speculative form.

The religious history of this race has been far from encouraging. In their normal state they would seem to have been merely heathen, with no proper sense of moral obligation, no rites of worship, no word even in their language to express the being of God. In Christian lands, as they become interwoven with the people, this condition of things improves, they gradually become church-goers, and sometimes devoted and even eminent Christians.

5.—*The Acts of the Apostles.* An Exegetical and Doctrinal Commentary by G. V. LECHLER, D. D., Leipsic : With Homiletical Additions, by the Rev. CHARLES GEROK, Stuttgard. Translated from the German, with Additions, by C. F. SCHAEFFER, D. D. Philadelphia. [Being Vol. IV. of Schaff's American Ed. of Lange's Biblical Commentaries]. Royal 8vo. New York : Charles Scribner & Co. 1866.

CRITICISM of commentaries upon the Bible should carefully respect the commentator's design. If that be to make an exposition on the plan of saying, not every thing, but much which may be said on any particular part of it, it would be unfair to judge of the result from the point of view which considers a class of helps to Holy Scripture, like Bishop Ellicott's, for instance, as the only ones admissible. What the linguistic expert may desiderate, in the way of an *apparatus criticus*, might be of no use to an ordinary pastor ; much less to an English reader only of the Bible. These respective kinds of books are alike simply in the one fact of being employed in elucidating the sacred text, but for quite different purpose, as in an altogether unlike method. They can not be combined in the same work without sacrificing that compact grammatical severity which is the chief value of the one. We have not thought it of much pertinence, therefore, when, now and then, we have found the present work disparaged for being too wordy and spreading. We have already said that some things might just as well have been left out, which are rather gossipy ; and so far as we have been able to look through this new volume, there seems to be less of this here than in the former. But it is quite out of the question to make a Comment-ary on the present plan without a large margin for excursions on the right hand and on the left. That the plan itself is a marketable one, the publishers are the best witnesses.

The Book of Acts is the great missionary record, and programme of the church. It is the guide-book of modern evangelization among the heathen. Our mission boards are following closely its methods, where the work is going forward with most success. Hence, this apostolic narrative is likely to become increasingly attractive to Christian readers as the Millennium comes nearer. It is also our chief authority in all questions of church polity; and so is of especial value to non-prelatic churches, as it is singularly innocent of the faintest hierarchical tendencies. It deserves, accordingly, the most scholarly handling. This, we are certified, it has received, in the volume before us, from the fact that Dr. Lechler has made this section of church history and its literature a special study for many years, with distinguished success; and that his associate in this Commentary, pastor Gerok of Stuttgard, to whom the homiletics was committed, is one of the foremost preachers of Germany; while the American editor and translator has brought a competent scholarship to the task of correcting, and supplementing with the results of later critical study, particularly of the Codex Sinaiticus, his trans-atlantic authors. It is not intended to overlay this work with a lumber of needless erudition, but to enrich it with the best exegesis of recent biblical learning; with a sufficient reference to various readings, doubtful texts, unauthorized interpolations, and whatever is of real use to the student. Pains have been taken with the chronology of this book, which has been much controverted; and the translator has been diligent also, in verifying and supplying references, much beyond the point attained in the original Commentary. We wait for the Gospel of St. John with unusual expectation. The eminently devout spirit of the work, thus far, assures us that this fourth Evangelist will not fail of a loving, sympathetic treatment. These Commentators are aiming to nourish the church in faith and affection, as well as in knowledge; mindful evidently of the truth that knowledge only puffeth up those whom charity does not edify.

6. — *An Examination of Mr. J. S. Mill's Philosophy; being a Defence of Fundamental Truth.* By JAMES McCOSH, LL.D. 8vo. pp. 434. New York: Robert Carter & Brothers. 1866.

It is well known that Sir W. Hamilton and Mr. J. S. Mill represent two widely different systems of philosophy. Hamilton was a vigorous defender of intuitive or a priori truth. Mill, though not entirely rejecting the intuitions, claims that our mental states or modes of thought are clearly derivable from sensations. That the mind is, in fact, a series of sensations firmly connected by association. The views of Hamilton are defended by a large number of zealous and loving pupils, while Mr. Mill, much to his advantage, can look quietly on, and shape his thoughts and system to meet the exigencies of each turn of the discussion.

Among the many who have taken this or that side in the discussion, is the author of the book under consideration. McCosh was not a pupil of Sir William, and consequently does not feel in duty bound to defend the great metaphysician, except when their views coincide. Nor is he a determined enemy of Mill, but frankly acknowledges our indebtedness to him for the clear exposition he has given of many important principles. He fearlessly combats, however, Mill's peculiar theory. He arraigns Mill for claiming to show that the mind is a series of feelings capable of being resolved into sensations, and at the same time, introducing the intuitions to sustain some of his favorite views. He shows how Mill admitted many intuitions, such as that there is an immediate and intuitive knowledge, and also that consciousness is a form of intuition.

Scattered admissions like these are collected, that the reader may see that Mill can have no desire to wholly deny the existence of intuitive truths, but only to wrest their application from the uses previously made of them, and turn them into new channels of thought.

McCosh is " not sure that any judicious defender of fundamental truth would demand a greater number of first principles than here allowed by one of the most important opponents of necessary truth."

In examining a system of philosophy, it is natural to expect a consideration of its distinctive feature or features. Accordingly we find an early examination of what Mr. Mill understands by sensations.

He considers sensations the earliest condition of our mental states, claiming that " sensations are states of the sentient mind," and also that " sensations are all of which we are directly conscious." It is claimed that they have accusative power, but are simple, undefinable and ultimate.

McCosh criticises this view in a way at once remarkable for clearness and precision, by showing what sensations are not, and that the sensational school have entirely overlooked the most essential element connected with sensations, namely, that they " can originate thought only by stirring up a mental capacity in the soul, which mental potency is to be regarded as the main element in the complex cause."

Mill's examination of the nature of mind is regarded as very unsatisfactory, that author considering it as " a something which we figure as remaining the same, while the particular feelings through which it reveals its existence change." McCosh claims that we do not refer to it, but that we know it in a particular state: that it does not reveal itself through feelings, but that we know it as a feeling: that we do not figure it as remaining the same, but that we decide the conscious self of to-day to be the same as the conscious self of yesterday.

The doctrine of externality becomes of great importance in considering this sensational philosophy. How we get from a mere sensation, or a series of feelings, to a vivid and intelligent idea of externality is naturally suggested, but with difficulty answered.

McCosh claims that Mill is guilty of a *petitio principii* in claiming that after having had sensations, we are capable of forming the conception of possible sensations, or, in other words, "that the human mind is capable of expectation." Mill also says: "The world of possible sensations succeeding one another is as much in other beings as in me; it, has, therefore, an existence outside of me; it is an external world." McCosh would admit this if we could only get out of ourselves, or out of the domain of consciousness, and get an apprehension of things thus beyond consciousness, n ot otherwise. He thinks Mr. Mill " has never logically got out of the shell of the egg."

He follows Mill through several succeeding chapters, often criticising, and often, as in considering his views on logic, commending him in the main. The chapter on the Tests of Intuition is a *resume* of some of the arguments for their solidity given in Intuitions of the Mind.

Mill's treatise on Liberty is considered as "stimulating in its spirit, but far from being satisfactory in its results." It is regarded defective concerning the regulation of the expression of sentiment, and as giving too much latitude to individuality at the expense of the interests of the community as a whole. The same treatise regards Christianity quite defective in some of the higher principles of morality, and hence the necessity of looking for such principles to other sources of truth. A Christian writer, like McCosh, of course, attempts to refute this, and adduces those searching scriptural truths which so clearly define man's duties, public or private, The chapter on Natural Theology deals with the views of the Positive school generally, since Mr. Mill has carefully abstained from expressing his views on so important a point.

The obvious consequences of Mill's doctrine of the mind being "a series of sensations aware of itself," are considered as showing the evident views of that writer respecting a belief in a Divine Being.

Many will regret that Mill's doctrine, that our idea of right and wrong may be traced to sensation and association, is barely alluded to, and not more fully discussed.

The spirit of these discussions is admirable. Fearless and courteous, McCosh never hesitates to bestow praise when merited, nor to attack a heresy wherever found. Much of the language is clear, sometimes elegant. It is a beautiful volume in type and general appearance, while as an unhesitating defence of some most important truths, it must enhance the reputation of its distinguished author.

7.—*Principia Latina.* Parts I. and II. By WILLIAM SMITH, LL. D. Revised by HENRY DRESLER, LL. D. New York: Harper & Brothers. pp. 187 and 375. 1866.

THESE two books are the beginning of a series designed to aid in the study of Latin. Part I. contains the necessary grammatical knowledge to enable a student to read Part II. The design of Part I. is to enable a pupil to fix in his mind the declensions, by giving him simple sentences to construct, and gradually increase his vocabulary. A prominent feature of this part is the special care taken to have the pupil drilled in quantity. The more simple rules of prosody are given from time to time, as the learner advances, and the quantity is indicated wherever it would not be inferred from the rule. Part II. contains Dr. Woodford's Epitome of Cæsar and L'Homond's Viri Romæ, with notes, chief dates in Roman history and a vocabulary. It also contains an article by Prof. Pillaus of Edinburgh, on the lack of juvenile Latin books. It is claimed that the Epitome is much better than the full text of Cæsar for beginners in Latin, as many of the more difficult passages are avoided and many particulars, uninteresting to youth, are left out. The notes are suggestions and not translations, while some intricate passages peculiar to Cæsar are made serviceable to the young student.

8.—*Hymns.* By HARRIET McEWEN KIMBALL. Large 12mo. Boston: E. P. Dutton & Co. 1866.

FOR a few years past, charming little gems of poetry have been finding their way into the reading world, until the name of this authoress has become familiar to at least a select if not a numerous circle of friends—fit audience if few. This is the way in which the best mental productions are wont to win their meed of fame. Great strokes of genius sometimes, by a sort of literary escalade, seize a triumph from the dazzled crowd—like Bailey's "Festus," shall we say, for example?—and after a while, like a burnt-out chimney, show that there was, after all, not much of the living fire to keep up the light.   If Milton's great epic could have begun its career like a volcano in full blast, the chances are that before this it would have shown a very cold, spent crater.   Miss Kimball may smile at our somewhat fuliginous exordium.   We mean to say, that her silver lamp, fed by the choicest of fragrant oils, bids fair to burn all the longer and brighter because so free from this smoky flare.

An exquisite delicacy of sentiment and purity of feeling are the marked features of these Hymns.   They are not designed for church service ; though some stanzas might be selected which would be very appropriate to such use.   They are closet hymns, fit companions, most of them, of the sacred hours of the "alone with God."   They breathe the spirit of a profound adoration of the infinitely holy and glorious One—a reverent, childlike prostration of heart before him whom the heaven of heavens can not contain ; and the spirit of a loving faith in Christ the only Mediator.   There is nothing morbid or mawkish in the expression of these devout emotions.   They flow naturally and healthfully from the inner fountain of worship.   They are not imitations of other hymnists : only once or twice have we caught a strain which seemed, for a moment, a faint echo of Keble's lyre.   The poet has lived through the experience of the emotions which she here embodies in the chastest language.   These poems are histories of her own heart and home.   In thus giving them voice, she will strike a responsive chord in many other souls, even " as face answereth to face in water."

Miss Kimball's melodies are mostly of the minor key, hymns of penitent sorrow, and clinging hope, and holy awe, and chastened consolation.   But once in a while her harp sounds out a more joyous chord, as in " The Two Cities," which discloses a vein of very precious metal that we hope she will work.   We have other evidence that she is capable of singing songs of the rosy sunlight, as well as of the dimmer hours.   She should give us another volume, in due time, of bright-winged lyrics, radiant with the hues of nature in its festal robes, and touched with the pencil of her own playful and blithesome fancy.   Will she pardon us for venturing to say that we should be glad to see in such a volume a merry little poem which now lies before us in her own handwriting, bearing date in one of the summer months of 1864, and which we should certainly have sent to some fortunate publisher, but for the most peremptory *non imprimatur* of the author.   We must not omit to add that the publishers have clothed these Hymns in a dress of fitting beauty ; especially are the artistic embellishments deserving of praise for their charming design and finish.   It gratifies us to remember that quite a number of these poems first met the public eye in the early volumes of our own *Review.*

9.—*Essays on Art.*   By Francis Turner Palgrave.   12mo. New York : Hurd & Houghton.   1867.

THE first hundred pages of this volume, taken up with criticism of the London Art Exhibitions for some years past, do not open a specially inviting door to the American reader.   Turning over to the end of the book we found a more pleasant, though less imposing entrance through a sharp stricture of modern British architecture compared with the "New Paris" style, that smacks of Matthew Arnold's spicy indignation at English Philistinism, which the present critic very honestly shares.   Our progress through this miscellany, thus reversely begun, has been entertaining and instructive.

The topics discussed are local and special, as the essayist addressed his readers through the *Saturday Review* and other weeklies, for immediate purposes of art-reform in sculpture, painting, building. The design is admirable, and its treatment vigorous and intelligible. His first law in art, both representative and decorative, is "appropriateness."   This includes place, subject, material, antecedents, surroundings and belongings of every kind—all of which are to be regarded and provided for, if art, whether useful or ornamental, is to be successful.   And so the study of the fitness of things becomes the first lesson and the constant one of all who would rightly execute or judge of these products of taste and genius : "that honest naturalness which is at the bottom of all good work as of all good art."

We thank the author for thus taking this matter out from the mistiness which has so generally beclouded it, and bringing it within the reach of the common understanding.   He aims at practical ends, and discriminates keenly, but candidly, between the genuine and the false.   His honesty is commendable.   " If," says he, " we are to have lives of poets, painters, or philosophers, we submit that there is no honest course open, but to tell the truth about them" ; and about every thing else, we say, as well, " either no biography, or a true one."   His estimates of Thorvaldsen, as a sculptor, will not escape dissent.   If his "Our Saviour" be not wholly satisfying, we demur to this—that " the apostles are pompous inanities."   They have not so impressed us, after hanging within sight of our study chair, in Goupil's fine copy, for a long time. Mr. Palgrave may have transferred a dislike of the Dane's character, which was none of the worthiest, to his works. But the critic is doubtless sincere, as he is frank. He writes not to make a sensation, but to educate the public eye and mind to a true standard of taste. While, therefore, his texts are mostly local, his discourses are of universal application, and the reprinting them for American readers is a good idea. We need very much a better style of architecture and ornamentation of public and private buildings, than is common among us. Our people are just in that aspiring and receptive state which exposes them to great blunders and wasteful expense in matters of this kind, and, at the same time, calls for the right sort of teachers. It is a gradual thing to cultivate the general sense of beauty and adaptation. What is beautiful in itself may be far from this in its actual relations. Of this we have instances to repletion. This book, if carefully studied, may do something towards decreasing their number.

10. — *War Poems.* By ELBRIDGE JEFFERSON CUTLER. Boston: Little, Brown & Company. 1867.

VIVID imagination, fastidiousness of taste, and a classic elegance of finish, are the more obvious excellences of these poems. The author, Professor Cutler of Harvard, seldom trips in putting his thought into the neatest expression, and he has the power to make intensely real to himself the scene or situation which he would represent. These short poems give the varying aspects of our late struggle, from the first arousing alarum —

> "Hurrah! the drums are beating; the fife is calling shrill;
> Ten thousand starry banners flame on town and bay and hill:
> The thunders of the rising war hush Labor's drowsy hum:
> Thank God that we have lived to see the saffron morning come!"

— to the four years later, which seem in the retrospect like almost as many decades—

> "The flag is folded; for the battle's din,
> The cry of trumpet and the blaze of gun,
> The thunderous rush of squadrons closing in,
> The stifled groan, the triumph-shout, are done."

With the varying fortunes of the strife as here depicted, the poet changes his measures, with a fine perception of the relations of spirit to form — the brilliant dash of the *Reveille* dying solemnly into the funeral tread of the

"Mourn for the young!
　Mourn for the brave!
　He sleeps beneath the sod,
　With all the stars of God
　To watch his grave."

The sentiment in these different expressions of feeling seems to be very genuine; yet the artistic care so manifest might sometimes possibly suggest, though we think unfairly, an artificial glow of passion rather than the true, deep-burning fire. It is a wise thing to discern between the "nascitur" and the "fit," in literature; and, in our judgment, it is a very unjust thing to decide for the last, because the fit is exquisitely exact. These poems are certainly eloquent; and they are also natural.

We do not hold the poet as endorsing what is a clearly untenable position, in "A Colonel's Last Words":

"I hold that he, the lawless, violent,
　When once he puts his country's armor on,
　Making his breast her bulwark, by that grace
　Compensates all a life of private crime."

On which principle, it would be quite impracticable to realize any sufficient answer to the impassioned prayer, on a former page:

"God give us Law in Liberty, and Liberty in Law!"

—a sentiment also which would necessarily render unmeaning the appeal to Deity—

"In His dread name whose throne is law."

We believe that the author has only reported an historical incident.

The war has flooded us with a great amount of poetry, or, at least, versification; some of it is in much the condition of many of our brave veterans who must limp on crutches to their graves. A fraction of it will live on as a part of our literary treasures; and to that part, this little volume, most elegantly published, will quite surely contribute several imperishable gems.

11. — *The Constitutional Convention.* By JOHN A. JAMESON. 8vo. New York: Charles Scribner & Co. 1866.

THE historical portions of this work are carefully elaborated from intelligent and faithful study of the origin of our local and general governments. This part of the task has never been better done; some of it has never before been attempted. Besides this and other connected topics, attention has been largely given to the fundamental questions which concern the fountain of power in summoning these bodies for the formation of governments; and the authority of Constitutions over States which have adopted them. On these points the author is strongly conservative, holding to a comparatively limited suffrage for the calling of conventions; and defending a rigid doctrine of the powers of a Constitution when formed. These subjects open political questions of great practical importance, particularly in such a day of constitution-making as the present in our country. The author's views will fail to meet the sentiments of very many of our citizens. But they are well reasoned, in clear, strong, argumentative method. If they do not convince all readers of their soundness, they can not fail to impart much valuable knowledge in a pleasing way; and may not be useless in checking a doctrine of organic changes too rapid and summary for the safety of the body politic. If the checks which Judge Jameson would throw around this machinery must, at times, impose annoying restraints on a community, it is a fair inquiry, whether their abolishment might not, on the whole, involve superior inconveniences. For we take the questions at issue here, to be not the settlement of ethical principles, but the ascertainment, through historical and logical guidance of what is most conducive to the stability and general welfare of a law-making and law-governed people.

12. — *Treasures from the Prose Writings of John Milton.* 12mo. Ticknor & Fields. 1866.

THE character of Milton's prose makes it more difficult to give him in fragmentary specimens than most writers. His strong and splendid sentences are so intertwined with elaborate trains of logic, that it is not easy to sever them from their connections. And this has been hardly attempted in this volume; for the pieces are mostly of considerable length. The topics are not very much in the run of modern thought. But the noble style of writing, the lofty inspiration of this foremost man of his day, must commend anything from his pen to the lovers of the highest literature.

13. — *Great in Goodness. A Memoir of George N. Briggs.* By WILLIAM C. RICHARDS. 12mo. Boston: Gould & Lincoln. 1866.

GOVERNOR BRIGGS was just such a man as we pray for, when we ask that our "officers may be peace, and our exactors righteousness." Will our young men, and particularly our young politicians, study this model? If some of them not young would do the same, and copy it, many good reforms would be the gainers.

14. — *A Summer in Leslie Goldthwaite's Life.* By Mrs. A. D. T. Whitney, author of "Faith Gartney's Girlhood," etc. Illustrated. Boston : Ticknor & Fields. 1867.

Mrs. Whitney has won some reputation as a sprightly, sharp-eyed delineator of young people's ways of thinking and acting : perhaps we should have said ' feeling' instead of thinking, for a large part of their thinking is rather with their emotional than intellectual nature. She discovers much earnestness to do her readers some permanent benefit, as well as to amuse them. She draws beautiful characters, as this of young Leslie, and throws her sympathies into them without stint. But there is also in her a kind of sympathy, or what looks like it at times, with the girlish brusqueness and sauciness of which we see so much in these mannish days. She would not say that she likes her "Sin Saxon" more than the gentle Leslie ; but it is easy to see that this well-named romp or rogue (as you please) is a *con amore* creation, which carries the author's imagination if not her judgment. We do not object to the zest with which the *petite diablerie* of the charming girl is described : it is very true to the life. But it ought to have been decidedly condemned in the doing of it, as well as generally shown to be improper in the rose-water finishing-up of the story. Sin Saxon will continue to be the model of our young misses who aspire to shine, unless something more is effected by our readable authoresses than just to show them how to play off this sort of bravado, with some half smiling—"you shouldn't be so naughty !"—attempt here and there to apply the brakes.

15. — *Open Communion: or, The Lord's Supper for the Lord's People.* By Henry A. Sawtelle, M. A. 12mo. Paper. San Francisco : Winterburn & Co. 1866.

The writer is a strict Baptist in everything save close communion. He contends against this on the ground that baptism is not scripturally enjoined as a pre-requisite to the Lord's Supper, any more than to the preaching of the Gospel ; and presses his brethren with the inconsistency, not to say, absurdity, of exchanging pulpits with ministers who are shut out from the Supper. We sympathize with the author's antagonism to so unchristian a custom as this which he opposes, and hope that he will go on to see that his notion of exclusive immersionism is equally anti-biblical, as is his repudiation, moreover, of the Abrahamic covenant. This *brochure* may do good in the denomination to which he belongs. Its members ought, at least, to be consistent enough to refuse all acts of Christian fellowship to other churches, until they are ready to remove this fence from around the communion table. Who would be the greater losers by such consistency, they can answer as well as their neighbors.

16. — *Orthodoxy: Its Truths and its Errors.* By JAMES FREEMAN CLARKE. 12mo. pp. 439. Appendix, pp. 72. Boston: American Unitarian Association, Walker, Fuller & Co. 1866.

MUCH of this volume shows an effort in the author to be candid, and he may even suppose he has been. We know it is no easy thing for one to define the position of his opponent fairly, but really one attempting it is obligated to come near to a success.

We must say, however, that no one can know what Orthodoxy is by reading this book. The author states some of its truths accurately, others imperfectly, others unfairly, and yet others so out of connection that they become untruths, while many are suppressed totally. The "errors" are seen from an opposing stand-point as our truths that the writer disbelieves. As a critique on Orthodoxy, the volume lacks symmetry, an understanding and appreciation of what Orthodoxy is, and a historical candor in stating it.

The logic of the book is equally imperfect. Orthodoxy is first defined by the philology of the term, but as there have been variations from Augustine down on minor points, it is concluded there is no such thing in book and fact as Orthodoxy. So his very subject is ruled out by the dictionary. So it may be shown that there is no Methodism, because all Methodists of to-day have not the identical methods of the Wesleys; and that there is no such thing as Unitarianism, because all the Orthodox hold to the unity of God, while that supposed denomination differs within itself vastly more than Orthodoxy ever did. Such treatment of a well defined system is unworthy, uncandid, unhistoric. The late National Council of our order affirmed, with but a single dissent, what Orthodoxy is, but this volume bears toward that creed basis the relation of a treatise setting forth modern astonomy, written from the Ptolemaic point of view. The book declares neither the truths nor the errors of Orthodoxy, and we see not how it could fairly come by such a title.

17. — *The New Birth: or the Work of the Holy Spirit.* By AUSTIN PHELPS, Professor in Andover Theological Seminary, Author of "The Still Hour." Boston: Gould & Lincoln. New York: Sheldon & Co. Cincinnati: Geo. S. Blanchard & Co. 1867.

WHATEVER is written by Prof. Phelps is rich in thought, in spirituality and in scholarship. This volume is a very valuable contribution to the literature of the subject under discussion. It seems to be founded upon the philosophy that man is a sinner in character rather than in nature, and that in regenerating the soul, the Holy Spirit changes this character instead of renewing this nature.

18. — *Morning by Morning : or, Daily Readings for the Family, or the Closet.* By C. H. SPURGEON. 12mo. New York : Sheldon & Co. 1866.

A PAGE a day of scriptural and devout meditation, less instructive and more impassioned than Jay and Temple ; more quaint, also, and sometimes fanciful in turns of thought. A selection of Hymns is added.

19. — *Rills from the Fountain of Life : or, Sermons to Children.* By REV. RICHARD NEWTON, D. D. 12mo. New York : Robert Carter & Brothers.

THERE are not sermons enough of this kind preached and printed. Adults would receive more of the Gospel if it were prepared for their children. We venture to say these twelve sermons had a more attentive and profited audience of grown up children than the most of the ordinary preaching of this eminent divine. We heartily commend the volume to pastors, as showing how a sermon for children can be made simple without becoming silly, and how the Gospel can be made plain, and yet be kept strong.

20. — *The Biglow Papers.* Second Series. Boston : Ticknor & Fields. 1867.

IT requires rare genius to trifle honorably with our good English tongue, as Prof. Lowell has in this volume. Whether success in this line should be regarded as a triumph for letters, is a question, as both the writing and reading of such productions must tend to vitiate a pure style. The sooner our provincialisms and vulgarisms and slang are purged away and forgotten, the better, and we regret that a keen wit and rare good thought, in which the Professor abounds, should have lent a kind of dignity to this low style.

The book has a most valuable philological and literary Introduction of eighty pages, tracing and locating the origin of many of our provincialisms in Old England. With a very poor grace, English writers deride us for expressions borrowed from them, as the most of our unfortunate ones were.

21. — *The Flower-De-Luce.* By HENRY WADSWORTH LONGFEL-
LOW. With Illustrations. Boston: Ticknor & Fields. 1867.

THIRTEEN beautiful gems of this favorite poet, set in the most
finished style of this well known publishing house. It must be a
favorite among the holiday books. Its title indicates only one of its
pieces, and that one shows how this author turns a trivial subject
into a teacher of rare taste and sentiment and morals.

22. — *An Essay on Temptation.* By E. C. WINES, D. D. Presbyterian Board of Publication. Philadelphia.

THIS treatise reminds us of the plain, thoughtful and godly essays of Flavel, Doddridge and Baxter. Its style is simple, rich
English, plain to the most unlettered, while the thought is practical,
suggestive and devout. It is a book for a meditative Christian who
earnestly desires to be more holy and useful.

23. — *The Authorship of Shakespeare.* By NATHANIEL HOLMES.
12mo. New York: Hurd & Houghton. 1866.

MR. HOLMES might as well undertake to make a Shakespeare out
of nothing, as out of Lord Bacon. Lord Bacon was learned, but
he was not a poet. Which is the easier, to account for Shakespeare's learning or his genius? And admitting his wonderful
genius, of which in its peculiar aptness and agility Lord Bacon
never gave the slightest evidence, his learning is no great mystery.
These six hundred pages prove how large a book a man may write
to vindicate an absurdity; how much industry and learning he may
foolishly throw away. We hope none of our readers will waste
much time upon this volume.

24. — *Agassiz's Geological Sketches.* Boston: Ticknor & Fields.
1866.

AGASSIZ's recent trip to South America and his lectures upon the
region of the Amazon since his return have added new interest to
these learned and yet quite popular sketches. In the direction of
scientific discussion, the *Atlantic Monthly*, from which they are
gathered, has done important service. It seems to us too, that
Agassiz has become more reverent toward the sacred record and its
Author.

25.—*The Riverside Magazine for Young People* (Jan., 1867), is the
title of Messrs. Hurd & Houghton's new Juvenile Monthly. We have
read its contents with great satisfaction. It evidently believes that
there are yet some " young " people left—some boys and girls not

prematurely forced into ungrown, unripe old heads without hearts ; and it has also ascertained that for such fresh, youthful spirits, a kind of reading is demanded which is not a writing down of adult literature to their comprehension, as if they could not comprehend as much as many of their elders, but is the genuine speech of souls as young and unhackneyed as themselves, with the advantage of a little more experience. This number, then, is not a diminished copy of a fashionable gentleman's or lady's magazine, but real boys' and girls' reading—racy, spicy, natural, not sensational nor silly, but entertaining and instructive. It is illustrated with taste and spirit, and is a specimen of elegant typography. Travels, history, biography, natural science, stories, music, in short, out-door and in-door life generally, will fill its ample and inviting pages. It is in the hands of managers who can safely be trusted with the Christian, as well as other interests of the young. Therefore, especially, we commend it to the homes of our friends and patrons, as just the kind of gift for the " young people " which will please them best, and, at the same time, do them substantial good.

26. — MISCELLANOUS. *Illustrations of the Shorter Catechism, for Children and Youth.* By Jonathan Cross. 2 Vols. Presbyterian Board. These volumes would be a great aid to our teaching or studying this invaluable manual of doctrine, and we receive it as one of the many evidences that the Westminster Catechism is finding its proper and important place again among our juvenile religious text books.

The same Board has also lately issued the following in their admirable "Series for Youth." They would be an excellent addition to any Sabbath School Library. *Amy Rivers: Little Nellie's Velvet Carpet : Asa and his Family : Jesse Thornton and his Friends : The Nevers : Golden Sands : Gold Filings : Ned Turner, or the Boy who said, " Wait a Minute": Blanche's Lesson, and Other Tales. Manna Crumbs for Hungry Souls,* is by the same, but for older minds. It is a happy compilation of thoughtful and godly sayings from that very excellent writer and preacher, the Rev. Samuel Rutherford.

The New York Tract Society has lately published *Phil Kennedy* and *Charlie Scott,* as Life Illustrated. The stories are made up of real incidents and beautifully told, having a good moral withal.

The Tabernacle, or the Gospel According to Moses. By George Junkin, D. D., LL. D., late President of Washington College, Va. Philadelphia : Presbyterian Board of Publication. A very judicious and excellent volume ; simple, intelligible and yet sufficiently learned and thorough.

Our Church and Her Services. By Rev. Ashton Oxenden, Rector of Huckly, Kent, England. Adapted to the Protestant Episcopal Church in U. S. A. By Rev. F. D. Huntington, D. D., Rector, Emmanuel Church. Boston: E. P. Dutton & Co. 1866.

For churchmen an excellent book; and for those who are not, it contains many profitable practical thoughts. The worldly element from every other church, said to be making its exodus toward the "true church," must feel the necessity of such treatises. Dr. Huntington is really the most important acquisition which Episcopacy has lately received.

The Character of Jesus Portrayed. By Dr. Daniel Schenkel. Translated and Edited by W. H. Furness, D. D. Two Vols. Boston: Little & Brown. To be reviewed.

The Brewer Family. By Mrs. Ellis. New York: M. W. Dodd.

The Brownings. A Tale of the Great Rebellion. Same Publisher.

Paradise Lost. New York: Hurd & Houghton.

Lalla Rookh. By Thomas Moore. Same Publishers. Good library editions of standard poems.

The Sanctuary. A Story of the Civil War. By Geo. Ward Nichols. New York: Harpers.

That Good Old Time; or Our Fresh and Salt Tutors. By Vieux Moustache. New York: Hurd & Houghton.

Stories of Many Lands. Grace Greenwood. Ticknor & Fields.

Frank's Search for Sea Shells. The Story of Zadoc Hall. By H. F. P. *Uncle Downes's Home.* By Glance Gaylord. Boston Tract Society.

Lyntonville: or The Irish Boy in Canada. Sisters and Not Sisters. By Mrs. M. E. Berry. *Sybil Grey: or A Year in The City. Jesus Christ's Alluring Love.* By Rev. George Flavel. New York Tract Society.

The College Days of Calvin. By Rev. Wm. M. Blackburn. Philadelphia: Presbyterian Board of Publication. An excellent book for young men.

Young Calvin in Paris. Same Author and Publishers. A companion to the former, giving fresh glimpses of this great man.

The Arithmetic of Life. By Sister Ruth. *Annie Lincoln's Lesson. Harry and His Dog Fidele. Bertie and His Best Things. Alice and other Tales. The Path and the Lamp. Lucy Clifton. Little Eppie. Isabel's Birth Day. Hugo and Franz. Kitty Dennison. Weeds and Seeds. Mary Raymond. A Week in Lilly's Life. Our Passover.* By Rev. Wm. J. McCord. Philadelphia. Presbyterian Board of Publication.

ARTICLE XII.

THE ROUND TABLE.

OUR SEVENTH YEAR AND ENLARGED PLANS. The change in our title indicates a change in our scope and aims. The National Council made our Denomination a unit in its doctrinal basis, and unless that basis be disturbed we see no longer a necessity for polemical discussions, as within the Denomination. The common enemy of evangelical truth should now engross the undivided attention of its defenders, and it gratifies us much to see a strong and growing tendency to union for this end.

The interests of our faith and polity have been too long sacrificed on minor issues among ourselves, and in an unwise indifference to our own growth. With all Christian good will toward other sects we think it not illiberal to say that we love our own ecclesiastical order best. All, therefore, that pertains to us as the Congregational Denomination of the country in doctrine, polity, Institutions, Societies and propagation, we mean now to advocate and press with what force we have and can enlist. Our purpose is to make the *Congregational Review* broad, manly, thorough and distinct for Congregationalism, as set forth by the late Council in both its faith and order. We shall know no school or party except such as may combine against the doctrine and polity adopted by that body.

While we intend to give a good proportion of our columns to general literature, and to the discussion of important and current questions, as related to morals and Christian faith, we mean that Biblical and exegetical studies, and an exposition of our church government and articles of faith, shall be the leading feature, as it should be, of a denominational Review. In carrying out our broader plans, we have added to our board of local editors two names, widely and favorably known, and are completing our arrangement for *Associate Editors* at distant and different points in the country, who, with an eye to sectional necessities, will help us in our endeavors to expound, defend and propagate the principles and interests of Congregationalism, as related to the church of Christ. And we intend that those, so to be associated with us in the editorial management of the *Review*, shall be such men as to assure all that our basis and scope are as broad as the Denomination. We expect to announce this arrangement in our next Number. With what strength we have we intend to unite and invigorate and urge forward our body, that, with other denominations holding a common faith, we may give to the people a sanctified literature and our land and the world to Christ and his church.

With these views and aims and plans, we ask a candid reception and a cordial co-operation.

CHRISTENDOM IN 1867. Dr. Cumming relieves himself of the failure of the past year to fulfil all his predictions, by telling us that eighteen hundred and sixty-six does not properly end until next March; and reassures himself in his old persuasion, by declaring that eighteen hundred and sixty-seven will most certainly exhaust all the remaining prophetic numbers. If this should not be the fact, it might be a two-sided question, whether the Doctor himself will be likely to be exhausted? Not entering upon this speculation, nor upon any prophetical arithmetic, we will take a look at the position of things in Christendom's moral and religious progress, as the New Year opens upon us.

The old doctrine of the balance of power in Europe has come to be something more than a political concern. It has suddenly loomed up into a question of the rights of the peoples thus balanced, rather than of the royal prerogatives and claims so involved. That balance was held in its old position by mechanical pressure, not by normal affinities and attractions. When, therefore, it began to lean heavily, it went over bottom-side-up like an iceberg in a thaw, with a tremendous swash, and an instantaneous re-settling in a very different shape. The fortnight Prussian and Austrian war was the summersault of European power. It shows us the unification of Germany under Protestant leadership, thus, in two weeks, answering the prayers of German patriots for generations gone by. This is a permanent triumph of civil and religious liberty. Not that Prussia is a free government in our sense of the term; nor that all the German States are Protestant. But Germany is now one nation under the auspices of the Lutheran Reformation; a first-class nation able to cope with any European power; stronger, in every way, now, than France; flushed with ambition to make a bold demonstration in favor of an advanced civilization, which is only what Christianity desires.

The great heart of Europe is thus beating true to human rights in the main. It is significant that, just at this moment, Russia comes forward to enter into a close alliance with the new German Empire, which places her immense prestige and prowess in the same line of advance into a worthier style of national development. The union of two such nations is ominous to French politics. France feels

herself to-day outranked by her continental neighbors.   Her Jesuit-
ism and her atheism have emasculated her strength.   Her flashy
culture and her spasmodic military exploits have not had a living
virility in them.   French glory is of the claptrap sort, and the
clapping is growing small.   Superstition and infidelity have cursed
her, and she is weak and faint when she needs to be the strongest.
Neither Germany nor Italy cares, at this moment, for French
friendship or enmity.

Italian unity, too, is at last a fact accomplished.   That land is no
more cut up into pieces to fatten the laziest, most worthless set of
temporal and spiritual princes which ever impoverished a people.
If its king is not a Protestant, he is the next best to it, an excommunicated Roman Catholic, not likely to forget his own grievances
from the Pope, nor yet those of the so noble, the high-spirited,
broken-hearted wife of Maximilian.   The Pope is a cypher in
European matters, without a home to call his own, living on the
charitable contributions of the faithful.   The "temporal power" is a
thing of yesterday, impossible to be regained.   The papal government does not expect it.   So much of the calculations of students in
prophecy has come to pass, as set down by Scott, Newton and
others, of the last century of expositors.

Concerning Austria, who asks what she is doing?   Her downfall reminds one of the terrible and sudden overthrow threatened to
the Babylonish "Lucifer, son of the morning," in Isaiah fourteenth.
She has followed Spain to an old age as premature as it is imbecile.

It certainly looks very much as if the political judgment-day of
Popery, at least, has come.   This of course, does not carry with it
the suppression of the ecclesiastical power of that hierarchy.   But
we incline to think it will weaken rather than reinforce this arm of
her strength.   Very much of her power over her unintelligent membership has come from the prestige of her temporal grandeur, her
regal consequence, at that old centre of imperial magnificence.   It
may, for a long time, have been only a sham; but shams have vast
influence until they are exploded.   Then the stroke is apt to be
severe the other way.   But this will be determined in due time.

The Turkish situation is critical.   It can not be long before the
Sultan must move his harem over into Asia.   His presence on the
west side of the Bosphorus is simply a nuisance.   Who will abate it
is the question.   If the young heart of Italy should throw itself into
this struggle, with the Greeks for allies in the crusade against the
Koran and its slavish followers, the world might again see what
would remind it of former deeds of splendid chivalry along those

classic shores and waters.   These kingdoms are all very near neighbors ; and the Candian revolt is not ended.

We have watched the progress of our own national fortunes with
the deepest interest, not to say solicitude.   It has not surprised us
that the termination of our war should have left the theatre of it in
a state of anarchical discord and wretchedness.   The destruction of
a false civilization is a shorter thing to be done, than the reconstruction of a true and healthy state of society.   To shove the latter,
as a ready made machine, into the former's place, is simply impossible.   It is not a thing to be built up, and imported from abroad,
like a train of railway cars and engine.   It is a tree to be grown
from a seed, a slow and careful process, even when you keep the
cattle from horning it, and the school-children from whittling it.
Considering what hinderments of both these kinds our tree of
Southern reconstruction has had to grow against, perhaps it looks
as promising as could reasonably be expected, which we fear, is not
saying very much.   The last year has, however, settled some results.   It is sure that slavery is extinct, beyond the hope of revival,
even at the South.   It is almost sure that the African race will be
enfranchised soon, as they have been emancipated.   They are no
longer slaves ; they are not yet citizens.   They are suffering, beyond description, from every sort of hardship and injustice, in this
transition state.   That is inevitable.

But it is not hopeless and endless.   We have no idea that enfranchisement will at once give them complete protection.   Neither
have we the slightest doubt but that this protection will, by and
by, be gained in a legitimate, satisfactory, and permanent way.
We never, for a moment, lost faith in our country's salvation, at her
darkest hour.   Now, we see many signs that the great cause of
"the government of the people, for the people, by the people" is assuredly to triumph.   We have settled several vital questions, both
in the State and General governments, which will not again be
disturbed.   We have passed the point of provincial insubordination
and of dictatorial danger.   Our future is most hopeful, and most
stimulative to philanthropic and Christian labor for the whole Republic.   We have a thousand fold better field to work in, than was
Europe after the disintegration of the Roman Empire.   That was a
more vitiated condition of society than any thing which we have to
contend with, while, instead of the rude hordes of Northern barbarians, who had that mighty reconstruction in charge, our appliances
for the task before us are the Christian forces of the highest civilization to which man has yet attained.

ANCHORED.

I'm anchored in my Saviour's love,
   The tides may come and go ;
I'm floating now with them above,
   I'm floating now below.

But still my anchor strong doth hold,
   Whichever way the tide ;
Through sun and storm, through heat and cold
   I shall securely ride.

The tide bears other barks apart,
   As up and down it flows ;
But still my moorings keep me fast,
   I find a sweet repose.

Some float all wrecked far out to sea ;
   And some are cast ashore,
With broken mast and sundered knee,
   And widely scattered store.

But there's no earthly wind or wave,
   That terror has to me ;.
For storm and tempest I can brave,
   Can I but hold in Thee !

CHURCH LITERATURE. Floating straws and other drift indicate a strong current setting in through the channels of some churches, which have not given much attention heretofore to the business of general self-education. A Roman Catholic Monthly, to keep out of the fold, thus fenced off, some other monthlies, is, to say the least, a sign of self-consciousness which is noteworthy. We doubt if it is likely to rival the interlopers, in literary ability ; for it is not an easy feat to spring a full armed Minerva into life out of any *caput mortuum*, be it even of a Roman Jupiter. But we are glad that the necessity of intellectual nutriment and growth is beginning to be recognized by our Papal fellow-citizens. If a relish for something really sharp and strong, as a mental diet, can be excited, then the feeders of that flock must provide for this new appetite, or it will seek food where it can find it ; for which it will not need to go very far, in this land   With the fate, however, of Dr. Brownson in fresh memory, we fear that the hope of any very great demand for a manly literature in that quarter, is not flattering. The genius of that heretical schism from the true church has directly opposed the progress of mental freedom for too many centuries, to make any rapid change, even in free America.

Our Protestant prelatic brethren are looking the same subject in the face with more than usual earnestness. They seem to be somewhat exercised by the activity of their Christian neighbors in furnishing the membership of their respective churches with denominational and religious publications; and are thus feeling the stimulus of a brotherly provocation to go and do likewise. It is hardly logical for that wing of " the sect " Episcopalian, which represents itself through the *Church Monthly* of this city, to slur severely the religious literature of other churches as " the offspring of a morbid revivalism," " the everlasting cant of learning that is not skin deep," when, whatever may be the short-comings or the extra-goings of this kind of reading, the best part of the books in common vogue among its own Low church people is much of the same sort—endorsed abundantly by " successors of the apostles " in the unfractured concatenation. But logic is at a discount in these days. Soundings, however, in supposed deep water are not always found to require the deep sea plummet; as, witness the Jesuit Professor Harper's recent exposure of Dr. Pusey's great ignorance of the very church fathers of whom he makes so much use in his Eirenicon. We sincerely hope that Dr. Pusey will be able to defend his scholarship against the erudite Jesuit's strictures of " unverified quotations," taken at second hand, " proved to be partly fictitious, partly corrupted, and not unfrequently falsified." [1] Passing this, we must risk the suggestion that there is enough of the same want of sympathy, in the Episcopal denomination, with a free movement of the mind, to which we just alluded in the Romanists, to block any considerable advance in the direction to which a few of their younger and fresher men would urge that church. It is, we apprehend, an organic, and, of course, a very chronic trouble that is in the way, and is quite likely to stay there. The men and women who are just now doing most to awaken a new intellectual thirst in that church, are generally late recruits from the outside " patched-up-irregularities," where they got their real intellectual culture and impulse, either in youth or riper years, which debt they should not too loudly ignore. So, in the best days of their church, which were a number of generations gone by, the men whom they and we delight to honor and to study, were men who had felt, to their souls' centres, the large inspirations of the Reformation on the Continent of Europe, and of the reawakenings of the English Commonwealth; and whose work in their own denomination was greatly energized by forces from without its pale. All this is history. We doubt if sub-

[1] *Peace through the Truth.* By the Rev. T. Harper, S. J. Prof. of Theology: London. 1866.

sequent influences of much power in that church have been favorable to the reappearance of any such mental vigor as produced those illustrious writers, and found for them appreciative readers. It will require a stronger motive-power than is at present visible in the field, to dispel such an intellectual lethargy, as a writer in the last September *Church Monthly*, who doubtless knows whereof he affirms, describes in more pages than we can quote ; but here is a sample :

" I do not believe there is one parish priest in ten who does anything toward encouraging a truly Christian literature. I do not believe there is one in ten who has ever taught his people publicly on the duty of having a religious newspaper in every family. I do not believe there is one parish in ten where there is even a decent parish library, or where the rector pays any attention to its circulation. The greater number of our clergy, even men of culture themselves, and even bishops among the number, have almost ignored the duty of a practical Christian education of their people in this particular, and with folded hands and piteous faces have wondered at the power of Satan in turning away the hearts of the people under their charge. Nay, these same clergy have carped at and given their influence positively against almost every effort to use the periodical press as a means of diffusing a knowledge of church principles. They have looked upon the press as the engine of Satan, and instead of turning his weapons into methods of church extension, they have only advertised from the pulpit his wonderful works. There is an apathy in our church, not only among the clergy but of course among the people, that makes those who believe that we are a true branch of the Catholic church, and that it is the bounden duty of the clergy, as Christ's servants, to make the Christian faith aggressive at every point, sick at heart ; though with the recent signs of life, we may now take some encouragement. It shows that in respect of Christian education our own people are half a century behind the age. There is a prejudiced narrowness among us in these matters which is unaccountable. Not the meanest sect in Christendom has so ignored the press as an aid to Christian work as the American church has done ; and the living example of our own Mother Church shames us into confusion of face. There is not a single church periodical in the country which is decently supported. The men who are at the head of the most successful, stay in their positions simply from a sense of duty and at personal sacrifice. Church publishers tell the same story, and the best religious books we have were first brought out by leading publishers of general literature, who could afford to run the very great risk of publication. When you visit the homes of our church families, you find, even among the best educated, persons of affluence and leisure, hardly any church literature, perhaps a single church paper, but hardly any of the current educational literature which we have. It is the exception, not the rule, to find them even decently informed on the progress of the church, and the questions which such laymen ought to consider."

We candidly say, that we are sorry for this state of things, and honestly hope that knowledge will spread among our brethren. Nor do we fear that this, if it be sound knowledge, will at all curtail the sway of those denominations who think " a church without a bishop " is no more a Christian anomaly than " a state without a king."

The Critics. These sometimes puzzle us not a little. We find ourselves almost inclined to conclude that much which is dignified with the name of criticism is only the repetition of fixed prepossessions, not to say prejudices, stirred into reiteration by some new chord or discord struck upon the critic's mind, from the pages which he may be perusing. What other key than this is there to the fact that men read history so differently, history so recent as that of our own New England of a half century ago : that intelligent scholars are at direct issue, whether, for example, "Dr. Johns" is a caricature or a portrait. Are we to suppose that its censors are "blue Puritans," and its apologists something else, and that this explains the discrepancy? Is literary criticism then an affair of church polity or creed, to be settled by the question where an author and his reviewer go "to meeting"? Are we coming to know how a writer will fare in this or that magazine, by just reading its name on the cover? These inquiries, of course, have two sides to them, and we propound them, as so many other things are now-a-days put forth, for the benefit of all concerned. We certainly ourselves are of this number, and like honest preachers desire to take our due share of the "word of exhortation."

Without consciousness of undue bias, the critic may easily read and write under the influence of some early accident, which has warped the judgment upon certain topics. It is a misfortune to have suffered any such injury, for it is next to impossible to rise above its power. Yet the true critic must do it. His balances must have no loaded weights ; his measures, no false bottoms. The critic, like the judge, must sit with bandaged eyes, so far as regards all mere personal considerations, because he is a judge ; and justice is blind to favoritism. He should do thus. But it is certain that this is not done ; else these sharp pens would not be clashing so often, like polished scimitars, over the same dead or living subject of their strife.

We are told that this is a critical in distinction from a creative age. This does not refer only to professional reviewing; for in history, and fiction, and general letters, the criticism of men and measures, of policies, ideas, systems of every sort, in life and art, is

busily going on. Every body is trying a hand at analysis and synthesis. Taking in pieces and putting together again is the
favorite pastime now, in authorship, even to the reconstructing of
theology itself; with a vast preponderance, however, on the pulling
down side of the business. We are literally nothing now, " if not
critical"—with some danger of a surplusage of Iagos. But the
periodical part of this profession is in the most danger, from obvious
causes. It has a mighty power, which there are strong temptations
to use in an illegitimate way, for personal or class interests or an-
tagonisms. A "good hater" has no more rightful place in the
critic's chair, than a fulsome eulogist. The criticism of depreciation, Saint Beuve has told us, plays the part of a detective. Yet
all detection is not depreciation. A good police is as necessary in
letters as in municipal affairs. But a New Orleans police is of
small worth in either. The criticism of appreciation, the same
authority adds, seeks the honors of a discoverer; to find out the
good things in an author more than the bad; the wheat, if this
there be, on the unthreshed floor, to which useful result some
wholesome thrashing is certainly not amiss. But the flail should
not be swung by a Thug or a Bohemian. The illustrious critic just
alluded to has one other suggestion (we are writing from memory)
with which we close: there is danger of dulling the power of
tasting the real quality of an author, through a habit of dogmatic
judging: whereas, the value of all criticism depends directly upon
keeping this power as fresh and sensitive as at the first. It should,
in fact, become more delicate by continuous exercise.

DISCE AB HOSTE. Old fashioned believers, who are tempted to
be ashamed of their faith, should remember the frank concessions of
its opponents to its value, as when Robespierre said, before the
National Convention of 1794, that "the idea of a Supreme Being
and of the immortality of the soul, was a continual call to justice,
and that no nation can succeed without a recognition of these
truths." The butcheries of the guillotine and the horrors of *sans-
culottism* were giving proof enough of the unwilling confession.
This is only a comment upon Voltaire's dictum, a generation before: "If there were no God, it would be necessary to invent one."
Conversing with a highly educated graduate of one of our Universities, upon whom it has conferred peculiar honors, he remarked
upon the utter weakness and inconclusiveness of Unitarian criticism
of Calvinistic theologians, observing that he had been reading carefully some of the latter, and that nothing impressed him intellectually so strongly, or so grasped his imagination, while he did not ac-

cept the system as religiously true. But the grand elementary facts of it, as necessity, freedom, sacrifice, and the like, it were vain to deny, for he found the response to them in his own consciousness ; and in a form that the philosophizing of the Liberal school fell entirely short of satisfying.

A few years ago, the *Westminster Review*, in a more sympathetic than flattering criticism of "Essays and Reviews," made some acknowledgments here, which deserve to be reproduced, as alike an encouraging and an admonitory paragraph for the times :

" Every religion which ever flourished did so by the strength of a body of doctrine and a system of definite axioms. Nothing else can give unity and permanence to its teaching. No collection of maxims or rules of life can last long, when deprived of dogmatic basis, and common intellectual assent. The whole teaching and influence of every religion has rested ultimately and entirely on cardinal propositions universally received as true. Nothing but such a basis can satisfy the mind of an inquirer, or give coherence to the social body. Moral principles have been found to lead to strife, when made the foundations of communities. Endless attempts have been made towards union in an ideal life. They have ended invariably in chimera and confusion. The moment one cardinal doctrine is surrendered as uncertain or even provisional, the whole intellectual framework gives way. All the repose, the unity, all the permanence which rest upon undoubted truths are gone. The unguided feelings, the variety and fluctuation of moral conceptions, take their place in endless agitation and discord. Such a work, indeed, undoes the labor of St. Paul, brought to perfection by the church. He taught faith, hope, and charity, insisting, indeed, chiefly on the moral truth, but resting it on a system of immutable doctrine. He preached a life of righteousness in this world, to be followed by certain glory in the next. He preached ' Christ and him crucified.' Once doubt the certainty of the story, or the reality of the sacrifice, and to what will the preacher appeal ? He will be left to the truism—' To be good, for it is good to be good.' . . . ., It is not this which can bring order out of the intellectual anarchy around us, control the whole moral energy of the present, and heal the deep diseases in society and states."

We are not concerned to account for the inconsistency of this most truthful utterance with the general tone of that mischievously able quarterly. If Saul is found among the prophets, let him explain this as he may. It is a noble tribute to the truth, as the church has, in all ages, taught and upheld it. We smile at the writers well put "truism." It reminds us of primary school exhortations and other juvenile addresses, on the "be good and be happy" text, *ad nauseam*. Yet this is about the highest reach of many a modern pulpit, the bottom of which has dropped out. Verily, such a ποῦ στῶ will never help any one's lever to move the world.

PROGRESS OF LIBERTY. We should be untrue alike to the history and instincts of Congregationalism, did we not thankfully record the advancement of the race toward a larger civil and political freedom, during the year past. In our own country, it is very apparent, that there can be no reaction or cessation of agitation, until impartial suffrage shall be accorded to all who bear God's image. We do not expect that the principle finally adopted will include woman as well as man. True woman does not ask it and would not accept it. When she does ask it, and when she feels prepared to accept with it all the duties of citizenship, that of bearing arms, the correlative of suffrage, included, it may be expedient, at least, to grant it. With the death of the rebellion, Napoleon's petty empire in Mexico has also expired; and it would not be strange if the Munroe doctrine should be so applied to that country, that no European power will hereafter venture to set foot upon it. Perhaps, the American eagle may soon be able to stretch the tip of one of his wings over it for protection. Austria and Prussia have had a short, but brilliant and decisive conflict, which has resulted in freeing Germany from the fatal ascendancy which has so long oppressed her, as well as Europe from the disagreable dominion of the French empire. The star of Napoleon III. seems to be on the decline.

> "What! did any maintain
> That God or the people (think!)
> Could make a marvel in vain?
> Out of the water-jar there
> Draw wine that none could drink?"

This interrogatory of Mrs. Browning is very significant in view of the recent policy of the French Emperor. The liberator of Italy becomes the would-be enslaver of Mexico. If "the water-jar there" seemed, at first, to hold "good wine," it is nothing but the stalest of water now. Italy had a hand in the European struggle of the year, but with indifferent success. It was "the needle-gun" that brought her unity, that drove the Austrians from that land of classic glory, as well as from Germany. One of the results also to her, was the re-acquisition of Venice, after almost seventy years of Austrian and French rule. The dreams of the British lion have been disturbed by visions of doughty Fenians fighting for a country, and he has been compelled to sleep all the year with half-closed eye, lest an insurrection might take place in some unexpected quarter. At this time, however, Irish patriotism seems to be paying extravagant prices for board in New York city, instead of leading armies to the field. The people in England are agitating for an increase of the elective franchise. Egypt has become a constitutional government, and Christians as well as Mohammedans share in its advantages. The temporal power of the Pope has been finally destroyed, and the world is at loss what to do with the successor of St. Peter. These are some of the grand forward movements of the people during the year 1866. We rejoice in them all, and pray for His advent, whose is the " kingdom, and the power, and the glory, for ever."

PARTON AS HERCULES. IT is remarkable to find the old myths of the ancients repeating themselves in modern times. Mr. Parton is an illustration of this; for he has evidently selected, as his *role*, the part of Hercules. Having in his Life of Aaron Burr brought Cerberus from the lower world, and having more recently cleansed the Augean stables under the charge of the New York city government, in an article on Beecher's Pulpit in the last *Atlantic*, he appears armed cap-a-pie against the hydra of Orthodoxy, which, according to Mrs. Beecher Stowe, Dr. Holmes or Donald G. Mitchell, has so long ravaged our fair New England. To prepare himself for the last labor, Mr. Parton actually attended church, one Sabbath, in Mr. Beecher's meeting-house and, wonderful feat! one evening's service in Mr. Beecher's lecture-room. Mr. Parton regards fashionable religion such as sits in Fifth Avenue churches and listens to expensive choirs with great contempt. But the people that worship (with) Mr. Beecher at twelve thousand dollars a year, and pay twenty-five thousand dollars for a splendid organ, are consistent enough Christians for him. According to Mr. Parton, Mr. Beecher is the grand bridge over which Orthodoxy is passing, with multitudinous tread, to where liberal Christianity sits in the polar regions of no-belief and infidelity. We have always regarded Mr. Beecher as pretty shaky, and now we are told the character of the abutment on the further side. It reminds us of one of Mr. Lincoln's stories about a bridge to the infernal regions.

THE LINES BEING DRAWN. The signs of the times for Christian Union are more and more obvious and ominous of good. The Master has said: " He that is not with me is against me." This line made but two parties of all men. Since that time his friends have been sadly subdivided, and often quite mixed in with the great opposing party. It is a goodly sight to see the change now going on to restore the one original line of Christ. The two great parties are drawing off in opposite fronts. Ritualism, rationalism and infidelity are falling into line over against Evangelism. The friends of a revealed religion and experimental piety, while they retain denominational names, are coming shoulder to shoulder for a common end. The Old and New School Presbyterians are thinking of better things than past issues, the Baptists are moving earnestly for open communion, and strong men and warm hearts in the Episcopacy are growing ardent and practical for church fellowship and ministerial exchanges, regardless of prelatical ordination and church organizations. Congregationalism is talking and working together, since her noble Council, to enlighten and sanctify the country. All these parties, feeling that they have the faith once delivered to the saints, can cease contending, except for the best gifts in doing the most for a common Lord. This is a good omen. We are coming evidently nearer to the time when the prayers of David, the son of Jesse, will be ended.

AMERICAN ART. There is no one thing in which the progress of our country during the last quarter of a century has been more marked than in the growing list of her distinguished artists. In landscape-painting and sculpture we have had for some time names which hold no second rank. If we have not yet seen our Sir Joshua Reynolds in portrait-painting, such names as Stuart, Alexander, Ames and Wight, are sufficient to save us from reproach.

To make a great artist, something more is required than a man to whom God has given all the necessary natural endowments. Great historical epochs contribute largely to the production of great historical painters ; and the artist must be in full sympathy with the epoch, or, even though he have the genius of Raphael or Michael Angelo, his success will be only partial. The last few years of our history have been wonderfully adapted to promote high historical art among us, and we shall be much disappointed if we have not the men who shall make the canvas speak to the coming generations of the men and deeds which have excited the surprise and admiration of the civilized world.

These thoughts have been suggested by the study of Mr. Marshall's masterly engraving of his own portrait of Abraham Lincoln. We first caught a glimpse of it hanging in the counting-room of a Boston merchant ; and, having never before seen any thing that answered to our idea of that remarkable man, our thought was, "That will do." We have studied it since, and it improves wonderfully upon every examination. It reminds us, more than almost any recent production, of the best things of Sharp ; and it will stand the same test : place it by the side of most engravings which have been pronounced good, and it will spoil them. Assuredly it needs not the high eulogium which the distinguished French artist Couture has pronounced upon it, " really superb," " most admirable," to draw to it the attention it deserves. We shall cherish it with national pride, and transmit it to our children, not only as an exceedingly beautiful specimen of highest art in line engraving, but as a faithful representation of that lamented man whose name will be encircled with a brighter lustre as the ages pass away.

OF THE JEWELS AND ADORNINGS OF WOMAN. The real ornaments of person are not visible objects. They are in the mind, the heart and the character. It is the soul shining through that constitutes the beautiful. It is a habit, a practice, a principle in action that constitutes the real ornament. She who glides in modest, silent haste along the paths of usefulness, shows better the graces of motion than she of the saloon of fashion. There is no article of jewelry for the hand so attractive and truly becoming as practical industry and works of mercy. The welling up of deep, pure, unselfish emotions gives the richest lustre to the eye, and those lips part nearest the line of beauty that speak right words to reclaim the erring, to console the sorrowing, to embolden virtue and confirm truth. True beauty forsakes the lips that flatter, deceive, curl in disdain at humble worth, or deny gentle words to the ignorant, the poor and the suffering. That ear is best jewelled that hears quickest the words of knowledge, the cry of human want. The bracelets that most commend the person are patience and perseverance, strengthening weary arms till a good work be done. The lockets to be treasured and worn as precious mementos are the mental and moral features of the wise, the good, the great. Diamonds of truth and gems of thought are the most ornamental of all the precious stones, and are the richest, most brilliant adorning of the head. That dress best becomes the person, and is nearest the highest style of dress, that has been diminished in cost, if need be, to make an unclad neighbor comfortable. The golden chains to be coveted for their real worth are those of such example, influence and character as bind over friends to a better life and lead admirers to a brighter world. The pearls that most adorn are of the heart, the Christian virtues in the beautiful setting of a symmetrical character. The perfume that is sweetest, richest, and most enduring in the apartments and walks of the true woman, is of the alabaster box broken in the honor and love of the Saviour. Its rare odors linger to delight many, long after she breaking it has passed through the gates of pearl.

Is the Race of the Giants Extinct? We know that Og, king of Bashan, and Lambert of Kentucky are dead, but has the Anak family wholly ceased? In younger days and nearer to College life, we remember how we hung on the lips and sentences of Webster, Everett and Choate, Clay and Benton. We recall the small hours of the morning, that the Lake poets, and poets quite opposite to Windermere, stole from our juvenile sleep, not forgetting that nearer neighbors on the Merrimac, Charles and Green Rivers, robbed us oftener, and fired our ardor more intensely. Knickerbocker of Sunny-Side memories, in more senses than one, and he of Abbottsford always carried us captive without parley.

No speakers, no authors, so rob our rest and fire our hearts in these later days. We looked up then and wondered, and enjoyed hero worship. We look abroad now and see no Anakim. Is the change in us, or in the race? New England rivers and mountains, surrounding our cradle home, have grown smaller in our estimation, since we have climbed the Alleghanies and paddled in the Missouri. The duodecimos of our early home library have become minimos to us, since we have made ourselves familiar with Harvard alcoves.

Yet the more we see of men the more we feel that those of our early days carried spears like weavers' beams. They were even then octavos to us, but since that time they have been growing to royal quartos.

Have the times changed to greater men and deeds, and we not changed with them? Are we spell-bound in a kind of Rip Van Winkle dream, or are our eyes open with nothing wonderful to be seen? We are in an inquiring state of mind.

THE

CONGREGATIONAL REVIEW.

Vol. VII.—APRIL, 1867.—No. 36.

ARTICLE I.

CONGREGATIONAL LITERATURE AS A PRESENT DENOMINATIONAL WANT.

DENOMINATIONAL Boards of Publication, as organs of denominational literature, are modern institutions. They are the legitimate products of the times. The printed page, as a moral force, has come into successful competition with the public address. The denominational press is, therefore, very naturally felt to be the necessary adjunct of the pulpit. Such a Board should be the exponent of the doctrines and life of the eccle siastical body whose name it bears. A Congregational literature should be the exponent of Congregationalism; of that system of doctrines, rites and polity maintained by our Puritan ancestors, who, to secure a deeper spirituality of life, and purer forms of worship, fled from persecution, and took refuge in the American wilderness. In the Fatherland they were divided into Nonconformists and Separatists, or Independents. In New England, after some slight modification of views, they coalesced, and became the founders of churches which may be called distinctively Puritan Congregational; and their biblical system, Puritan Congregationalism.

Puritan Congregationalism is a distinct scheme of faith and church polity, as definitely bounded as Episcopacy, Methodism, or Presbyterianism. As the river flowing in its own channel, smiling upon its own banks and swollen by its own tributaries, is the same stream, notwithstanding its enlargements ; so Puritan Congregationalism, though the product of different minds working in the same exhaustless mine of revelation, has a marked individuality ; and though it contain doctrines in common with other denominations, yet such is their logical combination and relative positon in the system, that it possesses elements of power entirely its own.

We not only affirm the system to be biblical in the general acceptation of the term, but more than this ; that the whole history of its disinterment from the rubbish of the Papacy and subsequent progress proves it to be the system of a sisterhood of churches, who take the Bible, interpreted by Christian experience or in agreement with the preferences of the renovated heart, as their only directory in matters of Christian faith and morality, of rites and worship, of church organization and government. We by no means present this as a discriminating definition radically distinguishing us from other denominations ; certainly not one which they will accept. We only state it as a fact which we believe demonstrable to impartial minds, and from which important practical inferences may be drawn illustrative of our subject. In other words, its system of scriptural truths flows harmoniously in the same channel with the experiences of grace in the soul.

Not that the Puritan blindly follows his sympathies or spiritual impulses. There are impressions concerning the truths of Scripture and Christian experience which are the mere offspring of a diseased fancy or feverish brain. We refer only to those sympathies and affections which are the production of the Holy Spirit ; and are, therefore, consonant to the dictates of reason and conscience. The same spirit which inspired the word of God illuminates the mind ; the light of one reflects light upon the other, and a rational sympathy is awakened between them. Sacred truth is " spiritually discerned." What is not fully comprehended, or seen logically connected, the Puritan receives because revealed by him whom his soul adores. Recognizing the difference between the experience of a Gospel truth and the comprehension of it in its manifold relations, he sits at the Saviour's feet, joyfully listening to his words, watching and waiting for further light ; in full communion with all who are hanging upon the same lips and treasuring the same words of eternal life, though they happen not to understand them precisely as he does.

Hence the Puritan scheme of doctrines and ecclesiastical usages. They are received because taught, and yet not simply because taught, but because loved. While they are the dictates of God's word, they are approved, even desired, by the Christian consciousness : so that the system is the joint production of honest study and of the heart reconciled to God.

A few specifications are sufficient for proof. The Bible represents the divine glory as the chief and ultimate end of all intelligent existence. The Puritans give this doctrine a fundamental position in their system. The regenerated soul is joyful in that glory. The Bible places God upon the throne as absolute sovereign, and he whose heart is renewed desires him to occupy it as such. He not only admits God's absolute ownership in his creation, and acknowledges him to be the universal lawgiver and judge, but rejoices to comply with his holy claims. Entire consecration he longs to realize. So absolute does he feel his individual responsibilities to be, that he can suffer no man to stand between himself and the divine claims; and must therefore obey God rather than man, though martyrdom be the result. The scriptural account of his entire moral depravity, of his need of a Saviour, of the necessity of the new birth, and of the unacceptableness of any works of his own while unregenerate, is confirmed to him by the illuminations of the Holy Ghost; and no logic can persuade him of their falsity. Such, indeed, is his deep sense of his inveterate corruption, of the purity and majesty of the divine law, and of the excellence of the divine glory, that he heartily responds to the declaration of Scripture that his atoning Saviour is, and must be, God as well as man, one who can fully sympathise with Jehovah's attachment to his own glory and immutable law, and at the same time, with man's infirmity and ruined condition. The doctrine of the saint's perseverance he deems an essential truth of the Gospel, and his holy, humble heart, can find no rest without it. He knows he ought to be holy as God is holy, and desires no lower standard of Christian attainment; yet, when he would do good, finding evil present with him, he is ready at every step of his progress to acknowledge with Paul : " By the grace of God I am what I am." He believes in infant baptism, not only because he finds its privileges a part of God's gracious covenant with the father of all believers, but because it is the yearning of his own parental heart. As he rejoices to dedicate himself publicly to God, he desires to dedicate publicly his child to him. Believing that God bids us worship him in spirit and in truth, he rejects all empty forms and ceremonies; the sweet communion of the soul with its creator, and with all who are like him, in social prayer and praise, being all the worship his renovated heart craves.

Thus it is with the whole circle of Puritan doctrines. The heart of the true penitent, burning like a seraph's at the feet of Jesus, can see no others appropriate to its needs. The Bible would not be his chosen directory were not its pages adorned by these brightest jewels from heaven.

The Puritan principle of church polity also grows out of this system of doctrines approved and craved by Christian experience. This is apparent from the fact

1. That human rights have their origin and foundation in God's rights. He has constituted every man with powers and tendencies qualifying him for activity in his service, and required him to employ them to his glory. Hence, no other being, man or angel, has a right to step in between him and his sovereign Lord, and prevent or restrain the full and free exercise of these powers and tendencies in the direction required. Every church is an aggregate of these individual powers and tendencies, and is a sacred confederation purchased by Christ's blood to show forth his praise. Consequently, no pope nor bishop, no hierarchy nor presbytery has a right to assume the prerogative of regulating its combined individual powers, or of interfering with its corporate functions. All men and churches must be left to stand unmolested in the conscious dignity of freedom, because God has a primary right to their service. The Congregational polity thus grows directly out of the foundations of the Puritan's creed ; God's sovereignty, the purchase of the church by Christ's death, and the divine glory as the chief end of man ; doctrines approved by Christian experience.

2. Equality among the membership is as decidedly the dictate of the Christian heart. The Scriptures represent the church of Christ as a band of brethren, vitally united to him, and one with each other in covenant, all standing on the same level, helpless in themselves, but strong in Christ, exercising mutual watch, and rejoicing together on their way to join the church triumphant; and this is just such a church as the Christian heart desires.   Then the union of the churches in a sisterhood for mutual advice and helpfulness is equally the craving of the renewed heart.   As Christian love goes forth to all personally in covenant with us, so it goes forth towards all Christians, so far as the relations of time, place and other circumstances allow.   There is not a principle or usage of Congregational polity which is not, or was not, in the circumstances in which it originated, the dictate of disinterested love to Christ and the brethren.   One in him, their heart's desire is to be one with each other.

Puritan Congregationalism may therefore be defined, the harmonious reception of the doctrines of the Gospel, held in that just balance which is promotive of all the Christian graces in their due proportion, and logically resulting in equality and freedom in church order and government.

We will briefly state its leading characteristics.

1. It is a practical system, practical in its broadest and most efficacious sense.   It contains not a doctrine or principle which is not influential in moulding character.   It moves every element of the human mind; arouses the reason, quickens the conscience, stirs the sensibilities, draws out the affections, and leads to the highest activity of all the powers of the soul and in their just proportions.   It renders the recipient trustful in God without presumption, zealous without fanaticism, independent, and at the same time humble and teachable, determined and persistent without rashness or obstinacy.   It thus subdues all that is carnal and low in man, energizes all that is manly and noble, and permeates his whole spiritual nature with light and love; thereby qualifying him to act at once with decision and prudence.

2. It is a system giving God and man their true relative po-

·sitions. It represents God as the self-existent creator making all things for his own glory, and constituting man to attain his development and blessedness in cheerfully promoting that glory both in his person and conduct. It enthrones Jehovah as the sole sovereign of the universe, the uncontrolled arbiter of all events, even swaying the hearts of men, so that they ever fulfill his immutable purposes of divine exaltation. It makes him also the undisputed lawgiver of his creature, giving him the right founded in the perfections of his being to require of them unconditional submission to his righteous sway. It places man on his footstool lost in sin, to be redeemed by the blood of his Son, and thereby to become his grateful worshipper, the witness of his truth, and his faithful coworker. It represents even the Christian as infinitely unworthy, the object of undeserved compassion ; as surrounded with perils, and struggling with difficulties from which he is delivered, and crowned alone by redemptive grace.

3. It is a self-renouncing system, demanding the spirit of Christ, who pleased not himself. It requires us to resign ourselves and all we possess to God, our rightful owner. It gives no place for self-seeking. It guarantees our happiness, but it is to be obtained by renouncing self, and growing into sympathy with God. He is to be first in our affections and purposes and actions. To live disinterestedly for his glory is to live for personal blessedness. In seeking the good of others it requires us to persuade them to enjoy God, to put him highest, to fix the eye on him as the chiefest among ten thousand ; and self-oblivious, to seek their happiness in God and in duty. That this was the essence of the creed of our Puritan fathers, and the spirit of their lives, their uncomplaining sufferings, their holy living and self-denying labors, abundantly testify.

4. It is a reformatory system. It was born of a reformatory spirit, and was named from its reformatory zeal. It is radically reformatory. Not simply aiming at reforming men manward, but God-ward, and reforming them man-ward through reforming them God-ward. As God is first in the system, God must be first in all reformations. The heart must first be turned to its Creator, and then it is turned of course to fellow-beings. The soul must be born again, and then by the law of

its regenerated being, it sends forth streams of love and good
will.   Thus it is radically and thoroughly a reformatory system ; never satisfied till the whole man, soul and body, is
bound to Jehovah.

5. It is a missionary system.   The last implies this ; its love
of God and holiness insures it.   Imitative of the Master, it
goes about doing good.   Misery, wherever existing, calls forth
its sympathy ; sin, wherever existing, calls forth its zeal.

6. It is a symmetrical system.   Its doctrines and principles
are symmetrical, revolving around one centre, God in Christ.
Love harmonizes them.   Love cements them.   The heart radiant with holiness perceives their just proportions and relations,
because it feels towards God and all beings as it should.   Christian experience, indeed, is the best logic in discovering and
arranging the great truths of revelation ; so that their combined
beauty may be appreciated, and their combined power realized
on the soul.   Hence, when attended by the Holy Spirit, the
system is fitted to inspire all the Christian graces in their scriptural harmony, guaranteeing a symmetry of Christian character,
as beautiful as it is effective.

7. It is an established, and yet elastic system, admitting
inquiry and improvement.   The human mind, and therefore
human knowledge, is progressive.   Hence, any system of
scriptural truth, so far as dependent on knowledge and experience, is improvable.   This, John Robinson and our fathers
maintained.   In his farewell address he says :

" I charge you before God and his blessed angels, that you follow
me no farther than you have seen me follow the Lord Jesus Christ.
If God reveal anything to you by any other instrument of his, be
as ready to receive it, as ever you were to receive any truth by my
ministry ; for I am verily persuaded, I am very confident, the Lord
has more truth yet to break forth out of his holy word.   For my
part, I can not sufficiently bewail the condition of the reformed
churches, who are come to a period in religion, and will go, at present, no farther than the instruments of their reformation.   The
Lutherans can not be drawn to go beyond what Luther saw ; whatever part of his good will our God has revealed to Calvin, they
will rather die than embrace it ; and the Calvinists, you see, stick
fast where they were left by that great man of God, who yet saw

not all things. . . . . I beseech you remember it, 'tis an article of your church covenant, that you be ready to receive whatever truth shall be made known to you from the written word of God. Remember that, and every other article of your sacred covenant. But I must herewith exhort you to take heed to what you receive as truth. Examine it, consider it, and compare it with other scriptures of truth, before you receive it."

This sanctions no bold speculations. Scripture must be carefully collated with Scripture.

The improvement of a system of biblical truth depends mainly on the progress of knowledge. (*a*) Respecting the laws of philology and of biblical interpretation. (*b*) Respecting the laws of logical investigation and of the moral affections.

It is important here to mark the distinction between improving a doctrine and improving a system of doctrines. A doctrine in itself can never be improved. It shines a fixed star in God's word, unchanged and unchangeable through every revolution of time. It may perhaps be rendered clearer to the mind by distincter statements, and the mists covering it dissipated by the brighter exhibitions of cognate truths, but the truth itself is as immutable as God himself; and will be for joy and praise to the righteous forever. But any human system of scriptural doctrine may be improved. Its nature proves this. It is a set of truths which the reason sees logically connected, or which the heart, warmed and instructed by the Spirit, feels to be essential to Christian growth and comfort. In such a system the logical connection between the doctrines composing it may be made to appear more consistent, or new practical bearings of them may be shown, bringing the whole system into clearer vision and pressing it with more power on the heart. In this sense a system may be improved while the doctrines themselves can not be improved.

There are, however, limits to improvement in any system of scriptural truth. The system must be held consistent with itself. Consequently, the alleged improvement must be consistent with the great constituents of the system. If any fundamental principle is left out, or any influential doctrine added, or any such doctrines essentially modified, so as to change their relation to other doctrines, or to diminish the gracious affections legitimately awakened by them, it becomes another system. Such an alleged improvement is rather a subversion. The improvements of a scriptural system must be such as will assimilate themselves to it, as the accretions of a shrub become one with it, or the food we take becomes, by a healthy process, assimilated to our bodies. This is emphatically the case with the Puritan system, which always harmonizes with, and is promotive of, Christian experience. Every improvement must therefore tend, in its legitimate workings, when attended by the Spirit, to originate or increase the Christian graces, especially those that are radical or determinative. Nay, as the humble submission of the whole being to God's sovereign will, leading the soul to depend alone on Christ for pardon and salvation, may be called the central grace, the heart of the Puritan system, from which all the life currents of its effectiveness flow, every alleged improvement which intensifies this assimilates itself to the body and may be accepted as an improvement. No additions of a contrary tendency surely did Robinson suppose possible improvements in that memorable passage above quoted. He was not all afloat in his doctrinal belief. On the contrary, he was firmly established in his convictions of fundamental truth, or of what constitute the determinative graces of the regenerated soul.

This is evident from his religious and mental character. His learning is represented as " great," his judgment " solid," his intellect penetrating, and trained to profound and accurate investigation. " He was never satisfied in himself till he had searched any cause or argument he had to deal in thoroughly, and to the bottom." " Though a man of peace, he knew when to speak, and on what side, and was ready to contend earnestly for the faith once delivered to the saints, though not without understanding of the matter and persons in controversy." He had carefully studied the questions in dispute between the Calvinists and Arminians; and " being very able," says Bradford, " none was fitter to buckle with them, as appeared by sundry disputes; so as he began to be terrible to the Arminians," " who stood more in fear of him than of any in the university." Two professors in the University of Leyden were elected in 1612, one, Episcopius, was the champion of

the Arminians ; the other, Polyander, of the Calvinists.   Robinson discerned the importance of the juncture, and determined,
according to his custom, to examine candidly and thoroughly
for himself.   He attended the lectures of both, and " became
thoroughly grounded in the merits of the controversy ; knew
the force of all arguments used, and the shifts of the adversary."
Such were his " singular abilities in divine things," such his understanding of the controversy, and the " decided stand " he
took in regard to it, that Polyander and the leading ministers of
the city requested him to engage in a public discussion with
Episcopius.   After much hesitation, he yielded to their " im-
portunity," and to " his own sense of the importance of the
occasion."   "And when the time came," says Gov. Bradford,
" the Lord so helped him to defend the truth and foil his adversary, as he put him to an apparent nonplus in this great and
public audience.   And the like he did two or three times upon
such occasions ; the which as it caused many to praise God that
the truth had so famous a victory, so it procured for him much
honor and respect from those learned men and others which
loved the truth."

Evidently Robinson was not in a state of uncertainty in respect to the doctrines of Calvinism.   When he said : " I am
verily persuaded ; I am very confident the Lord has more truth
yet to break forth out of his holy word," he could not have expected that Arminianism or Pelagianism, much less Unitarianism or Socinianism would ever break forth from the word of
God.   Unquestionably he had main reference to the " worship
and discipline " of the churches, the legitimate results of the
doctrines and religious experience of Calvinism, that which was
chiefly in dispute between the Puritans and the Church of England, and which must have been uppermost in his mind in giving farewell instructions to his departing flock.   Nor can his
language be interpreted otherwise, when he says : " The Calvinists stick fast where they were left by that great man of
God."   In point of doctrine, Robinson stuck in the same place.
He pretended to see farther than Calvin only concerning ceremonies and usages.   It is plain, therefore, if he referred to
doctrines at all, it was merely in relation to their mode of statement and defence, not to the doctrines themselves, a position

common to all true Calvinists. The spirit of our historical record, as well as the logic of Christian sense justifies, there-fore, the conclusion that whatever promotes and partakes of the life of the Puritan system ; whatever tends to absorb the will in the divine will, and to bring the soul into closer union to Christ, and thus to make men humbler, weaker in themselves and stronger in the Lord ; more earnest in the cultivation of personal holiness and in diffusing its blessedness, may be hailed as genuine improvements. But whatever has a diverse tend-ency, however much applauded by the ingenious and the learned, can not be deemed advantageous to the system. Chris-tian experience, guided by Scripture, is thus at once the test and limit of its improvements.

8. It is a catholic system. The cradle of persecution, in which its infancy was rocked, taught it catholicity. The sever-ities to which, in the years of its ripening growth, it was sub-jected by royal prerogative and priestly domination, further im-pressed the lesson. The essential doctrines of Scripture, man's utter depravity and the treachery of his deceitful heart, com-bined with his consequent moral weakness and liability to self-blindness, together with the fact that the Puritan has been trained to fix his eye on the practical bearings of Gospel doc-trines, all conspire to enkindle and cherish catholic sentiments. Hence the Puritan system is magnanimous, high-minded, over-looking minor differences of opinion, educational influences, local prejudices, social culture, and general habits of life. It makes large allowances for constitutional idiosyncrasies. It advo-cates exact statements of doctrine, and frames exact formula-ries, but allows verbal diversities ; adheres with an unrelaxing grasp to essentialities, but gives free scope to language. It will surrender the truth to no foe, open or disguised, but pre-scribes no fixed uniform to its soldiery. It is equally magnani-mous and charitable in view of varieties in Christian experience. The radical universal graces are insisted on. It believes in " the same Spirit," but in " differences of administration " ; in the same Lord," but in " diversities of operations." Hence, while Congregationalists earnestly defend their symbols of faith and modes of ecclesiastical polity, they are free from the ex-clusiveness and denunciatory spirit of sectarianism. Hume

testifies, that of all Christian sects, the Puritans were the first who during their " prosperity and adversity, alike adopted the principles of toleration." The Pilgrims of Plymouth never persecuted.

Such being the general characteristics of Puritan Congregationalism, its literature should be :

1. Biblical. The authors of Puritan Congregationalism were preëminently biblical men. They not only read the Bible ; they studied it ; fasted and prayed over it. It was their directory, not only in the pursuit of individual holiness, but in their domestic economy and civil responsibilities. To its teachings they bowed with the simplicity of children. They were not dreamy speculatists. Though of the Teutonic race, they were not like the modern Germans, intellectual theorizers or learned castle-builders. Their downright earnestness in the conduct of life and their deep piety prevented or checked such tendencies. They were always practical investigators of truth, serious, honest, devout listeners for the voice from heaven. Their great anxiety was to learn how they might please him who created and redeemed them to the praise of the glory of his grace. This sober, earnest, devotional character of our fathers should give character to the issues of our press. They should ever glow with Christian love ; be never cold and stiffened with philosophy ; never mere theories of Gospel truth, but Gospel truth itself. In a word, their aim should be to impress the solemnity of probation's work ; to hold up God as the Redeemer ; salvation, holiness, eternity, as the great realities.

2. A Congregational literature should be practical. The Bible is practical. Christian experience is practical. The sources of Puritan Congregationalism and its pervading spirit alike demand that a Congregational Board be practical. Its issues, solid with Puritan principles, should be written for the heart, the conscience, the life. While meditative and devotional, they should be stirring, energizing, rousing to duty. While they unfold the lowest depths of Christian consciousness, exhibit the sunshine and joy of " fellowship with the Father and with his Son Jesus Christ," the peace of pardon, the strength and triumph of faith, and the composure of submission to God's sovereign disposal, they should impress the conviction

that life is not a state of rest or of unsanctified pleasure seeking, but of toil, of vigilance, and of prayer, whose fruits are immortal. A Congregational Board of Publication can never be a mere doctrinal tract or book concern. Thus conducted it would be a standing falsification of its origin and life. Puritan Congregationalism, as a system of doctrines, contains none designed simply for the head or for the creed; all are central powers in the church, throbbing hearts, sending the warm life current through every line of daily conduct. Such should the books of the denomination be.

3. A Congregational literature should be historical. To comprehend a system of truth in its entireness, its practical workings, its true worth and efficiency, we must consider it in its source, and trace down its stream; mark its embankments, measure its width and depth, watch its rise and fall and ascertain their cause; in a word, take a survey of its past and present, and comparing the present with the past, gather up into one view its various historical developments and their contemporaneous influences on individuals and society. It is only by such a course that we can gain a knowledge of its vital powers and prospective usefulness.

To know the facts of Puritan history, such as are contained in a common school history, or indeed in any civil history, is of little moment. Nor is a bare intellectual conception of its theology or ecclesiastical polity of much more value. This generation need a deeper knowledge of our Christian ancestors; not only of the doctrines they believed and the logical processes by which they wrought them into a symmetrical system, but their *modus operandi*, their manner of wielding these great scriptural principles; how they pressed them on the heart and conscience; how they harmonized the different parts of their system so as to make them felt as vitalizing elements in every day life. It can not be too deeply impressed that he who would understand thoroughly the character of the founders of the New England churches must penetrate their inner life; not only analyze their intellectual conceptions and comprehensive views and plans, but explore the recesses of their inner being; comprehend them subjectively as well as objectively. We want to see them in their homes, around their family altars, in their houses of worship, and in their prayer-meetings ; we want to see them in their peaceful hours of meditation, in their conflicts with sin, in their prostrations of soul at the feet of Jesus, in their hopes of triumph through his death.   This can be done only by studying their practical and devotional literature, their sermons and their diaries, in connection with their theological and ecclesiastical works.

4. A Congregational literature should be aggressive.   It should be a leading aim to enlarge the borders of the denomination.   Fully believing our distinctive views to be the radical truths of revelation, it should avail itself of every opportunity to spread the savor of their influence.   This is necessarily neither sectarianism nor proselytism.   It is only obeying the solemn convictions of truth and duty.

5. A Congregational literature should adapt itself to the spirit and circumstances of the times.   Not that it is to float on the current of popular opinion.   Not that it should allow a vitiated literary taste at any time prevalent to blunt the point or dim the sheen of the sword of truth.   By no means.   Its mission is rather to correct the public taste and to lead the public mind. The true idea is to adapt itself to the spirit of the times so far and in such a manner as to make this its handmaid in furthering the designs of the Gospel.   It should always be finished in style, profound with sacred thoughts, glowing with apostolic fervor.   In this sense it should throb with the life of the times, enter into the current enterprises of the church, mingle in her current conflicts with sin, meet the various forms of error as they rise.   But in being up to the times, it should never sink below the Bible.   An organ of such literature should, therefore, be conservative as well as stirring and progressive.   It is to look down the future as well as back on the past.   It must earnestly defend the truth as it is in Jesus ; carefully observe the old landmarks ;   check all extravagances of views and measures ; endeavor not only to keep alive the spirituality of the living, but to elevate the unborn to higher communion with God and increased efficiency in the Redeemer's work.   In a word, adapting itself to the times is fashioning and fastening the link of steel which is to unite the future to the past.   Its vocation is not to encourage innovations, but to intensify life.

We are now prepared to consider the plans of the present Congregational Board of Publication.

It is the purpose of the managers of the Board to make it what, according to the views above expressed, a Puritan Congregational Board should be. They wish to occupy the same position in the denomination that the Baptist, Episcopal, and Presbyterian Boards of Publication occupy in their respective communions. To secure this noble object it is proposed :

1. To continue the publication of the works of distinguished Puritan writers on Congregational Polity, Theology, and Practical Religion. Their leading works on these topics ought to be reprinted on good paper, in clear, readable type, rendering them accessible to increasing numbers desirous of understanding the principles and the character of the Puritans. The republication of their devotional works we would make a specialty. The present generation are too much disposed to undervalue the worth of Puritan principles and the fervor of their devotional spirit. This misapprehension, encouraged by some who have swerved from Puritan doctrines, is working immense evil. It should be corrected; and the world made to hear of its correction. Men of the stirring present need to share in the deep and reverential piety, the profound religious experience of our fathers. The churches permeated by it would assume new life and vigor; the Christian activity of the age become holier and wiser.

2. It is designed, in the future as in the past, to publish the works, both theological and practical, of the leading divines of Congregationalism, who have lived since the time of the Pilgrims, and who have adopted their views and imbibed their spirit.

3. It is intended to publish the productions of living authors, short, comprehensive, and earnest works on the doctrines and precepts of the Gospel, books pervaded with its great determinative principles without dilution or equivocation. It is our conviction that Puritanism, when exhibited in its full proportions, moving all the elements of the human mind, and bearing on the several relations and vicissitudes of human life, is the most energizing and spirit-stirring system ever embodied in a human creed, and most transforming in its far-reaching influence on social and political organizations. The great doctrines

and principles of revelation are not mere dogmas or speculations, not truths to repose in the intellect, or to reign in creeds; but vital powers moulding the heart, determining, strengthening, and adorning the character.

We would bring the churches into closer communion with God in Christ, that they may feel him to be present, a power and a glory in the midst of them, sustaining, comforting, and commanding. There is no thought that moves the human soul like full and clear conceptions of the Triune Jehovah, clothed with majesty, the infinitely wise and powerful, the just, the faithful and merciful, promulgating law, and devising redemption, according to his sovereign pleasure. Man is truly man, only when God is dwelling in him, and he in God. We need a literature realizing this great idea; and therefore a literature full of God, full of his government and claims, full of Christ, the God-man Mediator radiant; with profoundest truths, not merely set forth in their logical sequences, linking them together in one golden chain, an object of delightful contemplation to the intellectual eye, but exhibited in their vitalizing power, kindling to a flame the heart on which they press.

While, therefore, we would publish practical books, we would not publish books bereft of doctrinal power, but those built upon the fundamental truths of the Gospel, pervaded by them, and holding them up in their varied experimental forms. Nor would we publish practical books in the costume of the sixteenth century merely, but those written in the earnest, vigorous, and accomplished style demanded by present literary taste, and beating with the life and stir and enterprise of the times in which we live. We apprehend that the piety of the age needs deepening; and this we believe can be done only in connection with profounder views of divine truth. To become strong established 'Christians, men must think. We would therefore circulate through our churches works combining contemplative with active piety, works on heart religion, home and closet religion, as well as social, books searching in their character, leading to thorough self-examination, and to profound meditation on eternal realities.

The times also demand works promotive of revivals, and distinguishing between the true and the false; concise, pithy treatises, laying open the depths of the whole subject in its theological and philosophical aspects, and permeated with the unction and fervor of the Pentecostal scene.

4. We wish the Congregational Board to be the representative of Puritanism in its symmetrical proportions, in its full healthful form, glowing with its flush of life, and radiant with divine power and beauty. We would sedulously avoid one-sided views. Presented with distortions, or with the undue proportions of some of its parts, Puritanism is a thing of ugliness ; but exhibited in its roundness and symmetry, every doctrine and usage in its right place and just proportions, it is a thing of beauty. Nor would we give undue importance to any one principle, or set of principles, on which the scheme is erected, but present them in their true scriptural aspects, as free as possible from philosophical explanations or theological theorizings. Nor would we explain and urge on the attention of the world the ecclesiastical polity of our fathers, separated from the doctrines which gave it birth. Without these we believe it as powerless to promote the kingdom of holiness as Episcopacy or Romanism. Unitarianism proves this. We have no sympathy, therefore, with zealots for the democratic principle in church order, who sever it from the vital truths out of which it grows. These, as we have seen, demand equality among the brotherhood. Theoretically, all are objects of equal interest and care. It allows no clerical order, or any other functionaries, to lord it over God's heritage. Nor, on the other hand, is all the power of the doctrines of Calvinism realized, separated from the Congregational polity. In consequence of this principle of equality, no scheme of church government so pervades and vitalizes the masses, none is so promotive of popular intelligence and true manliness of character, as Congregationalism. This constitutes in great part its superiority to Presbyterianism. Presbyterianism, by stopping short of the logical results of its doctrines relative to ecclesiastical polity, weakens its diffusive power. It neither interpenetrates all classes of society, nor develops the whole of manhood in any class, like Congregationalism. We would, therefore, present Puritanism as a systematic whole. one part supporting and giving life to another; the doctrines working

out into holiest activities, and these combined demanding the government of the brotherhood. In a word, we would present it as a doctrine, a polity, a life, one and indivisible.

5. It is our design to furnish indigent pastors with valuable libraries, either by gratuitous distribution, or at reduced prices. To render men successful heralds of the Gospel, they not only need books, but the right kind of books. The reading of a minister will give tone to his preaching, and his library give character to his reading.

6. Also to furnish our churches with parish libraries of a distinctive Puritan literature. A choice selection of Congregational books always on hand for consultation would not only be a source of Christian knowledge and edification, but a powerful conservative against the insidious incomings of error. We would especially make it our aim to supply with such libraries the churches erected, or to be erected, south and west, by the assistance of the church-building fund.

The reasons for a Congregational Board are :

1. The Puritan system of doctrine and polity is worth preserving. It is a system of inherent energy. Its doctrines may be stigmatized as severe, harsh, unlovely, repellant of the milder affections and gentler virtues which make society agreeable ; its advocates may be jeered at as austere, angular, uncompromising in character, vinegar-faced, devoid of every quality to win the popular favor ; and yet, wherever it has lived and thriven, it has been a mighty power, ameliorating the temporal and spiritual estates of men. Her childhood in her English home gave unmistakable indications of her spiritual royalty. Even in her cradle she evinced Herculean energy in throttling the serpents of ecclesiastical and political tyranny coiling their deadly gripe around her. Her influence in the English reformation is acknowledged ; but her influence on the civil institutions of England was no less transforming. Hume testifies that " the precious spark of liberty had been kindled, and was preserved by the Puritans ; and it was to this sect whose principles appear so frivolous, and habits so ridiculous, that the English owe the whole freedom of their Constitution." Carlyle and Macaulay, Bancroft and Palfrey, bear similar testimony. The system was equally promotive of public virtue when our

fathers were in Holland. The magistrates of Leyden " declared from the seat of justice": " These English have lived among us now these twelve years, and yet we have never had one suit or action come against them."

The moulding influence of the Puritan system in New England will not be disputed. Her free churches, her good morals, when Puritanism alone reigned within her borders, and her free political institutions, now just emerging from her last conflict with oppression, all spring from the seed in the Mayflower. The " social compact " entered into in Cape Cod Harbor, is indeed the root of that gigantic tree of liberty, whose branches now shelter the mightiest nation on the globe. When Puritanism stood alone, a rough shrub on the stony soil of New England, sturdy, but uncomely, it diffused its healing influences. Said an eminent minister in a sermon before the British Parliament : ' I have lived in a country seven years, and all that time, I never heard one profane oath, and never saw a man drunk in that land.' Up to the time of the American Revolution, the moral virtues and masculine piety of New England were unsurpassed. Besides, that cluster of missionary organizations which adorn the nineteenth century, and are scattering the darkness of heathenism, originated with the Pilgrims ; one of whose avowed objects in planting themselves in America was evangelizing the savages. The spirit of the Pilgrims may justly be called the spirit of missions. Thus, in its childhood and manhood, in the Old World and the New, Puritanism has ever shown itself a thing of life. Whether we can account for its vital energy philosophically or not, the fact stands. We believe it is owing to the fact that it is a system more in harmony with the teachings of Scripture than any other. This, we are aware, may be denied ; but the world-acknowledged fact can not be effaced from the annals of history. A system thus lifegiving is surely worth preserving. If New England is to continue to be the helm regulating the ship of our national government, the Christian doctrines which gave birth to her enterprise and solid virtues must be perpetuated.

2. The press is one of the most efficient agencies of the present century for diffusing truth, and for interpenetrating with it the public life. True, it is a still, quiet, unseen influence,

diffusing itself like the sunshine and the dew, but it is mighty to stimulate and control thought. God has created this prodigious engine of power, and put it into our hand; and shall we not employ it for the inculcation and spread of our denominational views, which we believe to be the eternal verities of God? Men of the world are wiser than the children of light. Every guild and professor, law, medicine, education, agriculture, horticulture. trade, mining, petroleum, etc., all employ the press to awaken the interest of the public. Politicians not only enlist the powers of oratory, but of the literary page. Why should not we do the same? Are we under no obligation to do it? Does not consistency demand it? We employ the academy, the college, the theological seminary, the pulpit, for denominational purposes, why not the press as well?

3. Other denominations are using the press for the perpetuation and diffusion of their distinctive views with a zeal worthy of imitation.

The Old School Presbyterian church has a Publishing Board with a fund of $200,000, besides a building in which to carry on their operations worth from $35,000 to $40,000 more. In 1865, they employed 129 colporteurs, and distributed over 374,000 volumes, and over 2,500,000 pages of tracts. The New School Presbyterian church has a Board with a fund of $50,000, and is in successful operation.

The Methodists support a Book Concern richly endowed, and circulate denominational books and tracts by millions. They say; " the ' Book Concern ' of American Methodism is now the largest religious publishing establishment in the world. From a borrowed capital of only six hundred dollars in 1789, it has since increased to $837,000. There are now four ' book agents,' twelve editors, nearly five hundred operatives, and between twenty and thirty presses in constant operation."

The Baptists are behind no other denomination in the earnest diffusion of a sectarian literature. The Episcopal church has two Boards. The Dutch Reformed, the Lutheran, the Freewill Baptist, and other sects, both evangelical and unevangelical, are successfully working the press for denominational purposes. It is believed that their families, while no more intelligent in other respects than our own, are generally far better informed in regard to their distinctive tenets. We need a Board of Publication therefore, as a means of self-preservation. We are like a little island, with the waves rolling in upon us from all sides, and unless we erect opposing barriers, we shall be submerged. We should be as far-seeing as our Baptist brethren. They say: " The American Baptist Publication Society had its origin in a deep conviction of the absolute denominational necessity for such an organization. Our fathers felt that private publishers could never be relied on to furnish the requisite amount of denominational literature. A Publishing Society for Baptists is an absolute necessity." For the same reason, is there not " an absolute necessity " that Congregationalists have a Publishing Board? Certainly, if other denominations are doing right in this regard, we are doing wrong.

4. A practical denominational literature is of inestimable importance to our stability and enlargement. Several considerations prove this.

(a.) The majority of mankind are conducted into the reception of the profound truths of Scripture, rather through the lead of the affections, than of the reason or by logical processes. They first experience them, or in their own consciousness feel the necessity of them. When thus felt the heart and conscience are in their favor; and when the heart and conscience are in their favor, they will be welcomed to one's creed though his reason fail fully to comprehend them. The great object, therefore, should be to enlist the moral sensibilities of our membership, and those worshipping with us, in our distinctive principles. This can be done only by so presenting them that they shall be understood and appreciated by the masses. Their necessity and uses in elevating the churches, and in saving souls, must be set forth. They must be discussed in their practical aspects and relations; illustrated by facts and analogies; by narratives demonstrating their efficiency; by the experiences of the great and good silencing cavils; by appeals; by solemn admonitions; by persuasives and encouragements; in a word, by every method fitted to warm the affections or awaken the sympathies. For only secure their apprehension by the light of these, and they will strike their roots deep into the soul ; they will be grasped with a tenacity which no counter influences will be likely to unloose. That the common people who are the sinews of our churches should be impressed with the vitalities of our peculiar doctrines all admit. But to compass an end so desirable, a practical denominational literature addressed to our emotional natures is indispensable. This lively appreciation of them by the bulk of our churches would exert a far-reaching influence. It would be almost certain to secure a Puritan ministry. "Like people like priest." There would be a common instinct in our congregations detecting error and guarding the pulpit from its intrusion.

(*b.*) A practical literature, in which our determinative doctrines, rites, forms of worship, and polity, are spoken of, alluded to as settled verities, as integral parts of the Gospel, would have a silent, but powerful influence in their favor. Indeed, such incidental and positive assertions with half of mankind, go for demonstration. While we have no such popular literature, and other denominations are systematically and energetically working the press for the production of a literature pregnant with their own peculiarities, and fitted to interest the common mind, our families and Sabbath schools will soon be found, indeed many of them are already found, abounding in books in which there are not only incidental allusions favorable to the distinctive views of other sects, but which contain insinuations and sneers against our own. Thus by our neglect, we throw open our doors to the stealthy entrance of our opposers, who are gradually sapping the foundations of our institutions.

(*c.*) By neglecting a popular denominational literature, while we zealously circulate an undenominational literature, we are insidiously undermining all just appreciation of our own distinctive tenets among ourselves. It is virtually admitting that they are not of essential importance ; all that is necessary for Christian growth and maturity can be attained without them. Said a good deacon to the writer, twenty years ago : " Why do you preach on God's sovereignty and electing grace ? The American Tract Society does not publish these doctrines, and they publish all that is essential to salvation." A member of one of our important churches recently remarked to the writer :

" I am a little afraid of denominationalism. I have thought the creeds of our churches might be reduced to the theological basis of the American Tract Society." Other denominations prevent such inferences by vigorously sustaining a denominational press. We can check the pernicious results of such inferences only by earnestly supporting a denominational Board, scattering through our families books and tracts unfolding the vital principles of our faith.

Besides, by neglecting a popular denominational literature, while we unite with other denominations in issuing one of a non-denominational character, and those with whom we unite are industriously circulating their own distinctive views in attractive forms, we indirectly support them. Certainly by forming such an alliance with the Methodists we negatively support Methodism. For take out the doctrines of God's absolute sovereignty, election, and the perseverance of the saints, and Calvinism has vanished, while Methodism remains in its strength. In the same way we are negatively sustaining the Episcopalians and the Baptists. Continue this process a few years longer, and the soil will be prepared for the seed of every evangelical denomination to take root, but Puritan Congregationalism. This will find little nutriment to give it growth. Thus we are guiding and winging the arrows that are drinking our life.

(*d.*) By such a course we are guilty of great inconsistency. We deem it of the highest moment that the doctrines embraced by the Congregational churches should be distinctly expressed in our formularies, proclaimed from the desk, and inculcated in the Sabbath school. We also deem it essential that our ministers be thoroughly instructed in them ; and we expend hundreds of thousands of dollars in founding theological seminaries for training them for their denominational work. All this we have considered of the first importance ; while we have felt that we were doing all that was necessary by the press in circulating through our families a religious literature from which all our distinctive peculiarities were expunged. Is this consistent? We wish our ministerial brethren and intelligent laymen would look thoroughly into this subject. Is a part of God's truth better than the whole of it to maintain the purity and efficiency of the church, and to convert souls? No believer in the plenary inspiration of the Scriptures will admit this. Indeed, we should be shocked at the thought of educating our ministry in the views of the Baptists, Episcopalians, or Methodists; or of having a committee composed of one from each of the evangelical denominations, appointed to examine the sermons of our pastors previous to their delivery, with authority to exclude from them whatever the committee might disapprove; so that the sermons to which our churches listen should be just as devoid of our distinctive principles as is the general undenominational literature which we now deem adequate for our families. Every thoughtful man must see that it is as important that the common people, who constitute the bone and muscle of our churches, be instructed in all the practical bearings and experimental workings of our system of doctrines, rites, and forms of worship, as that the ministry be thus instructed; and that as we found theological seminaries for the instruction of the latter, we should have an outspoken pulpit and the decisive utterances of the press for the instruction of the former. What theological seminaries are to the ministry, the Denominational Board is to the laity. The last is equally an institution of scriptural learning.

(e.) The non-denominational societies were not organized to furnish an adequate religious literature for our own families. They were designed for the waste places, and to reach those to whom the name of sect or denomination is offensive. True, the non-denominational publishing societies have issued many excellent books and tracts, and we rejoice in their circulation. We welcome them to our families. But because they have published many valuable books, is it certain that they have, or can, according to their constitutions, publish all that we need to develop the highest spirituality of our churches? Is it certain that they have not omitted some scriptural truths of vast importance in humbling sinners at the Saviour's feet, in promoting pure revivals, and in preventing spurious conversions?

We wish it distinctly understood that we by no means oppose non-denominational boards of publication. We only maintain that if we would vindicate the Gospel as we believe it; if we would advance and strengthen our churches, promote the richest Christian experience and the highest type of piety, we must have a denominational board beside the non-denominational which we support ; and the fact that we support non-denominational boards is a decisive reason for supporting a denominational board.

5. The pastors of our churches need a Congregational Board.

(*a.*) They need it that they may themselves imbibe the spirit of Puritan principles ; become identified with the denomination not only professionally, but in their modes of thought and habitudes of feeling. There should be an *esprit du corps* among our clergy ; and this can be realized only by their being imbued with a thoroughly biblical or denominational literature.

(*b.*) The publications of such a Board judiciously circulated by a pastor among his people would greatly strengthen his influence. They would constitute his detective corps, finding their secret way to every hearthstone and to every closet. The religious reading of the family should be in agreement with the sermon, the same in its doctrinal and practical teachings, the same in its solemnity and spiritual earnestness. As a denomination we have too much neglected the press as the handmaid of our pulpits. Employed by them as it should be, it would double or quadruple their efficiency. We apprehend that not half the power of the press has yet been realized. All its potency can be drawn out only in connection with the preacher or some personal agency. The printed page can never take the place of, or dispense with, the living voice, with the sympathy of face to face influences. But if, when the voice ceases to vibrate on the ear, the eye drinks in the same truth from the printed page, prolonging and intensifying the impression, or *vice versa*, the voice and the printed page, oratory and the press, walk hand in hand, augmenting incalculably the power of each other.

6. The Congregational Board is demanded by the prevalence of Romanism. Considered as a power antagonistic to this mightiest hierarchy of our world, Congregationalism occupies higher vantage ground than any other scheme of church government. Growing, as it does, out of the doctrines of Calvinism, it is an equalizing system. It denotes that all its members were alike dead in sin ; were alike regenerated by

sovereign grace; all lifted from the same abyss of corruption and adopted equally as sons. By consequence they stand on the same level, are all brethren, equally beloved by the Father. Puritan Congregationalism is thus most decidedly antagonistic to all hierarchies. In overthrowing that deadly upas which has been overshadowing and blighting the nations for more than twelve centuries, it will strike more vigorous blows than any other church organization. In the final encounter with this monster device of Satan, we apprehend its true position will be gained; its inherent efficacy, as inseparable from its vital structure, will be seen. That conflict is hastening on. This country will doubtless be the chosen field of the fiercest strife. The armies are rallying. The voice of providence is summoning Congregationalists to the encounter. The land should be occupied at once with the free spirit of Puritanism. Books and tracts of all forms and sizes, and adapted to all classes and ages, breathing the freedom of those who worship in spirit and in truth, who are combined in that simplest form of church order dictated by a conscious equality before God, and cemented by that love which is the realization of the unity of all in Christ, should be scattered systematically and wisely through every part of our country. Every argument for Congregationalism is a blow at Catholicism. Permeate the community with Puritan principles, and Romanism will be secretly undermined. The Congregational Board of Publication will be a most efficient auxilliary of the American Christian Union.

But this work can never be completed by a non-denominational literature. The Romanist is so habituated to a church organization, that when removed from one, unless he drop into infidelity, he must have another prepared for him, otherwise he will feel houseless. A non-denominational society may demolish Romanism. But its power is crippled in the work of reconstruction, because it can not point the convert from Romanism to an ecclesiastical home. The moment it undertakes this, it becomes a denominational board. The present aspects of Catholicism and its spread in this country demand a vigorous Congregational Board of Publication.

7. The influence of Congregationalism on civil liberty demands a Board of Publication. The kind and degree of free-

dom in the church determines the kind and degree of liberty in the state. The religious freedom of Puritanism pervading the churches of a nation will saturate the very soil, and gradually extirpate from it every germ of monarchism. This the two royal daughters of Henry VIII. and the Stuarts saw; and therefore, if the government of England was to be kingly, the church of England must be Episcopal. " No church without a bishop; no state without a king;" is a motto rooted in the very nature of things. English history proves that what royalty feared became true in fact. When there was no bishop in the church, no king occupied the throne. The free commonwealth arose. The commonwealth went down. Monarchy was restored, and Episcopacy returned. Thus it has been; thus it will ever be. Congregationalism as a scriptural verity must be a vital power. The too common argument for our church polity, drawn from its agreement with our republican institutions, is doubtfully used. Presbyterianism has an appearance of representative government as well as Congregationalism. But the inconclusiveness of the argument mainly lies either in the assumed principle that the government of the church should conform to the government of the state, or in the false position that freedom in the church grows out of freedom in the state. Whereas freedom in the church grows not out of freedom in the state, but freedom in the state is the fruit of freedom in the church. This ecclesiastical life-principle will impart itself to civil institutions. True, there may be a kind of political liberty, such as existed in the ancient republics, without freedom in the church, just as the moral virtues sometimes flourish without Christianity. But as Christianity existing in the heart will give birth to the moral virtues, so ecclesiastical liberty will give birth to political liberty. The habit of self-government in the affairs of the church will crave the right of self-government in the affairs of state. Would we then eradicate from the nation every remaining element antagonistic to human liberty, generated by slavery, or by any other cause; would we see the verdure and bloom of the purest civil freedom covering our country, gladdening with its fragrance the masses of the noble poor, and restraining the libertinism of the reckless, we should by every legitimate means spread the spirit and doctrines of Puritan Congregationalism ; making this great multitudinous people rejoice around the one grand centre of all the good, God and freedom.   This can never be done without creating and diffusing a Congregational literature adapted to every class of the community.

8. Our unsectarian spirit demands a Board of Publication. This catholicity is not a natural product.   It is heaven-born. It is the nobleness and unselfishness of angelic existence, indwelling in man.   It ought to be cherished and diffused through the world, vitalizing and elevating the nations.   Certainly, if we are the most catholic of the evangelical denominations, we ought to publish the fact, diffuse the spirit.   Merely to enjoy what has been received from heaven, to exult over it, and magnify ourselves on account of it, is neither gratitude nor high-mindedness.   It is mere self-gratulation and self-adulation. We should impart our wealth of principles as generously as our material resources.   If our system, wherever it has taken root, has always penetrated to the seat of the public life, has given the finest coloring to the fabric of society, and strengthened its texture ; if, as we anticipate, it is to work like the element of life, covering the earth with ecclesiastical and civil freedom, it becomes our solemn duty to avail ourselves of every facility to leaven with it the public life.   We should lift up our voice till the world listens.

Besides, who supports mainly our non-denominational enterprises ? Who moves the presses of the American Tract Society, scattering its leaves of varied beauty everywhere ?   The Congregational churches.   Who funish the funds of the American Home Missionary Society, and to a great extent, of the American Board of Commissioners for Foreign Missions ?   The Congregational churches.   Would we then keep the wheels of these beneficent organizations in motion, especially would we see them moving with increased velocity ;   or if we desire the American Tract Society to widen its sphere of operations, we must increase the number and elevate the piety of the Congregational churches.   If the light of these churches goes out, the light of all non-denominational societies goes out.

9. That portion of the population of New England who absent themselves from the public means of grace, amounting to more

than one-half, need the Congregational Board. To these the Gospel must be carried, and in part by the printed page.   Shall this work be left entirely to the non-denominational publishing societies? They can do much. But can they do all that a conscientious and prayerful Congregationalist desires? We wish these neglecters of the means of grace not only to become Christians, but Christians of the deepest, truest biblical experience, such as the great doctrines of Puritanism in connection with the Spirit's working are fitted to produce. We want them not only gathered into churches, but into churches most nearly harmonizing in form and life with those of apostolic organization. If New England is to continue to exert the influence she has in the past on the educational and civil institutions of the country, she must be filled with churches, not of other forms and influences, but of the true Puritan tone, giving forth no uncertain sound. We must have books and tracts to circulate among these absentees from public worship radically and thoroughly Congregational.

10. The West demands a Congregational Board of Publication.   Congregationalism is struggling there for extension. Other denominations are in the field fully organized and equipped. It is not so with Congregationalists.   Many even who went out from us, whose flourishing farms and comfortable dwellings adorn the banks of our inland waters, or are scattered over the broad prairies, men of strength and information, are exceedingly ignorant of Puritan principles.   They have forgotten the mother that rocked their cradles and taught their infancy to pray.   A gentleman of mind and intelligence, who had been for seven years on the bench, and for a long time deacon of a large Congregational church under the care of the Presbytery, when conversing with a Congregationalist, and showing him the Presbyterian Book of Discipline, näively inquired : " Is there any book on the Congregational polity?   I have never seen one, nor been able to find one." Multitudes are similarly ignorant.   Such men ought surely to have the opportunity of hearing of the Hookers and Cottons and Mathers of other days ; and of the Bacons and Mitchells and Uphams and Punchards and Cummingses of the present.   Little books and tracts tersely written, setting forth our distinctive

doctrines and polity, and their practical bearing on Christian efficiency, ought to be multiplied to a far greater extent than any private publishers are willing to do. Every Congregational minister in the West should be able to carry them with him and disperse them through the families of his congregation. Such an agency would exert a powerful influence in giving to the vast territories of the West an intelligent and working Christianity, rivalling New England in spiritual depth and enterprise.

11. The vast fields of the South, from which Congregationalism has been hitherto excluded, are now opening for the reception of Puritan views. Slavery and Congregationalism with its heaven-inspired equality, guaranteed by mutual covenant, could not co-exist. How could the haughty slave-master brook the idea of standing on the same level with his chattel, much less of being watched over and admonished by one who civilly stood no higher than his beast of burden. But thanks to "him who sitteth upon the throne of his holiness," this power, antagonistic to ecclesiastical freedom, is swept away. He has come in the storms of war, and slavery, red with gore in the combat, has gone down beneath his mighty arm. And though widows weep, and children are fatherless, and mothers are written childless, and sisters weep in solitude, yet we will praise " him who rideth upon the heavens," and doeth " terrible things in righteousness." More than this ; we will prostrate ourselves before him, saying : "Here, Lord, we are, ready to do what thou biddest us do by these righteous judgments."

In overthrowing slavery we have but begun our work. Its form only is in the grave ; its spirit still survives. A powerful shock has been given to old modes of thought and forms of society, but their roots yet cumber the ground. The sword is sheathed, but a moral war is upon us, a war demanding the highest type of Christian heroism and every appliance of the Gospel. The press, with its still, quiet influence gliding into every crevice and corner of society, has an important, though noiseless part to achieve in this fierce conflict. By neglecting it the battle may be turned against us. What the South now especially needs is a radical reform in principles. She needs, it is true, material aid, but with it she must have light. With all her "getting" she must "get understanding." The present up-heaving of her social strata invites labor in this direction. Other denominations, from the most liberal to Romanists, are availing themselves of the occasion. Congregationalists, under their broad banner inscribing "equality and love," should enter the field with their quickening doctrines. The past tells us that principles are not matters of indifference. The fomenters of the rebellion which has just agonized the nation acted according to their principles, principles which had been rooting in a soil watered by the tears and blood of slavery ever since the settle-ment of the country. These must be radically changed. New England principles must take their place. Said one of the speakers in Faneuil Hall on the occasion of the President's as-sassination; "We must send the South the New England Primer." Never was a sentiment uttered more truthful or timely. The North and the South must be animated by one religious spirit. This is indispensable if we desire to come to-gether and hold together. Political conventions and Congres-sional enactments are not sufficient. There must be a substan-tial unity in Christian doctrines and life. This can be secured only by diffusing over her broad fields the elementary ideas which have given vitality to New England society and shaped her institutions; and for this work we have abundant encour-agement. Many loyal Southerners of Northern birth are al-ready one with us in Christian sympathies, and are prepared to become one with us in church order. They only need instruc-tion. A lawyer connected with one of the newly formed Con-gregational churches in a Southern city, writes us: "Many, who love Congregationalism as the religion of their fathers and of their childhood, are not qualified to defend it or even to ex-plain it. They would gladly prepare themselves if they knew how. Such need your Board more than I can tell." As a fur-ther reason for the work of the Board he adds: "Here, and throughout the South, there is the most profound ignorance of Congregationalism, of its history, its doctrines, its tendencies." Surely, every son of the Pilgrims emigrating South should not only bear in his heart the love of Puritan freedom, but carry with him books and tracts explanatory of our faith and polity to put them into the hands of those willing to read them.   And we would that multitudes of our young men and women, thoroughly imbued with the self-sacrificing spirit of the Pilgrims, would make the South their field of labor, determining, so far as in them lies, to diffuse over those slave-blighted territories the free spirit of New England enterprise and manly equality. Especially should Congregationalists already in the field, the members of newly organized churches there, have the means, first, of informing themselves respecting their own principles, and then, of engaging in the work of disseminating them. They thus, and only thus, will become centres of Puritan light and liberty.

A Congregational Press may, therefore, be made an engine of immense power in sowing the seeds of Puritanism over the South, bringing it into harmony with the North.   Efficiently to work this engine is a solemn duty which God is imposing upon us.   We must not fail in its discharge.   Neglect is fraught with evil.   Even delay threatens peril.   This is the hour to scatter the leaves of truth.   It must not be unimproved.   To absorb attention and interest in other instrumentalities, to the disregard of this, is endangering our country's progress, and creating occasions for suffering and tears, when we, who now may prevent them, shall be at rest.

12. The best spiritual training of the Freedmen demands such a Board.   While we believe that the democratic form of church polity, disconnected from the vital doctrines of the Bible, is as powerless to promote the kingdom of holiness as Romanism or Episcopacy, we are equally confident that of all the forms of church polity, Congregationalism alone draws out the full power of the Pauline doctrines and presses them with their full force.   No other so leavens the masses, is so promotive of popular intelligence and true manliness of character.

When our Freedmen, therefore, are qualified, in the judgment of charity, to enter into church relations, we would have as many of them as are so disposed, brought into Congregational churches, where, under the instruction of a pastor, they may feel the responsibility of sustaining social worship, of watching with charity over each other, and of exercising, in the meekness of Christ, Christian discipline.   Nothing would so facilitate their growth in true worth of character and in all that is truly valuable in Christian civilization.

When they assume church relations they must of course be taught the principles of some church organization; and those of Congregationalism are certainly as easy of comprehension as those of any other. Indeed, we are told that multitudes of them are even now ready to receive them. The sweets of civil freedom have given them a relish for ecclesiastical freedom. Why should not the sons of the Pilgrims laboring among them as preachers and teachers, supported by the contributions of Pilgrim churches, imbue their hearers and pupils with the liberal views of our fathers? If we do devoutly believe our own sentiments, there is a solemn responsibility resting upon us, with the wisdom of the serpent and the harmlessness of the dove, to do it. We believe, therefore, that familiar tracts and books, explanatory of the great doctrines and ecclesiastical polity of the Puritan fathers, should be at once issued for this class of our countrymen. God's providence is bidding us wake to this subject. While Romanists are endeavoring to fasten upon this untaught people a mental tyranny not less ruinous to manhood than the civil bondage from which they have just escaped, how can we, believing ourselves possessed of the best, the most scriptural system of divine truth, be justified in idleness? It is to sit supinely still and see the worst of evils perpetrated on our fellows. Can this be innocent? We can not doubt that the time is coming when some of the strongest churches in our land will be those now being organized from among the freedmen; not the wealthiest perhaps, but of the truest spiritual power. We not only anticipate their efficiency in advancing the kingdom of holiness, but they will constitute, wherever they stand, strong pillars of political freedom. This work must be done now. It will not do to delay till they are brought into other church organizations. Then effort in this direction will be of little avail, and may justly subject us to reproach. Now we enter an open and unappropriated field, and we may glean with others without blame. Let, therefore, the press be at once put in motion for this purpose, and let all laborers among our freedmen, sustained by Congregational churches, diffuse kindly and wisely by its aid Congregational principles.

13.　We need a Congregational Board of Publication as a bond of union between our churches scattered, or soon to be scattered, over every part of our country.　In default of any ecclesiastical authority stretching its arms around them and holding them together, the greater the necessity for some moral and social bond.　Nothing can constitute such a bond like a living press with its appropriate appendages.　The commodious Congregational House soon to be erected at Boston and the large library of Congregational lore to be collected in it, may form, in part, such a centre of attraction and reciprocal influence.　But to make it a centralizing power, reaching to the extremities of the land, there must be in it a Congregational Board of Publication, which, like an electric battery, shall steadily send forth its telegrams of rich and essential truths to all our churches, confirming the principles and quickening the piety of the brotherhood.　This must be the vital element of such a power; without which its pulsations will never go forth to the limits, nor permeate the body, of the denomination. And in connection with this there should be a large Congregational bookstore where shall be kept on sale, not only the issues of the Board, but such old Congregational books and tracts as may be found in the market; and such works of current religious literature as a learned and judicious committee may deem important for the instruction and spirituality of our churches. Then, to disseminate and give efficiency to this central agency, there should be some safe plan by which our pastors shall become the colporteurs of our books, and thus workers together with us.　The denomination will then be a unit of moral forces.

Such a centre of mutual sympathy and influence we shall soon see in Boston, if the ministry, the churches, and munificent individuals will take hold of this enterprise as its intrinsic importance demands.

ARTICLE II.

THE SECOND ADVENT OF OUR LORD.

Christ's Second Coming: Will it be Pre-Millennial? By the Rev. DAVID BROWN, A.M., St. James' Free Church, Glasgow.

FROM a period soon after the publication of that wonderful prophetic book which closes the New Testament canon, and the death of its author, the last survivor of the apostolic college, there has seemed to prevail in the church at certain intervals a millenarian mania, seizing upon the entire marvellous element in the sacramental host.   We seem now to be in one of those periods.   Millenarianism seems to have taken on an epidemic form in the religious mind of this age.   Not that it is universal. The period is one of too general and too versatile activity.   Minds of a religious, and at the same time of a dreamy, poetic cast ; minds under the control of a strong materialistic rather than spiritualistic imagination, in this day are quite likely to be millenarians.   But all Christian minds are not such as these, and all Christians can not be led into this delusion.   Meanwhile candid and simple minded believers, who love and live upon the precious Book, and not upon illusive fancies, need to be on their guard against the plausible forms in which this pre-millennial theory of the second advent will present itself to, and claim, their attention.

To such, and to all who desire to be sufficiently informed on this subject, we can do no better service than commend to their careful study the work named at the head of this article.   The most that is needed is a knowledge of what this system really is, and a comparison of it with the simple word of God.   Few persons who have not specially looked into it have an idea of the radical errors and strange vagaries which logically inhere in it, and which its consistent advocates distinctly avow and defend.   In this point of view such a work as this of Mr. Brown is exceedingly valuable and worthy of general study.   He gives the main features of the system by means of full citations from all the leading and most respectable adherents and authorized expounders of it.   In short he fully states and fairly refutes the whole system.

In refuting the errors of millenarians, Mr. Brown gives his own views of the millennial prophecy in Rev. xx.   It is the view given in brief by Scott, Barnes and others, accepted by many now, and in earlier times.   Those who are satisfied with that, as in their judgment most in accordance with Scripture truth, may find here the clearest and best elucidation, on that basis, of the prophecies bearing on this general subject, which we have ever met.

We do not propose to give any analysis or minute description of this work.   Those who desire this will best obtain it by studying the work itself.   We propose rather to suggest some thoughts of our own on the millennial prophecy in Rev. xx.

We have an impression that many persons are millenarians from a supposed necessity of biblical exegesis.   The passage referred to contains a distinct prophecy announcing something seemingly very great and glorious.   They inquire what it is.   Their accepted expositors tell them : Nothing which may be expressed in the terms of the prophecy.   A period of time is to come of one thousand years, in which the visible power of Satan will be greatly repressed and restrained, and religious knowledge abound and prevail ; the prophesied resurrection is to be, not of persons, but of character.   The influential people of that period will be persons of a spirit and character like the holy martyrs, so that in their lives it may be said the confessors of old have risen from the dead.   Many readers of the Bible think that this sort of exposition fails to meet the demands of this text.   And as they never heard or thought of any other view as possible except this which, for distinction's sake we will call the figurative view, and the millenarian, if they do not accept this they are forced to that as the only alternative.

Now to destroy this alternative, to show that the rejection of either of these views does not necessarily involve the acceptance of the other, we propose to unfold, with as much brevity and clearness as we can, a third view of the prophecy.   We wish to show that there are more than two views of the prophecy, that we are not shut up to the acceptance of millenarian vagaries, if we find ourselves dissatisfied with that shadowy sort of analogical interpretation which is commonly opposed to them. We have farther to say that the view we shall offer, though not to our knowledge much canvassed in print, and wholly, so far as is known to the writer, thought out, as here presented, by himself, nevertheless has, in its essential points, long been held by many careful students of the Bible, who have rested quietly, so far as they could see, while waiting patiently for farther light on what they could not see. Indeed we have no doubt that every part of it has been held and promulgated by different Christian teachers in different ages of the Christian history.

This passage, at a first glance, seems entirely shut up in a unique and obscure symbolism. And so it would always be, if looked at as a whole. But if we scan it in its parts, we discover in the midst of this peculiar symbolism a familiar scriptural word, resurrection, and which it is not unreasonable to suppose may express a familiar scriptural idea. As it is qualified by a descriptive word, we may infer that it is not the resurrection of the dead, which is described by the sacred writers, as immediately preceding the final and general judgment. It is a resurrection, and is designated as the resurrection, the first, ἡ ἀνάστασις ἡ πρώτη. This very specific designation, the article twice repeated, would seem to point to some idea familiar to readers of the Scriptures.

This thought is strengthened by the declaration which follows : " Blessed and holy is he that hath part in the first resurrection : on such the second death hath no power, but they shall be priests of God and of Christ, and shall reign with him." Myriads of Christian readers have quoted this with a thrill of rapture, when they could not tell what the words mean ; only they were sure they mean some great and precious thing which the redeemed soul will experience, wherein he will be indeed blessed. And they must have been so far right, and justified in quoting it, though if asked for a definite exposition they had utterly failed. In conformity with universal Scripture usage, we must see that any blessing promised to a class of persons is limited to that class. The blessing is that those who have part in the first resurrection are holy or sanctified ones, that the second death hath no power on them, and as priests of God and of Christ, they shall reign with him.   It follows that on all others, as unholy and accursed, the second death hath, and must have power.   All the redeemed will sing the new song : " Thou hast redeemed us, and made us unto our God kings and priests."   But those alone can sing it who have part in the first resurrection.

What is this first resurrection ?   This is a question no less than of life everlasting and death eternal.   Can it be that such a matter can never be understood, but must be left to the unsatisfactory issues of curious and uncertain speculation ?   Can it be that it is so locked up as to require another revelation to make it plain ?   Nowhere in his word, unless here, does God set before men an unattainable beatitude.   If attainable, and if, as the very beatitude of escape from the second death it is our duty to strive to attain it, it surely must be possible to find out what it is.

What is this resurrection ?   It is the resurrection of the spirit of man, by nature dead.   The Scriptures teach us in several places directly,[1] and in several others indirectly,[2] that man embraces in his one personality three elements, body, soul and spirit.   In each of these three elements sin has brought, or will bring him to the experience of death, and if he ever attains to redemption from sin, he must in each of them experience a resurrection.   In respect to these three elements, the body, the corporeal element, needs no definition.   The soul, the psychical element, is the immaterial nature within, which constitutes man a rational, intellectual, immortal being, which animates and vitalizes the body, and which, apart from the body, may exist when death has turned the latter to dust.   The spirit of man is that element of his nature, whereby he may have communion with God, and in that communion, and by virtue of it, have spiritual life, as, in the want of it, and by virtue of that separation of the spirit from God, consists spiritual death.   In the spirit of the renewed man the Spirit of God dwells, and in his divine agency sometimes so identifies himself with the human spirit that the one agency can scarcely be distinguished from the other.   And hence we find the inspired writers some-

[1] 1 Thess. v. 23; Heb. iv. 12.
[2] 1 Cor. ii. 14, 15; Jude 19; Rom. viii. 4, 5, 16, 28.

times so using the word spirit, that we can hardly tell whether
they mean the Spirit of God, or the spirit of the renewed man.
In fact, it is the Spirit of God acting in and by the spirit of the
believer.[1] But the spirit of man is by nature and sin separated
from God, and is hence, as we have just shown, dead. The
resurrection of his spirit is the first resurrection which man,
dead in trespasses and sins, needs, and the first of which he
can have experience. And the text under consideration (Rev.
xx. 6) implies that whoever enjoys the blessedness attached to
the first resurrection, must now have part in it.

Let us now leave this passage, and inquire what is the first
resurrection of which the Scriptures give us any account? We
have it in the words of Jesus : " Verily, verily, I say unto you,
The hour is coming and now is, when the dead shall hear the
voice of the Son of God : and they that hear shall live." [2]
Here is a resurrection of the dead very plainly expressed. Its
title to the term resurrection, ἀνάστασις, is vindicated in the
manifest connection with the final resurrection in which Jesus
places it : " Marvel not at this : for the hour is coming in the
which all that are in the graves shall hear his voice, and shall
come forth ; they that have done good unto the resurrection of
life, and they that have done evil unto the resurrection of damnation." In the second chapter of Ephesians, Paul calls the
same fact of spiritual experience a resurrection. And we repeat, it is the first resurrection that the Scriptures give any ac-

---

[1] As an example of this, consider carefully the use of the word spirit in the following : Rom. viii. 9–11, 13–16, 23, 26, 27.   Perhaps the reader may inquire, What is
the real distinction between soul and spirit ?   Are they two distinct natures, entities
like soul and body ?   This is a question we are not careful to answer. The distinction is one of revelation, not of consciousness ; it belongs to theology, not psychology.
The Scriptures recognize it, but give no sharp definition of it.   Often in the Scriptures, as in common speech, spirit means soul; and perhaps, *vice versa*. Body,
i.e., flesh, sense, and spirit are the two opposite poles of human moral nature, between which lies the soul.   In the normal holy state, the spirit was in harmony and
communion with the Spirit of God, and in that state of holiness carried along with it
soul and body.   Man was spiritual.   The fall separated the spirit from the flesh ; the flesh
rose uppermost, plunged the soul into bondage, and now the whole man, soul and
spirit, is carnal, sensual, psychical.   Conf. Gr. of 1 Cor. ii. 14, 15., and Jude 19. And
on the other hand, the spirit separated from God is by that separation dead, and carries down to death both body and soul.   Indeed this distinction is implied in the entire evangelical doctrine respecting the fall, the renewal, the sanctification and
perfection of man, and especially in the doctrine of flesh and spirit in the renewed
man.   The depraved nature of man is called carnal from the body, and psychical
from the soul, but never spiritual.

[2] John v. 25.

count of, as within the ordinary range of human experience. If any resurrection may fitly be called the first resurrection, surely this may be. How truly may it be said : "Blessed and holy are they that have part in it ; on them the second death hath no power, but they shall be priests of God and of Christ, and shall reign with him."

What is the resurrection of which these Scriptures speak? It is the resurrection of the spirit of man. The spirit of man is that element of his nature whereby he may have communion with God. In the spirit of regenerate man, the Spirit of God dwells.[1] But by nature and sin, the spirit of man is separated from God, and in and by means of that separation is dead. The resurrection of his spirit is the first resurrection which man dead in trespasses and sins needs, inasmuch as death in his spirit is the first death he has any experience of. And the passage whose import we are seeking to find out, implies that whoever enjoys the blessedness attached to the first resurrection, must have part in it, in other words, must have experience of it now. "Blessed and holy is he that hath part in the first resurrection : on such the second death hath no power." But not a full experience ; that is reserved for the time when they shall be priests of God and of Christ, and shall reign with him ; which leads us to notice a second element in this great matter.

Man is soul as well as spirit. And sin will bring his soul to death, not less than his spirit and his body. When death seizes upon the body of the man who is already, in his spirit, dead in unregeneracy and sin, it at the same moment seizes upon the soul, and bears it away to the world of darkness and despair, the realm or prison of death, where death holds him for the second death. In this state the soul is dead ; not as being extinct, or unconscious, but as being in the world of death. David describes this when he says : "In death is no remembrance of thee : in Sheol who shall give thee thanks?"[2] "Sheol" is equivalent to "in death" ; it is the world or the prison where death holds the soul, which is therefore said to be in death. Heman the Ezrahite enlarges upon it in his mournful song : "Thou hast laid me in the lowest pit, in darkness, in

---

[1] Rom. viii. 9–16.   [2] Ps. vi. 5.

the abysses. Thy wrath lieth hard upon me. Wilt thou show wonders to the dead?" i. e., to souls that being in the world of death may properly be called "the dead," as the words immediately following show : "Shall the dead arise and praise thee? Shall thy loving kindness be declared in the grave, or thy faithfulness in destruction, [Abaddon]? Shall thy wonders be known in the dark, and thy righteousness in the land of forgetfulness?" [1]   This is the dreadful condition of the soul in the the world of death, under the reign of death, in Sheol, as in the Old Testament Hebrew, in Hades, as in the New Testament Greek, or in Hell, as in English. Dr. Dwight caught the idea with great exactness and expressed it in his well-known Psalm lxxxviii, "While life prolongs," etc.

> "In that lone land of deep despair,
>   No Sabbath's heavenly light shall rise ;
> No God regard your bitter prayer,
>   Nor Saviour call you to the skies.
>
> No wonders to the dead are shown ;
>   The wonders of redeeming love ;
> No voice his glorious truth makes known,
>   Nor sings the bliss of climes above.
>
> Silence, and solitude, and gloom,
>   In those forgetful realms appear :
> Deep sorrows fill the dismal tomb,
>   And hope shall never enter there."

Now, in consequence of what Jesus did in his own death and resurrection, it is provided in the dispensation of grace that he who in this life has part in the first resurrection, in other words experiences that quickening or resurrection of the spirit which is the immediate effect of regeneration, at the death of the body shall experience the resurrection of the soul. His soul will not be, when separate from the body, in Hades, as so many divines and theological teachers at this day are teaching the people. At death his soul will depart to be with Christ. Being absent from the body he will be present with the Lord, according to

---

[1] Ps. lxxxviii. 6, 7, 10, 11, 12. The use of the word "Abaddon," in the 11th verse, as the parallel of "grave," shows that "grave" is used for "Sheol." Com. Job xxvi. 6: "Naked is Sheôl before Him, and Abaddon hath no covering." Dr. Dwight, closely following his original, very manifestly uses the word "tomb" to express Hell.

the prayer of Jesus, John xvii. 24 ; as so well expressed by the
Westminster divines : " The souls of believers at their death
are made perfect in holiness and do immediately pass into
glory." When Christ ascended from Mount Olivet he did not
go into Hades.   He ascended to the right hand of the Father.
And his will is that those whom God has given him be with him
where he is that they may behold his glory.   And he is able to
secure this, for he is the resurrection and the life, and has declared, " he that liveth and believeth in me shall never die."
Dr. Watts saw this precise point in eschatology, and well expressed it :

> "When from the dead he raised his Son,
>   And called him to the sky,
> He gave our souls a lively hope
>   That they should never die."

This happy state of the redeemed soul when separate from
the body, is called by the Saviour a resurrection.   " The Sadducees, which say there is no resurrection," came to Jesus and
propounded the question of the seven brethren who successively
married the same wife.   Jesus answered : " As touching the
resurrection of the dead, have ye not read that which was
spoken unto you by God, saying, I am the God of Abraham,
and the God of Isaac, and the God of Jacob?   God is not
the God of the dead, but of the living." [1]   When that was
spoken to Moses from the bush, those patriarchs, though in a
sense dead, were in a more important sense living.   Their souls
were existing in a state of conscious blessedness.   That was so
far a resurrection and a pledge of their final resurrection.   If
when bodies die, the souls that animated them in life also cease
to exist, are exhaled as mere breath going from them not to return, as the Sadducees held, and as some millenarians now hold,
there could be no resurrection of the bodies, because there
would be no living beings to whom the bodies would belong.
This was the point of the Saviour's argument which so effectually silenced the Sadducees.   And this beatification of the redeemed soul with Christ, when separate from the body, is but
carrying out in respect to the soul what is begun in respect to
the spirit in regeneration.   As this experience of the spirit is

---

[1] Math. xxii. 31, 32.

" having part in the first resurrection," so that experience of the soul separate from the body is the first resurrection in its consummation.

We have now found in the instructions of Jesus an experience, that all the regenerate share in the present life, which he called a resurrection, and which is the first resurrection possible to human experience ; and also a happy state of all souls of believers after death, which is inseparably connected with that experience in life, to which Jesus applies the same term resurrection, ἀνάστασις. Let us now carefully note the prophecy in question, and see if what we have found does not precisely correspond with, and cover all, that is contained in it, in respect to this idea of the first resurrection.

We quote the passage, following Tischendorf's text, with whom agree all critical editors :

" Rev. xx. 4, 5. And I saw thrones, and they sat upon them, and judgment was given unto them, and [I saw] the souls of them that were beheaded for the witness of Jesus, and for the word of God, and whosoever had not worshipped the beast, neither his image, neither had received [his] mark upon their forehead, or upon their hand ; and they lived and reigned with Christ a thousand years. The rest of the dead lived not [οὐκ ἔζησαν, ' lived not ;' not οὐκ ἀνέζησαν, as *text. rec.*, ' lived not again'] until the thousand years were finished. This is the first resurrection."

" I saw," says the seer—what? The bodies of any part of mankind raised from their graves? Not a word of it. " I saw the souls of them that were beheaded for the witness of Jesus." If he intended to say : " I saw those who were beheaded for the word of God raised from the dead, living on this earth, and reigning with Christ," which it was necessary he should say, in order to express the millenarian idea, would he not have said it? Who has any right to put this idea into this text, which says nothing of the sort?

John was the prophet of the witnessing church. To encourage and strengthen them in bearing witness for Jesus, even to the extremity of being beheaded, he testifies to them what it was given him to see. " I saw the souls of them that were beheaded for the witness of Jesus." And how were they? " They were living and reigning with Christ." And " this " which he saw, viz., souls of beheaded persons, not dead with their dead bodies, but living and reigning with Christ, "made unto God kings and priests," and singing the new song, "this is the first resurrection." A very simple statement, yet one pregnant with the richest consolation, and one which, as we find corresponds precisely with what other Scriptures teach, will be true of all redeemed saints while their bodies lie in their graves. It is not the resurrection, but it stands in such inseparable relations to it, and at the same time to that spiritual resurrection which unregenerate man must experience to enjoy this blessedness of the dead who die in the Lord, that it may fitly be called, what the inspired seer does call it, "the first resurrection." It is the first resurrection in its consummation, which is begun in this life as a spiritual resurrection.

"They lived and reigned with Christ." Where? Expositors of all sorts, whether literal or figurative, have said, on this earth, putting it into the text, for it is not said. The thrones which John saw, occupied by these souls, are associated with the throne of Christ, for "they reigned with Christ." We have no account of any throne of Christ as a distinct person in the Trinity, except his mediatorial throne and his judgment throne. The latter will be on or near the earth. But it can not be imagined that the reigning of this text is any part of the solemnities of the last judgment. It only remains that these thrones are associated with Christ's mediatorial throne, and that these souls share, in some important respect, and to some important degree, in the mediatorial reign of Christ. But that throne is in heaven. And, therefore, these souls, living and reigning with Christ, are, and must be, in heaven. And this, too, we have found other Scriptures plainly and expressly declaring of the dead who die in the Lord : "Having a desire," says St. Paul, "to depart and be with Christ, which is far better" than "to abide in the flesh." "Willing rather to be absent from the body, and to be present with the Lord." Yet as the great triumphs of the mediatorial reign of Christ, are, and will be, on this earth, and as they share in that reign, they, too, "reign on the earth," thus fulfilling the new song, Rev. v. 10. They triumph before the throne in every triumph of grace in this world. " There is joy in the presence of the angels of God over one sinner that repenteth."

We thus find the seer of the Apocalypse comforting the tried saints of his time, and of all future time, with precisely the same considerations with which Paul comforted himself and others in similar circumstances, the truth which Jesus taught before either of them. He fitly follows it with the beatitude to which we have before referred, and which we quote again to show how completely it agrees with what we have found, and disagrees with either of the two prominent views which have been taken of the passage.

" Blessed and holy is he that hath part in the first resurrection. On such the second death hath no power, but they shall be priests of God and of Christ ; and shall reign with him."

According to both the millenarian and the figurative view of this prophecy, the first resurrection is wholly future. And how far in the future when the prophecy was written ! How could it be said of any one then living, or of any one now living, "he that hath part" in what was then so far, and still is wholly in the future ? But when we leave fancies and conjectures, and look at the first resurrection of which the Scriptures elsewhere contain an account, we find it, just as here, a blessing of which a partial experience, "hath part," must be enjoyed now, or there is no reason to expect its full consummation in the future, expressed in the words, " they shall be priests of God and of Christ, and shall reign with him." On him who has no "part" in it now, the second death even now " hath power." The second death, though future, even now has power, has a lien, so to speak, on every unregenerate soul. All who close probation as such, will, when the dread time arrives for the second death to assert its power, " be cast into the lake of fire, which is the second death."

We have now gone through this prophecy of the first resurrection in Rev. xx., with the exception of its connection with the millennial period, the thousand years, which we reserve for its proper place. And we have found the first resurrection, as here described, corresponding in every particular with a first resurrection revealed by Christ, taught by the same apostle to whom was revealed this prophecy, and by other apostles, else-

where in the New Testament.   Why should we not accept it as
a thread of inspiration given to lead us into the mysteries of a
prophecy confessed on all hands to be obscure and difficult?   If
we turn from this to the figurative expositors, we have, it must
be admitted, only conjectures and curious analogies.   If we go
from them to the millenarians, we have, with a pretence of
Scripture citation, that system of self-contradictory theories,
fancies and vagaries, of which we have found as yet, not a
trace in the passage under consideration.

Let us now consider some of the other points in this prophecy, and see if other Scriptures shed any light upon them.   We
will begin with the opening of the vision, the binding of Satan.

"And I saw an angel descending from heaven, having the
key of the abyss, and a great chain in his hand."

Before we can gain a comprehension of this prophecy it is
necessary for us distinctly to understand and bear in mind in all
our thought, that what we have here is the form of the prophecy, not its precise substance.   The substance is indeed contained in the form, and must there be sought ; but we must not
confound them.   The prophecy, like the most in this book, is
revealed in the form of a vision, i. e., something seen.   The
prophet in this case is a seer.   He saw a picture and describes
what he saw.   The first thing he saw was an angel descending
from heaven.   The being whom he saw appeared to be an angel.   Was it an angel?   Abraham on a certain occasion saw
three men approach his tent.   That was what he saw and it is so
written.   After a little he saw they were not men.   He saw
them to be angels, and then it is written so.   But at length he
knew that one of the three celestial personages was Jehovah, the
hearer of prayer, and the sovereign judge of all the earth, and
then it is written so.   And though the seer of the Apocalypse
saw this being as an angel, he was doubtless no other than the
Lord Jesus Christ, who had often appeared as an angel, as
could very easily be shown.   He had the key of the abyss or
depths of Sheol or Hades, called also the pit, Gehenna, Tar-
tarus, and repeatedly mentioned or referred to under one or
another of these names in both Testaments.   This corresponds
with what Christ said of himself (Rev. i. 18), "I have the keys
of death and of Hades."   He had also a great chain in his

hand.   The use in the vision of both these instruments is next stated.   "And he laid hold on the dragon, which is the devil, and Satan, and bound him a thousand years, and cast him into the abyss, and shut him up, and set a seal upon him that he should deceive the nations no more till the thousand years should be fulfilled: and after that he must be loosed a little time."

Now in seeking to learn what is here described, let us in the outset notice that all sober-minded expositors are agreed that this prophecy must not be understood to indicate a restraint upon Satan to such an extent that he shall have no power in this world as a tempter of men.   The world will always be one in which men will be liable to temptation, and that from the arch tempter.   This is very clearly shown to be Scripture doctrine in the work which furnishes the title to the present article. The prophecy will doubtless be fulfilled, if a period ever arrives in which Satan shall be deprived of the power of carrying on his grand wholesale operations, "deceiving the nations" as such, organizing error and iniquity so as to make them national and even continental in their scope, and so give them a power to sweep whole generations and nations down to death.

Let us distinctly apprehend another preliminary thought. This vision need not and can not well be understood as describing one single fact or event, performed at one point of time, viz., at the beginning of the period designated as one thousand years.   It speaks of not less than three and probably four distinct facts which are not necessarily contemporaneous, and which are not probably so.   These four facts are the following:

(*a*.) The angel lays hold of Satan and binds him for a thousand years.   That must needs be at the beginning of the millennial period.   When so much is done, he is then under restraint and in the power of the being by whom he was bound.

(*b*.) He casts him into the abyss.   The vision certainly places this after the binding or first restraint; in the fulfillment it may be centuries after.

(*c*.) He shuts him up. Here is another distinct point, an additional restraint following that which is described as casting in. It may be separated from it by a lapse of time which would be accounted long in-history.

(*d.*) He sets a seal upon him that he should deceive the nations no more till the thousand years shall be fulfilled. This follows the shutting up, and it may follow it, as the preceding, after a considerable lapse of time. It is the last act in the drama, the crowning work of the series to endure to the close of the millennial period.

Now our question is, whether the Scriptures contain any evidence that Christ has done any part of what he is represented in this vision as doing. If he has done any part of it, that is so far a fulfillment of the prophecy, and a pledge to our faith of its ultimate complete fulfillment, for which we may well with patience wait. To answer this question, we shall, waiving all guessing, all conjectures, all analogical reasoning, simply refer to a few plain declarations of Scripture prose.

Heb. ii. 14. "That through death he might make powerless [καταργήσῃ] him that had the power of death, that is, the devil." Christ by his death and resurrection, which necessarily followed his death, and therefore needed no separate mention, destroyed the power of the devil. Now if this plain didactic prose were to be translated into prophetic poetry, passing also as dramatic action before the vision of the seer, what could be more natural and fit than a representation of a mighty angel seizing Satan and binding him?

The seer of this vision had before declared, 1 John iii. 8, also in plain didactic prose : "For this purpose the Son of God was manifested, that he might destroy the works of the devil." He had also reported Jesus himself as saying, John xii. 31, 32, "Now is the judgment of this world; now shall the prince of this world be cast out. And I, if I be lifted up from the earth, will draw all men unto me." He was speaking of his own death. In connection with, and in consequence of, that great event, Satan, the prince of this world, would be cast out. Out of what? What but his princedom, this world? And into what, if not the abyss? When he cast out of the possessed Gadarene the legion of demons, they " besought him that he would not command them to go forth into the abyss," [1] which shows that the very thing they feared was what John saw in this vision.

[1] Luke viii. 31.

Consider the words of the Lord in Matt. xii. 29 : " How can one enter into a strong man's house, and spoil [make a spoil of] his goods, except he first bind the strong man? and then he will spoil his house." Here he declares his special work to be to bind Satan, as a necessary preliminary to making a spoil of what is in his palace or stronghold. It had been centuries before prophesied of Christ : " He shall divide the spoil with the strong, because he hath poured out his soul unto death ;"[1] and Paul tells us that by his resurrection Christ " spoiled principalities and powers, and made a shew of them openly, triumphing over them,"[2] the "powers," that is, of death and Hades, which was, especially, as we have seen, Heb. ii. 14, the devil. But before this could be, that is, before the triumph of his resurrection, he himself tells us he must needs bind Satan. His power to do this, and his purpose no less, he was then proving by his power over demons.

Now what we say is, and this is all that need be said or proved for the purposes of our exposition, it must be true, in some sense, that Christ did, in and by his death and resurrection, destroy the power of the devil, and was manifested for this very purpose ; it must have been true, in some sense, that Christ by his death and resurrection did take a decisive step to cast Satan out of his princedom, this world ; it must be true, in some sense, that Christ did, before his resurrection, bind Satan, as the strong prince of death and Hades ; for all this is literally said in the texts we have quoted. In other words, the very thing seen in this vision, Satan seized and bound, is in plain, didactic speech, declared to have been done when Christ arose from the dead.

Is some reader objecting, ' It can not be true that Christ has seized and bound Satan '? And is that objector a true believer in Christ? What security hast thou then, O purblind one, for thine own final salvation? What security hast thou that Satan will not yet prove an overmatch for the mighty Redeemer? Is the battle yet to be fought between Christ and Satan? Did Christ reckon without his host, when he said : " None," none, not even the roaring lion of Hades, " is able to pluck my sheep

[1] Isa. liii. 12.   [2] Col. ii. 15.

out of my hand"? It surely is not too much to believe that the Almighty Redeemer of men has bound Satan their puissant and malignant foe; that so much of this prophecy is fulfilled. And then what follows? We have, and the church has always had, a pledge that all the rest will be, the casting into the abyss, the shutting in, the sealing that he shall deceive the nations no more. We need not be too curious as to the time of the other acts in this great drama of the world's redemption. They will all come in their own good time, and in the best time. And when they come, the full triumph of the Gospel will have come, the bright vision of all holy seers of all the inspired ages, the latter day glory, when all the "ends of the world shall remember and turn unto the Lord, and all the kindreds of the nations shall worship before him"; when "the mountain of the Lord's house shall be exalted above the hills, and all nations shall flow unto it"; when "the kingdom and dominion, and the greatness of the kingdom under the whole heaven shall be given to the people of the saints of the Most High," "for the earth shall be filled with the knowledge of the glory of the Lord, as the waters cover the seas."

We have now shown what may be the nature of the facts revealed in this prophecy, the general trend of it. And this much must be conceded, so far as we have gone we are on safe and sure ground. We have propounded no new and startling article of faith, or theory of doctrine. We have found no necessity of revolutionizing the foundations of doctrinal or practical theology. We have not led the Scriptures, but have simply allowed the Scriptures to lead us. We have found revealed here, in a form indeed peculiar to this prophetic book, but in strict consistency with its general style, truths on which the faith of the church has ever rested, which have ever been its support and its strength; the sole peculiarity of our exposition being, that these familiar truths are contained in this passage, where so many sagacious and clear-sighted expositors have found something else.

There remains another quite important point, the millennial period, one thousand years. This at first sight will appear more difficult than those we have considered. Yet if we are

correct in the views we have already attained, we need not despair of a consistent solution of this.

Let it be observed here, that what we have so far found in
this prophecy is simply a form of statement peculiar to the seer
of the Apocalypse, of truths revealed elsewhere in the Scriptures in common forms of speech. It is not unreasonable to
surmise that this period of one thousand years, so called, is
but a peculiar form of expressing what is elsewhere plainly expressed.

We have here a prophetic period of one thousand years.
The first question is, whether this is a literal thousand years, or
is a prophetic symbol of a period of time fixed and definite in the
divine counsels, but not definitely revealed, as determinate time,
to us.   If we consult prophetic analogies, we shall say the latter.   All are agreed that the other prophetic numbers in
the Apocalypse are symbolic numbers ; as the time, times
and a half, the forty and two months, the thousand two hundred threescore days, and the six hundred threescore and six.
Why should this be an exception, especially when really
insurmountable difficulties environ the attempt to consider it a
literal period of just so many years ?   Our risen Redeemer himself turned our steps from all temporal investigations of this
sort in his emphatic declaration : " It is not for you to know the
times, or the seasons, which the Father hath put in his own
power." [1]   Surely the repeated disappointments, which all-dem-
onstrating time has brought upon many who were so confident
that it was for them to know the times, should be sufficient to
settle, for all sober-minded Christians, the point that this is one
principle on which prophetic numbers are not to be interpreted.

Not only does all prophetic analogy lead to the conclusion
that this is a symbolic, not a literal number ; the number itself,
if considered carefully, will demonstrate the same thing.   It
has in itself every sign of being a symbolic number.   It has
that peculiar artificial look which belongs to all symbolic numbers.   Yet in its structure it differs from all others.   It is an
exact power.   This is true of no other prophetic number.   All
prophetic numbers but this, are fragmentary, and they all ex-

[1] Acts i. 7.

press time in fractions of years, not in any round full number of years. It is not only an exact power, it is a cube. Its root, ten, is the most perfect number there is. It is the foundation of the decimal system, and is among all nations a perfect number. Like the king of Tyre among potentates, it "seals up the sum," [1] always completing a series in computation, always necessitating a return for a new series.

Next consider it as a power. A power is a geometrical conception. We shall see as we proceed, that the introduction of this symbolical number into geometrical conceptions, will not necessarily remove it from Scripture analogies. A single number, as ten, represents a line in geometry. A line is extension in one direction only. It is no figure and can include nothing. It is only the edge of something. A number repeated once as a factor, as 10×10, represents surface, which is extension in two directions, and is a figure. But it is only one side. A number taken three times as factor, as $10 \times 10 \times 10$, is extension in three directions; all the directions there are, length, breadth, and height. It is a complete figure. It includes and wholly encloses a definite portion of space, cutting it off from every thing else. In this number 1000, so composed, these three directions of extension are equal, making a cube, the most perfect geometrical figure, a figure embracing not only a complete, but also a perfect whole. Uniformly in the Scriptures the figure which represents the highest perfection, is a cube. The holiest of all, type of heaven, in the tabernacle and temple, was an exact cube. The perfection of creation, the holy and heavenly Jerusalem, "lieth four square." "The length, and the breadth, and the height of it are equal," [2] a geometrical cube.

We conclude that this apocalyptic chiliad, one thousand years, denotes a definite period of time with a definite beginning and end, but in respect to its length, beyond the range of human computation. The number which designates this period, a power of a root which is the most perfect number there is, the cube of that perfect number, the most perfect geometrical figure there is, can not denote anything that is incomplete or fragmentary. It can express nothing less than a full and complete period, having its beginning and ending, and its distinc-

---

[1] Esek. xxviii. 12.   [2] Rev. xxi. 16.

tive elements, within itself. Its beginning, *terminus a quo*, is distinctly defined in this prophecy. Its end, *terminus ad quem*, is not defined here nor anywhere else. "I saw an angel, . . . and he laid hold on the dragon, . . . the devil, . . . and bound him a thousand years." This symbolic period began then when Christ bound Satan, which was, as other Scriptures have shown us, at his death and resurrection. We have now only to inquire what period of time it was, which, full and complete, and having its beginning, and ending, and all its distinctive elements within itself, began at the resurrection of Christ; an inquiry which need not detain us long. It can be no other than the mediatorial reign of him who is the alpha and the omega, the beginning and the ending, the first and the last, a period of time which then began, and which is to continue till that day, which Jesus declared was known only to the Father, when, having destroyed the last enemy, death, he will deliver up the kingdom to God even the Father. During all this period, this symbolic chiliad, this millennium, as death gathers the redeemed home, their souls will be with Christ, beholding his glory, living and reigning with him, enjoying the blessedness of the first resurrection, and in that blessedness awaiting the close of the period, then to receive the higher blessedness not of the second resurrection, for the Scriptures make no mention of a second resurrection, but of the resurrection, the final resurrection from the dead.

We have now considered all there is in this vision which belongs to the millennial period of one thousand years. The prophecy however goes farther and speaks of a loosing of Satan at the end of that period for a short time expressed by the indefinite phrase "a little season," a gathering of the enemies of God under him to make war upon the saints, and the final issue of the attempt, followed by the solemnities of the last judgment. In regard to this we will detain the reader with only a brief suggestion.

In this vision all the dead, existing as souls separate from the body, are divided into two classes. First, those who as priests of God and Christ are living and reigning with him in the first resurrection; and secondly, "the rest of the dead" who it is said "lived not until the thousand years were finished." They exist, but do not live ; their existence is, as separate souls, in the world and state of death. Even in this life and in the body they are correctly said to be dead, (John v. 25, Eph. ii. 1) ; how much more might this be said of them when separate from the body, in the prison of death? When the thousand years shall be finished, their bodies reanimated in the final resurrection, they will " ascend on the breadth of the earth," ἀνέβησαν ἐπὶ τὸ πλάτος τῆς γῆς (v. 9) and so in a physical sense may be said then to live ; the only sense in which they ever will live. At the same time Satan, their great deceiver, being loosed from his prison, will be among them, their prince [1] and god [2] as of old. Besides, there is nothing in this prophecy in conflict with those numerous Scriptures which give reason to expect that the final resurrection will find many living wicked men upon the earth.

It is not inconsistent with any Scripture representation of the the last things to suppose some time to elapse between the resurrection of all the dead from their graves and the final judgment, which might be expressed as a "little season." What Satan may in that brief time do with that class of mankind, who were in life his willing slaves and dupes, is not for us to conjecture. We will only say that the idea that that may be the time of the war of Gog and Magog, though suggested to our mind solely by the study of the passage, is no new thought to the world. Gill published a full unfolding of it in his Exposition of the New Testament more than a century ago. Other millenarian writers, we know not how many, and quite likely antimillenarians, have followed him in the same view.

[1] John xii. 31.   [2] 2 Cor. iv. 4.

ARTICLE III.

HENRY TAYLOR'S PROSE WRITINGS.

The Statesman.   By HENRY TAYLOR, Esq.   Author of
Philip Van Artevelde.   London.
Notes from Books.   In Four Essays.   By HENRY TAYLOR.
Second Edition.   London.
Notes from Life.   In Six Essays.   By HENRY TAYLOR.
Third Edition.   London.

MR. TAYLOR'S reputation was won, and is maintained, by
those dramatic poems which have given " the author of Philip
Van Artevelde " as secure a place in English literature as that
of the author of Thalaba or Manfred.   There is a massiveness
and energy in his poetic thought and diction, which savors of
the older masters of our tongue, in the days when imaginative
vigor and wealth were not thought to be at war with strong
common sense.   Reading over his nervous dramatic creations,
one might naturally infer that it would not be very difficult for
this reflective and forcible writer to step into the prose-writer's
domain with advantage.   The volumes, whose titles are above
recited, are sufficient proof that this has been done.   We suppose that they are not much known on this side the Atlantic.
Those who have learned to admire Mr. Taylor's poems, may be
pleased to extend their acquaintance to his other publications.
Their contents are of sterling and permanent value.   They
have found a few appreciative readers among our people, as we
have been glad to know.   The first of the series, with annota-
tions, would well bear to be reprinted just now, as an excellent
manual of counsel for the rising public men of our land.   We
shall, consequently, review it with more particularity than the
others.   A very readable volume might also be selected from
these.

We are not aware that this writer has ever mingled in political life, but he obviously has been a close observer of public
men and affairs, and has thought wisely and patiently upon them.
The *Statesman* contains the results of this observation and re-

flection, in thirty four chapters, upon such topics as—education
for civil life; the age of commencing an official career; the
choice and use of instruments; getting and keeping adherents;
the value of literary merit to the politician; official style; false
reputations; the stateman's conscience; his married connections;
orderly habits and mental balance; the temper and the ethics
of public men; consistency, secrecy, ambition, decisiveness, as
qualities of the statesman; the evils of incompetency; the administration of patronage; a stateman's amusements, and manners; and the very difficult and common situation of the great
man of yesterday becoming the small man of to-morrow, at
least in the eyes of the time-serving crowd; that is, the statesman, and we presume other officials, as well, when out of office,
or as it might now be phrased—"out in the cold."

The conception thus taken of official life is elevated, and the
discussion of its adjuncts is fundamental.   But this is conducted
more in the way of pregnant hints than of exhaustive disquisition.   The whole book, in fact, is only a small one of less than
three hundred pages.   The author does not evaporate in glit-
tering or lack-lustre generalities.   He brings his topics down to
matter of fact details, and gratifies us by the homeliness as well
as the pith of his suggestions.   He thinks as little of public
men who have not served a faithful apprenticeship for office, as
the sailor does of the master of a ship who has stepped to the
quarter deck through the cabin window.   Young aspirants
should practice themselves early in public debate.

"Also the drudgery of an office should be encountered early,
while the energy of youth is at its height, and can be driven
through anything by the spur of novelty.   Nor let any man suppose
that he can come to be an adept in statesmanship, without having
been at some period of his life a thorough-going drudge.   Drudgery
is not less necessary to teach patience and give a power over details
to the statesman himself, than to enable him to understand the powers, and measure the patience of those who are drudges in his service.   And as ' trifles make the sum of human things,' so details
make the substance of public affairs."   pp. 10, 11.

Our author is far from belonging to the school of statecraft
which practically if not professedly lays its main emphasis on
the second half of that somewhat ambiguous word.   Yet he

understands that men must govern men through the use of much of that wisdom which seems particularly to characterize the "serpent" among the lower creatures. And as no one can do everything that must be done, *in sua persona*, it will always be true that real ability will show itself in the selection of allies for its work. "Therefore no man who contemplates a public career should fail to begin early, and persist always, in cultivating the society of able men of whatsoever classes or opinions they may be, provided only they be honest." That may be said of statesmen, says Mr. Taylor, which Dean Swift remarked of young ladies : "it would be well if fewer of them learnt to make nets, and more to make cages." This is not to be effected by cajolery.

"Excess of profession evinces weakness, and weakness never conciliates political adhesion. Willing to befriend an adherent, but prepared to do without him, is what a leader should appear to be ; and this appearance is best maintained by a light cordiality of demeanor towards him, and a more careful and effective attention to his interests than he has been led by that demeanor to anticipate. . . . . Shy and proud men are more liable than any others to fall into the hands of parasites, and creatures of low character. For in the intimacies which are formed by shy men, they do not choose, but are chosen. . . . Even coldness of character, without pride or shyness, will of itself tend to throw the head of a party into the closer connection with the more menial of his partizans. For the less menial will hold themselves more aloof, when they do not find the relation of political superiority to come qualified and recommended to them by feelings of personal friendliness." pp. 25, 27, 28.

This may commend itself as a shrewd study in human nature to some who may wonder at the author's old fashioned opinions on another point which, in our judgment, is of still greater importance. The ethics of this volume are not hyper-purist, but they are sound enough to teach that bad men are to be shunned in filling places of power and trust. If the choice must lie between talent without seriousness and worth, and good sense without ability, the last must be preferred, undesirable as such an election must necessarily be. It is quite impossible, just here, to repress the reflection, what a vacating of salaries there would be in most governments, if this doctrine could have way. We do not venture to conjecture the state of things which would supervene at our own seat of executive power. Did Mr. Taylor learn this truth by the inspiration of his own poetical nature? Nay, verily, we think he rather found it in an ancient book of political maxims, which many places in his writings show that he has reverently studied.

"But if there be in the character not only sense and soundness, but virtue of a high order, then, however little appearance there may be of talent, a certain portion of wisdom may be relied upon almost implicitly. For the correspondences of wisdom and goodness are manifold; and that they will accompany each other is to be inferred, not only because men's wisdom makes them good, but also because their goodness makes them wise. Questions of right and wrong are a perpetual exercise of the faculties of those who are solicitous as to the right and wrong of what they do and see, and a deep interest of the heart in these questions carries with it a deeper cultivation of the understanding than can be easily effected by any other excitement to intellectual activity. Although, therefore, simple goodness does not imply every sort of wisdom, it unerringly implies some essential conditions of wisdom; it implies a negative on folly, and an exercised judgment within such limits as nature shall have prescribed to the capacity. And where virtue and capacity are combined, there is implied the highest wisdom, being that which includes the worldly wisdom with the spiritual." pp. 30, 31.

It is refreshing to read such manly sentiments upon a subject which has almost ruled itself out of the pale of Christian morality, alike by its theoretical and practical Machiavelianism. It is disgraceful to the civilization of this age, that the science and the art of political management are a century behind the existing state of general education, in enlightened nations. Italian finesse carries it over Anglo-Saxon frankness and probity, in the best governments of the day. We stand aghast at the revelations of duplicity and every kind of mean adroitness which modern historians like Motley and Froude are unearthing from such hiding places as the archives of Simancas. But it is by no means certain that future writers upon our times will not quite as truly astonish our posterity with the disclosure of much the same viciousness, in the administration of power in the hands of Christendom's present rulers, however skilfully it may now be covered. The covering, however, is not long enough to hide the whole of this deformity from our eyes. The lupine extremities, and sometimes the Satanic, will crop out from the scant sheep skin which seeks to disguise the evil beast beneath it. Government is the noblest and loftiest employment of human energies to which any secular end can summon them. It is godlike, if pursued in its true spirit. The worst of the existing governments of the Western nations we suppose to be quite an advance on the old Roman and the mediæval tyrannies. How much room there is for further improvement, is an important question for those to study who think it about time for the enlightened world to put away childish and barbarous things.

The chapter on literary merit, as a qualification for official life, has some nicely discriminated thought. The author does not regard this as a very good preparation for the conduct of affairs. Indeed, it creates a decided drawback in this pursuit. Persons, who have cultivated particularly the imaginative and the philosophical powers, are thereby much disqualified for statesmanship. Both run into an idealism which is impracticable in real life : " because the business of a statesman is less with truth at large than with truths commonly received." Government must deal with what is, and make it as much better than it is, as the tools and material with which it has to work, will permit. But here it is of no use to spoil a horseshoe, by trying to make a watchspring, if the first is all that can be made. We have had, in modern states, examples of the incompetency of the imaginative genius to control political forces and issues. Lamartine is one : perhaps Disraeli may prove to be another. Also, the philosophic abstractionists have their illustrations, it may be, nearer home. Their error is, the attempt to extemporize the millennium without the preliminary educational and other processes of which it can only be the result. The mistakes of both are amiable, but mischievous. Yet there is a place for each of these qualities of intellect, and a measure of them is indispensable ; for " he can never be more than a second-rate statesman, into whose conduct of affairs philosophy and imagination do not in some degree enter." The point then is, to graduate rightly their proportions to other forces of the character.

The matter of a statesman's conscience might be thought a very intangible kind of thing to handle. What it should be may

detain us a moment.   Mr. Taylor thinks, that it should rather
be strong than tender.   The latter is apt to busy and burden
itself unduly with the lesser interests of a question of administration, as, in thinking more of a criminal under sentence of
death and suing for pardon, than of the responsibility of government to the public as its protector from crimes against its
very life.   From this false conscientiousness we have been
great sufferers.   The inmates of our state-prisons have been of
more consequence, in the eyes of "tender" rulers, than all the
outside population of law-abiding citizens.   Again, this kind of
conscience is prone to be insensible to the mischiefs of inactivity
and delay.   It becomes " all bridle and no spurs "; or, as we
might put it, all breeching and no whip.   It grows to be " a
quagmire, in which the faculty of action shall stick fast at every
step."   The reader will appreciate the truthfulness of this analysis.   A due adjustment of tenderness and strength is the ideal
of a public man's conscience ; intelligent and perspicacious ;
not the conscience of the heart only, but of the understanding,
as well, with a just sense of proportion between public and private objects which excite its action.   " It sometimes happens
that he who would not hurt a fly, will hurt a nation."

Would any one but a poet have thought of saying that a
statesman, as a bishop, should be " the husband of one wife "?
We catch a bright glimpse of our author's affectional nature,
and give him credit for much more practical sense than is
awarded, by common consent, to most of the "irritabile genus,"
from what he says of the elevating, purifying, rectifying influence of home life, and the picture which he draws of a true
wife for a public man.   She should have a character not lower
than his own.   She should not " idolize" her husband ; that
will only harm him : " for domestic flattery is the most dangerous of all flatteries."   A man who lives in the eye of the
world, be he minister of state, or minister of religion, needs a
wife, who in her strong, not weakly, fond affection, can be the
counsellor and even the critic of her husband, in many matters,
and who knows how to be this, so as to improve his nature and
to heighten his value among men.   Wealth is not to be despised
by a statesman, in making a choice.   We do not know that it
is ever to be, other things being equal.   Beauty is worth much.

" The taste goes deep into the nature of all men ; love is hardly love apart from it." Here speaks again the poet. And borne away by the congenial theme, he gives us the portrait of the woman whom he thus has idealized :

> " A love that clings not. nor is exigent,
>   Encumbers not the active purposes,
>   Nor drains their source ; but proffers with free grace
>   Pleasure at pleasure touched at pleasure waived,
>   A washing of the weary traveller's feet,
>   A quenching of his thirst, a sweet repose
>   Alternate and preparative ; in groves
>   Where loving much the flower that loves the shade,
>   And loving much the shade that that flower loves,
>   He yet is unbewildered, unenslaved,
>   Thence starting light and pleasantly let go
>   When serious service calls." p. 75.

When our author comes to the question whether the states-man is ever justified in using deception for public ends, he is constrained to step very cautiously and to confess the great in-tricacy of the topic. The point is, whether it is practicable to carry the principles of private life into public, " in all their dis-tinctness and strictness." To profess to do this, and yet not to do it, is a very hardening thing to a man's moral sense. To adopt the other view, is an equally, if not more dangerous one. It may be true that " falsehood ceases to be falsehood when it is understood on all hands that the truth is not expected to be spoken." Possibly this is the common understanding in politi-cal and official circles, though, we would hope, not quite to the extent as in the court of Philip II. of Spain, where, if any one wanted effectually to conceal a fact, he boldly published it in plainest terms. We submit whether the mendacity of courts and cabinets be not greatly chargeable to this very looseness in construing the demands of absolute veracity, and whether a thorough reform will be brought around until some Christian government has courage and conscience enough to stand by the truth as men must do in private life to have any character, though the heavens fall. Mr. Taylor does not decide the ques-tions which he raises. He leans to the side which would per-mit to statesmen what they " must necessarily take and exercise —a free judgment namely, though a most responsible one, in the weighing of specific against general evil and in the perception of perfect or imperfect analogies between public and private transactions, in respect to the moral rules by which they are to be governed." The morality of the state he would have to be above common opinion, but not so much above it as to have no attractive power upon this. The level of practicable virtue, he says, is high enough to stand upon, to work for its still higher elevation. We give the writer full credit for purity of ethical views, in his own understanding of his statements, while seeing that they are open to perversion. This he seems also to be aware of, as he candidly admits that, notwithstanding his cautiousness and well-meaning; " I may almost say that I have written this chapter with a trembling hand." It is a topic which demands a more thorough discussion, while there is no point in morals so difficult to handle satisfactorily as this, of misrepresenting in word or act the literal reality of things.

We can not specify all the subjects which come into the range of remark in the treatise before us. He advocates the culture of a self-protecting dignity which is the best guard against quarrels, a defence alike from aggression and aggressing. "A dignity which has to be contended for is not worth a quarrel ; for it is of the essence of real dignity to be self-sustained, and no man's dignity can be asserted without being impaired." A more positive condemnation of duelling would have better satisfied us. It is to be remembered, however, that this volume was written many years ago, since which time public opinion has greatly changed respecting this subject ; and very likely a stronger position would now be taken by Mr. Taylor upon it. The official world has been slow in reaching the truth in this matter ; slower, abroad, we believe, than in these Northern States, inasmuch as false notions about "gentlemanly" intercourse have prevailed there than with us. The duel belongs, in all its aspects, to the barbarism of the Middle Ages. It is utterly and always indefensible. Of course, its defence is not here attempted. Yet the implication is that sometimes it may be necessary, as society is at present constituted. There can be no necessity thus to imperil life and domestic rights, for any personal affront or offence.

Orderly habits are a *sine qua non* of official efficiency ; and the Sabbath rest is a boon to the wearied head and heart of a

man of affairs too precious to be thrown away.   Not only
should he set apart a sabbatical day each week, but a sabbatical
hour each day, for devotional purposes, and quiet thought, and
meditative studies.   He should have an eye, in this, to the
evening time of life when, if not sooner, he must pass back to
private life, for the rational enjoyment of which he should preserve the means, in a daily right self-culture.   Some admirable
suggestions are furnished upon a statesman's manners and
amusements.   Following the guidance of this mentor, we think
no one would find the days of retirement from office wearisome.
Mr. Taylor gives us Lord Bacon as a good illustration of graceful and dignified transition from public to private life.   When
his fortune turned, "then, though there was disgrace and a
tainted character to be contended with, his substantial greatness rose nevertheless like a monument over the shell that had
been buried."

We have not passed an indiscriminate eulogy upon this little
volume ; but we think it a very valuable repository of thought
upon a subject not often treated with systematic fulness, while
it is of the first importance in every free, self-governed country.
Notes from Life comprises essays upon the equally practical
topics (except perhaps the last) of money ; humility and independence ; choice in marriage ; wisdom ; children ; the life
poetic.   *Notes from Books* contains two elaborate review
articles on Wordsworth's poetical works ; another on Aubrey De
Vere's poems, and an essay on the ways of the rich and
great.   Beyond these volumes we are not aware that Mr.
Taylor has given to the public any considerable prose productions.   If he has, they have not reached us.

It has grown into a kind of common law in the republic of
letters, that the creative and the critical faculties do not naturally belong to the same intellect.   Yet we remember that
Southey spent a large part of his life in writing critical articles
for the *London Quarterly;* and here we have another of the
" creative " genius contributing to the same *Review* these careful critiques of two of his brother bards.   If the critical power
would hardly be denied these reviewers, it might be queried, at
least to save the theory, whether they could lay valid claim to
the creator's peculiar gift, in the sense which the above antith-

esis implies. It does not fall in our way to enter on this question. Our judgment of Mr. Taylor's poetical standing has been expressed in a former volume.[1] His estimate of Wordsworth is high, as might be supposed from the character of his own mind. And this respect for his subject leads him to a close study of the peculiarities of that originator of a new poetical school, which is by no means blind to Wordsworth's weak points. The philosophical spirit of this criticism is excellent. The writer is not content with surface views. He explores the roots of things. He weighs with steady poise the most delicate feelings. He puts strong thoughts into sturdy words, giving us a literary style in perfect keeping with that druidic head of his which a friend lately sent us—so thoughtful, reposeful, robust; a living protest against all effeminateness and sham. Thus, his direction respecting the language to be employed in poetic composition—a rule not absolutely, however, without exceptions:

" In general to use the same language which is employed in the writings and conversation of other men when they write and discourse their best—to avoid any words which are not admissible in good prose or unaffected conversation, whether erudite or ordinary—and especially to avoid the employment of any words in a sense which is not their legitimate prosaic sense."

It is to be regretted that all the popular writers of English verse have not better profited by such wholesome instruction.

Papers like these are not of mere ephemeral interest. They give us clear and tangible art-studies, like the demonstrations of the anatomist. They remind us that much of our best literature is to be found in the issues of the higher periodical press. In the hands of competent and conscientious men, this kind of writing is hardly second to any in pleasantness and usefulness. Take the observations here made on the love of nature to give poise and calm delight to "men of great excitability and a passionate sense of the beautiful"; who

> "———have learned
> To look on Nature, not as in the hour
> Of thoughtless youth; but hearing oftentimes
> The still, sad music of humanity,
> Nor harsh, nor grating, though of ample power
> To chasten and subdue:"

[1] *The Boston Review*, Vol. III., pp. 597, *et seq.*

Or, on the "sanative" influence of Mr. Wordsworth's severe and elevated style of thought and sentiment upon over-sensitive and self-distrustful spirits, as embodied in his Ode to Duty. These disquisitions are in the best vein of earnest, wholesome, reflection. And they are continually occurring. His keen perception of the likenesses and the differences of shades of thought, shows itself in what he writes of the subtile presence, in Wordsworth, of what looks almost, at times, like a pantheistic endowment of inanimate things with sentient life : and also, of the place in human intercourse for the legitimate exercise of "the harsher sentiments of our nature—anger, resentment, contempt." The critical remarks on Wordsworth's Sonnets are replete with these nice discriminations of ethical and philosophical truth. We would not say that, here and elsewhere, a judgment or opinion may not be open to dissent, though closer reflection has more than once relieved a statement of what seemed at first an error. The dissection is in a firm and honest, as well as practiced hand. It never attempts mere speculative display. We hardly think it possible for this writer to forget the practical, in any prose composition. How characteristic of him is the answer he gives to those who would have a poem one unceasing " mantling and sparkling of poetic effervescence " ; that, " it behooves " the artist " to apply himself from time to time to . . . . *transact the business* of his poem." (*sic ital:*) Mr. Taylor always treads on the solid earth, as critic and essayist, however he may soar in numbers. But there he never lays himself open to the stricture which he makes upon De Vere's writings ; that, while marked by rare excellences as works of genuine genius, they occasionally suffer from "obscurity and subtlety" of conception and expression.

On a former page of this article, we noted the lofty tone of Mr. Taylor's sense of the value of political morality. In his critique of the Wordsworthian Sonnets, he makes a stronger deliverance on this theme, in a passage which he clearly implies is applicable to his own country, and which we certainly know is applicable to ours.

"When the admiration of anything opposed to virtue is stronger than virtue itself in a people, that people is unfit for liberty, and the vital spirit of liberty is not in them. Through how much of politiical theory and practice ought this doctrine to be carried! Is there in this country any constituency to which what are called popular talents will recommend a representative notoriously profligate and reprobate? That constituency is unfit for its franchise; and whatever specious pretences may be made of supporting a public principle, and distinguishing between public and private conduct—as if the support of virtue was not a public principle—such an exercise of the franchise is tainting the very sources of liberty in the land." *Notes from Books.* pp. 144, 5.

It is bad enough that such men are placed in office when real ability can be alleged as some offset against vicious character. But when personal infamy is added to brutish stolidity, then indeed is the disgrace and the mischief superlative. This turns us from the reviewer of books again to the frank and judicious remarker upon life and manners.

As an essayist proper, Mr. Taylor has formed his style rather upon the older masters of this kind of literary work, than after the fashion of the more recent authorship. He does not sparkle with electric snap and flash, like the *Saturday Review's* disquisitions on social subjects. He is not idyllic and picturesque, like Alexander Smith; nor fantastical or flat, nor charmingly knowing and circumlocutory, like the varying moods of the Country Parson. He is pithy, perspicatious, sensible. If not volatile and flighty, he is never dull; sometimes caustic; never droll or humorous, but now and then giving a witty turn to his thought. He has told us " that nothing can be more unpoetical than a strong and vivacious spirit which is also hard and selfish." We find no trace of these alloys in his mind and heart—none of the metallic ring of the anvil which is iron of the best quality, and nothing else. Wholly free from the fawning tricks of an intellectual parasite and pander, he is companionable and sympathetic, a guide who will kindly help you up when you fall, as well as point you forward when fresh for your morning journey.

His essays are not written as a literary entertainment for an idle hour. With a theory even of poetic composition which demands that its more imaginative and aerial forms should faithfully subserve some useful end, and not expend themselves upon mere pleasurable excitation, we might expect that he

would carry this law yet more determinedly into prose literature.   He has written some important truth for the upper
classes of British society, as in his paper on " The Ways of the
Rich and Great."   While allowing for the intrinsic disadvantages of their position for the culture of the best character, he
does not hesitate to deal sharply with their sins against themselves and others.   Not only "the splash of newly mounted
pride," as Mr. Landor happily depicts the shoddyism of all
lands and ages, brings down our author's censure, but the lux-
uriousness, pride, cruel thoughtlessness, of the old aristocrats,
furnish themes for justly deserved reprimand.   The relations of
these to servants, to trades-people, to the community around
them, are discussed with a fine perception and independence.
He tells these rich and great people how much damage they do
to dependents by examples of wasteful extravagance ; to shop-
keepers, by not promptly paying their bills : to their own fami-
ilies and others, by aristocratic mothers so commonly refusing to
nurse their own offspring ; to sewing girls, by exacting the completion of their tasks so peremptorily for fashionable display.
It would be a small matter comparatively if the consequences of
this high life were only the self-dissatisfaction which finds that
" the art of carrying off a pleasure is not to sit it out " at a din-
ner table ; which learns, too late perhaps, that they who thus
try to draw up enjoyment " have let down a sieve into the well
instead of a bucket."   The relative evils of such living are yet
greater ; and we commend a passage, which we shall quote, to
our own " rich and great " as having its very sad illustrations
in the " upper-tendoms " of our own republic.   Having said,
that sewing girls' and women's lives are often sacrificed to the
" celerity which nothing but night labor can accomplish," he
goes on to a darker evil ;

"'The dressmakers' apprentices in a great city have another alternative : and it is quite as much to escape from the intolerable labors
which are imposed upon them in the London season, as from any
sexual frailty, that such multitudes of them adopt a vocation which
affords some immediate relief, while it ensures a doubly fatal termination of their career.   The temptations by which these girls are
beset might be deemed all-sufficient without the compulsion by which
they are thus, as it were, driven out into the streets.   Upon them

the fatal gift of beauty has been more lavishly bestowed than upon any other class—perhaps not excepting even the aristocracy. They are many of them probably the spurious offspring of aristocratical fathers, and inherit beauty for the same reason as the legitimate daughters of aristocrats, because the wealth of these persons enables them to select the most beautiful women either for wives or for concubines. . . . . They are thus possessed of exterior attractions which will at any moment place them in a condition of comparative affluence, and keep them in it so long as these attractions last—a period beyond which their portion of thought and foresight can hardly be expected to extend ; whilst, on the other hand, they have before them a most bitter and arduous servitude, constant confinement, probably a severe task-mistress . . . . and a destruction of health and bloom which the alternative course of life can scarcely make more certain or more speedy." pp. 263, 264.

In the essay on money, the writer talks to us like an experienced man of the world, on the getting, saving, spending, giving and taking, lending and borrowing, and bequeathing of this indispensable commodity ; with sundry hints concerning the dispensation of help to the needy, the right and wrong treatment of the embarrassed, and other collateral matters. It would be a good tract for young business men. So would, on choice in marriage, to any young man. Mr. Taylor touches this absorbing theme ethically, æsthetically and economically, with a poet's delicacy and a good man's heart. He has the manliness to say, that " there is no one of the burdens, vexations, dues and responsibilities incident to marriage, which will not be felt with tenfold force in concubinage. Such are the miscaculations of selfishness. A man thinks he has hung a trinket round his neck, and behold ! it is a millstone." *Notes from Life*, p. 60.

He endorses an early union : nearer twenty than thirty years of age for the female, as the rule. Beauty still holds his loyalty as a thing to be highly valued ; money far less. Disappointed love also has its uses. Marriages of the young with the old are a blunder if not "a moral malfeasance." Marriages of the old with the old are not deserving the ridicule which is apt to be showered upon them.

The essay on children is a lay sermon which should have

a large hearing.   In a vein of graceful irony the puerility is exploded, that the child should always be reasoned into obedience
and not controlled by parental will.   So, "the parent who
shrinks from inflicting just and proper punishment upon a child,
deprives that child not only of the rest to be found in duty and
obedience, but also of the blessings of a deeper love."   Equally
wise are the author's views of the evils of parental indulgence,
of the over education of the young intellect and conscience,
and of the religious culture of the child's heart.   On the subject of conscience, he says that this, in the child, " may easily
be worn out, both by too much pressure and by over stimulation."   He has known a child of such premature conscientious
sensibility that at seven, a slight fault committed would make
her ill from remorse ; but, though very carefully educated there-
after, at twenty, " she had next to no conscience and a hard
heart."   He adds, with an evident endorsement of another's remark, that children who are too good and clever to live, had
much better die.

   The concluding paper of *Notes from Life*, on the life
poetic, performs for the poet, in briefer compass, what the
book on the statesman has done for that profession.   It is a
most beautiful picture of what a poet's life should be, "contemplative, but not inactive, orderly, dutiful, observant, conversant with human affairs and with nature ; and though homely
and retired, yet easy as regards pecuniary circumstances."
These views are shaded in with many congenial thoughts, allusions, suggestions.   How firmly self-sustained is this sentiment,
and how illustrative of a noble spirit living so calmly above
the scuffle for present popular flattery ; breathing the very atmosphere of the sacred groves where dwells the choicest wisdom : " Nor is he worthy of the name of a poet who would
not rather be read a hundred times by one reader, than once by
a hundred."

   Mr. Taylor has a just idea of the superior value of the autumnal above the vernal products of true genius, both intellectual and affectional.   He sees a worthy field for the activities of advancing life, in the continued practice of literary art ;
and also in giving to younger men the critical helps of this
ripened culture.   He is not insensible to the liabilities of age

to an over fastidiousness, both in judging of others, and in amending its own earlier work. The old veterans of letters should be generous to the rising men of mark. "As the reflex of a glorious sunset will sometimes tinge the *eastern* sky, the declining poet may communicate to those who are to come after him, not guidance only, but the very colors of his genius, the temper of his moral mind, and the inspiration of his hopes and promises." These are hearty words—" notes," as we are sure, from the essayist's personal consciousness of the pleasant and rewarding evening of his own well-spent life.

There is another occasionally expressed opinion in the literary world, for which we have not more respect than for the one referred to some pages back ; it is, that successful poets can not write good prose. It is very true that many of them have not attempted it, preferring to give utterance to their thoughts in verse. This is apt to be attributed to a consciousness of incapacity for vigorous prosaic writing. There may be exceptional cases of this kind ; but, as the rule, we incline to regard it simply a matter of choice. For this there is an obvious reason in the fact that the number of good poets is always comparatively small ; hence, it is natural that they should thus exercise their gifts. A glance over English literature is enough to show that the poetic genius involves no necessary disqualification for prose composition. Dryden's prose is generally of a very superior degree of merit ; and Milton had already carried the art to as high relative perfection as he had reached upon the wings of the poetic imagination. If Wordsworth wrote nothing but poetry (which is questionable), Walter Scott excelled in both, beyond a doubt. Cowper could have given us, in prose, we fancy, something besides the choicest volume of letters we yet have in our mother tongue, as much excelling Robert Burns' in delightful archness and naturalness, as in their moral tone. If Coleridge is hardly to be brought into a comparison like this, Landor was unquestionably a master of each of these arts. In our own country, most of the better poets have also cultivated prose literature with success. Mr. Taylor has been sparing of his contributions to the press ; a half dozen volumes contain the fruitage of his husbandry so far as the public enjoys it. But he has given us enough to add another proof that a good poet can also be a good writer of prose, each being judged by a high standard of excellence.

ARTICLE IV.

THE BIBLE A BOOK OF FACTS, NOT OF MODES AND PHILOSOPHIES.

FACTS constitute the only reliable knowledge. These are ascertained and established, chiefly, in the four following ways : by experience, by experiment, by reason and by revelation. Experience confirms facts, and so establishes them; as that the presence of the sun gives heat, and its absence insures cold. Experiment establishes facts ; as the facts of agriculture, mechanics, chemistry. Reason establishes mathematical facts and many others. In mental philosophy it has its uses, but here its decisions are more unreliable. The facts are comparatively few which it so satisfactorily establishes, as to make them universally accepted and unquestionable. And, neither experience, nor experiment, nor reason creates facts, but only develops and confirms them. The Bible is a revelation of facts ; and this, and the book of nature embrace all the facts that are, or ever will be known in the present world.

Assuming that the Bible is a revelation from God, established by sufficient and satisfactory evidence, it is the object of this paper to state, not its facts in general, but some of its most important doctrines, and to vindicate these, necessarily in the briefest manner, as facts, every one of which is yet not fully comprehensible by a finite mind.

In regard to the doctrines of divine revelation, as in regard to many other facts, it is obvious that reason is to be employed in order to establish them. But how far may it be used? What is its specific province? Faith, likewise, has its place here. When facts have been duly ascertained by reason, acting within its appropriate and only legitimate sphere, the province of faith is to receive them as unquestionable, if the evidence for them is full; and if not wholly satisfactory, then according to the measure of the evidence furnished. Some passages of Scripture, formerly relied upon as proof passages of some of the doctrines are, by some of the late interpreters, rejected as unreliable; and yet it is conceded by the same, that if these passages are laid aside entirely, not a single doctrine would be without sufficient evidence to entitle it to the fullest credence.

Reason and faith have each their specific sphere in religion, and neither may rightfully trespass on the province of the other. Faith may not receive as true what reason, acting within its own sphere, does not establish; and reason may not encroach on ground which belongs exclusively to faith.

Reason, in regard to religion, is "man's natural faculty of reaching the truth without any supernatural assistance." Faith is "the assent of the mind to truth upon the testimony of God conveying knowledge to us through supernatural channels." This knowledge, thus conveyed, may be, and often, nay always, in a greater or less degree, is above reason, but never contrary to it. If it seems to be so, it is on account of our ignorance, or because it transcends the highest powers of our minds to comprehend it. It has been well said, "reason can not be the measure of our faith. We must believe much that we can not understand. We must use reason to reach the knowledge of what God means by his words, and what he would have us believe. But to understand the meaning of words is one thing, and to understand how the thing we believe exists in all of its relations, is entirely a different thing." If this be a correct view of the point in hand, then reason can never be the ultimate ground of our faith. Having established the fact by the proper evidence, that God speaks in his word, viz., "by the grammatical rendering of every text by itself, the careful comparison of Scripture with Scripture, the limitation of one class of passages by another bearing upon the same subject, and by an impartial deduction from all Scripture," having done this, we believe what he says simply because he says it. Whether it be reasonable in our judgment is not the question we should ask, but has God said it. If he has, that settles the question, and our duty is to receive it on his testimony. What else can we do? We surely can not disprove any of his utterances, except by denying their authenticity and authority. And this is what the unbeliever does, often to the setting aside of whole books and chapters, and repudiating almost every distinctive doctrine. Here, it should be remembered, that reason, in order to its best exercise, and to bring the mind to the safest results, should be " informed by a sanctified heart, and guided by the Holy Ghost." Many, without such a heart, and such guidance, have accredited the doctrines of the Bible, have acknowledged they are there, but reject them as unreasonable, and as not worthy of a divine origin. If such liberties are taken, and are justifiable, then plainly we have, and can have, no revelation from God, and we must have as many systems of religious faith as the benighted reason and the depraved heart of man may see fit to invent.

Facts then are what we need, and what we should seek after in religion as well as in every thing else ; and happily we have them, all that are useful and necessary, in the book of facts which God has put into our hands. Our religious knowledge must be based on these facts exclusively, and can be based safely nowhere else.

We have said that nature has its facts as well as religion. Our knowledge of nature is only a knowledge of facts. Let us look at some of the facts in both, which, as to a complete knowledge of them, can never be taken in by a finite mind. These are God's " secret things," and so far as they are secret, we have nothing to do with them.

Take the law of nature known as gravitation. What is gravitation ? We know so much as this, that it is the tendency of matter to a common centre. We know this from observation and experiment, and our reason, acting upon these, teaches us that, if there were not some other force acting upon matter besides this, all the matter in the universe, by virtue of this natural law, would rush together into one common mass. So much we know about gravitation. So much is revealed. But, what do we know about the intrinsic nature of that law or power which operates in this way ?

Take magnetism. It is a law of nature, known by long and extensive observation, that iron to which the magnetic power has been communicated, has the power to attract other iron ;

and also that a needle, to which the magnetic power has been imparted, when placed upon a pivot, always, if unobstructed, points to the north. So much we know. Is not all that concerns the intrinsic nature of this power hid within the impenetrable folds of the divine mind?

As to the vegetable kingdom, we know that plants grow, and that light and heat and moisture are necessary to their full and perfect development. But what do we know as to the manner in which plants are affected by light, heat and moisture? Why does one species grow in this form and another in that? Why does one tree bear sweet fruit, and another sour, and the same tree both sweet and sour? Why the varied hues of leaf and blossom in the rays of the same sun and in the same soil, and with the same heat and the same moisture?

What is matter? What, in its composition as to its original elements? How was it made out of nothing, as we are scripturally assured it was? We know much about it, and much more, doubtless, is to be known. But is there not a bound in respect to it, beyond which finite knowledge can not go? Here the most gifted mind is compelled to confess its incapacity and ignorance.

What is mind? We know its capabilities and operations to some extent. But what is it that operates, that thinks, and reasons, and remembers? What is the soul, and what is the nature of the connection of the soul with the material body, one of which dies, the other never? Who knows, and how the one operates upon and affects the other; for instance, how the will acts to lift the hand and to put forward the foot?

Questions of this kind might be greatly multiplied, but it is unnecessary. There are unknowable things in nature, things utterly incomprehensible by the human intellect, because the mind of man is finite and not omniscient.

Now, if there are inscrutable things in nature, why should there not be in religion? In nature certain facts are established by incontrovertible evidence. In religion certain facts are established by evidence, not the same, indeed, as that which establishes the facts of nature, but by evidence as clear and unquestionable. These facts, in religion, are established by the revelations which God has made in the Scriptures. The light of nature adds confirmation to some of these facts, but the Scriptures furnish the chief evidence.   God has revealed in the Scriptures certain doctrines as facts, and this revelation, authenticated as it is by satisfactory evidence, establishes their truth. We may, in a proper way, employ our reason about them. We must do this.   True, they are above reason, yet not contrary to it, incomprehensible because above it, because beyond its province.   Their truth, however, depends not on our ability to comprehend, or establish them by reason, but upon the simple declaration : "Thus saith the Lord."   These truths are not submitted to the test of human reason, as an arbiter in the case, competent and infallible to decide.   It is not competent to this. Reason was never designed to be used in this way.   What God says must be true.   His declaration settles the question, and puts an end to controversy, and indeed to argument.   Why argue when God speaks?   Can we make the subject plainer? Evidently there is no propriety in it.   Divine truth, when once ascertained, is solely subject-matter of faith.

There is a God.   Nature says so.   The Scriptures say so. There is but one God.   There need be but one infinite God. Two or ten thousand could be no more, nor do more than one, for he is possessed of every attribute that goes to constitute such a being, and is infinitely perfect.   God is a spirit.   What is a spirit existing as God?   Do we know?   We know the fact, for the Bible says he is a spirit.   Can we know any thing more, any thing as to the nature of an infinite spirit?   The unity of God.   What is it?   Unity in man, to some extent, we understand.   It is the union of a soul with a body, spirit with matter.   What is unity in God?   Can we decide that point before we can comprehend what an infinite spirit is, which we certainly shall never do?

The Scriptures reveal the fact that God exists in such a manner that there is in his nature or essence a foundation for a threefold mysterious, or, as it is usually termed, personal existence, as Father, Son, and Holy Ghost.   We can not comprehend the nature of this threefold relation of persons in the divine nature, the manner of this tripersonal relation.   This is as incomprehensible to us as the unity of God and the nature of his essence, yet no more so.   But, that God is one, and that he exists in tripersonality are facts revealed in his word ; disbelieved, indeed, by many, but accepted by all believers in the Scriptures, the whole Scriptures, as a divine revelation.

God is a sovereign, having the absolute control of every thing that takes place, of the thoughts, affections, and wills of his creatures, no less than of every event that occurs, even down to the falling of a sparrow.   This sovereignty is a revealed fact in God's book of facts, the Bible ; and our reason assents to it, because a right interpretation of the Scriptures, which interpretation comes within the province of reason, clearly teaches it. Reason, however, independently of the Scriptures, declares and accepts the doctrine of divine sovereignty.   "It is philosophically true," said a candid Unitarian minister, " but it is not safe and wise to preach it."   There are very few, who have looked at this subject carefully, who will venture to say as philosophers, much less as Christian believers, as one has recently said in a widely circulated religious newspaper : " It is impossible for the creator to create a free agent, and still retain the control of his mind.   In creating man, God necessarily parted with the control of his character in actions."   Then, in this respect, he made man independent of himself.   Strange language this ?   It belongs to a pseudo-philosophy, not to the Bible. Did God part with the control of human actions in the case of Pharaoh, and the murderers of Christ ?   And yet, did not these men do precisely what a sovereign God had " determined before to be done " ?

The free agency of man is a doctrine as distinctly taught in the Scriptures as divine sovereignty.   Our own consciousness is in agreement with this scriptural teaching.   Who doubts the perfect freedom of his actions, when under no physical restraint ? Here are two facts, seemingly contradictory, and by many asserted to be positively contradictory and irreconcilable, one established by the Bible, the other by the Bible and human consciousness.   Now, are they contradictory ?   By no means. God is never in contradiction to himself.   His word never contradicts itself, nor the universal consciousness of man.   The difficulty of reconciliation between the two lies in human incapacity to comprehend the consistency of the facts with each other.   Is it supposable that the mind, that is infinite in understanding, sees any inconsistency, or difficulty of reconciliation? The consistency of the one with the other is a secret which God, as yet, has kept to himself, for good reasons. If every thing, in respect to Christian doctrine, were made plain, there would be no room for faith, nor need of it. But one chief object of a divine revelation was to inspire faith in its author. It has had this effect with many, while too many more have presumed to sit in judgment upon these facts, and to condemn and reject them. It should be kept in mind, however, by such as do this, that, while they can not reconcile divine sovereignty and free agency, they can not disprove their compatibility.

The "Word of God," " made flesh," who once dwelt among men, is a mystery, as to the nature of the union of the divine with the human, but yet a plainly revealed fact. The union is affirmed, the manner of the union is not. In regard to the general subject of the mysteries of the Godhead, Professor Stuart remarks on the intimate connection between the Father and the Son, God and him who is called the Word of God:

" The connection is averred, the manner of this is not the subject of affirmation. When we assert that God is omnipresent, we assert a plain, simple, credible truth or fact. But do we assert, or know any thing of the manner in which he is so? When we assert the union of the soul and body which makes a human being, do we even pretend to know any thing of the manner of this? Even the blade of grass beneath our feet puts at defiance all our powers of knowledge, in regard to many particulars respecting it."

That sin is in the world, is a fact but too well attested by evidence from the Scriptures, and from human observation and experience. Do we know how temptation had power over the first parents of the race, in their state of holiness and purity, or over angels in theirs, so that they were seduced from their allegiance to their maker? We may imagine and speculate. We may construct and adopt specious philosophical theories, as many have done, and we may be satisfied with them as many are. So we may speculate respecting the connection between Adam and the race descended from him; when character begins, and why it is uniformly the same in the child as in the parent; whether souls are propagated as well as bodies; whether all human souls were created when the first one was,

or whether they are created when their bodies are ; whether sin
can be predicated only of the will, and whether the sinful will
is communicated to the child in connection with the body, by
the parents, a theory well presented in a preceding number of
this *Review*;[1] and whether sin may be accounted for on the
theory of federal headship.   These various theories, grounded
only on philosophies more or less plausible, have been adopted,
argued, and defended with zeal, ability, and confidence in their
correctness, during the ages, and by able and good men, but
neither of them has yet been established satisfactorily as a
scriptural fact.   But the fact of the universal sinfulness of the
race, including every individual of it, has been established by
the word of God.   The fact is of divine authority.   The methods of accounting for it rest solely on human authority.   And
if we are pressed with difficulties, and questions which we can
not answer, as St. Paul was, when the captious, unbelieving
Jews said to him : "Why doth he [God] yet find fault, for
who hath resisted his will?" we take refuge in the position of
the apostle, and say : " Nay, but O man, who art thou that
repliest against God?   Shall the thing formed say unto him
that formed it, why hast thou made me thus?"   This is always
the safest ground to take with cavillers ; for, with all our philosophies, satisfactory as they may be to ourselves, we never
satisfy them, because these are subject-matters of faith, and
faith they have not.

Some of these theories are plausible, and seem to be supported by reason ; yet the advocates of neither can say, with
certainty, we are right and you are wrong, for the reason of
each is fallible and not infallible.   Neither can say this is fact.
But when the word of God says : " Sin is in the world," "and
death by sin, and so death hath passed upon all men because
that all sinned," we have fact on ample and undoubted testimony, that can not be gainsaid or denied.   This is the end of
controversy.   If men will speculate, let them speculate, but
let them not foist in their speculations in the place of fact, and
require us to adopt their theories, or be set down as dull learners, and as decidedly behind the age.

[1] Vol. VII., pp. 1—20.

Difficult questions may be asked in regard to sin as well as to many other theological doctrines, questions which no man can answer, nor is bound to answer, because he has no light from reason, or from heaven, respecting it, except the fact of its existence, and the medium of its introduction, the fall of man. And, if theories were less regarded in preaching, and the plain, simple facts of the Bible more dwelt upon, and urged home upon the consciences and hearts of men, the cause of morality and religion would suffer no loss, and many more souls would be saved, which ought to be the great end of preaching.

Metaphysics have been invoked, and used most abundantly to explain and to maintain theories in regard to sin. Zeal worthy of a better cause has been displayed in doing this. Not a little acrimony has often mingled itself in the discussions. The weapons of sarcasm and ridicule, weapons of great potency in the hands of some men, and when used on some minds, have been employed with great effect. But what, after all our theories, acute and learned as they may have been, and positive as we may be that we have got the right one, the one that is true, and must be true without contradiction or doubt, what, it may be asked, do we know, know with certainty, except that all men are sinners? The fact of sin, and when and how it came into the world, and who are affected by it, we have, but what more have we respecting it that is reliable, for which we can bring a divine warrant? And, taking the fact of sin as a momentous and far-reaching one, can we render a better service to the world ruined by it, than to make it bear with all our power of argument and persuasion upon those, who if not relieved from its corrupting and condemning power, must bear it as a heavy and still heavier burden forever?

The Holy Spirit renews and sanctifies the sinful heart. This is a Bible fact. "Except a man be born of the Spirit he can not see the kingdom of God." Do we know the process of the new birth, how the Spirit works on the heart in renewal and sanctification, except as he uses divine truth in doing it? And, do we know how he uses this to make it effectual, effectual in some cases and not in others, the same truth convincing some of sin, and hardening others in it, and yet their moral liberty, their free agency not in the least impaired? "The wind bloweth where it listeth, and we hear the sound thereof, but can not tell whence it cometh, nor whither it goeth ; so is every one that is born of the Spirit." There is inexplicable mystery here, and yet fact; mystery as inscrutable, in the case of every man, as in the case of that master in Israel, who came to Jesus by night to be instructed by him in the things of religion, and who went away as ignorant of the Spirit's manner of regenerating the sinful heart as when he came. Jesus gave him the fact of the necessity of the new birth in his own case, and in that of every other man, and there he stopped with his instructions upon the subject. The fact was important, the manner of the fact was not.

The object of the Saviour, in the case of Nicodemus, was to convince him that he was a sinner, and that he needed moral justification, and that he could obtain this only through divine power. He went into no learned disquisition with him on human ability. This was not necessary. Nor is it necessary in the case of any man in order to his conversion and salvation. The fact of the necessity of regeneration and sanctification by the Spirit is what needs to be kept before the minds of sinning men ; and when they start difficulties, and cavil, and oppose, duty requires the fact to be stated, and urged and reiterated without the use of nice philosophical theories which only bewilder and never enlighten the mind nor persuade the heart. Respecting none of the theories of regeneration can it be said with positiveness, this one is true, and that one is false, because reason can not be appealed to as an infailible arbiter in the case. In labors then to save men, so far as human instrumentality is concerned in the work, the endeavor should be to bring them as soon as possible to feel that they are in the hands of a sovereign yet merciful God ; that they are helpless in themselves, yet through Christ strengthening them, they can do all that God requires of them. Never, till men despair of help from themselves, and from any other creature, will they cast themselves upon the mercy of God, and never will they or can they do this, till he disposes and inclines them to do it ; never will they begin to " work out their own salvation with fear and trembling till God works in them both to will and to do of his own good pleasure." Said a rejoicing Christian, after his conversion,

" in my self-despair, while anxious for salvation, I seemed to be like a single leaf on the outer extremity of a tree, in a gale which had swept away every other leaf, and as absolutely at my Maker's disposal as that leaf was in that furious blast. I saw my helplessness, and felt it, and then, and not till then, hope came to the relief of my burdened heart. He ' drew me with the cords of love, and then I ran after him.' "

The atonement of Christ, who died for " the sins of the whole world," and " tasted death for every man," is one of the prominent and important doctrines of the Bible. This is a fact clearly set forth on its sacred pages. Many deny and reject it, or if they profess to receive it, they make it to consist in something else than what the Scriptures teach it to be, namely, a sacrifice for sin. So, different theories of it are held by those who accept it as a sacrifice made that sin might be pardoned, a substitution of a divine sufferer in the place of those that deserved to suffer. It will not do to regard all these theories as resting on an equally solid basis, and yet aside from the fact of the atonement, and for whom it was made, and who will receive its benefits, we are not warranted to speak with entire confidence that we are right in the theories we entertain.

The resurrection of the body is a revealed fact. How God will raise the body, and how he will make a spiritual body out of a material one, and what a spiritual body is, and what are the laws of its existence and action, are things of which we know nothing. But the resurrection is a fact. " All that are in their graves shall come forth." .

A future judgment is a fact, and that is about all we certainly know of it, except that then a final separation will be made between the righteous and the wicked, and that its retributions will be just and endless.

Eternal future punishment for those chargeable with sin unrepented of, and unforgiven through atoning blood, is a fact clearly taught in the Scriptures. The precise nature and degree of that punishment, except that it involves great suffering, is known, on this side of the grave, only to " the Judge of all the earth." We may imagine what it is. We may form plausible, possibly, probable ideas, respecting it. Some assert, with much confidence, that " the worm that never dies, and the fire that is never quenched," are, and can be nothing else than the terrible upbraidings of a guilty conscience unappeased by a Redeemer's blood. But, future revelations, not the past, must bring satisfactory light on this momentous subject. It is probable from the tormentings of conscience here, that they will follow the wicked hereafter forever. We may even admit the certainty of this, and yet not be justified in believing and saying that this is the only punishment, because here the only One authorized to speak on such a subject, is silent.

There are revealed and unrevealed things in the divine administration of human affairs. Earthquakes, tempests, wars, revolutions, pestilences, by which multitudes are usually involved in calamities ; sickness, loss of friends, loss of property, and the various other ills of life, are facts cognizable by us. The reasons for these providential dealings God has kept to himself, except that he often uses them, as the Scriptures inform us, as chastisements, not punishments, for our good.

The point had in view in the foregoing discussion, viz., that the Bible is a book of facts, to be believed on divine testimony rather than to be comprehended by a limited understanding like ours, and that, too, biased by many evil influences, admits of a much wider range of thought and illustration ; but it is unnecessary now and here. The design of it will be readily seen, and its value, if it has any, will be duly appreciated by the thoughtful and believing, and by those who would rather have facts than fancy and philosophy, which, when they have done their utmost to enlighten, only leave the mind in mists and uncertainties. More is yet to be learned respecting the kingdom of nature. Facts in it are being developed continually. What further revelation of facts in religion, God will make in the future world, we can not tell. We have no reason to expect any thing further on this subject in this world. The canon of Scripture is closed. Nothing can be added to, and nothing can be taken from the inspired volume God has put into our hands, by the instrumentality of men, " who spake as they were moved by the Holy Ghost," without incurring guilt, as the closing book of revelation assures us.

Better methods of investigating and exhibiting the facts of the Scriptures may be found. The last fifty years have shown a marked advance on former years in this respect. But no new truth or fact can be brought to light from them, by any of these methods, for the Bible is a completed work, and has been investigated for centuries by the greatest and best minds. Our reason can add nothing to it of the least value, and our wisdom is "foolishness," when it is not in harmony with God's word. No new truth is it in the power of man, or of any creature to devise, that would be an addition of any value whatever to what we already have in our well authenticated book of religious facts. No creature can make truth. One can find out truths as facts to some extent, but he can not make them. God makes truth, and truth that is always credible and reliable ; credible though not always credited, reliable though very often disbelieved and rejected. " God is light, and in him is no darkness at all." Look at the idea of a finite, and especially a sinful man's attempting to supplement and improve a revelation given by the infinite mind. How preposterous ! How presumptuous ! Yet this right of sitting in judgment on God's plainly revealed and fully authenticated truth, of adding to it, and taking from it, many arrogate to themselves. And because they can not bring it down to the level of their reason, and that reason weakened and darkened by sin, they dare to reject it, and to assert that it is not truth, that it can not be truth, that it is unworthy of, and a dishonor and a disgrace to, the divine character.

What we need is just such a revelation as we have in the Scriptures ; no more and no less. It admits of no improvement. We should take it as it is and be satisfied. We must take it as it is, or grope our way in the dark, while all is light about our path, and we have only to open our eyes to see that light which is sufficient to guide to eternal day.

This is the chief impression, in regard to the subject presented in this article, which the writer desires to leave on the reader's mind, that should God audibly utter in our hearing what he has made known in the Scriptures, it would be no more entitled to our belief and cordial acceptance, and to be made the rule of practice by us, than it now is, in the revelation he has already given.

ARTICLE V.

THE THEOLOGICAL ANIMUS OF THE ATLANTIC MONTHLY.

VINET has said, that "to read only one book, is very often, however strong we may be, to place ourselves in the power of a book." Books are the most influential kind of companions. And when we take them into daily, closet intimacy, we can not avoid being affected, if not actually moulded, by them. They will modify our opinions, or our feelings. This is especially true of the issues of the periodical press. Let them come fresh from the printer, lively and sparkling, gossipy and imaginative, reeking with the fragrance of newness and originality, and they become a power over us. There are many men and women who take their opinions from paper or magazine, just as un-fledged birdlings take their food from the bill of their mothers. The fly they eat, the fragment of a worm they digest, they never caught. They have been snuggling in the downy nest of the home-circle, while some adventurous author or critic has chased the luckless insect through the air, or grubbed for him in the soil.

There is something very exciting about the regular advent of a popular magazine. Each member of the household, where it is read, wants to know its contents; wants to be the first to discover and proclaim its beauties; and so there is no rest until the whole number has been devoured and thoroughly discussed. It comes as a friend. The mind and heart are put into confidential relations with it. Parents read it to their children, and children to their parents. It is talked over in the family circle. It furnishes the mental and moral pabulum and recreation for many a leisure hour. In fact, it is easy for a stranger to determine what magazine or magazines are regarded as authoritative in any family, by the character and complexion of the sentiments and opinions which prevail among its members.

In this country, the power of the popular monthly is just beginning to be appreciated. It is no longer a mere vehicle for fine writing; a herbarium for pressed but crisp beauties. It is now employed to discuss great questions in politics, in morals and religion.   When this is done, openly and avowedly, no reasonable man can object to it.   " Uncle Tom's Cabin," that dramatized anti-slavery gospel, was perfectly proper in the columns of the *National Era.*   For this paper was established and maintained for the advocacy of just such views.   And, if a man knows that he is subscribing for a periodical established for the advocacy of one particular class of principles, he has no one to censure but himself, if its contents do not meet his approbation.   He receives just what he pays for.   The title-page of the periodical informs him to what it is devoted; for what purpose it is issued.

But when he has been induced to patronize a magazine because of the high literary character and reputation of its contributors, a magazine expressly devoted to general literature, and discovers that its secret tendency and drift are hostile to his most sacred religious views and instincts, as well as those which he would have his children cherish, then he may well be indignant at the course adopted to secure his patronage; he may well regard it as disingenuous, if not dishonest.   Which is the greater knave, the man who clandestinely undermines the foundations of another's dwelling, or of his most sacred religious opinions?

In a literary point of view, the *Atlantic Monthly* is perhaps the ablest magazine of its class ever published in this country. And why should it not be?   It has its home in the Athens of America.   Its authors walk in the shades, and wear the honors, of the Academus of America.   It can command the time and talents of the choicest and most highly cultivated writers which the nation has ever produced.   Bryant, Holmes, Longfellow, Lowell, Whittier, Mrs. Stowe, and many others of less celebrity, are stated and regular contributors.   These are names which every American delights to honor.   They are the names of this generation, which the world will not willingly let die. And these writers bring their choicest and mose costly offerings and lay them upon this shrine.   This magazine, too, is published by the literary publishers of America; the firm that hold the keys to the American pantheon of fame.   Published under such favorable auspices, it is not strange that it should gain the public attention.   It is not strange that the cultivated families of New England should heartily respond to a literary enterprise thus happily inaugurated.

The *Atlantic Monthly*, too, has been a most loyal periodical. It stood by the flag, and the oppressed, from the outset of the war. Its political articles had the true ring of freedom in them. It may be that in this particular, too, it departed from the true idea of a literary periodical. But it is one of its avowed departments; and the grand Puritan hymns of Holmes, and the caustic and trenchant leaders of Lowell, were to the people like draughts of water in a thirsty land. And a liberated nation will not forget that the literary spirits of the day, the scholars and professors and poets, not only allowed arms a great place among letters, but sent their own sons to the field.

It is a great pity that a literary enterprise, thus inaugurated, should not deserve and be able to command the continued confidence of all intelligent people. It is an enterprise in which every American must take pride. After the thousand-and-one failures in this direction, here, in America at last, is a living, active, enterprising literary monthly; here are men and women competent to write articles, in a literary point of view worthy of being read in every household in the land, worthy of being brought out in permanent forms. But there are many families in the land, that feel, to-day, that the *Atlantic Monthly* is an insidious foe to their purest and highest interests. It has lately been excluded from one of the most select boarding-schools for young ladies in this section of the country. No evangelical pastor, however highly he may regard it as a literary periodical, can but regret to see it longer upon the centre-tables and book-shelves in his parish. He knows that it is a wolf in sheep's clothing; that the wolf's ears and grinning jaws are becoming, every year, more and more distinctly visible. He had, indeed, no right to expect that it would be a religious periodical. To such a character it made no pretensions. But he had a right to expect that it would not be unfriendly to any type of the Christian religion, embraced and regarded sacred by any large class of its readers: and especially, that it would not lend itself, as the literary organ of New England, to a clandestine attempt at undermining what he regards it his commission from God to justify and maintain.

But no candid mind can examine the history and tendency of the magazine in question, without coming to the conclusion that it is, and has for some time been, conducted in the interest of rationalism, or a refined infidelity. Its leading stories have frequently, if not invariably, had an undisguised under-current of animosity towards truths regarded sacred by many of those into whose families it has always found an unchallenged admittance. It is more insidious, and therefore more dangerous, than any avowed organ of rationalism in the land. It is, in fact, the ablest ally which infidelity can boast here. It has been, and is still, doing a silent, but secret and certain work. Recall for a moment, the covert sneers, the sly wit, the sophistries and slurs directed against the doctrines of the Bible, in the past contributions of Dr. Holmes, Ik Marvel and Mrs. Stowe. "The Philosopher" and "Autocrat" is the modern rationalist. He is bent upon ridiculing whatever looks toward a scriptural view of life. Lively, ingenious, witty, beautiful, eloquent, he is still the infidel philosopher, the apostle of naturalism. In "Elsie Venner," he attempts to cover with ignominy the doctrine of original sin ; the statement of the Scriptures, that men inherit a moral bias to evil. "Dr. Johns" and his sister, too, are nothing but caricatures, with some slight element of truthfulness in them. Doubtless there may have been such characters ; but they are not, and never have been, representative ones ; and yet in "Dr. Johns," they are set forth as the natural and inevitable fruit of evangelical views, as taught and received in New England. The whole book is just what would harmonize with the views of "Young America," respecting parental government and true religion ; written, as it appears to us, with a pen dipped in the gall of a nature alienated from parental instructions by unbelief and sin ; from the reaction of having rejected the holiest influences of a Christian home ; of a home in the family of a Christian minister. And who can doubt the moral intent of the author of "The Minister's Wooing," where the old slander of "infant damnation" is revived by a child of Christian parents dedicated to God in her infancy?

It is notorious that the literary class, as such, are as irreligious as they are said to be irritable. "All literature," says Vinet, "is profane." There can be no Christian literature until the millennium; until Christianity controls the world of thought and of letters. Literary pursuits as such, have no tendency to make men reverent or devout. Literature is a kind of intellectual paganism, where the creature is more honored than the Creator; and where the creature's works are more regarded than the Creator's. Each successful *litterateur* is in some degree an idol, worshipped by his crowd of devotees; a prophetess, whose oracular utterances are eagerly sought by expectant throngs. We venture to say, that among those who pursue literature as a profession, and especially among those in the first rank of writers, the believers in the Bible, and the childlike students of it, the faithful observers of the Lord's day, the humble frequenters of the sanctuary and followers of the meek and lowly Jesus, are comparatively few. Fishing with Hawthorne in the Concord river, or discoursing with Emerson to the "yellow-breeched philosopher," indeed, any act of natural religion is much preferable to true spiritual worship of the Father. With most of such writers, the inspiration of the Scriptures is no more remarkable or authoritative than their own; the set place of worship is no more sacred than the grove, the Lord's day than any other day.

Revealed religion, too, is a world of facts. Literature is a world of sentiments and fancies. And men do not always admit that their prejudices and prepossessions are less truthful and important than God's facts. Revealed religion has great mysteries. It must have them. They may be easily ridiculed. But ridicule and innuendoes are fool's arguments. What a Chalmers can not understand, a ninny may turn into temporary contempt. The immortality of the soul is just as easily converted into a subject for ridicule, as the existence and government of God; as the doctrine of original sin. The men and women that consistently believe in it, are just as easily made the butts of the wit or the rationalist. The large majority of men love to see these great mysteries of the sacred writings flippantly and irreverently handled. Medical students sometimes delight to pellet with spit-balls their accomplished instructor who is discoursing upon the human lungs. But such an irreverent mode of procedure neither solves the mysteries of the subject, nor does away with them. We hope the facetious

Doctor will not lay this article to any of his "boys," or think
that we are in favor of irreverence toward teachers, whether
human or divine; but sometimes the *argumentum ad hominem*
is very convenient and convincing.

Could we reach the facts of the case, there is, doubtless, on
the part of the three writers above mentioned, a re-action, bitter
and malicious, against the truths taught by parental lips in early
childhood.   Dr. Holmes, the anatomist, is the son of Dr.
Holmes, the theologian.   And the anatomist has as little regard for his father's skeletons as for that of any other unfortunate subject. Harriet Beecher Stowe is the daughter of one clergyman, the wife of another, and the sister of five or six.   In
practical life, this gifted woman is known to reject some of the
fundamental doctrines of the Bible.   To a relation who dies
from drowning, with the language of profanity upon his lips,
cursing his associates for not coming to his relief, she inscribes
that beautiful, but, unless all men are to be saved, most inap-
propriate poem, "Only a Year."   Of another, who dies in
drunkenness, at a hotel in Boston, forsaken of all her connections, she says : "I think she was saved.   God sometimes destroys the body in order to save the soul."

Now, which is the noblest, the figure of old Dr. Emmons
standing consistently over the remains of his darling son, and
thus discoursing to his people : "He lived stupid, thoughtless
and secure in sin, until he was brought to the very sight of
death.   He was constrained to say : 'The world, the world
has ruined me.'   He was brought to give up all his vain hopes
and expectations from the world, and to feel the duty and importance of choosing the one thing needful.   But whether he
did ever heartily renounce the world and choose God for his supreme portion, can not be known in this world"; sacrificing all
his natural desires and impulses to the truth of God's word,
and to facts, or the act of that parent who seems willing to
overthrow the very foundations of the Christian fabric, rather
than believe it possible that a loved one can be lost?   We
frankly admit that the strength of the natural affections sets
against the doctrines of the evangelical system.   And we believe that the rationalism and infidelity of the present generation largely originate in these natural affections.   Whatever the

declarations of Revelation, men say : "Rather than one of my dear ones be lost, let the heavens fall !"

For the above, and other reasons, the leading writers above mentioned seem determined to employ the *Atlantic Monthly*, now regarded as securely established in so many of the evangelical families in the various portions of the land, as an organ for secret warfare against the time-honored religious views of the founders of this republic.   As Dickens sought to reform the abuses in boarding-schools and work-houses, by ingenious caricatures in novels, so would these writers disabuse the American mind of what they regard its false reverence for the truths of evangelical religion, by depicting ministers of the Gospel and professed believers, as such characters that they must be laughed at, if not despised.   The morality of this method, considering the general basis upon which this magazine has sought admittance into Christian families, may be thus illustrated : Let us suppose that Dr. Holmes, who is known to have very orthodox apprehensions of innovations in medicine, and who lately gave up one of his regular medical lectures to remonstrate with the Legislature against granting certain privileges to homeopathy, should discover that a magazine, which had been introduced into his family as a purely literary organ, was devoting itself to ridiculing the barbarisms, as they are sometimes termed, of his favorite allopathy ; how long would the very genial and funny little man endure the nuisance in his family? And what would he think of the integrity of the writer and publishers of such a magazine?   We say, if the *Atlantic Monthly* is to advocate the views of the self-styled liberals in the religious world, let it it be so announced on the cover, thus : Devoted to Literature, Science, Art, Politics and Hostility to Orthodoxy.

Take for an illustration of what the publishers of the *Atlantic* are sending with their imprint, into hundreds of evangelical families, chapters VIII. and IX. of " The Guardian Angel," as published in the number for March.   Think how ridiculous the statement, that in the year of our Lord, 1859, all the books that the heroine could come at in her home in a New England village, were " The Saints' Rest," " Pilgrim's Progress," " Robinson Crusoe," "The History of Deborah Sampson," " Rasselas" and " The Vicar of Wakefield." The Dr. has forgotten his chronology. He is depicting a New England family fifty, or one hundred years earlier. We would wager not a little, that in the year of grace 1859 there was not a single household in New England, with just such a collection of books as that. These forlorn spinsters must have owned " Uncle Tom's Cabin." It is the old insinuation of bigotry and want of culture, made against orthodoxy by an officer of a University founded by the dying gift of an orthodox minister, and bearing his name as an eternal testimony against the manner in which his funds have been perverted.

In this family, in the year of our Lord, 1859, on Saturday night, this choice writer of the liberal school seats his heroine between two maiden spinsters, to prepare "for the solemnities of the Sabbath." They select the 44th hymn of the 2d Book of "Watts' and Select," a hymn which contains a literal description of the place of woe, in which occurs the following stanza :

> " Eternal plagues and heavy chains,
>   Tormenting racks and fiery coals,
> And darts to inflict immortal pains,
>   Dyed in the blood of damned souls."

We have nothing to say in defence of such stanzas as poetry, or as fit to be sung. But, we do believe the Bible teaches the doctrine of eternal retribution, which Dr. Holmes means here to ridicule. And we would like to ask him, whether it bears the marks of probability, that when a collection of hymns contained such effusions as :

> " Sweet is the last, the parting ray,
>   That ushers placid evening in,
> When with the still, expiring day,
>   The Sabbath's peaceful hours begin ;" etc.,

and others expressly written for evening worship, such a hymn ever was selected for such an occasion. Was that the style sung in the parsonage of the Cambridge pastor, when Dr. Holmes was a little boy, thirty or forty years even before the time of this New England story ? It is a base slander to imply that in the families of New England orthodox Christians, the hour of devotion is so employed.

At the point indicated by the stanza quoted, Dr. Holmes's heroine thus breaks forth :

"I won't sing such words, and I won't stay here to hear them sung. The boys in the streets say just such words as that, and I'm not going to sing them. You can't scare me into being good with your cruel hymn-book." The author adds : "She could not swear ; she was not a boy." The language employed in the above stanza, however out of taste in a sacred lyric, is just as much the language of inspiration as of profanity. "He that believeth not, shall be damned," fell from the lips of our blessed Lord himself. And the spirit of profanity Dr. Holmes actually attributes to his heroine. For is it not implied, that had she been a boy, she would have sworn, and, according to the author's view, been justified in it?

The same violations of chronology appear in Dr. Holmes's allusions to the sacred tunes in use at the time of his story in this New England village of his creation. China, Bangor, Windsor, Funeral Hymn, etc., doubtless may have figured in "Old Folks' Concerts" in New England, in the year 1859. But that in any household or place of worship, they formed the staple of music, none but a very careless chronologist would ever intimate. Dr. Holmes ought to know that the line :

"To nothing fixed, but love of change,"

is the best description that could be given of the music sung in country congregations and families for the last thirty years. Every year has brought a new singing-book, as regularly as a new singing-master.

Dr. Holmes is a very difficult man to please. The grave delights him not, neither the gay. After a fling at the minors of the New England fathers, he describes the hymn :

"There is a land of pure delight,"

as "that most bacchant of devotional hymns, which sounds as if it had been composed by a saint who had a cellar under his chapel—'Jordan.'" It is perfectly shameful, that a true poet as Dr. Holmes is, and a man of such various accomplishments, should stoop to such an insinuation as this. The lively description of natural beauty which this hymn contains, is certainly warranted by the Bible ; but we suppose that Dr. Holmes likes the biblical description as little as this.   He is orthodox-mad. Whether the key be minor or major, he forthwith foams at the mouth.   The minors come neither eating nor drinking, and he says, They have a devil.   The majors come eating and drinking, and he says, Behold the gluttonous and wine-bibbers, the bacchants!

We have not space to allude to other germs of hostility to evangelical truth, and those who embrace it, which these two chapters contain.   The Rev. Mr. Stoker is an individual who preaches to men as " dreadful sinners," but yet is very familiar with young ladies.   Doubtless, thereby hangs a tale.   Perhaps the Doctor will regale the readers of the *Atlantic* with another Griffith Gaunt with the title Reverend prefixed.   Now we protest that this is the cheapest kind of calumny.   Would it be difficult, among the Doctor's acquaintance, to discover a clergyman of the liberal persuasion, who has proved untrue to his sacred calling?   But would the narrative of sin which might be unrolled, be regarded by him any fair exposition of the influence of embracing liberal views?   We protest against this abuse of the Christian public of New England.   We call upon every Christian editor in the land to watch the progress of this story, in which we fear Dr. Holmes, silkworm like, is winding up for burial his literary fame ; and to speak of it in the terms of reprehension which it deserves.   Some have already done so. We hope others will do likewise.   We can not close without reminding the Doctor that in his stethoscopic examinations of the breathings of orthodoxy, there may be an insect either in his stethoscope or in his ear ; and that possibly, this may account for the diagnosis of it which he puts into his stories.   We beg to commend to him his own sage counsel :

> " Now use your ears all that you can,
> But, don't forget to mind your eyes,
> Or you may be cheated, like this young man
> By a couple of silly abnormal flies."

ARTICLE VI.

THE FULL ENFRANCHISEMENT OF THE NEGRO.

THE negro is the inevitable man in American history.   We did our best to dodge and get around him, but he constantly stood in our path and met us at every turn and corner.   He furnished the way into the war, and he furnished the way out of it.   He led us into the mire and maze of reconstruction, and, in due time, will lead us on to the clear and solid ground of a right and lasting settlement.

Just here it is we have blundered, and just here the best skill of our statesmanship must be exerted.   We lost our providential opportunity, and now must find such an one as we can.

The time to have determined the condition of the different parties in the war was when we returned the sword to its scabbard ; but, unfortunately, we determined nothing.   And so, for nearly two years we have been feeling about in the dark for the key to our difficulties, which was all the time in our own hand. Had we simply decided to protect our friends at the expense of our enemies, if necessary, the way would have been plain. But instead we have sought to protect our enemies, if not at the expense of our friends, yet not to their advantage, to say the least. We have pardoned the rebels, given them back their lands and power, and then have taxed our ingenuity to save loyal blacks, left utterly destitute and helpless in their hands.   It is very clear that we have been working at the wrong side of the problem, and, of course, have worked at an impossibility.   Suppose it had been found necessary to impoverish aud disfranchise our enemies in order to make secure our sable allies, ought we to have hesitated ?   When the rebels laid down their arms they expected nothing less ; and would have been only too grateful had they been permitted to live and toil in obscurity.   But our generosity confirmed them in their hostility.   Unexpectedly it left them masters of the situation, with their ancient wealth and prestige, at liberty to meet us on the political arena with more hope of success than they have had on the field of blood.

Our help in these difficulties will again be found in that faithful race, which has yet to produce its first traitor to the flag. If we will use them, they will be a seed to regenerate, in time, the disloyal South. But we must use them fully, and give them every condition of development, and growth, and power. We are now laying foundations. Central principles and motives enter into our work, and nothing but thorough treatment will meet the case. We shall have it to do over and over, so long as we leave out the elemental forces of honor and right. We are dull scholars, if we need a longer tuition before we learn that the deepest law of this world is a law of righteousness. Henceforward no man must be either less, or more for his race, or color. Simple humanity must be the test of political equality.

The negro is not a common pauper asking for charity. His is the higher claim for manhood, for the opportunity to labor, for the privileges and immunities of other citizens. He stands at the bar of a great people, to whom he has made himself useful, and he asks simple justice at their hands. He wants no discrimination in his favor, but a fair chance for the prizes of life, and the same protection in person, property, rights, and happiness which white men enjoy. He will be satisfied with that, and he ought to be satisfied with nothing less. He is willing that " by-gones should be by-gones," but he would have a better future. Indeed, he can forget the past easier than we can, even as the memory of wrong-doing is the last to fade from the mind. And now that God is weighing men, and parties, and opinions, let us not seek to preserve what he shall find wanting.

By the stern wager of battle the negro was made a man, and by legislative enactment he has been declared a citizen of the Republic. And that citizenship rests on the most secure and substantial basis. By all the marks which can define the place, or the people, to which a man belongs, the negro is part and parcel of this nation. Whether the test be birth, or habitation, or loyalty, or toil, or suffering, or blood, he answers to them all.

And shall it be said that he asks too much, when he puts in his claim to a share in the government which he defended with his body, and helped redeem with his life? Surely our people have forever repudiated that atrocious sentiment, that " this is a white man's government, and that the negro has no rights here which a white man is bound to respect."

When an injury has been done, no duty is more binding and sacred than that of reparation. On this principle the debt which we owe the negro is great beyond comprehension, just as the wrong which we have done him is beyond expression. The horrors of the midnight surprise and capture, of the slave-ship and the middle passage, of the hounds, the lash, the thumb-screw, and the auction-block might have been palliated and borne, perhaps, had we left his manhood intact. But we did not, we unmanned him, we dehumanized him, we chattelized him. We merchandized him like the crops of the farm, the goods of the shop, or the wares of the market. He had no rights before the law, could neither buy, nor sell, nor own, could neither sue, nor be sued at law. Even marriage had no sanctity. Fatherhood and motherhood were a mockery, and the family relations an impossibility. Home, wealth, position, hope were not known in the dark vocabulary of the slave; we made his life bitter, quenched the light of intellect, the glow of the heart, and laid upon his faculties the blight of a killing and perpetual frost. As we stand revealed in the light of these acts it needs, at least, courage to call ourselves Christians. But whether Christian or not, the reparation we owe the race is none the less great and binding.

And then, again, the gains which we have made out of his unpaid labor, demand on our part an equal restitution. He has been a faithful and patient toiler, though he has toiled without reward and without hope. More than any other man he has produced the raw material out of which the wealth of the country has been created. For two hundred years he bowed himself to his tasks and had neither a share in his earnings nor in the rewards which they commanded. His labor has furnished the seed from which have sprung the manufacturing villages of the country. From the cotton raised by his hand, thousands have spun their fortunes; while every class and every industry among us has felt the quickening impulse, and the whole land has smiled under an unexampled thrift and plenty. Out of this material abundance which has flowed from the products of the plantation, everything else has been brought within reach of the people. Comfortable and tasteful houses have risen on every side. Capital has made sure returns, labor has become certain and remunerative. Intelligence has been made possible to the lowest, and elevation and culture have been brought within the reach of all. Disguise it as we may, we have grown rich by robbing the poor, and mighty by tasking the energies of the weak. "Behold the hire of the laborers who have reaped down your fields, which is of you kept back by fraud, crieth ; and the cries of them which have reaped are entered into the ears of the Lord of Saboath." To this hour, is not this the witness that is borne against us at the throne of eternal justice? Must other thousands fall, and other treasures be swallowed up in the great whirlpool of blood before we will deal equally with our fellow? We have had our Egypt, must we also have our Red Sea? If not, then shall we think our duty done by breaking off the negro's fetters? The earnings of his own life, and the earnings of his race, for generations, are in the hands of white men. And not only this, but all that he might have been in character, culture, position, influence, wealth of hope, joy, and power of good is to be added to the enormous sum we owe him. Give him back that of which we have robbed him, that which he would have been but for our injustice, and he is no longer a slave, or a dependent, but a man and a citizen.

But this debt, already so great, is to be multiplied by the aid which the negro rendered us in putting down the rebellion. It is a bright page in his history, but a stain and a blot on ours. Our treatment of him in the war was one of those dark and inexcusable acts which will be our perpetual shame and sorrow, like as the crucifixion of our Lord will be the endless reproach and regret of his betrayers and murderers. We repelled his aid, we drove him away from our lines, we gathered him out of our camps and sent him back, under the guard of the United States soldiers, to his masters, whose hands were lifted against the flag, and were exerting their direst might to destroy us. Neither party in the war meant any good to him. The South confessedly entered on rebellion that they might put him under a new Constitution a slave forever. And the North joined issue, not that they might break off his fetters, and introduce him to his manhood, but that they might keep him under the old Constitution a slave forever. For nearly two years we fought the battle on that line. And such years! the "Dies Iræ" of the Republic! They have not receded far enough, even now, tobe recalled without a shudder. The Bull Runs, the Balls Bluffs, the Chancellorsvilles, the Fredericksburgs, the whole peninsula campaign, how the mighty shades of our fallen, who struggled on unavailing fields, start up at the bare mention of the names. All the rhetoric of McClellan, before and after the battles, could not win victory to his banners. His defeats were overwhelming and felt to be due to something more than rebel prowess. If God did not fight against us we fought against ourselves, for we fought against conscience and humanity, and were half defeated before we went into the fight.

Indeed, the first real victory that we gained was not with the sword, but with the pen; not on the arena of war, but on the arena of righteousness and truth. It was the moral victory that Mr. Lincoln gained when he set his hand to that immortal instrument which gave liberty to four millions of slaves. And if this was our first victory, so was it the beginning of the last. For just as we went on, lifting up the weights that had crushed the slave, did God continue to smile on our banners, and give success to our work in the field. And when, at last, the people, in one of the most solemn and impressive acts in all the circuit of time, in their kingly way, said: "We decree that the slave shall be free, and we will make it good to the last man and the last dollar of the Republic," then God replied: "I give you the armies of the rebellion to scatter like leaves in the autumn winds." This, in a word, is the providential history of the war. We got on in our work precisely as we helped the negro.

The explanation is a simple one and is near at hand. In helping him we but helped ourselves, because we put ourselves on the side of God and man, and for that reason, and from that moment, we could not be beaten.

With what a willing love and ready aid he came to us has already gone upon the pages of imperishable history. How he served our living, nursed our sick, buried our dead, and now watches by the graves of our fallen, will be told when the long rolls of honor shall be made up. He was the scout and the spy of the Union army, putting his life on the hazard that he might warn our generals against surprise, or give them information which they might organize into victories. Our starving prisoners, escaped from their dens and hells of confinement and torture, learned that it was ever safe to trust him. No instance has been named in which he ever betrayed to his pursuers one of these hounded fugitives. With a matchless fidelity he concealed and fed them by day, and guided them towards our lines by night. And who that has any sense of honor or shame in his soul can help a blush as he remembers how differently we treated him in like circumstances. When years agone, escaped from his tasks, he came northward in hope of liberty and asylum and manhood, how we hunted him down in the name of the Union, and remanded back to his chains and his despair. God gave him the opportunity to make reprisals on us, principal and interest, for this enormous debt of cruelty and wrong. In what a godlike way he improved it !

Shall we forget how he stepped to the front, in the day of our calamity, two hundred thousand strong, and filled up our thinned ranks? On a hundred hard-fought fields he did as splendid and terrible work as any that wore the Union blue. Fifty thousand of them fell battling for the flag, their blood mingling with the blood of our own sons. They did a man's part freely, proudly, grandly, and now let them have a man's meed of reward. Especially is it fitting they should have that, since they asked none of the emoluments or the honors of the war. With a rare and magnificent heroism they fought for a country that had never done them anything but wrong. They fought without the hope of bounties or commissions, in the ranks where the leaden hail was thickest and deadliest, with the certainty that if they fell into the hands of their enemies their government would not protect them as soldiers of the Union. Such heroism should receive its patent of manhood, and such heroes should not ask in vain the rights of full citizenship.

And this debt, long overdue, is forever consecrated and made sacred by the prayers which this meek and suffering race offered up for the success of our armies. From the beginning of the war to its close, every aspiration of their hearts was for us. Night and day they knelt by the altars and bore us to God. They passed the hours of many a battle in crying unto the Lord that he would give victory to our hosts. The entire night, on which Grant made his final onset on Petersburg and Richmond, they spent in fasting and prayer that God would crown the attack with victory. It is possible that when we shall fully comprehend the moral forces that entered into the contest, and decided it in our favor, we shall then know that not the least among them was the prayers of the poor.

" Say, shall we yield Him in costly devotion,
  Odors of Edom and offerings divine,
Gems from the mountains, and pearls from the ocean,
  Myrrh from the forest, and gold from the mine ?
Vainly we offer each ample oblation,
  Vainly with gifts would His favor secure ;
Richer by far is the heart's adoration,
  Dearer to God are the prayers of the poor."

And those prayers have all been ours.

With such a memorial before him, will any one, who claims to be a man, deny manhood to a race that has given such abundant proofs of manhood? And especially will any man claim citizenship for himself, and yet deny it to those who have done a citizen's highest work and duty? If such meanness were possible, the negro could well be content to wait, for it could only dishonor us, it could not dishonor him. Let him still hold up the record of the past, and if we can afford to withhold, he certainly can afford to wait for justice.

But then, is our word to pass for nothing? Is national troth so poor and cheap? If the negro has nothing to expect from our gratitude and honor, must he learn that we only keep Punic faith with our allies? We promised them liberty, protection, and the rights of man. Mr. Lincoln promised it, the National Congress promised it, Mr. Johnson promised it, the people promised it, when they invited their aid, and clothed them with the authority and power of the nation's defenders. If we do not keep this promise, how shall we answer it at the judgment bar of public opinion? If we break faith with this confiding and desiring race, the world will fix upon us an infamy so deep and dark, that all the rains of time will not be able to whiten it, or wash it away.

If our only object were the vindication of truth, or the making out of a case, we should be content to rest our plea for the full enfranchisement of the negro on the ground of simple justice. But we are not merely pursuing an abstraction; this is the most vital and practical question with which the statesmanship of this generation has to deal. It is more important than tariff, or trade, or finance, or even the impeachment of the President. Questions pertaining to the moneyed interests of the country can all be answered by arithmetical rules of gain or loss, while the impeachment of the President might have its highest value in pointing a lesson of warning to men high in authority. But this question of fair deal with the negro is fundamental, and enters into the very life of the nation. It is a question of national prudence, and interest, and honor. So that as patriots, watching that "the Republic may receive no detriment," we must give it the most conscientious and thorough consideration.

How are we to save the nation, pacify the rebellious States, and unify the mind and heart of the people? Certainly not by leaving a weaker race subject to a stronger, a loyal portion to a disloyal. Equal protection to all loyal men, and the equal rights of all before the law is the least that can serve the purpose. And that protection can best be secured by putting the black into a condition to protect himself. If the white man needs the ballot for his security, not less does the black. And if the ballot is a constant stimulus to him who exercises it, to inform himself on the questions which he is called upon to decide, no man needs it so much as the black. And especially does he need it among a people hostile to his interests, and disposed to discriminate against him in their legislation. Would it not be a refinement of meanness to leave him in the power of his old masters, with feelings embittered against him to intensity, for the part he enacted in the war? As the ally of the Yankee, he shares in the bitter hatred which the very name excites in the Southern mind. And could we leave him to the consequences of such a feeling we should deserve the contempt of mankind.

If his ignorance is named as a reason for withholding from him the vote, it should be enough to reply that he knew the right and stood for the right when all the intelligence and wealth and power of the South were in the wrong. And yet we seem more ready to trust with the ballot that class which per- petrated the wrong, and hates more bitterly than ever the Union, than that simple race which constantly discerned the right, but never betrayed it. But should it be said that the negro enfranchised would be a tool in the hands of these wicked men to play their high games with, let the answer be found in his record for the last six years. He has opposed these men even to the death in maintaining his own convictions, and who is competent to say that he will not oppose them again ?

On three questions it may be safely assumed, the negro will be found true,—liberty, education, and religion. These are the central elements of a republican form of government. And if he can be trusted on these, it will make little difference which side he goes on the common questions that divide politi- cal parties. At any rate why should we fear to trust men whose instincts have led them right, and be willing to commit this high power to men whose education has led them wrong?

As a general principle we believe in limited or impartial suf- frage. But in this case it would evidently defeat its own end. The reason is a very obvious one. If suffrage were conditional, the whites having the power, would make that condition impos- sible for the black man to reach. Suppose the condition were a certain amount of intelligence, or property, it is not slander- ing Southern gentlemen to say that they would be likely to see to it that the negro never attained the required modicum of either. Practically, therefore, the only security in his case is universal suffrage. It would, doubtless, be attended with some evils, but with far less, we believe, than the opposite course.

But our interest as well as his, demands that he should have whatever is necessary to his complete protection. No half measures will do this. And for this reason we are opposed to any legislation which leaves him under political disabilities that do not appertain to white men, most of all are we opposed to any legislation that practically commits him to the power of his old oppressors. Hence we look with no complacency upon the Constitutional Amendment now pending before our legislature, unless other bills passed by Congress, as the military and the civil rights, shall render this harmless, as operating against the black. In its very terms it implies the superiority of the white, but indirectly furnishes a motive for lifting the black to a political equality. If accepted by the Southern States, and as a consequence, they were admitted to their full rights in the Union, the black would be left helpless, and he could only hope for the ballot when the interest, or the justice of the rebels might prepare the way. It would be an outrage to leave him to such precarious and uncertain justice. It is a most dangerous experiment. Once admitted to their normal condition, and these States could determine their internal policies. The black would be at their disposal. We should have no power to protect him, or to demand his protection. We should bind him hand and foot and turn him over to his enemies and ours. This would be something worse than a blunder, it would be a crime. For while we surrendered the negro, we should at the same time surrender all power of interference, or control in the revolted States.

In such an event nothing could prevent the revival of the worst passions and feelings of the rebellion. He must have studied that people to little purpose who can doubt that they would obliterate, as far as they were able, every thing northern. They would bring forth the Confederate flag from its hiding place and teach their children, who can doubt, to look up to it with rèverence and love, while they taught them to hate the flag of the Republic. They would fill their schools with disloyal teachers and disloyal books, and train their youth to despise and abhor the Union. They would keep alive by monument, observances, orations, literature, and song the memories of "the lost cause." They would hold forth the heroes and martyrs of the rebellion as models for their young men, and would exalt them as a perpetual inspiration and power. They would widen and deepen the gulf between the North and the South, would preserve every memento of the great struggle, and cherish with tender and sacred fondness its early promise and grandeur.

And no mere legislation can prevent such a result. We have already learned that laws will not execute themselves, and that the best of them may fail for want of a willing executive. We have been at a dead-lock for months because the President will not put in force such ordinances as are designed to pacify and save the country.   Indeed, nothing can be more visionary than the expectation that the feelings and the interests of the whole people can be fused into one, while the sentiment of loyalty and patriotism lies dormant in the Southern mind.   But we can operate on that mind directly, to create such a sentiment, only through the blacks.   They, in conjunction with the few loyal whites, will form a nucleus around which, in time, may be developed a thorough love for the Union.   But in any event, no reconstruction, or pacification can be useful and lasting that is not begun and carried on in the feelings and convictions of the people.

What is now needed, to allay the jealousies and animosities of the sections, is that the ideas and institutions which triumphed in the war should go southward and lead and control the Southern mind.   But they will not go of their own force, nor will the leading minds of the South willingly invite or receive them.   On the other hand, it rejects, with scorn, any thing which bears the Northern superscription.   It still clings to Southern notions, prejudices, ways of teaching, working, and living.   It cherishes, with undiminished ardor, the principles, heresies and abominations which the sword cleft and settled. It looks upon us as Vandals who trampled out an Arcadian simplicity, and a higher and better civilization which we could not understand.   It would be waste of time to offer New England ideas and institutions to such conceited Hotspurs.   They do not believe in either, and they are determined to have nothing to do with them.

There is but one course left.   We must turn to that portion of the Southern people that will accept the ideas which were tested and proved in the war.   While the white so proudly turns away from every thing northern, the black only too freely receives every thing northern.   He copies even our vices, because he believes in us with all his heart.   He is receptive to New England thoughts, welcomes New England teaching, and waits to be moulded to the New England pattern.   Through him we are to inoculate the white with our

culture, our industry, and our thrift.   It is clearly manifest that
the most effectual way to educate the Southern white, is to educate the black by his side.   For as schools are established for
the black, and he receives our letters, we compel the whites to
establish schools for themselves, or else be left behind in the
race for learning.   This is not a guess, we know it is practically true.

For example, the Superintendent of the public schools of
South Carolina, in his report to the Legislature last year, urged
that liberal provision be made for the schools of the State, because the blacks were being so rapidly educated that they would
very soon be ahead of the whites without such provision.
North Carolina was stirred up to the same duty for the same
reason.   In like manner the various religious bodies of the
South have been provoked to undertake not only the education
of white children, but in some cases the education of the black
children, also, to prevent their receiving the poison of New
England instruction.   Thus this work of lifting up the lowest
stratum of Southern society, is necessarily lifting up, at the
same time, all the strata above.

In the same way are to be propagated those great political
truths which now bear sway in the land.   The Southern white
will have nothing to do with them.   Our notions of freedom
and of the equal rights of all before the law, he regards as
rankest heresy.   But the black lends them a willing ear, and
he will defend them, at any cost, and at all hazards, because
his temporal salvation is wrapped up in them.   They are to
him the Evangel of a better future.   He has won his title to
them by blood, and he will be the herald to proclaim the glad
tidings of this new gospel to the ignorant and besotted millions
of the South.

It is vain to expect any right political action from men who
hate the Union.   The black is furnished to our hand, as their
counterpoise, to sap in time their pernicious influence, and to
leaven with the spirit of the Union the disloyal masses of the
South.   With rare exceptions, he is the only man in the rebel
States who is sufficiently loyal to those principles that had their
test and vindication in the war, and interested in the establishment of those institutions which brought deliverance to his race,

to be counted on in any reconstruction that would be either honorable or useful.

And why should we not use him as the man best fitted for
this purpose, and cease from trying to propitiate the favor of men
who have made up their mind to hate and oppose us?   We talk
continually about conciliating the South, and yet few of us have
thought what that South really is.   When, however, it is limited
and defined, it is found to consist in the four hundred thousand
slaveholders who made the war, and who, by their education,
and wealth, and position, wielded all the power and patronage
of the South.   The seven millions of poor whites, and the four
millions of blacks, had no voice in making the war, and thus
far have had no voice in settling the terms of peace.   The
South of our difficulties and troubles, therefore, is a haughty
and miserable oligarchy of a few thousands.   Were they out
of the way, the re-adjustment of our affairs would be a work of
ease.   And it is to be regretted that we failed to rid ourselves of
them when we had the opportunity.   It was a grave mistake.
As they had forfeited by treason, every right to liberty, property and life, under this government, they should have lost those
vast estates which gave them the power to rebel, and which now
give them the power for endless mischief.   Had this been done,
they would have been rendered harmless, their lordly acres
would have reverted to the government, and they would have
had enough to do to earn their bread without plotting other
"treasons, stratagems, and spoils."

The government then, would have been master of the situation.   It would have been in its power to have put upon the
soil of the South a loyal population.   It might have bestowed
the confiscated lands in bounties upon the soldiers who fought
its battles, or it might have cut them up into small farms and
thrown them into the market, to be preëmpted by poor loyal
men, white or black, that needed a home.   Had the government done this, it would have been a gainer in a threefold
sense.   In the first place it would have paid its war debt out
of rebel estates.   In the second place, it would have put upon
those estates a loyal population, who would have become its
best defenders, because the titles to their property would have
vested in the integrity of the government.   And in the third

place, it would have put upon them a producing class that would have added to the wealth of the country, in the place of the old consuming class that only impoverished the country.   Thus industry would have been secured all around.   Even the old idlers and consumers must have worked or starved.

It would have solved, moreover, the temporal support and independence of the negro better than anything else we can do for him.   What the negro wants is land ; give him this, and he will very soon provide for his physical necessities.   Now, it would seem as if there was a conspiracy among the land-holders to keep him out of land for the very purpose of holding him in subjection and dependence.   The master can no longer rent his slave for a hundred, or a hundred and fifty dollars per year, but the slave that was, must have somewhere to live, and so the master rents to him the old cabin for just about the same that he used to rent the slave for.   By this petty tyranny, the master is getting his support out of the negro, as truly as when the negro was his slave.   And there is no help for this, until the negro can become the owner of land.   If it is not too late, we could wish that the rebel estates might return to the government, and that out of them, homesteads might be created for that poor, but loyal race.   Could this be done, the race would no longer burden the charity of the North, while we should have forever baffled and disarmed the traitors, by lifting loyal men into place and power.

But whether we do this or not, the poor of the South are threatened by a kindred evil, almost as great, from the opposite quarter.   The planters, as a class, will be poorer before they are richer, and many of them will be compelled to part with their lands, either from choice or from necessity.   The reason is, they have no funds to farm them, and sooner or later they must throw them into the market.   In that event the danger is that speculators will bid them in, and either hold them at such a figure, or work them in such a way that the poor will get no benefit from them.   If the negro was obliged to choose between the Southern planter and the Northern sharper, it would not be surprising if he should prefer the former.

On the other hand, if benevolent men, with sufficient capital, would band together and buy up those Southern estates as they

are offered for sale, and hold them at just advance enough to
pay them a fair dividend on their outlay of money and trouble,
nothing could be more helpful to the negro, or sooner solve the
problem of his support.   A company formed for such a purpose, and wisely managed, would deserve well of the whole
country.   We throw out the hint to those to whom God has
given large means and large hearts.   Here they may at once
benefit themselves and, at the same time, confer measureless
blessings upon millions of the poor.

Nothing is of more importance to the country than that the
negro should have an opportunity to work to the best advantage for himself and for us.   As producers, they are worth,
twice over, all the rest of the South.   Physically there is no
finer body of laborers in the world, and they only lack intelligence and skill to make their labor most valuable and rewarding.   They have slumbering energies, that need to be awakened
and directed by education, in which we have immense interest.
They will wield the spade, and the sword, all the better for a
thinking brain.   The hand, guided by thought, will produce a
finer and richer material.   The Republic will be gainer every
way, by developing the minds of its laborers.   They will be
better citizens in peace and more able defenders in war.

And no time should be lost in prosecuting the work of education.   There are many reasons why it should be done now.
Chief among them is the fact that the race is now in its infancy,
and it must soon be determined what its future shall be.   The
race will become what the influences now operating make it.
We have everything at stake in the result.   If the negro is left
to a future of ignorance and vice he will be the heaviest weight
that ever dragged a nation downward.   But if his future be
made intelligent and virtuous and happy, if his mind be expanded
to the full measure of its capacity and controlled by right principle, he will be at once an ornament and a blessing to the republic.   Everything depends on the shape that is now given to
his mind, and heart, and will.   We can not be too eager, nor do
too much to secure the right result.   The future harvest will be
precisely as the seed that is sown.   And as the issue is in our
own hands we shall be inexcusable if it is not auspicious and
happy.   Nor should it be forgotten that it will be easier to se-

cure the right result now, than it will be if the work is delayed till a future time. "While men slept an enemy came, and sowed tares among the wheat." History is ever repeating itself. If we sleep over this matter, our enemies will certainly sow seeds of evil in the waiting mind of that race. Our safety is in pre-occupying their mind with the good seed of the New England school, and church, and culture. Do this and we need not fear all the wiles of our adversary. And there is no reason why we should not do this, for the negro is fairly in our hands, plastic and yielding, and waits to be moulded to our purpose. The waking up of his dullness and stupidity is like an inspiration, and his hunger for books is the marvel of the time. For them and for us it is the forming hour. We should be on the alert, watching our grand opportunity. We should quadruple the number of our teachers, and establish our schools at every accessible point, and pour in the light of learning until it permeates all the dark masses of the South and the whole land is flooded with its glory.

> "And all is well, though faith and form,
>   Be sundered in the night of fear;
>   Well roars the storm to those that hear
> A deeper voice across the storm,
> Proclaiming social truth shall spread,
>   And justice, even through thrice again,
>   The red fool-fury of the Scine
> Should pile her barricades with dead."

Thus far we have looked at this question as it would commend itself to a mind thoroughly in sympathy with justice, and imbued with the spirit of patriotism and humanity. We have purposely reserved the Christian view until the last, both because it is the most important, and because it properly rounds and concludes the argument.

In our opinion, no man comprehends the colored people, or can make the most and the best of them, who leaves out of the account the religious side of their nature. It would be a fatal defect in any system of education and reform, that had in it no provision for their religious wants, and had no means to take advantage of their religious impulses. To the colored mind, the school book would be cold and uninviting, that had in it nothing of Jesus. The school that was not daily consecrated by prayer, the reading of the Bible, and the Christian song, would rather repel, than attract, that sensitive race. Even the bread, that is given to the hungry is eaten with a sweeter relish, and the garment bestowed upon the naked has a warmer and richer significance, if given in the name of Christ.

As wise educators, therefore, it becomes us to use this deepest sense of the race as the great power to elevate and guide them. Our success, not unlikely, will depend on our ability to use it to the best advantage.

And this aspect of the subject may well lead one to feel that the negro is filling out some great providential purpose, as well by his enslavement on these shores, as by the new born freedom which he now enjoys. Let us hope that it is not more fraught with wisdom than it is with mercy to mankind. He has suffered, and we have suffered, and shall we doubt that both will be gainers in the end?

Perhaps our piety is to receive from him a new illustration and model, and so the world is to be the gainer. Perhaps he is to sit for the portrait of Christian character drawn by inspiration in the New Testament. Certain it is, that the specimens of Christian character which we have seen among the occidental races are, for the most part, cold and dwarfed, beside the New Testament models. We miss the gentleness, fervor, simplicity, patience, meekness, and forgiving love of the early disciples. Possibly we are to receive through this torrid race, an infusion of the oriental warmth, and richness, and power. They have already given us specimens of Christian simplicity, and faith, and zeal, that mock our low and meagre lives. Their meek, gentle, long-suffering patience would have disarmed the cruelty of any race, less hard and fierce than ours. Their forgiving spirit has passed into a proverb. What we find it so difficult to do—to forgive—seems to them but the most natural and easy thing in the world. Never a race that had so many wrongs to avenge, and never a race that forgave so many. Even the masters did not understand them. For when we first talked about arming the negro, they invoked against it the indignant protest of the world, affirming that the negro was a savage, and that, with his soul goaded and stung with the memory of such wrongs, it was not in human nature that his vengeance should not be dire and dreadful. But we put arms into his hand, yet he never used them save in lawful warfare ; and the women, the children, and the aged, never slept more secure than when they were at his mercy.

This, we are aware, might be put to the account of cowardice, if the race had not vindicated its courage on a hundred battle fields. The negro may lack the intellectual keenness and force of the Anglo-Saxon, but he has in higher degree the kindlier and better qualities, the moral, the social, and the religious. If we have more of pure intellect and will, he has more of sensibility and of the emotional. And this very distinction puts him into nearer communication with God, and is favorable to a high state of religious development. It may not be unreasonable, therefore, to expect that when he has received the best culture of our schools, and caught the deepest spirit of our piety, he will exhibit a Christian life so high, and warm, and full, that its attractions will draw us irresistibly nearer to God. We can not resist the belief that this is the plan of the Lord, and that, when it is wrought out, our piety will have received such an infusion of love, and faith, and zeal, as will fit it to become the conquering power of the world.

Nor will it be stranger than other works of the Lord, if it turns out that we have been preparing, through these sons and daughters of Africa, the redemption of that dark continent. Already, one of the features of our work among the blacks is the expressed desire, on the part of quite a number of the young men in our schools, to carry the Gospel to fatherland. As this work goes on, and intelligence deepens and broadens and means increase, it seems to be the most certain result to be anticipated, that hundreds of Africa's children will go from these shores to carry the glad tidings to their brothers and sisters of the sun. The field is white for the harvest. God offers no other to the American church so full of promise for the work required to be done. These millions speak our own language, have a form of piety, a love for truth, and a hunger for knowledge, which make the work inviting and easy. We have no years of preparatory work before us, ere we tell the story of redemption. God has prepared the way. and we have nothing to do but to preach the Gospel to eager, hungry souls. They wait to be fed, and hang upon the lips of our preachers, as if hearing for their lives. A dollar will go farther here, we believe, than on any other field that now invites Christian effort. It will be the simplest stupidity, the greatest recreancy to duty, the most stupendous lack of common sense, if we do not enter in and possess it for Christ.

And we should do this, not only because we are debtors to all mankind to give them the Gospel through the love we bear to Christ, but because we are debtors to them in particular, for having done what we could during two centuries to make them heathen. Now, with God's voice in our past history crying to us, we should not linger nor idle while they are asking what they must do to be saved.

If for no other reason, we must do this work in self-defence. Should we fail to do it our enemies will. The Southern people are not asleep. They will not yield control of the negro without a struggle. They know that the side which wins him, wins victory in the contest of ideas now going on. But a subtler foe is in the field, and one much more to be dreaded. The Catholics are moving quietly, but resolutely to gain the ear of the race. They will bring all the craft of centuries to the work, and they will give it up only when they find every point kept and guarded by the sleepless sentinels of a better faith. That conclave of Romish bishops, recently held at Baltimore, confessedly had this object mainly in view. Though the sessions were secret, yet enough has transpired to leave no room to doubt that the conversion of the blacks to Rome chiefly occupied the attention of the bishops. Already tokens of the invisible presence of their emissaries are beginning to be seen. Only a few days since a Christian laborer at Wilmington, N. C., found a Douay Testament in the hands of one of the blacks. On inquiry, it came out that a man had been quietly and stealthily circulating among the negro cabins, leaving these Douay Testaments. Of course he was a scout and a spy for Rome. About the same time it was announced in a public print that a cargo of Romish priests, sixty in number, had landed at New Orleans. Their forces are in motion and they mean earnest work.

We shall be a match for the man of sin, defeat his plans for the possession of the black only as we preoccupy the ground, throw out our teachers in advance, press forward the work of education, scatter the leaves from the tree of life and possess the mind of the people with the truth. If the blacks could be brought into the Catholic fold, and that dark church could wield them, as it now does the Irish, it would reach, at a stride, the goal of its ambition and rule supreme in church and in state. And such a result can be prevented only by urging forward every appliance of education and religion to take and hold that simple race for truth and Christ.

And now a closing word. Our country is still in danger. She has many and mighty enemies, and the battle for her rise or fall, who can doubt, is over the colored man. This nation must be saved. The redemption of the world hangs upon it. We neglected ourselves till we came to the verge of ruin, and now our first work and duty is for home and native land. God has brought the sons and daughters of Africa to our very doors, and for weal or for woe, our destiny is irrevocably bound up with theirs. If we would save ourselves, we must save them. And, so far as our denomination is concerned, the instrument of their salvation is the American Missionary Association. The National Council appointed it after mature deliberation, because they believed it was adapted to the purpose, and would do the work. That work it has undertaken with results which the most sanguine could hardly have anticipated. It has no lack of laborers, but of funds to send them forth. We verily believe the churches are not awake to the momentous issue. Many of them are treading the old, beaten track, working at the old programme, not seeming to comprehend that the last six years have changed their relations to the country and the world. Let them push their free and simple polity southward among the blacks, and not wait for its slow and uncertain adoption by the whites. This, we verily believe, is the true wisdom for our churches.

Let them come up now. There is no time to be lost. Our teaching and preaching forces should move forward at every point. Every patriot, every Christian, who would honor God, and save mankind, should join in a grand advance to possess the land for Christ and the church.

The battle for the nations is turning on this result.   If we win, we save, at least, two continents.   If the enemies of liberty and religion win, we lose our country, and defer, for untold years, the salvation of the world.

> " In the long vista of the years to roll,
>   Let me not see our country's honor fade ;
> O, let me see our land retain her soul ;
>   Her pride, her freedom, and not freedom's shade.
> Let me not see the patriot's high bequest,
>   Great Liberty ! how great in plain attire !
> With the base purple of a court oppress'd
>   Bowing her head, and ready to expire."

ARTICLE VII.

LIFE AND LETTERS OF JOHN WINTHROP.

Life and Letters of John Winthrop, Governor of the Massachusetts Bay Company at their Emigration to New England, 1630.   By ROBERT C. WINTHROP.   Boston : Ticknor & Fields.   1864.

Life and Letters of John Winthrop, from his embarkation for New England in 1630, with the Charter and Company of the Massachusetts Bay, to his death in 1649.   By ROBERT C. WINTHROP.   Boston : Ticknor & Fields.   1867.

WE agree with the writer of a review of the first of these volumes in the *Christian Examiner* for March, 1864, in saying :

" We have to thank the editor, the Hon. Robert C. Winthrop, for the care he has manifested in preparing this book. . . . . He has made a Life of his distinguished ancestor, which will remain as an authority and an exemplar to our historians.   There remains for him only to complete the task he alone seems competent to undertake, and to give us the Life of John Winthrop in New England."

This he has here done, and well done ; letting the subject of his history speak, mainly for himself ; and modestly doing little else than connecting the parts of the Governor's own writings, by necessary explanatory remarks. What we would try to do in this, our review of the volumes, is to make something of an analysis of the religious and moral character of the first Governor of Massachusetts, that all who read this part of the history of the old Commonwealth, may find occasion for admiration, gratitude and reverence.'

The key to the whole character and life of John Winthrop is found, we think, in two remarks of the editor in the beginning of the first and end of the second volume of the life and writings of his ancestor. In the first volume, he writes, truly, as well as eloquently :

" I hardly know of a deeper debt which any one can incur, or of a more binding obligation which any one can discharge, whenever circumstances may afford the means and opportunity of doing so, than to bring out from the treasures of the past, and to hold up to the view of the present, and of coming generations, a great example of private virtue and public usefulness ; of moderation in counsel, and energy in action ; of stern selfdenial, and unsparing self-devotion ; of childlike trust in God, and implicit faith in the Gospel of Christ, united with courage enough for conducting a colony across the ocean, and wisdom enough for building up a state in the wilderness."

And, in the last chapter of the second volume, in giving citations from " Winthrop's History of New England," and the last words of the History itself, the editor says :

" Here it ends ; and in beautiful consistency with his whole life, the providence of God, the blessing of prayer, and the keeping of the Lord's day, are the last topics which were touched by his pen."

We would ask attention to these two remarks, as giving what may be truly called the key to the character of Winthrop ; " a childlike trust in God, and implicit faith in the Gospel of Christ ; an habitual acknowledgment of ' the providence of God,' and ' the blessing of prayer.' "

The influence of a heartfelt conception of the God of the Bible, on the mind and acts of man, is a theme for thought, which no reasoning person can lightly set aside in reading the life and writings of John Winthrop ; and we are glad that the

---

¹ His early life, as unfolded in the first of these volumes was noticed in this *Review*, Vol. IV., pp. 248–57.

editor has exhibited the theme so clearly. We have read once in the discourse of a good man, that " every man is as his God is." We remember also, that Hume, in his history of England, cites one of the Puritans as saying in' Parliament, in an allusion borrowed from Lord Bacon, in his essay of Atheism :

" If a man meet a dog alone, the dog is fearful, though ever so fierce by nature ; but if the dog have his master with him, he will set upon that man, from whom he fled before. This shows, that lower natures, being backed by higher, increase in courage and strength : and certainly man, being backed with omnipotency, is a kind of omnipotent creature. All things are possible to him that believes ; and where all things are possible, there is a kind of omnipotency."

If we hesitate in affirming that there was " a kind of omnipotency " in the character of John Winthrop, we yet affirm with boldness, that there was a courageous strength in it derived from an affectionate, yet manly trust in a God who was, and is, omnipotent, which made him faithful, firm, persevering and successful, to use the well-chosen words of his descendant, in " conducting a colony across the ocean," and " building up a state in the wilderness."

In his conception of God the first Governor of our Commonwealth, though "childlike," was intelligent and philosophical. He regarded Jehovah as a personal being, "whose sovereignty is absolute" ; but whose purposes, though eternal, were so ordained with reference to the free acts of the accountable subjects of his government as to provide for the influence of their prayers on his own course of action respecting them ; and also for their entire freedom in devising their own way, while he directed their steps. This eternal purpose of God to answer true prayer is ever founded on the same reasons, which determine in any case his actual answer to it. So that, if we may suppose that he formed no eternal purpose, his decision in respect to any petition would not be different. And, we may say with Wollaston, as quoted in Gregory's Letters : "The prayers which good men offer to the all-knowing God, and the neglects of others may find fitting effects already forecasted in the course of nature :" [1]   Thus illustrating the gracious promise : "It shall come to pass, that before they call, I will answer."

Winthrop was therefore ever circumspect and diligent in the choice and use of the means necessary for the accomplishment of any object.   This trait of his character is finely exemplified in the care with which he considered, in writing, the several arguments in favor of his decision to come to America, as well as the objections against such a determination.

Nor was his reverence towards God, as a sovereign, thus continually expressed in prayer, and in trust in the divine providence, cold abstraction.   It was in words already cited, "a child-like trust in God, and implicit faith in the Gospel of Christ."   It was ever accompanied by an affectionate confidence in the divine love and mercy, which made his feelings tender towards God and man ; and which regarded the providence of God as ordered with reference to men, as an imperfect and fallen race, who needed to be chastened for their profit, that they might be partakers of the divine holiness.

It is under the habitual influence of such conceptions, that we see, in imagination, John Winthrop pondering the question, whether or not he shall embark for this land.   That pensive and fine countenance, with its mingled thoughtfulness and tender sadness so finely exhibited in the picture of the first Governor owned by the State, and so well copied in the engraving contained in the first volume of his life and writings, is strongly marked in all its features by intense thought.   It was like "the father of all them that believe" meditating on the command of God to leave his country, and kindred, and father's house, and go to a land which the Lord had shown to him.   The faith of the patriarch exercised and guided the soul of Winthrop.   It is at once interesting and instructive to notice the gradual manner, in which, noting the indications of providence, and communing with his own heart, he was at length brought to the conclusion to leave England for this country.   A severe illness, by which he was attacked in London in the latter part of the year 1628, seems to have been the beginning of the series of events, which led to this conclusion.   In writing to his wife, before he had re-

[1] Gregory's Letters, Vol. II., Letter 19th.

turned to her in Groton, and after she had encountered the inclemency of a journey in winter to London, to minister to his wants in sickness, and left again to preside at their home, there are frequent expressions of tender, yet exalted and pious sentiments which beautifully develop his dignified and heroic character.   They are such as these :

"The favor and blessing of God are better than all things besides.   My trust is in his mercy, that upon the faith of his gracious promise, and the experience of his fatherly goodness, he will be our God to the end, to carry us along through this course of our pilgrimage, in the peace of a good conscience."   "I know thou lookest for troubles here, and when one affliction is over, to meet with another ; but remember what our Saviour tells us : ' Be of good comfort, I have overcome the world.' "   "Let men talk what they will of riches, honor, pleasures, etc. ; let us have Christ crucified, and let them take all besides."   "There are very few hours left of this day of our labor ; then comes the night, when we shall take our rest.   In the morning we shall awake unto glory and immortality."

Then we meet with the expressions of a Christian patriot, sad at the evil state of public affairs in his country.   He writes to his wife :

"It is a great favor, that we may enjoy so much comfort and peace in these so evil and declining times."   "The Lord hath admonished, threatened, corrected, and astonished us, yet we grow worse and worse, so as his Spirit will not always strive with us, he must needs give way to his fury at last : he hath smitten all the other churches before our eyes, and hath made them to drink of the bitter cup of tribulation, even unto death."   "My dear wife, I am verily persuaded God will bring some heavy affliction upon this land."

It would seem that the mind of our first Governor passed through unusually sore trials at this period of his life.   Soon we find him writing again to his faithful wife :

"Our best comfort is, we shall rest in heaven."   And then : "For news I have but one to write of, but that will be more welcome to thee than a great deal of other.   My office is gone, and my chamber, and I shall be a saver in them both."

"It will be observed," writes the editor of these volumes, and with his very appropriate words we close this part of our review :

" It will be observed, that, in the letter of June 5, Winthrop says to his wife, ' I think my office is gone' ; and that, in a subsequent letter, without date, he tells her distinctly, ' My office is gone, and my chamber both.' We know not the circumstances under which he ceased to be an Attorney of the Court of Wards. His opposition to the course of the Government at this period, and his manifest sympathy with those who were suffering under its unjust exactions and proscriptions, may have cost him his place. Or, he may have resigned it voluntarily, in view of the new plans of life, which more than one of his letters would seem to indicate that he was contemplating. It is evident that he felt that a crisis was at hand in the condition of England, and that he was anticipating a personal share in the sufferings to which the friends of civil and religious freedom were about to be subjected. When he says to his wife, in the last letter but one, ' Where we shall spend the rest of our short time I know not, my comfort is, that thou are willing to be my companion in what place or condition soever,' we seem to find the first foreshadowing of the great decision which will be developed in our next chapter."

The editor refers to the decision of his ancestors to come to America.   He continues :

" The present chapter may be concluded like the last, with a little scrap from the private experience, which corresponds exactly to the period we have reached. ' July 28, 1629. My Bro. Downing and myself, riding into Lincolnshire by Ely, my horse fell under me in a bog in the fens, so as I was almost to the waist in water ; but the Lord preserved me from further danger. Blessed be his name.' New England may well say Amen to this blessing. That ride to Lincolnshire was on an eventful errand. Beyond a question, Winthrop and Downing were on their way to Sempringham to visit Isaac Johnson, and consult with him about the great Massachusetts enterprise."

As one contemplates such a character as Winthrop's, he is prompted to ask yet more particularly, how it was formed? And, what truths contributed to its formation? In replying to such a question, we would avoid the technicalities of theology, and say, in words which we think must commend themselves as true to the observation, and the conscience of every candid man, that the character was the result of a moral change in which one begins, habitually to exalt in his desires, feelings, thoughts, and acts, the personal God and Saviour revealed in the Bible,

above the objects and ends of earth and of time; not neglecting these, but in their use supremely seeking and serving
God.

We are fond of believing that there are those who have been
thus renewed from their earliest life, "sanctified," in the words
of the Scriptures, "before they came forth out of the womb."
We indulge the hope also, that such transformation and improvement among men, in early childhood, shall be more common as the Christian character and habits of the communities
of men shall advance in holiness.   We hold, moreover, that
this transformation is, in its essential nature, simple in its elements, and often, like a little leaven, or a grain of mustard seed
in its beginnings in the heart and life.   But, as men approach
towards this holier and happier state, it is a truth of unspeakable importance, and always to be watchfully borne in mind and
acted on, that every man must be born again, must be in Christ,
a new creature; must repent and believe the Gospel.   This
beginning of holiness in heart and life is essential to the commencement and growth of a godlike character in man.   And
the reality of it was fully believed and insisted on by John
Winthrop.   We may admit that in the words of our editor:
"His language must undoubtedly be taken with some grains of
allowance for the peculiar phraseology and forms of expression
which belonged to the times in which it was written, and also
for that spirit of unsparing self-examination and self-accusation
which was characteristic of all the Puritan leaders."   Nevertheless it expressed an essential and vital truth.   In his "spirit
of unsparing self-examination and self-accusation," he regarded
the exceeding evil of sin in its essential principle more than in
its outward form, as refined or gross, and this, instead of producing in him hard and censorious feelings towards his fellow
men, as transgressors with himself of the law of God, filled
him with a tenderness towards them, which, without excusing
or palliating the evil of sin, strove to reform them, and at the
same time clothed himself with humility as with a garment,
under the deep and habitual conviction that except he repented
he should likewise perish.   In the fine sentiment of Mrs. Bar-
bauld:

" Himself, through Christ, had mercy found,
   Free mercy from above ;
   That mercy moved him to fulfil
   The perfect law of love."

With these truths in mind, it is exceedingly interesting to read Winthrop's own account of the renewal of character and life, of which he believed himself to have been the subject, as this is given in his private record of "Christian Experience." " The merciful Lord," he writes, " notwithstanding all my stubbornness and unkind rejections of mercy, left me not till he had overcome my heart to give up itself unto him and to bid farewell to all the world, and until my heart would answer : 'Lord, what wilt thou have me to do?' "   This was an inquiry he evidently ever afterwards made in performing all his duties to God and man.   It made him watchful, prayerful, patient, persevering, courageous, in all his ways.   It led to his emigration from England.   It formed and finished his beautiful character and life.

It will be clearly seen by every attentive reader of these volumes, that his whole domestic life was greatly influenced by his religious principles.   His letters and journal show this in many very interesting forms.   His remarks on the early loss of his first wife show this.   And there are few accounts of the character and last hours of a faithful Christian woman so beautiful as that which he has written of his second companion.   The closing sentence is all that we can give : "Her loving and tender regard of my children was such as might well become a natural mother : for her carriage to myself, it was so amiable and observant as I am not able to express ; it had this only inconvenience, that it made me delight too much in her to enjoy her long."   The third of his partners for life, the noble, the affectionate, the energetic Margaret, daughter of Sir John Tyndal, was a worthy successor of her whom he thus mourned. When he left her and his eldest son, with others of the family, "behind for the present," to come to this country, she sustained and comforted him by her Christian firmness.   The editor, his descendant, well says :

" There is something of poetical beauty, as well as of pious sentiment, in the agreement, which is more than once referred to as having been made between his wife and himself, that they would remember each other every Monday and Friday evening, between the hours of five and six, and ' meet in spirit before the Lord.' "

She followed him. after more than a year had passed, with her little daughter, born soon after the departure of her husband, and buried in the sea, on her way to meet him. " Happily," writes our author, " she was not without the consolations which her pious fellow-passenger, the admirable John Eliot, was so well calculated to afford."

The letters of his son John, afterwards Governor of Connecticut colony, show that he too was worthy of his father; and that he felt and acted on the same exalted principles, as he expressed them in his first letter to that father, after having heard of his decision to come to New England. " In this business of New England, I can say no other thing, but that I believe confidently that the whole disposition thereof is of the Lord, who disposeth all alterations by his blessed will, to his own glory and the good of his ; and, therefore, do assure myself, that all things shall work together for the best therein." In short, hardly shall we find anywhere, out of the Scriptures, a clearer illustration of domestic movements in life, guided and controlled by intelligent religious motives and principles, than in the family history of the first Governor of our Commonwealth.

The same motives and principles guided and controlled his public life.   We hold that there is a close connection between religion and politics, though we do not favor any political union of church and state, but rather delight in the wisdom of Him who said : "Render unto Cæsar the things which are Cæsar's, and unto God the things that are God's."   Every one who obeys this precept, must and will, in the light of the great teacher by whom it was spoken, receive and act upon such truths in his own personal relations to God, as shall prompt him to apply them to all his conduct, public as well as private, towards his fellowmen.   In doing so, he must and will be influenced by that one, fundamental fact on which all the teachings and acts of Jesus proceed, that all have sinned, and come short of the glory of God.   In doing this a principle must be necessarily admitted and acted on, as essentially and invariably influential in all reasonings and acts in the government of men under human law, as the fact that all water-wheels are constructed on the principle that water flows towards the centre of the earth.   We mean the principle that men are imperfect beings, needing to be governed as such, by laws enacted and enforced under the influence of the great fact of Christianity, that mercy and truth should meet together, and righteousness and peace kiss each other, in the administration of human governments, as well as under the divine.   How often have we longed, of late years, under our own government, that these truths might be more profoundly regarded and acted on, than they sometimes have been.   Governor Winthrop did rely and act on them.   This is happily illustrated in those singular and, in themselves alone, almost trivial circumstances, which led at one time, through the power of popular prejudice and passion, to his own impeachment, and to his delivery, after his full and triumphant acquittal, of what he called so modestly, his "little speech" ; a speech which we commend to the attention of our readers, as containing what one of the most distinguished philosophical writers on " Democracy in America" calls "a fine definition of liberty."   We think it could be shown also, with great clearness, how the same influence of religious principles in their application to politics, so guided and prompted his acts, as to make him in the recorded declarations of John Adams, Quincy, Bancroft and Palfrey, a pioneer in promoting the blessings of religious and civil liberty in this country.   The last named writer, Dr. Palfrey, writes in his admirable history of New England :

" I do not forget that various agencies must be combined to produce an important political result ; but, to my view, the New England campaign of 1775–6, the movement of John Adams and his compeers for independence, eighty-four years ago, and, consequent upon these transactions, the later products of self-government in America, are to Winthrop's administration, something like what the fruit is to the blossom."

It is so pertinent to the name of this *Review*, that we can not pass in silence the influence of the religious principles and character of Winthrop on his course respecting the forms of church government and worship with which he united after coming to New England ; and the influence he thus exerted in favor of " freedom to worship God."   In that admirable address sent by him and his companions, "the Governor and his company late gone to New England," "to the rest of their brethren in and of the Church of England," it is affirmed with great clearness and beauty: -

" We desire you would be pleased to take notice of the principals and body of our company, as those who esteem it our honor to call the church of England, from whence we rise, our dear mother ; and can not part from our native country, where she specially resideth, without much sadness of heart, and many tears in our eyes, ever acknowledging that such hope and part as we have obtained in the common salvation we have received in her bosom, and sucked it from her breasts. We leave it not, therefore, as loathing that milk wherewith we were nourished then ; but blessing God for the parentage and education, as members of the same body, shall always rejoice in her good, and unfeignedly grieve for any sorrow that shall ever betide her, and while we have breath, sincerely desire and endeavor the continuance and abundance of her welfare in the enlargement of her bounds in the kingdom of Christ Jesus."

After this address of mingled tenderness and nobleness, nothing but a deep conviction of the influence of such a step on the advancement of true piety and religious liberty could have induced Winthrop to have united as heartily and actively as he did in forming the first Congregational church in Charlestown. We admire and reverence the exalted views of Christian truth and duty which prompted the act ; and we rejoice in believing that in performing it, he helped to fix "irrevocably" in the words of the late Hon. Josiah Quincy, in the Centennial Discourse before the citizens of Boston in 1830, "in the country that noble security for religious liberty, the independent [Congregational] system of church government."

This system is very closely connected with the whole form and working of our political, constitutional Union. The connection of each Congregational church, as exercising the power of self-government, with any general ecclesiastical council which may at any time be called in union with other Congregational churches, is strikingly analogous to the relation of each sovereign s ate in our political union, to the powers vested by our constitution in the national government. We are inclined to believe also that a patient study of both may, after all that has lately passed in our history as a people, aid us in arriving at highly satisfactory conclusions respecting the powers and the administration of each.

The catholic author of these volumes shows how fully he appreciates the Congregationalism of his ancestor, in the well chosen words of the closing paragraph of his work. After having alluded, in appropriate terms, to the action of the State respecting statues of its first Governor, he writes :

"Doubtless it would have gratified him to know that his services would be so valued more than two centuries after his death. But though he could not have been indifferent to the judgment which should be pronounced upon him by posterity, it may be safely said, that, above all other honors which could be paid to his memory, above monuments or statues or memorials of any sort, he would have appreciated the casual coincidence, that, on the very site of his residence, or certainly within the enclosure of his garden, should stands a consecrated edifice, in which, through a long succession of generations, should be gathered one of the chosen churches of Christ, worshipping God according to the faith and the forms which had been dearest to his own heart in his mature New England life. The Old South Church in Boston, as it is called, has many hallowed and many patriotic associations ; but it may be doubted whether any of them are more congenial with its sacred uses, or will be more cherished hereafter by its devout frequentors, than that it marks the Boston home of John Winthrop, its foundations resting upon the spot on which he dwelt in life, its steeple pointing to the brighter abode to which he ever aspired in the skies."

The people of Massachusetts should be forever grateful to God for the character of their ancestors, and particularly for the character of John Winthrop. It has been usual with many to attribute the differences which have been noticed between them and the more Southern citizens of our Union to the influence of slavery. And this institution, without dispute, must be admitted to have had great power in affecting, deleteriously, in many respects, the habits of the people among whom it so long existed. But there were also slaves once in the Old Bay State. And it has not been owing, wholly, to the influence of climate, that they have ceased to be held here. The religious and intellectual influences which have come down from the fathers more than climate, we are inclined to think, early cast off the incubus, and caused the energies of the people of all classes, to spring forth in manly and independent efforts for public and private good. The habit of exalting the value of man, because he has been continually contemplated as an accountable and immortal subject of the government of God, has always powerfully operated in New England and specially in Massachusetts, to produce and cherish a high estimate of the value of religious, political, and. personal liberty, as a necessary element in human improvement. The thoughts of the whole people, respecting themselves and others, have been happily affected by such influences. And John Winthrop did much to begin and continue the operation of such causes in the minds of his countrymen. We are glad, very glad, to see the spirit of the first of the family in this country still living and operating in his descendant, the author of these volumes. With no desire after anything like an order of nobility, but rather with a dread of anything of that kind, and its accompaniment, entailed estates, we have yet great and increasing faith in the influence of parents upon children, unto the latest generation, when purified and exalted by Christian character and life.

Mr. Winthrop has modestly said that his ancestor is now so far off from himself, by more than two centuries, and six entire generations of descendants, that he can scarcely call him his own. And he has happily and most appropriately cited the sentiment of a poet to sustain his position :

> Et genus, et proavos, et quæ non fuimus ipsi,
> Vix ea nostra voco.

But we hope that neither he, nor his countrymen will ever forget, or fail to emulate this bright example of the past.

ARTICLE VIII.

SHORT SERMONS.

"Who touched me? . . . . Jesus said: Somebody hath touched me, for I perceive that virtue is gone out of me."—*Luke* viii. 45, 46.

THE healing power for man, both for body and soul, is in the Lord Jesus Christ. This power he loves to use for the help of the needy, and his life was devoted to its exercise.

But he desires to be acknowledged as the redemptive agency, and to be credited publicly for what he does. For this reason he wishes to gather together in one public body all the witnesses who can testify to their personal benefit from his power. So their holy life will become an embodied declaration of what he can do in producing holiness. For their good, too, as well as for his own glory, he would do this.

It is in the light of these principles that the text finds its explanation.

This poor woman is in great trouble, and has been for twelve years. She has expended her estate on physicians, and yet is no better. She is well persuaded that Christ alone can help her. His aid she greatly wishes, but she fears to ask and receive it publicly. Like him who went to Jesus by night for fear of the Jews, and like the blind man who was to be cast out of the synagogue, if he owned the power of Christ, she felt her danger. So with a timid faith, she secretly snatched the mercy and sought to conceal it.

The Lord Jesus knew well what she had done, and why she sought to cover up his mercy and her love for him. But for her own good, and that of the multitude, as well as for his own honor, he could not allow this secrecy, and so he raises the question: "Who touched me?" He would bring the woman to a public confession of his kindness toward her, and of her faith in him. Hence:

The duty of publicly professing Christ, when we love him.

1. In the way of Gratitude.
2. On the ground of Friendship.
3. For the Good it may prove to Others, needing, but not yet receiving Christ.
4. For one's own Spiritual Good.

So we see that:

a. Trying to be secretly a Christian is not pleasing to our Lord and Saviour. "Who touched me?" "Where are the nine?"

b. Failing to make a profession of religion through the fear of man is dishonorable to Christ, and dangerous to his child.

"Let a man examine himself, and so let him eat of that bread and drink of that cup."—1 *Cor.* xi. 28.

THE Sacrament of the Lord's Supper is the purest, highest act of Christian worship, and of all the means of grace it stands preëminent.

It implies, in our observance of it ; (*a*) A confession of our sinful and lost state: (*b*) A total dependence on the Lord Jesus Christ for justification : (*c*) A cordial acceptance of him as our only Saviour: (*d*) A consecration of all we are and have to him: (*e*) A solemn covenant to become morally like him as far as in us lies : (*f*) And a hearty desire and plan to carry out his scheme for sanctifying and saving the world. When one comes to the Communion, he practically confesses and promises all this. It is plain, therefore, that at the table of the Lord one's heart and life should be in deep sympathy with Christ. Sitting thus with him, as it were socially, one must be presumed to be morally like him and practically with him.

The text suggests

The Self-examination required that one may come properly to the Communion Table.

The language of the text requires the examination to be very strict and trying. "Examine ;" δοχιμαζέτω, the word used to express the process for refining and proving ores and metals in the furnace. And the end sought in the Examination, as the context shows, is not whether one be a Christian, but what kind of a Christian life he is living.

This solemn and prayerful work should involve the following questions :

1. Am I strictly honest in all my business with others? Was the article sold as good as I said it was, according to the best of my knowledge? Have I kept my agreements in both their letter and their spirit? Since insolvency and chancery can not free me from moral obligation, have I done the best I could to pay any debts from which the law of man discharged me? Have I taken advantage of the ignorance of any, or by trick obtained any unjust gain?

2. Have I been strictly truthful in speaking of others? Has my

dislike of persons or things led me to misrepresent them? While
not obligated to like everybody and everything, have I been sacredly
careful to speak of them according to the rigid rule of facts? For
if I have intentionally varied from the truth in my speech, how can
I sit at the table with him in whose mouth was found no guile?

3. Is the law of kindness in my tongue? Do I allow myself in a
conversation that is sharply free, dissecting, depreciating, and scathing? Do I grieve, or trouble or vex others, when I neither design
nor convey any profit to them? Though I so speak, and say : " It
is my way," is it not a sinful way? Can I, accustomed to use
rough words, sit with him

"Whose lips with grace o'erflow "?

4. Do I bear ill feelings toward any one? Such a feeling is sinful, and foreign to communion with Christ. If I love not my seen
brother, how can I love my unseen Master? If unreconciled to
any, can my offering at the table be acceptable? "If thou bring thy
gift to the altar and there rememberest," etc. Matt. v. 23, 4. "Let
a man examine himself."

5. Are my Christian gifts and charities up fully to the rule of
Christ? I myself am not my own. I am bought by Christ. My
property, so called, is not my own. It is Christ's, and I am his
steward over it. He gave himself, and his whole mortal life to the
Christian cause. What are my theory and practice on charitable
and benevolent donations? If I am close and selfish with my
money, can I " eat of that bread, and drink of that cup"? I must
examine myself as to my pecuniary charities.

6. Do I use all my public means of grace? Do I occasionally
and without good reasons neglect the Lord's table? " This do in remembrance of me." Am I a constant attendant on public worship?
" He came to Nazareth, where he was brought up, and as his custom
was; he went into the synagogue on the Sabbath day." Luke iv. 16.
Do I surprise or grieve my Lord and his friends by frequent and unnecessary absence? What kind of causes keep me from the house
of God?

7. Can I come with Christ to his table as one faithfully working
for him? I have promised to do this, and I see great need of doing
it. He has kindly given me many opportunities for doing it. Do I
gain in my habits of industry, in work for Christ? How many,
since the last communion, have known, by my personal labor with
them, my love for Christ? " Let a man examine himself."

8. Am I on intimate terms with the Lord Jesus? Do I meet him
often in the prayer meeting? At the family altar? In the closet?

Have I been with him so little of late that he may look surprised to see me at his table?

9. Am I more and more like Christ? Am I more " holy, harmless, undefiled, separate from sinners," than when I last communed? I ought to grow in grace, and go from strength to strength.

10. Am I becoming fit for the heavenly communion? This may be my last here. Shall my next following communion be in the " church of the first-born"? Oh! I must examine myself, as if side by side with my Master.

ARTICLE IX.

LITERARY   NOTICES.

1. — *The Character of Jesus Portrayed.* A Biblical Essay, with an Appendix. By Dr. DANIEL SCHENKEL, Professor of Theology, Heidelberg. Translated from the third German edition, with Introduction and Notes. By W. H. FURNESS, D. D. Two Volumes. 12mo. Boston: Little, Brown & Co. 1866.

A RECENT Edinburgh reviewer gives us this generalization, which has about the average amount of the proverbial glitter : that the English mind approaches the question of Christ and Christianity on the ethical side ; the French, on the imaginative ; and the German, on the reasoning or rationalizing : the three typical exponents respectively of which he says, are Ecce Homo, Renan, and D. F. Strauss. Taking this scale of measurement, we should say, that the German doctor, whom we now have in hand, is considerably less unreasonable than that prince of unreason who, thirty years ago, thought to lay the axe at the root of the tree of Christian belief by turning the entire historical records of our Lord into myth and legend—the natural accumulation of the marvellous about a nucleus of fact, in an unhistoric age. But it so happened that the epoch of Jesus of Nazareth was just the reverse of such an age, lying plainly open to be seen and read of all men in the full daylight of Roman record and criticism, as unpropitious for the creation of the Straussian mythology as that of Napoleon I., or George Washington. This the German image-breaker has been made to see by the strictures which his work evoked : and in his late recension of the Life of Christ for " the German people," he takes the bold ground of charging a deliberate purpose to manufacture history, that is, to falsify facts, upon both the Master and his disciples of

the primitive age.   Dr. Schenkel, to his credit, rejects this last sui-
cidal and infamous notion, and but partially admits the mythical
theory of the formation of the Gospels.   With the fanciful romanc-
ing of Renan, he also has little sympathy, which he regards as
superficial and unsatisfying to the deeper want of our times.   He
proposes, then, not to write a Life of Jesus, which he thinks is impossible ; but to present " a genuinely human, truly historic representation " of that person's origin, development and character.

So far as the author's spirit can be inferred from these pages, it
is serious, reverential, earnest.   He professes, and we see not but
sincerely, a desire so to set Christianity, in its inception, before the
modern mind, that the tendency to anti-Christian radicalism may be
checked by a returning acceptance of what he considers the facts of
the sacred record, and a corresponding devotion to the essential
truths and beneficent aims of the Christian religion.   His scholarship is extensive, his style is clear, his sympathies are strongly democratic.   If the reader is startled, at times, by his bold positiveness,
he will not be annoyed by any Parkerian mockery.   The same is
true of the translator's elaborate additions to the text.   Concerning
these notes which run into lengthy essays, it is interesting to observe
that they differ almost always from Dr. Schenkel's conclusions in the
direction of more conservative views.   Dr. Furness has long had
the reputation of a progressive Unitarian ; but we are glad to see
that he finds so much fault with his author's more subversive criticism.

The author of Ecce Homo so carefully wrapped up his theology
of Christ, that his admirers are yet awaiting enlightenment upon
this vital subject.   On the contrary, our present author begins his
work by an explicit disclaimer of belief in the superhuman origin
of the Gospels, and by assuming that the dogma of the twofold nature of Jesus, his divine-human personality, places him beyond the
possibility of historical inquiry, as a being of whom no rational
conception can be formed.   His position is strictly humanitarian.
His theory of the four evangelists may be given in few words.
Mark, he considers the earliest of these writers, the most historic
and trustworthy.   Matthew came next, with more of unauthorized
tradition, and with " a literary purpose " — to convert the Jews by a
flattering use of Old Testament citations, which show more zeal
sometimes than knowledge.   Both of these books, he thinks, were
drawn up, in a previous form, in the rough, for immediate use ; that
by Mark dated as early as A. D., 60.   Dr. Furness is quite sure that
even before the crucifixion. and on the very spot where remarkable
incidents were occurring. memoranda were jotted down by intelli-

gent persons present, so thoroughly lifelike often is the style of the
narrative. Thus, written notes of Christ's doings and sayings were
in circulation from the outset of his career. Mark's Gospel, as we
have it, is regarded as the work of a later hand. What he prepared was done under Peter's eye, whose interpreter he was in
missionary labors. Matthew's Gospel is too Messianic to be accepted without considerable allowance. Luke had " richer materials " at his command than the two former, " some of them betray-
ing even more distinctly the increase of the fabulous element." The
fourth Gospel, as we might suppose, is entirely discredited as an
authentic and reliable historical document. It was written long
after the others, by some disciple of John, from " a philosophical
point of view," to exhibit "Jesus only in the brightness of his unbounded preternatural glory." p. 40. Dr. Schenkel gives us the
usual " internal evidence " that his critical acumen has not here
misled him ; as, that the fourth evangelist generally leaves out the
humiliating incidents and shadings of our Lord's life, which the
keynote struck in the first verse required him to do ; that it introduces a peculiar doctrine of Christ's theanthropic nature, is theological in its aim and speculative in its method, and in style wholly
unlike the spirit of the Boanerges whose fiery soul would have had
a much more natural expression in the volcanic explosions of the
Apocalypse. So thinks this biblical reconstructor. Of course, he
would deny the authenticity of the Johannean epistles. He further
contends that it is incredible that Jesus should have spoken so long
a discourse to his followers immediately before his arrest : or that
John could have omitted the account of the instituting of the Supper—therefore, that the fourth Gospel is not his. Neither could the
Bapt st have known enough of Christ to exclaim at so early a date :
" Lo ! the Lamb of God which taketh away the sin of the world ;"
when Jesus himself had not then come to the consciousness of this
office. All this in the critic's regard, belongs to the thought of the
next century. There is much of this kind of logic scattered through
these volumes, the fallacy of which is shown by the patent fact that
the " historic sense " on which it is based is about as various as the
individuals who attempt thus to use it—witness the author and the
translator of this book. Dr. Schenkel thus concludes his argument
upon the authorship of John :

" He has elevated into the region of eternal thought, and invested with
the transfiguring glory of a later century, a selection of reminiscences
from the Christian traditions, taken out of the framework of their history
in time. He has done this with an understanding of the interior being
and the loftiest aim of the life of Jesus, as it could not have been done at

an earlier, and, morally considered, narrower time. The fourth Gospel, therefore, serves as a really historical authority for the representation of the moral being of Jesus, but in a high and spiritual sense of the word. Without this Gospel, the unfathomable depth, the inaccessible height of the idea of the Saviour of the world would be wanting to us, and his boundless influence, ever renewing our collective humanity, would forever remain a riddle. In the several particulars of his development, Jesus Christ was not what the fourth Evangelist paints him, but he was that in the height and depth of his influence; he was not always that actualized, but he was that in truth. The first three Gospels have shown him to us still wrestling with earthly powers and forces. The fourth Gospel portrays the Saviour glorified in the victorious power of the Spirit over his earthly nature. . . . . Our portraiture of him must not disregard the natural, earthly foundation of the first three Gospels, if it aims to be historically real; but it can be an image of Jesus eternally true only in the heavenly splendor of the light which streams from the fourth Gospel." I., 46.

We have given this passage not merely as a favorable sample of this writer's temper and method; but also to say that, in our judgment, the " beloved disciple," softened, elevated, ripened in Christian grace, was inspired of God to compose this Gospel which bears his name, for the very purpose of exhibiting the Son of God in his transfigured, resplendent, divine ascendency over the flesh, and the powers of evil. If the old prophets foretold a triumphant as well as a suffering Messiah, why should we not have that side of his life portrayed as well as the other? We deny that there is any unhistoric self-contradiction in the conception which underlies such a portraiture. We claim its reality, and its necessity to meet the concessions even of this volume. The citation above made admits the moral truthfulness of the Johannean Christ. Can that be morally true which was actually false? Dr. Furness says, that " the intellectual, moral, and religious condition of the Christian world, is at this hour determined by the thoughts which men have of Jesus "; that, " after the lapse of twenty centuries, the great majority of the foremost communities on the face of the globe are accustomed to regard the young man of Nazareth as nothing less than Almighty God himself." Dr. Schenkel says : " It is quite impossible to *believe* in the Christ of the Rationalists. . . . . Rationalism lacks what is wanted in his person, in order to understand . . . the effect which he has produced . . . an original communion with the Divine, the Infinite ; the Divine does not appear as present in him." We maintain, then, contrary to these authors, that there is, and must be, historic as well as moral truth, in this dogma of the divine-human, and that this historic basis is laid in the evangelic narratives, not

alone in the fourth, but as really, if not as fully in the "synoptics."
We have, however, no common ground on which to argue this point
with those who deny the inspiration of these records. But we have
a foothold on which to meet the allegation of the recent and unau-
thentic origin of the fourth Gospel, as held by the school to which
this work belongs.

This Gospel, as written by John, is referred to and quoted from
by Jerome, Eusebius, Tertullian, Clement of Alexandria, Iræneus,
Origen, the Peshito, Polycrates, Tatian, Theophilus of Antioch,
Athenagoras, Apollinaris, the epistle to Vienna and Lyons, Justin
Martyr, Polycarp, the Artemonites, Marcion, Valentinus, Basilides,
the Ophites and Peratæ, and Celsus. These witnesses prove that
the genuineness of this Gospel was a universal tradition and belief
of Christendom so early as "the last quarter of the second century."
Dr. Schenkel labors painfully to set aside this evidence. But even
if he can invalidate some special point of it, nevertheless the fact
remains, that the church of the second century as generally received
this Gospel on equal footing with the other three, as that the enlightened world now believes in the genuineness of Shakespeare's
plays. That fact must be disposed of before such special pleadings as
we have in these volumes can produce conviction. The internal
evidence, supposed to militate with this testimony, can not negative
it, so long as every point of such structural proof is susceptible of a
fair refutation, and has abundantly received it at the hands of such
scholars as Bleek, Brückner, and Ewald. [1] It is a strong argument
for the affirmative of this controversy, that the character given to
our Lord in the fourth Gospel is in perfect harmony with that portrayed in the Pauline epistles, the genuineness of which is not dis-
putable. The main pillar, therefore of Schenkel's theory of Jesus
breaks down in his failure to confine the historical testimony upon
the subject to the first three Gospels.

With the fundamental question of the inspired or uninspired origin of the Gospels in debate between us, it is hardly worth while to
follow up the special criticism of these authors on the evangelic
narratives, as for example, the Jewish genealogies, the relation of
John Baptist and Jesus, the baptism of Christ, and the like. It is
curious, and if the text were an old Greek or Latin classic, it would
be amusing, to note the want of harmony on these points between
these two leaders of the sceptical school of biblicists. We will take
but one topic for an elucidation of this, the Resurrection of our Lord,

---

[1] For a condensed statement of this argument, see Prof. Fisher's Essays on the
Supernatural Origin of Christianity : Chap. II.

merely premising that the original contributor to this book denies the fact of a miracle, while his translator and annotator does not.

Dr. Schenkel finds a strong proof of the priority and superior credibility of Mark's Gospel, in that it makes no mention of the appearance of Jesus after the crucifixion. Our present second evangelist certainly does make this statement ; but the "Urmarcus," we are told, does not. Not having a copy of this at hand, we can not say. It is admitted, that Christ's grave was found empty on the first morning of the week : that Christ's friends were satisfied that he had been seen alive again : but the appearance is held to have been only as to Saul on his way to Damascus—a supersensuous vision, unreal corporeally, but real spiritually and efficiently for purposes of Christian motive, impulse and consolation. Our author thinks the dogma of Christ's bodily re-animation of no value as a foundation for faith either to the apostles or to us ; he discards the idea, but does not give an opinion as to where Christ's body was, after the vacating of the sepulchre. It must have been somewhere. Did the Jews, or the soldiers, or the disciples hold it in custody? What possible value could it have had to either of those parties?

But Dr. Furness comes to the rescue, with this confession :

"For my own part, I am free to confess that it is out of my power to resist the still further conclusion that this unknown person was no other than Jesus himself alive. I feel all the difficulties by which this conclusion is beset. The questions which it raises, I can not answer. Nevertheless, the fact that it was Jesus who was there, and who spoke to the women, is established by evidence, which to my mind is absolutely irresistible. . . . I can not resist the conclusion that Matthew's account must have been written down almost on the spot, and at the time, so visible to me in this narrative is the impress of this childlike simplicity and naturalness, so faithfully does it represent precisely such impressions as were likely to be among the first received." II., 325, 326.

This is creditable alike to the annotator's head and heart. But what shall we say again of the uniformity of the dictates of the "historical sense"? To conclude : we commend these volumes to orthodox students of the Gospels, as furnishing a readable and amiable statement of the position of a numerous body of people who reject the catholic doctrine of Christ's person and character, but shrink from the extreme denials of the ultra-rationalists.

2. — *Charles Wesley, Seen in his Finer and less Familiar Poems.* Riverside Classics. 16mo. New York : Hurd & Houghton. 1867.

THE title of this volume seems rather to invite attention to its author personally than to what he has here written ; or to this as an exponent of himself rather than of his poetical pretensions.   It is difficult, however, so to divide between "the joints and marrow." What strikes us first in these selections from the "above three thousand closely printed pages" of Wesley's poetry (so says the preface) is the vast inequality of their merit.   We pass from page to page of the merest prosaic and mechanical versifying, here and there suddenly to some of those sweetest hymns of devout affection and aspiration which have become familiar to us as our own name, and which have hardly been excelled by the sacred poets of any age or tongue.   But these bear a surprisingly small ratio to the whole ; and if the portentous bulk of the remaining thousands of pages is as chaffy as this, the "less familiar" they continue to be, the better for the author's fame.   We had rather know Charles Wesley in the "finer" specimens of our hymn books, than in this miscellany.

It is a riddle to us how the writer of "Head of the Church Triumphant" ; " Light of those whose dreary dwelling" ; "Hail the day that saw Him rise" ; "Jesus, lover of my soul" ; should ever have brought himself to indite the "Doctrinal and Polemic" contributions to these pages.   Without meaning to be offensive ourselves, we venture to say that there is nothing in the whole range of religious literature more offensive to the Christian spirit and truth, than the long strings of stanzas entitled "The Horrible Decree, and "Predestination."   The heated controversies of the times could furnish no sufficient apology for the utterance of such objurgatory rhymes as these : nor does the editor, in his note of a half dozen lines, at all mend the matter of this theological travesty :

> " The righteous God consigned
>   Them over to their doom.
> And sent the Saviour of mankind
>   To damn them from the womb ;
>   To damn for falling short
>   Of what they could not do,
> For not believing the report
>   Of that which was not true."

> " He gives them damning grace
>   To raise their torment higher,
> And makes his shrieking children pass
>   To Moloch through the fire ;
>   He doomed their souls to death
>   From all eternity
> " This is that wisdom from beneath,
>   That Horrible Decree !"

We omit the whole lines of italics and capitals which, of course meant much to the author in the way of the "thunder and lightning" which the preacher said could not be printed : and content ourselves with expressing our wonder that it should have been thought desirable, for the credit of Wesley, or for the sake of literature or Christianity, to bring up these "bloody bones" from the old theological *abattoir*, and to spread them all out before the public of this day, in this popular series of "classics." As curiosities of polemic warfare, they could have been found by the curious, in the complete editions of Wesleyan standards. We would rather their space had been filled, and so we think their author would *now*, with such excerpts from the "three thousand" and more pages, as this, which has as much poetry and much more sense :

> " What follies abound
> When reason is drowned
> By an heathenish nurse in a torrent of sound !
> When by Satan beguiled
> With sonnets defiled,
> She angers her Maker, to quiet her child."

3. — *Annals of a Quiet Neighborhood.* By GEORGE MACDONALD, M. A. 12mo. New York : Harper & Brothers. 1867.

A MIND accustomed sharply to see what is around it, and to look beneath and beyond the surface of persons and things ; a meditative and also a poetic mind—alike sensible and æsthetic, has filled these pages ; sometimes, however, with more words than the thought demands for its clear expression. This may be set down perhaps to the autobiographical shape which the story has taken, in the person, too, of an aged man, though it is our impression that this writer is not old either in years or authorship. He has a way of sentimentalizing occasionally about natural phenomena and religious feelings, which savors more of the vernal than of the autumnal cycle of life ; "for," as Lord Bacon writes, "there is a youth in thoughts as well as in ages." But, bating a little too much of this rather thin sweetishness, the book has substantial merit. It is Christian in a generally wholesome vein. It seeks to make Christ and the Gospels an every day power in society, a law of character and intercourse among people of all classes. The "annals" are of a country pastor's life among a plain but, it must be allowed, very peculiar set of parishioners. Some highly romantic and dramatic passages are drawn : of course, however, in an old country like England, it all might so have been, though we should hope, for the credit of hu-

manity and the comfort of relatives, there are not many Mrs. Old-
castles.

The writer gives some admirable bits of description, as of the old
mill and its cottage, the long rows of "pollards" seen from the village bridge, and the like. He has made his principal characters
also, very distinct, if not always very attractive. So much the better for the truth's sake. He puts a thought, now and then, in a way
which makes it stick like a burr. Thus: "for I never could believe
that a man who did not find God in other places as well as in the
Bible, ever found him there at all." So this; that "those with
whom the feeling of religion is only occasional, have it most when
the awful or grand breaks out of the common"; as in thunder, avalanche and storms; while, "the meek who inherit the earth find the
God of the whole earth more evidently present in the commonest
things—the quiet fullness of ordinary nature." There are many
fine hints here for a clergyman's guidance: this, among others, that
he "is not a moral policeman," to detect and punish all the wrong
things in his parish; not a policeman at all in the spirit of any part
of his legitimate work. And here is a sentence which strikes us as
worth pondering. The pastor is at the death-bed of a good woman
who has a great dread of being buried—its loneliness and decay.

" Here, let me interrupt the conversation to remark upon the great mistake of teaching children that they have souls. The consequence is, that
they think of their souls as of something which is not themselves. For
what a man *has* can not be himself. Hence, when they are told that their
souls go to heaven, they think of their *selves* as lying in the grave. They
ought to be taught that they have bodies, and that their bodies die, while
they themselves live on. Then they will not think, as old Mrs. Tomkins
did, that *they* will be laid in the grave. It is making altogether too much
of the body, and is indicative of an evil tendency to materialism, that we
talk as if we possessed souls, instead of being souls. We should teach
our children to think no more of their bodies when dead, than they do of
their hair when cut off, or of their clothes when they have done with
them."

There is some false exegesis in this book, as that the "witnesses"
in Heb. xii. 1, are fellow witness-bearers with us to the truth, instead of spectators of a contest, which last interpretation the allusion of the context to the stadium shows to be the right one.

4. — *The Tent on the Beach, and Other Poems.* By JOHN GREEN-
LEAF WHITTIER. 12mo. Boston: Ticknor & Fields. 1867.

OF all American poets, Whittier is rather our favorite. Not so
philosophical as Bryant, he is yet warmer-blooded, more human,
more earthly; not so musical as Longfellow, he is of vastly more

vigor and energy. Uneven and rough as many of his stanzas are, imaginative rather than fanciful, plain, straight-forward and practical, we like the Amesbury Quaker's verse-making.

This volume receives its name from the leading collection of poems which it contains; poems strung together upon the slight thread of having been recited, or by poetic license, having been supposed to be recited, as a small party spent together their leisure hours in " white tent, pitched where sea-winds blew." Most of them are of the narrative character. But in the " Grave of the Lake," the " silent, shy, peace-loving man," ventures upon great questions in theology, where he would, perhaps, have made shipwreck of faith, had it not been for a sweet womanly voice in the company, which checked his natural impulse to peer beneath the veil of the future. The same predisposition to rationalism appears in "The Eternal Goodness," which contains only those aspects of God's character, which are pleasing to minds unrenewed. Evidently, Whittier is looking after the Broad Church.

We transcribe from among many that might as well be taken from this volume, a portion of

THE CABLE HYMN.

O lovely bay of Trinity,
　O dreary shores, give ear!
Lean down unto the white-lipped sea
　The voice of God to hear!

From world to world his couriers fly,
　Thought-winged and shod with fire;
The angel of his stormy sky
　Rides down the sunken wire.

What saith the herald of the Lord?
　" The world's long strife is done;
Close wedded by that mystic cord,
　Its continents are one.

"And one in heart, as one in blood,
　Shall all her people be;
The hands of human brotherhood
　Are clasped beneath the sea.

"Through orient seas, o'er Afric's plain
　And Asian mountains borne,
The vigor of the Northern brain
　Shall nerve the world unborn.

"From clime to clime, from shore to shore,
  Shall thrill the magic thread ;
The new Prometheus steals once more
  The fire that wakes the dead."

Wild terror of the sky above,
  Glide tamed and dumb below !
Bear gently, Ocean's carrier-dove,
  Thy errands to and fro.

Weave on, swift shuttle of the Lord,
  Beneath the deep so far,
The bridal robe of earth's accord,
  The funeral shroud of war !

The poles unite, the zones agree,
  The tongues of striving cease ;
As on the sea of Galilee
  The Christ is whispering, Peace !

5 — *The Women of the Gospels, The Three Wakings, and Other Poems.* By the Author of the Schönberg-Cotta Family. 12mo. New York: M. H. Dodd. 1867.

THESE poems are well written, many of them devotional, and all of them of excellent moral and religious tendency. The author's genius is less abundantly manifest in poetry than in prose. Indeed, it is not the genius, but the high moral tone and apt scriptural allusions of this volume, which render it the most attractive. Here is a specimen which we venture to call

THE TRUE ECONOMIST.

Love is the true economist,
  Her weights and measures pass in heaven ;
What others lavish on the feast,
  She to the Lord himself hath given.

Love is the true economist,
  She through all else to Him hath sped,
And unreproved His feet hath kissed,
  And spent her ointment on his head.

Love is the true economist,
  She breaks the box and gives her all ;
Yet not one precious drop is missed,
  Since on his head and feet they fall.

In all her fervent zeal no haste,
  She at his feet sits glad and calm ;
In all her lavish gifts no waste,
  The broken vase but frees the balm.

Love is truest providence,
  Since beyond time her gold is good,
Stamp'd for man's wear "three hundred pence,"
  With Christ's "She hath done what she could."

Love is the best economist
  In what she sows and what she reaps;
She lavishes her all on Christ,
  And in His, all her being steeps.

6. — *The Baptist Quarterly*; January. Vol. I. No. 1. Philadelphia: American Baptist Publication Society. 1867.

In this new Quarterly we have another proof that an organ of this character is a denominational necessity. Some years ago, our Baptist friends suffered the *Christian Review* to die for want of support; since which time they have been trying to get on by neighboring with other publications of a similar order. But this has not been found to answer, and their Publication Board have now issued the first number of another serial which proposes to devote itself, first, to the special claims of that denomination; and, next to the general interests of the Christian cause.

This number is a fair beginning, and the work deserves the liberal support of the churches and people for whom it is specially intended. We must differ from its makers in the taste of its getting up, as we are obliged to do in some more important matters. The size of the page is largely disproportioned to what will be the thinness of the bound volume, if this instalment is an average one. The type, though just now in fashion, is neither winning or restful to the eye. And the heavy cornice-like ornament, across the page, at the head of each article, is singularly out of keeping with the prescriptive Quarterly style.

7 — *American Leaves*. Family Notes of Thought and Life. By SAMUEL OSGOOD. 12mo. New York: Harper & Brothers. 1867.

THE publisher of *Harper's Monthly* has gathered up from its pages this volume of a dozen or more essays on domestic and social topics. It is well that this kind of writing is winning upon the popular taste, if thus it may come to be somewhat of a substitute for the present voracity for fiction, to which Henry Taylor's description of modern reading-habits is emphatically applicable—" an ostrich racing across a desert." The subjects are common, and are pleasantly treated rather than profoundly, as the sub-title might indicate. They show one danger of magazine-writing—a needless dilution. Had these chapters been composed directly for a book, and not for a monthly, we think that the same ideas would have been compressed into two-thirds the bulk, much to the improvement of the whole. But writing on single topics without much, if any, intention of republication, with no special need of saving space, and perhaps at so much, the page, of a liberal rumuneration, an author is very liable to hold on to a thought much longer than its weight requires. Because novelists are expected, in these days, to know no bounds, it will hardly do for essayists to spin out their light or heavier fancies too verbosely.

Dr. Osgood gives much advice about children, young men and maidens, home-life, business-habits, with excursions into public affairs and church-interests, blending here and there personal incidents, and reminiscences from his own earlier years. Sometimes one mistrusts that the pulpit has helped fill out the essay, not because of any too much religion upon the page, but from the shaping and toning of the discourse. We will venture to say, just here, that we do not think the clerical culture is the best for a true essay-literature. It is apt to run itself into the sermon, if it have no text. An essay does not preach ; it converses. It would be an excellent discipline if clergymen would learn to break up or break down their written style into this easier habit. But, as a general thing, they have succeeded better in novel-writing which admits more of the rhetorical and oratorical—than at the essay ; no very great compliment to be sure.

8 — *The Complete Angler : or, The Contemplative Man's Recreation*, of IZAAK WALTON and CHARLES COTTON. Edited by JOHN MAJOR. 12mo. Little, Brown & Co. Boston. 1867.

ANOTHER edition of this expert and godly fisherman, and the more the better, if as good as this. It has twelve steel engravings, and seventy-four on wood, an elaborate Introduction of thirty-six pages by Mr. Major, the author's addresses to Offley and to the readers, with original and selected Notes, and the Various Readings and General Index.

We class Walton among the English Reformers, as one, who by practice and pen, did much to humanize and evangelize legitimate recreations. For we can apply to angling what Hugh Latimer so well says of shooting : "It is a goodly art, a wholesome kind of exercise, and much commended in physic." By following streams and shores, Walton found a vigorous old age, as he says when he made his will : "Being this present day in the ninetyeth year of my age, and in perfect memory, for which praised be God."

We commend this book to clerical vacationists in the place of any on logic, metaphysics, or the indestructible knots in theology ; and the manual exercises it teaches we commend from long personal experience, as the best gymnasium for dyspeptic, nervous, bronchial and Mondayish difficulties. We speak as a devout and constant disciple of St. Izaac, having been twenty two years in the ministry while we have lost but two Sabbaths from the pulpit in all the time by sickness. Yet we never spent a day at Newport, Saratoga or Cape May. Professional life, so frail and one-sermon-a-day and shortened, needs the out of door treatment of angle and gun and birch canoe. That staunch divine, Jeremy Taylor, states it well :

" Nature's commons and open fields, the shores of rivers and the strand of the sea, the unconfined air, the wilderness that hath no hedge . . . . in these every man may hunt and fowl and fish respectively."

9 — *Daily Hymns: or, Hymns for Every Day in Lent.* E. P. Dutton & Co. Boston. 1867.

GEMS from our best sacred poets, well selected and set for devout purposes. The mechanical execution of the book is very good, and the authors whose names adorn it, will carry the little volume to comfort and elevate many a Christian heart. We are always better fer reading again the choice things of Heber, Procter, Trench, Bonar, just now taking his new harp, St. Bernard, Xavier, Herbert and A. G.

10. — *Ned Nevins, The News Boy : or, Street Life in Boston.* By HENRY MORGAN. Third ed. 12mo. Boston : Lee & Shepard. 1867.

ONE does not care to criticize the literary execution of a book so full of humane and Christian impulses as this. Its impulsiveness is its literary fault—a nervous feverishness which is scarcely healthy. But this is more than excused by the developments of crime and misery which it thrusts upon our notice, as fouling and poisoning our own moral and enlightened metropolis. If the author, whose ministry has lain among this Black Sea of death for years past, shouts and shrieks its horrors into our deaf ears, as if he would wake even the dead, we can pardon his overwrought enthusiasm in so desperate a cause. He shows some skill in handling his materials, and some dramatic power in working up his effects. There is an excess of rhetoric in several rather ambitious attempts at literary display ; but the spirit of the book is thoroughly benevolent and Christian.

On this subject of vicious pauperism in our cities, there is need of light, and urgent appeal. How many thousands of religious and

philanthropic people are there in Boston, who have no conception of
the scenes which are daily and nightly passing within a street, it
may be, of their abode ! It is almost impossible to accredit the undeniable facts of the case. But their continued existence is a
grievous offence against God and man. Practical philanthropists
must take hold of this problem in a different temper than they ever
have, if the evil is to come under effective restraint. In our third
article in this number, a passage from a popular essayist is given,
as to this terrible curse in London, which deserves serious reflection : it is the same sad tale with variations. Meanwhile, such
earnest workers as Mr. Morgan are worthy of highest commendation and generous support in their labors to save these outcasts from
a deeper woe and ruin.

11. — *A Complete Manual of English Literature.* By THOMAS B.
SHAW, M.A. Edited, with Notes and Illustrations, by WILLIAM
SMITH, LL.D. With a sketch of American Literature, by HENRY
T. TUCKERMAN. 12mo. New York : Sheldon & Co. 1867.

A GUIDE to English literature is quite as necessary to the youthful explorer of its "broad land of wealth unknown," as is a handbook of Europe to its traveller. Such a guide should be judiciously
comprehensive and critical—the fruit of ripe, impartial scholarship,
not of one-sided or cliquish study. Mr. Shaw was an accomplished
and successful English teacher. Dr. Smith, who finished and edited
his manuscripts, is the well known author of the Bible and Classical
Dictionaries. The present edition is reprinted from the last and
emended foreign imprint. It is not a book of samples, but a continuous critical estimate of authors from the earliest Anglo Saxon
times. Mr. Tuckerman's supplemental sketch of our authors is
little more than a list of names and titles. His brief criticisms are
certainly not after the ultra-depreciative school just now so ambitious of notice. This kind of writing inversely against space can
not be very satisfactory however well intentioned. The latter part
of the volume is too crowded for great value. The remainder of it
contains, besides much useful information, a large amount of pleasant reading.

12. — *Gems for the Bridal Ring : A Gift for the Plighted and the
Wedded.* Compiled by Rev. J. E. RANKIN. W. J. Holland &
Co. M. H. Sargent, 13 Cornhill, Boston. 1867.

THESE carefully selected, with some original pieces, by the editor,
are a beautiful offering for the newly married. Pastors often wish

such a volume. It is small, yet large enough, and full of happy, suggestive, practical thoughts. A rare good taste has gathered the material from a wide range, and the making up of the volume is highly creditable to the publishers.

13. — *Passages in the Life of the Faire Gospeller, Mistress Anne Askew.* By the Author of "Mary Powell." New York: M. W. Dodd. 1866.

A CHARMING old time book written to-day. The dust of time and the quaintness of Anno Domini 1536 are well put on, and the Puritan seed-sowing in Old England, in "forcing beds" and for transplanting, is done up tenderly and lovingly. The book is a very enjoyable one. This assumed antique writing is a difficult feat in authorship; well done here, less dramatic than in "Mary Powell," but with fewer anachronisms, we think.

14 — *Dickens' Works Illustrated. The Posthumous Papers of the Pickwick Club.* By CHARLES DICKENS. With original Illustrations, by S. Eytinge, Jr. Boston: Ticknor & Fields. 1867.

THE reader of English for many generations to come will enjoy Dickens, and this neat diamond edition, with its many illustrations, will be popular. This author's vivid sketches of the middle, lower and street life of England, with so often a wrong exposed and rebuked, and a virtue cherished, make him a favorite as well as, in a measure, profitable writer. Few have taken a deeper or more abiding hold of the republic of fiction, and this we do not say in a "Pickwickian sense."

15 — *Six Hundred Dollars a Year. A Wife's Efforts at Low Living under High Prices.* Boston: Ticknor & Fields. 1867.

AN exceedingly interesting story of domestic life, showing how limited means, with economy, judgment, cheerfulness and a will, can give almost unlimited comfort to a humble family.

16. — *Studies in English, or Glimpses of the Inner Life of our Language.* By M. SCHELE DeVERE, LL.D., Professor of Modern Languages in the University of Virginia. New York: Charles Scribner & Company. 1867.

THIS work runs on a parallel with those of Müller and Marsh, and of course leads the reader into some of the misty regions of early English history. Briton and Celt, Dane, Saxon and Norman, come on the stage, and out of their polyglott jargon our good Queen's English takes its rise. It is exceedingly interesting to follow the author and watch this genesis of a language, till we see the strong, flexile and world-wide English. To one with any love of the antique, this volume must be fascinating. The style is simple and the drift and development of thought are well illustrated by free citations from old authors. The two chapters, Names of Places, Names of Men, interested us as joining in one so much of the historical, literary and curious; while to the young philologist, Living Words, that is, the chapter on verbs and how they are made, must give much information and excite enthusiasm in the study of our mother tongue.

We welcome the volume as one of the literary first fruits of peace in the Old Dominion. The book grows out of the provision made by Jefferson, in founding the University of Virginia, that the Chair of Modern Languages should furnish a course of lectures on the Anglo Saxon tongue.

17.—*Sermons.* By ALEXANDER HAMILTON VINTON. 12mo. Boston: E. P. Dutton & Co. 1867.

THIS collection of eighteen sermons was first published in 1855, and is now wisely reproduced. They are on eminently practical themes, in the simple, evangelical manner and spirit, so well known and loved in their author. *The Sinfulness of Sin: The Covenant: The Brazen Serpent: Repentance a Privilege: Holiness essential to Salvation: The Christian at Home,—in Church,—in Business,—in Amusements,—in Charities;* are topics that will never weary or become obsolete among Christian readers.

18. -- *The Restoration of Belief.* By ISAAC TAYLOR. A New Edition, Revised with an Additional Section. 12mo. Boston: E. P. Dutton & Co. 1867.

THIS house, so widely and favorably known, have rendered good service to the common interests of Christianity, by a re-issue of this most excellent work. This new edition is timely, when so many, yet craftily calling themselves Christians, are pressing a destructive and Vandal criticism, under the guise of rationalism, to the subversion of the first principles and fundamental facts of Christianity. Every evangelical minister should read this volume, specially its new Section, and then preach three or four sermons on modern theism and infidelity.

19. — *Steps in the Upward Way: The Story of Fanny Bell.* By MARY BARRETT. Boston: American Tract Society.

ANOTHER of this Society's fascinating books for the young. If our children do not read, and with interest and profit, it will not be the fault of this publishing house and their corps of tempting writers.

20. — *The Life and Times of Martin Luther. A History of the Huguenots.* By W. CARLOS MARTYN, Author of "The Life and Times of John Milton." 12mo. New York: American Tract Society.

WE shall never have too many forms of history and biography covering the ground of these two volumes. They are both a happy combination of history, local incidents and biography. In such a form, more than in the elaborate and massive treatise, the people gain a knowledge of the most critical times and leading persons in Christian history.

How much better for a religious press to issue such thrilling and true narratives, wrought into life around great principles, than feeble and ephemeral fiction.

21. — *History of England from the Fall of Wolsey to the Death of Elizabeth.* By JAMES ANTHONY FROUDE, M. A., Late Fellow of Exeter College, Oxford. Reign of Elizabeth. Volume I. 12mo. New York: Charles Scribner & Co. 1867.

MR. FROUDE has fully established his reputation as one of the greatest historians of the age. He surpasses Macaulay in some respects, and Hallam in others. Whoever read the first two volumes has waited impatiently for every subsequent issue, nor has expectation suffered the smallest disappointment. Mr. Froude occasionally reaches conclusions differing somewhat widely from judgments which have been pretty generally accepted, but he is so abundant and so accurate in his references to the best contemporary sources of evidence that, even where we find it impossible to agree with him fully, we are compelled to admit some modification of previous opinions. All historians are prejudiced and partial, doubtless, and so are all readers. Mr. Froude does not sympathize with the religious belief and aims of the great champions of Puritanism in the days of Elizabeth; it is not to be expected therefore, that his judgments of the men should be in strictest accordance with truth, even with the sincere desire and aim to be severely just, for which we give him credit.

It is evident from these volumes that Elizabeth herself was not so large a part of the great events which distinguished her reign as has sometimes been supposed. Perhaps she was all the better fitted for the place she occupied for the very reason that she vaccillated between Popery and Protestantism, and was undecided and hesitating frequently in regard to measures of greatest moment to the interests of Christianity. We must believe that God prepared his own instruments for the working out of his own purposes, even as he so evidently and so singularly balanced the Catholic and Anti-Catholic powers with reference to the same end ; compelling Philip II. of Spain, himself a determined and bitter Papist on the one hand, to help mightily the Protestants of England, by restraining their adversaries, and, on the other hand, to discourage and weaken the Irish Papists by thwarting their political projects ; projects as wise and as much entitled to sympathy and admiration as those which are causing slight inconvenience to the British Government and much damage to Ireland in the present year of grace.

While Elizabeth exhibited her peculiar strength, rather by resisting measures which would have been injurious to the cause of Protestant Christianity, than by directly promoting measures which would have advanced it, the wisdom and sagacity and masterly statesmanship of her chosen Secretary, Sir William Cecil, were every where felt and apparent, and the great moral forces which the Spirit of God had waked up among the people through the reading of Tyndale's Bible were suffered to work in the direction of the Reformation and religious liberty.

The change in the numbering of these volumes is thus explained by Mr. Froude, in the Preface :

" I have made an alteration in the form of the book, for which I must request the indulgence of the public. The accession of Elizabeth is the commencement of a new epoch in the history of the Reformation. There may be persons who, having gone so far with me, may not care to accompany me further; others may be interested in the later and brighter period, who may not care to encumber themselves with the earlier volumes : while the story therefore is continued without interruption, I have made the present publication the commencement as it were of a second work ; and the portion already before the world will be made complete as soon as possible, by the addition of an Index."

22.—*Household Reading. Selections from* THE CONGREGATIONALIST. 1849—1866. Boston : Galen James & Co. 1867.

This volume is highly creditable to the Weekly from which it is selected. Such writing as now goes to make up our religious newspaper press would have stood well beside the Spectator and Rambler in their day. The best authors and their best thoughts, as here seen, are thus made common property for our intelligent masses.

23. — *The Book of Psalms :* Arranged according to the original parallelisms for responsive Reading. New York : Mason Brothers. 1866.

A BROAD page, large and clear type, in Italic, Roman and Capital, and arranged for responsive use in an assembly, or the family. For such an end the volume is well prepared, and those wishing this feature in their church service would find this a book well prepared for them.

24. — *The Great Rebellion.* By JOHN M. BOTTS. 12mo. New York : Harper & Brothers. 1866.

AN egotistical, racy book, by one who was a staunch Union man during the rebellion. He professes to give the " secret history, rise, progress and disastrous failure of this struggle." Although it contains little that has not already been made public through the newspaper press, still the volume is a valuable contribution to the authentic history of the conflict of which it treats.

25.—*Manual of Elementary Logic.* Designed especially for the use of Teachers and Learners. By LYMAN H. ATWATER, Professor of Mental and Moral Philosophy in the College of New Jersey. 12mo. Philadelphia : J. B. Lippincott & Co. 1867.

THE best educational treatises are the productions of practical teachers. This is according to the proverb that " necessity is the mother of invention." And yet the number of even very successful teachers who are capable of producing a valuable text-book in their own particular line of things, is very small. To decide how much of a science should be included in a curriculum, so that the training of students in that department shall bear a proper relation to their acquaintance with other departments embraced in the course, demands a matured and sound judgment on the whole subject of liberal culture. It is just here that many makers of text-books for our High Schools and Colleges fail. Either they exaggerate the comparative importance of their own department, or they fail to consider how much it is possible to do in it without detriment to other branches included in the course. Hence they make too large a book, and so, frequently, a very important part of the work of the teacher is to decide what to use and what to omit. Not a few of our books in use in schools and colleges would be of greatly increased value if considerably reduced in dimensions, provided the reduction were made wisely.

This is what Professor Atwater has done in his " Manual of Elementary Logic." The volume contains two hundred and forty-four pages in beautifully clear, large type, and embraces all that is necessary for a text-book in our American Colleges. It does not profess to present any new contribution to the science of logic, or to be an exhaustive treatise on the subject, but, as the author very modestly says, " to present the great elements of the science in a form suited to the wants of teacher and learner." This the Professor has done, as we judge, most successfully. This " Manual" shows the hand of a master, and will speedily take its proper place, we believe, as a valuable contribution to the cause of liberal education.

26. — *The Rise and Fall : or The Origin of Moral Evil.* 12mo. New York : Hurd & Houghton. 1866.

THE solution of the existence of evil under the government of a wise and benevolent God, is here attempted by a novel process. The scene in Eden, according to the author of this scholarly book, who very modestly conceals his name, is in no proper sense a " fall," but a " rise. ' In it God presents to his creatures the query whether they will be free moral agents. By partaking of the tree of knowledge, they accept this proposed elevation. The author argues that moral agency was not needful to man at the outset ; that God might prefer to make this moral agency the consequence of man's own act ; that his moral agency at creation is never asserted in the Scriptures ; and then goes on in his attempt to show how his theory relieves the subject of difficulty. We can not say that he succeeds. By thus making the Creator's relation to the moral character of his creatures indirect, we do not see how this author's theory is essentially different from those usually held.

27. — *The Draytons and the Davenants : A Story of the Civil War.* By the Author of " The Schönberg-Cotta Family." 12mo. New York : M. W. Dodd. 1866.

THE Draytons and the Davenants are two families, one Puritan, and the other Cavalier, and the author weaves into her narrative respecting them many of the facts and scenes of actual history. We need not say that this is done with great skill and interest, and that the reader will be richly repaid for the perusal of the book. It is second only to the volume from which the author has derived her principal reputation.

28. — *Hopefully Waiting, and Other Verses.* By ANSON D. F. RANDOLPH. New York : Charles Scribner & Co. 1867.

THIS small volume is filled up with very simple and unpretending verses, by one who has done much to circulate the poetical effusions of others. By it religious feeling will be quickened, religious faith inspired, and the most delicate taste will not be offended.

29. — *Religious Poems.* By HARRIET BEECHER STOWE. With illustrations. Boston : Ticknor & Fields. 1867.

THIS is one of the most exquisitely printed and illustrated collections of poems which have come to us this season. We do not think that poetry is Mrs. Stowe's highest sphere. But some of these hymns and poems are exceedingly beautiful. "Knocking" is our favorite.

We admire Mrs. Stowe for her fidelity to the rights of man, and wish she had always been as true to what we regard the interests of evangelical religion. In this respect, we do not reckon her as " of us." Mrs. Stowe has been led by esthetic or other tendencies away from " the church without a bishop."

30.—*Home-Songs for Home-Birds.* Gathered and Arranged by Rev. WM. P. BREED, D.D. Philadelphia ; Presbyterian Board of Publication.

A VERY choice selection of hymns and poems about children and for them. The binding is very plain, and the book cheap ; put up for use and not at all for ornament. The only fault we find is, that the names of authors are in almost no case annexed to their productions.

31. — *Why Delay ?* By JACOB HELFENSTEIN, D.D. *Free Salvation.* By BENNET TYLER, D.D. *Conversion and Experience of President Edwards. Doctrinal Knowledge the foundation of True Religion.* By JACOB IDE, D.D. *The Bible on Baptism, or The Scripture Directory to Baptism.* By A LAYMAN. Congregational Board of Publication. Boston : H. M. Sargent.

PORTABLE little volumes, excellent in matter and convenient in form for travellers, and for those who go about doing good, in the footsteps of their Lord.

32. — MISCELLANEOUS. *The Blue Book Stories.* By Harriet F. Woods. Boston Tract Society. *Lucy and Bell, or, How they overcame.* Do. Interesting and good for our little folks. *Charlie Scott, or, There is Time Enough yet. Food for Lambs, or a Selection of Texts, for Young Children.* New York Tract Society. Two excellent Books to go on a catalogue of juvenile literature. The latter is an enlarged Daily Food for a child.

Anthropos. By the Rev. W. P. Breed, D.D. *The One Talent, and Other Tales. Emily Sherwood, or, The Girl who had a disagreeable Temper. The First Temptation, and Other Tales.* Presbyterian Board of Publication. The Publications of this House we are always able to speak of with commendation. "Anthropos" is a scholarly analysis of man in his nature, and relations to his fellow-men and God.

ARTICLE X.

THE ROUND TABLE.

OUR NEW PLANS AND NEW EDITORS. The inviting providences of God and the Holy Spirit, working in the hearts of Christians, are uniting the friends of Christ for a common cause. Less for sects and schools, and more for the Lord, is now happily the growing, leading thought among evangelical bodies. This feeling, almost universal in our own denomination, is marking the years just now as an epoch in Congregationalism. Yielding gladly to this new and, we think, divine tide in our religious affairs, we have undertaken to fit this *Review* to meet all the varied and wide-spread wants of our denomination, so far as a *Quarterly* may be expected to do it, and at the same time, keep its pages in harmonious co-working with all who labor for a pure faith, a holy church, a sanctified literature, and an evangelized land.

To do this, we are enlisting the best writers that can be had from all parts of our extended field, and we intend that all our local necessities, as well as general interests, shall be well observed and cared for. And that *The Congregational Review* may have a management as wide and as comprehensive as the denomination itself, we have added three strong names to our Editorial force. We take them from the West, because we well know that there are the hidings of power for the church of Christ in America. Happily we are permitted to associate with us men whose names only need to be mentioned: the REV. GEORGE F. MAGOUN, President of Iowa College, Grinnell, Iowa; the REV. A. L. CHAPIN, President of Beloit College, Beloit, Wisconsin; and the REV. H. M. STORRS, D. D., Cincinnati, Ohio.

CHURCH UNION. A strict Baptist once asked us, in a promiscuous crowd of by-standers, if we did not regard the apostolic churches as the model of all Christian churches? Divining his expected triumph, we promptly and flatly replied: "No—not the apostolic church, but the church in heaven, is the pattern for all churches of Christ, and there is no close-communion there." Our purpose was answered in turning the general laugh upon the over-confident and rather presuming interrogator. But, in proper circumstances, we should have no hesitancy in giving an affirmative to this question ; for we are thoroughly persuaded that no fair interpretation of the New Testament can afford any support to Baptist or Episcopal exclusiveness : which leads us to say, that the present attempt to bring about a visible unity of evangelical churches by interchange of pulpits, sitting together on platforms, and so forth, is entirely too superficial, so long as, on the one side, a monopoly of ordination-rights, and, on the other side, an exclusive church-title, are assumed. The basis of the real union, which our Lord prayed for, must be laid in the admission of ministerial and church parity, among his disciples, as organized bodies. This may not demand the giving up of denominational forms ; but it does demand that the denominations recognize each other's equal standing as Christian churches. Anything less than this only publishes, to intelligent observers, the inconsistency of the exclusives. If a Baptist pastor asks a Congregational neighbor to preach his ante-communion sermon, and then denies him the sacramental emblems, it may be a very good exercise of Christian magnanimity for the Congregationalist to accept the courtesy, and forget the affront which is real though not intended. If an Episcopal rector so far slips his neck out of the prelatic yoke as to be willing to exchange pulpits with a Presbyterian, while he would not receive the Lord's Supper from the hands of his brother because not " in the succession," it may or may not be well enough to make this pretence of an ecclesiastical unity, which may indeed be a unity of the spirit. But more than this it is not : we hardly see how, when it goes no further, it can be even this. These exclusive assumptions directly oppose a hearty love among brethren. This doubtless exists, but it is in spite of these hindrances.

We would not throw an obstacle in the way of those who are laboring to unite God's people in closer bonds. Perhaps this working on the outside of things may in time strike in to the centre, and effect that radical unification for which we contend. We must be one in the greater facts of our church-life, or these lesser fraternizations will not amount to much. Granted that we have the same Spirit of Christ, it is indispensable that no church organized under his authority shall lay claim to an exclusive right either to administer or to receive the sacraments of the New Testament.

We have designedly left the question of denominations open in these paragraphs, not that we consider it unimportant, but it is not vital as are these other considerations. It will be time enough to take up the subject of amalgamating the various evangelical churches into one polity and form of worship, when we shall have removed these preliminary barriers to Christian communion. Let us here say, that the recently advocated theory of our Baptist brethren in defence of their limited fellowship, which would divide this indivisible idea into " a Christian and a sacramental fellowship," is more ingenious than sound. The discovery is this ; that all believers in our Lord are to be admitted to the " Christian" degree of brotherhood, but that any church has the right, on what it deems a scriptural warrant, to establish an interior or " sacramental" degree of fellowship to which it will receive those who comply with its initatory formulas, and no others. This we regard as a mere special plea to save an indefensible point. We do not believe in any such " masonry" inside Christ's house. We find no hint of it in the Bible. It has, to our Christian sense, an exceedingly offensive look. Are we to adopt the notion that any sort of sacramental observance is a holier thing than a genuine experimental communion with Christ, the Head? This position must be taken, or else, going to the other extreme, it must be held that the Christian sacraments are only a kind of secret society pass words—the ceremonial of the locked and curtained lodge-room of the church. We see no third position ; and either of these are any thing but apostolical. We may have more to say on this new invention.

Since writing the above, we have alighted on the following recent deliverance of Albert Barnes, with which we rivet our protets :

" I am wholly in favor of *Union* in the church ; but I see no way to accomplish it, or to make any progress towards it, until the Baptists and Episcopalians *recede* from their exclusiveness, and recognize the ministers of other denominations as true ministers, and other churches as true churches, and *then* all will be clear. I think, therefore, the work must begin with them, and until this is done, I have no hope of any *real* union."

. NEGLECT OF THE LORD'S SUPPER. The indifference to this sacrament of Christ's enjoining, thus complained of by the *Christian Register*, does not surprise us. It may be taken, we suppose, as an average statement of Unitarian feeling and practice upon this subject.

" So long as this want of interest continues in our religious societies, the communion service can never be what it ought ; and if some change can not be made, if the many who refuse to join in the service, and yet are as interested in Christianity as those who do, will not come in and make it what, with their aid, it may become, will not the result be the abandoning the service altogether? The ministers are willing to help the people in any way in which the people believe they can be helped. But when only half a dozen out of every hundred in the churches join in this service, while three fourths of those who do not are just as well fitted as those who do, it is not strange that pastors become discouraged and dissatisfied. If so many of those without the service are able to come as near the Christian mark as do many others with it, it is not surprising that the question is asked: Is the service worth retaining?   Therefore, what this service is to be in the future depends, almost entirely, upon the people.   If it comes to be wholly neglected, it will be the fault of the congregation; for no earnest man ought to be required, or be expected, to minister to his people in a form or ceremony in which they see no life or meaning."

This would seem to be a direct and inevitable result of the doctrine held by that denomination respecting the person and work of our Lord.   He said: "Do this in remembrance of me."   In remembrance of what?   And it is answered: Of a very exemplary, truthful, heroic human life and death; through the moral force of which example of goodness and self-denial, men are to work out their own salvation.   A view of Christ like this, so nearly on a level with our valuation of the better class of earthly benefactors, necessarily lowers the idea of the church and its sacraments to little, if any thing, more than a human organization for hilanthropic ends, with one or two ceremonials of no special sacredness or obligation. A ritualistic formalism may keep up the observance of this ordinance as a mechanical means of grace; but a form of Christianity which relies upon spiritual agencies of sustentation and progress, must put into this sacrament the truth of a vicarious redemption; a discerning by its partakers of the Lord's body crucified for their salvation—if it is to have any strongly attractive power, any "life or meaning."   Inviting any body, moreover, who chooses to come to this communion, is the straight road to its desertion by every body. We do not wish to comment on this confession of our contemporary further than to call attention to its singular, yet not strange revelations.   It betrays a central and radical error in the Unitarian Christology.   It proclaims an absence of dissimilarity between the churches and the world, which is utterly irreconcilable, so far as we can see, with the essential nature of the Gospel.   If three fourths of those who do not join in this service are just as well fitted for it as "the half dozen out of every hundred" who do, what has become of the—"Ye are not of the world"?

THOROUGHNESS.   The old builders finished the inner surfaces of all their work as carefully as the outer; flower, leaf, and every ornamental device bearing closest inspection as far as chisel or eye could go; for they were building for the eye and the glory of God who sees all around and through every thing.   They did not believe in lath and plaster stone walls.

THE CIVIC CROWN.

In the ancient Roman state
Grandly noble, calmly great,
When in battle-hour, a slave
Did the life of warrior save,
Then for that, with gen'rous strain,
Did they break the bondman's chain.

When in forum he appeared,
Senate rose and people cheered ;
And they bound his head with bay,
Freed his father, old and gray,
Freed his children, freed his wife,
For that single rescued life.

Better is a Roman's life,
Than a nation saved in strife ?
Than a future proud, redeemed,
When the future hopeless seemed ?
Can a faithful state forget
Whom she owes this untold debt ?

Shall we to the vow be true ?
Less than Romans can we do ?
Wagner, Pillow ; shall each name
Publish treachery and shame ?
Shall the blood of outraged Shaw
This sweet vengeance fail to draw ?

Beat the false opinion down,
Give the man the civic crown ;
Be he red or be he white,
Be he black as blackest night,
Did our banner o'er him float,
Let him have the freeman's vote.

By the blood so nobly shed,
By the great unnumbered dead,
By the living and their woes,
Bring the conflict to a close ;
Beat the false opinion down,
Give the man the civic crown !

NOT THE RIGHT BECAUSE. In the opening paragraph of an able article in one of our recent evangelical Quarterlies, occurs a " because" which we are inclined to challenge : it is this :

" There is little resemblance between the theism of Theodore Parker, which rejects the Bible because it seems to make God less real and present among men than in the apostolic and patriarchal ages, and the deism of David Hume which denied all divine care and oversight."

Whatever may have been the difference between the scepticism of these persons, the cause above assigned to Mr. Parker's aberrations is new to us, and as we think erroneous. For, how could he or any one know any thing about the intercourse of God with men in "apostolic and patriarchal" times except from the Bible which he rejects "because" it makes God less, " less real and present among men" than—it does. This is not logic. Further ; Mr. Parker spent a large part of his force in reviling or decrying these very narratives of the patriarchal interviews with Deity : as, where he represents Jacob "driving a sharp trade with Elohim," in the vision of the ladder at Bethel ; and satirizes God as " dining on veal with Abraham." We do not see how Jehovah could be more "real and present among men" than here. If Mr. Parker had information of such increased familiarity over and above these accounts, which led him to disparage the Scripture records, one would like to know where he obtained it. Our opinion is that his deistic "'theism" did not spring from the fact that the Bible makes God too little " real and present among men," but *because* it brings him so closely around all our ways, in his " infinite, eternal and unchangeable being, wisdom, power, holiness, justice, goodness, and truth."

REMARKABLE DISCOVERY. Ours is an age of remarkable discoveries, but the most remarkable of them all, as we suppose, was announced in the January number of the *North American Review.* It is, that Daniel Webster was not a great man. We were pained in reading it, although we do not at all question that it was the duty of the discoverer to make the thing known. We intend to adjust ourselves and our ideas to the actual fact just as fast, and with just as good a grace, as we can. It is very important to know who are the great men, and, however unpleasant it may be to us personally, our pages shall always be open to set the world right in such a matter, and to keep it right. When a little man thinks himself to be great, as sometimes happens, that is of no particular consequence, though it may be amusing, because the whole thing will very soon be forgotten. But it is quite another affair when all the world thinks a man great, as was the case in relation to our countryman, and, lo, he is small, or, at least, only about middling, as this individual in the *North American Review* has discovered. We mean to comfort ourselves as well as we can, under this singular discovery, by two considerations: one, that the illusion, or whatever you call it, was very pleasant while it lasted ; and the other, that mankind generally were under the same. Daniel Webster certainly looked like a great man. Nobody can deny that. Even the arrogant and jealous *London Quarterly* said of him when he was in England, that his appearance was " striking, and even grand." Certainly it is very pleasant to think that where appearances are grand, realities are grand also. We are not old, yet we can remember when every body in our country believed Daniel Webster to be a great man, and when anybody who had called it in question would have been thought worthy of as much attention as if he had affirmed that Niagara was not much of a waterfall. He was believed to be a great lawyer, a great statesman, a great diplomatist, and a great orator. Even his enemies never called it in question. And it was just as readily conceded in England, and the States of Europe, as by ourselves.

Yet it was all a mistake! Daniel Webster was not great. We have it on the authority of this individual who writes for the *North American Review*. Neither does he simply assert it, but advances bravely to the proof. This is various, but, if we understand him aright, he rests mainly on the fact that, to the end of his days, Daniel Webster did not abjure the Puritan faith of his father and mother! He says (this writer in the *North American Review*) that all great men are doubters, and Daniel Webster was not a doubter ; therefore Daniel Webster was not a great man! Does he mean to say, that if our illustrious countryman had struggled his way through dark labyrinths of agonizing religious doubt to a full and joyous conviction that the faith of John Calvin was eternal truth, then his claim to greatness would have been vindicated, so far as that matter was concerned? Oh, not at all, for he talks about his having worn the "shackles" of his father's and mother's faith to the end of his days. Now we understand. Daniel Webster was not an infidel, therefore Daniel Webster was not a great man! Which is to say, the faith which shook England and the continent of Europe in the 15th century, which made and unmade kings, which changed the wilderness of New England to the garden of God, and gave to this entire American Republic all in which has ever consisted its truest glory and its greatest strength, the faith of Martin Luther and John Milton and Jonathan Edwards, is too narrow and weak to command the assent of great

minds! Such is the miserable puling cant of the men who deify
Aaron Burr, and Tom Paine, and Strauss and Theodore Parker,
while they pluck the crown from the head of Jesus Christ, and
change the Bible to a cunningly devised book of fables.

HISTORICAL INVENTIONS AND DISCOVERIES. It is becoming ex-
citing to follow our antiquarian experts. It is like watching an
Angelo chipping out a Moses from the rough limestone to see Mr.
Froude manufacturing a new Harry Tudor for the hero-gallery.
How deftly he finishes and polishes off the curves and angles. We
are thankful that he has not canonized either the Scottish or the
Bloody Mary. We had heard of some curious successes in this
line, abroad, upon such almost forgotten subjects as Cataline and
Cleopatra; there is still large store of material for similar exploits
among those old pagans. But it is startling to find such eleventh
hour conversions so near home. One begins to wonder at what
may not happen to some of our more modern Catalines and Clodi-
uses, by and bye. Possibly, however, the conversion may be the
other way. Macaulay's damaging of William Penn's character has
not yet been repaired; and Mr. Bancroft has made work of the same
sort for several families of indignant grand children, which is likely
to consume much ink and amiability. We even hear that a just now
quite popular magazinist of the biographical species has myste-
riously hinted that he has materials on hand sufficient to knock the
pedestal from under George Washington's fair fame, and drop that
national idol also into the dust of dishonor. Guard us, ye powers,
from such a Herculean club!

But whatever may be in store for our illustrious first President's
good name, a British antiquary seems to have demonstrated that
the currently accepted genealogy of his family, as given for instance
in Irving's Memoirs, is wholly erroneous: that, instead of coming
from the Sulgrave Washingtons of Northamptonshire, his pedigree
was of quite different stock. This is not so ominous as the other
adumbration; for, we presume a respectable ancestor will be found
in due time, for so famous a descendant. Yet the recent fate of the
Pochahontas-John Smith romance, of which not so much as "the
baseless fabric of a vision" seems to be left, tends rather to unsettle
faith in Old Virginian pretensions, it must be confessed. We little
know now what a new weekly, monthly, quarterly, or book will
bring forth: but the *mus ridiculus* family is certainly as prolific as
ever.

POPERY IN ECLIPSE. This church is undergoing the reverse of
the process which turned the winter of Gloster's discontent into

glorious summer. It is going into a very arctic eclipse. France is no longer its sun or its shield. Austria, Spain, Germany have not in them even the light or warmth of the moon for this shivering, withered, outcast " mistress" of kings and emperors. That word is her fearful condemnation. She thought to open a new source of help and power in Mexico through French machinations ; she hopes to, in Britain and in our Republic, through Protestant apostasies. But, whatever is in the future of Romanism, this is settled, that the Pope hereafter is to be a subject of the civil state ; whether in Italy, or in what other land he may take up his celibate habitation ; that he can no longer himself be a temporal prince, and fountain of secular law. Whatever promises to the contrary the Catholic powers may make him, they have not the means at command to fulfil any such pledges against the protest of reconstructed Italy. He comes down from the standing of a European king to that of a citizen-bishop. How much lower he may have to come, God alone knows. But, as we read the foreign bulletins now, we are struck with the prophetic foresight of the author of the Divina Commedia, six hundred years ago, who thus foreshadowed our current history of the events at Rome :

> " Thy city. plant
> Of him. that on his Maker turned the back,
> And of whose envying so much woe hath sprung,
> Engenders and expands the cursed flower,
> That hath made wander both the sheep and lambs,
> Turning the shepherd to a wolf.   For this,
> The Gospel and great teachers laid aside
> The decretals, as their stuffed margins show,
> Are the sole study.   Pope and Cardinals.
> Intent on these. ne'er journey but in thought
> To Nazareth. where Gabriel oped his wings.
> Yet it may chance, ere long, the Vatican,
> And other most selected parts of Rome,
> That were the grave of Peter's soldiery,
> *Shall be delivered from the adulterous bond* " [1]

Dante was a reformer, inside the pale of the Papacy, long before the reformation. He fearlessly told many abominable truths about that "mystery of iniquity" when it was at the height of its tyranny. Many more of its popes and bishops he found in the infernal and purgatorial worlds than in Paradise, where doubtless they still are. The last line of our citation, which we have italicised, is just at present being *italicised* in a way which would have given wondrous joy to the great poet's thoroughly Italian heart.

[1] Paradise, book IX. Cary's Translation ; who refers the " him," in line 2. to Satan ; and explains "the cursed flower"—of the Florentine coin, the floren ; " the covetous desire of which has excited the Pope to so much evil."

THE

CONGREGATIONAL REVIEW.

VOL. VII.—JULY, 1867.—No. 37.

—————

ARTICLE I.

JUSTIFICATION AND SANCTIFICATION.

WE have placed these two titles in this connection for the sake of indicating, with precision, the differences between the doctrines which they represent. These differences are not generally apparent to the popular mind, nor always to the theologically instructed. They are not speculative differences, but relate to distinct facts. They are not unimportant differences, but, on the other hand, of gravely practical character.

Both Justification and Sanctification respect the facts of sin and salvation. But they bound these, so to speak, on opposite sides. They alike belong to the Christian soteriology; but their relation in this is as antecedent and consequent, as the staple and its depending chain.

The very common confusion which regards these acts or experiences as substantially identical, has several causes. They both have the same final purpose, which is human salvation. They are not separated initially, in point of time, but are connected, as a river with its fountain. Each is a divine operation, in general terms. Thus they are taken to be the same, or parts of the same, thing. To these sources of confusion must be added a crude but extensive misconception of the essential law of the religious life—that it is making people better in physical development, personal habits, culture of intellect and taste, toning of the affections, control of the will; ed-

ucating them out of one stage of civilization into a higher. To
such a view of "the spiritual man," these biblical terms, which
we are discriminating, mean nothing more than a general reformation of manners and feelings. The first is wholly obsolete—
one of the dryest of the stuffed skins of the theological museum.
The second is kept as a convenient pietistic name of what after
all is considered a very natural transition ; to gratify good people who are mystically inclined, and to meet the occasional exigencies of stimulated religious sensibilities.

This obscuring of the motive forces and essential nature of
the Christian life, finds an ally in a somewhat prevalent dislike,
even among Christians themselves, to a close analysis of the
doctrines of grace. The unmeaning antithesis of which we
have heard so much—that Christianity is a life and not a doctrine, which is much the same as saying, that man is a soul and
not a body—has helped to confound yet more the justifying and
the sanctifying grace of God. The fashion is, to take salvation
in mass, and not to study its details ; to appropriate redemption
as a whole, without separating its action into its several stages.
This very unintelligent way of treating a subject of such explicit divine revelation, is little worthy the gravity of the theme,
however in keeping with the surface thinking of the day upon
all save material interests. Not to pause here upon this suggestive topic, there is one other cause of an indistinct conception of these correlated truths, which has a profounder root.

Theological science has approached the question of human
salvation through two main avenues : whether to find, in this,
a remedy for human guilt, or human corruption. Regarding
redemption mainly as an antidote for the corruption of the soul
through sin, the mind will fasten mostly upon the work of the
Holy Spirit as the agent of spiritual purification ; his re-creating
power will become its absorbing idea of the new life in man ;
and while it does not set aside the justifying act of God, it will
hardly escape the error of considering the soul's justification as
only the first stage of its sanctification, and as partly depending
on this, instead of the necessary introduction to its sanctification. This, as Professor Shedd explains in his History of
Christian Doctrine, was the mistake of Augustine, as it had
been of many of the Greek theologians. Not overlooking the

guilty perverseness of the will of fallen man, he was led, both from his own early profligacy, and by his controversy with the Pelagian dogmas of human native innocency and recuperative forces, more especially to contemplate the need " of the soul's renovation by divine influence. . . . The need of grace in the form of a renewing, strengthening, and purifying power, had been very vividly and painfully felt by him." Thus he came to confuse justification with sanctification through this attraction of his attention to " that side of the general doctrine of redemption which relates to the delivery of the soul from the power and pollution, as distinguished from the guilt and condemnation, of sin"; a defect which both Luther and Calvin detected and exposed in the writings of that theological leader of the Latin church, and from which a better understanding of Holy Scripture and fallen human nature saved his successor Anselm.[1]

This, then, is our guiding clue. Justification respects directly the bearing of our Saviour's expiatory atonement upon the guilt of man, the sinner. Sanctification respects directly the purifying influence of God the Holy Ghost upon the corruption of the human soul. Guilt is specifically the basis or cause of our condemnation as wilful violators of the law of God. It is that for which God's justice arraigns us at his sovereign bar, and on which the sentence of punishment has gone forth. Corruption is the taint, the contamination of moral evil in us. Guilt belongs to a wicked self-will opposing God's supreme will. Corruption inheres in the passions, appetites, affections —the sensuous nature thus vitiated into the sensual. It is the office of the Justifier to set us right on the point of past disloyalty, before the Lord, the King. It is the office of the Sanctifier to cleanse us from all impurity and iniquity.

---

[1] Thomas Aquinas, following Augustine, and advancing upon his positions, held that justification was not only the acquittal of the sinner from punishment, but also the *"infusio gratiæ,"* infusion of divine life into the soul. This shaped the Romish doctrine thenceforward. Among Protestants, Osiander (1498—1552) represented justification and sanctification as forming only one act; but, though the controversy was vehement for many years, and this view was ably defended, it gained no permanent foothold in the Reformed churches. Within the last century, the liberalizing of the Continental and Anglo Saxon theology, in many quarters, has again obscured or obliterated these distinctions. v. Hagenbach's History of Doctrines. Dr. H. B. Smith's Ed.: Vol. II. Index: "Justification."

To reduce this discrimination to yet minuter detail : Justification is a judicial or forensic *act* of God's grace, declarative of our re-instatement in his favor.   It is a single act, never repeated in the same person ; while sanctification is a continuous *work* of God's grace in the spirit of man once justified.

Justification rests upon Christ's righteous sacrifice in our behalf, as the Atoner, and upon this alone ; contrary to those primitive fathers who made the grace divinely produced in man a part of his justifying cause ; and contrary to the Papal doctrine which extends that cause to saintly intercessions, and the whole trumpery of anti-Christian self-righteousness.   Through sanctification, we become righteous by the help of the Spirit of God who dwelleth in us.   In justification, sin is pardoned : in sanctification, holiness is begun, and is increased as sin is subdued.   This distinction is not to be set aside because the after process of the subdual of unrighteousness in the believer, must be carried onward through frequent repetitions of forgiveness.   No subsequent act of pardon is like that first deliverance of the contrite soul from condemnation.

Justification is complete and perfect within itself.   Sanctification is never perfected until probation gives place to glory.

As related to associated doctrines, justification stands nearest, in this, to regeneration, that regeneration is the birth of the soul into the new life, and justification is the formal recognition of the fact.   Sanctification comes closer, in its nature, to conversion, which enfolds the human agency of this transformation, and, unlike regeneration, may be repeated in the soul's experience.   But sanctification, again, resembles regeneration in that the efficient agency of both is the inward moving of the Holy Ghost.   Regeneration, conversion, sanctification, coalesce at this point, and in this logical order.   Regeneration and justification, in like manner, harmonize in being single, finished, never repeated acts of God.   Faith, too, is essential to both justification and sanctification : to the first—not as any part of its procuring cause ; only, as a condition precedent of its reception : to the second, as an active means of its progress.   But the faith and the repentance, which are saving, are alike referable, in their origin, to the grace and gift of God.

The biblical authority for these definitions and distinctions, is found in a large collection of texts from the Old and New Testaments, compared with each other, and interpreted in the light of strict grammatical construction, and of the logical requirements of the citations. These scriptural references are furnished in the larger catechisms, and more complete manuals of doctrine prepared for churches, and for Bible-class study. As our purpose is rather a statement than an argument, we omit giving these references, and will now furnish the reader a few of the formulas in which these doctrines are expressed in the symbols of the churches.

The Westminster divines, who are followed by the Presbyterian and Congregational churches of this country, thus teach :

" Justification is an act of God's free grace, wherein he pardoneth all our sins, and accepteth us as righteous in his sight, only for the righteousness of Christ imputed to us and received by faith alone."

" Sanctification is the work of God's free grace, whereby we are renewed in the whole man after the image of God, and are enabled more and more to die unto sin, and live unto righteousness."

In this formula, the imputation of the righteousness of Christ to believers in him, is the affirmation that Christ's work of atonement is the sole ground on which the pardoned sinner is reckoned or accounted just before God.

The Heidelberg Catechism, which is the symbol of the Reformed churches of Holland and Germany, and of their descendants in the United States, is more paraphrastic.

" *Ques :* How art thou righteous before God?

" *Ans :* Only by a true faith in Jesus Christ . . . . God, without any merit of mine, but only of mere grace, grants and imputes to me the perfect satisfaction, righteousness and holiness of Christ; even so, as if I never had, nor committed any sin ; yea, as if I had fully accomplished all that obedience which Christ hath accomplished for me, inasmuch as I embraced such a benefit with a believing heart.

" *Ques :* Why sayest thou that thou art righteous by faith only?

" *Ans :* Not that I am acceptable to God on account of the worthiness of my faith ; but only because the satisfaction, righteousness and holiness of Christ is my righteousness before God, and that I can not receive and apply the same to myself in any other way than by faith only."

Professor Schaff, who has made this venerable Confession of
Faith the basis of the catechism which he has prepared for his
countrymen in America, thus condenses these doctrines of (*a*)
Justification and (*b*) Sanctification :

(*a*.) " The act of God, by which he pardons all our sins,
and applies to us the righteousness of Christ.

(*b*.) " Our continual growth in grace through the indwelling
and power of the Holy Spirit, until we attain perfection in
Christ Jesus." To which he appends this discriminating note :
" The grace of God is the efficient primary *cause* of justification, the merits of Christ the *producing* cause or (objective)
ground ; faith is the (subjective) *condition* on the part of man,
or the instrument and organ of its appropriation. Justifying
faith is not only a knowledge of the grace of God in Christ,
but also a hearty confidence in the same, and a living union of
the soul with Christ, so that we become partakers of his merits,
and all his benefits." [1]

The doctrine now more commonly received in New England,
regards " the satisfaction," rather than " the satisfaction, righteousness, and holiness," of Christ as the ground of justification :
maintaining that his sufferings rather than his righteousness, his
death rather than his holy life, is our expiation. Yet, as the Scriptures speak of his becoming " obedient unto death," it might
scripturally be held that his voluntary self-offering on the cross
was as really his righteous obedience as was his triumph over
Satan in the desert ; that his utter absorption in the will of
Deity in bowing his head and yielding up the ghost, was as essentially his holiness as was the spirit which held him in communion with God all night in prayer upon the mountain. The
Reformers took a distinction between Christ's active or living,
and passive or dying obedience,[2] in their generally accepted
doctrine of the vicariousness of his entire work in the flesh for
human redemption, which is the prevalent, but not universal,
teaching of the Protestant churches of the present day. It was

[1] Dr. G. W. Bethune, in Expository Lectures on the Heidelberg Catechism, gives
this interpretation of that symbol. " Thus the Catechism : ' God grants and imputes
to me the perfect satisfaction (that is, the expiation), righteousness (that is, the
obedience), and holiness (that is, the acceptableness) of Christ.' . . . God gives to
the believer the legal consequences " of this, " he has the benefit of it as much as if
it were his own." Vol. II. pp. 156—158.

[2] V. Hagenbach's History of Doctrines. Vol. II. 354, 355.

the original New England position.   In the Boston Confession
of 1680, adopted into the Saybrook symbol of 1708, it is ex-
plicitly laid down, that the basis of the sinner's justification is
" Christ's active obedience unto the whole law, and passive
obedience in his sufferings and death."   And again : " Christ,
by his obedience and death, did fully discharge the debt of all
those that are justified, and did by the sacrifice of himself, in
the blood of his cross, undergoing in their stead the penalty due
unto them, make a proper, real, and full satisfaction to God's
justice in their behalf : yet, inasmuch as he was given by the
Father for them, and his obedience and satisfaction accepted in
their stead, and both freely, not for any thing in them, their
justification is only of free grace, that both the exact justice
and rich grace of God might be glorified in the justification of
sinners."   So the elder Edwards, with strong emphasis ; but
less distinctly the younger Edwards.   In his writings appear
the beginnings of the departure from this ground, by our divines, which was fully made by the Hopkinsian writers.   While
discarding, on metaphysical grounds, the distinction between
Christ's active and passive obedience, President Edwards says :
" There is the very same need of Christ's obeying the law in
our stead, in order to the reward, as of his suffering the penalty of the law in our stead, in order to our escaping the penalty ; and the same reasons why one should be accepted on our
account, as the other.   There is the same need of one as the
other, that the law of God might be answered." . . . "As there
is the same need that Christ's obedience should be reckoned to
our account, as that his atonement," his death, " should ; so
there is the same reason why it should." [1]   But the second Edwards holds that, while by " his sufferings unto death," Christ
" made satisfaction to the law for sin," by " his perfect righteousness . . . he has exhibited to us an example ; has laid a
foundation for his own intercession " and rewards, " and for the
bestowment of justification and eternal life on his disciples." [2]
This is the doctrine of Emmons, that Christ's righteousness was

---

[1] Works of President Edwards.   New York.   1844.   Vol. iv.   92, 95, *et al.*
[2] Works of Dr. Jonathan Edwards.   Andover.   Vol ii.   69.

necessary to himself, to fit and to warrant him to suffer effica-
ciously for us a propitiatory death.

The creeds of the German churches give particular attention
to "good works," the synonym of Sanctification, as the proof
of a justified state : and these are defined to be : " Only those
[works] which proceed from true faith are performed according
to the law of God and to his glory ; and not such as are
founded on our imaginations, or the institutions of men." Thus,
the Heidelberg Catechism ;   on which Professor Schaff com-
ments : " Good works are just as necessary and indispensable
in the evangelical, as they are in the Roman creed, only not as
conditions, but as practical *fruits* or *evidences* of justification."

Turning to the Articles of the Episcopal church, we find
them entirely harmonizing with the foregoing under the heads
of (*a*) Justification ;   (*b*) Good Works ;   (*c*) Works before
Justification.

(*a.*) " We are accounted righteous before God only for the merit
of our Lord and Saviour Jesus Christ, by Faith, and not for our
own works or deservings.   Wherefore, that we are justified by
Faith only, is a most wholesome doctrine and very full of comfort.

(*b.*) " Albeit that Good Works, which are the fruits of Faith,
and follow after Justification, can not put away our sins, and
endure the severity of God's judgment ; yet are they pleasing and
acceptable to God in Christ, and do spring out necessarily of a true
and lively faith ; insomuch that by them a living faith may be as
evidently known, as a tree discerned by its fruit.

(*c.*) " Works done before the grace of Christ, and the Inspiration
of his Spirit, are not pleasant to God, forasmuch as they spring not
of faith in Jesus Christ ; neither do they make men meet to receive
grace, or (as the School-authors say) deserve grace of congruity :
yea rather, for that they are not done as God hath willed and commanded them to be done, we doubt not but they have the nature of
sin."

The early writers of the Reformation, in agreement with each
of these last cited paragraphs, considered that to make good
works of any degree a part of justification, was to give
them the power of satisfying, in part, the Divine justice.   Thus
Richard Hooker : " He which giveth unto any good works
of ours the force of satisfying the wrath of God for sin, the
power of meriting either earthly or heavenly rewards ; he which

holdeth works going before our vocation, in congruity to merit our vocation ; works following our first to merit our second justification, and by condignity, our last reward in the kingdom of heaven, pulleth up the doctrine of faith by the roots." [1]

The carefulness used in drawing these statements is apparent. They were designed to preclude mistakes in practice as well as in theory.   The distinctions above made between justification and sanctification, affect directly the estimate which we shall hold of the evil of sin.   We have seen that the justifying act of God points immediately to the expiatory sacrifice of Christ as the ground upon which human guilt is pardoned ; whereas the sanctifying work within us points to the Holy Spirit as its agent in freeing the soul from its remaining corruption.   Now, the evil of sin is most vividly seen in view of its guilt, not of its corrupting power.   That, then, is most fitted to deepen in our souls a sense of condemnation for sin, which charges home upon us the criminality of sin as an individual thing, rather than reminds us of the pollutions with which it has befouled humanity.   But the place of all others where to see the criminal nature of sin is the cross of Christ.   Looking upon him whom his iniquities are there piercing, the sinner gets his truest estimate of the enormity of being a sinner.   The anguish, in which the dying Son of God completed his satisfaction to the law and justice of God for human rebellion, is the grand illustration and demonstration of the inconceivable turpitude of man's wickedness as crime perpetrated against heaven's holy government.   That atonement, as a vicarious sacrifice in fact as well as in name, for mankind, must therefore be kept close to the mental eye, if sin is to be made to be " exceeding sinful." The doctrine of justification, if purely held, does this.   It confines the attention to the offering "finished" on Calvary, of the Lamb of God for the sin of the world.   It speaks of guilt, of crime, of condemnation, and of the pardon and removal of these for a sufficient cause—the righteousness and blood of Jesus Christ our Lord, without the reckoning in of any germ of holiness now springing in the heart, under Divine influence. Hence the fact which is not to be challenged, that the heaviest stress which is laid upon the sinfulness of man, the deepest

---

[1] Hooker's Works; Keble's Ed.   Sermon II. § 32.   Vol. II., 320.

views, and the sorest experience of its ill-desert, are to be found among those Christians who have held the strictest doctrine of a propitiatory atonement, and of the personal and complete justification of the penitent sinner who believes in Jesus.

Just as this position is left, a lessening off of this estimate of man's criminality for sin is disclosed. As sanctification is stretched over to take in justification as its incipient stage, and thus as forming a part of the ground of justification, and the eye is confused between the work of Christ in justifying, and of the Holy Spirit in cleansing the soul, the sharpness of its sense of guilt is dulled. This tendency is seen in the perfectionists of the day, with whom God's commandment is no longer so " exceeding broad," but that they can very easily compress it within the limits of their obedience. The enormity of sin is so diminished, the guilt and even the pollution of sin are so disguised, the claims of God are so lowered to man's convenience, by these religionists whose peculiar boast it is, that they are preeminently " the temples of the Holy Ghost," that they doubtless very sincerely think themselves to be keeping entirely Christ's two commandments, while it is often quite manifest that the *second* one, at least, needs to be much more carefully looked after.

We do not think that the importance can be exaggerated of preserving the utmost distinctness of doctrinal statement, and of the real differences between related doctrines. " When," writes Professor Shedd, " the popular feeling of a period is becoming less correct and healthy, nothing in the way of means does so much towards a change and restoration, as strict accuracy, which is the same as strict orthodoxy, in the popular creed." [1] The historical illustration which this author gives, upon the same page, of the reverse of this unquestionable truth, is impressive; it is almost appalling. " Perhaps, if the feeling of guilt in Augustine's mind had been as poignant and penal as it was in Luther's, or if his eye had been as penetrating and judicial upon this single topic, as was that of Calvin; perhaps, if this great theologian of the Patristic period had been as thorough and profound upon this side of the subject of sin,

---

[1] History of Christian Doctrine. Vol. II. p. 268.

as he was upon the other, a statement of the doctrine of justification by faith without works might have been originated in the fifth century, that by the blessing of God would have prevented the Papacy, and precluded those ten centuries of ' voluntary humility,' worshipping of saints, and justification by works." For that apostasy came in, as the church well knows, through the dogma, that the efforts of men to become holy may do something to expiate the sin from which they are toiling for release ; that is, that sanctification, which is a blended divine and human work, in part saves us, instead of Christ alone. " A keener vision, that could see the distinction between the guilt of sin and its pollution, would not have confounded the work of the Sanctifier with that of the Atoner."

ARTICLE II.

THE PIETISTS OF GERMANY.[1]

THE Reformation of the sixteenth century was one of those great and surprising events, which attract the notice of succeeding generations, and mark the periods in which they occur as epochs in the history of the world.   It sundered the chains of debasing ignorance, and inveterate superstition.   It broke the yoke of the most grinding moral and spiritual despotism.   It unlocked the long sealed fountains of knowledge, and gave the Bible to the nations.   In the course of a few years, it enlightened and emancipated half Europe.

In accomplishing this great work, human instrumentalities were, of course, employed ; earnest, appropriate instrumentalities ; but the power was of God. So it was felt to be, by those most deeply engaged in it. So it has been acknowledged to be, by succeeding generations. The reformation from Popery was no other than a great and general revival of true religion.

[1] The materials for the following sketch of the History of Pietism are chiefly taken from a work entitled *Pietas Hallensis*, prepared by the celebrated Prof. Francke of Halle, and published in London in 1705.

The Spirit of God accompanied the preaching of Luther and his associates; followed the reading of the Bible, and other good books; and hundreds and thousands were brought to the knowledge of the truth.

But this great revival, like most others which have been enjoyed on earth, was followed by declension. It was perverted to some extent by fanatical leaders; the reformers fell to disputing among themselves; the devil gained an advantage over them; and the Holy Spirit was grieved away.

The internal state of the Lutheran church was for the most part peaceful, so long as the great Reformer lived. His authority was sufficient to overcome opposition, and those who were unwilling to bow to it, had no alternative but to retire. But after the death of Luther, which took place about the middle of the sixteenth century, the peace of the church was much disturbed. Melancthon, though more than equal to Luther in point of learning, had not his firmness and strength of character, or his influence over the popular mind. For the sake of peace, he was disposed to yield certain points, both to the Catholics and Calvinists, which Luther would have preserved inviolate. Hence arose a bitter controversy between what may be called the strict and the moderate Lutherans, which detracted much from the spiritual life of the church. In the language of a cotemporary, "strifes and contentions, disputes and wranglings, grew to an excessive height, but the plain practice of piety fell to decay."

Then the thirty years' war in Germany produced, through the whole Lutheran church, a great degeneracy of morals, and a general prostration of discipline and order. Good preachers were not to be obtained, and the people were obliged to accept of such as were incompetent and worthless. Many of them were destitute of learning and piety; while those who had learning preached metaphysics and school divinity, rather than the pure Gospel of Christ. Their discourses were filled up with technical terms, distinctions, and subtleties, which the people could not understand, and in which, of course, they felt no interest. They combatted heresies, the very names of which were unknown to their hearers, but said little or nothing to arouse them from the sleep of sin, and bring them to newness of life and new obedience. Many of the clergy, perhaps the most of them, were confessedly unconverted men; and not only so, they insisted that conversion in the proper sense of the term, was not necessary for a minister of Christ.

It is not to be wondered at, therefore, that in the first part of the seventeenth century, the state of religion among the Lutherans was very low. The lamp of spiritual life, which had burned so brightly a hundred years before, seemed likely to go out in darkness.

Nevertheless, it was not entirely extinguished. There were those who sighed and cried over existing desolations, and who were moved to " lift up their voice like a trumpet, and show to the people their transgressions, and to the house of Jacob their sins." Foremost among these was the Rev. John Arndt, an eminent minister of Christ, and general superintendent of the churches of Luneburg. He was first a physician; but being visited with a dangerous sickness, he made a vow to change his profession to that of divinity, in case he should be restored to health. He wrote many books, the most remarkable of which was his treatise on True Christianity, which has been often translated, and has been the means of salvation to many souls.[1] Its influence in Germany, when first published, was not unlike that of Wilberforce's Practical View in England. It presented Christianity in a new light; not as a mere profession, a form, but as a great and solemn reality, which must be felt in the soul, and exhibited in the life, if men would be saved. On the one hand, it aroused multitudes from the sleep of sin, and put them upon a course of new obedience; while on the other, it excited a torrent of opposition, with the intent, though a vain one, to sweep both the book and its author away.[2] The excellent Dr. Worthington of England calls Arndt another Salvian,

---

[1] This work consists of four books. The first, Arndt calls the book of Scripture; the second, the book of Life; the third, the book of Conscience; and the fourth, the book of Nature. The first two books are the most esteemed, and were published, separate from the others, in Boston, in 1809.

[2] Among the opponents of Arndt was Lucius Osiander, a divine of Tübingen, who wrote a book against him in a most satirical style, called Theological Cogitations, of which he is said to have deeply repented, when he came to die.

"Whose business it was to convince men of their unchristian spirits and courses of life, and awaken them to the minding of true Christianity; that so they might not place the kingdom of God in meats and drinks, in mere opinions and outward observances, but might make it their great care to be a people reformed in deed and in truth, to crucify the old man in the affections of their souls, and rise to a new life, the holy and humble life of Christ."

Among the many who were savingly benefitted by the writings of Arndt, was a deacon of the church in Rostock, who, at his death in 1661, left in manuscript a tract, entitled The Watchman's Voice, which, ere long, was printed. This tract was the means of first opening the eyes of James Philip Spener, who soon became the leading spirit in this great revival movement. This eminent divine, who has been called not improperly "the Protestant Fenelon," was born in 1625, and acquired much fame as an oriental scholar. He was established in the ministry, successively, at Strasburg, Frankfort, Dresden, and Berlin. While at Frankfort, he published his Pia Desideria, Pious Desires, in which he set forth the great apostasy of the Lutheran church, with the abuses and corruptions resulting from it, and the remedies which he desired to see applied.[1] He also republished several excellent works of a previous age; as the Postils of Tauler, Theologia Germanica, and Thomas à Kempis on the Imitation of Christ. Later in life, he published sixty-six sermons on regeneration, and an important work on the divinity of Christ.

But it was not by his preaching and publications alone that Spener extended his salutary influence. After his removal to Frankfort, in 1666, he established, in his own house, what he called Collegia Pietatis, but which we should call meetings for conference and prayer. This was a new measure, at that time, in Germany, and it awakened a very deep interest. Multitudes flocked to these religious meetings, not only students and people in humble life, but ministers, professors, superintendents and officers of the government. More ample accommodations were provided, and other meetings were established on the same general plan. While many favored the meetings and were sav-

[1] This work was first published as a Preface to Arndt's Postils, afterwards it was printed separately, and entitled *Pia Desideria.*

ingly benefitted by them, others bitterly opposed and denounced them. They were said to be disorderly, fanatical, and, in many ways, of dangerous tendency. They were sanctioned, however, by some of the Universities and could not be broken up.

Spener was not contented with laboring only for the spiritual good of his fellow-men. He felt for the sufferings of the sick and the destitute, and, though opposed for a time by the magistrates, he succeeded in getting up a hospital in Frankfort for their relief.

In 1686, Spener was removed from Frankfort to Dresden, and became first court preacher to John George III., the Electoral Prince of Saxony. Here he continued the same course which had been pursued at Frankfort; and in addition to it, he commenced the work of assembling and catechising the children. For this he was censured by some of the nobility, and the University professors, who thought it unbecoming in a man of such great parts and learning, and occupying so high a station, to descend to the work of teaching children. But Spener thought differently. He regarded the youth of his flock as the hope of the church, and the most hopeful subjects of pastoral influence. "Older people," he said, "are for the most part inflexible, and unwilling to forsake their established opinions and practices. My greatest hope is from the children." The children appreciated the attentions of their pastor, and his catechetical exercises were thronged.

Spener had the misfortune, however, to be unpopular with the Prince Elector. He was a great drunkard, besides being addicted to other vices, and the plain dealing of the court preacher was offensive to him. He did not like his sermons; and still less could he endure his private visits, which were all of them of the most serious, searching nature. On one occasion, Spener addressed to him a respectful letter, reproving him for his vicious courses, and earnestly calling him to repentance, which gave great offence.

At the time of Spener's removal from Frankfort to Dresden, he had with him several theological students, among whom were Augustus Herman Francke, John Caspar Schade, and Paul Anthony, who now went to Leipsic, to pursue the study of theology there. In accordance with Spener's instructions, they established a private meeting for the study of the Scriptures, which they called Collegium Philobiblicum. At first, their exercises were chiefly critical.   Their method was, for one to read a select portion of the Old Testament in Hebrew, or of the New in Greek, and to expound the same; after which observations exegetical and practical were made by the others. As these meetings came to be known, and others wished to unite with them, they were removed to a larger place, and put under the direction of the Professor Extraordinary of Divinity in the University.   The leaders were in correspondence with Dr. Spener, who advised them so to conduct their meetings that they might tend more directly to Christian edification and growth in grace.   From this time, many were excited to an earnest love of the Bible, to the diligent study of it, and to a fervent breathing after spiritual life.   Their meetings were commenced and closed with prayer; and when the passage for the evening had been expounded, all were at liberty to make suggestions and remarks.   As the meetings increased in numbers and popularity, others of the same kind sprang up among the students, by means of which the study of the Scriptures was greatly promoted.   Mr. Francke opened one biblical school, and Schade another, and Anthony another, in which the truths of the Gospel were explained and applied.

These exercises necessarily drew away students from the University professors, whose lectures really were of little value. " The candidates for the ministry were bred up to a superficial smattering in divine things, and made little or no progress in true Christian theology.   They thought it enough to be able to fill a pulpit handsomely, and so to act the orator as to excite the admiration of a vulgar auditory."   Nevertheless, the old professors did not like to lose their scholars, and a violent opposition was raised against the new meetings and measures. The cry of heresy was raised; and because the students of the Bible had become serious and earnest in their religion, and endeavored to walk according to its precepts, they were, in derision, called Pietists.   Such was the origin of the name given to them.   It was, at first, a term of reproach, but was afterwards retained as one of honor.

Throughout the year 1689, the opposition to proceedings at

Leipsic continued to increase. The pulpits rang with the new sect of the Pietists; the Consistory took the matter up, and directed the University to make inquiry respecting it. From Leipsic the excitement spread through the whole of Saxony, and books were written and published on both sides. In the end the biblical meetings were abolished, and the leaders in the movement were driven from Leipsic.

We next hear of Francke and his associates at Erfurth, having been invited there by Dr. Breithaupt, Superintendent and Professor of Divinity in the University, and soon a great change was wrought in the city. The Pietists not only preached in demonstration of the Spirit and with power, but they undertook the catechising of children and youth, who flocked to them in great numbers. The revival which followed so alarmed the magistrates, the most of whom were Roman Catholics, that they procured a mandate, putting a stop to the new proceedings. Shortly after this, both Dr. Breithaupt and Mr. Francke were under the necessity of leaving Erfurth.

Nevertheless, they were not forsaken. The Lord had a more important field for them than any they had yet occupied. Through the influence of Spener, who was still at Berlin, Dr. Breithaupt was made Professor of Divinity in the newly established University at Halle; Francke was Professor of Oriental languages[1]; and Thomacius, a civilian, by whom the University had been projected, was Professor of Law. Paul Anthony was the Pro-Rector or President of the University; so that the whole establishment was in the hands of the Pietists, and under their influence. Francke was also constituted pastor of Glaucha, a village near Halle, where he subsequently established his Orphan House, and other schools. He first instructed and supported orphans and other destitute children, in his own house, in which he was assisted by benevolent citizens of Halle. But as the number of them increased, he found it necessary to provide more ample accommodations. In 1648 was laid the first stone of the buildings, which now form two rows, eight hundred feet in length. Sums of money poured in to him from all quarters; and frequently, when reduced to the greatest straits, the providence of God, in which he trusted, appeared

[1] Afterwards Professor of Divinity.

for his relief. A distinguished chemist, whom Francke visited and instructed on his death-bed, left him recipes for the compounding of medicines, which yielded him an income of from twenty to thirty thousand dollars a year. By this means he was enabled to prosecute his benevolent undertakings, without asking or receiving aid from the government. Francke's Institute, as it was called, embraced not only an Orphan House, but a system of Latin and Grammar schools, a valuable library, and a printing establishment, from which more than a million copies of the Holy Scriptures have been issued.

Spener, though advanced in age, was still living and laboring at Berlin, and rejoicing in the prosperity and usefulness of his former friends and pupils at Halle. He removed to Berlin in 1691, and died in 1705, "being sweetly translated," as Francke expresses it, "in a chariot of divine love and peace, and leaving his name as a fragrant perfume to posterity."

The interests of the Pietists now centred at Halle, and for the next half century, the new University, with its connected institutions, continued to be a fountain of good influences to Germany, and to the world. Faithful pastors were raised up here, to take the places of the worse than useless ones who had before possessed the land. And not only so, but faithful missionaries were sent forth to distant regions of the earth. As the spirit of religion and of missions is the same, we always expect, when the former is revived, to see the latter revived with it. And so it was in the case before us. In the year 1621, the King of Denmark came in possession of the town of Tranquebar, and a small adjoining territory on the coast of Coromandel, in the East Indies. For almost a hundred years, no attempts had been made to instruct the natives; but in the beginning of the eighteenth century, Frederick IV. of Denmark resolved to establish a mission there, with a view to their conversion.

But where shall he look for missionaries, who are ready and qualified, to go and devote their lives to this perilous undertaking? His own country did not furnish them; nor did England furnish them. The Christians of England were willing to assist the Danes in the support of missionaries; but there seems not to have been piety enough at that time in England, to raise up a missionary to go forth on a work like this. The only place in the Protestant world to which the King of Denmark could look for missionaries, was the Pietist University of Halle. Wherefore, a request was made to Dr. Francke, that he would recommend two or three from among his pupils, who were qualified to enter upon this important undertaking.

The first missionaries sent forth were Bartholomew Teigenbalg and Henry Phitscho, who sailed from Copenhagen, Nov. 29, 1705. They were followed at short intervals, by such men as Grundler, Schultz, Walther, Fabricius, and more especially Swartz. Swartz arrived in India in the autumn of 1750, and continued his labors there for almost half a century. The fruits of them remain to the present day.

In looking back upon this revival in Germany, we are constrained to regard it as a precious work of God, springing up in a season of deep declension, and shedding anew the blessed influences of the Gospel upon the land of Luther and of the other reformers. In its essential features, it strongly resembled more recent revivals, and especially that which took place in New England, near the middle of the last century. Like that, it came when it was most needed—when the light of life was burning dimly, and the holy example of a previous generation was likely to be lost. Like that, it was destined to encounter, at every step, a violent opposition, springing chiefly from a cold and selfish clergy, whose negligence the example of the revivalists reproved, and whose influence they curtailed. When Whitefield first visited New England, he found ministers not a few, who gave him no evidence of piety, who did not pretend to be regenerated persons, who even insisted that a renewed heart constituted no part of the necessary qualification of a minister of Christ. And just so it was in Germany, in the days of Arndt, and Spener, and Francke, and when told of their delinquencies, and urged to repent, they in both instances raised a storm of opposition, intended either to silence the reformers, or to drive them away. It was the same spirit which our Saviour encountered, in his reproofs of the Jewish scribes and teachers of the law: "Thus saying, Master, thou reprovest us also." In dealing with unworthy pastors, the Pietists of Germany were apparently more cautious and discreet than Whitefield, yet they did not escape reproach and persecution. They found, as faithful men have ever found, and ever will, that the offence of the cross had not ceased.

Near the close of our Whitefieldian revival, a fanatical spirit began to show itself, which gave occasion to opposition and reproach, and so it was in the time of Luther ; and to some extent among the Pietists of Germany. At any rate, we hear such things of them ; although the report comes, almost entirely, from those who had no sympathy with them, or their work. The devil knows how to manœuvre at such times. If he can not stop a needed reform, or a revival movement, he can enter into it, and spoil it. If he can not arrest the chariot of salvation, he can mount the driver's box, and seize the reins, and like Jehu of old press on furiously.

The Whitefieldian revival was followed by a long and sad declension, reaching through the French and Revolutionary wars, producing a marked division among the clergy of New England, and issuing in the Unitarian defection of our own times. A similar result issued upon the Pietist revival. Before the close of the last century, an infidel, transcendental, rationalistic movement commenced in Germany, which, in its progress, swept through the churches and universities, and corrupted and ruined the great body of the Lutheran clergy ; and what is most of all to be deplored, the noble University of Halle, which was got up by the Pietists, and worked by them, and accomplished, for a time, such a vast amount of good, was the first to be corrupted. Semler, the father of German rationalism, was a graduate of Halle. He commenced his career as a theological teacher there in 1752. He was a man of varied and extensive learning, but employed all his learning to unsettle the faith of his countrymen in the divine authority and inspiration of the Bible and in the most essential religious truths. Nor were his teachings without their legitimate fruits. The moral condition of the students at Halle, and even of the theological students, towards the close of the last century, Tholuck tells us, was deplorable. Those of them who resided in Dr. Semler's house were frequently seen abroad in a state of nudity. Bahrdt, who called himself a theologian, kept a coffee-house of his own, where he received his boon companions, and where, says Tholuck, "the waiting-maid took the place which belonged to the wife." Bahrdt died in early life of a vile disease, the result of his debaucheries.

We see in instances such as these, proof incontestable not of the bad influence of revivals, but of the inveterate corruption of human nature. Ours is a depraved, ruined world, in which the best things, if left to themselves, are sure to run down and become the worst.

Let us be thankful that a better spirit is now prevailing in Germany ; that her churches are recovering from the great gulf of infidelity in which they were so deeply whelmed ; and that a large body of her clergy, we hope a majority, are distinguishing themselves, not only for critical biblical learning, but for the inculcation of evangelical truth.

ARTICLE III.

THEORIES OF THE WILL.

THE discussion of this subject of the will turns necessarily on points of definition. Correct discriminations help to clear the subject of difficulties. Define the will as Coleridge defined it, to be the moral and mental starting-point in responsibility, and keeping to the definition, you reach a theory of the will corresponding thereto.[1] Define the will as Edwards defined it in his theological writings, as comprehending the entire moral nature of man, the moral sense, the emotions and desires, and you reach a philosophy of the will differing by certain shades from the theory above supposed.[2] Define the will to be the mind's power of decision that follows choice, as some recent writers have done, and the definition will essentially modify the

[1] We derive this definition from the drift of Coleridge's writings, rather than from any definite statements of the author. He followed M. de. Biran, Cousin, etc.

[2] President Edwards seems to have adopted a theory of the will in his ethical writings widely different from the one he combatted in his memorable Treatise on the Will.

ethical system founded upon it.¹   But define the will as modern writers and schools have defined it, with few exceptions, as
the mind's power to choose and resolve, and you have a philosophy of the will agreeing with systems or theories founded
upon different definitions, in scarcely a single point.

We lay the theory of Coleridge, of Edwards, of Hodge and
others, out of the question for the present, and proceed to consider questions of the will according to the theory now generally adopted, as being the mind's power to choose and resolve,
in the sense of carrying its choices into effect.

If it be asked what is the will in its ultimate principle, or in
the simplest idea of it, we answer, it is the mind willing, in
the sense of choosing and resolving, just as the affections are
the mind feeling, and the conscience the mind-perceiving intu-
itively the right or wrong.   The will, then, is the mind's power
of making choices and coming to decisions in the presence of
motives or that which challenges choice, or tends to this result.

The mind is not to be set off into parts or powers as the
checker-board is into squares and colors, or the map into countries and sections.   It is so constituted that it has the power to
act, now in this way or style, and now in some other way or
style; but it is the same intelligent, sentient substance that acts
in these different ways.   It is the mind, one and the same, that
originates, reasons, recalls, feels, resents and resolves.   It is
the same essence or unit that acts in these diversities of oper-
ations.²

The powers that can thus act diversely are styled functions
of the mind.   The mind as such may act in different ways and
come into different consciousnesses, so to express it, but it can
not rationally act in conflict with itself.   Each of its powers
has laws and limitations; so the soul as such becomes a self-
contained, self-moved, self-regulated unit, never in disorder or
derangement save as the laws by which it was made to be governed are violated.

¹ See Hazzard, Hodge, and others.

² An eminent writer has said, "The mind bears different names according to the
nature of its operations. Inasmuch as it contemplates, it is spirit, *spiritus*. Inasmuch as it comprehends, it is reason, *ratio*. Inasmuch as it recollects, it is memory,
memoria. Inasmuch as it feels, it is sentiment, *sensus*. Inasmuch as it resolves, it
is will, *voluntas*. But these are not divisions in its substance. The one soul acts in
these different ways." Alcuin, teacher and adviser of Charlemagne.

In this paper we shall briefly consider the will as the mind's power to choose and resolve in the sense of giving its choices practical effect.

It is natural to raise the question, has the will of itself a self-determining power? Has it the power of contrary choice? Is it capable of acting according to the weaker motive, or contrary to the greatest apparent good? We assume, if the will has either of these attributes or facilities, it has all of them; if it lacks either of them, it lacks all of them. They involve the same principles, and call into exercise the same elements of power and independence.

Let us, first, consider the power of self-determination as claimed for the will. If it exists at all, it must needs be a capacity in the will of acting independently of the other powers of the mind. It supposes a voluntary energy that could dispense with the conclusions of reason and the force of the affections in choice. It is claimed to be a *self*-determining power. It is alleged that the will acts, or has the power to act, from the force of its own inherent energies, and independently of any central law of the mind. We take this to be the theory asserted.[1]

Now the will, we have said, is distinct from the other faculties of the soul. It is the mind's power of acting in a specific way, namely, of making choices, forming decisions and carrying them into action. But the will, we affirm, can not act of itself, independently of the other faculties of the mind. It can not separate itself in its functions from the activity of the intellect and feelings. Difference here does not imply independence; nor does distinctness of activity imply independence. The will as a mental force has its own laws and ways; but it is not one of them to act independently of the other powers of the mind. It can not ignore them in its choices and resolutions. It has the condition of its activity, the ground of its choices, the data of its determinations in these authoritative powers of the mind. The intellectual operations and moral impulses enter into the account of the voluntary activity as an indispensable and enabling cause. The mental and moral processes and discriminations have to do naturally and necessarily with the laws that

---

[1] The will has power over its own determinations. Reid, also Hamilton.

regulate the will. They are forces concerned in its decisions; they are conditions pre-requisite to its action in any rational way. The will can not say to the intellect : I have no need of thee; nor to the conscience or the heart, I have no need of thee. It can not dispense with the light and laws that come to it from the sovereignty of the mind and heart in its operations. It can not but feel the force of the mental discriminations and moral affections in its decisions. The sovereignty of the mind is in these; while its executive efficiency is in the will. They are the sources of all legitimate and binding responsibility. If the will was in any proper sense independent of the intellectual and sentient nature, it would be a false guide in moral agency. If it could shut out the light that comes to it from the understanding and the conscience; or shut off the force of the sympathies and affections by any self-regulating activity of its own, it were a dangerous element in the soul. Who would feel safe for a moment with any such power between the moral nature and responsible activity? The will stands between the man and his actions. It connects man with his conduct. It is the last link in the chain of moral agency. It represents the mind at the bar of responsibility. It identifies the moral nature with moral agency and human behavior. It is the efficiency, not only, but the representative of the soul. It can not disconnect itself, therefore, from the rational and sentient nature; but connects these, at once, with personal activity and responsibleness. If the will could resolve itself into a condition of positive independence of the mind—its laws and powers, of what worth would it be in responsibility? What sort of authority would attach to its determinations? What shade of character would there be in them? What element of responsibility could be gotten out of them, or into them?

We desire to be explicit upon this matter of the alleged independence of the will. We said that, in the simplest idea of it, the will is the mind willing, or putting forth choices and decisions. How, then, can it be independent of the reason when it is the mind's own act in the form of volition? The affections are defined to be the mind feeling. Now we ask, how can the affections separate themselves from corresponding activity of the intellect? Can the heart be moved to sensibility

till the intellect has brought before it objects fitted to awaken
sensibility? What more preposterous than to set up for exclusive and independent activity on the part of the affections;
in other words, for the self-determining power of the heart?
The same, too, of the conscience; which is the mind, discriminating in view of moral relations adapted to awaken the idea
of right and obligation. But can the conscience act independently of the reason or understanding that presents these relations to the moral sense? Can it be claimed for the conscience
that it has any thing like the self-determining power? Can it
be claimed for either of the faculties of the mind, having sus-
ceptibilities of separate and different activities, that they are, in
any proper sense, independent of each other? No one power
of the mind can act independently of other powers. The action of the reason, affections and will is correlative action.
Hence the determinations of the will, if proper and reliable, are to be referred to the conclusions of the reason and
promptings of the affections. It can not rationally separate itself from these, in its activity. If it could do so, its decisions
would be lawless, groundless, reckless. It would not be such
a force in responsibility as one would wish to have, or as God
in his benevolence could give. It would be no guide in per-
·sonal accountability; it would be an unsafe element in moral
agency. Its action would chance to be irregular, contingent,
haphazard. No, the will can no more separate itself from the
affections and moral sense in its activity, than these can separate themselves from the understanding. As well claim that
the affections, or the fears, or the conscience, are self-moved
and independent, as that the will is so. If the affections were
to ignore the light of the intellect, and the conscience to shut
its eye to the moral relations unfolded by reason, what reliance
could be placed on them in moral responsibility? The mind,
in that case, were as well off without these faculties or functions
as with them, as to any proper harmony in itself, or any right
moral ends. Why, then, should we assume to give to the will
a liberty which could not be given ·to the other powers of the
mind? What sort of necessity that we do this? What safety
would there be in its decisions, if it were to act independently of
the general government and harmony of the mind?

The will, then, has need to go out of itself to get proper grounds or data for its action.   As with the other powers, so with this, its action is a related action, a dependent and in some sense, mutual action.   Its choices, if rational, result from proper discriminations and proper affections ; else they would be unfit representatives of the moral nature, and would form a treacherous ground of moral obligation.   The will can not set up a court of its own in the soul, as a sort of star-chamber, without presumption.   It would cease thus to express properly the mental and moral operations.   It would cease to indicate obligation to activity, or to connect the moral nature with personal conduct.   It would not be a true index of the soul ; and could not properly determine or indicate accountability.

Such is not the nature of the will.   It has not the power of self-determination.   It can not assume any thing like vicegerency in the soul without usurpation.   In such case, its action would be irrelevant, abnormal, irresponsible, blind.   Moved by no ray of reason, no rule of conscience, no force of affection, it would be a demoralizing element of activity within, and would turn the whole rational scene into confusion and chaos.

We then dismiss this claim for the will, as founded on no mental analogy, demanded by no moral principle, favored by no rational experience, and made necessary by no moral exigency.   No such power exists in the moral constitution of man. No such right of secession or independence inheres in the government of the mind.   The claim, therefore, is not allowed.

What then, secondly, becomes of the theory of contrary choice, as claimed for the will ? This doctrine of contrary choice follows from the theory of self-determination as a logical sequence.   It goes to the ground if that theory fails.   The power of contrary choice has no possible basis save in the absolute independence of the will or voluntary nature.

What is this doctrine of contrary choice? It assumes that the will can create or reverse its own decisions of itself, independently of the other faculties of the mind.[1]   It assumes that the will can come to a choice the opposite of the one actually made,

---

[1] In the will there is an alternative power, or pluri-efficient power. Whedon on the Will.

and this by virtue of its own self-determining power. It can do this without any regulating process of the higher moral faculties of the soul. It can do this without any change in the mental or moral status of the one choosing. It can elect with or without reasons, or contrary to them. It can choose according to motives, or contrary to them; according to supposed interests and rational considerations, or against them. · It can make choices alternately that clash with each other, and without any change, moral or mental, in the one choosing. It can adopt the alternate or opposite choice with the same readiness and facility that it did the one it actually made. It can choose either way, any way, or no way, at its own option, and by virtue of its own inherent independence. So we are taught to believe.[1]

There is then in the will a sort of sovereignty or absoluteness that fits it, as is claimed, for the special exigencies of responsibility. It can ignore the authority of reason and the moral nature. It can reverse motives at option, and veto the laws of judgment and rational decision according to its own caprices. It can always decide otherwise than it does, and without any change whatsoever in the circumstances or moral condition of the agent.

Now we deny that the will has of itself as a function of the mind any such power. We said the will is the mind choosing and determining. We would have more properly said, it is the mind and heart, the rational and moral nature, acting thus. It can not, therefore, dispense with the laws that govern rational action. It can not swing loose from the reason and the affections in the process of coming to a decision. No one power of the mind has any such independence or separateness from the other powers of the mind, much less the will that represents the rational and moral nature in responsibility. It would imply one of two things, either that the will has some element of reason and affection of its own distinct from the natural reason and affection, or else it has power to act without any reason or

---

[1] Prof H. P. Tappan says in his review of Edwards on the Will, (we quote the substance of his statements): The will can take the side of the reason against the sensibilities, or of the sensibilities against the reason, or it can take sides against them both. President Mahan takes the same ground, and others of greater or less note.

affection whatsoever.   If the will has not reason and sensibility
of its own, and if it is capable of acting independently of the
natural reason and sensibility, it must needs have power to act
without any such regulating influence or motive as these, in the
crisis of decision.

But we ask, has the will anything like intellect or sensibility
of ·its own apart from the higher reason and sensibility?   If so,
what of the will's reason and affection?   What relation do they
hold to the natural reason and affection?   And in what sense do
they differ?   And then, it would be obvious to ask : What were
the use of such duplicate endowments?   What need of a twofold reason, one of the mind, and the other of the will ; or of
complex sensibilities, one class belonging to the mind, and the
other to the will ; or of a confused conscience, one sort in the
service of the mental, and the other, of the voluntary nature?
The supposition would involve singular mental phenomena,
and would necessitate a somewhat crude and crooked mental
philosophy.   The theorist will then be forced to take the other
point of the dilemma, namely, that the will must have power to
act without any reason or affection or moral influence whatsoever.   For if it does not possess these of itself, and can act independently of them in their natural sphere in the mind, it
must be able to act without them in any and every sense.

We are forced to set such a theory, involving a dilemma,
either point of which is so irrational and unnatural, out of the
question at once.   Have we need to combat a theory that assumes the possibility of a divorce of the rational from the voluntary nature, that makes the latter independent of the former,
that separates the will from the reason and the moral nature, in
its choices?   But the theory in question does this.   Certainly,
if the will has not these as an endowment of its own, and has
power to act independently of them in their natural relations to
the soul, it must needs have power to act without them in any
form or sense conceivable ; that is to say, it has power to act
arbitrarily, irrationally, contingently.

But as this theory of contrary choice is contended for with great
ability and from the highest sources, we will bestow upon it
still further attention.   What is choice?   Answer :   The determination of the mind in preferring one thing to another in view

of rational considerations. One comes to a divergence of roads. He pauses, and considers, and determines to take the right rather than the left. That which brought him to this decision was the power of choice, or that element of the will which we denominate as such; and that which brought him to this choice was the supposed reasons in the case. But on the theory of contrary choice, he could as well have chosen the left as the right, and with no change of reasons or motives in the case.

Take a different illustration, where moral character is involved. One is invited to a drinking saloon. An alternative is before him, to remain at home, and enjoy one kind of happiness; or go to the house of dissipation and enjoy another kind of happiness. Either course has its allurements. The charms of vice or the charm of home must prevail. It is the former. He chooses perversely and goes the way of death.

The question narrows itself down to this: Had that man power to do otherwise than he did? In this form of the question we answer affirmatively. He had the power of reflection, of counting the cost and the consequences. His soul is a harp of many strings, every one of which is sensitive to each breath of influence, and every chord in this divine instrument touches, terminates in the will.

But the exact question here is, has the will alone, of itself, acting independently of the moral nature, or vibratory action of the sensitive spirit within, any power to act otherwise in the circumstances than it did act? We admit that the soul with its furniture of faculties, its complete equipment for moral agency, has this power. It belongs to the soul comprehensively, but not to any particular function of the soul. The theorist on the other hand, endows the will with a sort of a sovereignty over the soul in moral action. It is self-determinating, he tells you. It has no need to await the tardy action of reason and sensibility in moral emergencies, but can seize the reins of responsibility, and act authoritatively, independently, absolutely, and at once.

But we may be told here, in the way of a compromise of opinions, that this power of contrary choice is of the nature of a special endowment of the will, and would need be used only in extraordinary exigencies, that the will in ordinary affairs is, indeed, regulated by the reason and moral nature. Something like a latent force, or reserved power, we will suppose to be claimed for the will here, in the use of which it can seize the helm of the mind, and put the ship of responsibility against wind and tide and sea by its own strong right arm. It is in the use of this special power, therefore, reserved for unwonted occasions, that the will can set aside the authority of reason and motive and assume the sovereignty within.

But we do not see that this helps the case at all. If the will has this power at all, it would be natural to use it at its own option, and we do not see by what law it would be limited to special occasions. And then, if it be in the greater matters of responsibility that this power of absolute independence is to be used, the difficulty and danger still exist in all their strength. We say danger, for if the will has power to choose contrary to choice, to prefer against preference, to decide against decision, and determine against determination; if it can refuse what on the whole it prefers, and can choose what is not actually desired, and this with no change whatsoever in the scale of appreciable motive or of moral considerations, what safety is there in human responsibility? What guarantee has conscience or virtue or character? We ask, again, in order to be perfectly explicit upon this point : Can one prefer a thing exactly the opposite of the one he desires, and with no change whatever in the circumstances or moral conditions in the case? Can he do so by the will alone? Can the will regulate its own choices of itself absolutely? Can it arbitrate in the crisis of decision without reference to reason or conscience or the moral nature? We want to ask precisely this : Can one choose a course, or a thing, and at the same instant, have the power to choose oppositely, or adversely to the choice made? The doctrine of contrary choice teaches that one can choose as he does, or as he does not ; what he desires, or does not desire ; and this, by the force of the self-determining power of the will. The will of itself effects or accomplishes this alternateness of decision! Choices are mere playthings of the will, it would seem. It can create them, and annihilate them, at its own option. It can veto its own determinations continuing such, we are told. For if they have ceased to be choices by the quick intervention of reason or the arbitration of the higher moral powers, the question is changed, the theory falls to the ground; no room is left for doubt or controversy. But the doctrine or theory supposes an existing choice, an alternate or opposite one to the prevalent choice, that so suddenly supercedes and vanquishes the other.[1] Now it is admitted that this may be so, where there are reasons or causes of the nature of motives, summoned to the bar of the will by the higher nature. But all such processes our theory excludes. It makes the will all-sufficient in the case, yea, self-sufficient. It gives us an effect without reasons. It gives us action with no rational ground of action. It gives the will a veto power upon the choices and decisions remaining such, and a creative power to originate new ones out of nothing, that antagonize against those vetoed. The choices are called up, and put down; are made to come forth, and disappear, as mere automatons of the will. And motives, if allowed any weight at all, can be made to change places instantly by this innate sovereignty residing in the voluntary nature.[2]

It is fair to state here, that the theory now in hand is put forth no doubt as a supposed necessity to save the doctrine of moral agency. It is urged in the interests of moral freedom, aud to give just ground for human responsibility. The will must be free, it is said, or man is not responsible. But this does not follow, if we are to attach to the doctrine of freedom such notions as we have just considered, and as are strenuously taught. The statement is very sophistical and unsatisfactory. The truth is here: The soul must be free, or man is not accountable. The spirit as a unit has this attribute. We say, then, that the soul of man is, in the proper sense of the word, free.

---

[1] "The will has unrestricted power to put forth a counter volition in the same unchanged circumstances. Whedon."

[2] It may be objected that the will must have power to act in cases where there can be no preference or choice whatever; as when either of two things, equal in amount and quality is offered; or when two roads are before you with no appreciable reason for taking the one rather than the other; or when two courses of conduct present themselves, with an apparent balance of motives or reasons for taking either. But in cases like these the choice is not between the things presented, but between acting and not acting in the case; or between taking one, without care as to which, or neither of them. Such suppositions give no strength whatever to the theory in question. We would say generally that to be without choice in a moral exigency, if the thing were supposable, would be of itself a sin.

But soul and will are not identical. The words are not synonyms.[1]

The will is a function of the soul, but not the soul itself. It shares in moral responsibility, but does not monopolize it. It has the reactive, as well as the recipient capability. It has its portion of endowments belonging to moral agency, the other faculties have their portion also. It has its place and play on the moral scene; the other powers have theirs too. The sovereignty is federal, and not sectional. In order to the proper freedom of the will, it has no need to be independent of the other powers of the mind. Such independence were destructive of true freedom. It were as the arm taken from the body; or the eye unorbed from its sphere. The will is free in the freedom of the other powers, but is not free from them. We might as well have no freedom at all, as one into which no element of reason or responsibility enters. It were an aimless, useless, worthless freedom, unhinged from moral relations, or moral restraint. Such liberty would be of the nature of licentiousness and utter recklessness. Divorce the will from the moral nature, that it may be free, and man accountable! If man had such a will, he would not be free nor accountable; he would not be rational; or could not, indeed, act rationally. Such divorce were enthrallment, it were derangement. Who would trust for a moment the caprices of a mental force that could ignore all the rules of reason and moral restraint? Such freedom of the will would overthrow the freedom of the soul. It would be but another name for bondage or despotism. So far from being an element of liberty in man in the interests of moral agency, and just accountability, it would effect the overthrow of all true liberty of the soul. It were liberty in particular, for thralldom in general. Such freedom were had at too dear a rate. It would be a sort of secession from the government within. It would do the work of ruin in the moral nature. This power to lead off in responsibility, it may be against the remonstrances of reason and the moral sense, would reduce the soul to a state of chaos and anarchy. Is it

[1] We use the terms soul and spirit to mean the same, though not unaware that in systems of moral philosophy, a distinction is made. We mean by soul, the whole spiritual nature of man.

said, this would not follow? But forces are likely to assert themselves; endowments rarely lie dormant; faculties are for use; power for evil is a fearful thing in perverse nature.

We would say once more, the rational and moral powers have need to express themselves through the will in order to proper accountability. How else are the results of reason and the moral nature to indicate the character at the bar of responsibility? If the will can veto these, or contravene their verdict or promptings in the crisis of action, what confidence can be placed in its decisions? In what sense does it represent the mind and the heart? But what other representative has the mind and heart on the scene of responsibility? If the will does not represent them, they have no way of expressing themselves in the crisis of action. They are without a representative in the court of responsibility.

We now proceed to the third point raised in the discussion. Has the will the power to act contrary to the greatest apparent good, or under the influence of the weaker motive?

Motive is that which induces choice and decision, or tends to this. It is objective and subjective; from without and from within. There must needs be something *ab extra,* that appeals to the desires and tastes within, to induce choice and action; so there must needs be that within also, in the form of inclination or susceptibility, to which the outward object appeals. The outward object is called a motive, the inward affection is called a motive. Neither of them would be a motive without the other; it takes both the outward and inward motive to fulfil the condition necessary to action. In the apostasy the apple was the objective motive, the appetite or aspiration the subjective. In state, the honor or crown is the objective motive, restless ambition is the inward or subjective motive. The outward object or motive must needs take on the complexion or coloring of the inward affection, so to speak, in order to influence the conduct. Our responsibility has to do with subjective motives, that have their sphere in the soul. We are not accountable for that which appeals to us from without. But we are always accountable for the response which the outward solicitation awakens within. And then we are to consider motives with regard to their intrinsic weight or value, in opposition to their apparent or seeming power. In other words, motives are to be considered in view of their intrinsic character; and also in view of their actual or effective influence. God regards motives intrinsically; man regards them as they seem to him. God looks upon them as they are; man as they appear. A motive may be strong as intrinsically viewed, that is powerless in view of the one acting. A motive may be powerful as regarded from a grovelling standpoint, that would seem weak and worthless from the standpoint of high moral principle. The same thing viewed by the holy and the unholy has an opposite tendency, and is an opposite motive.

Now if the question be, whether one can act according to the weaker motive intrinsically viewed, or not, it is easily answered. We would say, man ordinarily acts thus, till he comes to act from principle. The weaker motive properly viewed offers to the depraved man the greater seeming good, while the stronger motive intrinsically regarded offers to such the least apparent good. When the sinful man acts according to the greatest apparent good, and under the influence of that which is to him the stronger motive, he acts contrary to the greatest real good, and according to the weaker motive, as regarded by the pure and the holy. That which seems the stronger motive is really the weaker motive; and that which seems to such the greatest good, is, in fact, no good at all, but a positive evil.

So the question is not, whether the will can decide contrary to the greatest real good, or the stronger motive intrinsically viewed. There is no doubt here. It is the way, the habit of a perverse will to act thus. It ordinarily does this, till it comes into harmony with moral law. But the question is this; whether the will can of itself, independently of the other powers, choose contrary to the greatest seeming good, or the stronger motive as viewed by the one choosing. Let us examine this matter for a moment.

Choice implies comparison, which calls into action the intellect and desires. We can not conceive of an act of choice where there has not been this process of comparison, and also the stirrings of desire in the heart. Now in what sense can a thing be said to be chosen, which has, in the view of the understanding, and in the scale of the affections, fewer points of attraction and desirableness, than the thing rejected? We would ask the same with respect to different courses of conduct to be decided upon by the will. How can a motive be said to preponderate in decision which had, on the whole, in view of the person, fewer attractions and less influence than the one set aside? In other words, how can one prefer a lesser good to a greater, himself being judge in the case? How can one prefer a thing, or a course, that offers him less happiness than the one rejected? Why prefer it, if it be a lesser good in his own esteem, and when the other and greater good was equally attainable? We ask how this can be at the time of the choice, without change in the one choosing, and as a pure act of the will itself. When one makes a choice, can it be said that the considerations that brought him to the decision were literally weaker in his view than those that failed to do it? Did he act as if it was so? Did he feel that it was so? Was it so? Then why the choice in the case? Indeed, was it a choice at all? Let the advocates of the theory answer.

We would add, if the will has the power claimed above, to act against preponderating motives and moral considerations, and this without change in the thoughts or heart, it has power to dispense with motives altogether external to itself. If it can act against them, it can act without them. If it can act in spite of motives to the contrary, it can act when free from them.[1] Motives in such case were an encumbrance or embarrassment in the act of choice; so that advantage would be gained to the will in point of freedom, if they were taken away. If the will can choose what it does not want, and set aside what it does want, it is done by virtue of a power to dispense with motives altogether. It can laugh at reasons; spurn inducements, and set up for itself in responsibility; and do this lawlessly, absolutely, recklessly. If one can choose that which seems to him less desirable than that which he rejects, or has power to set at nought a greater seeming good and adopt the lesser one in its place, he must have power to act independently of motives, and in the absence of them. The will were as a wheel within a wheel, running lawlessly in the general movement, and to the destruction of the

---

[1] "Is volition dependent on motive?" Prof. F. H. Newhall.

general harmony.   It would be a dangerous force in responsibility, leading to irregularity and absurdity in action, and would be
subversive of all moral ends.

As we have said, the above theories have been adopted, no
doubt, in the interests of moral freedom, and to avoid the hand
of iron fatalism.   Good men have supposed that the doctrine
of moral agency necessitated the hypothesis above considered ;
and rather than give up this doctrine, they have started theories
that necessarily overthrow it.   Relief here is not found in the
will as a will, but in the soul as a moral unit.   It is not
found in a fraction of the soul. but in the unity and harmony
of the soul.¹   We admit the sovereignty of the soul as a whole
in a proper dependence on divine power, in every exigency of
human life.   In such dependence rightly exercised, the soul, not
the will, has the self-determining power, the power of contrary
choice, and to arbitrate in the presence of motives.   We do not
object to the statement that the will has this power, if you connect it rightly with the soul, and make it the proper expression
or representative of the soul, if it be regarded, in other
words, as the sensorium, or focal point of the spiritual nature.
The soul thus considered and regulated has a sovereignty over
motives, external and internal ; it can regulate and control
them and arbitrate between them ; it can adjust itself to exigencies instantly ; it can make the weak motive strong, or the
strong one weak.   With its full furniture of faculties, it is
sensitive to every moral influence and inducement and interest ;
it can summon from all sources and worlds considerations to
act upon the will and induce a rational decision.   We are not
shut up to a single faculty or force in the great affairs of moral
agency.   That agency calls into play a moral system, an
order of faculties, mutual and harmonious, in the proper use
of which the great ends of life are reached.   The will has its
play in these, but can not act independently of them, much
less can it monopolize the moral sense ; it does not control
the moral faculties ; it is not absolute in moral agency ; it in-

¹ "The moral ideas that are given by reason, in the light of which we choose and
act, through which indeed the will is a rational rather than a brute will, are quite as
necessary to personality as the power of choosing and acting."   *President Hopkins'*
Lectures on Moral Philosophy.

dicates, expresses, represents, and connects the moral powers
with the conduct in responsible action ; it has freedom in their
play, but in not playing free from them ; its freedom is one of
harmony rather than of independence.   Moral freedom is not
in the reason, nor the conscience, nor the affections, nor the
will alone ; but in their synthesis or harmony.   Free agency,
therefore, is not of the voluntary nature as distinct from the
moral ; but it is in and from them both.   Freedom, it is true,
is essential to just accountability ; but it is not the will's freedom or independence of the rational and moral nature.   These
constitute accountability.   The will is free, not from the soul,
but in the soul ; not of the moral nature, but as its exponent.
It has no independence of its own that frees it from rational
distinction or moral restraint.   It is a symptom of insanity when
the will obeys no law of wisdom or reason.   But man is so endowed that he can summon considerations instantaneously to
influence his conduct through the will and thus regulate the
choices so as to conform to moral law.   On this ground moral
freedom is safe, and no place is left for necessity or fatalism.
The power of contrary choice and of regulating the motives, the
soul of man certainly has.   It belongs to the moral nature as
a whole, but not to the voluntary nature in particular.   This
attribute of freedom in the soul, properly distributed among the
powers, holds the key to accountability. How different this from
the freedom claimed for the will exclusively, that gives it independence of the rational and moral faculties !   Such freedom
would destroy moral liberty in its largest sense.   It would be
of the nature of " State rights," as absorbing the general sovereignty.   It would be liberty for a part, but slavery in general.

But the view we have taken relieves this question of responsibility entirely.   It puts the attribute of liberty where it belongs.
For what though the will has not independence, if the soul in
its completeness has it ?   What though the will as such has not
authority or power against prevailing motives, if the soul itself
possesses a mastery over them ; can recall, create or regulate
them according to a felt sense of their weight, and the force
of obligation in the case ?   Is not the freedom here claimed for
the will a broader and better freedom, more natural and relia-

ble than could be had by any assumed sovereignty or independence of its own? The will has just this freedom, not of itself apart from the moral constitution, but as growing out of it, and acting in accordance with it. The will is free only as the soul is free. It is free because the soul is free. The soul can not be in bondage, and its functions or powers be free. The will is in some sort the instrument of the soul, the short arm of the mighty lever, acted upon by the controlling powers of the mind.

Thus furnished the soul has the attributes of perfect moral agency. It can summon considerations that lead to rational conclusions instantaneously, or can banish them as soon if seen to be faulty. Is it said that the will does this? How does it do it, and why? Independently of the soul, or as its representative, its efficiency? The moral man, thus endowed, can trample temptation in the dust, and by the force of reasons and motives adapted to do this. Moral freedom, like moral agency, has a broad basis, and a wide field. These come of the completeness of the moral furnishing or the endowment of the soul as a whole. The soul has no bondage save that which is self-imposed or freely allowed. Responsibility rests here, is reasonable; and retribution or accountability following is just.

The bearing of this discussion upon questions of Christian doctrine is plain. We will notice in particular its relation to the question of sin, as to whether it is limited to the will, or affects the whole moral being. It would seem that limiting it to the will merely is to take an inadequate view if it. The theory is contradicted, we think, by a correct philosophy, and the plain teachings of the Bible. Out of the heart proceed evil thoughts, adultery, fornication, murder, theft, etc. Can we limit the motions of sin or evil to that which is but an expression or exponent of the moral being? Are we to look for sin in that which follows the affections, rather than in the heart itself? Is there not somewhat in us that is not expressed through the will to any positive result? The heart's choices are not always the actual decisions. Man is often prepared morally for much that he does not dare to do practically. The surface volition or snatch resolve does not always represent the deep moral character.

We are restrained from much evil doing and purposing by our surroundings and our fears.

To limit human sinfulness, therefore, to the voluntary nature, is to fail to get the full inventory of it.   Sin is a deeper thing; its roots run below the purposes or choices.   It has its seat and reign in the moral nature.

It needs scarcely be said here that taking the broader definition of the will, as embracing the whole moral nature, as in Edwards on the Affections, or as the active responsible agent, according to Coleridge, it would follow that all sin is of the will.   Hence, those adopting these definitions affirm this, and do it consistently with themselves and with the truth.[1]   With the most thorough views of the sinfulness of man, they say nevertheless, all sin is of the will, meaning here that it lies in its death-forms in the deep moral nature of man.   But, to express this truth, they use the same terms that those use who hold different opinions of the nature and guilt of sin.   Both schools in philosophy and theology hold that all sin is of the will; the one meaning by the will a part, the other the whole of the moral man.

With great respect for those who differ from us, we are brought to the conclusion that whatever philosophy of the will we adopt, whether we make it a function of the soul, as in this paper, or the substance or foundation of the soul, with Coleridge and others, we shall be brought to the result that human sinfulness and responsibility extend to the deep moral nature of man.   This nature is the man himself morally.   No part of the moral being is exempt from the claims of God, or the scrutiny of the last judgment.

It belongs to this discussion properly, to notice the relations of the will to the subject of ability, and inability, to questions of regeneration and the Spirit's influence.   It reaches questions also that relate to responsibility under moral government and the sovereignty of God.   It enters into the whole subject of practical religion, as well as of Christian theology.   But we will not pursue the subject farther.   These relations will be suggested to the reader without argument.

[1] See article on Imputation in this *Review* for April, 1867.

ARTICLE IV.

PREACHING FROM WITHIN.

In an interesting book, which we have recently been perusing, entitled, " My Ministerial Experiences," written by a pious
German pastor, this passage is found :

" If we distinguish among poets between those who make verses
and those in whom verses are born, we may with equal justice distinguish between those sermons written according to rule and with
infinite trouble, and those that gush forth from the preacher's
inner life. All preaching springs from the word of God, and nothing more is necessary than to live upon the Gospel. It is essential
that the preacher should place himself under the power of the text
and with prayer and self-examination seek to discover how it applies
to himself; what reproof and consolation, what warning and nourishment it contains for his own soul. He will soon find that the
experience of his own heart will win its way to the hearts of others.
As painted victuals can not satisfy the appetite, so putting imaginary
cases and speaking from without, is powerless and lifeless."

As we read these forcible words, they suggested to us what
may be reckoned one of the peculiar perils of ministers of the
Gospel, and the only security against it. The peril is this,
that on account of the constant necessity laid upon them of
producing sermons for their congregations, they will often
preach and say what their own hearts do not feel, or have not
proved by actual experience. In other words, the danger is
one of affectation, of speaking from without, instead of from
within, after an inward realization of the truth. For instance,
the Sabbath is approaching, and we have, as yet, nothing prepared for our congregations. We open our Bibles and seek
for a text upon which to base a sermon. We find one, guided
in our choice by some recent event of general interest, or the
religious impressions of the season of the year, by a conversation had with some of our people, or by what seems to be mere
chance. We then see what we can make out of it, what doctrine of faith, what lessons of conduct, what encouragement
and what consolation. The sermon, which is the result of our

study and meditation, may be a natural and legitimate out-
growth from the text, like a plant from its seed, or it may be a
forced and artificial product, obtained by some ingenious method
of accommodation, analogous to grafting in fruit culture. However this may be, all our study and labor are directed to the end
of composing a sermon with which to meet our congregations
the next Sabbath. We are liable, therefore, to look at the
truth as it applies to them, and not as it also relates to ourselves. We subject it to the examination of the head, without
always taking care first to test it by trial of the heart. We
consider it critically, and not experimentally.

Such a practice carries with it a double danger. First : that
of subsiding into a low state of personal religion, where one will
have no growth in spirituality. Secondly : that of giving erroneous instruction. Let us take into consideration each of these
specified particulars, that we may know how real is the danger
alleged. Christian ministers, as a class, ought never to forget
that they are sinful men as well as their hearers, and as much
need the instruction and enlightenment of God's word. As it
is written of the ancient high priest, that he needed to offer
up sacrifice daily, first for his own sins, and then for the people's, so it may be said of the ministers of the Gospel.

He must apply the means of grace to his own heart as well
as to the hearts of his hearers. If all Scripture is profitable to
them for doctrine, for reproof, for correction, for instruction in
righteousness, it is equally so to him. He is a fellow pilgrim
with them, and needs not only to point the way, but to walk in
it himself. The word which he ministers is a lamp to his own
feet as well as to theirs. He is not, therefore, to stand still,
contenting himself with throwing forward the light over the
way they should tread, but carrying the lamp in his hand to go
in it himself before them, as their leader and guide. If they
need to watch and pray lest they fall into temptation, he needs
to watch and pray for the same cause ; if they must abstain from
fleshly lusts, beware of covetousness and not be conformed to
this world, he must do these things for the same reasons as he
gives for their doing them. He is compassed about with infirmities as well as they.

When a physician is sick, if he is not an imposter, he will

take the remedies which he prescribes to others afflicted with the same ills. And the family cook, being subject to hunger, must take of the food which she prepares for others. But while this seems to be a very obvious truth, to which no one would find any difficulty in assenting, we apprehend that in actual practice it is sometimes forgotten.

In the stress laid upon us of providing spiritual food for our congregations, we are in danger of neglecting to take it ourselves. While constantly engaged with their infirmities and wants, and ever devising remedies for them, we may overlook the fact that we, being also children of infirmity and want, require the same. We not unfrequently observe something like this. The censors of society, who make it their business to detect and rebuke the faults of their fellow-men, are often found possessing the same, seemingly unconscious of inconsistency. Where one's business is to care for others, it is a sort of natural consequence that he should neglect himself. Thus one may acquire great keenness in detecting the mote which has lodged in his brother's eye and skill to extract it, while a beam of the very same kind imperceptibly forms in his own. We once heard of a good minister whose sermons upon the duties of patience and gentleness were excellent, but he himself was often known to be very querulous and irritable, so that his listeners secretly smiled to think that he did not any better take home in self-application the admirable teaching of his discourses.

Where one looks at truth principally in its application to others rather than to himself, the truth after a while loses its operative force upon him. This is what Robertson meant when he spoke of " the hardening influence of preaching upon ministers," and warned them to guard against it. The danger is a real one and such as we are not altogether unacquainted with. We know how perilous it is to one's moral and religious safety, to listen to truth which he does not practice. We often warn our impenitent hearers against it, exhorting them to beware of neglecting the truth too long, but after awhile they become insensible to its power.

The apostle Paul describes the fearful result by two expressive words : " Past feeling." And what is it to be past feeling in the sense indicated ? To have the religious sensibilities grown callous to the impressions of divine truth, so that one can feel no motive leading him to repentance and godly living. His perceptions remain clear and true enough, and he is able to see what his duty is with sufficient plainness, but he feels no impulse towards it. The propelling force is gone. It is death in life, like a paralysis which affects the working hands, though all the remaining members of the body are alive and sound. And this direful condition results from being familiar with the truth without obeying it. The only safeguard against it is to act promptly and appropriately whenever the truth is perceived, and the duty to which it calls is ascertained.

It is obvious, therefore, that if for any cause, we direct our attention more to the exposition and inculcation of truth, than to acting upon it ourselves, we are exposed to the danger under consideration. Thus it may sometimes happen, that while his knowledge of the Scriptures is far superior to that of any of his people, a minister's real piety will fall behind that of some of them.

With more to feed his faith and quicken his ardor and kindle his devotion, he is surpassed in these very particulars by some humble child of God, whose knowledge in comparison with his is but small. His mind is like a clayey soil, which is impervious to the rain that falls upon it. Though the rain descends in floods, as it does not sink into the ground, but runs away elsewhere, the verdure is not so thick nor the flowers so abundant in that spot as in places having a porous soil, though there they have scarcely more than the night dew to water them. The case is not wholly singular or without a parallel elsewhere. We have often been told that policemen are sometimes found to be wicked and profligate in character. As it is their business to look out for rogues and law-breakers, one might suppose at first thought that, on this account, their reverence for law, and regard for the well-being of society would become so enhanced that they would be the most scrupulous of all men in their careful observance of what was right and orderly.

But holding a place in relation to civil law, analogous to that of ministers with respect to the Christian religion, they are prone to carelessness as regards a strict observance of them. It seems that while jealously exacting from others a due respect for those laws, they themselves sometimes trample upon them. Prompt to ferret out evil-doers and bring them to punishment, they indulge themselves in a criminal laxity with respect to the very same things.

It looks as if they regarded the whole field of public welfare, which is fenced in and guarded by civil statutes and penalties, somewhat as an English squire or nobleman regards his park, a place where he himself is at liberty to pursue his game at pleasure, but no one else can do it without being arrested and punished as a poacher. Such treatment of the majesty of law by its authorised guardians is like that said to be rendered by pagan priests to their idols, who require of the people in their behalf an awful reverence and scrupulous worship, punishing with death the least breach of propriety or profane touch as a sacrilege ; but they themselves, secluded in the privacy of the temples, buffet, scrub, and roughly handle them with the most irreverent levity. The fault of these public servants is that they do not carry their zeal far enough. They should not be any less intolerant than they are of infractions of the law ; they would be justified in the most rigid enforcement of its every demand, but they should regard themselves as subject to it, and be no less stern in exacting from themselves as true an obedience, and as conscientious a respect for its authority as they insist upon in another. To do otherwise is demoralizing. Every improper liberty which they take ; every unlawful transgression allowed in their own practice is sure to blunt the moral sense, and deprave the heart.

Men suppose that one's growth in personal religion will keep even pace with his attainments in religious knowledge. It is perhaps a just and reasonable expectation. But when the fact is otherwise, and the conscious heart is aware how far short it comes of that piety which is imparted to it, because of its advantages of knowledge, the man feels convicted of a fault, as though he were acting a part, walking in craftiness and handling the word of God deceitfully, rather than by manifestation of the truth commending himself to every man's conscience in the sight of God.

If it comes to this, one is in danger indeed. He stands almost on the threshold of infidelity. Not realizing an inner life accordant with the truth which his head has attained, he is tempted to doubt that truth, or whether the results commonly accredited to it may not arise from a mistaken fanaticism. If the causes of the decline of the German churches into rationalism and infidelity, in the beginning of the present century, were known, we suspect this would be found to have been one of them. They had previously sunk into a dead formalism, and the transition from that to the other things was easy and natural. Men can not easily endure the constant sting of self-reproach which attends a low state of spirituality. If they can not get rid of it by attaining to a higher and better state, they may do so by plunging into unbelief.

We now come to the other danger referred to, as resulting from not speaking from the heart, viz. : That of giving erroneous instruction. We might dismiss this division of our subject with the pertinent question of Christ : "How can the blind lead the blind ?" or with the dictum of Anselm, which has ever commanded the assent of the living church : *Qui expertus non fuerit, non intelliget :* He who has had no experience can not understand, and not understanding of course is incompetent to instruct. But perhaps it may be well to linger upon the point awhile for the sake of illustration and enforcement. With the writer quoted at the beginning of the essay, we believe that one who would truly preach the Gospel "must live upon the Gospel," or, as he further on says, that "the preacher must first place himself under the power of the text, and with prayer and self-examination seek to discover how it applies to himself, before he can successfully explain and enforce it upon others." His sermons should impress his hearers like narrations of experience, rather than as conclusions of the intellect. The thoughts which compose them should seem spontaneous, not artificial ; offered, not sought for. They should gush from a natural spring, and not be brought up by wheel and axle. They should flow from the heart as from a brimming fountain, not be drawn from the head as from a forcing pump. The sermon should have the characteristics of truth and life, and not of unreality and death ; it should be a growth and not merely an ingenious or elaborate composition. It is related of the celebrated Welch preacher, Christmas Evans, that when he was to prepare a sermon to preach, the first thing he did was "to take his text up into his heart," as he phrased it. He did this by prayer and intense reflection. Sometimes this effort of previous verification was like wrestling with an unseen antagonist. He appeared to strain every faculty of soul and body. He had throes of spirit like those of one in birth pangs. But when the hour of preaching came he was calm and serene as the unclouded sky, and his discourse was the speaking of one who knew whereof he affirmed. It fell upon the ears of his hearers as the speech of one who had talked with God, or just come from the eternal world, and was familiar with its realities. It produced swift conviction and had great effect. Men felt that one could not preach as he did unless he preached the living truth, and feeling this they submitted to it.

The effect on his congregation of a revival of religion upon a minister's preaching has often been remarked. A new warmth and vitality are infused into it, so that it seems as if it came from another man. His people say of him : "How earnest he is, and his words are as goads, driving us to duty." If there was ever any doubt of the sincerity of his convictions there is none now. His tones tremulous with emotion, his eyes with their look of entreaty, the natural eloquence of voice and look and gesture, joined with a more direct and pointed style of address, form a product that can not be counterfeited, and carry with them convincing evidence. This new energy and animation in the preacher is not the mere effect of the unusual excitement which exists at the time. Neither is it wholly due to the encouragement and elation which the success of his labors is having ; but to the fact of his being more frequent in prayer at this time, and having his heart quickened by feeding it more abundantly with the truths of the word. He renews and deepens the religious impressions of his soul by carrying them to that word, and subjecting them again to its power.

The effect of this upon his thoughts, feelings, and entire spirit is to give them a freshness, vividness, and warmth which are refreshing to all who come within the reach of his influence and teaching. It is like what occurs when the old, defaced, worn-out coin of our money currency is recalled from circulation back to the Government mint, that it may be recoined and appear again bright, clear cut, and having its original weight.   A man who constantly is renewing in this wise the impressions and experience of his heart by daily intercourse with divine truth, and a faithful application of it to himself will always preserve the freshness of his thoughts.   His preaching will remain as vitalizing at the last as it was at first.   It will never degenerate into hollow cant, or seem stale or lifeless.

Among the other eminent services which the late J. W. Alexander rendered to the American church and its ministry, especially the younger members of it, we reckon that not the least, by which he insisted that the best, and only way, in fact, in which a minister could maintain the freshness and interest of his preaching was by the constant, reverent, obedient study of God's word.   Whoever will give heed to it, is not likely to be shelved from the ministerial work on account of dulness as he grows old, but he will improve and ripen with time, and his later preaching will be as much superior to that of his early ministry, as a ripe, mellow peach is better than a green one.

We have said that one who preaches what he has not first verified in the experience of his heart is in danger of teaching error.   The error will consist in impression, perhaps, more than in the matter set forth.   The latter may be theoretically correct, the doctrine of the sermon may be theoretically sound, but as it is merely a fabrication of the head, its impressions will be no other than that of a fabrication, that is, it will not have the thrilling, convincing effect of truth.   That this may be obtained, he must first take it up into his heart and live it.

Let us attempt an illustration from nature.   There are various natural substances, the elementary composition of which has been accurately ascertained by chemical analysis.   But it is not possible to manufacture those substances by purely artificial processes from their elements.   One can not make sugar, for instance, by combining carbon and water, its components, even though he combines them in exactly the same proportions as they are found in the natural product.   No one tasting the mixture would call it sugar.   The only way in which this can be produced is to throw these elements into the laboratory of nature, and allow her to produce it in accordance with her laws.   To be sure, men assume that it is an article of manufacture.   But how or in what sense is it such?   Only as they have been able to produce it by strict obedience to the conditions which she has imposed.

"The powers of nature, or, in other words, the properties of matter, do all the work when once objects are put into the right position.   This one operation, of putting things into fit places for being acted upon by their own internal forces, or by those residing in other natural objects, is all that man does or can do.   He only moves one thing to or from another.   He moves a spark to fuel and it ignites, and by the force generated in combustion it converts into sugar the cane juice which he has previously moved to the spot.   He has no other means of acting on matter than by moving it."—Mill's Political Economy.

The composition of a tree or plant may likewise be discovered by the same mode of analysis.   But one can not by any amount of ingenuity manufacture one or the other.   The only way is to drop the seed in the ground, and let nature develop it by the action of sunshine and rain, heat and moisture, into the proper product.

It is somewhat so with all right preaching.   It is not enough in order to make a sermon, that one have an intellectual acquaintance with the truths that should enter into it, or mingle them in just proportions.   The heart must vitalize them after having been first quickened by them.   They must be transformed into living forcible verities, as nature transforms her elementary substances when she binds them together by some living principle of growth.   Art can not do the work of life. She may construct a figure in which every bone and muscle, vein and artery of the human body shall be accurately represented ; but, after all, it will be but a manikin.   She has no power to send the blood coursing through the veins, to set the lungs agoing, and convert it into a living, moving, thinking man.   Life alone can do that.   No more can mere art produce good, effective preaching.   However admirable and orderly the work, the instincts of man will pronounce it a counterfeit.   It will not afford spiritual nourishment.   It sets before them painted victuals, and not the real bread of life.   They will say of a man who speaks from no deeper knowledge, that he talks about his subject, but he does not talk it.   He speaks of the kingdom of God from hearsay, not from his own personal knowledge and recollection. He seems to tell them of what others have seen, but not what he himself has seen.

It remains to consider briefly : What will save us from these dangers. It has been already implied in what has gone.before. We must take heed how we read and study the word of God. We must not read it merely to obtain material or suggestions for sermons and exhortations, but always and chiefly for spiritual edification. We should absorb the truth before we venture to give it forth. After it has enriched our own hearts and wrought its due effects upon ourselves, then we may proceed to apply its teachings to others. As the earth drinks in the rain and dissolves into it the various substances which the plants require for food ere she yields it up again for their nourishment, so should we first receive into our own souls the word which we study, and impregnate it with the evidences of self-conviction and reality, before we attempt to use it for the edification of others. By a change of figure we might regard ourselves as performing for our hearers the work of a telescope with respect to the truths which the Bible contains. That is, we endeavor to bring those solemn verities more distinctly and vividly home to them, so that they shall be fully impressed with their importance and inclined to conform themselves to them. But it is not enough that the rays of light fall on the object glass of the telescope ; they must pass through it ere a magnified image of the object looked at can be presented to the beholder. So must the rays of truth, shining forth from the word of God, penetrate the heart of the preacher and be brought to the focal point of a clear recognition in him, before a clear and stirring impression of it will be likely to be had by the hearer. Better than such elaborate imagery, perhaps, is the plainest statement of the case. If we would successfully persuade men to piety, we must be men of piety ourselves. Our success in preaching the Gospel will be proportioned to the faithfulness with which we live it, and not to the learning and skill with which we expound it. It is all comprehended in the advice of St. Paul, who next to his divine master, was the greatest of preachers, to Timothy : " Take heed [first] unto thyself, and [then] unto the doctrine ; . . . . for in doing this, thou shalt both save thyself and them that hear thee."

By such a personal self-application of the word, the preacher will gain, not only in respect to the force and truthfulness of his sermons, but also in respect to the ease with which he can produce them. For it has the effect of vastly increasing the productive power of the mind. He will write from an overflowing soul, and the difference between composition in such a state and one that is spiritually dull and uninspired by the inward revelation of the truth, is the difference of drawing from "a well of water whose waters fail not" and a cistern which contains no more than what has been poured into it.

De Quincy divides literature into two classes; the literature of knowledge and the literature of power. "The function of the first is to teach; the function of the second is to move. The first is a rudder, the second is an oar or sail." The one informs or communicates something new; the other, without perhaps imparting any thing new, excites, inspires and exalts. To the first class belong encyclopedias, scientific treatises and books of discovery; to the other, poetry and the forms of eloquence, whatever aims to affect men through the imagination and the heart. Paradise Lost, the tragedies of Shakespeare, the orations of Burke and the sermons of Massillon are examples of it. Following this fine classification, the Bible must be placed in the literature of power, and it is not merely a sample, one book among many, but the very highest in the class. It stirs the depths of our being more profoundly, quickens into life more and higher faculties than any other. In its operation upon the spiritual nature it stands single and alone. No other book in literature can do its work. But whether it fully accomplishes this depends upon its being absorbed into the soul. There is no possibility of realizing the deep moving impulse and spiritual awakening which it is fitted by divine appointment to produce, but by passively submitting the heart to its influence, any more than it is possible to feel the power of noble music without a surrender of the soul to its operation. When, however, the power of divine truth has thrilled through the depths of man's spiritual being, and revealed him to himself, its effect does not end there in a mere transient sensation; the light which it flashes through the consciousness is not simply a flash like that of lightning in the night, whose illumination is but for an instant, and then succeeded by a deeper gloom. The thrilling touch awakens the dead soul to a permanent life; the sudden light is the breaking of a spiritual dawn which grows brighter and brighter to the perfect day, instead of operating as a galvanic shock, which can only impart a momentary and hideous semblance of life to what is dead. It acts like the touch of Christ upon the ruler's daughter, by which she was made to arise and walk in actual existence. In other words, it evinces its right to be classed in the literature of power by awakening faculties capable of exerting an independent power of their own. As health gives vigor to a sickly, languid frame, and makes what once might have required painful and even impossible exertion, become a joyous play and easy exercise, so does the spiritual life, elicited by the operation of divine truth upon the heart, produce an increased ability to handle the themes relating to that truth, and change to a pleasure what otherwise were a drudgery.

For such reasons as these we feel that the importance of giving careful attention to the religious discipline of the heart, so as to make it the seat of a truly vital, growing piety, can not be too strongly urged upon those engaged in the work of the Christian ministry. That we shall care enough for the cultivation of our minds, there is little cause for fear. The incentives to do this are too immediate and pressing to allow us to neglect it. The faults of the head, though not so disastrous, are more open to observation than those of the heart; we therefore make haste to correct the former and delay to do so with the latter. These may wait too long. There is danger of the evil becoming inveterate and irremediable if suffered thus to remain uncorrected. It would be a better plan to reverse the usual order of our care, so as to be more anxious to have the heart right and to feed it with the truth it requires. Our reading of God's word should rather be for self-improvement than to find matter for talk and sermon making. We should not find our material for the latter purposes at all diminished by this course, but largely increased. The quickened heart would discover ten thoughts suited to its need where but one was found before, and all would be more effective than any thing which the skilled head alone could devise. For then a description by St. Paul of the effect of true preaching will be verified to us. "And thus are the secrets of his heart made manifest; and so falling down on his face, he will worship God, and report that God is in you of a truth."

ARTICLE V.

THE ENGLISH CONGREGATIONAL COLLEGES.

An American in England, going up to Oxford and Cambridge to see those venerable institutions for himself, realizes, what he had dimly learned before from printed accounts, how different the English universities are from American colleges, and how different are the idea of a college and the idea of a university in the two countries. If he also visits the "dissenting" colleges of England, for example, the Congregational, he becomes acquainted with another class of institutions, differing from the Oxford and Cambridge colleges in not being organically connected with any national university, and differing also, as they do, from American colleges, in this, among other things, that they impart both what is called in this country collegiate, and also what is called theological education. He hears them called "theological colleges," a name quite unknown in his native land. Since the day in August, 1807, when Madam Phœbe Phillips of Andover, "relict of Samuel Phillips, Esq., late Lieut. Governor," etc., and John Phillips, Jun., "son of the said Samuel and Phœbe," and Samuel Abbot, Esquire, established and endowed "a public theological institution in Phillips Academy," using the word "seminary" throughout the constitution they signed, all such institutions have been known among us as theological seminaries. The English Congregationalists have one institution under the name at Hackney.[1] Its sixty first report lies before us. It does not differ particu-

[1] "Hackney Theological Seminary." There are besides, six "private theological seminaries" where ministerial candidates are prepared for college

larly from the colleges, so called; the classics, mathematics, mental and moral science, rhetoric and logic are taught, as well as Hebrew, biblical criticism, theology, homiletics, and church history. "It was designed originally to prepare suitable men for itinerant service; but the course of education has been so raised and extended as to place it in all respects on a par with the other colleges."

No class of Christians in Great Britain, indeed, makes the distinction between college and theological seminary which is so familiar to us. The terms are in that land entirely interchangeable. Our well-defined distinction between them seems almost impossible to the English mind. In the universities the clergy of the Establishment have always received from one corps of teachers both secular and ministerial education. So in the Congregational colleges. Several of these have but two professors, viz., Rotherham, Brecon, and Western Colleges, one of whom is professor of classics and mathematics, the other is a theological tutor. At Spring Hill, (Birmingham), Lancashire (Manchester), and Cheshunt, founded by Lady Huntingdon at Talgath, with which Newport Pagnel is now incorporated, there are three professors. In two of them the mathematics and classics are divided, and in one exegetical theology is taught by one professor, and dogmatic and general theology and philosophy by another; while in one of them philosophy and Hebrew are put into the same department, and in another mathematics, philosophy, and Hebrew.[1] Airedale has four professors, one of theology, one of pastoral theology, one of classics, and one of mathematics and philosophy. New College, St. John's Wood, London, formed by the consolidation of Coward, Highbury and Homerton,[2] has a faculty of five, a teacher of Greek and Latin, Dr. Wm. Smith of the dictionaries, one of metaphysics and logic, with the English language, one of German and Hebrew, one of mathematics, natural philosophy, and ecclesiastical history, and one of theology, Dr. Robert Halley, with a lecturer on chemistry and natural his-

---

[1] In Lancashire college, Henry Rogers, author of "The Eclipse of Faith," teaches theology and moral philosophy.

[2] There is still a Homerton college, Rev. W. J. Unwin, LL.D., Principal; but it is a training institution for teachers in infant and juvenile schools.

tory.   Of course, any thing like the thoroughness of our separate college and seminary courses of study is quite impossible.
At Airedale, Lancashire, and New Colleges, there is the nearest
approximation to this, the whole term of study being five years,
and in the last institution the curriculum being divided into a
literary course of two years and a theological course of three
years.   The same division obtains at Spring Hill, the theological course, however, occupying but four sessions.   How long
these sessions are we can not discover from documents either
personally gathered in the country or kindly sent to us, but we
presume they are of three months each.   In all, there are thirteen ¹ Congregational colleges in England, Scotland, and Wales.
The Hebrew and Aramæn languages are taught at Spring
Hill ; the Hebrew and Chaldee at Western College ; the Hebrew, Chaldee and Syriac at Airedale.   The modern languages,
as well as the English, are in the curriculum of several of the
institutions.   By only part of them is anything more than
a good English education required of candidates for admission.
At Airedale, which stands high among them, applicants must
pass an examination in the first book of the Æneid, the first
book of Xenophon's Anabasis, and the first book of Euclid's
Elements ; "but the committee have power to modify this rule
in the case of pious young men of decided promise as preachers, whose previous educational advantages have not been great."
At Rotherham an examination is had, partly oral, partly written, in the English language and history, arithmetic, Paley's Evidences, and in a general knowledge of the Scriptures.   At Lancashire an acquaintance with the elements of Greek and Latin
is required, with an examination in the first two books of the
Æneid, the Gospel of Luke in Greek, the principles of arithmetic, and the first book of Euclid.   At Spring Hill candidates
are examined in the sixth book of the Æneid, the first of the Anabasis, the first of Euclid, "and arithmetic and algebra as far as
fractions."   At Bala, North Wales, "the candidate must not
only be conversant with the Welsh language, but with arithmetic and the English tongue also."   Brecon requires more.   At

---

¹ Mission College, Highgate, in connection with the London Missionary Society,
is not here included.   Here "the missionary students spend the last year of their professional training, pursuing studies peculiar to missionary life and labors."

New College, London, which perhaps stands highest, "each candidate is examined respecting his literary knowledge, religious history, and general aptitude for study and ministerial labor." At Western College, Plymouth, "he must submit to examination respecting his religious principles and purposes, as also respecting his literary attainments and mental resources." Something like these requirements, but varying in each, obtains in other institutions, while in some no previous examination is had. In several of them the period of study is lengthened to supply defects of elementary education ; at New College students are allowed to devote a part of their time, during the first year, to preparatory studies, for which elementary classes are formed whenever necessary ; at Lancashire a separate preliminary course is founded ; at the Theological Hall of the Congregational churches of Scotland, which most nearly resembles our American theological seminary, though it has but two professors, "the students, for the most part, attend the University of Edinburgh for their general learning" ; "in cases where elementary education is required, a fifth year may be added."

In the Scotch universities, if we may judge by Aberdeen, the requirements are not so severe as to imply great proficiency in those who pass from them to theological study. "The matriculative examination is a very easy one," says a statement we obtained in Scotland, "and there is seldom an instance of a boy being rejected. It is enough to be able to translate and construe a chapter in Cæsar's Commentaries. Less Greek is looked for, and if a boy have some acquaintance with τύπτω he will pass. The standard has been raised a little lately." The first session at Aberdeen is devoted to Greek and Latin ; the second and third to the same studies, with mathematics and natural history, the proportion of classics in the third being less ; the fourth to mathematics with logic and moral philosophy. Sir William Hamilton, as is well known, withdrew for many years from the Senatus of the University of Edinburgh because no other accepted so little knowledge for the degree of A. M. "The Church of Scotland was neither the offspring of learning nor of power : it was the choice of an unlearned people, established by a revolution." "Theological learning remained superfluous, if not unsafe." Classical education he represented as still more depressed. Dr. Leonard Schmitz, on retiring from the rectorship of the high school of Edinburgh, (1865) complained that the universities still include an amount of elementary instruction which is wholly disgraceful. " After all that has been done of late years in the way of amendment and elevation," says the *North British Mail*, "the Scottish universities have not yet risen" (the University Reform Act notwithstanding,) "to a much loftier part, at least in some branches of academic learning, than that of upper schools." The evil is ascribed to the defects of the preparatory schools, and the lack of a national board of university examiners. In the United Presbyterian Church the principal defect of their training of ministers is acknowledged to be "the want of an efficient, impartial, and uniform examination of all candidates for admission to the theological hall, which shall preclude the entrance of any who do not possess competent talents and attainments." Many of the deficiencies of the British pulpit in all denominations are unquestionably owing to defects of preparatory training, before the study of theology is commenced. In that the old country remarkably resembles the new.

At a college conference held in London twenty two years ago, the late Dr. W. H. Stowell, then of Rotherham College, objected to candidates for English pulpits resorting to American seminaries, on the ground that equal advantages could be well found nearer home, as "in London, Edinburgh, Glasgow, Halle, or Bonn." Dr. Stowell admitted, however, that "the advantages of an American theological seminary are these : the instruction of distinct professors, a sifted result of German studies, the fruits of some learning, of approved piety and of reverent freedom in theological inquiry, together with boldness of conception in connection with public service." The late Dr. H. F. Burder, then of Bala, North Wales, arguing for special attention to theological learning in the latter years of the collegiate course, and for two full years [1] of study in theology, commended emphatically the order and distribution of the Scottish universities and theological institutions.

[1] Dr. John Pye Smith, after forty years' experience at Homerton, said three for "the almost exclusive study of Bible interpretation, divinity and church history." He intimated that the time then afforded was less than two years

"After passing through the grammar school, the student is usually placed under the professors of Latin and Greek for about three years; he is then engaged in the study of logic, of rhetoric, of mathematics, of mental, of moral, and of natural philosophy, for three years more; and if he is destined for the ministry in the established church, he pursues the study of theology, and of related subjects, during four additional years. If he belongs to the Secession church, he is placed, after his graduation at college, under the professors of their divinity hall, and his attention is entirely directed to those studies which have the most important bearing on the Christian ministry. This arrangement, recommended by long experience of its advantages and efficiency, as well as by the order of nature, can not be disregarded without serious injury."

Dr. William Smith, then of Highbury, late of New College, pleading for adequate preparatory training, stated that it had been the practice, till very recently, to admit young men into the English colleges who possessed hardly any acquaintance with the first elements of the subjects taught. He insisted upon an accurate knowledge of Latin and Greek grammar, and sufficient acquaintance with the vocabularies of the languages to enable a student to read an easy author in each; a clear idea of the nature of mathematical reasoning, with the mastery of the first book of Euclid, fractional and decimal arithmetic, and algebra as far as simple equations; and also some facility in the use of English, with an acquaintance with the elements of Greek, Roman, and English history, these matters to occupy one year of study under the tuition of some competent minister, the expense to be borne by the colleges. This plan was preferred to that of preparatory teaching in the existing colleges or the founding of a preparatory institution. Even in the five years' course, said Dr. Smith, "less than two is left for the exclusive study of theology." Evidently it is quite impossible to make needful improvement in either preparatory, collegiate, or theological education, where all three are undertaken in the same institutions, and the time of attendance is limited to four or five years. Evidently nothing like the advance we constantly see in our own country is to be expected. Dr. Robert Vaughan, in his Notes on the United States since the War, published after his return from the Boston National

Council,[1] commends, with qualifications, the diffusion of the higher education among us.   Alluding to the common school system, he says : "Each State, moreover, has a number of efficient grammar schools dotted over it, where an education preliminary to entering the classes of the colleges or the universities may be obtained, also free from cost.   These universities or colleges are so called, because their object is to secure a general collegiate training.   In this respect they are distinguished from the theological seminaries and the medical colleges."   He estimates the total attendance in 1864 at fourteen thousand ; Students in theological seminaries, Catholic and Protestant, a little above one thousand.

"The reader will see that this network of instruction, spread over the whole country, is something extraordinary.   What is the result?   I shall not attempt to answer.   The reader will call to mind the names of Americans who have distinguished themselves in science, in history, in philosophy, in poetry, and in general literature.   Still, in proportion to a population of thirty one millions, the *athletæ* are few and far between.   Nor should this surprise us.   America has done well to have done so much.   She is still in her seed-time.   English booksellers know that for the best books in all departments of learning they have had no customers like America for thirty years past.   In history, in patristics, and in theology the libraries of the United States are rich beyond anything commonly supposed in this country.   If there are few professors in their theological seminaries who have made themselves felt in England as they should have done, the learning and the ability existing among the men who fill those offices are highly creditable to them.   English Nonconformists greatly need a few such theologians as Professor Park of Andover."

At the late College Conference in London in 1865, the following question was proposed by the Committee who called it together : "The establishment of a theological college for students who have already completed a satisfactory literary curriculum."   One of the essayists, Rev. J. M. Charlton of Western College, suggested that all the colleges save one should become

[1] *British Quarterly Review*, Oct. 1865, pp. 433—497.   Dr. V. was formerly Principal of Lancashire College.

" Preparatory institutions, that is, affording classical, mathematical, and scientific training, in preparation for a more extensive and
special divinity and ministerial college, wherein all biblical, dogmatic, ecclesiastical and homiletic studies might be more efficiently
conducted ; to which the students from the others might be at length
transferred ; and from which, as from a common centre, all young
ministers might finally go forth to take those stations in the churches
for which they might be found fitted."

Dr. Falding of Rotherham urged the adoption of the American plan, substantially, for the more complete ministerial training of advanced students. "The increased amount of attention
paid to literary studies makes it increasingly difficult," he observed, " to do justice to studies theological." No action, however, has followed these suggestions. One essayist suggested
that a change might come when the sectarian restrictions at
Cambridge and Oxford are removed ; adding : "The revolution
which this plan would produce in our collegiate system is
enough to make one tremble." It is widely felt in England
that there are too many colleges [1] and none of sufficiently high
character ; propositions for combining two or more are often
started ; but the questions, which shall cease to be, and which
shall go on, which shall be elevated, and which depressed,
present insurmountable difficulties. It is an illustration of the
fixed ways of English life, and of the improbability of reform
and advance, even among Dissenters, that four of these institutions are half a century, and four more a century old, and no
theological institution, as such, yet exists in England.

The limited number of students in these institutions is a matter of surprise to an educated American. One of the things Dr.
Vaughan notices in his account of that network of instruction,
which he pronounced extraordinary, is this : "The number of
students in each in 1864 varied from twenty in some, to between
eight or nine hundred in others." At the late London Confer-

---

[1] More than twenty years ago Prof. B. B. Edwards said in the *Bibliotheca Sacra*
(Vol. III. No. XII., p. 777), "The number of these academies is thought by many of
their patrons to be much too large. By the building of railways in every direction
much of the supposed necessity for some of these institutions has been taken away.
Birmingham, for example, is only three or four hours from Manchester. Still it is
found to be very difficult to amalgamate them. In some cases local feelings and
prejudices in favor of particular institutions are very strong. In other instances legal
difficulties stand in the way." All the difficulties have been increased since Prof.
Edwards wrote.

ence, Dr. Vaughan said : "Up to within the last seven years the
great want of our colleges had been, for some while past, the
want of men. Since then, from some cause which I hardly
know how to explain, the quantity has increased so that all our
colleges have been full." It has diminished since that time from
four hundred and fifty five to two hundred and ninety three.
New College, which has had the largest attendance, has increased from fifty two to fifty three ; the Congregational Institute, Nottingham, from forty two to fifty three ; the Glouces-
tershire Institute, Bristol, from thirteen to sixteen ; Cheshunt
from twenty seven to thirty one ; and Hackney from twenty to
twenty one. But Brecon has declined from forty five students
to thirty three ; Bala from twenty one to fifteen ; the Theological Hall, Edinburgh, from twenty to twelve ; Airedale, from
eighteen to fifteen ; Western, from seventeen to fifteen ; Lancashire from forty three to thirty two ; and Spring Hill from
thirty to twelve. In the Presbyterian college, Caermarthen,
Wales, the number of "Orthodox Independent students for the
ministry" has decreased from thirty four to twenty one. We
are not sure whether the attendance at this college is included
in both of the aggregates given above. In former years it has
been named in the tables of Congregational colleges in the
Year Book. It was once a Congregational seminary ; but
some of the tutors became Arians and Socinians, and the Independents withdrew and established Brecon College. Caermarthen was originally formed by the union (1719) of a local institution with the old Tewksbury Dissenting Academy where
Bishop Butler and Archbishop Secker had their first training.
It is now owned and controlled by the Unitarians, the management being in the hands of the London Presbyterian Board.
There is, however, a fund for the education of Orthodox Independents, the income of which is about five hundred and thirty
pounds per annum. There is a Congregational theological professor, Rev. William Morgan, who teaches moral philosophy,
natural theology, the evidences of Christianity, biblical criticism and interpretation, homiletics and the composition of
sermons. "Systematic theology is not taught professionally
in the college, the students seeking instruction in that department from ministers in their own denominations." The relative

number of students is : Congregational, twenty ; Welch Methodists, (Calvinistic) three ; Unitarians, two ; Baptist, one. If any one finds it difficult to account for this small aggregate of students per annum, since both collegiate and theological students are taught together, let it be remembered that many candidates for the Congregational ministry in England commence their study elsewhere. Since the establishment of the London University metropolitan students have pursued the study of the arts and sciences in connection therewith, receiving degrees on examination.[1] The list of ministers in the Year Book is plentifully embellished with titles, from B. A. and LL. B. upwards, received from the English and Scotch universities. Every list of degrees conferred at the universities contains the names of students of the Dissenting academies. Our impression is, however, that these are counted in the college tables of numbers each year.

The cost of educating English Congregational ministers, estimated by the cost and expenses of the colleges, is much greater than in this country. At one of them, "where there are not more than ten or fifteen students," wrote Prof. Edwards in 1846, "the salaries of the professors amount to five or six thousand dollars." The financial reports for last year furnish the following comparisons : Western College, two professors, expenditure about six thousand dollars ; Rotherham, same faculty, expenditure a little less ; Hackney, the same, expenses between six thousand and seven thousand dollars. Spring Hill, Nottingham, Hackney, and Cheshunt, with three instructors each, expend from eight to ten thousand dollars each. Lancashire with four costs per annum about fourteen thousand dollars. New College with five, is carried on at an expense of about twenty one thousand dollars. Our estimates are made on the old basis of five dollars to the guinea ; at the recent ratio of exchange, these statements should be very much increased. The cost of the buildings, grounds, etc., is many times greater than in the case of American institutions with many more instructors, and several times as many students. The style of furnishing is also far more costly and luxurious. Probably the style indulged in at the universities has had its effect. We looked in

[1] So in the Theol. Hall, Edinburgh, mentioned ab)ve.

upon students' rooms at Lancashire and Spring Hill, which would make the eyes of young theologians and collegians in our land, especially at the West, open wide with amazement. The taste and elegance of architecture, the beauty and cost of grounds which we noticed there, and at New College, London, made us remember with a sigh many a bleak campus and many a pile of "barracks" in our native land. Usually, as at the universities, the family residences of the faculty are in the buildings. There are but few heads of American Congregagational colleges who are so fortunate in their condition that they would not envy the quarters of Principal Barker at Moseley, or Henry Rogers at Manchester. A gentleman from Canada lately undertook to show a community in Iowa, of somewhat aspiring tendencies in respect to education, that "a college could be established as easily as an academy." It would take the funds and subscriptions of half a dozen of our Western colleges to found and set in operation one of the Dissenting colleges of England.

The students also are far better provided for than among us, in the amount and quality of accommodations. At Spring Hill each student has an attractive and convenient study-room to himself on the first floor, and a separate single bed-room, spacious and pleasant, in the second story, directly above. All board within college walls, eating together in a handsome refectory on the first floor, front, beneath the library, and opposite the chapel. The edifices which we saw show the influence of college architecture at the universities. Some of them surround three sides of a rectangle, a striking and beautiful form of structure, with a central front tower over the principal entrance. Inside the rectangle, under the first floor, is a covered walk running round the whole building for exercise, the story sheltering it being supported by massive stone arches. Board is furnished in some instances, if necessary, at the cost of the college; in others, students board and lodge out of college with families, or in houses, approved and registered for the purpose. At Lancashire, Spring Hill, and New College, there are scholarships for those to whom they may be awarded for merits and "exhibitions," or charity provisions for those needing aid.

Some years ago it was proposed in Yorkshire to unite Airedale and Rotherham. The whole number of students would be about thirty ; the increase of advantages and economy would be considerable. The same obstacles prevented it which our Methodist brethren in Iowa have encountered in attempting to make two struggling seminaries, Cornell and Fayette, into one of a better class. The friends of union in England argue that it were better every way if the newer schools were preparatory institutions, enlarging the number and improving the scholarship of students sent to the older ones. The necessity of building anew for both the Yorkshire colleges has revived recently the question of union. The premises are old, inconvenient, and much too small.

"On the ground of expense alone," says the *London Patriot*, "we should be sorry if the needless cost of maintaining two collegiate institutions should be permanently bound upon the Yorkshire churches, when they have such a large industrial population rising rapidly around them, which appeal to the most liberal sacrifice of money and effort in order to spread amongst them the vital and saving influences of evangelical truth."

The Yorkshire colleges grew up by the association of students in olden time with some able minister apt to teach, as did our first theological schools ; and when, from imperfect means of travel, but a small district could look to any one source of supply.

"But the change which has come in education," says the *Patriot*, "shows the folly of perpetuating small institutions, which local necessities formerly occasioned and justified. If twelve or fifteen men were trained by a minister who was full handed with his work, he could train no more, and their education cost but little. But now the educational demands are greater, tutors are called to give their whole energy to their proper work. The cost of education has thus grown excessively, and the question arises which has escaped consideration. If the work of education now requires the continuous and entire devotion of men separated to it and qualified for it, should not more students be gathered to receive the benefits of this unremitting labor? And if the cost of education has been immensely increased by the just increase of the tutors' salaries, should it not be reduced by the enlargement of their sphere of usefulness ; the increase of the number of their students? We are most firmly assured that by this means not only would the cost of education be

reduced, but the education itself would be improved.   The tutorial
staff of either Yorkshire college would teach more efficiently and successfully some thirty or forty students, combining the number in both
colleges, than the small half-number they are now privileged to
teach.   By their very qualifications for their high office, we desire
for them this noble sphere of influence.   And it is plain that with
the more animated and masterful discipline which larger numbers
would evoke, the cost of the improved education would be reduced
one half.   Nor does the reduction of expense end here.   All conversant with the working of institutions know how great the working expenses are.   It can not but be improvident to maintain two
institutions to do what one would do more effectively."

These suggestions acquire force from the fact that Rotherham
is between Airedale and Nottingham, about forty miles from
each.   It is now proposed to rebuild both the Yorkshire colleges, but for different purposes, Airedale to remain what it is,
and Rotherham to become "strictly and solely a theological
hall," after the American fashion.

" It would thus be lifted out of all competition with all existing
colleges," says the *Patriot*, "and appeal for its support to the whole
country, as meeting a special want of our denomination, and raising
up a special class of men for its service.   Students might pass from
them to it who desire a more lengthened theological curriculum ;
and only those students would be received into it whose previous education warranted their entering upon its higher and specific course.
There can be no doubt that this scheme commends itself to a prevailing feeling that more specific theological attainments are to be de-
siderated in our young ministry, and that the age preëminently demands such theological training and scholarship."

Some inferences touching the multiplication of small colleges
on the same field in our own land, draining the resources of the
charitable, dividing the interests involved, and keeping the institutions poor and feeble, may be drawn from the fact that
Airedale and Rotherham are situated in a county of immense
wealth from mining, manufactures and shipping, as well as
from agriculture and trade, with a population sixteen years
since of nearly two millions, being about twenty five hundred
to the square mile.   And the suggestion that there can not be
any over-multiplication of colleges in our Western States, at

least, on account of constant increase of population, loses much of its apparent force when we remember that the population of England increases at the rate of one thousand a day.

One very singular peculiarity of Congregational education in Great Britain, closely allied to all that has been stated in this article, is the practice, so different from our own, of discouraging the association of candidates for the ministry with students contemplating the other professions in the literary and scientific course. With our fathers and with us it has always been a very precious feature of our American colleges that our young pastors, lawyers, physicians, teachers, etc., have been educated together, receiving from Christian instructors a training and culture moulded and inspired by religion. With our fathers and brethren over the water it has been entirely different. A published paper of the Rev. Francis Watts, 1845, now before us, argues elaborately for "the admission of youths not preparing for the ministry into our divinity colleges." No other young men, however, than " the sons of evangelical Dissenters" are contemplated in the argument, and only some of the colleges, those affiliated, or to be affiliated, to the University of London. And the condition understood was " that the number of such general students do not exceed a fourth, or, perhaps a fifth of the whole body of students in any college." With these very important, and un-American limitations, Mr. Watts proceeds cautiously, as one who expects to encounter fixed views and formidable prejudices, to show " that the admission of such young men, under the conditions, is likely (1) to prevent the decay of piety and nonconformity in Dissenting families ; (2) to promote the influence and usefulness of the Congregational ministry ; and (3) to increase the efficiency of our colleges as theological seminaries." On the last point it is urged that the secular students would retain an interest in the colleges in after life, and that the income received from their board and instruction would support an increased number of candidates for the ministry, and enlarge the means of instruction. On the second point it is represented that useful friendships would be formed between the two classes of students, and the well-educated Dissenting gentleman, merchant, or professional man would cease to regard Dissenting ministers as, "with some exceptions, a meanly educated class." On the first point it is stated as a known fact, that the younger members of influential Dissenting families very frequently abandon the ministry under which they were brought up. It was asserted some years since, in the *Quarterly Review*, that "Dissent seldom retains its hold on the same family for three generations." This is accounted for by common worldly motives, and by the fact that literary honors were to be attained only by going to Scotland for an education, or conformity, at Oxford or Cambridge, to the established creed and worship, while the moral dangers of the universities were fearfully destructive of piety. The writer meets the objection from the sad decline of piety and doctrinal soundness in the students at Northampton and Daventry, by showing that this came not from the mingling there of secular with ministerial students, but from the absence of discipline and the training of unconverted men for the ministry; both points in respect to which Dr. Doddridge, with all his zeal for evangelical religion, was in serious error, theoretical and practical. An interesting note is added to the essay, in which the writer

"Ventures to express his deep and firm conviction that the academical isolation of · our theological students, is, on the whole, rather unfavorable than otherwise to the formation of a complete ministerial character. He is of opinion that the admission into our colleges of a limited proportion of young men, early trained to those habits of social order and propriety, of which our most influential Nonconformist families exhibit some of the happiest examples in the land, would be decidedly favorable to the tone of morality as well as exterior cultivation of our students for the ministry; and that the occasional interchange of thought with young men of honorable principles, contemplating the learned professions, or preparing for the higher walks of manufacturing or commercial enterprise, would be of immense advantage in enlarging the moral perception, expanding the public spirit, and giving completeness and finish to the practical aptitudes of our young brethren. He believes this, even supposing, what, however, is practically most improbable, that none of the general students were professedly pious; and so strong is his conviction on the subject, that he would dissuade any young friend of his own from entering one of our colleges, were it not that their academical seclusion is favorably modified by the journeys and visits which attend the occasional preaching engagements of the students, and by the long summer vacations. The human mind requires some relief in order to its healthy development; and the greater the object upon which its energies are to be concentrated, the greater is the necessity of moral support by enlargement of views *ab extra.* The preacher or pastor who, *cæteris paribus*, will be the most efficient, is he who, without ever deserting his own high position, has the faculty of throwing his mind, upon occasion, into the point of view of other men and other classes."

In accordance with these suggestions, "lay students" have been since admitted to some institutions, though others exclude all who do not contemplate the ministry. At Spring Hill, for example, "lay students, of good moral character and respectable position, are admitted on liberal terms and under special regulations." At New College, "lay students above fifteen years of age are permitted to attend the literary classes, and by special agreement, the theological." There are thirteen lay students here besides the fifty-two theological. At Western College, "lay students intending to enter as ministerial students, can attend the classes without the payment of fees." The number of such at present is two. This college is open to young men of all denominations, of approved moral character, as lay students. The fee for each class is three pounds and three shillings (three guineas, or fifteen dollars) and half that amount to the sons of ministers.

The question how to maintain the highest type of piety through the whole term of study, seems to have been thoroughly considered by the friends and instructors of the English colleges. The late John Angell James regarded the plan of the Wesleyan Methodists, appointing a chaplain in each of their theological institutions to care for the piety and ministerial character of the students, but not to teach, as an improvement on all other systems. This failing, he urged a closer intercourse between aged and eminent ministers and candidates for the sacred office while pursuing their studies. The Rev. J. B. Paton, M. A., of the Institute at Nottingham, in a published essay before us, treats this spiritual charge as laid upon the Faculty of each institution, who are selected for

"Their formative, stimulating, inspiring force of character." "If these tutors have this power, then they must feel how entirely it lies with them, personally and inalienably, to maintain a high tone of piety in their students." "To this end, all the tutors of a college should combine, and, as do the tutors of our large schools, confer occasionally with one another, as they should confer always with God, in reference to the spiritual condition of each of their students. A worldly minded tutor, or one whose spirituality is questionable, will work the greatest detriment upon the souls of the students, and all the greater in proportion to his fame, energy, and vivid, friendly, sympathetic disposition. But if all must conspire to fulfill the chief end of a college training for the ministry, it forms the special and paramount object of the principal. Upon him devolves, in a peculiar sense, the care of the morals of the college, and this with us means Christian morality, or spirituality. He stands *in loco parentis*, and though a father may commit separate branches of learning to other masters, the character of his son is his own charge. I suggest, then, that in fulfilment of this charge, the principal of every college should devote one hour a week to a pastoral address to his students, or to simple, earnest conversation, with the view of nurturing their faith and zeal. These lectures should show them that he has a pastor's care for them."

It is recommended that an hour of the Sabbath should be taken for them; and besides that one whole day in every month should be counted holy unto the Lord, in which the students should "give themselves to fasting, devout meditation, and the reading of the word, and all of them should appear before the Lord in the assembly of the church in their college, for the breaking of bread." This ordinance is recommended to be celebrated regularly every month "in a full and solemn religious service, in which all the tutors take part, thus consecrating themselves and their students by the eating of one bread and the drinking of one cup to a fellowship in the sufferings and ministry of our crucified Redeemer." In New College "all the students of the Faculty of Arts receive religious instruction, chiefly of a practical nature," every Thursday from ten to eleven o'clock, A.M., from the principal, or president, Rev. Dr. Robert Halley.

It is also urged that no class should assemble or separate without prayer,[1] and that all students should be required to per-

[1] One is amazed in the Protestant theological lecture rooms of German universities to hear not a word of prayer offered, as at Heidelberg, for example.

form some mission service among the poor.   Our English brethren are not quite agreed as to the value, for training, of this kind of service ; such men as Principal Fraser of Airedale, for example, contending that an institution can not give experimental acquaintance with evangelistic and pastoral work.   But our opinion is, though we can not now verify it, that some kind of Christian work is everywhere carried along with study. At Hackney there is a Village Itinerancy Society, whose report for 1864 ascribes to the ability and faithfulness with which the Hackney students have proclaimed Christ in the villages supplied "the very large demand made upon the services of the students as supplies."   The open-air worship and preaching, in which England surpasses other lands, are largely maintained by their labors.   At Nottingham one day a week, besides a large part of the Sabbath, is devoted to home missionary efforts and evangelism.   At Bristol the students are required to engage in city and village mission work, as far as practicable, throughout their course, and the first five years after it is completed the graduates are under the control of the college committee or trustees.   This same singular provision for laboring at the outset under direction prevails at Edinburgh, extending to one year after leaving the Theological Hall, balanced with a provision for aid, if necessary, from the funds of the Hall. Some of our English brethren insist strongly upon labor with the study from the outset, as indispensable.   The Rev. R. W. Dale, successor of John Angell James at Birmingham, says :

"Though probably I attach as high a value to the royal science of dogmatic theology as any, and believe that it is equally presumptuous and dangerous for any one to despise the aids to the formation of his doctrinal creed, afforded by by-gone controversies, I believe that on the great doctrines which immediately underlie our preaching, a man is far more likely to arrive at the truth, if while he is studying the systems of the great masters of theological thought, he is earnestly endeavoring to save the souls of men."

Mr. Paton, quoted above, affirms that

"The real conditions that test religious opinion, that clear up difficulty and unfold the truth, are not to be found in the speculations of the study, but in the application of religious truth to the great religious needs of men. The chief source of heresy among religious thinkers is the abandonment of that one criterion which the experience of an evangelist alone supplies."

ARTICLE VI.

BENJAMIN F. HOSFORD.

A Memorial of the Life, Character, and Death of Rev. Benjamin F. Hosford. Cambridge : Printed at the Riverside Press. 1866.

THIS Memorial was prepared, as the preface informs us, for "Mr. Hosford's own intimate friends," and so it was " printed at the Riverside Press," not published. Yet in the hearts of many strangers what a profound and tender interest has its perusal awakened. That a character of such a peculiar and varied strength and opulence and beauty should have lived and labored so long, almost in the very heart of Massachusetts, and yet should have been so little known outside his personal friendships and the limits of his pastoral charge, has excited surprise. God makes but few such men, and he intends them to shine and glow in a limited sphere, as trees of most delicate organization and sweetest fragrance are set, not on the broad mountain tops or in the great forests, but in " a garden enclosed." So far as the influence of such a man is considered, there is no cause for regret that he did not stand more prominently before the community while he lived. That very circumstance, as it was one of the conditions of the singular beauty of his character, so neither, when rightly viewed, does it involve any limitation of his influence. If that influence was extended over a smaller surface, it reached to lower depths. There was something wonderful in the love which he inspired, and that with as beautiful an unconsciousness as that of the lily or the morning star. When the final and hopeless failure of his health had rendered inevitable the severance of the tie which had bound him so strongly and tenderly to the one flock that had called him pastor, and he was struggling with the sadness awakened by the thought of quitting forever the pleasant parsonage where his happiest days had been spent, where his children had been born, and his darling Mattie had closed her eyes in death, he was surprised to find that another cheerful house, on the sunny slope of one of the hills which he loved, was already prepared to receive him and his family. The house and garden had been purchased, out of mere overflowing generous affection, by four friends, and there he dwelt, in a peace and thankfulness unutterable, to the end of his days, and there the widow and fatherless children are dwelling still. Benedictions on the head and heart and storehouse and barn of the men who have given us so beautiful a deed to think upon !

Mr. Hosford was born on the 11th day of November, 1817, in Thetford, Vermont ; and there, amid the blended lights and shadows of an uncommonly rich and varied landscape, his first years were passed. It was the right place for Benjamin Franklin Hosford to be born in. His spirit was indigenous to the region, as much so as the magnificent elms and sugar-maples which cover its noble hill-sides, and stretch out their branches to the sky. He needed no master to help him see and appreciate the many fine pictures which reflected the sunlight of that sweet mountain home. Through all his subsequent life the memory of those bright pictures was a joy to his heart which language could only very feebly express. "I feel," he wrote in 1849, "as if the whole warp of my soul's fabric would be taken out, were I to lose the remembrances and influences of a virtuous, industrious, peaceful home among the ever-varying scenery of the country." p. 7.

"His early life," the Memoir says, "was one of rare exemption from the common foibles of youth, and of amiableness, cheerfulness, and seriousness, blended in a character of remarkable maturity and symmetry." The true explanation of this, doubtless, is contained in that simple and touching account of his religious experience given on the occasion of his uniting with the Congregational church at Dartmouth College, in the nineteenth year of his age : "I grew up into piety by baptism, religious training, and the grace of God." He graduated at

Dartmouth College in 1838, and entered at once the Theological Seminary at Andover, where he graduated in 1841, being twenty four years of age. Then he went forth to preach, with no "great sermons" in his hands, and no disposition to secure for himself a position and influence by the display of those powers which he was fully conscious of possessing. He made such exhibition of himself in the pulpit as comported with his own severe notions of the simplicity and dignity of his calling. With a faith and patience not less than his modesty and humility, he chose to bide his time. And well was his patience rewarded. After nearly three years' journeying in the wilderness, he came suddenly to a place of rest where his wanderings were speedily forgotten, and where, to the close of his ministry and his life on earth, God gave him such joy in his people's love and. confidence, and in a very beautiful and happy home, as is given to but few. He was invited to supply the vacant pulpit of the Centre church in Haverhill, Mass., and the congregation discovered at once his superiority and the peculiar qualifications they desired in a pastor. The interest was mutual, decided and profound. He loved the people, and the people loved him, from the very first. The effect of time and intimate acquaintance was only to give to that first warm affection a strong foundation of respect and confidence ; and so the affection grew continually, as his fine character developed and matured, year by year, in the preacher and the pastor, in strength and beauty, and the flock grew, under his loving and faithful instruction and guidance, in knowledge and faith and spiritual understanding. There was a mutual content and joy through all his lengthened pastorate of nearly eighteen years. The people desired no change, and the pastor desired none, and when, at length, the Master called him to his rest and reward, after long and painful sickness, and many alternations of hope and fear, the sorrow of the bereaved flock was much alleviated and soothed by the consideration that God had so directly and obviously disposed the whole matter of their mutual relations, in his peculiar grace, from the happy commencement to the mournful close, appointing his peaceful sleep in the beautiful cemetery whither so many members of the flock had gone before him, and where he had so often wept with the survivors by the open graves of their dead.

Mr. Hosford was ordained on the 21st of May, 1845, and on the 28th of July, in the same year, was married to Mary Elizabeth, daughter of Luther and Mary Eaton Stone, of Saxonville, Mass. Then commenced that beautiful life in which the holy ties and responsibilities of pastor, husband, father and friend, were interwoven as God has wisely and mercifully ordained, for personal growth in whatever is purest and most elevated in human character, and for largest communication of good to others. In the bereaved home and in the church of God, that life still exhales a fragrance which seems to come laden with benedictions.

Few spots are more beautiful than Haverhill, rising from the banks of the crystalline Merrimac to the noble heights from which magnificent pictures are spread out on every hand; and few pastors are as happy as Mr. Hosford was, among his generous, affectionate and appreciating flock. He dearly loved the proper duties of the Christian ministry, and discharged all with a peculiar grace, which gave him a constantly increasing hold of the confidence and affections of his people. Comparatively, for a New England parish, his labors were not arduous. Yet his heart seemed always yearning for his Green Mountain home, as the heart of a child yearns for its mother; and his frequent complaints of weariness, bodily and mental, from his Sabbath labors, might suggest a doubt as to whether he should have entered the ministry at all. "Were not Providence somewhat concerned in placing me here," he says, "I should feel like asking for a location where duty would be consistent with delight, and usefulness in my calling be cheered by a daily luxuriating amid the beauties and still more beautiful associations of a mountain home." p. 8. And again after a visit to his native Thetford:

"The fields still smile, never more lovingly, but the hands that once tilled them are dust. The brook still murmurs its sweet soothing music across the farm, but the more musical voices of those who used to play with him [me] along its willowy banks or among its smooth pebbles are silent forever. Under the same shady trees where he and his schoolmates played, and around the same cool spring where he and they knelt to drink, other merry children drink and sing, who perhaps never heard the name of the stranger who stands weeping at the sight." pp. 9, 10.

When only thirty two years of age he had a presentiment of an early death, and even fancied that he might be gazing for the last time on the beautiful hills of his beloved Thetford. Almost from week to week, we find in his Journal such entries as the following :

"Monday eve. Nervous and sensitive to-day, as is quite common, from the excitement of yesterday. It consumes my life, I am quite confident, and yet 'tis not without its advantages. What a luxury it is to read good poetry in such a frame! Coleridge's Hymn and Apostrophe to Mont Blanc wellnigh overcame me. This may be considered as one of the prerequisites of my calling, perhaps not too dearly bought by the deadness that is apt to succeed." pp. 41, 42.

His constant longing for that "sweet, green, birdy, flowery country home" of his childhood, and the painful prostration which so frequently came after the services of the Sabbath, were both the result of that exquisite sensibility which constituted one of the sweetest charms of his character, and one of his peculiar qualifications for the work of the ministry. Exquisite sensibility can not be, without exquisite suffering. He understood this law and was content. When he had been especially happy in the services of the sanctuary, had poured out all the fulness of his heart to God in intercession for his flock, and to that beloved flock in preaching, there would ensue, when night had closed around, and he sat with only his family and his books about him, and the heavy burden of care was lifted from his soul, a condition in which all the faculties of his understanding, and every affection of his heart was quickened to an unwonted activity. Then the great Christian poets afforded him unutterable delight, and he seemed to penetrate, almost with the vision of a seer, the profound mysteries of the Faith. As all disposition to sleep was far from him, he would linger often by the hearth-stone quite into the small hours of the night, taking no note of time, giving full play to thought and fancy and feeling, and beyond measure happy in his own soul and in the dear society of her in whom all his soul found truest ap-

preciation and tenderest sympathy. He was accustomed to say
that he found a full equivalent for all the suffering which his
sensitive nature caused him, in the high enjoyment which came
to him through the same channel ; and that, while it distressed
him much to think that his children should suffer when he was
gone, yet, balancing one thing with another, he was more than
willing that they should resemble their father in this respect.

His delicate and highly nervous physical organization and
the weakness induced by impaired health, had, doubtless, not
a little to do with the peculiar sufferings of which we have
spoken, and many others to which he was subject through
the whole course of his pastoral life ; and yet, of all earthly
callings that, beyond the shadow of a doubt, was the one best
suited to him, not more when considered with reference to his
usefulness, than to his truest present happiness, and length of
days on earth. That his days were prolonged by his studies
and labors in the Christian ministry, is a conclusion which
all the data, as we judge, would go to establish ; and that, with
all the abatements in his case, he was one of the happiest, most
joyous men, diffusing sunlight wherever he came, they who
knew him best will bear witness. When one of a band of
brothers has been suffered to leave his father's farm and go to
college, for the reason that he, of all his father's sons has not
the physical strength to do a full day's work on that farm, and
has entered the ministry and toiled hard in it for half a century,
and has outlived every one of those stronger brothers, and has
still been full of energy and intelligence at fourscore, he has
simply supplied an illustration of well-known laws. The student lives longer than other men. All the professions are
abundant in very remarkable illustrations. Among the liberal
vocations, the clerical is decidedly most favorable to longev-
ity, as statistics clearly show. Partly, and, as we believe, in
large part, this is owing to the fact that, of all earthly callings,
no other is so happy as that of the faithful minister of Jesus
Christ. Happy, we mean, in the sense that it embraces the
conditions on which a man's peace and contentment and joy do
most largely depend.

We speak what we do know in this matter. It happened to
us to be counted in a numerous family of brothers and sisters,

whose father was a poor country minister. A new garment was a most important event, from childhood upward, and a new school book was a prize which glittered in our view as few things have glittered since. We have likewise had lengthened experience ourself in the pastorate, and have fought with beasts at Ephesus. And now, looking back over all, from a point in the journey at which human judgments are supposed to be sober and deliberate and matured, our very decided testimony is, that if the journey were to be commenced by us once more, we would willingly be the son of just such a father of a numerous family ; that we would choose the Christian ministry in preference to any other earthly vocation, and, if we had ten sons and seven daughters, we would rejoice exceedingly to have them all ministers, or the wives of ministers.

That Mr. Hosford completed his appointed time on earth, and accomplished his appointed service for the Master, we know. That his life, though not long, and in spite of bodily weakness which would have conquered other men, and kept them out of the ranks altogether, was beautiful and brave, a picture in which joyous sunbeams struggled everywhere with deep shadows, a garden by whose bright flowers, and fragrance, and precious fruits, many hearts were made glad, this most fitting Memorial shows. His richest graces were so closely blended with God's fatherly chastening in that hopeless and ever increasing weakness, that one is afraid to wish anything changed, lest the wish should savor of irreverence for God, who, we must believe, finds a pleasure worthy of himself in fashioning the plan of every good man's life. It is an unspeakable relief to the sympathy which his sufferings awaken, and the deep sorrow caused by his death, to think how all his sufferings wrought in him, through the divine mercy, to fit him for heaven, and how beautiful and happy he must have been on his first entrance there. If we could believe fully, and remember, that heaven, and not this sin-stricken and blighted earth, is the scene of Christ's completed triumphs, and that his people are kept here chiefly that they may be prepared for translation, in a glorious perfection, to the mansions he is preparing for them there, many of our judgments would be reversed, as regards their temporal condition. We are not more than half believers as to the things in which true blessedness consists. Few are quite willing to walk with Christ in his pilgrimage of sorrow, not considering that for us, as well as for him, that is the appointed path to the heavenly felicities, the crown of glory. There is another view of the subject which deserves to be deeply pondered. The minister of Jesus Christ suffers for others. It is an indispensable part of his qualifications for his work. " And whether we be afflicted, it is for your consolation and salvation, which is effectual in the enduring of the same sufferings which we also suffer." In this sense, whoever will be a faithful pastor enters into the shadows with Christ.

Christ suffered for us in a double sense. He met the divine justice, and satisfied all its claims on our behalf. He suffered the penalty of violated law, thus providing a free justification for sinners, and maintaining the honor of the Divine government. In this stupendous work he stood alone, the Creator of the universe becoming the Redeemer of fallen men. The mightiest angel, all the angels, could not have relieved him of the very smallest particle of that great sorrow and travail of his soul. He must tread that winepress alone. Only God can be a vicarious Saviour. To claim any participation for sinful man, or sinless angels, with Christ in such sufferings, is either to exalt creatures to the throne of God, or to bring God down to a level with creatures. It is most consolatory to remember that there is another view of Christ's sufferings on which the Bible lays much stress, as having a very important relation to his great work, as the Redeemer of his people. He suffered that he might sympathize. He bore with him to heaven, when he ascended, the heart of the " man of sorrows," the same human heart whose unutterable tenderness was poured out in tears at the grave of Lazarus. Thus when we pray in the agony of our grief, we come not to the invisible and incomprehensible Jehovah, clothed in awful majesty, and terrible to us by reason of his pure spiritual nature, but unto the Lord Jesus Christ, who suffered on earth for us, and then for us ascended to the glorious heavens in the same human nature in which he suffered, and there ever lives to intercede for us, and to extend to us a sympathy, in which the remembrance of personal human sorrows is strangely blended with a love and power that are infinite.

In this sense he says to all whom he calls to the ministry of the Gospel : " Ye shall drink of the cup that I drink of, and with the baptism that I am baptized withal shall ye be baptized." The mystery of many a deep sorrow laid upon the faithful servants of Christ has its beautiful solution here. It is appointed and necessary, not only that they guide the footsteps of the flock, but that they bear their sorrows. A momentous responsibility, and a most exalted honor ! Who is sufficient ? The young pastor, as he stands up in the house of God, and looks upon his charge, of all ages and conditions, and remembers how multiplied and how various, ere many years are past, will be the afflictions in which he, as the faithful shepherd, will be called to bear a part, may well be troubled in spirit as he says within himself : "I have a baptism to be baptized with, in order that I, like the Master, may be prepared to weep with them that weep."

In this view of the life so beautifully presented in the Memoir before us, we are constrained to admit and to glorify the wisdom and the grace of God. The heart of Mr. Hosford was a fountain, a deep, unfathomed well-spring of truest, tenderest sympathy for the sorrows of his flock. There are those in that flock who can not remember his form, his face, his voice, without a tear. " He spoke to us words of tenderness in our affliction, he prayed with us by the bedside of our sick, he sat with us in silence and wept, in the chamber of our dead."

The minister of Jesus Christ bears the sorrows of his people in this sense, and carries their griefs ; and for this special work a training is required which the colleges, and schools of the prophets can not give. It is a baptism of suffering. Thus did God himself prepare our brother for his appointed work, imparting a strange charm to his character, and giving to his ministry a power that reached to the lowest depths of his people's hearts.

It was an innate quality, developed and fashioned by his peculiar personal experiences into a fitness for the work he was to do. It is not every good man who can be wrought by the grace of God and much affliction to the pattern of Christ as a friend of the sorrowing. We have seen a man who was singularly true and sincere and kind, but who could not weep with those who wept ; and when his own beautiful and beloved child died, we marvelled that he seemed to stand in so little need for others to weep with him.   Such a man excites confidence, respect, esteem ; but has little power to awaken love.   He is not the good man for whom, peradventure, some would even dare to die.

It is a fact worth careful study, that conscience has a much broader, fuller play in a man of strong and tender sympathies. He imputes to himself as grievous sin, sin which causes life-long, bitter sorrow, and which he can never forgive, an act which another would hardly remember.   We know a man of brilliant talents, and distinguished reputation in the republic of letters, who declares that he can not remember without harrow-ing remorse having once, when a boy, made a black girl in his father's house cry by a single act of harshness.   Can it be necessary to say, that all his life long his sympathies and his conscience have been prompting him to deeds of generosity which many men who are called good would pronounce foolish-ness ; just as their ethics would write down that act of harsh-ness to the poor black child as an instance of boyish thought-lessness, instead of a sin.

A touching incident in the life of Mr. Hosford illustrates the same law.   When he was a boy an elder sister whom he ten-derly loved came home to die of consumption.   It was a cold December, and a part of Frank's daily duty was to bring in at night the wood to keep the sick chamber warm.   Once, when his coasting or skating had suffered some abridgment or inter-ruption, he was betrayed into an expression of impatience and fretfulness in his sick sister's hearing, which his mother noticed, and said to him in a low voice : "You wont have to bring in wood much longer for poor Lucy !"   The next Sabbath evening he was called into the room to see her die.   Seventeen years after he wrote : "That one act has cost me more sorrow than any other act of my life.   It seems as if God punished me every day for it ; for every day I think of it, and it makes me unhappy."   pp. 2—5.

That the severity of his self-judgment was according to truth, we believe, as we believe that out of it God made to spring a rich and abundant harvest of tenderness and sympathy and tears for the sick and sorrowful, through the whole course of his beautiful life. How gentle and loving and full of solace his pastoral attentions must have been, is made plain by his own frequent reference to the afflictions of his people. At the funeral of a little child,

" I was impressed," he says, "with the idea of the great amount of joy that Christian hope has distilled from tears, and the many beautiful things (like flowers) that have sprung up from the graves of children. Verily Christianity sheds a light on little graves." p. 37. Again, "To have come to this scene from the sick-bed of an aged person whom I could address only through a trumpet ; and then to hurry from it to the funeral of a poor colored girl, who had died homeless and friendless, but who in her last hours, expressed a desire to see her brothers, who were, she knew not where, only that they were far off amid the sorrows of slavery ; and then to go from this last to the funeral of a little child ;—th's has made out a day's labor, which, if it could impress others to whom I ministered as deeply as it has worn into my own body and mind, would be a day long to be remembered." pp. 39, 40.

It was twelve years later, and when he was drawing very near the promised land, that the great sorrow of his life fell upon him, in the death of his darling child, "little Mattie." With a crushed and bleeding heart he laid her in the grave, and two years later his own worn out and wasted frame was laid by her side. It would seem that he hardly needed the terrible discipline of this affliction to qualify him for his work ; yet he was not suffered to lay down his burdens until it had borne very precious fruits. To friends under a like visitation he wrote :

" You will now understand. better than before, the depth of my affliction ; and will not think it so strange that it should follow me so long, with a freshness ever new. U——'s bursting out into loud cryings when he came unexpectedly upon little Frederick's hat, some months after his decease, is reënacted here almost every day of our lives ; and not unlikely you will also learn what this is, and what it means. Oh, to have such a shadow settling over everything earthly, all relishes so deadened, all ambitions so tempered down, all joys so modified ; and to have all these great effects flow from the death of a little child, it shows what mysterious possibilities we are living among, and what powers of joy or sorrow we are bearing about in these souls, oftentimes without knowing or suspecting it! Poor little Arthur's suffering seems to have been worse than Mattie's, unless the disease paralyzed his sensibilities in part. Oh, her great, cool eyes looking up to us with more than human understanding, and silently pleading for that breath which we could not give! I pray I may never be compelled to witness it or its like again. But I need not tell you this, which, in its substantial elements of sorrow, is so like what you have passed through. I trust the deep baptism of grief, (and you can now see how grief for a child may be deeper than any other, or at least tenderer, for love goes downward rather than upward;) I trust these recent, and to us new griefs, will help us in the higher experiences of the Christian life. We ought now to find it easier to live unworldly and unselfishly, and easier to leave the world when our turn comes. The invisible world is much more a reality, and a nearer and much more precious reality, now that I have such a personal treasure in it. Indeed it does seem very near to me, since I daily talk with one in it, really in it, conscious and blessed, though I see her not with the bodily eye. . . .

"And now, having lived over my afflictions anew in this fresh outgoing of sympathy for you at home, I turn away to other duties.

" Much of the little flesh that was clinging to my bones has been dissolved by the corrosion of silent grief, wearing upon it night and day. Still I work on with a secret conviction that I shall not bear up under it many years." pp. 161, 2.

The chief design of this overwhelming sorrow was to prepare him for the higher scenes on which he was so soon to enter. And here we may note the exceeding tender pity of God, in keeping back that terrible stroke till so near the end. How powerfully it wrought in him toward the accomplishment of the merciful design, is evident. When little Mattie had been lying five months in the grave he wrote to his wife:

" I went this morning to church, but I was thinking most of the time of dear departed Mattie, as I have been, indeed, ever since you left Oh, how many times of late has the thought of her melted my heart and moistened my eyes. And from her, I turn thought back again to you and the remaining children, and get comfort in the hope and expectation that God will help hold you up by means of them. Oh, how deeply you lie in my heart, so very deep, indeed, as to make few ripples on the surface, so deep that no earthly experiences can shake you out, no, not even the deep experience of death.

"Now, dearest, go on your toilsome, lonely way, cheerfully and rejoicing, and I will try to do the same. The 'Cross Bearer' is my daily counsellor.

"Oh, how deep down it has driven thought and search! How utter the humiliation which it naturally begets! I have recently learned some new things about myself. But must I be utterly bruised and dissolved, in order to know the whole? And if so, can I ever be brought to say, 'As God wills'? Can I look on you and our children, and still say, 'As God wills'?

"Read the 'Cross Bearer' yesterday, with prayers and tears. Heard fine music in the afternoon. Alas, alas, dear Mattie! Half my life has already gone after her, and the other half remains out of regard to you. May the Heavenly Mercy pity me, and take care of you all." pp. 162, 3.

How great the happiness must be in the enjoyment of which such afflictions seem "light" and "for a moment." That the deepening shadows of his closing years tended to make his "deliverance out of life" a morning of transcendent light and glory, who can doubt; and who would have wished to detain him another day amid the thickening gloom of his sorrows?

We are not quite sure that such a word as "gloom" should be used in connection with his name. Certainly he was never a gloomy or even a sad man. Naturally cheerful as the morning bird, and genial as a summer day, with a charming wit and humor, which all his sufferings only chastened, his pleasant sallies, suggested by his books, the furniture of his sick room, the prescriptions of the doctor, surprised his friends, and softened for a moment the keen edge of their grief, even to the last, like flowers which bloom late into autumn. But, withal, he was a man of a profound Christian faith and a most cheerful piety. His soul rested on Christ as the rock of ages, and basked in his love as in the fulness of noon-day. His deep and overwhelming convictions of personal guilt were the counterpart of the joy unspeakable which he found every day in the hope that Christ's righteousness was imputed to him for justification. All his sorrows and sufferings were, to his serene, unwavering faith, the dispensations of a wisdom that was perfect, and a love that was infinite. He knew that the shadows extended but a little way, and that all beyond was the brightness of eternal day, as the sun shines full and clear on the mountain-tops, when clouds and tempests lie on the valleys below. His vision reached that perfect day, its glories were the theme of his pleasant song in the house of his pilgrimage. So have we seen at midday, in the dense and tangled forest, whose deep shadows were in sympathy with the awful stillness, a beautiful bird singing a song in which the plaintive and the cheerful were strangely blended, while a single bright sunbeam had made its solitary way through the thick foliage, and was pouring all its sweet light upon the plumage of the little songster, and apparently inspiring its lay.

Few men have so keen a delight as Mr. Hosford had in the many beautiful and precious things which are saved to us out of the primeval wreck. He loved the great, rough mountains, and the smooth, grassy meadows, and rivers and brooks and trees and skies and flowers and birds, with an affection as tender as a little child has for the pleasant things of its home. He sketched them, too, with an exceedingly delicate pencil :

"And then the woods—the old, stately, and historic woods— the cool, mossy, flowery, and sweet-scented woods ; in one part as silent as the place of graves, and in another as social as all heaven's sweet songsters can make them, ' God's first temples,' his latest and his best, in which the worshipper is both awed down and lifted up by an atmosphere of divine presence." p. 93.

How skilfully he turned all to account for the instruction of his flock, those who heard him will not soon forget. Thus in a sermon on the transfiguration :

"A memorable Sabbath in our history was one spent in the Glen at the foot of Mount Washington. Our fellow-worshippers were not of human mould or stature. During all the day clouds and darkness were round about the sovereign mount. The hoary head of the prince of that group was not once visible. We saw him only by the eye of faith. Oh, how deep thoughts concerning him were stirred by the very fact of his being veiled! A little before sunset the hoary summit broke through its envelope for a few minutes, and then all was mystery again. But soon a rising breeze swept the whole cloud-drapery aside, and there stood the glorious king in serene majesty and beauty. The rain had so washed the atmosphere from its impurities as to show every outline of the mountain with almost incredible distinctness ; and all this majesty was then flooded in the

golden rays of the setting sun.   A sight it was to be remembered
through life ; yea, death itself can not wipe it out of the memory,
save by wiping out the very fabric of the soul.   The unusual beauty
of that sight was all due indirectly to the preceding clouds.

" So do dark providences screen from clear vision the benevolence
of our God.   So does this obscurity quicken our inquiring souls to
an unusual intensity.   So then do the clouds break, and give you a
momentary but clear view of the paternal countenance." pp. 89, 90.

Mr. Hosford's love of science would have made him a master in that department if it had been his chosen vocation.   His
literary tastes were various, and, taking into account his conscientious and assiduous devotion to all the duties of his ministerial and pastoral charge, we are no less surprised at the opulence than the severity of his culture.   The best poets soothed
him in his weariness, and refreshed him like new wine.   His
powers as a writer made him a most welcome contributor to
the leading issues of the periodical press.   Whether he wrote
for the daily or weekly newspaper, the magazine, or the quarterly review, he was equally at home ; nor was it easy to say
in which he excelled.   He meddled with a wide range of subjects.   Natural scenery, science, music, criticism, his country,
the great war, theology ; on all these he essayed his powers,
and left papers on all, in which strength and beauty of thought
are embodied in a style of singular transparency, and of a
classic elegance.

In sparkling humor, and keen, withering satire, it may be
safely affirmed that Mr. Hosford had few equals.   These were
not things which he sought, or on which he plumed himself,
but spontaneous, irrepressible, a part of his very nature, like
his tender sympathy, or love of woods and mountains.   His
wit played forever in delicate coruscations about that which was
innocent, while his satire, like a Damascus blade, cut deep into
the heart of foolishness and sin.   Many of our readers will remember, as instances of the latter, his series of articles upon
" Great Sermons," published in the *Boston Recorder* in 1857,
and " A New Professor in Old Theology," in the same paper
in 1859.   The articles on "Great Sermons" were republished in
England.   A great multitude who never saw Mr. Hosford, but
who had derived both instruction and delight from the produc-

tions of " Cecil," sincerely mourned when that genial heart ceased to beat, and that right hand forgot its cunning.

One thing more would seem to have been necessary to complete the beautiful harmony of the character which we have very imperfectly drawn, and Mr. Hosford had it in high degree—a love of music. He was richly endowed by nature in this respect, and his gifts were largely cultivated, so that his whole soul was filled with an intense, unutterable delight in listening to the sublimest compositions of the great masters. How he should have found time, need excite no more surprise than that the towering pine tree finds time to be aromatic, or to sigh in the wind, as well as to be beautiful and strong. It was a part of his nature, and a constant growth through all his years from the time when he used to climb upon his father's knee in Thetford, to hear him sing " Thousands of thousands," and his mother charmed the little ones by singing plaintive airs and simple ballads at her little wheel and loom, and all in the happy home were made happier by listening to the strains of the Æolian harp. As his friends now remember him, what a strange blank would there be in that exquisitely rounded character, if music were left out ! It was not a sentiment or a passion, but a healthy appetite of his spiritual nature. Its indulgence brought repose and healing and elevation. His soul was fed on ambrosia. It was his training and growth, in part, for the blissful day when he should stand among the hundred and forty and. four thousand on the Mount Zion above. Thus he says :

"I am sure I have struck at the very soul of music. No man could describe, I could not myself, its effect on my highest culture, intellectual and religious. All I can say is, that I have been permitted to enter the ' Holy of Holies,' in this respect, for which I give most humble and hearty thanks. The Bible gives every intimation that music will in some way form part of the worship of heaven. So this preparation of soul will not be lost." p. 104.

This was written, it will be perceived, after his return from a grand musical banquet.

We must speak of Mr. Hosford as a preacher. When he had been more than two years out of the Seminary, and no church had called him to be its pastor, he was troubled in spirit, and feared, lest, after all, he lacked the necessary qualifications for the high vocation to which he had looked forward with intense desire. But he possessed his soul in patience and in cheerfulness. He was neither broken in spirit nor soured. During the third year of his patient waiting he wrote those genial and sparkling articles which many readers of the *Boston Recorder* still remember, over the signatures respectively of "Luke," "Joseph," and "Mark"; and entitled, "The Unsettled Minister to his Brethren," "A Dream of an Unsettled Minister," and "Hints to Destitute Churches, by an Unsettled Minister." With what a peculiar ability he acquitted himself in the pulpit, there is abundant evidence to show. His biographer has sketched him in a passage as beautiful as it is just:

"Those who have known and appreciated him, are the best judges of his character as God's public ambassador. And it is not too much to say, that, in their estimation, Cowper's familiar and oft-quoted lines are rarely applied with more exact appropriateness to a modern New England preacher than to him. Never did a man more heartily abhor pretension, claptrap, and noisy emptiness in the pulpit than he. Never did a preacher more thoroughly despise the substitution of ' philosophy and vain deceit, and oppositions of science falsely so called,' for the simple Gospel, or the putting of self in the place of Christ. Cordially and strongly, as well as intelligently attached to the old doctrines of the Reformation and of the New England Fathers, which, in his inmost heart, he believed to be the doctrines of Paul, and, better than all, of Christ, he never swerved in defending them against all attacks and all threatening dangers on the right hand and on the left. Yet he never did this roughly nor coarsely. He was always the gentleman, as well as the ambassador of God, both in the pulpit and out of it. Simple, yet original; quiet, yet often very striking; earnest, yet ever kind; keen, yet always delicate and dignified; pointed, yet never rudely personal, his sermons were deeply impressive, and always full of useful and serious practical lessons." pp. 70, 71.

It was in the pulpit, above all other places, that Mr. Hosford desired to excel, and to his weekly preparations for the pulpit the best of his strength and his most patient, earnest efforts were given. To this all other pursuits, however highly valued, were strictly subordinate in his view and in his conduct. How well the variety and affluence of his gifts and attainments contributed to breadth of treatment and beauty of illustration and strength of argument and force of appeal in his preaching, they can best bear witness who listened year after year to his voice, with an ever increasing interest and profit, and with a not infrequent astonishment at the rich abundance of the " things new and old " which he brought forth.   That there would be " beauty and tenderness in his language, when speaking of the future world, of heaven as the home and rest of believers, and the consummation of the interrupted joys and plans of this life," it is easy to believe.

" Who that has heard him often can not recall the light which shone from his eyes, and the meaning which animated his tones, as he dwelt upon these lofty themes?   On such occasions we felt lifted above the level of our wonted experience on the wings of his faith and spirituality, and permitted for a time to breathe the air of the heavenly city." p. 73.

The Memoir informs us that he "particularly excelled" in " the tenderness and apposite beauty of his illustrations of truth," yet never knew it, and was always longing to possess the gift. (pp. 73, 4.)   There was another remarkable power as a preacher which he possessed in a high degree without being at all conscious of it, and that was the power of extemporaneous speaking.   He dared not attempt it on the Sabbath, but in the lecture-room on a week evening, when he had well digested some grand theme, and had arranged the things he wanted to say upon it, and his own heart and soul were filled with it, and he surrendered himself without fear to the strong current of his thoughts and emotions, he soared to heights of eloquence which surpassed his best written efforts.   We state this on the testimony of a competent critic, a very intelligent member of Mr. Hosford's church.   We are reminded to say here, that we had hoped ere now to see the announcement of a volume of Mr. Hosford's Sermons and Essays.   Such a volume would possess an interest and value quite beyond the circle of those whose happiness it was to know him personally, as pastor or friend.   There was another rich gift for the pulpit in which our brother was preëminent, and that was the gift of prayer.   Many who heard him in public and on private occa-

sions, have testified that few men prayed as he prayed. Says
Professor Shedd :

> "The prayers of a Christian man, when he is in a praying mood,
> reveal his inward nature and traits more than any other mental pro-
> ductions. Those of Mr. Hosford were oftentimes strangely search-
> ing and intensely supplicatory. When under the strong impression
> of eternal realities, his petitions reached a sphere that was wholly
> unearthly. I remember, and shall always remember, a prayer
> which he offered beside the open grave of the late Dr. Dimmick.
> We had followed his remains, as a clerical association, to their last
> resting place in the cemetery, and with us were the weeping kin-
> dred, the weeping parishioners, and the saddened townsmen. Mr.
> Hosford was called to give voice to the reflections and emotions of
> the hour. His own mind had been deeply smitten by the very sud-
> den death of a most respected and beloved father in Christ : and
> there rose from his burdened but confidently believing soul such
> a supplication as lifted, and strengthened, and comforted us all.
> Once again, in the privacy of his own home, and under the anguish
> of a bereavement that seemed to tear away a part of his own heart,
> I heard him offer a prayer that was awful for its spirituality, its
> resignation, and its rooted trust in God." pp. 257, 8.

Mr. Hosford was dismissed from his pastoral charge, in compliance with his own request, on the twenty sixth day of October, 1863, when it had become only too plain to himself and
the sorrowing flock, that God had already brought his labors in
the ministry to their appointed close, through the hopeless failure of his health. In less than ten months from that day the
Saviour came and received him unto himself, when he had
calmly spoken words of benediction and tender farewell to all,
had, with an unclouded mind, according to his own earnest
wish and prayer, borne his last emphatic testimony to the divine love and faithfulness, and endured as seeing Him who is
invisible, in the fearful agony of dissolution. He died the tenth
of August, 1864, in the forty seventh year of his age. "On
the southern slope of an embowered hill, from which there is a
charming view of the Merrimac," our dear brother sleeps.
"Little Mattie" is sleeping by his side. He had chosen it for
her place of rest, and, may we not believe? hardly less for his
own.

The monumental stone bears the following inscription :

" BENJAMIN FRANKLIN HOSFORD,
For Twenty Two Years a
Minister of Christ.
Born November 11, 1817 ; Died August 10, 1864.
' I know in whom I have Believed.' "

The storms of three winters have swept over his grave, and the early birds and flowers of the third summer are already disappearing from the magnificent landscape which lies around that peaceful " city of the dead"; but many years must come and go before that hallowed spot will cease to draw the footsteps of those who remember the words which he spake while he was yet with them, and to move their tears.

And now we have to ask pardon of Mr. Hosford's friends for having had the temerity to attempt what we have so inadequately performed. Our portraiture is not for them. We have felt that such poor tribute as we could pay was due to our affectionate homage for one of the most beautiful characters we have ever known, and who, in addition to delightful personal fellowship, stood to this *Review* in the relation of one of its ablest and most valued contributors. We are content to occupy a humble position among those who bring flowers to deck his grave. It is most pleasant to think how little our services are required. This unique and singularly elegant volume is a fitting and graceful expression of love. Its reception was an agreeable surprise. Who could doubt that it was another fruit of that quadruple alliance of " brotherly kindness " to which we have already made allusion. In the manufactory of one of the parties the paper, so exquisite in texture and thickness and ample size, was prepared expressly for this Memorial. Let it be received as a part of the tribute due to the beloved name of Benjamin Franklin Hosford, if we write along with his, the names of Hale, Nichols, Tyler and Warren, the four friends whose hearts the transcendent beauty of his character moved to deeds of such generous benefaction.

ARTICLE VII.

MODERN PAGAN WRITERS.

History of the Rise and Influence of the Spirit of Rationalism in Europe. By W. E. H. LECKY, M. A.
The Radical.
North American Review.
Christian Examiner.
Atlantic Monthly.

WE could never think of being so tedious to our readers as to give a very long list of the modern pagan writers; we instance the above as affording curious illustrations for those whose business it is to know the depravity of man. We have specially to do with Mr. Lecky's book, intending to take note of the spirit of the writer, his historical prejudices, and the effect of the book; illustrating our remarks by reference to the other writers named. Mr. Lecky's assault on the Christian doctrines, his attempt to divorce morality and doctrine, and his substitute for doctrine, may be suitably taken up in the same manner at some future time.

This work has been now for a considerable time before the public; long enough to find many readers among those curious in such literature. The copies in public libraries are well worn. The book is an attempt to prove that all the improvements in modern society came about through secular forces and, in the main, in opposition to Christianity. This secular movement is called rationalism; " a secular, that is to say, a rationalistic standard." We suppose that this was the definition Mr. Lecky had in mind when he called his book a History of Rationalism. This differs from the orthodox use of the word, which represents rationalism as the secular spirit in its opposition to Christianity. Mr. Lecky treats of the secular spirit in general, taking the best things he finds in history, and asserting that they are the fruit of rationalism; he shows indeed how this spirit has opposed Christian errors and doctrine, and he claims that the secular spirit is the true Christianity. Taking the word rationalism in its orthodox use, Mr. Lecky has not written a history of rationalism; he has written a book in which he cites certain historical facts to sustain certain theories calculated to undermine the Christian doctrines, and he has called this a History of Rationalism.

There is something very vague about Mr. Lecky's use of terms, which indicates an inexperience in close writing. "The spirit of the age." What is it? He uses the phrase : "the guilt of error," but we question a long time before we find out whether he means an intellectual wandering, or the wandering of the will from the path of rectitude; it is by a comparison of several uses of the term that we at last find out. It is certainly a grave error, a serious mistake of the intellect, to prepare so big a book without stating more definitely what the author would be at. The animus of the book can not be mistaken. It is opposed to revelation, and in more than one place it definitely takes the ground that the conscience of man is revelation enough from God. What the author says on page 182 of the first volume (Eng. ed.) is to the point, and in various places he appears to know definitely what rationalism is, and what it is not, in its leading principles. Now this is the position with which he ought to have set out if he meant to give a history of rationalism; here is something definite, easily done. But instead of being thus clear, he is very vague, as indeed he needs to be after pages 18, 19, Introduction, in which he gives altogether a different definition of rationalism, or rather no definition at all. He there denies that rationalism is anything definite in doctrine or criticism; but it is "rather a certain cast of thought, or bias of reasoning, which has, during the last three centuries, gained a marked ascendency in Europe," and that "the nature of this bias will be exhibited in detail" in the book. Then follows a partial intimation of his real views, that biblical dogmas are subordinate to reason, and that they only indicate the religious wants of the universal race, that conscience is the only moral guide, and that nature accounts for "all kinds of phenomena." All this he calls "a mental tendency," "the spirit of the age."

This vagueness allows the author to put into his book any fact or theory he pleases, baptizing all as "the spirit of the age," and calling it that all this is somehow indefinitely connected with the history of rationalism in Europe. Anything that ever happened in Europe can be treated of under the title the spirit of the age; and whenever the author has anything to say that is not connected with the subject announced in his title-page, he intimates that rationalism and the spirit of the age are the same thing, and then goes on to tell his story. This vagueness in the outset allows frequent wandering from the real point in hand, all through the book; or rather the point that ought to be in hand, for the author is sometimes pointless. This vagueness of definition allows frequent misapprehension of the real points at issue. Many and many pages of the book would fall out of it if they were asked how they came there, by an honest proposition put forth in the outset. Is this book a history of the religious, or irreligious movement which has denied the Christian assertion of an infallible written revelation, and which, on the other hand, has asserted the sufficiency of the conscience as a revelation from God? Apply this proposition to the book, and the book would about go to pieces. The paragraphs would leap out in squads. This book is not really the history of rationalism, according to the author's own definition of the term, though this may by some be said to depend on which of the author's definitions we take. This book is not even a " history of a mental tendency " in Europe; it is merely a book which sets forth the mental tendency of the author. In setting forth his own mental tendency he has massed a great many facts, which are more or less classified, and he makes all exhibit his own mental tendency with great clearness. This is the key if you will understand this curious book. It is not worth much as a history of anything in Europe, but it is curious as exhibiting Mr. Lecky's mental peculiarities. We said that the author is sometimes pointless; this is true if we try to find a history of rationalism in the book; but he is always to the point in making known his own infidel wanderings. He has read much; he cites a great many very curious facts; he propounds a great many very curious theories; he makes all bend to one point, incidentally setting forth his intense opposition to the leading doctrines of Christianity, but primarily his intense opposition to the cardinal doctrine of the plenary inspiration of the Bible.   The whole book is designed to overthrow the leading Christian doctrines, and with them the Bible itself.

With such prejudices he has misread the history of Europe, seeing all things darkly through his peculiar glass, and writing what he thinks he has seen.   For example : The Reformation under Luther has made modern Europe ; without it, the revival of classical learning, the printing press, the discovery of America, and the invention of the steam engine, would have only aided the development of the depravity of man.   But Mr. Lecky, looking through his " mental tendency," and affected by his bias of reasoning, thinks that his peculiar cast of thought has made Modern Europe.   The book is very curious.   It is a psychological curiosity.   It is honestly and earnestly written, and it is very plausible.   The man evidently believes that rationalism is the saviour of the world; and this view leads him to turn all facts to substantiate his position. It would be difficult on this account to review the book in detail without making another book as large as his ; it would take a page of truthful history to offset or upset a page of his singular theorizing.   His facts and theories need the modifying presence of other facts which he has left out of sight.   Laying aside these peculiarities of the author, the book is well written and entertaining.   While he appears to have a subject he does not always stick to it, or he does not know what the vague thing is, and so wanders pleasantly ; he does however stick to his obvious object, which is to undermine Christianity.

The assumption of the man is wonderful.   Under cover of a quiet and dignified style there is simple boasting.   But we are not surprised ; this is nothing new ; these boasting words, this quiet assumption, this vanity, this self-conceit, are nothing new. We detect at once the family to which Mr. Lecky belongs. Bombast, baptized or unbaptized, is accustomed to attack the Bible and the biblical theology.   Paine was a little vulgar. The self-conceit of Mr. Theodore Parker, however, bordered on the sublime ; he intimated that he had better thoughts for men than Jesus Christ had.   Christ is often patronized by the " most highly cultivated" writers of New England.   And if Jesus Christ was a mere man, why not patronize him ?   And,

while you are about it, why not abolish God? Is there any
blasphemy in the thought? " There is no need of the hypothesis of a God," said Laplace. Says Mr. J. Stuart Mill : " We
venture to think that a religion may exist without a belief in a
God, and that a religion without a God may be, even to Christians, an instructive and profitable object of contemplation."
Abolish God, and yet call yourself a Christian? But this
is all right, for long ago men called themselves Christians,
though they had abolished Christ. If the Lordship of Christ
has been scouted as a fetish which Unitarian churches are
bound to get rid of, and if the use of the title Lord in that
connection is objected to, it is no wonder that they now talk
about getting rid of God also. It is said that you can be just
as good a Christian whether you believe in God or not. Says
the *North American Review* for April :

"We arrive at the conclusion that the nature of religion justly
conceived, consists not in the acceptance of any special opinions,
such, for example, as those concerning the existence or non-exist-
ence of God, nor in the performance of any special acts, such, for
instance, as prayer or worship, but in an attitude of the will. . . .
But in more exact terms, we may define religion as a man's devotion, that is, the complete assent and concentration of his will, to
any object which he acknowledges to have a right to his entire service, and to the supreme control over his life."

That is, the object of his choice, whatever it is, is his god ;
and his service is true religion. But a man is a god to himself ; for this New England writer scorns the notion of any authority above man. " The principle of authority is indeed contrary to the very nature of religion, properly understood" ; the
writer holds to " the responsibility of every man to himself
alone " for the opinions which he may hold. And yet this
writer calls himself a Christian, and says that Christ taught " a
conception of religion wide enough to embrace the spiritual aspirations and endeavors of mankind."

That is, a religion which will endorse all the religions of the
race.

" Such a conception of religion as this is alone consistent with that
spiritual liberty, that freedom of thought, which is the prerogative
of every individual, and without which religion is but a form of

superstition." "In such a view of religion as that which has now been set forth, theist and atheist, Christian and infidel, find ground for union in mutual charity, confidence and help; for common labor in the endless work to advance mankind in virtue and happiness."

We can not but agree with this singular *North American* writer that "this now seems bad doctrine," and we wonder whether he himself has not "misread the words of Christ." It is a fact that the "theist and atheist" and "infidel" will "find ground for union" with such a Christian as this; the sentence would, however, have been more complete if he had inserted the word "pagan." All the pagans will agree with this writer.

The natural man is in heart a pagan, find him where you will. The highly cultivated heathen Thoreau, sailing on Sunday on Merrimac River, believed in Jupiter as much as he did in Jehovah:

" Jehovah, though with us he has acquired new attributes, is more absolute and unapproachable, but hardly more divine, than Jove. He is not so much of a gentleman, among gods, not so gracious and catholic, he does not exert so intimate and genial an influence on nature, as many a god of the Greeks."

Thoreau calls Jehovah "the almighty mortal, hardly as yet apotheosized"; and adds :

"In my Pantheon, Pan still reigns in his pristine glory, with his ruddy face, his flowing beard, and his shaggy body, his pipe, his crook, his nymph Echo, and his chosen daughter, Iambe ; for the great god Pan is not dead, as was rumored."

Is not this paganism? Is it not possible to find Modern Pagan Writers even in New England? There is nothing harsh in applying the term pagan to the "Brahmin class," who make an open boast of pagan sentiments. The development theory finds advocates among "the first scholars" of the age. There is a natural tendency in unrenewed men to fall back into heathenism of a base type. The process is all the time going forward. There are highly cultivated heathen in India. We need not wonder to find them in England or America. The process is gradual. In the first generation the total depravity of a literary man may lead him merely to ridicule his father as an orthodox bigot of very narrow mind ; but in the next genera-

tion the son will say : "My father was an ape." A sad ending
this for the "three-decker brains" of the "first writers" of New
England.

Mr. Lecky has all the marks of this highly cultivated heathen
race, though his culture is above the average of the tribe as it
appears in America. He resembles them most in his disposition to think more highly of rationalism than he ought to think.
Country clowns are not more boastful than the members of the
high literary circles of our American rationalism. Mr. Lecky
has all the assumption of his class. Not yet given over to the
work of doing away with God, he quietly goes through the history of Europe as blind as an atheist. He sees only the development of man, and "the spirit of the age." To him
there is no God in history. His eye is blind to the appearance
of a kingdom of God in the world. Christianity itself is
deemed divine only as one of many religions, one form of the
development of the religious nature of man. And all
through his book he grandly assumes that rationalism is taking
the place once occupied by Christianity. Mr. Parker is the
only writer who approaches him in the grand dignity of this assumption. What appears to be a considerable knowledge of
history supports his theories. An appearance of fairness, and
magnanimous charity, tends to give the reader confidence in the
writer as a man of large mind. Does he not take a fair view
of the historical field? And is it not the deliberate conviction
of this comprehensive mind that Christianity is failing, and that
rationalism is coming to occupy its place as a religious power?
For example, he asserts that once those forsaking the Roman
Catholic church became Protestant, but now they become rationalists, and that " the general current and bias of the intellect of the age is in the direction of rationalism"; and that
" there is a strong predisposition to value the spiritual and
moral element of Christianity, but to reject dogmatic systems
and more especially miraculous narratives"; and that " intellects unshackled by" the " traditions " of " dogmatic Protestantism " "will never embrace " it, and it seems " plausible " that
" the current of civilization must ultimately transform or overthrow " it. In all this he sees the rising glory of rationalism
with its " sublime synthesis " of " all the past forms of human
belief."

But in all this we see only the fact that under the influence of the Protestant movement infidelity is free to have a "continous and uninterrupted development." Men are free to indulge in "the guilt of error." Protestantism has made open, outspoken rationalism possible. Infidelity rose and fought Christianity in the early ages, as soon as there was any Christianity to fight. During the Roman Catholic dominion in Europe, all heretics and infidels were repressed by physical violence if need be ; secret infidelity remained secret. And when the Reformation under Luther broke up the Roman Catholic power, infidelity began to work again. The mere frankness which comes of freedom will make it appear that there is more infidelity than once. One half of the Unitarian ministers in America, according to Dr. Bellows, are preachers of infidelity. This handful of preachers have a few adherents. We have a few people in America who really think with Mr. Lecky that the world is all running after rationalism. Preachers who do not believe in an atonement, or in regeneration, readily fall into this rationalistic notion of doing without a Bible altogether. So far as concerns these hundred and fifty Unitarian churches, the movement is more of a success than the infidel worship that was set up in the French Revolution ; but this is because these congregations have mostly formed the habit of going to church under the name of Christianity, most of them even now thinking that they are the best Christians in the world. But the number of these infidel teachers is so ridiculously small when compared with the evangelical ministry, that it is evident that the number of infidels is not really greater in proportion to the Christian church than once, though the freedom of the age may make them more outspoken, and by loud boasting it may be made to appear that they have become a great power in the world. This Mr. Lecky has his head so full of this insignificant "modern spirit," that he can hardly discern what the ancient spirit really was. He can see only rationalism in the past. He thinks rationalism has been the great instrument in affording light and hope to Europe. So a fly on a coach wheel knew not what raised the dust, the fly or the wheel, but thought on the whole it was the fly that did it. This Mr. Lecky has become so involved in the "traditions" of unbelief that he can not even see the grand movements of Christianity. "One conclusion we may most certainly and most safely draw"; " it is that the general current and bias of the intellect of the age is in the direction of" Christianity. Never before has Christianity had such singular power as in this very period in which it has seemed to Mr. Lecky to t e powerless. Never before has Christianity exerted so mighty an influence on the nations of men, modifying society, and introducing Christian ethics, thus giving "strength and nourishment" even to rationalism. Never before has Christianity made such conquests as in the present generation. Christian dogmas, as the basis of morality, have made a wonderful advance within the last half century. Men begin to see the truth of the system. Never before has vital godliness, the very spirit of Jesus Christ, been so great a power on the earth as to-day. Regeneration, the submission of the will to God, submission to the guidance of the Holy Ghost; faith in the atonement of Christ; an earnest spirit of self-sacrifice, holiness, love to being : these principles of vital Christianity are the great powers in the world to-day. And if Mr. Lecky can not see it, it is because he is subject to the dogmas of rationalism. It is this delightful unconsciousness, or delightful conceit, of the fly on the coach wheel that makes this History of Rationalism in Europe one of the curiosities of literature. The author seems utterly to ignore the Christian stand-point in looking at the history of Europe. He sees Rationalism, and Voltaire, and Hobbes, and the spirit of the age ; but the yellow primrose of Christianity on the border of "the great movement," "the moral and intellectual development," is to him only a very yellow primrose ; it looks pretty enough, but it makes small show by the side of the great infidel sunflower. Yet there are some very amusing passages in Mr. Lecky's Introduction, in which he utters many beautiful and poetic sentiments concerning the importance of divesting one's self of prejudices, and thoroughly understanding the position which even the enemies of the truth occupy, and seeing things through their eyes ; a little more dignified in form, but in spirit not very unlike the noisy pretense of fairness and liberality and freedom from bigotry, put forth by the most bigoted sect in New England.

So much for the spirit of the book, now for the subject matter. How easy to leave out of all account certain facts, and then deny the existence of such facts. So owls have been represented as shutting their eyes in the face of the sun, and hooting: "Where is it?" Mr. Lecky's prejudices have led him utterly to misapprehend, and thus to misstate history.

For example, he takes it for granted that the heathen masses of Europe have been influenced by true Christianity, and then proceeds to imply that the fruits of a heathenish state of society are the fruits of Christianity. But, as a matter of fact, Christianity as a scheme of doctrines and morality has never obtained any great degree of power over the masses of Europe even to this day. There has been a nominal Christianity which has rendered the people better off than the so-called pagan nations, but the true spirit of the Gospel has at no time affected any considerable part of the population. The number who have seemed to understand and obey the Gospel has been greater within three hundred years past, but even now the properly Christian element is small compared with the actual populations of the countries. The history of Europe as a whole before the Reformation and since is a history of total depravity in Europe. Christianity has made some show, but much less than some imagine. Read the history of Europe since the conversion of the Northern nations, and it is a history of men very little under the control of the Gospel. Nations were perhaps called Christian, and so counted in the books; but the bulk of the people were still heathen, practically heathen, unbelievers in the Bible sense, having little of the kind of religion set forth by Christ and by Paul. Even in the height of the Papal power, taking the census of Europe, and going to the people as individuals, it appears that the great part of them were, to all intents and purposes, heathen, not habitually attending religious service, the greater part of the time not even under the direct influence of the priests. They had no religious knowledge to speak of aside from the baptismal formula; and no religious experience beyond being wet in baptism. So long as they confessed at suitable intervals, and paid money to the priests, and were guilty of no heresy, they were not disturbed. There was always a rabble in the towns, and a vast class of peasantry who, for three hundred days in the year, had no more religion than so many brutes. That this was true of all the people appears all the more clearly since it is to so great an extent true of the present population of Europe. We can not pretend that the lower classes before the Reformation were, to any great extent, under the practical influence of the religion of Christ as it is taught in the New Testament. Among these there must have been much more infidelity than is usually supposed. Superstition and unbelief go hand in hand. Go to heathen countries, even where Christianity has not shaken the superstitions, and intimate acquaintance with the secret life of the people will show a considerable number who are infidels. The depravity of the human heart is such that men will not be practically much affected by religious motives, if they have any scheme of iniquity to carry out. Such practical infidelity is always accompanied by more or less theoretical unbelief, even though little is said about it. If the true history of Europe could be known, it would be found that at almost any given period a great body of infidelity existed in the Roman Catholic church, and that practical heathenism prevailed. Primitive Christianity raised the rank and file of the church. The Reformation began to move the church back to the primitive experience ; it began to elevate the masses.

It can not now be shown that the leaders of Europe were much more under the influence of true Christianity than the common people. If many of the leaders had been much better the people would have been elevated. At the Synod of Trosley in the beginning of the tenth century, the bishops said ;

" In the churches many are found sunk in the lowest vice, and multitudes almost without number of every sex and order, who, to years of old age, have never obtained so much correct knowledge of the simple faith, as to be able to repeat the words of the confession of faith, or of the Lord's prayer."

These were the churches : if there were, besides these, outside barbarians, it does not appear what character they bore. But history abounds in statements concerning the clergy, as men caring "for nothing but horses, flocks of sheep and fields," and appearing "with the marks of intoxication at the altar."

There were devoted men among the clergy but the larger part of the priests and people were heathen. In the eleventh century Hildebrand told the Romans, Longobards, Normans, that they were worse than the pagans, and said that the bishops were

"Opposed to everything which serves to promote religion and the cause of God. Casting your eye over the west, south or north, you find scarcely anywhere bishops who have obtained their office regularly, or whose life and conversation corresponds to its requirements, and who are actuated in the discharge of their duties by the love of Christ and not by worldly ambition."

Take the morals of the monks in Geneva, Germany, Italy and England, before the Reformation, and it appears that most of the so-called religious teachers were shockingly irreligious men. They also knew how false and mean they all were. They knew that the vicar of God was a knave, and that the mother church was the mother of many knaves ; though perhaps some deluded themselves with the idea that they were ideal Christians. But the hypocrites were infidels ; practical and theoretical infidelity abounded. The dogmas of Christianity had little influence upon the lives of the priesthood.

The working of a purer Christianity for three hundred years has not yet brought the nations of Europe into subjection to the Gospel. In the first century of the Reformation little could be done in eradicating the errors of the masses. The gigantic superstition of witchcraft, and the fearful persecution of heretics, were the offspring of the pagan mind, the offspring of unregenerated man, the offspring of rationalism. Rationalism gets on without a Bible ; rationalism believes in following out the passions of the natural man ; all Europe was in this sense rationalistic when the persecution of heretics and witches prevailed. Europe despised the Bible and the Bible doctrines, and merely took up the teachings of a so-called church which taught whatever accorded with self-interest. This can be proved beyond all peradventure, that the persecutions which arose under the papal power, and which for a time affected the Protestant church, arose from what is now called rationalism, though the name rationalism was not then used to describe that evil "spirit of the age." Europe was then what the rationalists

want it to be now, a continent ignorant of the true spirit of the
Bible, despising the authority of the Bible, and mindful only of
the development of original sin. The early Protestants were
so involved in this rationalistic spirit of persecution that they
found it difficult to break away. If any Christian writer will go
into history with the zeal Mr. Lecky has shown, he can easily
make out the case, showing that the precepts which governed
the persecuting Roman Catholic church and the precepts of
modern rationalism are substantially the same. The substantial
unity of error is a tempting theme for thirty years' study and a
book. Rationalism and Romanism can be shown walking hand
in hand; they agree, rejecting the word of God, and merely
developing the evil heart of the natural man. The main difference is that Romanism is a church, while rationalism is trying
to become a church. The horrors of the French Revolution
exhibit the infidel spirit when it has power; a spirit as fiendish
as was ever displayed by the Roman Catholic church. This
fiendish spirit is found in the natural man.

Now it is absurd for Mr. Lecky to suppose that the dogmas
of the church had really much weight in originating the persecution of heretics or witches. Total depravity did it: the total
depravity of all Europe did it: and the church dogmas were
only the tools the bad men used. It was convenient to use
these dogmas. We know that there were some true Christian
men who fell in with all these movements, but it was because
they were in these points influenced by " the tendency of the
age"; such would naturally urge Christian doctrines to support
the infamous practices they thought the Lord endorsed.

In looking at the history of Christianity in Europe, it can
not be borne too constantly in mind that the so-called " conversion" of Europe was merely nominal. A king was baptized,
therefore all his subjects were baptized and called "Christian,"
but they were pagans as much as ever. For example: France
has never been in any proper sense "converted" to this day. A
vast population in France are as truly heathen as the Caffres.
Lamartine once said of the French people, that lack of conscience was the fatal defect in the French character which made
a permanent French republic impossible. Guizot once said:
"The thoughts of this people are not the thoughts of a civilized

race ; their imaginations are those of a savage tribe." This is true of vast numbers in all Europe. Dr. Arnold called special attention to this mere nominal conversion of the nations as an explanation of the present state of Europe. The Roman church accommodated Christianity to heathen ideas, and then called the heathen "Christians." So the *North American Review* calls its heathenish ideas of religion by the name "Christian." Said Andrew Fuller of the Jesuit missions in China : "They had a great many converts such as they were ; but thinking people looked upon the missionaries as more converted to heathenism than the heathen to Christianity." So "liberal" Christians, in despair of bringing men over to them, at last conclude to go over to men, and accommodate their religion to "theist and atheist," "infidel" and pagan ; but would not the sharp-eyed Andrew Fuller question whether the *North American Review* is not "converted to heathenism"?

But now we come to inquire how the most gigantic vices of the papal pagans in Europe were removed. Mr. Lecky implies that rationalism broke up the persecution of heretics and witches, and gave rise to the grand commercial, intellectual, and moral movements of modern Europe. His theories show a wonderful perversion of a really remarkable inventive spirit. The revival of letters, the religious reformation, the grand discoveries of printing and the mariner's compass and of America, and the rise of commerce, were remarkable movements. Mr. Lecky takes all these things into account, and calls all "the spirit of the age," and uses this as synonym of rationalism ; and says that rationalism, "the spirit of the age," broke up superstitions, witchcraft, religious persecutions and torture. The religious reformation was a rationalistic creation : "The reformation was created and pervaded by the modern spirit." This is the way it is made out : The revival of letters, the study of the Latin classics in the twelfth century, and the fall of Constantinople and the diffusion of the knowledge of the Greek classics and the Platonic philosophy, gave students something to think about and broke up the nightmare under which they had been sleeping in the dark ages ; the intellectual habits of Europe were changed, and hence the religious feeling changed ; and after that Europe was divided between the Roman Catholics, the

Protestants and the rationalists, the determining causes of the locality of each faith being found in political, social and geographical causes. Mr. Lecky evidently thinks that the revival of learning did really more for Europe than the revival of religion; or, at the least, he vastly overestimates the value of the new-born zeal in the study of the classics. As a matter of fact there was no vital or redeeming power in it. It indeed brought the ancient history face to face with the romantic legends which had taken the place of verities; but its only real service was in promoting philological study, as a preparation for the study of the Bible in the original. The knowledge of the ancient nations brought to light did not rouse the best part of man's nature; it did not result in more profound thinking; and the shallow students were content to imitate the old heathen in their immoralities as well as in their literary culture. The revival of learning did not result in anything very useful till Erasmus turned men's attention to the study of the Scriptures in the original tongues. It was the opening of the Bible which reformed Europe. Mr. Lecky sees the classics and Plato, and the tendency of the age, and the development of blind society, guided by " many special political or social, or even geographical considerations "; but he takes no knowledge of the prayers of " the friends of God," no knowledge of the appearance of the Bible in the common tongue rousing the masses like a new revelation fresh from heaven. He does not see that the revival of learning was only a preparation for the study of the Bible in the original, and that the study of the Bible renovated Europe, and that the discoveries of printing and of the mariner's compass and of America, and the rise of commerce, were only grand servants raised up by Providence to aid the Bible in its work. Not till within three hundred years has the world had a Bible. Before the flood, and for more than eight centuries after, men tried this experiment which Mr. Lecky would have tried again, a world without a Bible. Then the Bible was sixteen hundred years making. Then it worked a few years on a few people. Then for hundreds of years a few thinking men studied the Bible more or less, and learned something of its doctrines; but the masses knew nothing of it: men were left to try the experiment of having a church without a

Bible; and it appeared that a church without a Bible was little better than no church. About three hundred years ago, the Bible began its great career in reforming and saving the world. The printing press and the rise of a new hemisphere, the rise of learning and the rise of commerce, waited on the Bible. Mr. Lecky evidently understands nothing of this. He does not know that the Bible has been a great reforming power, awakening a spirit of inquiry, stirring the minds of common men in the common life, rousing enterprise and love of freedom, and leading men to shake off superstition like a cloak. Mr. Lecky does not understand it. He can understand that Voltaire and Hobbes were influential writers; he can understand that mediæval priests had evil dogmas and led evil lives; but he can not understand that the diffusion of the Bible among the common people had any great influence in renewing the character of society. He can never know just how modern civil liberty came about. He can understand the influence of the contests in the fifteenth century between general councils and the papal authority, and the influence of the ancient classics on a few minds in awakening a love of freedom; but he does not appear to know how the multitude of Bible readers were agitated by the teaching of this book, and how far the conflict for religious freedom aided in gaining civil liberty. A large part of the history of Europe he knows nothing about. The religious reformation, a reformation based solely on the Bible, is the source of the best part of the civilization of modern Europe; and yet Mr. Lecky appears to know little about it, save that one Servetus died at the stake, and certain Scotch ministers believed in witchcraft. He gives, however, some credit on the score of civil liberty.

It is not common for the enemies of the Bible to give the reformers the credit that is due for the work they did in establishing the inductive method of philosophy, which has done so much toward making modern Europe. It is not needful to ask whether Bacon learned the inductive method of Luther. But the fact is that Luther applied the inductive method to theology before Bacon applied it to science; the method was tried on God's written revelation before it was tried on his revelation in nature. To the religious reformers belongs the honor of intro-

ducing the inductive method.   They were the first to make it
a power in the world.   It is true that individuals had suggested
this method before, as all great inventions have been heralded
by solitary and powerless prophets; but the reformers discovered the method all new, and used it till a new era rose on the
world.   The early church studied the Bible and drew life from
it; but the Papacy nominally relied on the fathers and on church
authority, though really relying on the ingenious spirit of base
men in the church; so that when Luther and Calvin and Zuingle and Knox succeeded in reëstablishing the church on the
Bible, deciding all questions of doctrine and polity and morality by the inductive study of the word of God, and when
men began to push the process, and especially when the
printed word began to move through the world so that men
could study the Bible inductively and know for a certainty the
mind of God, then rose a new era in the world.   Now when
we take into account the different causes which have operated
upon Europe in forming modern society, and especially in making modern England, which is the best part of Europe, we find
that the work of Luther, Zuingle, Calvin and Knox, has done
more to make all that is worth having in modern Europe than
any other operative power.   Religious and civil freedom, without which inventive and intellectual life can never attain the
highest development, arose directly in connection with the work
of the reformers; that is, the work of the reformers was the
foundation.   Take England, and it may be further affirmed
that the influence of the Bible has been felt all through the
work of building on this biblical foundation, and that if this
influence were now withdrawn it would be like taking down the
national structure and then taking the bottom out.   Without
the Bible, England would literally fall through into China; that
is, become like China.   Our Christian civilization is not a mere
natural wisdom springing from the experience of the natural
man.   Asia and Africa and the isles of the sea also have an
experience of forty centuries since the flood; why do not they
also have "political economy" and all the modern improvements? Have the Hottentots improved any for centuries? This
writer, Mr. Lecky, is only one of many, still half pagan in
spirit, who are sighing to get loose from the influence of the

Bible, and who want to try over again the old heathen experiment of a natural development of "the spirit of the age." Why do they not all go to China or India or Africa, and "develop"? They want to get along without a Bible; and there are countries enough where there is no Bible. With all the world before them, why do they stay in Old England and in New England, where the Bible has the most power? If they are philosophers very earnest to improve the world, why do they not develop in a savage country, and create a "spirit of the age" in some heathen nation? Why do they leave all this civilizing work to the friends of the Bible?

But we can not close this part of our subject without alluding to that other great religious reformation in which our rationalistic friends appear ambitious to figure so largely. If we may believe Mr. Lecky and kindred writers, we are now just entering on a new era. Rationalism is held to be a power which will bring in a reform more glorious than that three hundred years ago. Is not this the beginning of a higher and nobler Christianity, a Christianity with all the doctrines left out? Dr. Bellows, in the *Christian Examiner*, November, 1866, announces that the Unitarian church is the grand reforming party engaged in " the great work of correction and purification of the common faith of the church." All who go with them will soon take " a vast step onward and upward." This is the step "which the moral and spiritual interests of humanity wait for and sorely need." Some of our kind country pastors, who have been steadily minding their parish cares, and who have never thought of looking into the *Christian Examiner* and *The Radical*, and who have rarely looked into the *Atlantic Monthly* as into a glass to see how vicious and bigoted they are; these poor, innocent, maligned men have very little idea of the storm that is gathering about their heads. But there is to be another Reformation. Our modern Protestantism is to be swept away. We are on the eve of a great movement. Do we not have heroes all around us? There are men who are trying to do more than Luther and Calvin did. The Unitarian church discovered some years ago that the world had been mistaken for at least "fifteen centuries," in regard to the character of Christ. They are now fully bent on making the most of this

discovery. They have a mission to rectify this mistake. They
have given notice that they mean to do it. They have raised a
hundred thousand dollars, and they have had several respectable
sermons in a Boston theatre. The great movement has begun.
All Christendom is on tip-toe. In the language of Mr. Hepworth : "We are on the threshold of a new and fresh commencement." These reformers claim (*Christian Examiner,* Nov.
1866,) that "the fundamental Unitarian protest, denying the
deity of Jesus Christ" is a "revolution" of a "radical character."
This is true, for if their position is correct all who believe in the
deity of Christ are idolators; we are the pagans if Unitarianism is true, and we need not wonder if they look upon us as
we look upon them. The "Unitarian protest" is "radical."
"No such other step remains to be taken in Christian theology
as Unitarianism took. It can not be exaggerated in height and
depth." To deny the deity of Jesus Christ is

"To deny the fundamental idea on which the theology of the
Christian church has rested since the fourth century, is to dig up the
very corner-stone and to undermine the whole structure of the popular theology, both of the Catholic and the Protestant church, for
fifteen centuries. If that denial be made good, and successfully
established, the very key of the church position and creed is taken;
and it is only a question of time, when every other characteristic dogma of what has called itself Orthodoxy so long must be
formally surrendered or silently abandoned as untenable."

The Unitarian body has surely begun a great reformation. Its
mission is to "undermine the whole structure of the popular
theology." It has begun by an attack on "the very key of
the church position and creed." Dr. Bellows and Rev. O. B.
Frothingham and Rev. Theodore Parker are the true successors of Channing; they are only following up the attack. If
Christ is not God then the whole Christian system falls.
Buckle, Lecky, Schenkel, Renan and Strauss, are all fellow-
helpers with our Unitarian friends. Whoever tries to "undermine the whole structure of the popular theology" is a fellow-
helper of the Unitarian "church." The great No-church is
invited to prove that the Christian dogma of the deity of Christ
was a fable of "the fourth century"; and that the Gospels
were composed of exaggerated legends, and that they were not

written by eye-witnesses, by the men whose names they bear,
or written at the time commonly pretended.   Every shallow
author who will venture to attack the received faith is heralded
in the Unitarian press as a profound student.   The learning of
the world is said to be overthrown in an hour by most puerile
and inconsistent theories put forth by men thoughtless and unlearned, or by men who have gone to work to study the facts
with their minds all made up as to what the facts should be
made to prove.   These men are all engaged in the great religious reformation of the nineteenth century.   They aim at first
to tear away the Christian doctrines.   The next logical step
after this will be the overthrow of Christian morality.   It is
true that many of these reformers make a great cry in regard
to morals ; but their morality rejects the authority of the Bible.
They have no infallible standard of morality ; they leave every
man free to be " moral " after his own peculiar style.   They
leave it to every man to do as he pleases ; and there are enough
already who assert that no conduct is seriously displeasing to
God ; and they will soon go over to the ground of denying the
distinction between right and wrong, some, in fact, standing
there now.   Dr. Bellóws (*Christian Examiner*, Nov., 1866)
fears this as one of the effects of the overthrow of the doctrine
of the incarnation.   He fears that amid the " general scepticism " there will be " a disposition to deny " the " moral and
spiritual authority " of Christianity.

This, then, is the great reformation of the nineteenth century.   The reformers look upon the Protestant church as
Luther and Calvin looked upon the papal power.   Dr. Bellows
(*Christian Examiner*, Nov., 1866) says that " transubstan-
tiation and the worship of Mary, or the worship of images,"
and " the Athanasian and Nicene creeds and the worship of
Christ," " are mere degrees of the same kind of superstition."
" That same spirit which later made the mother of our Lord an
object of Catholic idolatry, earlier made her holy son an object
of divine worship."   The *Christian Examiner* looks on the
Protestant church as the Protestant looks on the Catholic.
The incarnation is " as essentially incredible, absurd and self-
contradictory a proposition as the human mind, in its wildest
flights of religious fancy, ever imagined."   This hideous doc-

trine is represented as standing in the way of the progress of
the race.   The incarnation is ·set forth as merely a "mythical
dogma" united with "the worship of the Virgin," and attracting "the faith of the common people in superstitious times."
It is declared that "the time has come when Christian faith
staggers under the load of this venerable assumption; when
the Gospel is hampered and hindered by its supposed responsibleness for such an hypothesis."   Mr. Lecky's book is an attempt to show how these Christian doctrines have hindered the
progress of the race, and how they have caused all that has
been horrible in Europe for hundreds of years.   Even Dr.
Holmes must put in his little pen and tells silly stories about
immoral Orthodox ministers.   The fact is that the world has
stood Orthodoxy about as long as it can, and now there is to
be a "great reformation."

We can not but admire the spirit of these reformers.   Some
of them have been out West; they think that it is a goodly
land in which to sow their seed.   They are talking about missions.   Already some of them begin to despise the petty and
self-satisfied spirit of what *The Radical* calls The Hundred
Thousand Dollar Broad Church.   Mr. Hepworth describes
the Unitarian church as "horridly respectable," "folding their
arms over their littleness and their stinginess."   "We have
lived in the frigid zone."   "We have been cold, unsympathiz-
ing and terribly stingy."   Our Unitarian friends are talking
about receiving the Methodists to their fold.   But we fear that
if the Methodist brethren had been present in Music Hall to
hear Mr. Hepworth tell these truths, there would have been a
general "Amen" all over the house.   If Mr. Hepworth had
added that as a denomination they lacked "piety," in the Methodist sense, and lacked a creed, he might have accounted for
part of the lack of spirit in the denomination.   Their Methodist friends, whom they hope to win over, will tell them that
men who never "experience religion," and who do not believe
anything in particular, are not the men to promote missions.
Dr. R. L. Collier, the Unitarian convert from Methodism,
who retains much of his Methodist fire, and we trust no small
share of his Methodist religion, says that if the Unitarian denomination is not now ready to enter on a new movement, it is

because it is "not quite dead enough to have a real resurrection." We gladly confess, however, that we are pleased with any signs of a revival of religion in the conservative part of the Unitarian church.   An infidel said of the public meeting of the American Unitarian Association in Music Hall in Anniversary Week, that it was "like a Methodist meeting," or a meeting of some other evangelical denomination.   Orthodox clergymen present certainly rejoiced to hear so much plain truth well put.   Said Dr. Collier: "We mean now more than the Orthodox dream of.   We mean to take the world and convert it to primitive Christianity."   We say, Amen.   He advised the Unitarian denomination to leave theological discussion and go to work to "save the lost."   While we noticed more of a sectarian spirit in the Unitarian meetings of Anniversary Week than we found among the Orthodox, we were made glad by hearing some earnest words well spoken for the honor of Christ and the salvation of man.   It was said that many of our Methodist brethren are about going over to Unitarianism; but we earnestly pray that the conservative Unitarians may go over to the Methodists.   The only salvation for a dying church is found in an unselfish life.   Let the conservative Unitarians give themselves thoroughly to earnest missionary work, not to propagate a sect, but to save the perishing, and they will find new life as a body of Christians; though they can never hold what they gain till they have a Christian creed recognizing the word of God as infallible, and confessing man's need of a divine redemption.   Our Unitarian friends have little idea of the intense earnestness of the Orthodox church in its work to save the fallen.   While the Unitarians are self-complacently talking about "infant damnation," the evangelical churches are quietly sending the Gospel all over the world.   There are so many Christian men in the Unitarian ranks that we can not but hope that there will be a re-formation in that body.   Unquestionably within a little time the conservatives must enter on Christian missionary work in earnest, and draw nearer to the evangelical denominations, or the denomination, as such, will go over to mere deism.   The beginning of the end has come, unless the Christian men in the denomination rise and make a new beginning on a more thoroughly Christian basis.   The logical tendency of Unitarian teaching is now appearing. The greater part of the denomination is now going over to open infidelity. Many of them will still call themselves Unitarians, and will still make it appear that Unitarian and infidel are synonyms; but many will reject even the name Christian, and call Christ Leader, not Lord; and some will even reject the leadership of Christ, and follow the pagans.

Twenty years ago Mr. Parker wrote concerning Unitarian anniversaries: "The Unitarians are getting shockingly bigoted and little; their late meetings were windy, and they meet to ventilate their narrowness; yet how contemptible must be a sect who only deny the divinity of Christ, affirming a denial, their life the development of a negation!" But if Mr. Parker had lived in this year of grace 1867, he would have been gratified with "the tendency of the age." He would have found the best men in the denomination earnestly protesting against deism, trying in vain to stem the tide of open infidelity that is sweeping away the denomination. But he would also have found among our "religious" anniversaries in Boston this year, a public meeting "to consider the condition, wants and prospects of free religion in America." This is really a split of the radical from the conservative Unitarians. It was distinctly set forth by the chairman of the meeting, Rev. O. B. Frothingham, that the movement originated with "Unitarians," or those having "their root in Unitarianism." It was distinctively a Unitarian movement, but it was an openly infidel movement. The design was to unite the enemies of Christianity. The name Christianity was spurned by many. The "absolute religion," the religion of the natural man, open paganism, was advocated. The meeting was not opened by prayer. The only prayer made was made near the close by an insane man, who declared even their "freedom" to be a "chain." This Association is to become one of the features of Anniversary Week. This first meeting was, on the whole, rather tedious. Three manuscripts were produced, one of which occupied fifty minutes. Every speaker stood for himself, and most assailed the others. It was "Individualism gone to seed." The meeting was a striking illustration of the intellectual confusion and practical folly arising from the efforts of man to draw spiritual life from a depraved heart

and a head unilluminated by the word of the living God.   Such
definitions of religion, and such metaphysics, and such definitions of morality do not often appear in well-dressed companies,
unless indeed in the congregations of some of these curious
" ministers of the Gospel."   Yet this little meeting, so contemptible in appearance, is undoubtedly a grand era in the rationalistic church.   Said the reverend chairman : " The time
for a new religious departure has come."   " The great exodus
has long been going on."   Egypt is left behind, and after
passing the wilderness the promised land will appear.   The ambition of these men is wonderful.   They act on the teaching of
Mr. Parker that Christ by no means knew so much as the moderns.   Says *The Radical :* " It is perfectly possible that Jesus
and his Jewish disciples, being among the earliest, were, in
some respects, the poorest fruit of this indwelling divinity."
We have come, therefore, to a new reformation, at least as important as that under Luther, and by some held to be as important as the Exodus and the Christian era.   This is a great
reformation.   Was not Channing an Erasmus?   Was not
Parker a Calvin?   Is not the editor of the *Christian Examiner* a Melancthon?   Perhaps, however, we are mistaken
about Erasmus.   A writer in *The Radical* for April, seems to
bear away the palm in this new revival of learning.   In advo-
cating infidel missions to the West, the writer says : " It is
possible to use the Unitarian divinity schools"; but first, it is
needful to make the " instruction more free and broad";
" some relics of superstition, such as the pious investigation of
Israelitish heathenism in the original Hebrew, need to be
pruned away."   It is not very generally understood outside
rationalistic circles; but we are living in a most remarkable
era ; and these " highly cultivated " men around us are reformers.   In a little while they will be famous.   Perhaps we ought
not, however, to say that they will be like Luther and Calvin
and Knox, for these were all narrow, bigoted men ; rather we
compliment them by comparing them with the great names
they love, Voltaire, Hobbes, Hume and Paine.
     It might be suitable at this point to enter somewhat more
particularly into an account of the singular system of pagan-

ism which these reformers propose to introduce in the place of Christianity. But we reserve this theme till cooler weather.

It is suitable, however, in this connection to follow out our purpose to say something of the effect of Mr. Lecky's book. The book will unquestionably confirm rationalists in their views. Any man who has become involved in the doctrinal teachings of the " Christian " opponents of Christianity, will, by reading this book, be confirmed in his dogmatism, and will be more fierce for his sect, and more intolerant of the Orthodox heretics than ever. We can not say that we consider this a serious mischief: it is to be regretted ; but the regret reaches further back : original sin is to be regretted ; total depravity is to be regretted ; and it is seriously a sad thing that any should become voluntarily so blinded by passion, or by prejudice, or by training, or by circumstances, as to be unable to see the beauty and glory of the Christian system and the infallible word of the Lord. But since men do in great numbers reject the truth, we may not wonder if they are confirmed in it by all who see things from this peculiar standpoint ; and we may not much regret it since decision of character is desirable in the moral world, and all things tend toward the valley of decision. We need to know what is truth and what is error ; and God hasten the day of battle. We need to have just such books as this to lead men to take sides and to stand up to fight. Here have been " Christian " teachers of vital error ; some of them really Christian men, who have fed on the sincere milk of the word, who have known more about milk than meat, and who have known very little about the bones of the Gospel, but men who, nevertheless, have had a " bone theology," a theology of the feelings and not of the intellect and of the sense ; yet teaching vital error, taking out the doctrines of the Bible, denying the full inspiration of the Bible, and opening the way for the savage Theodore Parker and the genial Mr. Lecky. In one of the early numbers of the *Spirit of the Pilgrims* it was shown that the term infidelity, as it has been applied to the English deists, was equally applicable to many men concealing themselves under the name Unitarian, since the infidelity of both consisted merely in denying the full inspiration of the

Bible.   The Unitarian denomination has, like the charity it so freely claims, covered a multitude of sins and sinners, in that it has given shelter to a multitude who have covertly or openly attacked the plenary inspiration of the Bible.   We will allow no one to surpass us in praising the truly Christian spirit of some who call themselves Unitarians.   We confess that we admire the frankness and zeal with which some of them stand up for the truth as they understand it, and who hold that the truth is for use as a missionary power in saving men from the power of sin.   But we will allow no one to surpass us in condemning the theological errors taught by the Unitarian church.

If you deny the entire sinfulness of man, if you deny the deity of Christ, if you deny that his death on the cross was needful to furnish a way of salvation for man, if you deny the need of divine power in regenerating man, if you deny the plenary inspiration of the Bible, you may perhaps, in spite of your nominal unbelief, really believe, and be a Christian ; but your theology leads logically straight to paganism, a mere natural religion in which the natural man develops his evil heart and calls the "development," whatever it is, a "religion" acceptable to God.   Theodore Parker is the logical result of the teachings of Channing.   "To put Dr. Channing and Theodore Parker, differ as they did in theology, into opposite categories, is a mistake in every way."   So says Dr. Bellows.   But they did not so greatly "differ in theology."   Mr. Parker merely carried out the principles taught by Dr. Channing.   Professor Stuart long ago said that it would come to this.   In this, Unitarianism has done infinite mischief.   It has prepared the way for open infidelity.   Infidel books establish and confirm many, who still flatter themselves that they are Christian, in their opposition to the peculiar teachings of the Bible, and in their opposition to the Bible itself as the infallible word of God.   There are many now who were in childhood trained up under influences which have made them bitter in their opposition to all that is Orthodox, and their opposition is so great that it seems morally certain that they will never receive the Orthodox dogma that the Bible is the infallible word of the living God.   Now such eagerly snatch at Mr. Lecky's book, and say : We now feel perfectly sure that Orthodoxy is the same in spirit with the Catholic church, and both are failing, and we are triumphing; we take the morals of Christianity and leave its dogmas and superstitions behind; we tear out the Sermon on the Mount and throw away the rest of the Bible; we are developing into a millennium after our own fashion. So Paine also taught. He had a "respect for the moral character of Christ," and praised "the most excellent morality" of his teachings, though he could not understand the doctrine of turning the cheek to him who would smite you, and despised the "feigned morality" of "loving enemies." But we hail the day of decision when Paine shall have his own followers; a day for the crumbling of a baptised infidelity. Let the angel of light show hoof and horn.

Let us hope that another effect of this book will be to quicken men in the study of history. We commend the study of history to the rank and file of our rationalistic friends. The study, if it is profound enough, may enlarge their minds. A shallow knowledge of history may mislead you. History is so full of matter that it may be made to support the wildest theories. Suppose you want to make a book: There are so many facts on record that all you need to do is to go through the centuries, taking the facts that can be made to sustain any particular theory you may happen to have, and, meantime, carefully avoid citing or even seeing the facts that militate against the position; and you will be then prepared to make a sensation. Ignorant men will read your book and say: Surely this man has the ages to support his statements. It is in this way that the History of Rationalism is written. A vast array of facts show that Mr. Lecky is in the right; and a still greater number might be arrayed to show that he is all wrong. The evidence against him is as overwhelming as an avalanche. He can not stand a moment before a fair, truthful presentation of the history of Europe. See how easy it is to write an untruthful history; see how easy it is to cite facts. Here are facts: Abraham lied; Jacob was dishonest; Moses was angry; Aaron made a golden calf; Gideon was covetous; David was a murderer; Peter denied Christ, and John called for fire from heaven to consume his enemies. Do not cite any more facts in regard to these men or the time in which they lived: now draw your inference, and say that the church of God has been made up of rascals. All this it is easy enough to do; and it may be that very ignorant men will be deceived by your statements. But then if you want to know the whole truth, you need to know all the facts in regard to these men; and after you have found out these facts, you are not yet able to make up your mind about the character of these men; you must compare them with the other men in the generation in which they lived. This is the only fair way of judging their characters. Compare Abraham with the Sodomites; Jacob with Laban and Esau; Moses with Pharaoh; Aaron with Balaam; David with the Philistine champions; Peter and John with Pilate and Nero. Do this and then you will infer, not that the church of God has been made up of rascals, but that the Scripture phrase is true which represents the church in the world as a lily among thorns. Mr. Lecky would have made a very much more truthful book if he had been blessed with a more comprehensive mind, and if he had learned to generalize. An inability to generalize leaves the mind a prey to almost any error that may try to seize it. The whole Universalist denomination, so far as it pretends to rest on the Bible, is based on a few isolated texts; the denomination takes no comprehensive view of the Bible. Spiritualism is based on one class of facts; other facts are ignored. Unitarians, so far as they pretend to take the Bible, do not deal much with the mass of texts relating to the atonement, only as illustrations when they exhort men to self-sacrifice. So the rationalists take such facts as suit them and leave out others. They claim to take the universal religion, but they leave out the most vital doctrines. The universal religion believes in the endless punishment of the wicked, and in the need of sacrifices; but these are left out by the rationalists. They do not comprehend the universal religion. Rationalists are narrow men.

It does not take much to make a rationalist. Take a substratum of native depravity, and set a man to acquiring the universal religion, that is, let him read what he pleases, believe what he pleases and do what he pleases; and let every man blow his own trumpet, and if possible blow a little for neighboring rationalists. Talk a great deal about culture and taste, and show your taste by frequent inuendos against your mother's religion; hate the Orthodox with the hatred of a bigot; be sure you call yourself liberal; and make it appear that there would be found many men of like spirit if you could be induced to be so vulgar as to count. It is easy to make a rationalist. It is easy to make an ism. It is easy to make rationalism. It takes few men. There are vast multitudes of irreligious men in the world, men who hate the truth, and who are disobedient to it; they would about as soon be called one thing as another, provided they are not called Puritans or Orthodox; some of them would just as soon as not be gathered into pretty meeting-houses to hear men of " culture " talk of taste or political economy. If a few men agree to call this company rationalists, or liberal Christians, or Unitarians, what is the harm? And if considerable many people do not object to the name, but on the whole feel rather proud that now they have a " religion," where is the harm? Does it not stand in proof then that rationalism has wonderfully increased? It is a little amusing to consider the narrow grounds of the assumptions made by rationalists. It is assumed that the tendency of the age is fast undermining Christianity. But there was never a time when the Christian faith stood firmer in the world than it stands to-day. There are always irreligious men enough in the country, and it makes little difference whether you baptize them and call them Christians, or whether you call them rationalists, or, the enlightened public, or what not. It is nothing more nor less than the same old human sinfulness that Christianity has been battling so long. It is easy to boast; a few men can boast. It takes only a few men to make a great fuss. Our neighbor from the forest says that half a dozen wolves in the night will make so much noise that you think the forest is full of them. Read the writings of our " Brahmin class," and you will find that they make great use of each other; but the reputation of some of these fine writers will not be worth much in three hundred years. A very small and select mutual admiration society can praise each other in print. It can be printed, on tinted paper if need be, that A. B. is the most profound philosopher of the age, and that B. C. is a great poet, and that C. D. has a fine style, and that D. E. is a genius to be remembered forever, and that the works of these great writers will be immortal, and that rationalistic " culture " thrives. A very few men can say that Orthodoxy is tumbling down. Almost any man can read history little or much and gather up a number of isolated facts to make it appear that infidelity is about to triumph, and there are ignorant men enough among the Brahmins to read and believe and praise. It is easy for a few men to manage to get colleges and churches into their hands, and to use literary magazines for infidel purposes. But Orthodoxy did not mind losing Harvard College, or a few churches ; and nobody cares much if the *North American Review* and the *Atlantic Monthly* go over to open Unitarianism or open infidelity. " If they will only say so," adds our neighbor. But they have said so ; and let them go. The loss will not be very profoundly felt by anybody. Other churches and other colleges have arisen ; and it is possible that at some future time there may be intellect enough in New England to carry on other reviews and magazines. It may be that "culture " and " style " and " mutual admiration " will be lacking ; we could not think of having these things ; but we are a plain, puritanical sort of people, and we can get on without such stuff. Meantime we would suggest to the publishers of the *Atlantic* that a salaried gossip, kept in pay to slander Orthodox ministers, is a very valuable contributor to a purely literary magazine. Slander is good as a mere matter of taste. It is also cheap. Almost any foolish old woman can be hired to write such stories, and to do it well enough to secure the applause of the highly cultivated Brahmins who are supposed to read the *Atlantic Monthly.*

But seriously we would recommend these cultivated men to the profound study of facts. Let us hope that one effect of Mr. Lecky's book will be to excite men to take hold of historical studies. Orthodox and rationalist may be greatly edified by this sort of work. What does history teach ? What is the tendency of the age ? It is childish to boast. Give us the facts. Let the thing be tested. Is Christianity decaying ? Are the Christian doctrines giving way ? Is rationalism about to sweep the earth ? In the first half of this century one of the New England States showed an increase of evangelical church members in proportion to the whole population threefold. Such facts abound. All history is full of matter to show the development of the power of Christianity, and to show that Christianity alone affords hope to a race cursed by sin. If, then, a man rises and says that the old institutions of the devil were the children of the church, and if he undertakes to prove his assertion from history, let him be met by history. But most men are so ignorant of history that they are related to a historian as Dr. Kane's readers were related to him ; a man who had never been to the North Pole could hardly dispute anything the Doctor might say. There are few men well read in history ; and if infidelity professes to make profound discoveries in that field, we shall be glad if Christian men also feel compelled to explore that unknown region. The science of history is in its infancy. While the leading facts are known, many of the facts and the theories are obscure and confused. But well-established history affords the most striking proofs of the truth of the Christian system. The time is coming when far greater attention will be paid to this branch of study. Clergy and laity are yet to take to this work. Masters will abound when pupils multiply. A thorough study of history is a great and crying want of the present generation. Can we not have a new zeal imparted to this study ? The field is so vast that it needs to be occupied by an army of Christian men. One man can do but little. Who can gain an accurate knowledge of the eighteen Christian centuries ? Who can theorize without a knowledge of the facts ? There must be a profound study of the sources of history. Men must plunge into the obscure recesses of the early and the middle ages. The true history of the Reformation is by no means commonly understood. This is specially true of the Genevan reform. Few are very well acquainted with Scotch and Puritan movements. The greater part of our people are not familiar with the history of the church even since the Reformation. The history of the formation of doctrine is not popularized. The relation between doctrine and morality needs to receive searching study. There is to be a battle just here. This is a fine subject for years of study : to show from history the connection between doctrine and morality. The adaptedness of the Bible doctrines to man can be shown. The Christian apologists of the coming generation will draw more material from history than from any other source. Says the *Christian Examiner:* "History is being rewritten in our generation under the inspiration of Liberal Christianity." The enemies of the truth study history and announce that Christianity has had its day, and that in important respects it has done incalculable mischief as well as a certain good. The Christian doctrines are assailed from the historical standpoint. It is asserted that Christian dogmas have perhaps for a time done good service in the early days of Christianity, but their mission is now done, and they only hinder the progress of the race. Facts are gathered from history which seem to enforce these statements. Unless these statements are met by Christian men who know whereof they affirm, unless Christian men know history, unless Christian men popularize the true history of the church, incalculable evil will be done. Let Christian men pursue such courses of study as shall make them strong to defend the faith.

In some points we would commend Mr. Lecky as a model for Orthodox clergymen. Sometimes, indeed, his style is foggy, but usually the style is good, and sometimes marvelously good when compared with the style of some sermons. A clear, ringing style in the pulpit is better than a bell in the church tower to get people out to meeting. Mr. Lecky is remarkable for his apparent moderation. His style is restrained. He does not appear to exaggerate. Too much can not be said in praise of his urbanity. His sentiments are often atrocious, but he is a gentleman. His culture is evidently far superior to that of any American rationalistic writer. But, besides his style, he has ideas. He has managed to mass a great deal of matter in his plan, much of it irrelevant, but much of it supporting his subject. He has made an elaborate book. It is the result of long study. Half of the book is light reading; the other half you want to think about. If you read the book questioning every paragraph or sentence, asking, Is this true, or false? you will find that you have more ideas when you are through the book than when you began. The book is eminently suggestive; and in this respect is commended to all sermon makers. But another point is this: Mr. Lecky has evidently run in no rut in his study. He has made wheel-tracks in many directions. He has read infidel writers, enough of them, and some of the Orthodox. The variety of information brought to light in the text and in the notes hints of long hours in the study. We hope that Mr. Lecky will find readers among our clergy, and that we shall have many among us who love to see ourselves as others see us, and who love to find out what the enemies of the truth say, and who love to go over the Christian evidences again and again in the face of the enemy. The man who loves to pray over his studies, and who loves to mingle intense pastoral work with his studies, will be in no danger of falling from the faith by reading infidel books; but on the other hand, the perusal may establish him in the faith, and make him stronger for meeting the people of his own parish. We must know books in order to know men. We must know men or we can not save them. We must know the truth and know it, or our knowledge of men will be useless. The great use of having infidels in the world is to teach Orthodox ministers to think. Christianity must go to school to her enemies. We get the main part of our thinking by going to God; but if we turn aside now and then and examine the devil and his lies, we shall then more than ever before know that we hold the very truth of God.

ARTICLE VIII.

SHORT SERMONS.

"And when he was in affliction, he besought the Lord his God, and humbled himself greatly before the God of his fathers, and prayed unto him: and he was entreated of him, and heard his supplication, and brought him again to Jerusalem into his kingdom. Then Manasseh knew that the Lord he was God."—2 *Chron.* xxxiii. 12, 13.

KINGS are but men. Birth, position, distinction, do not relieve a man from personal responsibility to God. Histories of such are recorded for general admonition or encouragement or both. In the history of Manasseh the chief interest should be to discover his moral character and the influences which contributed to make it what it was. It may be divided into two periods.

Under the first period of Manasseh's history may be noticed,

1. His great natural advantage by virtue of a godly parentage.
2. His misfortune in being orphaned at twelve years of age.
3. His misfortune in being surrounded by evil counsellors; and
4. His inexcusableness in yielding to them.
5. His aggravated degeneracy. (*a*) Disregarded his father's good instruction and example. (*b*) Dishonored his father's good reign by undoing his work. (*c*) Dishonored himself by reigning as badly as possible.
6. The savage form of his idolatry. 2 Chron. xxxiii. 6.
7. His amazing credulity. Spiritism. xxxiii.
8. His profanation of the temple of God by enthroning an image.
9. His seduction of his people.
10. His scorn of God's terrible threat. 2 Kings, xxi. 10–16. He grew worse and worse. The bane of his own realm.
11. His downfall. The nation heathen, vicious, idle, weak, a tempting and easy prey to the invader. His captivity and exile.

Under the second period of his history may be noticed

1. The good effect of his adversity; as leading him (*a*) To renounce his idolatry, (*b*) To acknowledge God, (*c*) To repent of his sins, (*d*) To pray for pardon, and for restoration to his throne.
2. The mercy he found: (*a*) God had compassion, (*b*) And heard his prayer, (*c*) And restored him to his kingdom.
3. The results of his reformation. (*a*) He fortified the holy city. (*b*) He destroyed the images; in spite of shame, and cavils, and prejudices. (*c*) He restored the true religion. Repaired the sanctuary, reorganized the Jewish worship, put away his spiritism as an abomination, and sought the reformation of his people, which latter was a slow and difficult work.

What a contrast between the first and the second period of his history! in his character, acts, and influence. Eminent in wickedness, and afterwards in piety and good works. Ruined many, and perhaps was instrumental in saving many. Learn:

1. That grace is not inherited.
2. The danger of once departing from the course of rectitude.
3. That evil counsellors should be avoided.
4. That the sons of the most godly men may become the foulest slanderers and most bitter enemies of evangelical religion and evangelical men.

5.   That spiritism is contrary to the word of God, and loathsome to a truly converted man.

6.   That individuals and the state may be corrupted much easier than reformed.

7.   That the most abandoned may be saved by grace.   Manasseh, the prodigal son, the thief on the cross, Saul of Tarsus.

8.   The godly life of those who have been renewed out of great wickedness is a striking proof of the reality and power of Christianity.

"And they said one to another: Did not our heart burn within us while he talked with us by the way, and while he opened to us the Scriptures?"—*Luke* xxiv. 32.

The resurrection of Christ was as essential as his death, in order that sinners might be saved.   1 Cor. xv. 17–19.   His death is universally admitted, though the sacrificial nature of it is often denied. But because the denial of the expiatory value of his death is accompanied by the denial of his eternal Sonship with the Father, his resurrection is by many denied even as a historical fact.   The report of it by his disciples was immediately denied by his enemies. Though their denial of his resurrection is inconsistent, and completely refuted by the Scriptures, it is still accepted as true testimony by many who regard him as a model man; as if his own claim to his resurrection, if false, were not a fatal detraction from the transcendent human excellence which they ascribe to him! Perhaps some, who dare not deny the inspired record, are still perplexed with doubts and questionings concerning a fact so miraculous, so entirely beyond the power of mere human philosophy to account for.

There is, however, another kind of testimony to the resurrection of Christ, which the more candid unbeliever may respect though not fully appreciate, which the infidel does not care to recognize and is utterly incompetent to deny.   This testimony was referred to by those two disciples who asked each other the question recorded in the text.   It is

The testimony of Christian consciousness to the resurrection of Christ.

The first element of this testimony is the believer's conscious peace.   (*a*) Peace with God.   God no longer condemns. Rom. v. 1; viii. 1.   (*b*) Peace with conscience.   Conscience no longer condemns.   1 John iii. 21.   (*c*) The constant and growing serenity of soul, which results from peace with God and peace with conscience. Isaiah xxvi. 3 ; Rom. xv. 13 ; Phil. iv. 7.   This threefold peace is the result, not of a mere compact, but of acceptance with God through the merits of Christ on the one part, and of acquiescence in the atonement which satisfies divine justice and the sense of justice in the heart on the other.   And this is not peculiar to the individual believer, but common to all believers.

If the resurrection of Christ were not a vital part of the divine plan of salvation, such peace were impossible.   Without expiation as a basis no mercy could be shown to a sinner ; and the acceptance of Christ's death, by the Father, as an expiation for sin, involves his resurrection as the condition to his ascension and priesthood.   Heb. vii. 24, 25 ; viii. 4, 5, 6 ; ix. 11–15.   But the believer's peace is peace in believing, and faith in Christ as an atoning Saviour is impossible except on the ground of his resurrection. 1 Cor. xv. 17, 19. Rom. iv. 24, 25.   The believer's peace is thus a testimony to the resurrection of Christ, which no false testimony can destroy.   The burning heart of the disciples, whose perplexity at the report of Christ's resurrection he, as a stranger, relieved by opening to them the Scriptures, shows that they now believed in him as risen.

The second element of this testimony is the believer's conscious delight in communing with Christ. (a) Communion is between the living. Matt. xxii. 31, 32.   Christ is the Son of God in human nature, and therefore must still be living in that nature in order to be in communion with the believer. (b) The believer communes with Christ by thinking of him, speaking of him, addressing him.   The burning heart attests such communion. (c) The believer communes with Christ by communing in spiritual things even with the stranger who bears Christ's image.   The " stranger " himself, with whom the two disciples on the way to Emmaus communed, was the risen Jesus.   Their burning heart proved the fact to themselves.   This is incontrovertible testimony.

A third element of this testimony is the believer's delight in laboring for Christ. (a) He serves a living Master. Heb. xiii. 8. (b) He does good to his Master's disciples.   As soon as their eyes were opened to know him, the disciples of Emmaus forgot their weariness, and felt no desire to sleep, and hastened back to Jerusalem to bear witness of the resurrection of Christ to the disciples there. They arrived late, but " found the eleven gathered together," and others with them, equally eager to bear witness that Christ had risen. (c) He seeks to bring the impenitent to Christ.   Christ was sure of Paul " as of one born out of due time," and Paul could not but preach him as the Saviour of the lost.   1 Cor. ix. 16. (d) His delight to labor for Christ converts secular into holy time. The disciples of Emmaus began their labor as his witnesses on the first day of the week, thus consecrating by their labor what he had consecrated by his resurrection, the first day as the Christian Sabbath.

In the Christian consciousness, then, there is a testimony to the resurrection of Christ, before which doubt, denial, and destructive criticism must yield.

Let Christians learn to trust the testimony of their own consciousness. It is the counterpart of the word of God. Christ delights to commune with believers who commune together concerning him. The absence of the burning heart may be very easily accounted for.

Communion with the risen Jesus is the secret of Christian efficiency.

Unbelievers should learn to be very modest in opposing any experimental truth of the word of God.

The way to learn whether any good thing can come out of Nazareth is to come and see. As man believeth with the heart unto righteousness, trial of the truth as it is in Jesus is the true way to test it.

ARTICLE IX.

LITERARY NOTICES.

1.—*The Progress of Doctrine in the New Testament, considered in Eight Lectures delivered before the University of Oxford, on the Bampton Foundation.* By THOMAS DEHANY BERNARD, M. A., of Exeter College, and Rector of Walcot. From the second London edition, with improvements. Boston : Gould & Lincoln. 1867.

THIS is an attempt, not to prove the reality of a progressive development of doctrine in the New Testament, a fact now generally recognized and admitted, but to ascertain its true character. The position defended in these lectures is that this gradual unfolding of particular doctrines, instead of exhibiting the incongruities and inconsistencies of a merely human conception of the Gospel, does, in fact, illustrate the wisdom of that presiding Mind which gave the revelation this form, as best fitted for permanent and universal use, that there can be traced, throughout, the unity of a divine plan and the continuity of a divine purpose, and that this divine teaching reaches its perfect stage of development as a revelation in the Scriptures of the New Testament, and coincides in extent with those Scriptures.

The subject is a very important one and is extremely well handled. The attention of the reader is held, and his assent secured, while the successive stages of development are traced through parable and history, epistle and prophecy, from the manger in Bethlehem to the city of God, until the revelation stands before him rounded and complete. It is not a new vein of thought which the author has opened, but we must give him credit for having worked it more thoroughly and with richer results than any who have preceded him. His style is remarkably pure, transparent and animated ; his thinking is fresh, logical and vigorously sustained. His treatment of his subject is candid, thorough and scholarly, while his spirit is profoundly earnest and reverent. It is rare that we meet with a book of the kind so readable. We welcome it as a contribution of real strength to the defences of Christianity. Though not controversial in form, it grapples manfully and successfully with some of the subtlest objections of the recent sceptical criticism. Its method of doing this illustrates the tendencies of the time to rely more on the internal, than the external, evidences of Christianity, while its success confirms our faith in the impregnable strength of those evidences. But it is not alone in this aspect of it that the book is a valuable one. We turn from the perusal of it to read the New Testament with increased interest and satisfaction.

To many readers these lectures will suggest much more than they directly reveal. If the author would enlarge the plan of his work so as to include the Old Testament, and trace the progress of doctrine from the beginning of the creation onward to the consummated glory of the kingdom of God, he would lay the Christian public under new obligations.

2.—*Notes, Critical and Explanatory, on the Book of Genesis.* 2 Vols. By MELANCTHON W. JACOBUS, Professor of Biblical Literature in the Theological Seminary at Allegheny, Pa. New York : R. Carter & Brothers.

THIS is a clear, practical common sense commentary, serviceable for the masses of readers. It is learned and profound where necessary, still it is simple, and the reader is not burdened by its erudition, or confused by labored explanations.

The first volume, which extends from the creation to the Abrahamic covenant, is preceded by an Introduction of forty six pages, covering the authorship and credibility of the Pentateuch. In this the learned author passes in close review the various sceptical theories and supposed scientific difficulties that modern infidelity has thrown around these five opening books of the Bible. An epitome of objections and defences as to the six days of creation is well given, the internal evidences of the book to its own genuineness are collected, as well as the testimony of the New Testament for the Old. Geology, philology, ethnology and universal history, are summoned as witnesses. A very useful code of laws for historical interpretation is introduced and used with effect. The exegesis, explanation and practical remarks are brief, plain and to the point, and the difficult passages are rather met than shunned; so that we can heartily commend the work as one of the very best hand-books for ordinary students of this part of the Scriptures.

The second volume, from the covenant with Abraham to the end, is worthy of careful study, and is a publication eminently pertinent, in these times when notions are so vague and erroneous on the origin, nature, unity and perpetuity of the church of God in this world.

3.—*Memoirs and Correspondence of Madame Recamier.* Translated from the French, and edited by ISAPHENE M. LUYSTER. 12mo. Boston : Roberts Brothers. 1867.

A LADY, whose fascinating qualities have put in requisition the critical and commemorative labors of Guizot and Sainte Beuve, who numbered among her crowd of devoted friends Chataubriand, Bernadotte, De Toqueville, Madame De Staël, and who had self-respect and decision enough to repel the political and amatory advances of even the first Napoleon, at the zenith of the empire, certainly deserves the careful editorial study bestowed upon her in this inviting volume. Mme. Récamièr was one of those queens of society, charming in private and influential in public life, of which France seems almost to have had the monopoly. In her day, she was the most beautiful woman in Europe, the belle of the Parisian *salons.* But no one seemed to regard with jealousy her unrivalled ascendency in the fashionable world, such was her artless or her exquisite tact in disarming hostility. Her coquetry, if not too amiable to inflict severe wounds, had a singular power to soothe their pain. Those who did not escape it seldom could refuse her their lifelong friendship.

This volume, a condensation of the bulkier work of Mme. Le-

normant, is full of the sprightly, gossiping interest of the familiar
life of its subject and her friends, as given us in their letters to her ;
of hers, there is an unprecedented scarcity. Her letters are supposed to have perished by some unexplained mishap. The salient
points of a state of society, as unlike our own as is easily conceivable, are thus presented to us ; anecdotes, sketches of people and
things, habits, opinions, pleasantries of great variety and brilliance,
which sometimes remind us of a condition of morals that by no
means commands our approval. But for a study of life and character, which we have no wish, indeed, to see reproduced among
ourselves, the book is well worth perusal. The plentiful sprinkling
over its pages of names which made illustrious the court and camp
of Bonaparte, is enough to entice the reader who is curious to
know the unstudied, unobserved side of great people's histories.
That great man's petty malice towards the noble woman who would
not fall down and adore him, shows how short also may be the distance from the *magnifique* to the contemptible.

4.—*Benedicite :* Illustrations of the Power, Wisdom, and Goodness
of God, as manifested in his Works. By G. CHAPIN CHILD, M. D.
Two volumes in one. 12mo. New York : G. P. Putnam &
Son. 1867.

NATURAL theology, pursued under Christian light and motive, is
a noble science. Substantially the Psalmist so contemplated it when
the heavens were telling him the glory of the Lord. Undevoutly
and atheistically studied, nature only makes pagans of our philosophers. The work before us is not open to this grave condemnation.
Taking up the various topics of the hymn, *Benedicite, omnia opera*,
the author discusses, in a fine vein of religious sentiment, what is
revealed to us of God in the manifold forces and operations of the
material world — sun, moon, stars, seasons, light, darkness, waters,
clouds, winds, heat, cold, mountains, oceans, beasts, birds, swim-
ming creatures—their laws of action and of life, in recondite as well
as more obvious manifestations. His scope of illustration is wide,
and his knowledge various and sound. His thought is fresh, and
his argument clear and well sustained. His work, though full of
curious inquiry, tends to something much better than the gratifying
of a mere curiosity. It ministers strongly to the culture of pious
feeling and character. We take leave at this point, to express our
protest against some criticism which we have lately seen, in some of
our American imitators of the smart and captious *Saturday Review*,
depreciating, if not ridiculing the class of literature which the
"Bridgewater Treatises" made conspicuous, several years ago, and

to which the book in hand is a worthy contribution. It is not wonderful that those, who have no patience with revealed religion,
should wish to expel from our confidence the natural revelation of
"The Great Architect," and to leave us literally a world without
God. But when men talk of the puerility of such studies as have
tasked the strength of writers like Paley and Chalmers and Brougham and their noble co-laborers in Natural Theology, they must expect to be told, without apology, that their criticism is worse than
puerile ; it is the utterly contemptible cant of the thinnest, slender-
est, however pretentious, pseudo-philosophy. Meanwhile we welcome this elegant volume, and without endorsing all its teachings,
we commend it to the "wise who understand," and to the as yet
not wise, who have not made up their minds to know nothing which
they ought to know concerning God.

Here and there a slip occurs ; as, "the elephant has got a skin"—
where *got* is superfluous and ungraceful. Also "the mission of the
Kangaroo" (293), and "the summer mission of the wasps" (295),
is a little wider extension of the missionary field than we think to
be in the best taste. If this be an Americanism, our English author has certainly quite outrun our usage. But generally his volume
is marked by great carefulness.

5.—*History of England from the Fall of Wolsey to the Death of
Elizabeth.* By JAMES ANTHONY FROUDE, M. A., late Fellow
of Exeter College, Oxford.

Reign of Elizabeth. Vols. III., IV. New York : Charles Scribner
& Company. 1867.

THESE two volumes extend over a period of seven years, from the
beginning of the year 1567 to the close of 1573. The tragedy of
Kirk-a-Field occurred on the night of February 9th, 1567, and on
the morning of the 15th of May following Mary Stuart became the
wife of Bothwell, whom Mr. Froude characterizes as "the foulest
ruffian among her subjects" ; his own wife having been divorced with
all possible haste after the murder of Darnley, to prepare the way,
on his side, for the shameful union. It was one of the strangest,
most humiliating infatuations which history records, the passion of
that most brilliant and most beautiful of women, a Queen in her
own right, the daughter of a king, and presumptive heiress
to the crown of England, for that "thick-limbed scoundrel"
Henry Bothwell, a man whose whole life had been notoriously an
unbroken career of foulness and shame ! The interest which the
life of Mary Stuart has awakened is largely owing to the fact that

she stood related closely to grand historic events in which all the civilized world was concerned. The murders of Rizzio and Darnley were, in themselves, incidents to excite little notice, such was the character of the age, so abounding in every species of evil deed. This is so well put by Mr. Froude, in a passage of great force and beauty at the opening of the first of these two volumes, that we are tempted to quote it:

"Enormous crimes are not subjects on which it is desirable to stimulate curiosity, and had the assassination of Darnley been no more than a vulgar act of wickedness; had the mysteries connected with it and the results arising from it extended only to the persons, the motives, and the escape or punishment of the perpetrators or their accessories, it might have remained a problem for curious speculation, but it could neither have deserved nor demanded the tedious attention of the historian. Those events only are of permanent importance which have either affected the fortunes of nations or have illustrated in some signal manner the character of the epochs at which they have occurred. If the tragedy at Kirk-a Field had possessed no claim for notice on the first of these grounds, deeds of violence were too common in the great families of Scotland in the sixteenth century to have justified a minute consideration of a single special act of villany.   .
But the death of the husband of the Queen of Scots belongs to that rare class of incidents which, like the murder of Cæsar, have touched the interests of the entire educated world." Vol. iii., p. 1.

This passage, as strictly true as it is eloquent and philosophical, presents but a sorry picture of the state of morals among the nobility in the age of John Knox and the Puritans. Yet the Ormistons, the Powrys, the Hepburns and the Lady Buccleughs of that stormy period, surpassed the great of other times and countries, not so much in the extent of their wickedness as in the unrestrained violence, or the unblushing coarseness of its manifestation, while the good were perhaps no better than the men whom God has raised up in every age to bear witness for his name.

Mr. Froude paints with a terrible distinctness. He sets his reader down at Holyrood on the morning after the murder of Darnley, and makes the successive acts of the dark tragedy with its thrilling incidents, great and small, pass before him as in a moving diorama. There is no possibility of mistake as to the part of Mary Stuart and Bothwell in the crime, or the infamous end which they sought.

Elizabeth had a most difficult part to act, and she performed her part on the whole with consummate ability. Largely as her wisdom consisted in a caution which was sometimes carried so far as to have the appearance of cowardice, she never lacked the courage to pursue with utmost decision and firmness the course which mature deliberation and sound advice dictated. Her sympathy for Mary was the result mainly, no doubt, of her own prerogative as a crowned head in the true succession, and her extreme jealousy of any popular manifestation that might seem to trench on the *jus divinum.* Yet she would not express that sympathy in such a way as to call in question her deep abhorrence of the crime which had been perpetrated, or involve her in the most distant complicity with Mary's guilt.

Mr. Froude's opinion of Mary is expressed in his own brief and pungent way, as follows:

"Nestled in the heart of England lay the bosom serpent, as Walsingham called the Queen of Scots, with the longing eyes of the English nobles fastened upon her as their coming deliverer. There she lay, deserving, if crime could deserve, the highest gallows on which ever murderer swung, yet guarded by the mystic sanctity of her birth-claim to the Crown." Vol. iv., p. 118.

It is pleasant to remember that the sixteenth century was not less remarkable for good than for evil in human character and conduct. Jeremiah's two baskets of figs represented a fact which was to be perpetual in the history of man under Christ's providential government of the church and the world. Of the Puritans in the days of Elizabeth our author says:

"But there was another form, quieter, purer, nobler far, in England, in which the new ideas were developing themselves, and that was Puritanism." Vol. iv., p. 108.

And again:

"If the young Puritans, in the heat and glow of their convictions, snapped their traces and flung off their harness, it was they, after all, who saved the church which attempted to disown them, and with the church saved also the stolid mediocrity to which the fates then and ever committed and commit the government of it." iv., 114, 15.

Among the illustrious men who helped to shape the events of that period and to save whatever was of chiefest value from threatened destruction, there was no one to whose greatness and goodness posterity will more cheerfully and unanimously yield its homage than to John Knox. He was a man of giant intellect, profound sagacity, and the loftiest Christian heroism, a man whom no bribes or flatteries could seduce, and no dangers could appal. How dearly he loved his country, and how much more dearly the kingdom of Jesus Christ! The character and designs of Mary Stuart he read as easily as a book, and could not be swerved a single hair-breadth from his clear and fixed judgment by all the world. There was a grandeur and force in his eloquence which " stirred his countrymen, ' like ten thousand trumpets,' " and its influence was felt for God and his country to the last.

Very touching and very beautiful is the account of the passing away of the great man, " the one supremely great man that Scotland possessed—the one man without whom Scotland, as the modern world has known it, would have had no existence"—from the earth on which he had acted so illustrious a part:

"On the 17th of November [1572] the elders of the congregation came to his bed to receive his last instructions. He went over the chief incidents of the last year with them 'He had done his best to instruct them,' he said, 'and if at any time he had spoken hardly, it was not from passion or ill will, but only to overcome their faults. Now that he was going away, he could but charge them to remain true—to make no compromise with evil—especially to yield in nothing to the Castle—rather to fly with David to the mountains than remain at home in the company of the wicked.'

"Two days later, the 19th. Morton came, and Ruthven and Glencairn; and to them he spoke at length, though what passed none ever knew. Afterwards some fine lady came ' to praise him,' to flatter him in a foolish way for the great things which he had done. 'Hush, hush !' he said; ' flesh is ower proud, and needs no means to esteem the self.'

"He was rapidly going. On the 23d he told the people that were about him that he had been meditating through the night on the troubles of the Kirk. He had been earnest in prayer with God for it. He had wrestled with Satan, and had prevailed. He repeated the Apostle's Creed and the Lord's Prayer, pausing after the first petition to say, 'Who can pronounce so holy words !' It was the day on which a fast had been appointed by the Convention for special meditation upon the massacre. After sermon many eager persons came to his bedside, and, though his breath was coming thick and slow, he continued to speak in broken sentences.

"The next morning the end was evidently close. He was restless, rose, half-dressed himself, and then, finding himself too weak to stand, sank back upon his bed. He was asked if he was in pain. He said ' it was no painful pain, but such as would end the battle.' Mrs. Knox read to him St. Paul's words on death. ' Unto thy hand, O, Lord,' he cried, ' for the last time, I commend my soul, spirit, and body.' At his own request she then read to him the seventeenth chapter of St John's Gospel, where he told them he first cast anchor.

"As night fell he seemed to sleep. The family assembled in his room for their ordinary evening prayers, and ' were the longer because they thought he was resting.' He moved as they ended. Sir, heard ye the prayers?' said one. 'I would to God,' he answered, ' that ye and all men heard them as I have heard them, and I praise God of the heavenly sound.' Then, with a long sigh, he said: 'Now it is come.' The shadow was creeping over him, and death was at hand. Bannatyne, his secretary, sprang to his side.

"'Now, sir,' he said, 'the time ye have long asked for—to wit, an end of your battle—is come; and, seeing all natural power fails, remember the promise which oftentimes ye have shown me of our Saviour Jesus Christ, and that we may understand ye hear us, make some sign.'

"The dying man gently raised his head, and 'incontinent thereof, rendered up his spirit.'" Vol. iv., pp. 455, 6.

It was a fitting end for such a man, and a beautiful illustration of the text, "Precious in the sight of the Lord is the death of his saints." It was the clear and glorious setting of the sun, after a day of alternate brightness and storms, during all which he had kept his steady course in the heavens. So have died the faithful servants of the Lord Jesus Christ in every age, and only they. The death of Mary Stuart differed not so widely from that of Elizabeth as both from the death of John Knox.

Of the character of the great reformer Mr. Froude says:

"The full measure of Knox's greatness neither he [Morton] nor any man could then estimate. It is as we look back over that stormy time, and weigh the actors in it one against the other, that he stands out in his full proportions. No grander figure can be found, in the entire history of the Reformation in this island, than that of Knox. Cromwell and Burghley rank beside him for the work which they effected, but, as politicians and statesmen, they had to labor with instruments which they soiled their hands in touching. In purity, in uprightness, in courage, truth, and stainless honor, the Regent Murray and our English Latimer were perhaps his equals; but Murray was intellectually far below him, and the sphere of Latimer's influence was on a smaller scale. The time has come when English history may do justice to one but for whom the reformation would have been overthrown among ourselves; for the spirit which Knox created saved Scotland; and if Scotland had been Catholic again, neither the wisdom of Elizabeth's ministers, nor the teaching of her bishops, nor her own chicaneries, would have preserved England from revolution. His was the voice which taught the peasant of the Lothians that he was a free man, the equal in the sight of God with the proudest peer or prelate that had trampled on his forefathers. He was the one antagonist whom Mary Stuart could not soften nor Maitland deceive; he it was that raised the poor Commons of his country into a stern and rugged people, who might be hard, narrow, superstitious, and fanatical, but who, nevertheless, were men whom neither king, noble, nor priest could force again to submit to tyranny. And his reward has been the ingratitude of those who most should have done honor to his memory." Vol. iv., pp. 457–8.

Mr. Froude is a believer in the necessity and the immeasurable value of the Reformation in which Knox bore a hand, and sees in him the mighty power but for which "Mary Stuart would have bent Scotland to her purpose," and in Knox and Burghley, the two men who together saved Elizabeth from being " flung from off her throne," or going " back into the Egypt to which she was too often casting wistful eyes."   Mr. Froude thinks also that the Papists of to-day are greatly changed as compared with the Papists with whom Knox contended and subdued them, because their power to kill has been taken from them!   Doubtless with the restoration of that power, these " forbearing innocents " of the nineteenth century would speedily manifest all the peculiar attributes which characterized the Papists of Philip II., and Mary Tudor.

We are of those who believe that eternal vigilance is the price of the liberty which was achieved in the sixteenth century, and that it behoves to note with exceeding jealousy every movement of the Papacy in our country.   We confess ourselves afraid of the female seminaries under Roman Catholic direction so multiplied among us of late, and utterly amazed to see so many Protestant fathers and mothers, and even members of evangelical churches, sending their daughters to these seminaries !   Such fathers and mothers should read history.

In our perusal of Mr. Froude's successive volumes we have had a constantly increasing conviction of their exceeding value. He invests with wonderful fascination the grand events which he delineates, so that the reader must be dull indeed who is not both interested and instructed.   We are boasting all the while of our unequalled public school system, and the remarkable intelligence resulting.   It may be so, but we want to see some new tests applied.   According to our standard no young man can claim to be intelligent who is not familiar with the principal characters and events of the " history of England from the fall of Wolsey to the death of Elizabeth."   Certainly no American young man can comprehend the history of his own country otherwise.   How many of our " intelligent " young men are purchasing these successive volumes of Mr. Scribner's superb edition as they appear, and placing them on their book shelves when they have read, marked, and inwardly digested them ?   All the light literature and *Ledger* stories that have been published since the beginning of the century are not worth a thousandth part as much for the education of a young man as this one work of English history.   Our earnest hope is, that it may be the means of greatly increasing an interest in historical studies among our scholars, as well as our young men generally.

6.—*Old England;* Its Scenery, Art, and People. By JAMES M. HOPPIN, Professor in Yale College. 12mo. New York: Hurd & Houghton. 1867.

BOOKS upon foreign countries, made up like this from the recollections of travel, have some advantages over the jottings of a tourist upon the wing. If the latter has the greater freshness and dash of first impressions, the other has the chance of a riper reflection, a better toning, and a more finished treatment of the various topics introduced. A large amount of rawness and some measure of positive inaccuracy may be forgiven to the manifest disadvantages of the flying notes which form the staple of our current touring. Even what is copied out of the guide-book may be quite unreliable in point of fact. We take up then a volume like Professor Hoppin's with a comfortable feeling that we are not about to make a lunch of green apples or halfgrown grapes. Our present author will not disappoint that hope. He has digested his material thoroughly, and has given us a book worth its shelf-room for permanent reference. It is a good exposition of British life and work, thoughtful, critical, well elaborated. Mr. Hoppin is fond of quiet beauty and pleasures, though alive to the sublimer attractions of nature. He writes purely and with a fine insight of his subject. Setting forth to show why our ancestral country should receive more attention from our travelling people, and not be used so much as a mere point of departure for Continental travel, he has well executed this very sensible design.

7.— *Works of Charles Dickens.* Globe Edition. *Nicholas Nickleby.* Four volumes in one. 12mo. New York: Hurd & Houghton. 1867.

FOR easy, pleasant reading—inviting type, right size (except a trifle too thick), flexible opening, fair paper—we give this edition of Dickens our preference. Eyesight to us is worth more than any other *diamond.* We are sorry to see the double-columned, microscopic fashion in books coming round again. In the end, it is too expensive, *me experto.* The "Globe Dickens" promises a happy combination of the good points of a book for every body. This duodecimo of more than twelve hundred pages (two volumes would have been better) is firm, elastic, tasteful. The illustrations are excellent. It is too late, we suppose, to criticise Mr. Dickens' swearing so much, by proxy, in his low characters, and higher ones, sometimes. It is lifelike enough, doubtless: but a kind of life which however "artistically" portrayed, is offensive and corrupting.

This Dickens-mania among our publishers may very likely put
money into their pockets ; but we augur no good from it either to
the taste or morals of our people, while by no means insensible to
the better qualities and strong fascination of many of these stories.

8. — *Lectures on the Study of History, delivered in Oxford*, 1859
—61. By GOLDWIN SMITH, M. A.,Regius Professor of Modern
History in the University of Oxford. To which is added a Lecture delivered before the New York Historical Society, in December, 1864, on the University of Oxford. 12mo. New York :
Harper & Brothers. 1866.

HISTORY is so broad a field, that any book is warmly welcomed
which will facilitate a survey of it either as a whole or in any of its
parts. Life is too short for any man to gain any very extensive
and profound knowledge of general history, except by reading with
definite purpose and with method. That method is doubtless the
best, which traces the natural development of a subject from its
seminal principle onward. But the detection of that principle, and
the tracing of its development, are just the problems which the
reader desires to know how to solve. The title of this book promises aid in this direction. How well the book redeems the promise,
is a question which different readers might answer differently, according to their appreciation of the subject of method in general,
and their agreement with the author.

Whether history is a science, whether it is governed by such laws
that, the factors being given, the result might be substantially determined beforehand, is a question in debate. Professor Smith rejects
the doctrine of the necessarian, yet accepts that of historical progress. In his view, the fact of the moral freedom of man precludes
the possibility of a historian's becoming so scientific as to show with
tolerable certainty what shall be hereafter. He writes with sharp
though brief criticisms upon the theories of those who would ascribe the progress of the race to anything rather than to Christianity. But whether he himself clearly distinguishes between "the
law of sin and death," under which man's boasted moral freedom is
essentially moral bondage, necessitating in the main a development
from bad to worse, and "the law of the spirit of life in Christ
Jesus," which frees man from moral bondage and impels him from
bad to better ; and that, only when the various forces of this latter
law interpenetrate and check and overcome the forces of the former—what his real views are, is not so obvious as it might
have been had the entire volume been made up of lectures strictly

appropriate to the title.   The book, however, is written in popular style, and is interesting and valuable, not only for its suggestiveness in regard to the philosophy of history, but also for the view it gives of the University of Oxford.

9.—*Ecce Deus, Essays on the Life and Doctrine of Jesus Christ.* With Controversial Notes on Ecce Homo.   Boston: Roberts Brothers.   1867.

HE who read Ecce Homo will want to read this companion volume.   It is well written, not, as we think, by the author of Ecce Homo, nor with so much genius; but in some parts with the same irreverence for the Bible.   In the main, it agrees with the views usually regarded orthodox.   The chapter on eternal punishment is a very happy grouping of the arguments in favor of the doctrine. There is a perfect rage for Latin titles, and now Deus Homo follows in the wake of Ecce Deus.   The special consideration given to the character and office of the Messiah is a forcible illustration of what men regard the great central doctrine of the Bible.   They are still attempting an answer to the question, "Whom do men say that I, the Son of man, am?"

10.—*Lange's Commentaries.*   Critical, Doctrinal, and Homiletical. The Epistles of James, Peter, John, and Jude.   Vol. IX. of the New Testament.   New York: Charles Scribner & Co.   1867.

DR. SCHAFF, the American editor of this voluminous German serial, has found an able co-laborer for the present volume, in Dr. Isador Mombert, who translates and annotates these shorter epistles.   The general characteristics of the work, as explained in our former notices, are maintained in this section of it.   The salient points in these apostolic letters, such as the doctrine of James upon good works, the canonicity of the second epistle of Peter, the relation of this epistle to that of Jude, the Johannean doctrine of Christian sinlessness, are handled with care and scholarly fulness.   The critical questions thus raised are settled according to the generally accepted view of the church, and, as we think, upon satisfactory grounds.   At the same time there is no attempted concealment of the difficulties involved in these fields of inquiry; they are fairly stated, and the reader is referred to the sources where he can examine more at length the opposite conclusions of other investigators.

The eminently practical character of the epistles here presented, their application to the condition and wants of the church in all ages, gives a very great richness to these pages.   The different transatlantic writers of this volume, and their American translator and editor, have brought out affluently the teachings and the literature of this part of holy writ, thus making a noble treasury of truth for the nourishment of the reader. Some of the best minds and maturest Christian experience of the Christian ages have explained and illustrated these general epistles ; and it is only necessary to turn these leaves to see how diligently the gleaners have here followed these reapers, gathering whole sheaves of ripe knowledge and holy wisdom into this garner. We answer a question which was lately asked us, when we say in closing, that this series of volumes is quite as well adapted to lay reading and study, as to that of our clerical friends. It ought to have several regular purchasers in each of our churches.

11.—*Ministering Children.* A Sequel. By MARIA LOUISA CHARLESWORTH. New York : Robert Carter. 1867.

THOSE who read the previous book by this title will be likely to read this. They may not think it any better, but they will find the same admirable and instructive qualities. The Carters' make gain of godliness in a sense in which this is proper ; serving the public and the Christian's Master at one and the same time.

12.—*Lectures on Natural Theology :* Or Nature and the Bible from the same Author. Delivered before the Lowell Institute, Boston. By PAUL N. CHADBOURNE, A.M., M.D., Prof. of Natural History in Amherst College, etc. New York : G. P. Putnam & Son, 661 Broadway. 1867.

A BOOK at once religious and scientific. The author, a devout and enthusiastic student of God's works is also a devout believer in his word. Prof. Chadbourne has put the Christian public under obligations to him by bringing out these lectures to a larger audience. The publishers have done their part in admirable style.

13. — *God's Word Written ; The Doctrine of Holy Scripture Explained and Enforced.* By the Rev. EDWARD GARBETT, M. A., Incumbent of Christ Church, Surbeton ; Bayle Lecturer for 1861, 1862 and 1863 ; Select Preacher to the University of Oxford in 1862 and 1863. Am. Tract Society, 28 Cornhill, Boston.

THIS is a reprint from the London Religious Tract Society, and is a very able, direct and succinct re-statement of the argument for the plenary inspiration of the Bible, with such further arguments and illustrations as the times demand. The volume concludes with a valuable recapitulation and summary, chapter by chapter. An internal argument for the verbal inspiration of the Scriptures, the author thus felicitously states :

" It is possible for us to gather the sense out of the words of the text, and yet find, nevertheless, that the words have a power of their own like the fragrance of some sweet flower that we lay next our hearts. The soul seems to imbibe from contact with the very words a certain indescribable tone and spirit, as if the mind in its prayerful meditations goes into the text, and through the text came into contact with the mind of the inspiring Deity. What Christian man has not repeated the words of a text over and over again, as if they were a strain of sweet music,—a breath fresh from the other and the better world? " p. 356.

14.—*Longfellow's Poems Complete.* Diamond Edition. Boston: Ticknor & Fields.

HERE they are, from " Voices of the Night" to " Flower-De-Luce," a wonderful series of titles to volumes and poems, the very reading of which does one good. How finished and chaste and elegant and scholarly a poet this Longfellow was and is ! And here is a French poem addressed to Agassiz, which even Beranger might have been proud of; though since it is so free and easy in its temperance principles, we are glad it is in its appropriate tongue. We trust the wine sent was in "original packages."

Here from the " Birds of Killingworth " is one of those terrible creatures, which according to the *Atlantic Monthly* once made New England quake with their tread.

" The Parson, too, appeared, a man austere,
  The instinct of whose nature was to kill ;
  The wrath of God he preached from year to year,
  And read with fervor, Edwards on the Will ;
  His fav'rite pastime was to slay the deer
  In summer on some Adirondac hill ;
  E'en now, while walking down the rural lane,
  He lopped the wayside lilies with his cane."

Shade of gentle Harvard ! on what have these professors, that walk the shades of modern Harvard, fed, that their and thy clerical brethren must always throw them into such paroxysms ! Even the golden-tongued Longfellow hath the bitter speech ! Belonging to the clerical class ourselves, we hope we shall be forgiven for quoting a text, that seems possibly applicable :

"And when he saw Him, straightway the spirit tare him ; and he fell on the ground and wallowed foaming." Mark ix 20.

15.—*Dickens' Works Illustrated.* David Copperfield and Nicholas Nickleby. Diamond Edition. Boston: Ticknor & Fields. 1867.

VERY fascinating little volumes, just what one wants to take into the country in vacation and read under shade-trees, if he dares risk his eyes for such a feat. The illustrations, by S. Eytinge, Jr., are full of truth and action, and equal to anything of the kind we have ever seen. We propose to regale ourselves again with these creations of Dickens' genius; although, as already intimated, we fear that some of the diamond points of the printer may leave pangs in our eyes.

16.—*Annual of Scientific Discovery :* or Year-book of Facts and Science for 1866 and 1867. Edited by SAMUEL KNEELAND, A. M., M. D., Fellow of the American Academy of Arts and Sciences. Boston: Gould & Lincoln. 1867.

ALL who would keep up with the progress of scientific discovery must own and study such a volume as this. It is prepared with apparent accuracy and care, and has a full index. David A. Wells, U. S. Com. of Revenue, who has edited the previous issues of the work, introduces it with a prefatory note; and his portrait embellishes the volume; the face of a man who would look sharply after figures and facts, or we are deceived.

17.—*The Market Assistant.* Containing a brief description of Every Article of Human Food sold in the Public Markets of the Cities of New York, Boston, Philadelphia and Brooklyn; Including the various Domestic and Wild Animals, Poultry, Game, Fish, Vegetables, Fruits, etc., with many curious Incidents and Anecdotes. By THOMAS F. DE FOE, author of "The Market Book," etc. New York: Hurd & Houghton. 1867.

AFTER this long descriptive title-page, little remains to be said about the volume itself. Mr. De Foe in his meat-stand is presented in the frontispiece, sketched by himself. And never clergyman with robes and bands ready to be daguerreotyped, appeared more self-complacent. As a "market assistant," we do not regard the book as having especial value; but, as a compendium of useful and interesting information, it certainly possesses many good qualities.

18. — *The Open Polar Sea: A Narrative of a Voyage of Discovery towards the North Pole, in the Schooner United States.* By Dr. I. I. HAYES. 8vo. New York: Hurd & Houghton. 1867.

THOSE who followed Dr. Kane among icebergs and through Arctic winters, will be sure to want this volume. There is a fascination, a contagion for adventurers and readers on the Arctic Ocean. One book or expedition only prepares the way for another; and it is highly creditable to the scientific and commercial enterprise of our country, as well as to the energy and daring of our discoverers, that we have followed up the idea of an open polar sea with so much perseverance to success. The declarations of Morton have become confirmations with Hayes. The problem is solved.

In this volume, the story is told with all the witching excitement of the best Waverly novel. The labor of organizing the expedition, the departure, the icebergs, fogs, snow storms and breakers, the ice-pack, the winter quarters and long winter night, dog-teams, reindeer and bears, Arctic midnight, a new summer, the terrible sledge expedition, and the Open Sea at last—it is all intensely interesting. The book would energize a sluggard. Dr. Hayes is a good descriptive writer, and his style, as well as facts, carries the reader. Here he writes out mainly the story. His contributions to science, drawn out in official reports, are in the hands of the Smithsonian Institution, and it is to be hoped will some day be published, though there seems to be much delay about it.

The work is ornamented by a very fine steel engraving of the author's likeness, and nine illlustrations with thirty " tail-pieces."

19.—*Rural Studies, with Hints for Country Places.* By the Author of " My Farm at Edgewood." pp. 295. New York: Charles Scribner & Co.

ANY thing from the pen of Ik Marvel is well worth reading, and these essays, many of which have appeared already in the serial press, are of special interest and value. It is an occurrence of every day in the year, to spoil what might have been a very beautiful place, by building the house first and making it immovable, and then consulting the landscape gardener or his book; whereas this should always be the first thing. To locate a house properly is one of the fine arts. Or if it has been already located it is a fine art to give it the proper horticultural embellishments, of lawn, tree, shrub and flower. No other outlay is a hundredth part so productive in making a home beautiful. Mr. Mitchell has a fine taste and judgment in this direction, and moreover has made the thing a study:

his book, therefore, is of special value to those who have homes to embellish or are expecting to have, while it is full of entertainment and instruction for all who love the country. A growing love of horticultural ornament is among the most gratifying indications of the advancing civilization of our country. Our wide forests supply trees and shrubs in the largest and richest variety, and we have land enough. It is a great piece of folly to pay an enormous price for a quarter or an eighth of an acre of land, and put a house on it close to the noisy, dusty street, and shut in by other houses, near the centre of things, when by going a short distance a man can have two or three acres, furnishing ample room for shade trees and lawn, and fruit, and for the blue bird, robin and wren to build and sing. We would like to say a good deal more, but if our readers will get Mr. Mitchell's book, that will be better still.

20.—*Classic Baptism.* An Inquiry into the Meaning of the word BAPTIZO, as determined by the Usage of Classical Greek Writers. By JAMES W. DALE, Pastor of the Media Presbyterian Church, Delaware County, Pa. 8vo. pp. 354. Boston: Draper & Halliday. Philadelphia: Smith, English & Co. Chicago: S. C. Griggs & Co. 1867.

A WORK of great research, scholarly fidelity, and immense labor. Going back of all lexicons and commentaries, the author has consulted the original sources, where the meaning of a word is determined by its use. In this labor, Mr. Dale has consulted and quoted, with references to work and page, thirty two Greek writers in their use of $\beta\acute{a}\pi\tau\omega$, and thirty seven in their use of $\beta a\pi\tau\acute{\iota}\zeta\omega$. Twelve Latin writers are quoted to show the use of *tingo*, and seventeen to show the use of *mergo*, and about fifty eminent English authors to illustrate the force of the English related words. Every known case of classical usage is adduced, and the quotations cover a period of about a thousand years. The words dip, plunge, immerse, immerge, submerge, whelm, bury, drown, sprinkle, dye, imbue, and all those other that commonly go into a discussion of this question, are analyzed most sharply and delicately in their structure, import and use.

Mr. Dale takes up this question of the last two or three centuries, with the opening inquiry, what results the Baptists have reached since they claim to have arrived at the absolute truth. They claim to have demonstrated that $\beta a\pi\tau\acute{\iota}\zeta\omega$ has but one meaning in all Greek literature; that $\beta a\pi\tau\acute{\iota}\zeta\omega$ and $\beta\acute{a}\pi\tau\omega$ have precisely the same meaning, with the one exception of dyeing: that they both express the definite act and mode, to dip. To prove these claims many leading

Baptist writers are cited, by which it is seen that they differ much among themselves as to whether baptism is an act, or a mode, or a state. The Baptists are allowed to speak freely for themselves, about twenty are cited, and are seen to be far from a unit in their claimed demonstration. Mr. Dale's treatment of Baptist authorities is comprehensive, liberal, critical and dissecting, and their claims to demonstration are thrown out on the showing of their own want of harmony among themselves. Their one meaning to βαπτίζω, definite, clear and precise, and translatable by the one word, immerse, is shown to be a declaration only and not a demonstration.

All this is preliminary, occupying about one hundred pages, and before the author comes to his investigations proper within the classic field. As the unwarrantable conclusions and unfortunate confusion among themselves are attributable very much to the error of the Baptists in making βαπτω and βαπτίζω synonyms, the first step of our author is to show " that they are radically different in meaning." Almost sixty pages are given to the import of βαπτω as shown in the classics. pp. 137—195. These pages are a beautiful specimen of scholarly, controversial and kind writing, approximating to what is so often miscalled exhaustive. This subject, so *dry* in one sense, the author gives sprinkled, and even at times, immersed in the good humor of his nature and style. His conclusions on the word, βαπτω, are that it means to dip, moisten, wash, dye, stain, paint, gild, temper and tincture, with more of dyeing than dipping, though ten or twelve words are required to render all its classic meaning into English. So this word must be rejected as the same in import as βαπτίζω, first because no one word can express it, as the Baptists claim for the other, and secondly, because it is radically different. Mr. Dale then proceeds to devote the rest of his noble volume, one hundred and fifty pages, to the meaning of βαπτίζω.

Immerse, *mergo*, is outlined in its import by quotations most abundant from ancient and modern writers. Then several meanings are shown to pertain to βαπτίζω, from the very varied and abundant quotations from scores of Greek authors.

1. Intusposition, or condition of the object without regard to the action baptizing it. 2. Any act, or number of acts, securing this condition of intusposition, constitute a baptizing action, while the baptism is in the condition of the object, and not in the agency. 3. βαπτίζω is without limitation of power, object, or duration, as the sea baptized the shore, the sun himself in the ocean. 4. Some baptisms influence the objects baptized, as " the soul being baptized

very much by the body," Alex. Aphrodisias.   5. Some are baptized for an influence.   As, "One, saved by the voyage, whom it was better to baptize," i. e., drown.   6. Baptisms without intusposition or mersion.   As, "Baptized by such a multitude of evils," "Baptized by an anger," "Misfortunes baptize us," "They do not baptize the people by taxes," Diod. Siculus. "The events still baptized you," "Baptized by diseases," "Baptized by the affairs of life." And many more cases from the Old Greek Writers Mr. Dale quotes, where the Baptist notion of immersion would find a dry baptism indeed, in "wantonness," "debts of fifty millions," "diseases," "evils" and "taxes."   7. Physical mersion is not necessary to baptism.   As, one may be baptized with wine—be drunk, or by any opiate, or by any trouble. That which brings the object under a controlling influence is said, by the Greeks, to baptize it.

"Give what explanation you will, the stubborn fact, the truly important thing remains; that the Greeks daily effected baptisms by a draught of wine, by a bewildering question, and by droppings from an opiate. Accumulate around these baptisms metaphor, figure, picture ,and what not, I make my argument with finger pointed to the cup. the question, and the opiate drop, and say, the old Greeks baptized, through a thousand years, by such things as these." p. 79.

8. Baptism is not a definite act of any kind, as to immerse or dip, sprinkle or pour.   No form of action is justly involved in any proper inquiry into the import of baptism.   Baptism, in its deepest meaning, is a complete change of condition, physical, mental, moral, or ceremonial.   The element in which, and the mode, are of no account.   The condition of the object or person baptized is all of the classic idea of baptism.   Completeness in the changed condition of the subject, with or without a physical envelopment, that is baptism.

This book must take its place preëminent in the alcove as an arbiter among scholarly disputants on this question.   It comes in as Blucher at Waterloo, and this *bellum philologicum* ought to cease.

21.—*Bible Pictures; or Life Sketches of Life Truths.* By GEORGE B. IDE, D. D.   Boston: Gould & Lincoln.   1867.

HERE are twenty sketches, lively and familiar as an address, on as many interesting biblical scenes.   The style is the flowing, open style of the more popular form, and is easy for the reader. By such volumes many of the more practical thoughts of the preacher work out, through the press, among the masses.   Of course we read, this warm weather, the chapter on Deep Sea

Fishing, but were surprised to catch carp, pike and bass, in the lake of Gennesareth. Did they furnish the good haul for Peter when " the net brake?"

22.—*The Book of Proverbs, in an American Version, with an Intro-duction and Explanatory Notes.* By JOSEPH MUENSCHER, D. D. Printed at the Western Episcopalian Office, Gambier, Ohio. 1866.

WE welcome almost any exegetical work on the Old Testament. It has been too much neglected by the writers of biblical handbooks. Specially may this be said of the Book of Proverbs. Glances at this work of Dr. Muenscher satisfy us that he has done a good thing for the laity, as well as the clergy. The new translation was needed in places, and throws fresh light.

23.—*History of Congregationalism, from about A. D.* 250, *to the present time.* By GEORGE PUNCHARD. Second Edition, Rewrit-ten and greatly enlarged. Vol. III. pp. 455. New York : Hurd & Houghton. 1867.

IT was a pleasure to us to give a very favorable notice of the two preceding volumes of this most excellent work, Vol. V., pp. 413—14.

Mr. Punchard has shown great patience in research, and great scholarly accuracy and zeal in gathering his material. He has been in no hot haste to publish an uncertain work, and time and labor he has put far below fidelity and fulness in the handling of his great theme. It is in the light of such protracted and care-ful study in authorship that we get a new meaning in the proverb : Beware of the man of one book. We should be very slow to con-tradict Mr. Punchard in this field of ecclesiastical history.

This volume opens with the distinct separation of the Puritans from the English church, 1575 and following. A careful outline of the head of the Brownists is given, and of many of his co-martyrs, Copping, Thacker, Gibson and others ; and of the leading Congre-gationalists we have minute and exceedingly interesting accounts, as of Barrowe and Greenwood, their imprisonment, examination, suffer-ings, execution and writings. Two chapters are given to that dis-tinguished martyr, Penry. The strength of mind, biblical knowl-edge and firmness of those men, and their broad, deep principles of church government and Christian liberty are a marvel to us, and a sorry thing it is for our church that they must wait so long to have their history written.

After the death of Penry, Mr. Punchard takes his reader through the last days of Elizabeth and of Burleigh, the friend of the Puritans. Then come James I. and the Hampton Court Conference, John Robinson, the first Congregational church in England, the Scrooby Manor, and flight to Holland, with fast following, mingled and stirring events in the early history of our order, down to the emigration to America. On the settlement and opening of New England, Mr. Punchard lingers a little till he finds that our Congregational fathers have founded a State " memorable in the annals of the world " with " a name and a fame which are likely to endure while the world shall ᵳtand," and there he leaves them.

But we hope only for a time. It remains yet to be told, by a careful historian, how much of the thinking and writing and working to found the colonies of the North and secure independence and establish the Federal Government, was done by this same Congregational church. Also it remains yet to be told how this church stands related to the benevolent and Christian enterprises that now characterize the age. Particularly should we like to see a bibliographical history of Congregationalism, that it might be seen how much our libraries are indebted to this church for its theological and religious, educational, civil, historical, literary, scientific and other works. We think not a few who now flout at the Puritans would find empty shelves in their alcoves, if not empty heads also, if all the volumes written by those despised ones were withdrawn. "There was a little city, and few men within it, and there came a great king against it and besieged it, and built great bulwarks against it. Now there was found in it a poor wise man ; and he by his wisdom delivered the city," and we wish Mr. Punchard to write one more volume and tell us about it.

24.—*Speeches and Addresses.* By HENRY WINTER DAVIS, of Maryland. Preceded by a sketch of his Life, Public Services and Character, being an Oration of the Hon. J. A. J. CRESSWELL, U. S. Senator from Maryland. New York : Harper & Brothers. 1867.

HENRY WINTER DAVIS will one day be regarded as one of the greatest ornaments and honors, as he was one of the most loyal patriots of his native State. "Of Maryland !" Yes, of the true, faithful Maryland that loved the Union ; not of the false, treacherous Baltimore stamp, that our Massachusetts soldiers encountered on their way to the relief of Washington. An orator, ready, quick and vehement, sometimes a little florid and artificial, he always magnetized his audience, and held them at his fingers' ends ; a lawyer, well versed in the technicalities of his profession, skillful in chopping logic ; a political leader, of a keen sense of right and wrong, loyal to the right, and willing to make sacrifices for it ; a man not infallible, but never to be bought or sold ; this is the man whose speeches are, here gathered.   It will do an aspiring young man good to read them, and to imitate their author.

25.—*Recent British Philosophy.*   By DAVID MASSON.   New York : D. Appleton & Co.   1866.

THIS book is written in a clear style, and contains much valuable thought and information.   The substance of it was delivered in lectures, at the Royal Institution of Great Britain.

26.—*Life and Works of Gotthold Ephraim Lessing.*   From the German of Adolf Stahr.   By E. I. EVANS.   Philadelphia : D. Appleton & Co.   Two volumes.   Boston : Wm. V. Spencer. 1866.

IT takes this biographer a long while to get under way ; but the book increases in interest toward the end.   Whether Lessing was such a benefactor to man, or his native country, as here claimed, we very much doubt.   That his influence upon its literature, and that of the world, has been very marked, all must admit.   The translator seems to have done his work well, and the book is brought out in admirable style.

27.—*History of the Christian Church.*   Ancient Christianity. Vols. I., II. and III. Rev. P. SCHAFF, D. D.   C. Scribner & Co. 1867.

THIS is the best church history we have ever attempted to read.   It is readable, learned, carefully prepared, candid and independent. Dr. Schaff has put American scholars in this department under lasting obligation to himself.

28.—*Studies in the Gospels.*   By Archbishop TRENCH.   C. Scribner & Co.   1867.

THIS learned divine is at the head of biblical critics ; and this is a collection of expository lectures upon many of the difficult subjects in the New Testament.   It is curious, critical, suggestive, and can not be read without advantage.

29.—*The Redeemer : A Sketch of the History of Redemption.*   By EDMOND DE PRESSENSÉ.   Translated from the second edition. By Rev. J. H. Myers, D. D.   Boston : American Tract Society. 1867.

WE have here twelve chapters, beginning with the Fall and ending with Jesus Christ as King.   It treats of the promise of redemption, and the preparation for the coming of Christ among the nations, Jewish and heathen, and also of the nature of our Lord and his plan in coming; his teachings and miracles and sacrificial work. It is less labored, but more systematic than Edwards' History of Redemption, and has the advantage of a lively style, as if made up of addresses, but the author tells us it was first written for the press, and not for an audience.

30.—*Ornithology and Oölogy of New England*, etc., etc. By EDWARD A. SAMUELS, Curator of Zoölogy in Massachusetts State Cabinet. Boston : Nichols and Noyes. 1867.

AUDUBON'S splendid work was never within popular reach, and Wilson and Nuttall are out of print. There was a vacancy, a need, in this department of our natural history popularized, and therefore this work of Mr. Samuels is timely.

A bulky octavo of nearly six hundred pages well illustrated with life-like and accurate plates of all our more noted birds, and the eggs of many of them drawn in the natural size, the volume is tempting to the eye. To the reader who loves nature, it is fascinating. Mr. Samuels has a good descriptive style, and he gives minute and enlarged views of all our woodland favorites. Their songs and sounds, habits, nests and rearing of young, with their times and seasons and localities, are sketched in a delightful way for the common reader, while the scientific ornithologist finds the claims of science honored in the structure of the book.

In one or two instances, where Mr. Samuels has followed others, he has been misled, as in speaking of the Pinnated Grouse or Prairie Chicken. This bird is found in New England only on Martha's Vineyard, and one or two other islands, and so the author had not been able to study its habits.

He quotes Wilson as saying : "Old gunners have reported that they have been known to trespass upon patches of buckwheat, and pick up the grains." A Western farmer would smile at that statement, when they are such a serious enemy to all his grain fields, and often visit them in flocks of hundreds. "The flights of grouse are short." After the coveys are broken up, in October or November, we have seen them make flights of many miles when put up, while at sunrise and sunset they fly back and forth from three to twelve miles between the open prairies, where they delight to spend the night, and the grain fields.

Some of the plates are very spirited and true to life ; and we can not refrain from speaking specially of the group of Spruce Partridges, or Canada Grouse, on p. 378. It takes us back to the

forest between the Magalloway and the Middle Dam on the Andros-
coggin, where we first saw and ate this beautiful bird. Its flesh
was sweet and tender then, in September, though commonly bitter
later in the year, from the spruce bud, from the eating of which it
takes its name. Of the utility of the robin, so well argued on pp.
155–163, we are profoundly sceptical. But we are writing in the
strawberry season, and our specimen berries are sadly mutilated by
this quarrelsome, imperious, sharp-toned thing.

Mr. Samuels has most happily combined the scientific and popular in his book. This is an admirable feature. And he has carried
the oölogy of some birds with much interest farther than any writer whom we can recall.

We are exceedingly glad that our author has thus put the feath-
ery tribes of New England and a fascinating style of ornithology
within the reach of our young people. It opens to them a study
and recreation at the same time ; following it will improve and make
delicate their taste by such constant and varied familiarity with nature, while the general effect will be good physically, mentally and
morally.

31.—*The Jesuits in North America in the Seventeenth Century.* By
FRANCIS PARKMAN, author of " Pioneers of France in the New
World."   Boston : Little, Brown & Co.   1867.

THE fields of literary research are constantly on the increase, like
our national domain, and Mr. Parkman has in this case opened a very
inviting and long-neglected one. His History of the Conspiracy of
Pontiac, and of the Pioneers of France in the New World, led him
naturally to this volume, as also to the next now in promise : the
French Discovery and Occupation of the Valley of the Mississippi.

Mr. Parkman is to be greatly commended for his patient, faithful
and painstaking discovery and examination of original documents.
We can fancy the immense amount of manuscript, old letters, jour-
nals and memoranda, in miserable handwriting and worse French,
that he has overhauled, noted and abstracted. Monasteries, convents, Jesuits archives, State departments, the files of the De Prop-
aganda, and Antiquarian Libraries must have had their venerable
dust not a little disturbed.

How much easier for our author to have made his facts as he
went along, like our most voluminous and popular tale writers, and
escaped all this dust and drudgery, and with a richer pocket too.

This volume has an interesting and labored Introduction of about
seventy pages, dividing, naming and locating the Indians of the
seventeenth century in New England, the Canadas, and the North

West of the great lakes.   In this part of his work he gives account
of their houses, fortifications, habits, arts, trades, feasts, politics,
superstitions and religion.   It is the best summary of this Indian
matter that we have ever read, in the same space.   The volume
proper, as a history of the missionary Jesuits in this country, opens
at Quebec in 1634.   Thence, and to the end, it is a wilderness romance, all true and real.   The Jesuit system is outlined theoretically, and then illustrated practically.   We have the wigwam, the
Indian scholars, summer and winter encampments, forest life with
its perils, savage incantations and conversions, the reverses of the
missions and their enthusiasm, visions, tricks and miracles.   While
the book is a history of religious labors, it is at the same time a
treasury of Indian history, antiquities and customs, and very few
readers will begin to read it who do not finish it.   It fascinates
while it instructs, and we shall await the next work with a deeper
interest.   The volume furnishes a lesson for our modern deists that
ought to profit them.   Some are now saying and teaching, indeed
they call it often preaching, that we can have a Christianity without Christ ; a revelation without inspiration, and even religion without God.   This is a free religion, a liberal Christianity of the
radical wing, a natural religion.   In this book Mr. Parkman shows
what and how much this means, and so what these men, wiser than
the holy men of old, who spake as they were moved of the Holy
Ghost, would give us.   We quote :—

"Close examination makes it evident that the primitive Indian's idea of
a Supreme Being was a conception no higher than might have been expected.   The moment he began to contemplate this object of his faith,
and sought to clothe it with attributes, it became finite, and commonly
ridiculous."   "In the primitive Indian's conception of a God the idea of
moral good has no part."   "In no Indian language could the early missionaries find a word to express the idea of God."   "The primitive
Indian, yielding his untutored homage to One All-pervading, and Omnipotent Spirit, is a dream of the poets, rhetoricians, and sentimentalists."
"Would the Iroquois, left undisturbed to work out their own destiny, ever
have emerged from the savage state?   Advanced as they were beyond
most other American tribes, there is no indication whatever of a tendency
to overpass the confines of a wild hunter and warrior life.—*Introd.* pp.
65-89.

Indeed, the world by wisdom knows not God, and this kind of
wisdom that reduces religion to a naked deism, is not yet extinct.
What it would do for us this volume shows.   These same wise men,
deists, scorn the idea that by a divine and unerring inspiration,
"life and immortality are brought to light in the Gospel."   They
think the light of nature and of reason sufficient.   We commend

them to a study of the experiment, recorded in this volume, of their predecessors in the same theory.

"The primitive Indian believed in the immortality of the soul, but he did not always believe in a state of future rewards and punishment. . . . In the general belief there was but one land of shades for all alike. The spirits, in form and feature as they had been in life, wended their way through dark forests to the villages of the dead, subsisting on bark and rotten wood. On arriving, they sat all day in the crouching position of the sick, and, when night came, hunted the shades of animals with the shades of bows and arrows, among the shades of trees and rocks. For all things, animate and inanimate, were alike immortal, and all passed together to the gloomy country of the dead."—*Introd.* 80-11.

31.—MISCELLANEOUS. By the American Tract Society, New York. *Paul Venner; or the Forge and the Pulpit.* One of those fascinating stories, in which the facts of every day life are made to teach lessons of gentleness, industry and piety. So taught, of course Paul Venner, the blacksmith boy, comes to honor, and "is now known as the learned and dearly loved president of a celebrated college." *The Bible Reader's Help : Pastoral Reminiscences*, by the late Rev. MARTIN MOORE ; *A Mother's Legacy ; George Wayland, the Little Medicine Carrier ; The Cinnamon Isle Boy ; Times of Knox and Mary Stuart.* These small volumes are good additions to our juvenile reading. The *Times of Knox* is written in the lively, diary style, full of incidents, facts, and conversation, and must be sure to carry the reader along through those stirring days and events. By the Presbyterian Board of Publication. *The New Boat.* Our boys must read this. *The Cloud and the Sunbeam ; Two Terms at Olney ; The Little Priest.* This is by the Rev. W. P. BREED, one of the best writers for this Board ; *The Martyr's Daughter ; The Little Norwegian* and *The Young Woodcutter.* By the American Tract Society, Boston. *Friendly Words to Fellow Pilgrims.* By JAMES WILLIAM KIMBALL. Mr. Kimball has made his initials familiar to the Christian public through the columns of the religious newspaper press. He is a man of very decided opinions, and often expresses them very clearly and forcibly. We think this little volume calculated to do good. *Glimpses of West Africa, with Sketches of Missionary Labor.* By Rev. SAMUEL J. WHITON. We like this style of book : fact, incident, history, geography, Christian work and the lives of good men, all worked in together, and all known to be true. This book pleases us for this reason. *The Sister's Story. Rich and Humble : or the Memoir of Bertha Grant.* By OLIVER OPTIC. Boston : Lee & Shepard. 1867.

The name of the author will carry this interesting story everywhere among our young people, for whom it was written. The writer knows how to tell a story well, and the little folk will not soon forget him. Works of Robert Carter & Brothers : *Binding the Sheaves, Cripple Dan.* By ANDREW WHITGIFT. *Father Clement.* A Roman Catholic Story. *The Story of Martin Luther*, edited by Miss WHATELY. *Wanderings in Bible Lands.* By the author of the "Schönberg-Cotta Family." *Heaven Opened.* A Selection from the Correspondence of Mrs. Mary Winslow. Edited by her Son, OCTAVIUS WINSLOW, D. D. The Wanderings in Bible Lands, by a well known and graceful pen, is full of light for any reader or student of the Bible. Not technical and professional, like ministerial books and helps on this theme, the ordinary scriptural reader will enjoy the volume. Heaven Opened is a book that ought to be much read and loved. It is more like the "good books" of our earlier days, that helped our sainted parents and aged friends into glory. The books of this House can be trusted by the devout followers of Christ. *The Church Hymn Book.* A. D. F. Randolph, New York. J. P. Brown, Burlington, Iowa. Root & Cady, Chicago. 1867. Seven hundred and ten hymns, followed by one hundred and fifty tunes, with the usual Indexes, and one of tunes and hymns as adapted to each other. The paper and type are good, as the form, and the page is welcome to the eye. It will be difficult to find more of the choice hymns and tunes that Christians love to use in worship, in the same compass. Mr. Slater shows an excellent selecting and condensing power.

ARTICLE X.

THE ROUND TABLE.

WHO AND WHERE. "Who publish your Congregational works, and where are they kept ?" It was a humbling, mortifying question, and thinking we ought to do penance unto humility, we replied : They are not published anywhere, and they are not kept by anybody. Our denominational authors have been obliged to go into the market and sell their manuscripts as if they were strangers in the home of the Pilgrims. Their volumes have been left to a simple trade interest for sale and circulation, and the expositions and defenses of our peculiar tenets have gone out into the world like orphans and foundlings.

We take up the catalogue of the Episcopal Society for the Promotion of Evangelical Knowledge, and a hasty perusal of a part of it, guided by titles only, shows us about sixty works of their own devoted to their peculiar denominational features. A similar notice of the catalogue of the Baptist Publication Society shows us about forty of the same kind. The books of this class published by these societies is probably two or threefold the numbers specified, and the Presbyterians and Methodists have the same wise and energetic policy. An author of their own ranks, and defending their faith and polity or peculiarities, is furnished a standing within their own lines.

Mr. Punchard's History of Congregationalism, Bertha and her Baptism, Dr. Dexter's Congregationalism, the Papers and Records of the National Council, and a hundred other denominational works issued within a half century, should have been thrown off at the press and offered on the counter of a Congregational Publishing House. Instead of that they have found as many publishers as they had authors, and now lie about loose, like the leaves of the Sybil.

Not only so, but the same is true of our undenominational works on practical godliness, in memoir and essay, narrative and fiction. Organized boards of other branches of the church, and private enterprise of the dollar and cent aim have been the medium of communication for our most worthy and sterling authors. And because we have shown as little interest in saving our old authors as in cherishing with a warm feeling our modern ones, we have lost already much of their dust through lack of an urn in which to deposit it. Congregationalists can build churches and colleges and seminaries, union and even sectarian for others, but have not yet a fireproof closet five feet square in which to make safe any old record or relic from Scrooby, Leyden or Plymouth. Congregational money keeps scores of Hoe's latest patent presses going day and night for others, but no organization of the church, so far as we know, owns a pound of small pica. They owned the first press, and printed the first work on the continent, and ought now to be doing in this line more as a denomination than any other in America. It is to our mortification and reproach that the authors we have mentioned should be obliged to enter the literary world as private adventurers.

OUR APRIL NUMBER. Our friend Tilton of the *Independent*, who, if he has not that Grecian cut profile which the *Post* attributes to him, has yet the Toledo cut to his pen, writing with the truest kind of abandon in slashing cavalry style, gave our April number nearly a column among his literary notices. We were more than satisfied, both with his likes and his dislikes. He thought our Article on *The Black Man*, just the thing. We think he is a good judge in that department. He thought our Article on *The Atlantic Monthly* very much aside from the mark; a sign that we are yet in " the Middle Ages." Here we think his judgment at fault. In theology we are several centuries back of mediæval times. We confess it. Our motto is *Sanctos ausus recludere fontes*. It will take more than 'three months' to bring this department of the Review down to the standard of our cotemporary. In fact, we do not intend to come down. We hope, however, to be always ready to strike hands with men of whatever persuasion or complexion or age in all proper efforts at reform.

The Round Table, too, from which we have received the most appreciative notices, hitherto, resenting our crowding into its peculiar domain, that of finding fault with things in the world of letters, takes us severely to task for what we said of Dr. Holmes's misrepresentations of orthodox Christians. We can only refer the editor to an extended notice of " Dr. Johns," in which the same view was taken by that periodical of Ik Marvel's portraiture of the same class. And we say, if for *his* representations Ik Marvel deserved censure, a thousand times more Dr. Holmes!

By the way, we find the following in our portfolio, which may as well take its place in this connection :

LOOKING AT HOLME (S).

" I am afraid I shall have to square accounts by writing one more story, with a wicked physician in it. I have been looking in vain for such a one to serve as a model." *Dr. Holmes before the Mass. Med. Society.*

> I have been prying round about,
> Inspecting people lean and stout,
> To make a reg'lar villain out,
>> And mark him in my book like Cain.
>> Among the doctors all in vain
>> Are my labor and my pain :
>> Sure, our profession's free from stain ;
>> Wherefore ' Stoker?' 's very plain.
>
> We're glad to learn, immac'late Doctor,
> Of morals pure, high priest and proctor,
>> That in your guild's whole warp and filling,
>> You can not find a downright villain !
> A hint or so may help your knowledge ;
> Near Cambridge bridge there is a college ;
>> Have you forgotten, gentle fibster,
>> The gibbet of Professor Webster?

De mortuis, if you reply,
  Looking affronted, curt and stern,
  Then to the quick let us return.
The eye can never see the eye :
  A physiological fact you know.
  To find the man no further go !
Neath Harvard's classic shades he roams ;
  Try introspection ; *look at Holme (s) !*

Not Parallel Cases.   De Quincey, in his acute historical criticism of "the Cæsars," with his usual sharpness looks into the causes of the terrible and utterly indiscribable corruption of the Romans in Italy, as early as the last of the Julian emperors, A. D. 68.   The first and chief source of this deterioration from the old Republican virtue, he finds in the almost total change of population which had come in on the heels of the revolutionary devastation of the late times.   In a single century, almost every masculine and noble trait of the nation had sunk down into an effeminate disso-luteness paralleled by nothing but the Babylon of Belshazzar.   This was not the apostasy of the Roman stock so much as the importa-tion of foreign races.   "Not one man in six," in Nero's day, was probably of native descent.   Blackwell, quoted by De Quincey, tells us : "Those of the greatest and truly Roman spirit had been mur-dered in the field by Julius Cæsar : the rest were now massacred in the city by his son and successors ; in their room came Syrians, Cappadocians, Phrygians, and other enfranchised slaves from the conquered nations."   These took the place of the former inhabitants, filling Rome and the whole peninsula with Asiatic people and manners.   " In a single generation," says De Quincey, " Rome became almost transmuted into a baser metal. . .   The taint of Asiatic luxury and depravity," nameless vices of Antioch and Alex-andria displaced the sterner morals of the Tiber.   The effect was like murrain among sheep.   Social and domestic virtue, none too exemplary for some generations precedent, absolutely perished. When the Emperor Augustus compelled one of his nobles to give up his young wife, in most delicate circumstances, to become a royal bride, what could be expected universally but unlimited excesses? Our author says, that " for the first four hundred years of Rome, not one divorce had been granted or asked, although the statute which allowed of this indulgence had always been in force."   Others place the first Roman divorce in the year of the city 520 ; an almost incredible fact, on either chronology, yet the general truth of the statement is undeniable.   But now, parties married and were un-married to suit the whim or the profit of the moment.   A woman's fortune went with her by law, and sold her to successive husbands yearly and oftener, in numerous instances. After this "we need little wonder at the assassinations, poisonings, and forging of wills, which then laid waste the domestic life of the Romans."

Not further to pursue this historical inquiry, what we have written is enough to suggest a thought concerning our own national prospects. At first sight, there seems to be a strong resemblance between the picture thus drawn and ourselves. We are going through great organic changes ; some, as the London *Times*, insist that these are rapidly revolutionary. But whatever they may amount to, we think they are not in the direction of Cæsarism. Immense accessions of foreign immigrants are changing very much the quality of our population, and certainly for the worse. Our manners and morals are becoming shockingly "Asiatic," in the large cities, if not in the rural districts. The early republican virtue and piety have sadly fallen off. We concede the melancholy facts. Yet, we do not feel disposed to accept any such conclusions as that we are going down the grade which swept the Roman power and civilization into ruin. There is not sufficient likeness in the cases to justify this deduction, while there is enough to arrest the mind, and to point a very serious warning to our countrymen.

Our foreign population, as a mass, are vitating to our social and national life. But not as in Rome, they come to blend themselves with an enlightened and Christian people. The Rome of the Cæsars was religiously divided between utter atheism and a maudlin superstition. Intellectually it was a desert. De Quincey gives an illustration of this, that while the whole world was ransacked, under imperial orders and bounties for the strangest animals for the conflicts of the amphitheatres, where tens of thousands were exhibited and slaughtered annually, Roman authorship does not furnish a book on Natural History after the age of Pliny, though the best opportunities were thus afforded for these studies. We stand at the opposite pole from such mental and spiritual torpidity. Our social condition is not a cess-pool to turn every thing to corruption which is flung into it. Hence, with a due vigilance, we may hope to elevate the material, which is coming in upon us, to a higher level, instead of subsiding to its lowness. Popish subserviency, continental materialistic infidelity, and the spread of domestic license are our worst demoralizers. But we have an invasive and an aggressive Christianity girding itself anew for the close grapple with these infernal principalities and powers. The emancipated slaves which also flooded Rome were as debauched by every kind of vice as were their masters. Ours, if uneducated, are not rotten to the heart with crime. While the freedmen of Rome sunk her civilization into an Oriental barbarism of sensuality and cruelty, our freedmen stand ready to be converted into, it may be, the saviours of the Republic.

It strengthens our argument to note that, so early as the reigns of Hadrian and the Antonines, A. D., 130—180, the Christian religion was making itself felt as a purifying force, even in that weltering sea of Italian depravity. Its traces are seen in the efforts of those emperors to mitigate the atrocities of the public games and shows. The valuation of humanity was rising when these reforms were undertaken, shielding men, so far forth, from the degradation and barbarity of these fightings with one another and with the wild beasts of the arena. Our author ascribes this to "the contagion of Christian standards and sentiments then beginning to pervade and ventilate the atmosphere of society in its higher and philosophic regions." The inference is that, if in those circumstances, Christianity could do any thing to improve the horrid customs of an immemorial paganism, it can surely do for us, if faithfully used and applied, all that is necessary to fuse into a friendly whole the discordant and the malignant elements of our population, and to leaven it with the righteousness and the freedom which, from the first, have theoretically been our birthright.

BEHIND THE INDIANS. Some of our profound thinkers, progressive beyond all biblical limits, have dispensed with the creation of man, and developed him from the monkey. Yet others, greatly gifted with an inner sight of things, are learned and powerful spiritists, and all the ghostly world is subject to their rap and beck, single or in pairs. These are the men of "progress," thought and discovery, pioneers of the race who, in their Jehu gig, leave the rest of the world behind, old fogies and foot-pads. But it is a little singular that the North American Indians knew all about these discoveries and this wonderful progress of modern *savans*, long before white men came to this country. They had the "development theory" of man from the animal in far better state than our modern scientists. These tell us that man sprung from the ape, and they almost prove it by specimens. The theory is good for some among us, since they are evidently quite imitative, apish in habit, manner and opinion. Yet others show other animal traits, and so an animal pedigree. Now the Indian theory of development covers all kinds of men, and so is more philosophic than this of the modern theorists. Mr. Parkman in his recent work, the Jesuits in North America, says :—

"A belief prevails, vague, but perfectly apparent, that men themselves owe their first parentage to beasts, birds, or reptiles, as bears, wolves, tortoises, or cranes." "Each Indian was supposed to inherit something of the nature of the animal whence he sprung."—*Introd.* p. 68.

Our men of science in the apine line must go back to our Indians *for* the supplement, or rather complement of their theory. Some men are evidently not developed from apes. They are original grizzlies, savage and solitary. Others are foxy, and of vulpine descent, full of low cunning and trick. Some are quick of eye and motion, with a soft graceful hand, and gloved claws, feline surely in their pre-existent ancestry. Some of our fat office-holders, we suppose, sprung from the tortoise family, and our expressmen from pigeons and antelopes. Those who live for dress, and in gay colors, and before the public, sprung from butterflies, the peacock, and bird of paradise. The Indian theory systematized and connected us perfectly with an appropriate parentage in the preëxistent world.

We like this notion better than the modern and partial reproduction of it, as more comprehensive and more discriminating, and having more of a show of common sense in it when we look at men. For the origin of some people is perfectly obvious. And quite as obvious it is that they did not spring from monkeys.

Such a scheme of preëxistence, moreover, is worthy to be studied together with the one now before the public. We think the Indian theory could be made to help the other into favor if united with it ; and illustrative specimens could be cited, as the bovine, ursuline, vulpine, angelic lapsed, etc.

These Indians understood and practised spiritism far better than the moderns. According to Mr. Parkman's account of their theory, inanimate things as rocks, trees, and lakes, as well as animals, had spirits dwelling in them, and these became the companions, mediums, of men. The land of spirits was often the very neighborhood of the wigwam, specially was it for the spirits of the old and of the children, who were too feeble to get off to a full heaven.

"The sorcerer [or spiritualist] by charms, magic songs, magic feasts and the beating of his drum had power over the spirits. . . . There was a peculiar practice of divination very general in the Algonquin family of tribes, among some of whom it still subsists. A small conical lodge was made by planting poles in a circle, lashing the tops together at the height of about seven feet from the ground, and closely covering them with hides. The prophet crawled in, and closed the aperture after him. He then beat his drum and sang his magic songs to summon the spirits, whose weak, shrill voices were soon heard, mingled with his lugubrious chanting, while at intervals the juggler paused to interpret these communications to the attentive crowd seated on the ground without." *Do.*, pp. 84, 85.

"Here we have the "circle," "medium," "shrill voices" of the spirits," "communications," and the interpretation of them to "the attentive crowd." This is original spiritism, and, we submit, better than the corrupted modern article, inasmuch as voices are more sensible means of communication than rappings and table-tippings.

Truly this is an age of profound and original investigation. In the new theories of preëxistence, the development of man from the ape, and spiritism, our deep thinkers and men of progress have almost come up with the North American Indians.

SUNSHINE IN THE CATACOMBS. Among all that has been written of the spiritual beauty of the early Christian character and life, we know of nothing more attractive than this surprising testimony which we have somewhere found—that, amidst the innumerable inscriptions of the Roman Catacombs, no word of bitterness, vindictiveness, or sorrow is seen on those monuments, although the Christians were driven thither by fiercest persecution, to find alike a place to worship and to be buried. So cheerful was their habitual temper, that they wreathed Christ's head with a monumental crown of flowers instead of thorns, in representing his dying anguish ; and funeral days were scenes of holy thanksgiving.

HOW WOULD IT WORK? We notice that many of the churches paid their pastors through the war, and still pay, the nominal sum of their contract. With the increase of prices, this is paying about fifty *per cent.* (a little less) of what they promised, since their promise was a specie and an equity promise. Many pastors are likely still to be half paid in reality, though fully paid nominally.

But ministers are scarce, while many of the churches are talking of the plan of one sermon a day. Why not give a pastor two churches? He could preach one sermon a day to each, and by the united salaries of each, on the old rates of contract, he might just live, as he managed to before the war.

THE

CONGREGATIONAL REVIEW.

VOL. VII.—OCTOBER, 1867.—No. 38.

ARTICLE I.

THE PREACHERS FOR THE TIMES AND THEIR TRAINING.

CHRISTIANITY casts contempt on all human wisdom and power. That which to human reason is forever impossible it accomplishes by agencies which reason pronounces foolishness and weakness, and that not in contempt, but in all sincerity. According to all the decisions of human reason, Christianity *is* foolishness and weakness, as the overthrow of Jericho by the blowing of rams' horns was foolishness to the military science of Julius Cæsar and Charlemagne.

The first Christian preachers were regarded by the world of philosophy either with a proud indifference or with ineffable scorn. They were babblers, fools, madmen; only deemed worthy of notice when they stirred up the common people, and so were inconvenient; and then to be put out of the way like other fools and madmen, by the scourge, the prison, or the public executioner.

When Christ said: "Lift up your eyes and look on the fields; for they are white already to harvest," what did he mean? Was the world sick of its idolatries, disgusted with its blind guides, convinced of its own foolishness, and ready to welcome the preachers of the Gospel? No! Its delirium was at the height. The recoil of its sated passions was still followed by increased devotion to all the gods of its idolatry. Learning, philosophy, eloquence, art, were panders to its pride, handmaids to its licentiousness. Its very despair of deliverance from the miserable thraldom of evil was an incentive to the wilder rage of its lusts, its still more reckless transgression of law. It was a moral chaos, inconceivably more dreadful than that on which darkness sat in the primeval day, and to all human view more hopeless. With all that human reason could accomplish, the world was on the verge of utter destruction.

Then were the fields white already to harvest. A better theatre there could not be for Christianity to display its power. Now shall it be seen, that the foolishness of God is wiser than men; and the weakness of God is stronger than men. The greatest and best of the Greek philosophers has utterly failed in his most strenuous endeavors to win the young men of Athens to the practice of sobriety. The voice of the Christian preacher is lifted up, and lo, the power of evil is suddenly and strangely broken; chains, which had seemed of adamant, snap asunder and fall off; the votaries of debasing passion, transformed by an unseen, mighty power, turn away in disgust from that which is evil, and walk in the image of God. The darkness which has long brooded so disastrously over the whole face of human society is rolled back, and in many a humble village and many a proud and voluptuous capital, throughout the Roman Empire, that is fulfilled which was spoken by the prophet: " The wilderness and the solitary place shall be glad for them, and the desert shall rejoice and blossom as the rose."

There is but one possible conclusion from this; and it is, that the Christian pulpit is the great power of God for the regeneration of human society, and that all possible or conceivable obstacles are so many foils to its triumphs; since it is in its very nature and design, that it should shut the mouths of lions, quench the violence of fire, subdue kingdoms, pluck up mountains and cast them into the depths of the sea.

Is it supposed that the Christian pulpit has already achieved its greatest triumphs, because the world is no longer arrayed in open hostility to the Gospel? Since Christianity has been taken under its patronage, and Christ admitted to a seat among the gods many and lords many of its Pantheon, is the Christian preacher therefore to conclude that now he has only to travel at ease over the leveled and smooth highway of the King to receive his crown?

A graver mistake there could not be. The hostility of the world to Jesus Christ has not ceased. Its manifestation may be changed, its spirit is ever the same. A glance at the present aspects of the Christian world will make it plain that there has been no day in which there existed greater necessity for the preacher to take unto him the whole armor of God, and gird himself for earnest, uncompromising warfare. The evils with which he must contend are manifold, subtle, and fraught with deepest peril. We may note, as one of these,

Indifference to Christian doctrine. This is an evil of far greater magnitude than the teaching of positive error. If the inspiration of the Bible, or the proper Deity of the Lord Jesus Christ, is assailed openly, there is nothing to fear. The result can only be the confirmation of the truth. But when some grand article of the faith is simply left out, men slumber, and its foundations are loosened. If the main pillars of a house are wanting, the house can not stand. Without completeness of doctrine, the entire fabric of Christianity must be weakened, if it does not fall. Even Luther's *articulum stantis vel cadentis ecclesiæ*, justification by faith, when separated from the principle of daily obedience to Christ, as Lord of the church, runs into religious sentimentalism or antinomian delusion. The grand symbols of Christian doctrine are not the productions of cold speculative men, smitten with a passion to reduce all things to logical form; but the statement of the truth of God as wrought into the profound convictions of spiritual men, and demanded, in stormy periods, to strengthen the heart of the faithful, or resist the assaults of infidels. Augustine and John Calvin were not more distinguished for clear, massive intellect, and brilliancy of genius, than for warm affections, and exalted communion with God.

Closely allied with indifference to Christian doctrine, is a rationalistic temper, the deification of human reason.

The rationalists are men of progress. Creeds and dogmas, which to illustrious Christian Fathers have been as the armor of God, are no more to them than cerements of the long dead.

It is their high prerogative to see truth as God sees it, directly; and whatever is not clearly and indisputably true to their spiritual vision—the reason or intuitional consciousness—they reject, even though God himself should seem to declare it.   The Bible is a revelation, or, at least contains a revelation, and Christianity is true: but not a single fact or doctrine is to be accepted as truth because the Bible in direct terms asserts it.   The reason is supreme, infallible judge.   To suppose that God, who created the human reason, should reveal to that reason mysteries of faith, to be implicitly received, though impossible to be understood until seen in the light of eternity, is held to be a pitiable weakness or fanaticism.   Thus a full and sufficient cause for the rejection of the doctrine of original sin, or the trinity, or the atonement, or regeneration, or justification, or the resurrection, or future punishment, is found in the fact that man's reason pronounces it absurd.

This is rationalism, in its temper and essential elements, however it may seek to hide itself under a professed reverence for God and his revelations.

We note also, as one of the prominent characteristics of the age, a tendency to exalt man.   We do not mean by this a disposition to lift him up from his degradation and guilt, in a conformity with God's gracious plan, but rather to set a crown on the head of fallen humanity, ignoring the sad fact of its fall, its debasement, its ever-accumulating ill-desert and misery; investing this fallen, debased humanity with rights and immunities which trench on the prerogatives of God.   It is not because man was made in the image of God, and is still dear to the heart of God; not that Christ came to redeem and restore.   Of God and Jesus Christ this spirit of the age takes little note.   Neither is it to a humanity redeemed from what is low and earthly, and lifted up to the highest moral and intellectual strength and beauty of which man is capable, that its homage is accorded—man fitted to command respect, to determine questions, to be, in human society, as the head among the members; to rule.   Of principalities and powers and prerogatives it is intensely jealous.   It denies their right.   It refuses its reverence.   It demolishes the Corinthian pillar; it breaks rudely the polished mirror; it profanes the beautiful temple.

Humanity is the object of its reverence, the god of its worship. It speaks great swelling words, having men's persons in admiration, because of advantage. It tramples on authority; its own will is law; it dethrones God and revels in a practical atheism, uprooting, in the end, and by an inevitable rule of sequence, all the foundations of order, and debasing itself, even unto hell.

There is a disposition in the spirit of the age, to put philanthropy above the Gospel. The apostles were not schoolmasters. They preached the Gospel, and when men were converted, however rude and ignorant, even the most abject slaves of pagan masters, they gathered them into churches and gave them ordinances of Christian worship. That made the first Christian preachers the greatest civilizing power which the world ever saw; though civilization, let it forever be remembered, was not the object which they sought, but the spiritual renovation of men. This was the divine method, and the result was a countless multitude of souls washed from their sins and saved forever. The wisdom of the present day has changed all this. The multiplication table is better than the ten commandments; mechanical skill is before morality; the schoolmaster takes precedence of the preacher, liberty is above salvation. It is a fatal mistake, in any point of view, as all history shows. The Jesuits were a mighty power for good, so long as they kept close to the original design of the order, and preached. Whole communities were reformed in an incredibly short space of time. The intrepid Francis Xavier, in the ten years of his apostleship, "planted the faith in fifty two kingdoms, preached the Gospel through nine thousand miles of territory, and baptized more than a million persons." But when they sought for themselves chairs in the schools of theology, and made alliance with princes, and contended with the Sorbonne, and aimed to extend the influence of their order by secular plans and agencies, their glory departed.

Another peculiar feature of the religious world in our day is, an increasing demand for brilliant orations on the Sabbath, in stead of simple Gospel sermons, and musical performance in the place of worship. "My house shall be called the house of prayer for all nations," said Christ; and both Christ and his apostles stood up on the Sabbath to preach repentance to the people, to rebuke their sins, to excite their fears ; not to please their taste, and win their admiration.   How are men to be saved if the pulpit is changed to the tribune, and worship is perfunctory ; or if Massillon and Bourdaloue are the preacher's models, in stead of Wycliffe and Hugh Latimer and Richard Baxter ?

It is hardly to be considered a step further in the same direction, when men run a church as they run a lyceum.   The case is only too common at the present time.   It is the operation of a law of political economy in religious things.   The supply is suited to the demand.   A fine orator in the place of the Christian preacher ministers delight, and so long as his theme, or at least his text, is taken from the Bible, however far away his conclusions may be from Bible conclusions, men easily persuade themselves that they are religious in going to hear him, and so they are willing to pay, and the enterprise is a success, albeit no place is found for the poor in the pews, and little Gospel is heard from the pulpit.

The building of splendid churches for the rich and fashionable is another marked tendency of the age.   If it were a disposition to honor Christ by bringing rich gifts to his altar, that would be well.   The Lord accepts with approval the most costly offerings of a love which delights to bring the best of all that which is already his own ; whether it be the alabaster box of very precious ointment, or the goodly stones and golden vessels of the temple.   He sees through the hypocrisy and cant which erects a mean house for him, and then seeks to cover up the meanness under the name of Christian simplicity.   But how much better is it, when a swelling pride lavishes its wealth in the erection of magnificent edifices, not that the rich and poor may meet together there, and Christ, to whom both are equally dear, may be honored in their comely fellowship of praise, but for vanity and self-aggrandizement?   Such a process may seem to save to the ranks of a denomination the votaries of fashion and elegance and polite culture ; but it is too sure a sign that spiritual life is departing.

The absence of the true spirit of Christian fellowship is an element of weakness in the piety of the present day.   This,

assuredly, is not a matter to be regulated by the customs of
society. " As I have loved you," are the terms which Christ
employs to define the duty of his people to each other.   Such
language means *something*. In him it was a *flame*, which many
waters could not quench, nor floods drown.   Has the obligation
ceased?   Is the law abrogated?   Was it meant only for the
primitive ages, or for days of persecution?   Does Jesus Christ
attach less value to his people's love for one another, and
its appropriate manifestation now, than when he was himself
on the earth?   Or is it any less required, as an argument for
the truth of Christianity, when infidelity, in new and most
subtle disguises, is laboring everywhere for the subversion of
the faith?   If the spirit of conventionalism reigns with as
supreme a sway in the church as in the world, and if the fellowship of those whom Christ has redeemed and separated for
his service is to be regulated by social affinities, and earthly
distinctions in rank and condition, then it is high time that one
give us a new exposition of the old law, and tell us what advantage in this respect Christianity has above paganism.

It may sound strange to hear it said that the Lord Jesus
Christ has not the place to which he is entitled in the views of
the Orthodox at the present day : nevertheless we affirm it,
and in this fact we find the germ of all the evils at which we
have glanced.   It is not enough that Christ be the central
point in our creeds, to be folded up and laid away ; not enough,
that we see him dimly, in his person, his offices, his teaching,
through the mists and shadows of eighteen centuries. This is not
according to truth.   He is present with his church to-day.   He
comes to us, as it were, from the sorrows of his cross.   He
talks to us of those sorrows ; their dreadful necessity, their
transcendent results.   He gives us doctrines fresh from his lips,
and the lips of inspired men.   He binds us, by an oath of allegiance, a covenant sealed with blood, to his service.   He
gives us ordinances and sacraments, to be most religiously
observed ; he constitutes us depositaries of his truth, and witnesses for his name, to the men of this generation.   Our whole
life is to be ruled by a supreme regard to his will, an unutterable gratitude for his love, the spirit of implicit obedience to his
commands ; as though he had but now left the earth, still

stained with his blood, and might return again to-morrow. Do the heart and life of the church answer to this?

And now what, in view of these peculiar characteristics of the age, is the province of the Christian pulpit? We answer, that it be true to its high commission. That commission is directly from the Lord Jesus Christ, and is simple, well-defined, and clear. " Preach the Gospel!" The Gospel is the same which was preached in the beginning, and admits no change so long as the great facts of God and human depravity and redemption are the same. God is dreadful in his majesty, perfect in his holiness, strict and immutable in his justice, the supreme and only Law-giver and King to the intelligent universe. Man is fallen and utterly depraved, full of all wickedness and madness, in a most determined rebellion against God, under a condemnation declared and irrevocable; and absolutely hopeless in his misery. Christ, the Divine-human, the God-man, in fulfilment of an eternal covenant with the Father, has made atonement by his death, has suffered the penalty of human guilt, has satisfied, to the last tittle, the demands of justice, and so has solved the problem of infinite difficulty—how God can be just in justifying the ungodly. Thus salvation, full and free, is offered to all, on condition of repentance and faith. Man, in the pride of his heart, treats the offer with indifference, or with contempt. The Holy Spirit, by an operation of sovereignty and grace, subdues the will and changes the heart of those whom God will save; all the rest are incorrigible in sin, and perish forever.

This is the old Gospel, with its related facts and truths. To deny that the Bible teaches it, is flagrantly to violate all the laws of human language, and to make language an impossible vehicle for the communication of truth. To keep it back, or to modify it, under pretence of philosophical adaptation and the conciliation of human pride, is to incur the triple guilt of treason to the Lord Jesus Christ, complicity with rebellion, and eternal death to human souls.

This has been the faith of the church and the armor of God in all the ages. Paul and his coadjutors the apostles preached it, and the strongholds of sin fell everywhere before them, in an age when philosophy and eloquence and poetry and art were in impious league with a universal voluptuousness and rejection of God. This made Claude of Turin mightier than the thunders which reverberated along the valleys of his native Alps, when all his contemporaries wore the badge of the woman in scarlet. With this, Martin Luther carried stronger gates than those of Gaza, and opened the spiritual Bastile of dark ages, that imprisoned souls might come forth. Wycliffe and Knox and Hugh Latimer and Whitefield made impious Belshazzars tremble at the hand-writing on the wall, sent dismay to the heart of Satan, and filled heaven with joy over countless multitudes of repenting sinners, only because they were armed in this panoply of God.

This old Gospel the modern preacher is required to proclaim, in the exercise of a simple reliance on the mighty power of the Spirit of God. Without it, his life must be a mournful failure. The multitude may be charmed by his eloquence, and may loudly applaud his fancied wisdom : but not one sinner will ever be saved by his doctrine. He may as soon heal a leper or raise the dead by the sound of a lute or the fragrance of flowers.

At the same time that we claim for the Christian pulpit that it must remain unchanged through all the ages in its essential features, we affirm, with almost equal earnestness, that it must adapt itself to the peculiar character of every age, and each particular community. This is common sense, the wisdom of the serpent, sound philosophy, in relation to the things of the kingdom of God. So Paul was made all things to all men, that he might by all means save some. Paul at Athens preaching, and Paul in a synagogue of the Jews at Thessalonica, was quite another man. But how another? Not that in either case he substituted speculations, conceits, dogmas, dialectics, for the truth of the Gospel. Not he ; but he suited himself to his audience, in his selection of weapons from the divine armory, and in his method of assault. With the Jews, his starting point was their own acknowledged Scriptures : with those acute, yet pagan philosophers on Mars Hill, an inscription on one of their altars of religious worship. The conclusion in either case was alike irresistible, and the result in both substantially the same. Some believed ; and as for the rest, the Jews, impulsive, bigoted, and unbelieving, got up a mob and made an assault; while the philosophic Athenians, unbelieving also, wrapped themselves about with the dignity of ineffable scorn, and mocked.

There are two faults in our day, which lie on either side of the course pursued by Paul. The one is that of the men who affect a peculiar wisdom in the adaptation of their ministry to the age, and find such adaptation in softening, or modifying, or dropping out of view altogether, the old and offensive doctrines of the cross. Every thing is shadowy and indistinct. A mist is over all the landscape. God's revelation becomes vague and unintelligible. Not even men as trees walking do we discern; and what we took for mountains on their everlasting foundations, and rivers, and lakes, and mighty waves of the sea, and temples and towers of a great city, in God's glorious sunlight, is all a deceptive, mocking mirage. There is wisdom still, but it is found in a universal doubting and darkness and uncertainty. Paul, with his certitudes and positiveness and strong asseverations, would find himself altogether behind these times.

These are the paganizing preachers. They come to us with old darkness, and, with a wonderful simplicity, expect us to receive it as new light. They put all the candles of the tabernacle under bushels, or into lanterns, so that one can not distinguish a man from a brazen altar.

We have said there are two mistakes of the pulpit at the present day. The other is that of those who hold fast the old doctrines, and preach them with all the decision of a profound and rooted conviction, but with little power to compel the attention of an intensely materialistic and sensuous age. They are as honest as Paul, and as fearless; but they have not Paul's masterly skill in the great Gospel warfare. They stand still, in their consecrated temples, and utter the old oracles in the old way, while the world without goes rushing madly by, not knowing that they are there. They are right in their theology, but wrong in their tactics; orthodox, but not philosophical. If the age was serious and earnest, and would go up to the house of God from fixed habit and traditional popular sentiment, then the oracle might utter itself within the walls of its temple, clad in the robes of its proper dignity, and its influence would be felt and acknowledged afar. But the grand problem for the preacher of the age is, how to arrest and hold the attention of a pleasure-loving, irreverent, atheistical generation, and to do it in a legitimate way ; in other words, to compel the attention of men to the old and unwelcome truths, which the men of every age have hated to hear, and in a time when the externals of the Gospel awaken small respect ; when mere official dignity goes for nothing, if not even for less than nothing ; when there is a strong and growing disposition to challenge and profane things which the fathers of this generation held as reverend and sacred. We must not shut our eyes to the fact that this is a great and a very difficult achievement. Neither, on the other hand, must we set it down as an achievement impossible to be accomplished.

The thing demanded is, that the preacher of Christ's Gospel exhibit the same broad common sense and keen sagacity and fertility of expedients and indomitable will, in his own particular line of things, which are every where seen in all other departments of human skill and enterprise. He must command the respect of his generation ; must be a master in intelligence and tact and prudence and the power of adaptation. Paul was all that, or his ministry, with all the strength of his giant intellect, and all his varied learning, would have been, comparatively, a failure. If any man thinks that, because he has been duly qualified, according to established and venerable routine, has been properly accredited and received all the stamps of his professional career, therefore the men of this age will stand up and do him reverence, or even listen to his message, it is a mistake, and the sooner he becomes a fool that he may be wise, the better. He must be willing to put himself, in this respect, on a level with men in the secular professions ; men at the bar, on the platform, in the senate. No man expects to be listened to there on account of his credentials. All the honors of all the universities can not help him, and there could not be found a court-room or deliberative assembly of modern days that would not laugh him to scorn if he dared assert the smallest claim based on any such qualifications. He knows this, and accepts the conditions : and more, he knows that the strongest batteries of criticism and satire and sarcasm are planted against him when he takes the field, and if he can not stand before them, he must fall.

What we assert is, that the temper of the present age will subject the preacher to much the same rough, yet healthful ordeal. And we say, that if, having the armory of God from which to draw his weapons, having the everlasting Gospel, whose proclamation was the glory and strength and triumph of the angel of the Apocalypse; if, having these, and, back of them, the credentials of God and the promised aid of the Holy Spirit, he can not arrest and compel the attention even of the men of this arrogant and irreverent age, then he deserves to fail. There is no sufficient reason, human or divine, why a preacher should not fight his way to success through all the obstacles which lie in the path of any other man. It is effeminacy and cowardice and pitiful cant to claim for him a special dispensation.

Such is the ministry which the circumstances require. How is it to be secured? Two things are necessary. First the right men. God provides these. A preacher is a creation. That which constitutes his marvellous power came with him when he came into the world. It is the power by which a man moves other men by speech, making them see with his eyes, and hear with his ears, and feel what he feels: a more wonderful thing to do, some one has said, than to dance amid a thousand red hot ploughshares blindfold, and not be burned. God furnishes such men in every age. To doubt it would be to impugn his wisdom in the providential government of the world, and to assert that the Lord Jesus Christ has less regard for the peculiar needs of his own redeemed church than for the relief of men's wants through the exercise of natural gifts in the mechanic arts. Yet is not the number of such men large in any age. The churches of New England are paying the penalty to-day of the mistake into which they fell in the revivals of thirty years ago; that of pressing every converted young man into the ministry, without pausing to inquire whether God meant him for a minister. This error has wrought much mischief. It has robbed the community of not a few good farmers, mechanics and tradesmen; and, peradventure, of merchant princes, physicians, lawyers. Moreover, it has kept a very worthy class of men poor and discontented and miserable, through their undertaking the duties of a calling for which God never designed them.   This evil has been aggravated, and the discontent and misery of these men intensified, by the severe censures heaped upon them because they, good men and Christians, have not kindled and glowed on the great themes of God and judgment and eternity, when there was no fire in them to kindle on any thing.   They have been fain to make reprisals, by accusing the churches of a wicked fastidiousness, simply because they could not be enamored of dulness, try they never so hard.   By an inevitable reaction, again, the churches, wearied with coldness and deadness and platitudes, and thirsting for a pulpit ministration that can stir their emotions, have been too ready to accept the natural endowment without the spiritual grace ; and unconverted fluency has carried it against converted dulness in the preacher ; and Christ has been dishonored and his doctrine disparaged, and the ranks of the church have been filled with worldly men, and souls have been lost.

There is still another evil resulting from that strange error of thirty years ago, and it is not small, however we may consider it.   This is a fearful floating dead weight of unacceptable and uncalled ministers.   They may be very good men, but nobody wants to be there when they try to preach.   Their life, consequently, is a failure ; and, since failure sours a man, and stirs up whatever uncomfortable tempers his mother may have given him, and he will be ever blaming others, rather than his own incompetency, and will envy and decry those who succeed, these preachers who can not preach become eminent for one thing, and that is, as troublers of the churches with their pastors and deacons, giving rise to the slanderous assertion that no other man is so much to be dreaded in the parish as a retired minister, whereas it is true only of the ministers who are not preachers, and so have had very small things to retire from.

Christ exercised his sovereignty, doubtless, when he elected those twelve plain men to be his apostles.   But does any one doubt that they had natural gifts which had to do with their success as preachers, and gifts which God has not bestowed on every man ?   Therein Christ exercised an intelligent judgment, and the churches and schools of the prophets must do the same.

The men are in the churches, created and specially endowed by God for the work of the ministry. They are in our schools and colleges; in the banking and mercantile establishments of the cities; in the printing office; on the farm and in the black-smith's shop, in remote, out of the way sections of the country; or leading the rough life of a sailor, on far distant stormy seas.

What is the other thing required? Plainly, that these men have an opportunity to grow into faithful pastors and able preachers of the word. Has there been no mistake among us, as to what the preacher is, and how he is produced? We have thought to construct him; he is a development: we would build him, like a house, with square and compass, and axes and hammers; he is a growth, like a tree, from a creation and a new creation of God. You can make a house, but you can not make a preacher any more than you can make a tree. God makes him, and next to God he makes himself.

We believe in the theological seminary; but it is not a divine institution, neither is it indispensable. The world has never seen a nobler race of preachers than the Puritans in the days of Elizabeth. Their theological seminary was in those district meetings which were held for the training of the young preach-ers in the knowledge of the Bible, promptness and accuracy of thought, and fluent extemporaneous utterance. New England did well also in the days when her theological seminaries were the studies and parishes and pulpits of her active pastors.

All this is not to decry our own venerated schools of the prophets. We affirm, on the contrary, that they ought to give us the best race of preachers the world ever saw. Unless they shall be found to do, in some good measure, this great work, the churches may choose to dispense with them, and therein may do wisely.

It must be kept in mind, by those to whom is committed the direction of our theological seminaries, that all their processes should have a direct reference to the pulpit. They are ex-pected to send out PREACHERS. Scholars, theologians, elegant writers, let them be if possible; it is a thing to be desired, doubtless, that the Christian ministry should be, as, to a large extent, it always has been in New England, a priesthood of learning. But *preachers* they *must be.* The pulpit is the tower of their strength. Scholars, theologians, elegant writers, and much more in the same direction, they may be; prepared to excel as editors, professors, secretaries, yet fail in the pulpit, where God made them to be preëminent. Nay, your Greek and Hebrew and theology and canons of logic and canons of rhetoric, and making of sermons, invaluable to the preacher, as they undoubtedly are, may, standing alone, even bury so deep the fountain of eloquence, that it will never come to the surface. We have called the preacher's peculiar and marvellous faculty divine. So is a tree; but a tree must unfold and develop into strength and symmetry and beauty, in favoring circumstances. The theological seminary must be a nursery where the preacher grows toward the fulness of his power.

It should never be forgotten for a day, from the time a man enters the seminary to the end of the course, that his vocation is to be public speaking : that it is a grand vocation, demanding the exercise of a wonderful, God-given power, for which the multitude are always thirsting, and from which they will never turn away. It should never be forgotten that this wonderful power, innate, God-given, is susceptible of indefinite development ; and that, wherever, in any age or among any people, it has been exhibited in the highest degree, it would not be easy to say whether more was due to nature or to art, to original endowment or lengthened and severe training. A slender, pale young man takes his place by the forge and anvil, and a few years later, we find there a man with broad, full chest, and muscular arm. But who believes that the slender *voice* can become, under proper training, full and deep and sonorous, like the sound of a trumpet? This, too, is a matter very much of muscular exercise and development ; and the training which secures all the finest qualities of the human voice, will, at the same time, expand the chest, and impart color to the cheek and fire to the eye.

The crowning acquisition of the preacher is the power to clothe his thoughts in words, and let them flow forth upon an audience, on a torrent or in an atmosphere of earnest and fervid feeling. This is a gift so rich, we are sorry to be compelled to say, so rare, that the man who shuts himself up in caves, or walks day and night by the roaring sea, or travels through distant lands to attain it, shall confess himself a thousand times repaid for all his toils. What needs most to be insisted on to-day, and here in New England, is, that this gift may be acquired by every man who ought to think of entering the pulpit as his vocation; not by every man in an equal degree, but by every man in such degree that an intelligent audience will find it a pleasure to listen to him. Because a man has now and then flamed up into an orator, not only without any special training in that direction, but in spite of many unfavorable influences, the conclusion has been extensively accepted that eloquence is altogether a predestinate thing : that if nature designed a man for an orator he will be an orator, without any help from his school-masters; and that, on the other hand, if he does not show himself eloquent by nature, all the aid of school-masters will be in vain. A more palpable absurdity could not be entertained. It is most true, indeed, that if a man is not eloquent by nature, no amount of training will make him so. But it is equally true, that a man who is eloquent by nature, will never become eloquent in fact, without an amount of training somewhere which demands almost incredible toil. The best possible proofs and illustrations of this are the very men to whom the world is forever pointing as natural orators. Demosthenes, without his training, would have been excluded from cultivated Athenian circles, because of the clumsiness of his speech. Cicero traveled far, and submitted himself to many instructors, and triumphed over personal defects apparently insurmountable, before he electrified the senate and people of Rome, and sent his name sounding down through the ages as the synonym of eloquence. Henry Clay attained his matchless fluency and musical cadence, by the frequent and painful training of himself in private. Robert Hall broke down utterly in the pulpit, and more than once, in his earlier attempts to preach to a Bristol audience. Great orators have their secrets of the cave, which they do not like to disclose. But if there is any one thing which the history of true eloquence demonstrates, it is, that in no department of human attainment is excellence more largely the result of continuous and well-directed training, and no where else is less to be expected without such training, however great may be the measure of natural endowment.   We say, therefore, that in a seminary which proposes, as its one object, to send forth preachers, all its methods should have reference to the pulpit.

Especially should such a seminary foster and encourage and cultivate incessantly by all the means in its power, a fluent and earnest utterance, as that without true eloquence can not be.   That which we wish to affirm here, with special emphasis, is, that, through the entire preparatory course, fluency is to be preferred to correctness : and that, not only because all the world prefers warmth and fluency to accuracy in an orator, but because, by a law of nature, the attainment of fluency belongs to an earlier, and of correctness to a later period.   If correctness be put first, as the manner of the schools long has been, in accordance with the canons of the doctors, there is no little danger lest, by the constant plying of the young men with rules and principles and unmerciful criticisms, as to style and method and language, you utterly crush out and kill all true freedom and earnestness, without which you can no more have real eloquence than you can have the sparkling, leaping, foaming river in a leaden pipe.

Lord Henry Brougham, himself a prince among orators, and a philosopher too, in writing to the father of Macaulay in relation to the education of his son, insists, with special earnestness, that the power of easy, fluent utterance should be acquired first of all.   "Let him first of all learn to speak easily and fluently," he says ; " as well and as sensibly as he can, no doubt, but at any rate let him learn to speak."   He gives two reasons for the advice : one, that this is the true foundation on which to build, if a man is to be a public speaker, and the other, that it can only be acquired early in life.

For mental discipline, biblical learning, theology, and the writing of sermons, the regular course of training for the Christian ministry in our American colleges and seminaries has distanced all competition.   For securing preachers, it has exhibited no special adaptation ; which is not to say that we have not had in New England a succession of men of great pulpit power, who have used all these advantages with consummate skill.   To march and counter-march a man, in morning and evening drill, for a fixed term of years, through the prescribed courses of stately seminaries, and then, at a time appointed, when he has been duly laden with Greek and Hebrew, and canons of logic and canons of rhetoric, and dogmas philosophic and dogmas theological, and church history and polite litera- ture, solemnly to license him to preach! the very thing which of all others he feels he can not do, and for the doing of which you have given him no proper training; if the thing were not an institution, would it not be a cruel satire? It is proposed to teach a man to swim. There is placed before him a painted water, and the wall is covered with diagrams; then he is plied with a lengthened course of instructions, how to carry his head, his chest; how to move his arms, his legs; how to turn the palms of his hands, how to lie on his back, and how to float with the stream. He is permitted to go through some of the proper motions, and all his mistakes are severely criticised. All this for two years. Then, on a set day, he is brought to a real water, where the channel is deep and the current strong, and with a multitude on the shore, who are to watch every movement and laugh at him if he fails, he is solemnly licensed to swim, and bid plunge in. What will he do? Why, when he feels the cold water, which he did not feel in the painted river, and struggles with the dashing wave, and remembers that the water is deep, and that many are looking at him from the shore, expecting to see the grand results of his long and expen- sive training, he will pant; and then throw up his arms; and then—sink! So many a minister has done, when, if he had been trained according to the principles of common sense, his life might have been, not a failure, but a brilliant success.

Can it be necessary to say, that, having direct reference to pulpit power in the best and highest sense, the Bible should be the grand classic and magazine and handbook of the entire course? It should be read and pondered, day and night, un- til its histories and facts and doctrines and precepts become as familiar as household words. To discourse of these things in the pulpit is the one life-long vocation of the preacher. They are themes high as the throne of God, vast as eternity. They will wake up the intellect, and move the heart to deep feeling and the tongue to eloquence, as no other themes can. Sentiment, poetry, flowers of rhetoric, questions of philosophy, splendors of diction, are trifling and impertinence in comparison. The thorough mastery of Paul's single epistle to the Romans will work out a better theology for the pulpit than the study of all the systems of divinity ever written.

Passing by all which might be said of the value of a familiar acquaintance with the Greek and Hebrew Scriptures in relation to this point, we do but repeat the language of secular men, when we say, that there can not be found in all the wide range of English literature any thing which can be brought in comparison with the Bible for the student in eloquence. For simplicity, force, elegance, pathos, power, our English Bible stands alone and preëminent, and contains in a single volume all the richest treasures of eloquence, and much more than all which can be culled in a thousand years from all the poetry and history and oratory which have been preserved to us from the days of Chaucer to the present time. A constant and diligent study of the Bible will give to the preacher a better style for the pulpit, and for effective oratory, than the most familiar acquaintance with all the best uninspired models of ancient and modern times. Daniel Webster owed more to the Bible in this respect than to Quintilian and Cicero and Demosthenes and Edmund Burke.

There is one other qualification for effective pulpit eloquence in comparison with which all that has been named sinks into insignificance. It is earnest piety. There is a power in the pulpit which consists in voice, manner, originality of thought, strength of argument, splendor of diction, brilliancy of genius : but it is not the highest. George Whitefield was an immeasurably greater power in the kingdom of God than Massillon, and Charles Haddon Spurgeon is greater than Bourdaloue, though in natural endowments immeasurably inferior. That is one point. There is another which deserves attention in our day, and it is, that a profound and earnest piety tends directly to the highest development and strength of all a man's natural powers. To aim at intellectual excellence, as the main thing, therefore, is to miss the mark every way. When Paul has fought with beasts at Ephesus, and gained the victory, animated and sustained by the sublime hope of the resurrection ;

when Luther and Bunyan have contended with foes temporal and spiritual, more terrible than the raging waves of the sea, and have conquered by faith and prayer, then it has been given to these men to see visions of God which have made all earthly things fade away into the faintest shadow of a shade ; and eternity and judgment and heaven and hell have been to them realities, stupendous and awful, and they have preached with an irresistible power to the heart and conscience of dying men.

Few men can have the experiences of Paul and Martin Luther and John Bunyan : but all men can pray, and obtain wondrous answers to their prayer.   What Luther wrought out in storms and revolutions which sent dismay to the hearts of tyrants, and gave a reformed Christianity to Europe and the world, our young men aspiring to the high vocation of the preacher may demonstrate, first within the quiet precincts of the theological seminary, and afterward amid the most peaceful scenes of pastoral life. *Bene orasse est bene studisse.*   Then, whatever other attributes of the preacher they may possess, this will secure to them a new and wondrous force and energy ; and it shall be even as if one were risen from the dead, or angels clothed with the power of God had come down to men.

It must not be forgotten that, as this is immeasurably the most important of all the qualifications of the preacher, so, by a great law of analogy, it is immeasurably the most difficult. Coleridge has said, that to swing on hooks thrust through the body, or to walk with shoes having nails driven through the soles and pointing upward, is easier than to reflect.   But to have all the natural powers cultivated and improved in the utmost possible degree, and then to account all these as nothing in comparison with deep and earnest personal piety, this is infinitely a more difficult thing.   Build, with vast expense and mighty toil, a splendid mansion ; decorate the ceiling, fresco the walls, hang it all full of richest tapestries and costly pictures ; and then with your own hand set fire to it, and stand and gaze, with folded arms, and without emotion, till only ashes are left. This, too, would be easier far than the thing for which we plead.   And yet that thing is possible by the Spirit of God.

The distinguishing characteristic and crowning excellence of our modern schools of the prophets then, should be found in their constant endeavor, above all things, to cultivate in the young preachers the spirit of an earnest, manly piety ; accounting that without this the highest intellectual power, with all possible human culture, can only result in mournful failure as regards the great end for which Christ has instituted the ministry of the word.

If Christianity is destined to assert any new power over the nations, and to give to society a higher enfranchisement than has been realized hitherto, it can only be, as we judge, through a signal revival of the power of the pulpit.   Nay, is not this indispensable, in our own country at least, to arrest the progress of social evils of which we are more afraid every day, and to save us from a frightful moral degeneracy?

This is the question of the churches.   Let them look to it. If they discern the signs of the times, and have formed already a deliberate and fixed judgment as to the order of preachers which the pressing exigences of the times demand, let them see to it that the demand is met.   The field is white already.   If our nation is to be saved from perils greater than all we seem to have escaped hitherto, if we are to have, in the generations to come, a Christian Sabbath and a family compact, a free government and a loyal people, then, doubtless, the pulpit, out of weakness made strong, must assert and maintain its supremacy, must take to itself all its proper attributes, and wield with a skill and effect which even wicked men will be constrained to admire, the sword of the Spirit, making its irresistible appeal to the understanding, the conscience, the heart.   Then the reason will be compelled to bow to inspiration, and philosophy will stand abashed before the cross.   The primitive spirit of Christian fellowship will be restored.   The temples built for God, whether simple and inexpensive, or costly and beautiful, will scarcely be remembered by the spiritual worshippers, bringing their hearts' oblation to Him whom the heaven of heavens can not contain.   Then God will be seen to be greater than man ; eternity greater than time ; and the salvation of a single soul of infinitely more value than all the immunities of liberty and civilization and material prosperity secured to the entire human race for ten thousand years.

All this, and much more, that simplest of agencies, the Christian pulpit, is divinely adapted and ordained to accomplish. It will draw the multitudes everywhere to hear the Gospel, even as they followed Christ into the wilderness. It will make the wicked tremble, and fill the saints of God with joy. It will give to the oppressed of every land the only true enfranchisement. It will set the crown on the head of Jesus Christ.

ARTICLE II.

JEWISH BAPTISM IN THE TIMES OF OUR LORD, AS RELATED TO HOUSEHOLD BAPTISM.

"Teach all nations" : make disciples, proselytes of them, to my religion [μαθητεύσατε]. "Baptizing them." What is that? The term is not explained. It has no qualifying words as to mode or subjects. Without comment or enlargement, do the Apostles know what the ascending Master means? Shut out all history between now and then, go back beyond the Book of Acts and the day of pentecost, hear for yourself that command, and what will you do? "Baptizing them." What is the thing to be done? To whom is it to be done? Is there any antecedent or surrounding light to guide you? You can not consult the Book of Acts and the Epistles, the Councils, the Fathers, and Christian history. Is there any sacred service or ceremony of the times that can explain the command? Evidently our Lord assumes that the Apostles know what he means, without an explanation. And they do know. You, set back so far, and under that command, would at once recur to John's baptism for explanation and guidance. That would be your principal if not only aid, and it would be enough.

Back then in Judæa, in the year thirty-three of our Lord, and under this commission for baptizing, what are you going to do? You would make a careful study and digest of John's baptism, and follow it strictly as your interpreter, except where divinely authorized to vary from it.

Our teacher and example, when we have thus gone back, is one whose raiment is camel's hair, whose girdle is leathern, whose spirit and power are as of a prophet. As when we by sudden discovery bring forth a painting from the dust and cob-webs of a convent cell, the gem of an old master, glorious in the costume and colors of an elder and better day, so he stands among the wondering multitude as one of the old prophets risen from the dead. "All the people are in expectation, and all men muse in their hearts whether he be the Christ or not." The times are full of this expectation of the Messiah. Men are studying promise and prophecy, and they watch and wait. When, therefore, the prophecy of Isaiah is answered in "the voice of one crying in the wilderness : Prepare ye the way of the Lord," the multitude flock about the mysterious preacher as the harbinger of the Christ. And when he preached to the people repentance, and urged a cordial preparation for the com-ing Lord, and an acceptance of him, they were eager to seal these promises of reform and undergo a ceremonial purification, as about to be subjects in "the kingdom of heaven," now at hand under a new dispensation. So there "went out to him Jerusalem and all Judæa, and were baptized of him in Jordan, confessing their sins." Mt. iii. 5, 6. So general was that ex-pectation of the Messiah, and so ready were they to prepare the way of the Lord, that this baptism was almost as the baptism of the populace, so extensive was it.

The import of the rite is obvious. It was performed on a circumcised people, the chosen of God. They had broad no-tions of discrimination between the clean and the unclean. When Aaron and his sons were consecrated for the priesthood they were washed and made clean, and when Israel was about to receive the dispensation of Moses and of Sinai they were required first to wash and be clean. Baptism has the import of purification and dedication, and so now, when "Jerusalem and all Judæa" are about to receive the Christian dispensation, this rite is administered to them as purifying and preparatory and dedicatory. Indeed we find that this High Priest himself is inaugurated by the same rite of consecration. So it became him to fulfil all righteousness ; and so "when all the people were baptized, it came to pass that Jesus also was baptized."

This, then, was not Christian baptism. That was first administered a few years afterward to those three thousand Christian converts on the day of pentecost. It was not a baptism representative of "the washing of regeneration." For some of the subjects of it thirty years afterwards had "not so much as heard whether there be any Holy Ghost." Acts xix. 2. And then the Master himself received it, in whom it could represent no such regenerating work.

It was administered to church members. It was a ceremonial purification and introduction of the church to a higher and holier dispensation. The baptism of John was a formal purification of the people, preparatory to the inauguration of Christianity. He "called upon his countrymen to prepare themselves, by repentance for sin and reception of baptism as a symbol of a changed mood, to enter into the Messianic kingdom, now on the point of being established."[1]

The baptism, as an act, does not seem to have created any interest, as if it were a strange custom in Judæa, introduced by John himself. Indeed in all the hostility to John and his work there is no accusation that he had assumed to create another and novel sacred service; and in all the hostility of the Jews to the Christians in their innovations in religious teachings and ceremonies, it is nowhere implied that the Jews regarded baptism as a new rite, springing up with this new sect.

On the question of household baptism some are troubled to find any recognition of it in New Testament times. So it is hopefully inferred that the baptism of children is only a human invention, that came into the church among other innovations in the second Christian century. For it is agreed that in the middle of the third, at the council of sixty six bishops at Carthage, A. D., 253, the rite was so well established as to give rise to a lengthy discussion whether an infant could properly be baptized before the eighth day, thus assuming, as both duty and usage, that it ought to be baptized sometime.

The baptism of John, preceding Christian times, is also conceded, but when the question is put: "The baptism of John, who received it?" like those first troubled by the question, "Whence

[1] Guericke's Ch. His., Shedd's Ed. p. 36. See also Mosheim's Commentaries, Murdock's, Ed. 1: 89.

was it?" they answer: "We can not tell." Yet they add: It did not include infants. They know a negative, a denial, only.

A tolerably fair ecclesiastical history covering the period between the return from the captivity and the apostolic pentecost remains to be written, and when written will close the controversy on the disputed rite. A single link only remains to complete the chain of historical argument. That link is furnished by showing the object of John's baptism, and the subjects of it: whom he baptized, and for what purpose he did it. Without any good reason this field of inquiry has been abandoned, and so the question of infant baptism has been lost in many minds simply by default. Some practice it without knowing why, some because it will do no harm, and very many in our church neglect it wholly. So doing, the constitution of the church of God is very greatly misunderstood and mutilated.

We enter, therefore, in this paper, into a historical inquiry as to the use that the Jews made of baptism before and during and immediately after the times of John the Baptist.

When baptism was introduced among the Jews is not definitely settled; it is of very ancient if not unknown antiquity. The Septuagint says that Naaman, the Syrian, was baptized in Jordan for the curing of his leprosy: ἐβαπτίσαντο ἐν τῷ Ἰορδάνῃ. 2 Kings v. 14, and that unrighteousness baptized Isaiah: ἡ ἀνομία με βαπτίζει. Isa. xxi. 4. If Alexandrian Greek, in the year B. C. 285, could properly describe acts as baptisms that took place among the Jews seven hundred and nine hundred years before the Christian era, we can easily presume that baptism was a rite of very great antiquity among them.[1]

One thing is evident. In the times of our Lord the rite was national and common among the Jews. So Jost[2] says: "Jesus also, knowing the national custom, received consecration from him." Jost's Gen. His. of the Israelites. Vol. 2. B. 8, c. 6.

"The first use of baptism was not exhibited at that time" of John the Baptist, says Lightfoot, "For baptism very many centuries of years backwards had been both known and re-

[1] We find twenty and more cases of the use of βάπτω and βαπτίζω, and their related words, in the Septuagint.

[2] Jost "a learned Jewish Rabbi, who has devoted his life to the investigation of such subjects, and who is considered by intelligent Jews as the most profound historian of the age." Rev. James Murdock, D. D., Bib. Repos. 14: 174.

ceived in most frequent use among the Jews, and for the very same end as it now obtains among Christians, namely, that by it proselytes might be admitted into the church; and hence it was called baptism for proselytism." And he refers to the Babylonian Talmud for his authority. Lightfoot's Works, London 1684. Vol. 2: 117.

He also adds that it was an axiom among the Jews: "No man is a proselyte until he be circumcised and baptized." And so he says: "You see baptism inseparably joined to the circumcision of proselytes." Works, Vol. 2: p. 118.

So Maimonides, one of the very best ancient Jewish historians, whom they call "The glory of the East," "The light of the West," says: "In all ages when an ethnic is willing to enter into the covenant, and gather himself under the wings of the majesty of God, and take upon him the yoke of the law, he must be circumcised, and baptized, and bring a sacrifice, or if it be a woman, be baptized and bring a sacrifice." Wall's His. Infant Bap., Cotton's Ed., Ox., 1844. Vol. 1: 5. By this last remark of Maimonides it will be noticed that female converts to Judaism received the ordinance of baptism. The authorities are full on this point.

The Talmud says: "We find concerning the maidservants, who were baptized, but not circumcised," that they are proselytes. "One baptizeth a heathen woman in the name of a woman; we can assert that for a deed rightly done." Lightfoot, 2: 117–18.

Yet again: "When a proselyte is received, he must be circumcised, and then . . . . they baptize him in the presence of two wise men, saying: Behold, he is an Israelite in all things: or if it be a woman, the women lead her to the waters," etc. Wall's His. Inf. Bap. 1: 7.

But what should be more carefully noted as bearing peculiarly on our inquiry into the import and scope of John's baptism, if the parents were baptized the young children were included as a matter of course. The law of baptism held all who were held by the law of circumcision, and went beyond, including females. From the abundance of testimony to this point we give an item or two.

Says Lightfoot: " For so was the custom of the Jewish nation in their use of baptism, when a proselyte came in, his children were baptized with him : and all this upon this ground, that all that were related to the parent might come into covenant." Works, Vol. 2 : 1128.

And to the same effect he quotes the Babylonian Talmud and Commentary thus : "They baptize a little proselyte according to the judgment of the Sanhedrin. If he be deprived of his father, and his mother bring him to be made a proselyte, they baptize him, because none becomes a proselyte without circumcision and baptism, according to the judgment of the Sanhedrin, that is, that three men be present at the baptism, who are now instead of a father to him." Do. 118.

As to the age under which a child may be the proper subject of infant baptism, they had this rule :

" Any male child of a proselyte, that was under the age of thirteen years and a day, and females that were under twelve years and a day, they baptized as infants, at the request and by the assent of the father, or the authority of the court, because such an one was not yet the son of assent, as they phrase it, i. e., not capable to give assent for himself. But the thing is for his good. If they were above that age they consented for themselves." Wall. 1 : 17.

This usage of infant baptism among the Jews is farther illustrated by one of those mercies that cropped out over the barbaric roughnesses of their time. The practice of the heathen to expose their infants to death is well known, and such were often found by the Jews and adopted into their families either as children or servants. They did the same often with infants that came into their hands by victory on the battle field. For the treatment of these, the Jerusalem Talmud thus prescribes :

"Behold one finds an infant cast out, and baptizes him in the name of a servant. Do thou also circumcise him in the name of a servant. But if he baptize him in the name of a freeman, do thou also circumcise him in the name of a freeman." Wall. 1 : 20.

The statement of Maimonides is also to the same purpose : "An Israelite that takes a little heathen child, or that finds an

heathen infant and baptizes him for a proselyte, behold he is a
a proselyte." Wall. 1 : 20.

These are but a few of the very many specific and direct
declarations of the practice of baptism by the Jews in the times
of John the Baptist.   It is not needful to multiply these quotations.   But there are certain incidental, or wayside items,
that have a peculiar force in illustrating this practice.

Maimonides says that when any offered themselves as proselytes for baptism, "they make diligent inquiry concerning such,
lest they come to get themselves under the law for some riches
that they should receive, or for dignity that they should obtain,
or for fear.   If it be a man, they inquire whether he have not set
his affections on some Jewish woman, or a woman, her affection on some young man of Israel."   Maimonides makes mention, also, of many minute circumstances that must attend the
ceremony of baptism.   It must not be on the Sabbath, nor on
any holiday, nor by night.   There must be three witnesses of
the ceremony.   Circumcision must precede it, and a bloody
offering accompany it.   Yet in times of revolution or dispersion
the sacrifice may be omitted.   The sacrifice must be a burnt
offering of a beast, or of two turtle-doves, or of two young
pigeons.   It was also a rite never to be repeated on the same
person.   Nor were the children born to proselyte parents after
their baptism to be baptized.   For baptism by the Jew was
regarded as a purification of the race, or family stock.   The parents once purified, all their unborn posterity was made pure too.

Here is the fittest place to mark the sharp distinction that
the Jew made between baptism and circumcision in their uses.
Baptism constituted one a Jew, while circumcision constituted
him a church member. Wall. 1 : 5–45.

The side allusions to this usage, scattered through the best
Jewish authorities, show baptism to have been as surely an ordinance among them, as circumcision or sacrifice.

Now we see well the reason for these strong and confident
declarations of Dr. Lightfoot, a man so scholarly in the writings of the Jews concerning their doctrines and antiquities:
"Baptism was well enough known to the Jews, and both John
and Jesus Christ took it up as they found it."   "Christ took up
baptism as he found it in the Jewish church, and they baptized

infants as well as grown persons." "Think not that baptism was never used till John Baptist came and baptized. It was used in the church of the Jews many generations before he was born." "Baptism of men, women and children was no new thing among them when John Baptist came baptizing, but a thing as well known as with us now." " Christ took baptism into his hands, and into evangelical use, as he found it, this only added, that he might promote it to a worthier end, and to a larger use. The whole nation knew well enough that little children used to be baptized. . . . . . . Nor do I believe this people, that flocked to John's baptism, were so forgetful of the manner and custom of the nation, that they brought not their little children also with them to be baptized." "We suppose, therefore, that men, women and children came to John's baptism, according to the manner of the nation in the reception of proselytes." Lightfoot's Works, Vol. 2 : pp. 1129, 1133, 1040, 119, 122.

In these historic inquiries into the baptism of John we find several important facts.

Baptism as a religious ceremony was in common use among the Jews in the time of John the Baptist. Why introduced among the Jews, and how long before, and by what authority, are questions not pertinent to the unfolding of our one topic. It is enough here to know the fact that baptism was in general practice among the Jews before and during the time of John. It was used as an introductory rite to a new religion. The Jews esteemed the pagan gentiles an unclean people. Yet they were constantly drawing converts from them. When one came over to Judaism, he received the baptismal cleansing. The act made him a Jew. It initiated him into a new religion. It did not admit him to church membership. This was the office of circumcision. When the father of a family received it, the rite was also administered to his children of thirteen years and under. If an adult female became a proselyte, she also received baptism. So was the ordinance both national and common. When John the Baptist entered on his work as the forerunner of Christ, and as introducing a new religious dispensation, he found this proselyte baptism in common use. His work was to persuade the Jewish populace to receive a higher and holier religion, to proselyte them to another system. This proselyte baptism was precisely the rite he needed to indicate the purification of his converts, and to seal them over to this new religion. This baptism John practiced during the years of his ministry, and so successful was he that it became a national proselytism. There "went out to him Jerusalem and all Judæa, and all the region round about Jordan, and were baptized of him in Jordan, confessing their sins."

So much for the usage, facts and subjects of John's baptism. It may be objected that we have quoted mainly from Rabbies, and Talmuds, and Jewish authors and traditions, and that these are not to be trusted. We submit that all ecclesiastical and exegetical writers on the sacred authors and ceremonies of the first century, make free use of the authorities we have quoted, when there is nothing manifestly untrue in the quotation they would wish to make. We use Josephus in this way, trusting him when he is not self-contradictory, or contradicted by manifest fact. Rawlinson convicts Herodotus of very grave mistakes, but we rely on Herodotus nevertheless, in every point where we do not convict him. In the same way it is manifestly just to use Jewish witnesses. It is a huge assumption and an assault on the canons of historical criticism thus to reject this historical account of Jewish infant baptism in the times of our Lord, and without specific objections to the specific passages.

Look at it. Very early in the Christian centuries, as early as 200 A.D., the Jews, as all agree, baptized infants. With the Christians the custom was old and well established, all agree, as early as A. D. 253. When did the Jews adopt it? He rejecting these statements of its use in the times of John, is obligated to tell us. Did the Jews borrow the rite from the Christians? A Jew borrow a sacred rite from a Christian! The Jerusalem Talmud, one of the authorities we have quoted, was probably written before the year 200 A.D., and contains a vast amount of nonsense. Yet its simple, often puerile detail of rites and ceremonies and religious notions is to be as fully trusted as any other history not absurd, or opposed to known fact.

The pædobaptists have committed a grave error in yielding this historical evidence from Jewish writings so readily on an opposing assumption, a mere dictum. Their history of infant baptism among themselves is the uninspired preface to the inspired history of household baptism in the Book of Acts. It is as reliable as any chapter in Grecian or Roman history, written a century or two after the events.

"Go teach all nations baptizing them." Was that a new word then, pointing to a new ceremony? If so how could "the eleven" understand it? It is not explained in their commission. If baptism was not then common, they might well say : "What is this new thing we are to do?"

In pursuing the inquiry, who, according to this last command of our ascending Lord, should be baptized, we need, not so much a lexicon to define the word, or a commentary to give the opinions of the learned, as a view of the times when the Lord Jesus issued the commission. For it is one of the first principles of interpretation, in gaining the import of an old law, to ascertain how it would fall in with the times when it was given, how it would suit the circumstances of that day, and how those to whom it was given would naturally understand it. The time and the place of the giving of a brief and doubtful command are two admirable expositors. They are as the "two great lights" that God made in the beginning.

Let us, then, place ourselves with " the eleven " when they were commissioned for this baptismal work. They are in Judæa, and near the close of the first third of the first Christian century. Judaism is as yet the religion of the land. Its religious forms, rites and ceremonies are · daily seen on every hand. The eleven are commanded to go and make disciples to Christ, or proselytes to the Gospel. This is the import of that word, " teach," and is so given in the marginal reading in the English version. The eleven understood this duty. They saw such religious labor in the daily life of the Jews around them. Those Jews were compassing sea and land to make proselytes, and the disciples understood that with a deeper ardor, and for a vastly holier purpose, they were to imitate them in proselyting.

Then, when by their teaching they had gained a disciple, a proselyte to this new religion, they were to baptize him. This ordinance was no novelty to them. It was from the olden time in the holy land. As zealous Jews formerly themselves, they had labored to gain gentile converts, and bring them to this purifying rite.   And often had they seen it administered.   The Lake of Merom and the Sea of Galilee, as well as waters more limited, had witnessed the dedication of many a proselyte. What multitudes had they seen thronging to John's baptism at Ænon, and along the Jordan, while probably they themselves received the same baptism.   Then what they were commanded now to do was no new and strange thing.   The mode and nature of the ceremony were familiar to them, as common usage in their native land.   True, they were to exact a more spiritual and radical preparation for it, and were to attach a deeper significance to it, but the rite itself was to them an old and familiar rite.

They had seen adult females receive, as proselytes, this ordinance, and so become members of the commonwealth of Israel.   They saw them in the mixed multitude that gathered so eagerly to John's baptism.   So when they made disciples and baptized them, they would as a matter of course, include the females, though we do not find any specific order to this effect.   As a matter of recorded fact, we find that they did thus infer their duty, and did baptize women.

The eleven also saw that proselyte parents, coming over to Judaism, brought their little ones with them to baptism, and made them over to the new religion with the same ceremonial seal of water.   They knew no case where a proselyte parent had kept back his infant child from baptism.   To the male infant of a gentile, thus coming over to Judaism, they knew that baptism was as much a matter of course as circumcision.   Each was inevitable.   "The whole nation knew well enough that little children used to be baptized."   It was as persistently exacted as the other ceremonies so tenaciously held and rigidly enforced by that ritual people.   It was an integral part of the idea of proselyte baptism, as held and practiced in those times, that it covers the child as well as the parent.   This the eleven knew, and saw illustrated, and very like had practiced, as Jews.

This was the usage and the history of those times.   These were the surroundings of the disciples, when commanded to baptize their converts.   An ancient and common rite, that, coming on the head, invariably covered the members of the household, they were to administer.   There is no qualifying word, no intimation, that in the new use of an old rite, there is to be any change as to the sex or age of the subjects of it.

Place yourself, now, in those times, and in those circumstances, and, receiving that command, whom would you baptize? How would the sentiments and usages of the times concerning the rite of proselyte baptism, interpret the command to you? The Jews around you, your neighbors, are industrious in making proselytes; and gaining the head of a gentile family, they baptize the household. You are commanded to make proselytes and baptize. You have no command or intimation to draw a dividing line between the parent and the infant child in administering the ordinance. The command is simply to baptize, as if from all you know of usage, and all you see in practice about you, there could be no need of describing more specifically who should be baptized. You are left, therefore, for an interpretation of the command to the practice of your proselyting neighbors, the Jews. They followed the rule as the Talmud records it. "Any male child of a proselyte, that was under the age of thirteen years and a day, and females that were under twelve years and a day," should be baptized. In those circumstances could the eleven do anything otherwise than baptize believers and their households? What was there to suggest to them in those times any other course? What was there to give to them the notion, so foreign to all the teaching and practice of the day, and of the Jewish church from Abraham, that the infant of the believer was to be passed by?

And here it should be said that we are not to mark out a course, or provide an interpretation for the eleven, from the views and feelings of this day. We may not make up a creed and course of conduct out of our present denominational material, and carry it back to them for acceptance and use.

Out of the material for a judgment of duty that they then had, in the traditions, teachings and practices of their times, what line of obedience would they naturally, and as a matter of course, mark out for themselves? As this command of our Lord is a brief and unexplained command, the import of it must be made up from the views and uses of baptism that prevailed when the command was given. As a matter of course, therefore, the eleven would proceed, even as Jews, to baptize the children of proselyte believers.

It is now in place to notice certain common and plausible objections. So long as these very important facts, now stated, are unknown or unadmitted, there are some objections to infant baptism that must lie with much weight. If the Jewish usages of baptism be kept out of the argument, and the history of Jewish religious ceremonies in the times of John the Baptist be excluded, then objections to pædobaptism may have a peculiar force. But it is a force that they only seem to have, while material facts are absent.

1. It is objected that the command is to baptize only believers. And so it may be correctly said that only believers in Judaism were to receive the circumcision and baptism of a proselyte. Yet when that proselyte had children, even so young as to be unable to believe, they were to receive these rites. The rite among the Jews in baptizing proselytes was to baptize only believers. An adult believer must be found, according to the command of our Lord, before baptism could be administered, but when found, his infant children were to be reckoned as natural adjuncts of the man. They were regarded, ecclesiastically, as parts of his personal responsibility, and so were not to be dissevered from him in any total dedication of himself and all his to God. The ancient policy of God was to build up his church by family additions, and ever regarding, as he did, the family as a unit, he embraced all when he specified the head. So when the parent believed, the children were held to be believers also by presumption and anticipation. The policy of God was not like that of too many parents, who presume on the child's being an unbeliever, and expect it, and so treat it negligently and hopelessly, and thus make out a parental insurance and foreordination of unbelief. Unlike this unnatural process, having the seeds of death in it as an organic law, was the encircling bond of mercy and of gracious expectation in which our Heavenly Father enclosed his accepted ones. How often in his covenants of mercy do we find the phrases, "children's children," "a seed to serve him," "a generation." On this principle his church was built at the first, having not an individual but a family basis, and this policy was

actively in practice in the times of our Saviour. He continues it in the command to baptize only believers. As a matter of theory in the church from time immemorial, and as a theory in full practice in the church to which they were to make prose-lyte additions, the Apostles would, as a matter of course, gather in the little ones with the parents. To have done otherwise would have required, first, a radical reconstruction of the church, and then a specific order to exclude children.

When one objects to infant baptism by saying that baptism is a sign and seal of saving faith, and that saving faith should precede it, he is obligated to explain a difficulty that his sweep-ing objection creates. Circumcision is called "a seal of the righteousness of faith." Rom. iv. 11. Yet infants received this seal before they were old enough to have faith. On the same principle, whatever it be, they may receive baptism. By the same exegesis and principles infant baptism and infant cir-cumcision stand or fall together. The objection to the former, that faith can not precede it, as a seal of faith, is valid against the latter. So the objection is an objection against fact. It is an objection to what actually took place, that infants, who were not old enough to exercise faith, received the seal of faith.

It is an objection against fact. Adult and believing parents "were baptized of him in Jordan, confessing their sins." Their infant children were baptized at the same time without confess-ing their sins, just as they were circumcised without confession.

Moreover, if want of belief should prevent infant baptism, why should it not prevent infant salvation? For it is said: "He that believeth not shall be damned."

This rigid exegesis, demanding belief precedent to baptism, not only subverts the divine theory of circumcision, but makes the salvation of infants impossible. The exegesis is as unscriptural as the conclusion is abhorrent. We hope that in the sacred memories of coming ages we shall not become that traditional Calvinist, preaching, when long dead, what he was never known to have preached when he was alive, that there are infants in hell not a span long, because they were not old enough in this world to believe and be baptized.

2. It is objected that there is no command in the Bible to baptize infants. In the light of the facts now before us there

would be no need of such a command to the Apostles.   The objection goes on the assumptions that the Apostles are about to
organize the church of Christ as a new institution, and that the
nature of church membership is now to be determined for the
first time, and that the rite of initiation is a novel one for the
times, and not interpreted and limited, in the extent of its application, by precedent and daily use.   But the church of Christ
is one from the days of Abraham and continues through all
the ages.   No new church is formed.   David and Paul and the
Christian converts on the day of pentecost are members of the
same church, having the same creed.   The ancient principle
of membership embraced the children of the adult believer.
Changing one characteristic in the seal of membership would
not change this ancient principle, any more than changing the
motto on a government seal would change the import and power
of the seal.   We have seen, too, that our Saviour took an existing and common rite, by which the Jews admitted proselytes
to Judaism, and promoted it to be the introductory rite to the
Christian church.   When the Jews used this rite, initiating a
gentile parent, they invariably applied it to his little ones.   So
far, then, this would be a happy ordinance to come in the place
of circumcision, since it embraced the children of believers, as
circumcision had done.

When, therefore, Christ commanded his Apostles to baptize,
what need was there to command, in an especial manner, the
baptism of children?   Instead, therefore, of allowing this objection any force, it really turns on those moving it.   Considering all the circumstances in the times of the Apostles, there
should have been a special command to exclude children from
baptism, if it was not designed to have them included.   For if
nothing were said, the presumption would be totally for their
baptism.   So the very silence of our Lord, that is made the
ground of this objection, is virtually an affirmation of an existing command to embrace the children, and an approbation and
adoption of an existing practice that did embrace them.

3. It is objected that baptism is a seal of personal righteousness, or true piety, and so an unconscious infant can not properly receive it.   The objection misapprehends the nature of the
ordinance.   Baptism is more a rite of dedication than of con-

fession.   The person or thing receiving the ordinance is thus
sacredly set apart for God.   As when one is baptized in the
name of the Father and of the Son and of the Holy Ghost,
the name of the sacred Trinity is called and set upon him, as a
mark of new ownership.   It is also a purifying rite, ceremo-
nially expressive of the fact that what is about to be given to
God should be first purified.   It is also a rite representative of
that inward purification in which the Holy Spirit in regeneration
dedicates the subject acceptably to God.

Now as baptism served as a rite of dedication, as well as for
other purposes, it will at once be seen that an unconscious babe
may be the subject of it.   For a believing father or mother has
the right to dedicate a child to God.   All Christian parents
agree in this.   They differ only in the mode of doing it.   One
mode, and as we think, a mode appointed of God, is baptism.
God asks the gift of the child, that it may be his and bear his
name.   And as a child is above all other wealth and worth,
how fitting, when one makes a complete dedication of all he has
to God, that the only immortal gift in the collection and total
offering should be dedicated with a peculiar ceremony and seal.

4. It is objected that in infant baptism the child has no understanding of the rite, and gives no assent to it.   This is true,
even as it should be.   In a proper, Christian state of society,
where all heads of families are converted and professing Christians, baptism is an ordinance not to be understood or as-
sented to by the subjects of it.   Strictly and properly, baptism
in the Christian church belongs only to an infant, as circumcision in the Jewish church.   In the normal use of baptism
it is a parental duty by which an immortal is dedicated to God.
It classes among those duties that are to be done for another,
and not by the person receiving the act.   Adult baptism is a
necessity created by a failure in parental duty.   The parents of
such an adult ought to have been godly, and to have given their
child to God in this ordinance.   Failing in this, the adult baptism is a necessity to cover a defect.   It is irregular and abnormal.   The case of circumcision sets this objection in its true
light, and shows the true time and place for baptism.   The
only regular and proper subject of circumcision was an infant.
It was no rite for him to understand, or assent to.   It was a

parent's duty to God for the child; and had the whole family of man become the people of God before circumcision was abandoned, adult circumcision would have been impossible and unknown. In its original and legitimate design it did not belong to adults. Its application to them was an exception to the law. So the objection that infant baptism is without the understanding and assent of the person lies equally against circumcision. By covering too much ground it destroys itself. It is an objection to a principle that underlies circumcision and baptism, and a thousand other acts that we perform for a child, the principle that we may and often must act for the child without its assent. Baptism, when properly administered as to time, that is, in infancy, is simply and only the act of a parent, and it is no more necessary that the child comprehend and agree to it than that it comprehend and agree to the many duties that God requires us to discharge to our infant children. Adult baptism is a remedy for a defect, just as naturalization is, in constituting foreigners citizens under our government. Were there no more who could become immigrants, there could be no more naturalization. What it gains would be gained as a birthright, without knowledge or assent. And when infant baptism, even as circumcision, has its proper place among parental duties, as God originally designed, there will be no place for this irregular and remedial step of adult baptism. So the objection that the infant can not understand and give assent to its baptism is not only invalid in this specific case, but it is subversive of a fundamental principle in both the divine and the family government.

5. It is objected that infant baptism deprives one of the privilege of making a profession of religion for himself. This objection is founded on a false assumption. It is assumed that a profession of religion is made in the administration of the ordinance of baptism, and that a profession of religion can not be made unless this rite is administered at the time. Here is a confounding of two things that differ. Baptism is a rite of dedication. It is performed for a person. In the act the person is the passive recipient. He is the subject. But in making a profession of religion he is the agent, the actor. The profession is made through a creed, confession and covenant. One may be the

voluntary or the involuntary subject of a dedication to God, but a profession of religion is a cordial consent to such a dedication. It is the personal declaration of one's religious faith, feelings and purposes. In baptism one is given to God. He may be conscious of being given, as an adult, or unconscious, as an infant. If the former, he is not a professor by receiving the ordinance unless he has made a declaration of his religious doctrines, experiences and purposes. Our Baptist brethren agree to this. If an unconscious infant, it remains for the child to ratify the dedication in coming years, and give in his adhesion to Christ and his Gospel. When he does that, he makes a profession of religion. He is already dedicated, and bears the seal of the act.

The objection, moreover, lies on the strange assumption that all who come into the church, on a profession of faith, having received only infant baptism, are not professors of religion by any personal act of their own. The bare statement of such an assumption refutes the objection. All nominally in the Christian church, having received none but infant baptism, are reckoned and held as professors of religion in fact and form, because they made a public profession. By the one voice of common consent they are called professors. Yet they were not constituted such by infant baptism. Though baptized in infancy, if they had made no personal confession of Christ when they came to years of discretion, they would not be regarded as professors of religion. They became such by a personal and a subsequent act. There are many ten thousands in our congregations who were baptized in infancy, and yet no one calls them professors of religion. They have been solemnly given to God by their believing parents. They have received the appointed rite of dedication. They properly belong to God and are in the generation of his people. But they have not confessed into the faith of Abraham. They have not publicly received Christ as a personal Saviour, and his teaching as their rule of life. When they do this they will make a profession of religion. The public and common voice of all denominations will say that in that personal confession of Christ they made a profession of religion. Now all this common and public judgment shows two things. First, that infant baptism is not regarded as a profession of religion, and secondly, that it does not stand in the way of making a profession, when an adult inclines so to do. So the parental duty of infant dedication does in no way interfere with the personal duty and privilege, in conscious and adult years, of professing Christ.

We obtain in this discussion on John's baptism the additional light needed fully to understand the cases of household baptism mentioned in the New Testament. Already they are clear almost to an absolute certainty. But some doubt, reading only the New Testament.

Let us come down into Christian history to the Council of Carthage, A.D., 253. Here we find the rite of infant baptism established beyond a question. It only remains for those sixty six bishops to answer the question of Fidus, whether an infant may be baptized before it is eight days old. The usage is conceded without a word, and within one hundred and fifty years of a living Apostle, and the closing of the New Testament canon. Cyprian's letter to Fidus in answer to his question reduces the number of doubters very much. Yet some doubt still.

Let us now go on the other side, the far side of the New Testament, to the times of John the Baptist. Here we find him baptizing households, believers and their children. "For so was the custom of the Jewish nation in their use of baptism, when a proselyte came in, his children were baptized with him." And when our Lord commissioned his Apostles to baptize he left them to learn what was meant, by leaving them to the teaching and influence of this custom. They, going about their work, baptized households, as that of the jailer, and Lydia and Stephanus. Can any one longer doubt what household baptism means in the New Testament? Infant baptism common in the year 30, A.D., and common in the year 253, A.D., and in doubt what household baptism means in the times between! Infant baptism common in the year 30, A.D., and doubtful whether it was allowable and possible and probable in the year 53, A.D., when the households of Lydia and the jailer and Stephanus were baptized! Between John the Baptist and these sixty six bishops, both which parties baptized infants, we have a range of two hundred and twenty three years not covered absolutely by historical evidence. The opposers of this rite, to make their position good, must show that the Apostles did not follow the example before them, when Christ, without explaining, commanded them to baptize; and then show how the rite could have crept into the church and become established beyond a question or opposition, within one hundred and fifty years of the times of the Apostles.   Surely it would be easier to lean tenderly toward the children, as our Lord did, when they were rudely excluded, and give them the benefit of any remaining doubts, by giving them as good a status in the Christian dispensation as they had in the Jewish.

ARTICLE III.

THE CYCLES OF HISTORY.

. WE have sometimes imagined the wonder which Adam would have felt could he have seen fully mapped out before him the history of his posterity for these six thousand years.   Such a multitude of tribes and nations; such diversities of character, language, forms of government, arts, manners and religion; such collisions and conflicts; such breaking in pieces of old systems, and springing into life and vigor of new ones, would have filled him with astonishment and perplexity.

At first sight, and without the clue which Christianity gives, the history of the world looks like a chaos.   Empires arise, strong, well-compacted, splendid; they fill the world for a time with their renown; and then they are crushed by more powerful rivals, or are dissolved by their own weakness.   Conquest succeeds conquest, and change follows change, as the waves roll one after the other, and break and are lost upon the beach.

But is there no divine law to be discovered in these changes? Has there been no true progress in the vast and varied movements which history records?   Are we no nearer a goal than at the outset, or has mankind been going round and round the same weary road, like the horse grinding in the mill?   And must we believe that the world is doomed to a never-ending succession of cycles like those she has gone through, new formations of society on the ruins of the old, new growths out of the soil of a perished vegetation? Are we, for instance, to build up a new American civilization, radically different from that which was transplanted here by our fathers from the old world, itself to be superseded in its turn by something newer in the revolutions of the ages?

This we know, that no nation, no age, has been the mere repetition of another. Each has had something peculiar to itself. And it is not boastful to say that the civilization of the last three centuries is in some respects higher than had been known before, and this as the fruit of the labors of the preceding ages. We must believe that a divine purpose has been accomplished in all the changes through which man has passed. They have not been like the eternal roll of the ocean, issuing in nothing, reaching no haven, repeating from age to age its monotonous motion and roar; but rather like the course of the stream, which, though it may wind hither and thither, and sometimes may seem to flow back upon itself, and though its waters may partly stagnate in the swamp, or be swallowed up in the sands of the desert, yet has a living current still, which rests not till it finds its way to the ocean. And our object in the present Article is to show that the past ages of the world's history have not followed each other in blind succession, but have been linked together in a divine order, and that there has been a real progress towards the great end for which all things were made, the bringing in of the kingdom of God. We shall seek, especially, to prove that the great historical nations before the Christian era did not exist in vain, and that it was truly in "the fulness of times," in that ripe time for which all preceding ages and events had been the necessary preparation, that Christ was born into the world. There is a process of education for the race as truly as for the individual, and in obedience to the same great laws. There is an order which God observes in the training of mankind answering to that which regulates the development of infancy into manhood.

The spiritual powers and faculties of man may be divided for our present purpose into the moral and the intellectual, and the latter class again into the imagination (with which we associate the reason in its highest natural form as the organ of intuitive truth) and the understanding.   The moral powers imply conscience, or the faculty which discerns between right and wrong ; and faith, which lays hold of truths that belong to the invisible and supernatural realm.   In a well ordered system of education, these are the first to be awakened and cultivated.   It is found that if the moral training of a child be neglected, it is almost impossible to supply the defect in after years.   We must begin early to awaken the conscience, and to enlighten it that it may distinguish the good from the evil, the false from the true.   We must from the start seek to develop those ideas of God and immortality, of freedom and responsibility, without which man were no better than the brutes, and which lie wrapped up in our spiritual constitution as our very birthright.   Moral culture should always precede intellectual.   The foundation for the noblest character is laid in the quick discernment of moral distinctions, the strong feeling of obligation, the spirit of obedience, the purity which shrinks from a stain, and the early reception of those great spiritual mysteries which the heart of a child can lay hold of in faith, though no created intellect can fully comprehend them.   Every wise system of education recognizes this principle and is constructed upon it ; in every well ordered family it is put into practice.   The Christian mother teaches her child to have faith in a being whom it can not hear, nor see, nor understand, and calls out its feelings of love and adoration towards him, long before she would task its faculties with a problem in arithmetic, or try to make it relish the beauties of a poem.

Next after the conscience, the imagination and the reasoning powers are developed.   The one is the mind's faculty of picture-making, which shows itself very early in childhood in the transforming and coloring of the objects around it ; as when the girl sees a queen beautiful as Cleopatra in her misshapen doll, and the boy a palace in his cobhouse, and a war horse in the stick which he bestrides.   The imagination does not rest satisfied with the every-day world, nor much trouble itself about the literal truth of things.   It uses these as suggestive of something higher and more wonderful.   The mountain path, that turns away from the beaten highway, may, to the mind of the child, lead to Tyre or Babylon; and a distant hillside with its dark and shaggy forests may be the foreground and symbol of an unknown world.

A little later, and that faculty of the mind will be roused into activity which speculates on its own ideas, and is drawn to those sciences which are created by itself, such as the harmonies of numbers, the relations of the figures of geometry, and the laws of the human intellect. Youth and early manhood have always delighted in such intellectual exercises.

Afterwards comes the time for grappling with the real problems of life, the time for the understanding and the will to prove themselves in dealing with things as they are, and getting the mastery of the actual world. As youth ripens into manhood, realities take the place of dreams and speculations? from "cloudland" and the regions of the ideal, we come down to the solid earth, and build houses, and till our farms, and show our ingenuity in our workshops, and seek to guide, and rule, and bless the world. We give up theorizing, and become practical; action is henceforth the business of our lives.

We know that this is the order in which the human faculties are generally developed. And the same law has been observed in the history of the world. The preparation for Christianity was made chiefly in three nations, the Jews, the Greeks, and the Romans. It was in their languages that the title of Jesus as King of the Jews was written on his cross, as if to show that they, above all other nations, would have to do with the planting of Christianity. They were eminently the historical nations of antiquity, because from them alone has any permanent influence passed over to the modern or Christian ages. Babylon, Egypt, Assyria and Persia, have contributed nothing, or next to nothing, to the religion, or philosophy, or civilization of Christendom. They were outside of the true line of progress; it was not in them that the education of the world went forward. Whatever end they answered in the scheme of God's government was only for the time; nothing Babylonian, or Egyptian, or Assyrian, has entered as a perceptible element into our institutions, or laws, or modes of thinking.

The Jews were selected and separated from all other nations

to receive a moral and spiritual training, such as should be suitable to the people amongst whom the Son of God was to be born. A narrow strip of land along the southeastern coast of the Mediterranean was given them, not well situated for commerce or for conquest, nor so rich as to tempt to indolence, but fruitful in the best productions of the temperate zone; a land of hills, and valleys, and springs of water, of bold mountains, and broad and fertile plains, suitable to the vine and the olive, and to the pasturage of flocks and herds; and separated from Egypt and the region of the Euphrates by sandy deserts, and from Syria by the mountain-chains of Lebanon, and so a fit country for a people who were to dwell alone, and not to be mixed up with the surrounding nations. They were to be kept apart, like children at school, that their education might not be interfered with. For the end which God aimed at was not to train up a warlike people who should march through the world, trampling it into submission, nor a commercial people whose fleets should whiten every sea, nor an intellectual people who should excel in art, and science, and philosophy, but a people who should live by faith in the unseen God, the creator and governor of men, and in whom the moral affections should blossom and bear fruit. Their history is to be read in the light of this idea; otherwise, it is unintelligible. But if we bear in mind that it was the conscience and the spiritual faculties of man that were to be educated, and this in the infancy of the race, we shall see the necessity of the supernatural interpositions of divine power which marked their progress, and the wonderful wisdom of the system of laws under which they were placed.

The great danger of the ancient world was the being brought into bondage to nature, which they saw lying all about them and above them in its vastness and beauty, full of productive and destructive energies; now winning them by its bounty and its soft caresses, as in the flowers and fruits of summer, and the gentle gales of spring; and now overwhelming them by its terrors, as in the storm and the earthquake. All the nations of antiquity, save the Jews, yielded to the mighty spell; and they would have yielded but for the power and severity of God's discipline. All of them idolized nature in some of its elements and powers, and under some of the many symbols by which these were expressed. The Persians looked with adoration upon the sun, glorious in his brightness, from whose golden fountain the light that gladdened and the heat that fructified the earth flowed forth in endless streams. The Egyptians saw in animals the representatives of the unseen forces of nature, and to these they paid their worsh'p; while the Greeks, excelling all others in artistic skill, carved, out of the marble, images full of majesty and grace, and brought offerings and incense to their shrines. From all these, and from every other form of nature and creature worship, the Jews were to be kept. They were to have no object of worship but the living God, who is above nature, and may never be confounded with it; the eternal Spirit, by whose will the creation was brought forth, and by whose wisdom and power it is guided and sustained.

This being the end of God's dealings with them, what a fitness do we see in all the steps of their history! When the time arrived for them to enter on their national existence, they were slaves in the mightiest kingdom of the world. A wild and trackless desert, without food or water for such a multitude, separated them from the promised land. They were without laws and institutions, except of the simplest kind, such as masters might allow to a subjugated race. It needed some extraordinary interposition to emancipate them from bondage, conduct them in safety across that inhospitable wilderness, and plant them in their own country an organized nation, capable of fulfilling all the functions of national life. In the ordinary course of events, this would have been impossible to an ignorant and undisciplined people, whose manhood had been well nigh crushed out of them by oppression. Hence the necessity for that succession of stupendous miracles which accomplished and accompanied their deliverance. An unseen hand dealt the strokes of judgment which broke every fetter; an unseen hand opened a path through the Red Sea, brought water out of the rock, and made the heavens to rain down bread; and the same unseen hand gave to them from Sinai laws and a national constitution, and bound together that confused and timid multitude into a well-ordered host. Their first national lesson was that the power, in whom they were to trust, was outside of the world

and independent of it.   And so they were led into the depths
of a savage desert, far down between the two arms of the
sea ; and there, amidst the wildest and most terrible desolation, as of the earthquake and the volcano, and from the
summit of a mountain wrapped in mingled darkness and fire,
and trembling to its foundations under its creator's footsteps,
they received that national code, the holiness and righteousness
of which were worthy of its sublime delivery.   Its moral superiority over all other ancient systems of laws was well nigh
immeasurable.   No other code was ever so just, so pure, so
merciful as this.   None ever defended the family by such strong
bulwarks from disorder and pollution, or so mitigated the hardships of servitude, or made such generous provision for the
widow and orphan, or so guarded from abuse the administration of justice.

But its great power lay in this, that it reached to the roots of
the conscience, and brought the inward as well as the outward
life into subjection to itself.   It educated and disciplined the
moral faculties of the people, and made them feel the fundamental, eternal distinction between right and wrong, as no other
nation of antiquity did.   This gave them their noblest national
characteristics.   They did not excel in the arts and sciences ;
they had no painting, no sculpture, no philosophy.   Their glory
lay in their purity of life, their moral integrity, their lofty faith,
their strength of manhood, their wisdom outrunning logic, and
those depths of love and tenderness which ofttimes opened
themselves in their rude life like springs of water among the
rocks.   Men of finer intellectual culture, of larger and more
varied accomplishments, were reared in Greece and Rome, but
no where did humanity, the man within the man, blossom in
such beauty, and bear such fruits of noble action.   Where shall
we find a statesman and leader of the people, to be compared
with the great Hebrew lawgiver?   One so disinterested and
self-sacrificing, so patient in bearing with the caprices and perverseness of the people, of such penetrating sagacity and far-
reaching and lofty aims, and with such power of organizing
men, and bringing them under the dominion of law?   We are
accustomed, and justly, to speak with admiration and reverence
of our Washington's farewell address to his countrymen ; but

let any man read the last of the five books of Moses, which
contain his parting counsels to the people whom he had been
guiding for forty years, and say whether lessons of deeper political wisdom, or warnings of truer patriotism, ever fell from
a statesman's lips.   And take, as another specimen of the rich
and noble character of the old Hebrews, that sweet singer,
warrior, and king, all in one, whose songs have been chanted
in Jewish temple and Christian cathedral for more than three
thousand years, and have stirred more hearts with joy, and
comforted more sorrowing spirits, than all the poetry of the
world besides.   There was a man as bold and adventurous as
one of the knights of old, winning his place as the great champion of his country in the very bloom and tenderness of his
youth, yet loyal to his king to the last, though hunted by him
from rock to wilderness as the foresters hunt the wolf, and
lamenting over his death in that plaint of sorrow in which all
remembrance of injury is swallowed up in shame and grief that
the beauty of Israel has been slain, and the shield of the mighty
vilely cast away ; a man who bound his friends to him with a
love passing the love of woman, and who, saving one great
crime which he sorrowed for with as great a repentance, filled
a long life of the wildest viscissitudes with all that was heroic
in war, and gentle in domestic life, and merciful in rule : while
his harp ran from depth to height through all the compass of
human feelings, and breathed forth its divine melodies for all
generations.

And what glimpses do we get here and there of the social
life of the Hebrews, vales of greenness and beauty lying em-
bosomed amidst much that was stern and savage !   Who, in
reading the story of Ruth, has not wished that he might have
lived amongst a people where all hearts were moved towards
the widow returning from her long exile, where the poor
gleaned in the harvest field after the reapers, and such mutual
love and respect bound together all ranks and classes, that the
rich man met his laborers with the salutation, "The Lord be
with you," and was answered by them, "The Lord bless thee,"
and where poverty was not considered a reproach ?

But we have said enough to show what purity and nobleness
of life were the fruit of those old Hebrew institutions, and that

the cultivation of the moral powers was one great end for which they existed as a nation. A people were thus prepared amongst whom Christ could be born and educated for his work. In no other country could a holy virgin have been found worthy to be the mother of the Lord, and to have the training of his infancy and childhood; nor national institutions and forms of worship suitable to be the moulds of his human character and earthly life.

We come next to speak of the Greeks. On the north side of the Mediterranean, there runs far up into the land the Ægean Sea, studded with countless islands, and bordered on either side by a deeply indented coast. The air is pure and exhilarating, the sky most often a cloudless blue, and the temperature that which most braces up the body and the mind. Even more than Palestine, it was broken by mountain ranges which gave endless diversity to its scenery, blending grace and majesty in every form of exquisite combination. Its physical character was such as to give the highest stimulus to the activities of the people. A bright and sunny land, with a climate neither stern nor enervating, it was well suited to awaken and give scope to their intellectual energies, which also worked the more intensely from the number of small commonwealths that naturally arose from the nature of the country broken into many distinct parts, suggesting and easily leading to political divisions. The Greeks never formed one nation, except for a brief time under Alexander the Great, and that was after their noblest triumphs had been won. Each considerable city with the territory around it formed an independent state, and there was no stagnating under the overshadowing despotism of a huge central power. The Greeks were, physically and intellectually, the noblest race which the world ever saw. Noble in form, athletic, full of grace in every movement, they were unrivalled in all the manly games and exercises which at once task and increase the strength and agility of the body. Their language was never equalled in flexibility, richness and melody; the philosopher found it adequate to express his subtlest distinctions, and the poet to give to his loftiest imaginations "a local habitation and a name." And never were a people more quick-witted and versatile, more thoroughly trained to every intellectual exercise, or more ready to appreciate every beauty of thought, and every grace of utterance in their great orators. The arts and literature of Greece were the noblest fruit of mere intellect that the world has given birth to. The mind of man seems to have reached there the utmost limit of its capacities, apart from the truths and influences of Christianity. More subtle reasoners than Aristotle on every problem of logic, and ethics, and the philosophy of the mind ; more lofty thinkers than Plato ; more delightful historians in simple and charming narrative than Herodotus, or of greater power in condensed portraiture than Thucydides ; or poets in whose majestic verse the whole outward world lies more truly and gracefully mirrored than in Homer, we shall not probably see again. Greece became the home of beauty in all the forms of art. You saw it in the porticoes and cornices of temples and museums, in statues which wore the ideals of the human form, and in the daily life of the people, in drapery, attitude and movement ; and you felt it in the music of the language, not only as it flowed from some master's lips, but as you heard it in the streets and from the laborers of Athens. The cycle of Grecian history was especially marked by intellectual development. Inferior to the Jew in moral integrity, in purity of life, and in the faith of things unseen, the Greek had a far higher culture. His language was better fitted to be the vehicle of Christianity, for it was more the language of reasoning. The Hebrew was not fitted for argumentation, such as Paul uses in his Epistles, but for the simplest narrative, for epigrammatic writings like the Proverbs, and for lyric poetry like the Psalms and the prophets. The Greek, therefore, was chosen to be the language of the New Testament ; and one of the providential ends for which Greece existed was to prepare this noble instrument for the service of the church. At the time of our Lord's birth, Greek was spoken very generally throughout the civilized world. The conquests of Alexander had spread the knowledge of it to the farthest east, and it is now held by some of the best scholars that it became the common language of the Jews, and was used by Christ and his disciples. The Greeks could not give to the Lord his birthplace and his training ; that was an honor belonging to the Jews ; but they gave to Christianity the language in which its glad tidings were first carried forth, and by which its earliest triumphs were won.

But besides the conscience and the pure intellect, there is in man the understanding or the faculty of adapting means to ends, which, when joined to an energetic will, is the practical part of our nature. This found its highest development amongst the Romans, a people whose forte was not speculation but action, beyond any other nation of antiquity. The Italian peninsula, on the western side of which, not far from the Mediterranean, the city of Rome was founded by a band of robbers, if we may credit the old traditions, when Greece was fast rising to the heights of its civilization, was well situated to be the seat of a great empire. By sea it had easy access to almost every part of the then known world, while the Appenines so far cut it off from communication by land with the rest of Europe, as to serve as a barrier against the northern barbarians, thus giving the Romans time gradually to consolidate their institutions. Nor were there any such natural divisions of the country as in Greece, breaking it up into distinct and separate territories not easily bound together under one government. It is one of the mysteries of humanity how diversities of national character originate; but we know that they are as striking and permanent as the diversities of expression in the human face. The Romans were raised up to conquer and to rule. Their mission was to subdue the world, and to bring it under the dominion of stable law. A robust, truth-telling, straightforward people, they conquered one nation after another in fair fight, and when they had conquered them, they legislated for them, and established one uniform code through the empire. They had as great a genius for legislation as for war. It has been well said that

"The Roman law grew into such perfection with the progress of the nation that at last it civilized a world, and its principles outlived that fabric of society, and are recognized still, even where its forms and perhaps its very name are forgotten. The laws of the Greek legislators are cabinet curiosities, and no more. They formed nothing beyond their own short-lived republic. The reason of the difference is that while the one was created as a whole by the effort of one man's thought and diligence [a product of the pure intellect], the other was evolved by time, and sprung up with the living plant of human society, existed for the wants and exigencies which actually occurred, and therefore was profitable in its principles and most of its provisions, for all the exigencies to which all human societies must to the end of the world be liable." [1]

It was because their turn of mind was more practical, and they knew better how to deal with things as they are, that they so far surpassed the more intellectual Greeks in the framing of laws.   They adapted them with greater wisdom to the circumstances of each case, and did not strike out systems at a heat, as the chemist experiments in his laboratory.   They excelled in what the English call round-about common sense, the faculty which takes large and just views of things, looks at them on all sides, and will have nothing to do with mere theories.   Their language was simple, strong, austere, fit for plain and true men, not so good for poetry and philosophy, but the very language of legislation and war.   Cæsar's *Veni, vidi, vici*, was never surpassed in brevity and force.

The work which the Romans were raised up to do was not so much in the world of ideas, in the region of the intellect, like the Greeks, as in this matter-of-fact, every-day world of ours ; no fine play of the imagination, or excursion of the reason, but downright, sturdy blows as with an iron hammer, to break in pieces the barriers which kept the nations apart, and so to prepare a highway for the Lord.   It was to make distant lands accessible to Christianity by binding them together into one empire, and subjecting them to wholesome laws.   It was to tame and refine the barbarian tribes, and extend the blessings of peaceful and well-ordered society into regions where the cruelties of savage warfare had been unrestrained.   And so through seven centuries they went on conquering nation after nation, till their dominion reached from the Atlantic to the Euphrates, and embraced almost every country that has been famous in history. And where they conquered they civilized.   They filled every land with works of lasting utility.   Massive bridges, the arches of which survive to this day, were thrown across rivers as distant from Rome as the Tagus and the Danube.   Broad highways, built on foundations of solid granite, reached from the

[1] Sermons by the Rev. William Dow.

Forum to the most distant frontiers. Aqueducts, parts of which still remain unimpaired, conveyed water to all the chief cities and towns ; and public baths contributed to the health and enjoyment of the people. The Romans have been well called the Anglo-Saxons of antiquity, for they showed the same practical talent, and the same unflinching courage and perseverance, which have made of foggy England a terrestrial Paradise, and are fast transforming our own wildernesses into fruitful fields.

Such was the three-fold preparation for the introduction of Christianity, and can any one believe that it was not with divine forethought and purpose that the birth of the Son of God into the world was delayed until the divine institutions and training given to the Jews had prepared a people amongst whom he could find fit entrance, and Grecian intellect had provided a language in which the new Gospel could be carried forth, and Roman conquest and legislation had thrown the world open to apostles and evangelists? Who can help seeing in these three great cycles of history, a wonderful providential arrangement to prepare for and to facilitate that mighty change in human affairs which was to be the effect of the Incarnation?

At length, when all was ripe for it, that great event, for the sake of which the heavens and the earth had been brought forth, and which had been the goal of all human history, was accomplished. *God was made man.* The second person in the adorable Godhead was born into the world in the true nature of our race, and linked his own interests and destinies indissolubly with those of humanity. He passed through all the experiences and changes of human life, and gave therein the first example of unspotted holiness in fallen manhood. By his expiatory death, he blotted out sin and reconciled the world unto God, making peace through the blood of his cross ; and by his resurrection from the dead, he redeemed the body from the curse, and opened a new and endless career of blessing for man. He was then exalted into the glory from which he had come forth, but not as he came forth ; for he came as the Son of God, but he returned as the Son of man, carrying the nature which he had redeemed from its ruin to be glorified in indissoluble union with the Godhead. And from the throne of glory in which manhood, in his person, was thus crowned with

honor and invested with dominion, he sent down the Holy
Ghost, to be the link of union between himself in the heavens
and his disciples on the earth, and to convey to all that would
receive him the fruits of his wonderful work and victory.

Christianity is the product of two facts : the Incarnation, and
the giving of the Holy Ghost. By the first, including in it all
the acts and events of our Lord's personal history, the human
nature and, potentially, the human race were redeemed ; by
the second, the blessed results of this redemption were, actually, communicated to believing men. These transactions were
the most stupendous of all history, and their effects upon mankind could not but be most transforming and ennobling. A
new peace and joy took possession of man's heart when he
knew that he was forgiven through the blood of Jesus. There
was a new hope born for him out of the grave of the risen
Christ. A new feeling of love and pity entered into his spirit,
when he saw the love of God toward his enemies manifested
in the cross of his Son. New possibilities of holiness were
disclosed to him in the spotless life of the Man of Nazareth,
tempted in all points like as we are, and foregoing every advantage of his Godhead in his perilous warfare, because he
must fight lawfully, as man, and not as God ; but ever prevailing to present his entire humanity a spotless offering unto his
Father.

The world had never before seen such an example of self-
sacrificing love, and lowly humility, and willing obedience ; and
a new life was breathed into men, which had power to overturn the old foundations of society, and rebuild it anew after the
law of a new creation. But we can do no more than sketch in
mere outline the characteristics of the Christian cycle, and this
chiefly as they are connected with the social and political life of
Christendom. When the church entered upon her work, she
had to deal with, and appropriate to her use, the three elements
which we have described, not by any wholesale transplanting
into her own realm of Jewish institutions, and Greek philosophy, and Roman laws, she being a purely spiritual organization,
in the world, but not of it ; but by taking up into herself, and
subjecting to her own higher laws, whatever of good the world
had thus far been able to produce. Springing into life in the

bosom of Judaism, Christianity retained all its purity of morals, its spirit of order and reverence, and its strength of faith. The sacred books of the Hebrews became the sacred books of the church. Their songs were sung in her worship, and the words of their prophets were the theme of her teachings. Then she conquered to her service the acuteness and culture of the Greek intellect, and the treasures of its philosophy, using them in developing her doctrines and defining her faith with such skill that the Eastern church has left us, as one has well said, "a metaphysic at once Christian and scientific, every attempt to improve on which has hitherto been found a failure." And on the other hand the Western church inherited the genius for legislation and rule which had characterized the Roman Republic and Empire, and showed equal firmness of purpose and power of organizing men in carrying on her spiritual (alas! that they should have become in later ages her worldly) conquests.

Christianity could not save the Roman Empire, although its effects upon society were great and wonderful. It infused the element of mercy into legislation, gave new dignity to man as man through that common relationship to Christ into which rich and poor, the monarch and the slave, alike were brought within the church, and so it gradually loosened the bonds and mitigated the evils of slavery. But the corruption of the Empire was too far gone when the church entered upon her work, for the building up of a true Christian national life. It was like grafting a vigorous scion into a decayed and worn-out stock. She needed better materials than those effete nations, enervated by luxury and vice. And such were brought to her in those German or Gothic tribes which came pouring forth from their northern fastnesses in the fifth and sixth centuries, and shattered the old civilization to its centre. Savage they were in their manners, and cruel and vindictive in their feelings, but a strong, resolute, and untainted race, truthful and honest, holding woman in respect, and even reverence, and guarding jealously the sanctity of marriage. These were the new materials which the breaking up of the old Roman Empire furnished to the church; and out of them, she reared, step by step, through centuries of toil and strife, and not without many and great failures of her own, the wonderful structure of Christian society.

Christianity has given freedom to nations, and made despotism, as we see it in the oriental world, all but impossible. This it has done by introducing the counterpoising spiritual authority of the church, and thus making kings to feel their responsibility to One higher than themselves. It is probable, too, that the principle of representation, one of the great safeguards of popular liberty, was learned from the church, in which the election of the clergy has been, more or less, a law and usage from the first. In the very beginning, the Christian people chose their deacons, to whom the collecting of her revenues, and the dispensing of them to the poor, were committed; and there is a remarkable analogy between them and the lower house, or third estate, in most European countries, and in our own, which is looked on as the proper representative of the people, and to which the origination of money bills belongs. No Christian king or governor could be as absolute as a Pagan monarch, because he was continually confronted by a spiritual authority higher than his own. Henry VIII., ferocious despot as he was, was not so despotic as he would have been had there been no Latimers bold enough to give the monarch a New Testament with the leaf turned down at the words, "Thou shalt not commit adultery."

Another fruit of Christianity has been to give to family life a sanctity, dignity, order and joyousness which it had not even amongst the Jews. The true meaning of marriage was first fully disclosed when the Son of God incarnate entered on the work of redeeming and forming his church. Then it was seen that the earthly relationship was a symbol of a mightier mystery, the union between Christ and the bride whom he had ransomed by his blood, and with whom he would share the glory of his kingdom. In the church alone can woman be brought into her true position. It is as representing the wife of the Lamb, that she attains her true dignity as the beloved and honored partner of man, to whom she is yet subordinated as the church to Christ. Polygamy died out as Christianity came in, not so much from any express command, as because it is at war with the whole spirit of the Christian religion. One wife for one husband, is the expression and counterpart of the one church wedded by indissoluble bonds to the one Lord and Saviour. The beauty and blessedness of the family, as seen in Christian lands, are the fruit of the light which Christianity threw upon its relationships, and of the new and divine life imbreathed into them. These acquired a higher meaning, and became guarded by more sacred sanctions, and were made channels of deeper and purer joys, where the church faithfully did her work.

The influence of Christianity on the intellectual culture of Christendom has been scarcely inferior to its moral and spiritual influences. The building up of literature and art, though not the direct aim of the church, has been the indirect result of her labors. Christianity has to do with the whole being and life of man. It has the profoundest truths to present to the understanding, the most moving appeals to address to the affections and conscience, and the sublimest mysteries, and the most majestic symbols to stir and guide the imagination. Every part of our humanity is ennobled by it. It is not surprising, then, that as soon as it found a suitable vehicle in the languages which gradually grew up out of the ruins of the empire, and favoring circumstances in the condition of the newly formed states, it should have produced a literature deficient, it may be, in form, as compared with the Greek and Roman, but immeasurably surpassing them in depth and power, in the range of its ideas, and in the purity of its spirit. Homer may have pictured the outer world, and the movements of man's external life, whether in the council-chamber, in the banqueting hall, or on the battle-field, with greater distinctness and vividness than Milton; but who would think of putting them on the same level as to the thoughts which wander through eternity? Or could the dramas of Shakespeare have been the product of any but a Christian land? Is not Christianity the hidden root of what is noblest and most beautiful in that wilderness of life which his imagination has created? Could such forms of character have existed any where but in the bosom of Christian society? But it is not our purpose to dwell on this.

The Christian cycle is the last in the world's progress this side of the resurrection and the kingdom of God. It is the preparation for the true *novus ordo sæclorum*, in which the whole groaning creation is to find deliverance from its bondage, under the manifested rule of Him who became man that in him the Creator and the creature might be made one forever.   The Jewish, Greek, and Roman cycles existed to prepare the way for his first advent into the world, and for the subsequent gathering of his church; the Christian cycle exists to make ready for his second and glorious advent, when he shall judge the world in righteousness, and cause the prayer to be fulfilled, "Thy kingdom come; thy will be done in earth, as it is done in heaven."   Christ will be the second Adam of the new creation, and he will have a second Eve, the counterpart of her whom God formed out of the flesh and bones of Adam, and brought to him to be the partner of his dominion.   The gathering and training of the church to be the mystical bride of the Lamb, is the one great work of the present cycle or dispensation; and the next thing in order will be the setting-up of the kingdom of God in the earth, and the administering of its rule by this royal company.   Not the subjugation of the world to Christ, but the taking out of an election for him, is the work which God has now in hand.   This is the key to the otherwise insolvable riddle of Christian history.   The early falling away of the church, and her continual failures can be accounted for only on the principle that this is not the time for the glory of the Lord to fill the earth, even as the earthly and mortal life of Jesus was not the time for him to set up his kingdom.   Those who are to reign with him, must be trained and disciplined for their royal dignity by experiences of toil and sorrow such as he himself underwent.   The law of the present dispensation is: "They that live godly in Christ Jesus shall suffer persecution"; "If we suffer with him, we shall also reign with him"; "In the world ye shall have tribulation."

This great truth as to the end for which the Christian cycle exists, must be borne in mind if we would meet the infidel objection that Christianity is a failure.   It is a failure, if it has no other immediate purpose than to civilize and christianize the whole world.   But if its purpose is, as St. James declared in the council at Jerusalem, to take out from the gentiles a people for his name, it is not a failure.   It has prevailed to gather an innumerable company out of almost all the families of the earth, by whom, in the next age or cycle of human history, the rule of God shall be administered, and his blessings dispensed, and the promised destiny of humanity shall be gloriously realized.

The greatest strength of infidelity at the present time, lies in its promise of a golden age, conjoined with the manifest weakness and perplexities of the church.   Men are turning away from that which has so little power to mitigate the evils everywhere pressing upon human society, and opening their hearts to the lie of the tempter, "Ye shall be as gods," which promises a paradise to the disobedient.   Humanity, weary of waiting for redemption from him who will not deliver from curse where he can not wash away sin, and where he is not suffered to rule, is striving to be its own redeemer.   Christianity is being rejected as effete.   It has accomplished its work, and its day is over.   A new Gospel, sweeter in its accents to the ear of fallen man, with no harsh and discordant notes of sin and curse to mar its melody, is sounding forth throughout all Christendom. "God has deceived you," is the serpent's plea with the disheartened nations; "his methods of blessing have miserably failed; trust in him no longer, but follow me, and I will lead you to the paradise you seek."   And they are following him.

Lusting after a larger liberty than God would give them, and drunken with self-conceit, they are sweeping away the restraints of the old Christianity, and beginning to reconstruct society after their own lawless devices.   The corruptions of the church have given too much occasion to this infidel work of destruction, and it is in those lands where her failure has been the greatest, that she is now exposed to the most imminent peril.

But in every country, and especially in those which are most highly civilized, the faith and institutions of Christianity are being thrust aside to make room for the doctrines and schemes of the fallen intellect; and there are already foreshadowings (as in Mormonism and Spiritualism) of a still darker day, when all that has upon it the stamp and sanction of God shall be supplanted by the ordinances of hell.   St. Paul (2 Thess. 2) gives warning of the revelation of the Man of Sin, the Lawless One, whose coming shall be "after the working of Satan, with all power and signs, and lying wonders"; and in whom the rejection of God and the deification of humanity shall be consummated, for he shall exalt himself above every thing that is called God, and shall sit in the temple of God, pointing himself out as God. This is a form of wickedness beyond the abuses of the Papacy, though this, by its corruption of Christianity, has prepared the way for it. To exaggerate and distort truth, or to adulterate and defile it, have been the sins of past generations; but the crowning act of rebellion will be the utter rejection of all that comes from God and testifies of Christ. There is a double duty resting on the church at this time, to stand up for every divine truth and ordinance which have come down to us from the beginning, and to put to shame the lying promises of the infidel by the full exhibition of the glorious hope of the Gospel. The highest measure of blessing attainable in the present dispensation must be the fruit of Christianity filled with the life and power with which it entered on its heavenly mission, and holding with clear insight and unyielding grasp "the faith once delivered to the saints"; but the utmost perfection of humanity can only be reached in the resurrection at the coming of the Risen One, and in the glory of the kingdom which follows it. The first aim of the enemy is to get rid of what Christ has already done for man in his cross and from his throne; the next will be to put an usurper in his place. The rejection of all authority professing to be derived from God and his anointed Son, whether in church or state; the denial of inspiration to the Scriptures; the decrial of the mysteries of Christianity; the elimination of the supernatural element from revelation; the relaxing of the marriage tie; the magnifying of the rights of fallen man, apart from the redemption that is in Christ; and lax views of sin and of expiation, are unmistakable tendencies of the present age, and are ominous of a time when, for the full manifestation of human wickedness before its utter overthrow, ungodliness shall, for a little season, be allowed to triumph. But the purpose of God shall stand, and the earth, which he has promised to his Son for a possession, shall see his salvation, and be filled with his glory.   The present cycle of its history shall not come to an end till it has furnished to Christ the full number of his elect, and that which shall follow it shall bring rest and peace to the sore-burdened creation.

ARTICLE IV.

THE MEETINGHOUSE AND THE MINISTRY.

THE practical power of the church is to be developed, very largely, in connection with two central ideas, viz., the meetinghouse and the ministry.   The meetinghouse, as the home and muster-room of God's people, where they are to come for comfort as well as for discipline in their heavenly work, and the ministry, as the living and authorized instructors of his people into the labors and responsibilities of their high calling. The local church must needs have, on the one hand, its house of worship, and, on the other, its acknowledged head and guide to press forward its appropriate work.

How shall the meetinghouse answer its highest uses, and how shall the ministry best accomplish its design?

It is not proposed to answer these questions fully, but if we may submit a few observations that may help in their solution, in however slight a degree, we shall do all that we anticipate.

And at the outset, it seems necessary that we form a clear and precise idea of the meetinghouse; for the idea, whatever it is, will determine not a little the uses that we make of it. There are two passages of Scripture which may aid us to a just conception of the vital thing we seek, the first in the Old Testament, the second in the New : "My house shall be called of all nations a house of prayer," "Compel them to come in that my house may be filled."   Taking these as our guide, it would be essential to a proper idea of the meetinghouse, that God's ownership should inhere in it.   "My house" is the term which the Scriptures employ on this subject. It is not only a house built generally for religious purposes, and specially controlled by religious people, but it is a house in which God's ownership is so involved that it can not be alienated to other purposes than his service and worship. The Scriptures never teach differently from this; at the same time the history of the meetinghouse demonstrates that the primary and prevailing idea of it has been that it is God's and not man's.

In this regard, the temple may be taken as the representative house of its kind. Its sacred character was never questioned, and the ownership of it was vested in God, both because it was built under the divine direction, and because it was forever consecrated to his worship. If it belonged to the nation of Israel in a peculiar sense, it was simply because the nation accepted and held it in trust for God. Solomon was not more divinely moved and commissioned to build "an house unto the Lord," than he was to dedicate it to him by solemn prayer and sacrifice. There was no fiction, and no pretense in that transaction. The house was really and entirely given to God. And so abiding was his presence there, that no man might enter it without careful ceremonial washings; the common people into the outer courts, the priests within the temple, and, once a year, the high priest into the Holy of Holies. No man in Israel ever dreamed that the temple belonged to any body but the Lord, or that the rights of one man in its blessings and privileges could be superior to those of another. The king and the beggar met there together, and neither could claim any advantage on account of his worldly position. And not only the Jew, but every man of every nation who would keep the law, and who would worship God, had a right to come to his house. Within its hallowed walls there were no distinctions of birth or wealth. Rich and poor were invited to the same provisions of grace. In their Father's house they were equals, and sharers alike in its infinite mercies and joys.

After the temple came the Jewish synagogue, answering a more limited, and somewhat local purpose, but just as strictly maintaining the idea of sanctity in its services, and of divine ownership in every stone and timber of its structure. It was built ordinarily for the accommodation of a town, or city, or district so remote from the temple that but occasionally they could avail themselves of its advantages.   It stood to the temple, very nearly in the relation of the chapel to the church, a smaller, easier, freer house, but no less sacred, and no less a house of the Lord.   It opened its doors to the stranger as to the Jew, and offered its blessings to all, on the simple ground that it belonged to the common Father of all.   And this idea that the house of worship was God's was never modified or limited among the Jews.   So simple and controlling was it that the Jew never attempted to make social distinctions in the house of God.   Come from what quarter he might, from traffic in remote cities, or from his vineyards, or his herds on the hills of Judea, or on the banks of the Jordan and the Euphrates, wherever he saw the synagogue, or whenever he came to the temple he recognized his Father's house, and claimed the privileges of a son.

The Christian meetinghouse of the first centuries, which took the place of these Jewish houses, adopted the idea of sacredness and of God's ownership without the slightest change. Neither the New Testament, nor the early Christian fathers furnish a hint that the house of worship was in any way secularized by a modification of its rites of worship.   With the introduction of Christianity the whole ceremonial of divine service was changed to forms simpler and more expressive, yet the object of worship remained the same, and holiness was still written upon his house.   The Christians of the first few centuries ever speak of the house of worship as God's, his peculiar property and dwelling.   It was reserved for modern times to speak of it in any other way.   It was an unheard of thing, until within the last century, that a Christian temple should not be absolutely the Lord's, and that it could ever be alienated to any secular use.   The cross, crowning the church, was the symbol of its consecration to God, and whenever the disciples saw it they recognized their home, and entered it as children of God. And, as in the temple, all were equal in God's sight, so, much more, in the Christian church there was neither bond nor free, male nor female, rich nor poor, but all were one in Christ.

And this idea of God's ownership in the house of worship has traversed all the Christian centuries, and has come down to us as fresh and vital, almost, as in the beginning. The Catholic meetinghouse, or church as they would call it, touches the meetinghouse of the first Christian ages, and has preserved with wonderful tenacity the original idea of the house of the Lord. In Catholic countries one could hardly fail to be impressed with the simplicity and power of this idea. In many of the larger churches, oftimes without seats, will be seen kneeling upon the pavement, side by side, the prince and the beggar. It is a most impressive lesson of the levelling of all human distinctions in the house of God. These houses, too, are open night and day, as if the common Father kept open doors, that his children might ever have access to his presence. In such houses there is not only nothing to suggest man's ownership, but man's ownership is expressly disclaimed; they are simply held by the church in trust for God. It matters not, therefore, where the devout Catholic may wander, to our own shores, or to the ends of the earth, wherever he sees the steeple, or the turret of a house, surmounted by the cross, he recognizes the house of God and the Christian's home. And without waiting for anybody's invitation, or saying, " by your leave," he goes inside, crosses himself with the holy water, and falls upon his knees in the nearest slip. O, what a power the church of Rome has in this simple idea that all her houses of worship are God's, and the homes of the faithful. It need not excite wonder that the Catholic clings so tenaciously to his church, when he finds a home in every house that bears the emblem of his faith.

In outlining this history of the meetinghouse, we next come to the English parish church. And split off, as it was, from the Romish church, it need surprise no one that it took away with it the original idea of the house of worship. The convulsion which tore the one from the other, left intact that fundamental principle of divine proprietorship in the sanctuary. If every man must pay his church rents, every man has equal right to church privileges. In this respect the noble has little advantage over the peasant. Both are beggars in the house of the Lord, and both are suppliants of a common mercy. There is no idea in the English mind that is more pervading and powerful than this. We are very confident that this fact goes far to account for the Englishman's love for his church, and for that subtle power which ever holds him true to her articles and forms. No man can come, thoroughly, under the influence of that idea without feeling its subduing and ennobling grace. Settle it that the meetinghouse is the Lord's, and that within its sacred walls human distinctions are merest shadows, and how you consecrate the brotherhood of man, and exalt the common nature of the race. Let the poor kneel beside the rich, the weak beside the strong, and both look up and say, "Our Father which art in heaven," and there will be melting of hearts, and blending of sympathies into fraternal oneness. And because the church of England, in her houses consecrated to God, teaches this prayer and this lesson to all her children, they guard her with sleepless jealousy, and hold her in ceaseless affection. And we shall see, that just as we weaken the idea that the meetinghouse is the Lord's, and the free and common home of the people of God, shall we lose power to draw the people within the sanctuary, and hold them loyal to our creeds and polity.

Up to this point, the idea of the meetinghouse is simple and uniform. The evidence is unvarying that it was accounted as God's and not man's. But we come now to the Puritan church, or the New England meetinghouse. And here, for the first time, we discover a contracting of the idea which, from the temple to the English church, obtained on this subject. The Puritan church was not so much the Christian's home, as the home of those who reared it. But still the old idea was not lost ; only a little obscured and narrowed. The house was still dedicated to God, and a high character of sacredness was still attached to it. It was built in such a way that all the people, within certain limits, had equal rights and privileges in it. Frequently it was built with funds provided in the original charter of the town, or else by a common tax upon the town, or precinct, for all the inhabitants within their borders. It was not till a much later day that a few persons, or a single individual, built and controlled a meetinghouse as they would a private dwelling, or a factory. The first meetinghouses of New England were without pews, most conclusive evidence that there could have been no distinctions of rich and poor inside of them. In time persons got leave to put in private seats for themselves

and their families. And, at length, the whole house was furnished with seats at the public expense. It was a long while
after this the churches and pews came to be owned and controlled by a few proprietors. In that early day, one citizen of
the town had the same right in the meetinghouse that another
had. And although the strict idea of God's house had somewhat departed, yet as a house open to all within the town,
without distinction, it was perfectly unlimited and free.

After the New England meetinghouse came the Methodist
chapel. The theory in regard to this was, not so much that
the ownership of it vested in God as in the Methodist denomination, and was to be used for Methodistical purposes. It preserved the original idea of the sanctuary only to this extent,
that it was absolutely free to all who chose to enter it for purposes of worship. For seventy five years Methodism kept open
houses. It had all things in common. It reserved no pews
for men of wealth and position. Wealth had its place in the
denomination, but no place in the house of worship. Here all
classes shared alike, and illustrated a practical equality before
God. Under this system the denomination went ahead with
unparalleled rapidity, far outstripping all other modern sects in
the race for denominational extension. And one must be blind
to evidence not to see that the free chapel had not a little to do
with this surprising success. And it is worth while to note,
that just so long as Methodism kept open house, it led the
other denominations, and its prosperity was unchecked. The
tide turned when the denomination began to imitate other bodies
that were building houses for themselves, owning their own
pews, and taking rent for sittings. And unless the denomination shall go back to the free chapel, we predict that all the
enthusiasm of its centennial year, and all the millions of its centennial fund, can not arrest the backward flow of its early
successes.

The modern meetinghouse of the different Protestant
churches, is the bane of Christianity. It is the property of the
parish, or of a few individuals combined into a society, and in
no sense belongs to the church, or is controlled by the church.
In a general way, it is built for religious purposes, but its
pews are bought, and sold, and rented like any other household

property.   Such houses are called houses of the Lord, and go
through a form of dedication to his service, but they are as
strictly owned by men, and admission to them secured for a
price, as a concert hall, or a lecture room.   They are not even
owned by the denomination, as the Methodist chapel was, and
used for the purposes of the denomination, but, at best, are
owned by individuals of the denomination, and are devoted to
individual interests and uses, so that one, as a member of the
same denomination, would feel no more liberty to enter one of
these houses unasked and unbidden, than he would to enter a
private dwelling.   What a departure from the original idea of
the house of the Lord!   What a mockery to God's children to
call it by such a name!   In the cities, especially, almost every
church employs a person, commonly called the sexton, an important part of whose duty, by some singular fiction, is said to
be the seating of strangers.   In reality, however, his duty is to
keep strangers and others out of the seats until the owners are
accommodated.   When this is done, those who have patiently
waited may be shown to a place.   But the whole transaction is
so ungracious that no person with any sense of delicacy, or propriety, will be willing often to repeat it.   If the meetinghouse
were God's and felt to be so, would not every Christian feel
such right to go within, as a child does to enter his father's
dwelling?   While the Catholic, or the Episcopalian, roam where
he may, finds a home wherever he finds his denomination, because the sanctuary is the Lord's, the Congregationalist, e. g.,
has no home out of his own town, and outside of his own
meetinghouse, because the sanctuary in which he worships belongs to men and not to God.   In all this there is not a trace
of the original idea of the church.   We have lost it as effectually as if we were living under a new dispensation.   And along
with the idea, it is not strange that we have lost, so generally,
the sacred associations, and so have ceased to feel the best and
highest power of the house of God.   Instead of giving it to
God, and making it open and free to all who would worship him,
we have rather made it common to such uses as the lecture, the
concert, the exhibition, until we have stripped it of almost the last
vestige of sacredness that may have lingered around it.   Is it
a surprising result that our houses are being emptied, and that

so many of the children are forsaking the denomination of their fathers? This process will go on until Ichabod is written upon our churches, or else we shall come back to the primitive idea, and build houses for God, and homes for his people.

In this country the tendency is to estimate all values by the standard of our decimal currency, as well men as things, as well character as principles. In the rawness of our national life this is not so surprising. With no nobility of blood, or rank, with no aristocracy of learning or genius, or fame, money has become the badge of distinction and honor. Our great man is the millionaire. The poet, the painter, the orator, the scholar, without money, are lacking the one thing to touch our hearts most deeply. No matter whether a man has mind, or character, or worthiness, so he has money he has a passport to the best society, and to the highest positions of trust and profit. And these men, finding their money so potent to secure preëminence everywhere else, can see no reason why it should not do it in the house of God. Even the Catholic and Episcopal churches among us are beginning to feel the pressure, and it is not at all certain that they will be able to withstand it. Indeed, there are signs of yielding already. For while they hold their churches, as God's, sacred, and forever consecrate to him, we learn that they are beginning to adopt the system of pew rentals like ourselves, and, in some cases, the ownership of their sittings. It is plain to see that the drift is in one direction. The meetinghouse, in this country, has broken from its moorings, is dragging its anchors upon a sea swept with storm and danger. We must bring it back to the old anchorage of the centuries, and fasten it with the old twisted cables with which God launched it in the beginning. It is not a human contrivance for which we plead. Nobody could have less confidence in any thing of that sort than we. But we plead for a divine idea, and a divine form, in the line of which, we believe, the success and the safety of our churches will be found.

And now, if we have given the true account of the meetinghouse, it is very plain that, as Congregationalists, the lesson has varied and important applications to us. Out of the meetinghouse grow all of the questions pertaining to a settled ministry, and to the establishment and maintenance of religious institutions at home and abroad.   Make the meetinghouse man's, and the ministry, in some sense, must be man's to correspond.   If the house is built with an eye to gain, the minister will be put into it for the same end.   That is, the minister will be chosen to sell the pews, and to sell them to the highest bidder.   And so, on the other hand, the minister will serve where there is the best pay.   Practically, therefore, ministerial talent will be in demand just in the ratio of its power to fill the house and profit the pew-holders, and it will be held and sold at just its market value in dollars and cents.   And then, too, on this principle, the meetinghouse would invite to its sittings not the poor, nor those, even, of moderate means, but the rich, who could pay large rents, so as to enhance, at once, the value of the house and the amount of its dividends. This process would not need to go on a great while before the churches would be left in possession of the rich, and the poor would be left outside.

If these statements seem too strong, let an appeal be made to the facts.   If what is called a first class pulpit is vacant, what sort of a man does it seek?   A man that will draw, that will sell the slips, that can attract the wealthy who can pay good rents.

And then, again, what sort of men seek such pulpits?   Just those who think they have the talent to draw, and who wish to share in the profits that may accrue.   A vacant pulpit of this kind will have its eye on about every attractive preacher of the denomination, not to say that all these preachers will be floating around that pulpit like moths around a candle.   A preacher of talent recently sought the good offices of a western gentleman to introduce him to a good pulpit, but was told that it was of no use, that there were ten men for every such pulpit, but that if he wanted to take an ordinary, or second class pulpit, he could introduce him to a hundred.

If the churches and the ministry come out of this ordeal unharmed, it will not be because the danger is not great and threatening.   It would seem the most natural result to be anticipated that the high moral tone which should ever characterize both would be gradually lowered to the common transactions of the street, and the market.   Fortunate will it be for both, if, having timely warning, they retrace their steps to the safe and solid ground of the fathers. But for the hour, the omens are not auspicious. The evil, it is to be feared, is rather increasing than diminishing, and where it is to end, the wisest can only conjecture. One thing, however, is certain, we are going in a wrong direction, and sooner or later, must meet disaster.

And the meetinghouse is almost wholly responsible for this state of things. It has made both ministers and churches fickle and uneasy. It is, at least, a singular coincidence that churches and ministers have been growing more restless, from the time the parish tax ceased to be assessed and collected by authority of the State. While the meetinghouse belonged to the town, nobody sought to make gain out of it, or thought of a minister to sell the pews. But when the meetinghouse and the support of the Gospel became voluntary, both were made articles of traffic, houses were built to rent, and ministers were sought to draw and pay. This is the simple account of the present condition of our Congregational churches.

It would seem the plainest dictate of reason, then, that we return to the old paths. We do not mean to the Puritan Fathers alone, but especially to the original, and, we believe, divine idea of the house of the Lord. We must rescue this from its secular uses and associations, and clothe it again with its sacred quality. Nothing but this will touch and hold the heart of our people. We are weak, because we have no places hallowed by the special presence of God. We shall continue to send out recruits to other denominations, whose ideas on this subject are better than ours, until we establish sacred centres around which the reverence and the love of our children shall perpetually revolve.

But this can not be done so long as we build churches as we do machine shops and stores. The only right way is to make the meetinghouse an out and out gift to God. No distinctions of birth, or rank, or wealth should be known within its consecrated walls. It should be free to all comers. Like the Gospel itself, it should invite all, who will, to partake of its privileges without money and without price. The spirit of our holy calling, as well as the nature of God's house, forbid the setting of a price on the preaching of the Gospel. We degrade the sanctuary when we open its doors with the same golden talisman with which we open the doors of the concert hall or the lecture room. Every Christian child has equal right in his Father's house, and none may determine for him what offering he shall bring to the altar.

No man, and no body of men, have a right to erect a house unto the Lord for "their set." God's house, in its very nature, can not be exclusive. And yet the fact is all the other way. There is just now a mania for fine churches. This is the natural result of our increasing wealth. A few men band together to build a splendid house for those on the same social plane. And then to pay the running expenses of it, such enormous rates are asked for the sittings that the poor are as effectually excluded as if a guard stood at the door to warn them back. Such houses may serve the ends of pride, but can never serve the purposes of our holy religion. What a burlesque on the words of our Saviour : "Unto the poor the Gospel is preached." Had we set ourselves to keep the Gospel from the poor we could hardly do it more successfully than we are now doing, by making it so expensive a luxury that only the rich can afford to enjoy it.

Nor do we mean by the poor, the absolutely destitute, but we include in this number thousands and thousands of mechanics and laborers, who, by economy make comfortable livings for themselves and their families, but have nothing to expend for luxuries. For this great working, thinking, middle class to take seats in our fashionable churches is out of the question. They can not afford it, it costs too much, the Gospel so preached is only for the rich.

It may be said, we know, that free churches have been tried, and have failed. It is enough to reply, not such churches as we plead for. In New York, some years since, there were opened a number of what were called free churches, but they did not succeed, and for the very best of reasons. The rich, with but a few noble exceptions, kept their places in the aristocratic churches, and left the free churches to the poor. Of course they failed, they ought to fail. God never meant to have the distinctions of rich and poor enter his house, least of all that they should occupy separate houses. It is bad enough to have "poor slips" in our churches, which nobody will occupy, but to build churches expressly for the poor is a crying shame to God and man. Our people are so educated into notions of independence, that they will never consent to be discriminated against in the house of God for what is, at best, their providential lot of wealth, or poverty. "A man's a man for a' that." So they will insist, and if there be no other remedy they will leave the churches to fashion, and folly, and pride. The prospect is simply appalling. If this process goes on for another generation, the middle and lower classes will be outside the house of God.

And all efforts that are now making in the direction of home evangelization by the churches, and the Young Men's Christian Associations, will not prevent, nor much hinder such a result. It is very well to carry the Gospel to the neglecters of the sanctuary, into the saloons, dance halls, upon the wharves or streets, or wherever they may be found. More or less interest will attend these efforts, and more or less good will be done. But no permanent hold will be taken upon this class, and no permanent inroads be made upon its numbers or strength, until they are gathered into the churches. The meetinghouse is an organizer, it must accompany the successful preaching of the Gospel any where, and in any place. A man, like Whitfield, may produce a great religious excitement, perhaps reformation, but without the meetinghouse to fix it and hold it, it would spend itself and be lost, like a wave on the sand. The meetinghouse is in the way of the evangelization of the masses. They will not come to it, if to be made to feel their lowlier lot, and to see how wealth claims place and puts on airs before God. We can not reach the masses without the meetinghouse, nor, as at present constituted, can we with it. When God's house is free, and the rich are willing to meet the poor on a common level, multitudes will crowd the gates of Zion.

We do not wish to convey the impression, however, that the poorer classes are all eager to attend public worship, for it is not true. Multitudes of them are not only indifferent, but they are haters of divine things. Nor do we wish to convey the impression that a large number of these absentees from the house of God are not able to pay for a sitting, and to attend worship if they chose.   For they are.   They are inexcusable for neglect.   They have a foolish, wicked, devilish pride almost. Nevertheless, this does not lessen the evil of their non-attendance, nor render our duty less plain to remove every obstacle which a departure from the divine models has thrown in their way.   We have made distinctions in the house of the Lord. Wealth has commanded advantages, and fashion and display have flaunted themselves in the faces of those in humbler circumstances until they have painfully felt their inferiority, and, as the easiest way to save their self-respect, have finally remained at home.   We do not justify this.   We are dealing with facts.   As Christian men, we are anxious to get at the source of the evil and remove it.   And our duty will not be done until we put public worship on to the ground where God puts it.   And nothing to us seems plainer than that this will not be until the meetinghouse is God's, and its doors are thrown open to the world.   And we have so much confidence in God's plan, that we do not believe failure is possible.

An illustration of this is found in the Methodist churches of Brooklyn, N. Y.   They have, we are told, some twenty houses open and free, thronged every Sabbath, and four or five owned by proprietors and rented, which have, on the same Sabbaths, a beggarly account of empty seats.   In Boston, Tremont Temple, open to all, is literally crammed two or three times on the Sabbath to overflowing, while her stately and exclusive churches can show, in the morning, a barely respectable congregation, but, in the afternoon, more vacant than filled seats. Tremont Temple is doing more to preach the Gospel to the floating and unsettled masses than any ten, very likely any twenty, wealthy churches in the city.   The tide of human life surges and rushes past these houses from sun to sun, every Sabbath day, but they have no power to arrest it, or to draw it inside.   Would they but throw open their doors, level human distinctions, and invite a desiring multitude to a free Gospel, the lips of the ministry would be touched with a new fire, and they would have power with God and with man.

But it seems to us that we have prosecuted this discussion far enough to see certain fixed facts, or principles, in regard to the meetinghouse, e. g. :

1. That it is God's and not man's.

2. That it is the free and common home of the people of God.

3. That it knows no classes with peculiar privileges.

Assuming that these are established principles, it would follow that men essay a divine prerogative who claim to own a house of worship, and who dare to rent it for purposes of gain. On the principles enumerated above, men are forbidden all traffic in God's house. They may neither sell its privileges, nor may they exclude any from participating in them. They are merely trustees of the sanctuary, and are bound to administer it impartially to all classes, or they incur the divine displeasure. [See James, 2d chapter.]

But what right have Christian men to provide nice little snuggeries for themselves and their families, while the great outside world, orphaned and homeless, is drifting to the pit? "Go ye into all the world, and preach the Gospel to every creature," is their royal commission. They are debtors to the Greek and to the barbarian, to the wise and to the unwise, to give them the Gospel of their ascended Lord. The meetinghouse is involved in this obligation, for the very obvious reason that its organizing power must go along with the Gospel, or preaching would be in vain. For what other purpose does God give large means to any of his people but that they may build sanctuaries unto him, where the word of life may have free course, and the weary, and the stricken, and the sinning may find a home? But blindness seems to have happened to our moneyed men on this subject. Thus far they have shown little aptitude to invest in anything that does not bring back a dividend in kind. But a change must come. These men are to learn that instead of using all their gains in building railroads, and steamships, and factories, they are to use enough of it to furnish free churches to all the people of the land. Would they use but a tithe for such a purpose, there should not be a man, woman, or child in Christendom, unprovided with a sitting in a Christian sanctuary.

We are not unaware that free churches would affect the

question of ministerial support, quite likely would change the manner of it completely. But that would be no objection, provided the support were made legitimate and sure. It is to be presumed that with the coming of free houses, the parish anomaly would cease to exist. The worldly element, which now controls in the settlement and dismission of ministers, would be eliminated, and only the church would have a voice in the decision of such questions. In that case the church and the parish would be identical, the members of the one would be the members of the other. In these high matters the church alone should direct. Worldly intermeddling here is evil, and only evil continually. The sooner the separation comes the better, so the church will assume all responsibilities connected with the sanctuary, and with preaching the Gospel to the world.

But it is asked if the house is made free, and the parish is destroyed, how will the ministry be supported? In the same way that the ministry of the early church were, by the freewill offerings of the people. The difficulty is only apparent, not real. A tax on the parish, per capita, or on the pews, to meet the parish expenses, is just as truly voluntary as a contribution gathered by passing the boxes in church. There is this simple difference, that in the one case the man assesses himself, while in the other, he permits himself to be assessed by his fellow. But societies are continually resorting to shifts and expedients to raise their money, because men are not willing to be taxed. The annual sale of the slips is just now the most common, and, perhaps, the most popular way to do this. But this, aside from the objection to vending God's house, is very unequal in its operation, the burdens frequently falling upon those who are least able to bear them. We are aware that the subject is, practically, a delicate and a difficult one, and we do not speak confidently. We are clear as to the main principle, while the application of it would necessarily vary with the character and circumstances of different communities. If the church were willing to assume the support of the ministry by a direct tax on its own members, pro rata, that would be just, and there need be no objection to it. Or if the church were willing to assume the responsibility of the minister's support, collecting the money among themselves, or outside, that might be legitimate. Or if, upon the first day of the week, every member of the church, or of the congregation, should lay by him in store as God had prospered him for the support of the Gospel, and that were collected at the close of every service by passing the boxes, it would be scriptural, and so would bear the divine warrant of success.

But, whatever method is adopted, let it distinctly embody the principle that both the church and the ministry are divine institutions, and that the means necessary to sustain them should neither be given grudgingly nor of necessity. The scriptural duty in this regard should be made so plain that he who runs may read. And then every man should be left to his own sense of honor, as to what is fit and right in the offering which he shall voluntarily make unto the Lord. It seems to us we have no warrant to go beyond this. Nor do we need one, for this is not only all we want, but the best we could possibly have. It disenthralls churches and ministers, leaving the one free to preach the word, and the other free to support it.

Let this be done, and the ministerial vocation would again became high and holy. The ministry would cease to chaffer for a price, and be only too glad to leave their temporalities in the hands of the people who would flock to the courts of the Lord. Some, indeed, might not be willing to trust to a support so spontaneous and unenforced. But others, we believe, who preach because they must, would hail the deliverance from the parish as a new gospel. We know of many a good man, who has felt so humiliated by what was required of him in order to secure a place, that he has been ready to throw up his commission in disgust. These men are ready to preach the Gospel, but they are not ready to surrender their independence. The course we propose saves both. The man is no longer tempted to preach smooth things, lest some rich sinner might interfere with his means of support. He will preach with a new freedom, and boldness, and power as one sent of God.

But some one, who accepts our main proposition, asks; "Could a church so constituted hope to succeed in these times?"

It could not fail, if it was right. God will see that it succeeds. Every true thing is immortal, as every false thing carries in itself the sentence of death. All that belongs to man, sooner or later, perishes; but God's plans, and thoughts, and works are as enduring as himself. The house of worship, as man's, is smitten with mortal weakness; as God's it is endowed with perpetual vitality and power. The strength of the early church lay, very much, in making its house of worship the house of the Lord, the Christian's home. It is still, largely, the strength of the Catholic church, of the English church; was of the Methodist church. Our weakness lies, largely, in building men's houses, misnaming them houses of the Lord. We offer the Gospel to men as we do the lecture and the fair. As a business operation this may be well enough, but as a plan of evangelization nothing could be more short-sighted. A wealthy parish, not long ago, exchanged a minister to whom they paid a salary of fifteen hundred dollars, for another to whom they paid three thousand. A member of that parish remarked that it was a capital speculation, for so many wealthy families were drawn into the church, in consequence, that it considerably reduced the taxes on the old members. Besides, the value of the sittings had been so raised by the change, that they were now sought after by business men for safe and profitable pecuniary investment. This looks strangely on paper, and yet the strangest thing about it is, that it is true. What a charming church that must be for the poorer classes! A man is brought in, the salary doubled for the very purpose of increasing the value of meetinghouse stock, drawing in the rich, and necessarily excluding the poor. Such an operation is in the line of State street, or Wall street, but it does seem out of place in the committee room, or the vestry of a church, where the spiritual and eternal interests of undying thousands are discussed and decided. If gain and godliness are identical, this may be perfectly legitimate, otherwise it is on a level with the operations of the stock board, or the exchange. The evil is great and threatening, and the wonder is that Christian men can be parties to it, especially that Christian ministers can be used for ends so hostile to the kingdom of our Lord. It is becoming a serious question, as to whether the Congregational churches in New England can hold their own. Certain it is they are not making the advance that a healthy organization demands, or that they might make with an open meetinghouse,

and a Gospel adapted to the masses.   If Congregationalism has
any future, it will be because it has a ministry to the masses.
All strong and permanent religious movements have begun
with the common people.   Our Saviour began there, the Apostles began there, Luther began there.   The English Reformers
began there.'   Our Puritan Fathers began there, the Methodists
began there, and we must begin there, or fail.   If we are to
be satisfied with fine churches, artistic singing, and classic sermons, we have had our day, and are out of place in these grand
times of God.   Others will do the work, and take the honor.
It is to be seen whether Congregationalism, with the finest opportunity ever given to a denomination to spread out and grow,
has any conception of the time, or any power for the work.
Eleven millions of poor in the South, and as many more in the
West and the North, stretch out imploring hands for succor
and aid.   Here are the living stones with which we are to build.
Whoso uses them will come into sympathy with the Master-
builder, and success is sure.

And what is to prevent the denomination from undertaking
this work among the masses?   She is eminently fitted for it
both by her polity, and by her history.   Facile, rapid, pliable,
at home anywhere, adapting herself to any circumstances,
it would seem as if God had intended her for this very time.
The fact, too, that her freedom banished her from the South,
and so, of all the denominations, saved her from the complicity,
or guilt of slavery, seems to mark her as the church that is to
go southward and westward, heralding that Gospel which she
has ever spoken with unmuzzled lips.   Episcopacy may covet
the favor of the great, and seek her conquests in the high
places, but be ours the humbler, though surer, and more enduring work among the common people.   Here is the most depth
and richness and vitality and power, and here the divine seed
will spring to the most abundant harvest.

For such a work we need no theological *dilettanti*, but genuine, earnest men, who can endure hardness as good soldiers,
and in whose ears there is ringing a wo if they preach not the
Gospel.   The only question is as to whether our ministry are
equal to the work, whether the young men in our divinity
schools are fitting for a profession, or for a work unto which

they are called of God.   Whether they are fitting for pulpits, or for ministering the word of life to the perishing.   Give us two things and we will solve the problem of home evangelization.   Houses of worship, open and free, and a ministry who preach simply to save souls, and the Congregational church shall go forth as the morning, fair as the moon, clear as the sun, and terrible as an army with banners.

ARTICLE V.

JOHN HOWE'S
BLESSEDNESS OF THE RIGHTEOUS OPENED.

WHOEVER has taken a journey in New England, or in any other region, must have remarked the different impression a town or village makes on the observer from the different time and direction in which he approaches it.   If he enters it in a beautiful season of the year, after a refreshing shower, from an eastern course, in face of a setting sun, and all the fields clothed with a transcendant verdure, it makes the most favorable impression, especially if his own spirits share in the exhilarations of nature; but if on a hot day, under a burning sun, his own spirits depressed with languor and fatigue, and all the fields blasted by a continuous drought, the description in his note book is almost reversed by the circumstances, and though the place be the same, yet the earth mourneth and languisheth; Lebanon is ashamed and hewn down; Sharon is like a wilderness; and Bashan and Carmel shake off their fruits.   On something like this depends the impression which eminent authors make on us.   Our receptivities, our circumstances, the mood in which we approach them, concur with their qualities to shape our estimation of them.

The way in which we met the author of the Blessedness of the Righteous, was peculiar.   We met him in a tranquil afternoon, under the mild light of a setting sun, with every field flourishing around, after long hearing of his fame, and with the most excited but deferred expectations.   It so happened that we never read a word of the famous John Howe until we had almost completed our seventy-eighth year.   By the current writers around us he is sometimes mentioned, but very rarely quoted.   The theologians of New England seldom mention him.   Edwards, Hopkins, Emmons, Dr. Dwight, Stuart, Dr. Woods, rarely use his name ; never appeal to his authority. We seldom find his works in our popular libraries ; to us (speaking individually) he has been like the Southern Cross, no doubt a brilliant constellation, but hid behind the horizon ; and shining over distant seas which we never expect to navigate. We have often asked theological men what they know about him, and the uniform answer has been, we have heard of him by the hearing of the ear, but our eyes have never seen him. Then comes the question : What is the character of that spring, remote in the desert, of which no traveller ever drinks, though gushing with crystal waters and surrounded with fruits and flowers ?

John Howe was born in Loughborough in the year 1630, and was the son of the officiating clergyman.   But his father was driven from that place by the persecuting zeal of Archbishop Laud.   Finding no place of rest within the limits of that prelate's ecclesiastical tyranny, he went over to Ireland and carried his son with him.   The war and massacre in that unhappy country forced him back again into England, and he settled in Lancashire.   There his son acquired his classical knowledge, and was sent early to Cambridge.   After continuing some years in that university, and taking his first degree, he removed to Oxford, where he made considerable progress in literature, commenced Master of Arts, and was elected Fellow of Magdalen College.

Soon after taking his second degree he was ordained by Mr. Herle of Winwick, assisted by the ministers of the chapels in his very extensive parish.   On this account he used pleasantly to observe that few men in modern times had a more primitive ordination than himself.   The field of ministerial labor to which he afterwards removed was Great Torrington, in Devon, and his abundant services were crowned with considerable success.

Business calling him to London, he had the curiosity to go to the chapel at Whitehall.   Cromwell, whose eyes were everywhere, thought that he saw something extraordinary in this country minister, and sent a person to say that he wished to speak with him when the service was over. When Mr. Howe came, he was requested, with much earnestness, to preach there the next Lord's day. He did everything he could to be excused, and begged to be permitted to return home to his flock, but in vain. He was constrained to comply with the wishes of one who would take no denial. After officiating one Sabbath, he was obliged to do so a second and a third; and the consequence was that nothing would satisfy the Protector but Mr. Howe must come to Whitehall, and be his domestic chaplain. With very great reluctance he was compelled to gratify a man who would have his own way.

His conduct in this difficult situation was that of an eminently wise and prudent and good man. Such was his disinterestedness that once when he was applying for a favor, the Protector said: "Mr. Howe, you often come to me in behalf of others, but you never have asked one benefit for your own family; how comes it that you do not rather seek to advance their interest?" At one time he gave great offence by preaching against a favorite notion, "the efficacy of a particular faith in prayer," which was then in great vogue at court. But he was a man of unalterable fidelity, and nothing could move him from the path of duty. After Oliver's death, he continued about three months in the service of his son Richard, and then went down to his old people at Torrington, and labored among them till the act of uniformity took place. Soon after the Restoration he was accused by one of those time-serving men with whom every country abounds, but whom none but bad governments encourage, of having uttered something seditious, if not treasonable, in his sermon; but by the testimony of more than twenty of his most judicious hearers, he was cleared from the malicious charge.

Nothing, however, could free him from the effects of the Bartholomew act, and he retired from the station of a parish minister to be a silenced non-conformist. He must now steal opportunities of usefulness, and preach the Gospel in secret, as if he were a thief, offending God, and injuring man. For several years he was an itinerant preacher in the habitations of his friends.   In the course of the year 1665, he endured an imprisonment of two months in the Isle of St. Nicholas. When released, he continued in the West, exercising his ministry from place to place as times would allow.

Seeing no prospect of extensive usefulness at home, he accepted an offer from Lord Mazarine to be his chaplain, and went over with his family to Ireland in the year 1671.   The mansion of his patron was in the neighborhood of Antrim. The demon of uniformity does not appear to have obtained so full a possession of the Irish as of the English bishops of that age; and Mr. Howe, while he continued in that country, statedly officiated in the church of that city, and was admitted into the churches in the neighboring towns.

From this situation he was, in the year 1675, on the death of Dr. Lazarus Seaman, called to be pastor of a church formed of persons who had belonged to his congregation; and he returned to London to exercise the office of the ministry, but in a state of things how changed since the time of his former abode in the metropolis, and to an audience how different from that which he had served before.   For ten years, and some of them peculiarly unfavorable to religious liberty, he labored with extraordinary acceptance in the service of his people, among whom were not a few eminently distinguished, not only for their piety but their talents, their education, and their respectability in social life.

In the year 1685, when tyranny was come to its height, he complied with an invitation from Lord Wharton to travel with him to the Continent; and after visiting many foreign parts, as the door was still shut against public usefulness at home, he took up his residence at Utrecht, and continued there for a season, greatly respected by all ranks of people, preaching statedly at his own house, and frequently in the English church.

In the year 1687, when King James changed his maxims of government, and gave the dissenters full liberty of worship, Mr. Howe returned with pleasure to his flock, and took the benefit of the indulgence.   In an interview with the Prince of Orange, just before his departure from Holland, he had been advised not to thank King James for dispensing with the penal laws; and he, and a great majority of the dissenters, complied with the advice.

After the revolution Mr. Howe continued to labor among his people in Silver street, who are said to have been a society peculiarly select.   He took an active part in every thing relating to the concerns of religion, and ever appeared the powerful advocate of truth, of piety, of moderation and liberality.   In every part of his conduct his entire devotedness to the service of his Master shone forth; and in the end he exhibited a resemblance of the sun in a summer evening setting in mildness of glory.   He died the second day of April in the year 1705, in the seventy fifth year of his age.

Mr. Howe's person was the index of his mind.   He was above the common size : there was a dignity in his countenance, and something unusually great and venerable in his whole deportment, which struck even strangers with reverence.   His talents were of the highest order.   The God of nature endued him with a soul capable of the most vigorous exertions, and the most exalted degrees of improvement.   The capacities which he possessed he did not suffer, through inglorious indolence, to remain inert.   His application to study was close and unremitting ; and his faculties were roused with their utmost energies in order to attain every branch of knowledge which could conduce to improve and aid the researches and pursuits of a divine.

His sentiments in theological matters were such as would lead men to call him a moderate Calvinist.   In his writings he scarcely descended to the minuter parts of divinity ; but chiefly confined his literary labors to the great and fundamental principles of religion, and set himself to illustrate those important truths in which Christians are agreed.   The manner in which he formed his creed is not unworthy of notice.   By his skill in languages he was able to examine with accuracy the originals of the sacred code.   He perused the writings of some of the fathers and of the schoolmen.   He made himself master of the systems of theology drawn up by the reformers and divines of the former age.   He formed an intimate acquaintance with the works of the heathen philosophers.   Above all, he studied the sacred oracles, and from an attentive, serious and repeated perusal of them, drew up a system of theology for himself, which in the course of his long life he never saw reason to change.

Unfeigned and exalted piety filled the soul of John Howe. It would be difficult to say, if ever there was a better man in England. The principles of the Gospel were felt by him in their utmost energy, and he was wholly devoted, both in heart and life, to Father, Son, and Holy Ghost. His great end in living was to please God, and to advance his glory; and it would not be easy to find a man equal to him in love to all the disciples of Christ, in universal benevolence, and in that purity and humility which adorn the character of a man of God.

While deserved praise is given to Mr. Howe for personal religion, there are two qualities in which he was preëminent.

In integrity of heart he yielded to no man who ever trod on English ground. There was an honesty in him which nothing could shake. He had an uprightness of soul which could not be bent from the straight line of rectitude by promises or threatenings, by the hope of worldly benefit or the fear of temporal evil. What appeared to him a duty, nothing could allure or deter him from performing; what he conceived to be a sin, neither earth nor hell could induce him to commit.

The other excellence is magnanimity; and it may well be questioned if there was ever a man in the British isle superior to him in this respect. There is in some characters a certain sublimity of both mind and heart. A Roman writer says of Scipio Africanus : *nihil nisi magnum unquam nec sensit, nec dixit, nec fecit.* The God of nature may have endued that man with an innate greatness of soul. But in forming the character of John Howe, the God of nature and grace united the combined energies of both. A greater measure of intellectual, moral, and spiritual sublimity than were united in him, where shall it be found? He had his sentiments as to lesser points in religion, and as to church government; he acted according to his own judgment, and would be guided by no other man's opinion. But his soul appears to have been filled with the great principles of Christianity, and with them alone. He loved all good men, and loved them according to their goodness, without considering to what communion they belonged. To promote pure religion was his grand aim, not the interests of a party. In his own soul, the great fundamental principles of the Gospel reigned, and formed the character of a catholic Christian above all sects and parties, uniting and willing to unite with all good men of every church, who were united to Christ, following him and devoted to him.

Some unusual displays of divine love this man of God had received ; and near the close of his ministry, while he was dispensing the Lord's Supper, the grace of Jesus, his Saviour, affected his soul in so powerful a manner, that it was feared he would have expired, while giving the bread and wine to the members of his church, and discoursing to them on the infinite greatness of redeeming love. With those who visited him as he drew near the gates of death, he conversed as one already in the celestial state. There was something in him so spiritual and dignified, that they could not help regarding him with the veneration due to an inhabitant of heaven. His views of future blessedness were exceedingly exalted, his hopes steadfast, and his desires intense. While his earthly tabernacle was fast hastening to decay, he said to Mrs. Howe :

" I think I love you as well as it is fit for one creature to love another ; yet, if it were put to my choice, whether to die this moment, or to live this night, and the living this night would secure the continuance of my life for seven years to come, I would choose to die this moment."

Such was the chaplain of Oliver Cromwell. It has usually been conceived that his preachers were contemptible fanatics. Whatever men, and some of them high in ecclesiastical office, may have said to their disadvantage, we venture to assert, that for greatness of talents, unfeigned piety and goodness, the true learning of a Christian divine, a thorough understanding of the sacred Scriptures, and skill and excellence in preaching, none of the rulers of the house of Tudor, of the house of Stuart, or the house of Hanover ever had a chaplain superior to John Howe.

His works, in the estimation of the public, have deserved the first place in the theological library. For the last three score years, no books in divinity have uniformly sold for so large a sum as his two folio volumes. Not a bishop's, nor archbishop's writings, though there be a charm in titles, have been marked in catalogues at so high a price.

One of his most celebrated pieces is the " Living Temple." The former part has been considered by adepts in metaphysical reasoning as unequalled at the time : the latter part has been the delight of judicious Christians as a luminous illustration of the Gospel of Christ.   His "Blessedness of the Righteous " is a first rate performance, and contains a vast extent of thought, of learning, but especially of piety.   It displays the author's acquaintance with the writings of the ancient philosophers, that he had their sentiments so much in his mind as to communicate a tinge of the Platonic system which was then much in vogue at the universities.   Mr. Howe, among others, appears to have been fond of it, and to have estimated it far above its real value ; and he sometimes introduces it in his works, when it might better have been omitted.   His "Delighting in God" is one of the purest treatises of practical theology to be found in the English language ; and demonstrates Mr. Howe to have been not only a superior writer but a most eminent Christian.   "The Redeemer's Tears wept over Lost Souls," and "The Redeemer's Dominion over the Invisible World " contain a strength of reasoning, a sublimity of thought, and a pathos which it will not be easy to find elsewhere in an equal degree.   Indeed what did he write which does not bear the evident marks of a master's hand ?   No man appears to have understood the Scriptures better, or to have possessed equal skill in throwing light on a passage, by two or three words. These brief illustrations are like a sunbeam.   And there is scarcely a writer in the whole compass of English theological literature, in whom a greater number of new and uncommon, but useful thoughts are to be found.

His style is, in many places, stiff and involved, and in some obscure ; but it has a dignity, an energy, a splendor, and a sublimity which produce the most powerful effects on the reader's mind.

Besides the two folio volumes, consisting of treatises and sermons, which were published in his lifetime, there have since appeared two in octavo, the one on love to God and our neighbor, and the other on miscellaneous subjects ; two on the work of the Spirit, the one, in particular persons, and the other on his influence in producing the glory of the latter days ; and a duodecimo volume on family worship. All these discourses were taken from his lips by a short-hand writer, without having been ever committed to paper by Mr. Howe, who possessed the talent of forming and retaining an extensive plan in his mind, and was accustomed to preach wholly from premeditation, and the thoughts suggested in the time of delivery. But they bear the stamp of their author's superior genius, and are such as, none but a great man could preach. It is remarkable that in his posthumous works there is a perspicuity of style and a simplifying of ideas which are exceedingly striking and which the reader of his former pieces could not have expected to find. With all their disadvantages they are valuable remains of one of England's greatest men, and confirm the ancient adage, "that the gleanings of Ephraim are better than the vintage of Abiezar."

Perhaps it may be considered as no unfair test of intellectual and spiritual excellence that a person can relish the writings of John Howe; if he does not, he may have reason to suspect that something in the head or heart is wrong.

A young minister who wishes to obtain eminence in his profession, if he has not the works of John Howe and can procure them in no other way, should sell his coat and buy them; and if that will not suffice let him sell his bed and lie on the floor; and if he spends his days in reading them he will not complain that he lies hard at night.[1]

Dr. Watts' has strung his lyre in his praise. He wrote in 1704 an ode to the Rev. Mr. John Howe, *laudatus a viro laudato*, of which the following stanzas are the close:

"A puff of honor fills the mind,
    And yellow dust is solid gold;
Thus, like the ass of savage kind,
    We snuff the breezes of the wind,
        Or steal the serpent's food.
            Could all the choirs
            That charm the poles
        But strike one doleful sound,
'Twould be employed to mourn our souls,
Souls that were framed of sprightly fires
    In floods of folly drown'd,

---

[1] For the substance of the above outline of Mr. Howe's Life we are indebted mainly to " The History of the Dissenters," by Bogue & Bennett.

Souls made of glory seek a brutal joy :
  How they disclaim their heav'nly birth,
  Melt their bright substance down with drossy earth,
And hate to be refined from that impure alloy !

"Oft has thy genius rous'd us hence
  With elevated song ;
Bid us renounce this world of sense ;
Bid us divide th' immortal prize
  With the seraphic throng :
' Knowledge and love make spirits bless'd ;
Knowledge their food, and love their rest ;'
But flesh, th' unmanageable beast,
Resists the pity of thine eyes,
  And music of thy tongue.
Then let the worms of grov'ling mind,
Round the short joys of earthly kind,
  In restless windings roam :
Howe hath an ample orb of soul,
Where shining worlds of knowledge roll ;
Where love, the centre and the pole,
  Completes the heav'n at home."

The "Blessedness of the Righteous" is one of the sweetest, though not the most thoughtful, of the works of Howe. It seems to be the blending of a series of sermons or lectures delivered by him to his people on the felicities of the heavenly state. The original form is lost in the unity ; it is a kind of informal system, assuming a central truth around which he contrives to hang a whole system of divinity. Baxter's Saint's Rest probably originated in a similar way. The text is from Psalms xvii. 15 : "As for me I will behold thy face in righteousness : I shall be satisfied when I awake in thy likeness." He considers this life as a kind of moral and intellectual sleep, a benumbing of our faculties, a dream, an empty show from which there are three consecutive wakings. Fist, at our regeneration ; second t our death ; and third, at our glorification after our resurrection, each of them increasing in intensity of feeling and clearness of vision. Then comes the full vision of God. What is it? We can form but poor conceptions now ; we must wait for the glorious experience. But these three wakings, those successive steps, at once give us anexalted idea of the final state, not only by the degrees, but each step helps us to conceive the next.

Every Christian knows what regeneration does for him; grace prepares for glory and the disembodied state for the final heaven.   Then he assails the chief difficulty of his subject. What is the vision of God, the beatific vision, and what are its joys?   He divides it into three parts.   I. The vision of God's face.   II. The assimilation to him.   III. The consequent satisfaction.   Each is considered absolutely and relatively.

As to the vision, he first considers the seeing and secondly the glory seen.   Let us quote his remarks on the glory seen:

"As to the nature of this glory, 'tis nothing else but the conspicuous lustre of divine perfections.   We can only guide our present conceptions of it by the discovery God hath already given us of himself, in those several excellencies of his being, the great attributes that are convertible and one with him.   When Moses besought him for a sight of his glory, he answers him with this: ' I will proclaim my name before thee.'   His name, we know, is the collection of his attributes.   The notion, therefore, we can hence form of this glory, is only such as we may have of a large volume, by a brief synopsis or table; of a magnificent fabric, by a small model or platform; a spacious country, by a little landscape.   He hath here given us a true representation of himself, not a full; such as will secure our apprehensions, being guided thereby from error, not from ignorance.   So as they swerve not in apprehending this glory, though they still fall short.   We can now apply our minds to contemplate the several perfections which the blessed God assumes to himself, and whereby he describes to us his own being; and can in our thoughts attribute them all to him, though we have still but low defective conceptions of each one.   As if we could at a distance distinguish the streets and houses of a great city; but every one appears to us much less than it is.   We can apprehend somewhat of whatsoever he reveals to be in himself; yet when all is done, how little a portion do we take up of him!   Our thoughts are empty and languid, strait and narrow, such as diminish and limit the Holy One.   Yet so far as our apprehensions can correspond to the discovery he affords us of his several excellencies, we have a present view of the divine glory.   Do but strictly and distinctly survey the many perfections comprehended in his name, then gather them up and consider how glorious he is!   Conceive one glory resulting from substantial wisdom, goodness, power, truth, justice, holiness, that is, beaming forth from him who is all these by his very essence, necessarily, originally, infinitely, eternally, with whatsoever else is

truly a perfection. This is the glory blessed souls shall behold forever." Chap. III.

No doubt this language will appear mystic and unintelligible
to the man of the world. What satisfied the Psalmist will per-
plex him. But Christ has told us that the pure in heart shall
see God, most probably alluding to the beatific vision. This
is the sum of what is promised in the second and third chapters
of Revelation to the seven churches, to eat of the tree of life,
not to be hurt of the second death, to eat of the hidden manna,
to have the morning star, to be clothed with white raiment,
to be a pillar in the temple of God and have a new name,
to sit with me in my throne, all mystic terms and full of
meaning. Perhaps it may conduce to the justification of Howe
in the use of such expressions to remember that even Bishop
Butler, the coolest Christian and the most cautious reasoner,
lays aside his severity and almost becomes an enthusiast on
this theme.

"In this world it is only the effects of wisdom and power and
greatness, which we discern; it is not impossible that hereafter the
qualities themselves, in the supreme Being, may be the immediate
object of contemplation. What amazing wonders are opened to
view by late improvements! What an object is the universe to a
creature, if there be a creature who can comprehend its system!
But it must be an infinitely higher exercise of the understanding,
to view the scheme of it in that mind which projected it, before its foundations were laid. And surely we have meaning to
the words when we speak of going further; and viewing, not only
this system in his mind, but the wisdom and intelligence itself from
whence it proceeded. The same may be said of power. But since
wisdom and power are not God, he is a wise, a powerful Being;
the divine nature may therefore be a further object to the understanding. It is nothing to observe that our senses give us but an
imperfect knowledge of things; effects themselves, if we knew
them thoroughly, would give us but imperfect notions of wisdom and power; much less of his being in whom they reside. I
am not speaking of any fanciful notion of seeing all things in God;
but only representing to you how much an higher object to the understanding an infinite Being himself is, than the things which he
has made; and this is no more than saying that the Creator is superior to the works of his hands." Sermon on The Love of God.
XIV.

But the vision of God is connected with our assimilation of him when the vision is enjoyed.   Here our author meets with a new difficulty.   Some of the attributes of God are such as we ought to imitate and resemble; such as his goodness, justice, mercy, condescension, truth, and long-suffering.   But there are others, which we can not imitate, and it would be presumption to make the attempt.   His omniscience, his power, his sovereignty.   Here our author with wonderful skill maintains the categorical unity of his leading proposition.   Where there is no possibility of assimilation there are certain correlatives and correspondencies which even his highest and most inimitable excellencies demand from the human heart.   Thus man must be assimilated to the glory of God.

" The soul's perfect assimilation unto that revealed glory, or its participation thereof; (touching the order the things themselves have to one another, there will be consideration had in its proper place), and this also must be considered as a distinct and necessary ingredient into the state of blessedness we are treating of.   Distinct it is, for though the vision now spoken of doth include a certain kind of assimilation in it, as all vision doth, being only a reception of the species or likeness of the object seen; this assimilation we are to speak of, is of a very different kind.   That is such as affects only the visive and cognitive power, and that not with a real change, but intentional only, nor for longer continuance than the act of seeing lasts; but this is total, real, and permanent.   And surely it is of equal necessity to the soul's blessedness, to partake the glory of God, as to behold it; as well as to have the divine likeness imprest upon it, as represented to it.   After so contagious and overspreading a depravation as sin hath diffused through all its powers, it can never be happy without a change of its very crasis and temper throughout.   A diseased, ulcerous body would take little felicity in gay and glorious sights; no more would all the glory of heaven signify to a sick, deformed, self-loathing soul."

But the most incommunicable attributes demand their correspondencies; that is, they ought to make their parallel impression.

" For instance, is he absolutely supreme, inasmuch as he is the first being?   The correspondent impression with us, and upon the same reason, must be a most profound, humble self-subjection, disposing our souls to constant obedience to him.   Again, is he simply independent, as being self-sufficient and all in all? The impression with us must be a nothingness, and self-emptiness, engaging us to quit ourselves, and live in him. This is the only conformity to God, which with respect to his incommunicable excellencies, our creature-state can admit. It may be also styled a likeness to him, being a real conformity to his will concerning us, and his very nature as it respects us. We may conceive of it, as of the likeness between a seal and the stamp made by it; especially, supposing the inequality of parts in the seal to be by the protuberancy of what must form the signature. In that case there would be a likeness, *aliquatenus*, that is, an exact correspondency; but what would then be convex or bulging out in the seal, would be, as we know, concave or hollow in the impression. Such is the proportion between sovereignty and subjection, between self-fulness and self-emptiness. Whereas, a similitude to God, in respect to his communicable perfections, is as that between the face and its picture, where no such difference is wont to appear." Chap. IV.

The vision of God, with the consequent assimilation, is intended to explain the nature of celestial happiness, to bring the conception nearer and make the exalted state a positive idea, and the meditation of it an influential principle, a perpetual motive to increase our virtue and deliver us from sin. We are blamed by Howe and Baxter for not meditating on them more, increasing our faith and kindling our devotion. But here we must confess to one difficulty, whenever we have endeavored to carry out their directions in our own experience. The subject is too sublime, the object is too refulgent for weak mortals to carry the great idea into an articulate development. For a long meditation there must be more for the intellect; there must be components and parts; there must be springs and branches for the mental bird to light on or he can not sustain his aerial flight. Even the eagle can not soar above the atmosphere, nor the flame of love burn without some intellectual fuel. You enter a garden: there must be walks and alleys; there must be streams of water and beds of flowers to exercise our thoughts and detain our attention. We must honestly confess that an objective heaven, whatever impression it first makes on the mind, is not the best aid to a correct conception or to the quickening of our hearts.

How then shall we conquer the difficulty? Meditation is our

duty, and heaven a blessed reality. We say at once it must be subjective, not objective. We must look into ourselves. We must find the temper which craves heaven, and is prepared for heaven. When you have such deep repentance that your sorrow is delightful, when all your past sins are turned into present monitors, when a sense of condemnation makes the cross delightful, when you go to it yourself and long to draw others with you, when your afflictions only increase your patience and every provocation prompts you to forgive, when approaching death forecasts a shadow of heaven, and every duty, springing from love, increases your delight, then you experience heaven in the preparation of heaven. The sun that you see reflected in the pool is really above the clouds. The instrument is in tune and you have nothing to do but to begin your everlasting song :

"Worthy is the Lamb that was slain to receive power, and riches, and wisdom, and strength, and honor, and glory, and blessing. And every creature which is in heaven, and on the earth and under the earth, and such as are in the sea and all that are in them, heard I saying : Blessing, and honor, and glory, and power, be unto Him that sitteth on the throne, and unto the Lamb forever and ever."

After discussing the satisfaction which arises from the vision of God and assimilation to him, the author proceeds to a large number of inferences, all of them natural and all important, constituting a beautiful system of divinity, the most important article of which is the necessity of regeneration. How impossible it is that the man who has never communed with God on earth should derive his eternal happiness from communion with him in heaven !

The style of Howe is not wholly secure from critical objections. He uses too many dictionary-words. He talks of the complacential fruition the soul has ; that the resurrection will connaturalize them to a region of glory ; of the primordia of this glory of God's most aspectable glory, etc. In using this learned diction he certainly has not the facility of expression and the nicety of meaning which marks the learned terminology of Sir Thomas Browne. But his most recondite words appear to have occurred to him spontaneously. What would have been pedantry in others was simplicity in him.

His use of the classic writers was peculiar and worthy ot notice. He was a Puritan and lived in the age of puritanical rigor. Some of his learned contemporaries among the Puritans thought it necessary to quote the classic authors with a cloud of distrust and a note of disapprobation. Howe, it seems to us, hit the true medium. Let the reader compare him with Gale in his Court of the Gentiles. Gale, in adducing their best authorities, always uses a tone of severity. But Howe quotes them as a Christian scholar. He uses their authority as Paul might have done. His argument is generally *a fortiori*. If beclouded pagans could soar so high, how much higher should enlightened Christians soar !

Perhaps one of the most curious uses that we can make of this enlightened author is to summon him from his sepulchre to make him bear witness of his judgment on some of those most earnest controversies which have existed in New England long since his death. Fortunately it is the very subject on which he has providentially spoken. It is well remembered among us that Dr. Hemenway and Dr. Hopkins had a controversy on the use of the means of grace, and Dr. Tappan and Dr. Spring a similar controversy on the same subject ; and these controversies have had a great influence in shaping New England theology. Even now, though the rock has fallen from the mountain's summit and has sunk beneath the surface of the waters, the whole lake is still shaken by the mighty agitation. What would John Howe have said had he been alive and a spectator to the scene? He could not have spoken more clearly had this been the fact. After stating that the sinner will allege his imbecility as an excuse for the non-performance of his duty, he says :

" If you were serious in what you say, methinks you should have little mind to play the sophisters, and put fallacies upon yourselves, in a matter that concerns the life of your soul. And what else are you now doing? For sure, otherwise one would think it were no such difficulty to understand the difference between the *esse simpliciter*, the mere being of any thing, and the *esse tale*, its being such or such, by the addition of somewhat afterward to that being. Though nothing could contribute to its own being simply ; yet sure when it is in being, it may contribute to the bettering or perfecting of itself, even as the unreasonable creatures themselves do; and if it be a creature naturally capable of acting with design, it may act designedly in order to its becoming so or so qualified, or the attaining of somewhat yet wanting to its perfection. You can not be thought so ignorant, but that you know the new creature is only an additional to some former being; and though it be true that it can do no more to its own production than the unconceived child, as nothing can act before it is, doth it therefore follow, that your reasonable soul, in which it is to be formed, can not use God's prescribed means in order to that blessed change? You can not act holily as a saint; but therefore can you not act rationally as a man? I appeal to your reason and conscience in some particulars. Is it impossible to you to attend upon the dispensation of that Gospel, which is God's power unto salvation, the seal by which he impresses his image, the glass through which his glory shines to the changing souls into the same likeness? Are you not as able to go to church as the tavern; and to sit in the assembly of saints as of mockers? Is it impossible to you to consult the written word of God, and thence learn what you must be, and do, in order to blessedness? Will not your eyes serve you to read the Bible as well as a gazette or play-book? Is it impossible to inquire of your minister, or an understanding Christian neighbor, concerning the way and terms of blessedness? Can not your tongue pronounce these words, What shall I do to be saved? as well as these, Pray what do you think of the weather? or, What news is there going? Yet further; is it impossible to apply your thoughts to what you meet with suitable to your case, in your attendance upon preaching, reading or discourse? Have all such words a barbarous sound in your ear? Can you not consider what sense is carried under them; what they import and signify? Can you not bethink yourself, Do the doctrines of God and Christ and the life to come, signify something or nothing? or do they signify any thing worth the considering; or that is fit for me to take notice of?"

In a word we can heartily recommend this work, indeed all the works of Howe, to the young men of our theological schools. If they do not sell their coats or jackets to purchase his volumes, happy will they be if generally they think with him and stop with him, but certainly if they imbibe his spirit.

He was the best man to write on the Blessedness of the Righteous.

ARTICLE VI.

THE DOUAY OR CATHOLIC BIBLE.

NEVER, perhaps, was there a more interesting congregation than that to which the Apostles preached on the day of pentecost. It was gathered from nations more widely separated than the Euphrates and the Nile. Never was there a more wonderful spectacle presented, than when " cloven tongues like as of fire appeared, and sat upon the Apostles, and they began to speak with other tongues," and preach to every man in the tongue in which he was born.

And as significant as wonderful. God was showing those teachers of the nations that he would have the revelation of his will made to all men in the language they can best understand.

He had taught the world the same truth before. He inspired Moses and the older prophets to write the greater part of the Old Testament in their own, the Hebrew language. After the return from the captivity, however, and when the Jews had so far lost the knowledge of their native tongue as to be unable to read it, the Levites, it is said, " read it distinctly in their hearing, and gave the sense, and caused them to understand it." And Ezra, and Daniel, accommodating themselves to the state of the people, now acquainted with the Chaldee tongue, wrote to some extent in this dialect.

Again, when the New Testament was written, the Hebrew was becoming a dead language. The Greek was the popular dialect of Palestine; not pure Greek, but the Greek as modified by the Hebrew which it had supplanted. The New Testament writers were therefore inspired to write in Hebraistic Greek.

So careful has God been that the people to whom the successive portions of the Scriptures were given should have them in a form to them the most perspicuous and intelligible.

And no doubt, when the Apostles went out, and came in contact with different nations, they preached, as on the day of pentecost, " to every man in his own tongue," as far as they were able.   Possibly they commenced the work of translating the Scriptures into the dialects of Western Asia.   Their immediate successors certainly did this, if they did not ; for Eusebius, writing only two hundred and fifteen years after the death of the Evangelist John, says that " The Scriptures were translated into all languages, Greek and barbarian, where the Gospel had gone."   In the middle of the fifth century, it was declared to be " impossible to corrupt the Scriptures, because they were already translated into the languages of seventy two nations or tribes."

But the church became corrupt, began to think lightly of the inspired word, and to exalt the traditions of men.   Long centuries of darkness settled down upon the race in consequence, more and more concealing the Scriptures from view, until only here and there a copy could be found.   A few disciples proved faithful ; and in cloisters and caves of the earth they preserved the ancient manuscripts, that in later days, and some in our own day, have been brought to light.

In multiplying copies of the Scriptures by successive translations, it will necessarily follow that the different versions will have various degrees of accuracy and merit, according to the circumstances of their translation.   The early manuscripts made by the Apostles, or their immediate successors, will always remain the true test of their genuineness and value.

It is rare that the translation of any work comes up to the spirit and fulness of the original.   It is more difficult to make a satisfactory translation of the Bible than of any other book, because here is an infinite fulness of meaning to be reproduced under new forms of thought.   To be able to do this perfectly implies higher qualifications even than the inspired writers themselves possessed.   They did not comprehend the length and breadth of the truths they uttered.   They gave themselves to the diligent study of their productions, just as we do, "searching what, and what manner of time the Spirit that was in them did signify."   It is reasonable to expect then, that every translation will be, to some extent, imperfect . rendered so, not so much perhaps by incorporating positive error, as by failing to reach the breadth and depth of the inspired original.   Other things being equal, the greater the number of minds engaged upon a given version, the more extensive their knowledge of language and literature, and the greater the time spent upon it, the greater will be the accuracy and value of the translation.

Trench, in his work on the revision of the Bible, has placed the difficulties attending the successful translation of the sacred Scriptures in so clear a light that we quote from pages 49, 50.

" How many questions at once present themselves, many among them of an almost insuperable difficulty in their solution, so soon as it is attempted to transfer any great work from one language into another!   Let it be only some high and original work of human genius, the Divina Commedia, for instance, and how many problems, at first sight seeming insoluble, and which only genius can solve, (even it being often content to do so imperfectly, to evade, rather than to solve them,) at once offer themselves to the translator. The loftier and deeper, the more original a poem or other composition may be, the more novel and unusual the sphere in which it moves, by so much the more these difficulties will multiply.   They can therefore nowhere be so many and so great as in the rendering of that Book which is sole of its kind ; which reaches far higher heights and far deeper depths than any other ; which has words of God and not of man for its substance ; while the importance of success or failure, with the far reaching issues which will follow on the one or on the other, sinks in each other case into absolute insignificance as compared with their importance here."

Again, if the first translation is liable to be defective, the version that is made from that will be necessarily more so ; and so on, as the departure is greater from the original manuscripts. Every remove will lessen the value of a translation, and there will be no means of testing its worth, as being an embodiment of the mind and will of God, but by comparing it with the best early copies extant.   Manifestly therefore, these ancient manuscripts, in Hebrew, Chaldee, and Greek, are the ones from which every translation must be made, to have the highest claims to regard, although reference may be had in the work, and very properly, to the labors of all previous translators. Every version furnishes an individual judgment, of greater or less weight according to circumstances, which a judicious translator will respect.

Premising these general principles of interpretation, which are as applicable to the translation of the holy Scriptures as of

—

any other literary production, let us look at the origin of the
Douay version, the only one approved by the Roman Catholic
church, compare it with our own, and consider some of its
prominent characteristics. These inquiries will have a direct
bearing upon the value of the version, and its claim to our regard.

The Saviour and his Apostles, in addition to the ancient Hebrew Scriptures, had in their hands the first translation that
was ever made of them into another tongue, the Greek version,
commonly called the Septuagint. Respecting its origin we
know little that is satisfactory, though it doubtless originated at
Alexandria, in Egypt, about two hundred and eighty five years
before Christ. It was universally received by the Apostles and
early Christians, it was quoted by Christ, who gave in this manner the most unequivocal sanction to the work of translating
the Scriptures into the vernacular dialects of the different nations of the earth. Respecting the value of this version, Robinson remarks, in his edition of Calmet's Dictionary :

" The character of this version is different according to the different books. It is easy to distinguish five or six translators. The
Pentateuch is best translated, and exhibits a clear and flowing
Greek style ; though it seems to have been made from a different
and interpolated original text. The next in rank is the translator of
Job and Proverbs ; he indeed often misses the true sense, but still
gives everywhere a good idea, and his style is like that of an original writer. The Psalms and the Prophets are translated worst of
all ; often indeed without any sense. The version of Ecclesiastes is
distinguished by an anxious literal adherence to the original. Indeed, the real value of the Septuagint as a version, stands in no
sort of relation to its reputation. All the translators engaged in it
appear to have been wanting in a proper knowledge of the two languages, and in a due attention to grammar, etymology, and orthog-
raphy. Hence they often confound proper names and appellations,
kindred verbs, similar words and letters, etc., and this in cases
where we are not at liberty to conjecture various readings. The
whole version is rather free than literal ; the figures and metaphors
are resolved, and there are frequent allusions inserted to later times
and later Jewish dogmas."

If such is the character of the Septuagint translation, it is
easy to see that it is totally unworthy to be adopted as the basis

of a new version. And yet it is the source from which the Old Testament of the Douay Bible is in large part derived, after suffering a still further perversion in passing through the Latin.

The Gospel was early preached at Rome, as we know from the Acts of the Apostles, and the Epistles of Paul. To meet the wants of the western Christians, the Bible was early translated into the Latin tongue. Numerous versions indeed were made, for Augustine observes: "Those who have translated the Bible into Greek can be numbered, but not so the Latin versions. For in the first ages of the church whoever could get hold of a Greek Codex ventured to translate it into Latin, however slight his knowledge of either language." There is no evidence that the entire Bible had been rendered into the Latin tongue, at that early age, by any one translator. But in process of time entire versions were completed, each one doubtless fragmentary in its origin, and the work of several minds. Hence they differed very materially from each other. To one of these Augustine, Jerome and others gave the preference. It was called the Itala. Writers are not agreed respecting the meaning of this title, nor is it known by whom it was made. Parts of that version are still extant. Jerome twice revised it, and afterwards undertook a new translation of the Old Testament from the original Hebrew. This he accomplished only in part, leaving the remainder of the Bible, which included all the New, and portions of the Old Testament, as they stood in his revision of the Itala. These two versions, the one a recension of the Itala, and the other in part a new translation, both from the pen of Jerome, were in common use from the latter part of the fourth century to the time of Gregory the Great in the seventh. For he testifies that in his day "the apostolic see made use of both versions." Subsequently, the version containing the translation of Jerome became the standard authority. But it is said to have been "sadly corrupted by a mixture with the old version, and by the uncritical carelessness of half-learned ecclesiastics, as well as by interpolations from liturgical writings and glosses. In fact, the old and new versions were blended into one, and thus was formed the Vulgate of the middle ages."

This corrupting process went on until the changes had become so numerous, and the variations of the copies extant so great, that it was felt to be an impossibility to recover the true text. Roger Bacon declared that " every reader and preacher changes what he does not understand ; their correction is the worst of corruptions, and God's word is destroyed."

The invention of the art of printing, and the multiplication of copies from different manuscripts revealed these corruptions in their true light. The work of revision could now be carried on with better helps, and better success. Numerous versions were collected, corrections were made by the thousand, but who should say, amidst the multitude of renderings, which was correct, so long as they turned away from the unchanging originals, the Hebrew and Greek? While matters were in this unsettled state there assembled one of the most important councils that was ever convened, the Council of Trent. And in the month of April, 1546, they passed their famous decree respecting the Scriptures, in which these words occur :

" The most holy Synod, considering that no small advantage will accrue to the church of God, if from all the Latin editions of the sacred books which are in circulation, it should determine which is to be received as authentic, decrees and declares, that the ancient Vulgate version, which has been approved in the church by the use of so many ages, should be used in public readings, disputations, sermons and expositions, as authentic, and that none is to presume to reject it under any pretence whatever."

But a difficulty at once presented itself : Which one of the editions that had appeared should be adopted as the authorized text? This the Council of Trent had not decreed. " The ancient Vulgate version which had been approved in the church by the use of so many ages," was protean in form ; each of its numerous editions differing from all the rest. It is difficult to see how the identity of the old Itala, or of the translations of Jerome, could have been preserved. No one of the existing versions was considered satisfactory. Accordingly the Council of Trent raised a committee to prepare a new edition. But the Pope interfered. They did not execute their commission. New editions however continued to appear, and in 1590 one was issued from the Papal chair, accompanied with anathemas against all who should use any other version. The successors of Sixtus V., however, found this work so inaccurate that they suppressed it. Soon after Clement VIII. issued a new edition made by his predecessor Gregory XIV., declaring in the preface, in order to save the doctrine of the Pope's infallibility, that the errors of the former edition " had crept into the press." The Clementine edition was published in 1592, and is the basis of all subsequent ones.

It will be seen by this hasty review of the origin and history of the present Vulgate Bible, that it is impossible to determine its paternity. Almost numberless hands have added something to bring it into its present form. Its basis was the Itala, a translation from the Septuagint. It has come to us through the revision of Jerome in which he introduced, in parts of the Old Testament, translations of his own from the Hebrew. It underwent almost endless revisions and alterations before its form was established by Papal authority.

If therefore, as we have seen, the Septuagint was not worthy to be made the basis of a translation, still less can the Vulgate be so esteemed. It is largely a translation of a translation, and has had a history which of itself is calculated to bring it into discredit.

If it be said that the authors of the numerous recensions had reference, in the performance of their work, to the original Hebrew and Greek manuscripts, it will be a sufficient answer to say, that Belarmine, in his preface to the Clementine edition, assigns as one reason for the use of the Vulgate, " the ignorance of the original languages, which prevailed in the church, instancing the Council of Ariminum, where, out of four hundred bishops, not one knew the meaning of ὁμοούσιος, all exclaiming, " not Homoousios, but Christ." And Dr. Robinson says, (Calmet, *Art. Language*,) that, " among Christians, during the first twelve centuries after the Apostolic age, the knowledge of Hebrew could scarcely be said to exist."

With this ignorance of both Hebrew and Greek, the frequent revisions of the Scriptures could accomplish little except to add to the already numberless readings that existed. The process was corrupting rather than purifying.

When now it became apparent that the Bible could no longer be kept from the common people, concealed in a dead language, but that they were having access to the translations of

Wiclif, Tindal, Coverdale, Archbishop Cranmer and others, Rome, although she had burned the bones of Wiclif, and brought Tindal to the stake for the crime of rendering the Scriptures into their vernacular, yielded to the necessity, and caused a version to be made in English for use in the Roman Catholic church. But not from the original Scriptures. The Council of Trent had decreed, that " whosoever shall not receive as sacred and canonical all the books, and every part of them, as they are commonly read in the Catholic church, and are contained in the old Vulgate Latin edition, let him be accursed." This decree determined the basis of the new translation. It must of necessity be " the old Vulgate Latin edition," with all its defects, as no other, not even the original Hebrew and Greek, were tolerated. The Council of Trent has exalted the Vulgate above them both.

By unknown Professors at the Catholic College at Rheims the New Testament was rendered into English. At another Papal Seminary at Douay a few years later appeared the English translation of the Old Testament. These versions were brought together, and constitute the basis of the Catholic Bible, as now received wherever the English language is spoken.

The foregoing remarks will make the title page of this edition intelligible.

"The Holy Bible, translated from the Latin Vulgate: Diligently compared with the Hebrew, Greek, and other editions in divers languages; The Old Testament first published by the English College at Douay, A. D., 1609 : and the New Testament first published by the English College at Rheims, A. D., 1582. The whole revised and diligently compared with the Latin Vulgate."

Now, even without instituting a comparison between this version and the original Scriptures, it will be evident, if the principles laid down at the outset are correct, that it must be imperfect. The Old Testament has come to us through three translations into different languages. And the New is removed by two such translations from the original Greek. If to this we add, that the last translation was made by men of no reputation, or special fitness for the work, we shall see that nothing could have preserved the truth from being corrupted, save the pres-

ence of the Spirit of inspiration, at every step of this long departure from the original sources of truth.   And we shall find
little evidence that this aid was granted, when we come to study
it.

That the foregoing judgment respecting the Rheimish and
Douay translators is not uncharitable, we will cite the testimony
of the Catholic Brownson, in his Review of Oct, 1861.

" The version called the Douay Bible was made under great disadvantages by Englishmen exiled from their own country, living,
and in part, educated abroad, and habitually speaking a foreign language.   They were learned men, but they had to a great extent
lost the genius and idioms of their own language, and evidently
were more familiar with Latin and French than with their mother
tongue.   Such men could not produce a model translation. . . . . .
In literary merit it can in no respect compare with the Protestant
version ; compared with that it is weak, tasteless and inharmonious."

Similar to this is the testimony of that judicious Protestant
critic, Trench :   "The authors of the Rheimish version seem to
have put off their loyalty to the English language with their
loyalty to the English crown."

If these criticisms are just, they had no suitable preparation
for the work they undertook.   With their imperfect knowledge
of the English, they could not have made a translation of the
Vulgate into their tongue, either elegant or accurate.

For the sake of comparison let us glance briefly at the history
of our own version, commonly called King James' version, because made during his reign, and with his sanction.

The middle of the fourteenth century witnessed the dawn of
the Reformation.   " Wiclif appealed from the Pope to the word
of God," says D'Aubigné.   In doing so he rekindled the light
of truth in England and on the continent.   The greatest work
of his life was the translation of the entire Bible into the English tongue.   Our Saxon forefathers had translated portions of
it, Wiclif achieved the task of rendering it all into their vernacular.   But he was not learned either in Hebrew or Greek.
The Latin Vulgate was the basis of his translation, while he
made free use of such versions as had appeared before him.   In

this translation, imperfect as it necessarily was, thousands read "in their own tongues the wonderful works of God."

Persecuted by the monks, deprived of his office by the Archbishop of Canterbury, Wiclif was nevertheless allowed to die in peace.   But after his death every copy of his manuscripts that could be found was committed to the flames.   And twenty eight years after his death his bones were disinterred and burned to ashes, to testify to the malignity of the hatred of that age for an open Bible.

At the opening of the sixteenth century God was moving the heart of William Tyndal to undertake another, and, if possible, a better translation.   "I defy the Pope," said he to a Romish divine, "and all his laws ; and ere many years I will cause the boy that follows the plough to know more of the Scriptures than you do."   Four years from this date he published the New Testament, as translated from the original Greek. This translation, afterwards revised by his own hand, is said to be "surpassed in point of perspicuity and noble simplicity, propriety of idiom, and purity of style, by no English version that has since been made."   He entered upon the translation of the Old Testament from the Hebrew, but before the work was completed he was burned at the stake.   " Lord, open the King of England's eyes," were his dying words.

The art of printing had just been invented.   Efforts for the suppression of the Scriptures in the language of the common people were therefore ineffectual.   " So the word of God grew mightily and prevailed."   " We must root out printing," said the vicar of St. Paul's Cross, " or printing will root us out."

Meantime the King of England has come into collision with the Pope, and Tyndal's prayer is answered.   His version of the Scriptures, completed and edited by John Rodgers, is " set forth with the king's most gracious license."

While these things had been transpiring in England, Coverdale, on the continent, had been engaged upon a new translation from the original Hebrew and Greek.   This was dedicated to the King and Queen of England, Henry VIII. and Anne, and was freely circulated.   Soon after this Cranmer published another version by royal permission, which for half a century was regarded as the authorized version.

During the reign of Mary, Protestant preaching was suppressed. Ministers and their flocks fled to the continent. At Geneva in Switzerland, a number of Protestant divines undertake a new version from the original Hebrew and Greek. Among these we find Coverdale, Whittingham, John Knox, the Scottish Reformer, and John Bodleigh, the founder of the great Oxford Library. This version is known as the Genevan edition, and is still in use, to some extent, in England and Scotland.

Under the reign of Elizabeth, the Protestants were recalled, the Bible was publicly read again in the churches, and by fifteen bishops, appointed for the purpose, a new translation was prepared which was denominated " the Bishops' Bible," published with the Queen's imprimatur, its title-page embellished with the British coat of arms, and provided with maps, portraits, etc. It was for a time regarded as the standard edition, though less faithful, as a translation, than the Genevan that preceded it. These several translations preceded, and prepared the way for our own incomparable version.

Meantime the original Hebrew and Greek manuscripts remained, the fountains of spiritual truth, the standard of appeal in all questions touching the worth of any translation. And before the minds of scholars, and in the hands of the church there were six English versions, each having its merits and defects, according to the circumstances under which it was made ; viz., Wiclif's, Tyndal's, Coverdale's, Cranmer's, the Genevan edition and the Bishops' Bible. All, except the first, had been translated from the original tongues.

The materials were now at hand for a more labored, more accurate version. The age abounded in men of ripe and rare scholarship. It needed only that their attention be enlisted, and their labors be directed to this end. It was done.

In the spring of 1603, James I. ascended the throne of England. By petition of the Protestants, a conference was assembled at Hampton Court for the discussion of matters relating to the church. It was moved by the President of Corpus Christi College, Dr. Reynolds : "That, inasmuch as the existing translations were manifestly incorrect, there ought to be a new translation of the Bible." The proposition was entertained. The project pleased the king.   It was undertaken.   Fifty four learned men were appointed to execute the work, and provision was made for their support.   Every facility needed was placed at their disposal.   Forty seven of them actually participated in the work.   For the sake of convenience they were divided into six committees.   Every man was to make a translation of the whole Bible.   And, as often as they desired, the members of a given committee came together and compared their labors, and from them all adopted a version which was presented as their own.   This was then sent to each of the other committees for examination, criticism, or approval.   Doubtful points were then discussed in a committee of the whole.   "By this arrangement, every part of the Bible was most closely scrutinized at least fourteen times."   By a process so thorough, and continued through a period of about five years, the work was brought to a close, the most important work in the line of translation that was ever accomplished.   It was printed in 1611, with the following title :   .

"The Holy Bible, containing the Old Testament and the New ; Newly translated out of the original tongues : and with the former translations diligently compared and revised ; by his Majesty's special commandment.   Appointed to be read in the churches."

Two centuries and a half have passed since this work was completed, during which the original languages of the Old and New Testaments have been most carefully studied ; Bible lands have been explored by the ripest scholars ; Bible customs and manners have been diligently compared with the stereotyped habits of the Orientals ; and the literatures of ancient peoples have been deciphered, putting the work of these translators to the most searching tests.   But not one grave or essential error has been detected.

It will not be pretended that the work is faultless, for it is human.   It can not be supposed that it represents all the fulness of the original.   This no translation, probably, can do. But it is believed to come nearer to it than any other translation that has ever been made.

Taking the labors of the Dean of Winchester, Richard Chenevix Trench, in his work on " Bible Revision," as the test of what faults the ripest scholarship can find in it, they appear singularly few and comparatively harmless. Having shown that the translators fell into some few grammatical errors, failed occasionally to adopt the best rendering, even when it was before them in some previous translation, and in a small number of instances " wholly or partially mistranslated," he bears the following unequivocal testimony to the faithfulness, accuracy and worth of their labors :

" There is often a sense of something ungenerous, if not actually unjust, in passing over large portions of our version, where all is clear, correct, lucid, happy, awaking continual admiration by the rhythmic beauty of the periods, the instinctive art with which the style rises and falls with the subject, the skilful surmounting of difficulties the most real, the diligence with which almost all which was happiest in preceding translations has been retained and embodied in the present, the constant solemnity and seriousness which, by some nameless skill, is made to rest upon all ; in passing over all this and much more with a few general words of recognition, and then stopping short and urging some single blemish or inconsistency, and dwelling upon and seeming to make much of this, which often in itself is so little. For the flaws pointed out are frequently so small and so slight, that it might almost seem as if the objector had armed his eye with a microscope for the purpose of detecting that which otherwise would have escaped notice, and which, even if it were faulty, might well have been suffered to pass by unchallenged and lost sight of in the general beauty of the whole. . . . In respect of words, we recognize the true *delectus verborum* on which Cicero insists so earnestly, and in which so much of the charm of style consists. All the words used are of the noblest stamp, alike removed from vulgarity and pedantry ; they are neither too familiar nor on the other side not familiar enough ; they never crawl on the ground, as little are they stilted and far-fetched. And then how happily mixed and tempered are the Anglo-Saxon and Latin vocables ! . . . . One of the most effectual means by which our translators have attained their happy felicity in diction, while it must diminish to a certain extent their claims to absolute originality, enhances in a far higher degree their good sense, moderation and wisdom. I allude to the extent to which they have availed themselves of the work of those who went before them, and incorporated their work into their own, everywhere building, if possible, on the old foundations, and displacing nothing for the mere sake of change. It has thus come to pass that our version, besides having its own felicities, is the inheritor of the felicities in language of all the translations which went before."

If to this testimony we add that of the Catholic Brownson already quoted, we shall have no occasion to doubt the incomparable superiority of this translation over that of the Rheimish and Douay translators.

In his Lectures on the English Language, George P. Marsh remarks respecting this version, that

" It has now, for more than two centuries, maintained its position as an oracular expression of religious truth, and at the same time as the first classic of our literature, the highest exemplar of purity and beauty of language existing in our speech. . . . . Most successful were the translators in making it a summing up of the linguistic equations solved in three centuries of biblical exposition, an anthology of all the beauties developed in the language during its historical existence."

The truthfulness of this testimony respecting the language of King James' version has been very generally acknowledged, not only by Protestant but by Catholic writers. And in the particulars here referred to, it stands out in very marked contrast with the Douay version, whose very frequent and prominent defects led Trench to affirm that the authors of that version "seem to have put off their loyalty to the English language with their loyalty to the English crown."

It can not be affirmed, of course, that the " authorized version " is perfect in all respects. This would have required a miracle at every stage of the work. It would be strange if the accurate and scholarly criticism of two centuries and a half had not revealed some blemishes in it, notwithstanding the care and learning of the translators. But like the spots on the sun's disc, they by no means obscure its brightness. We need not close our eyes to them. It is a laudable desire to have them removed. And for a few years past that desire has been gaining strength, and the question of a revision of the existing text has been much talked of.

None but those who have denominational interests in view will think of remedying the existing defects by a new translation. " To attempt a new translation of the Bible," says

Marsh, "in the hope of finding within the compass of the English language a clearer, a more appropriate, or a more forcible diction than that of the standard version, is to betray an ignorance of the capabilities of our native speech, with which it would be in vain to reason." But a revision in the spirit of the translators of our version, though by no means as extensive as theirs, would remove some acknowledged defects. They say of their work : " We never thought from the beginning, that we should need to make a new translation, nor yet to make a bad one a good one, but to make a good one better, or out of many good ones one principal good one, not justly to be excepted against ; that hath been our endeavor, that our marke." A revision removing acknowledged blemishes would employ itself, as Trench has shown, in correcting some minor errors of Greek grammar ; in adopting in some instances preferable renderings, many of which were suggested by the translators themselves, and are already in the margin ; in substituting more modern words for those that have become obsolete since the translation was made, numbering as Marsh estimates not over two hundred and fifty ; and in correcting a few words wholly or partially mistranslated. Of these last Trench has selected the prominent ones, and they are less in his judgment than a score, only one of which inculcates any doctrinal error. Respecting this passage, Col. i. 15, " Who is the image of the invisible God, the first born of every creature," he remarks : " This is one of the very few renderings in our version, I know not whether the only one, which obscures a great doctrinal truth, and, indeed, worse that this, seems to play into the hands of Arian error." But this rendering, which seems to include Christ in the creation of God, is corrected by the passage itself which affirms that he was " before all things," and that " by him were all things created."

In respect to the class of words which are imperfectly rendered, it will sometimes happen that the Romish translation is preferable to our own. This we are most happy to acknowledge. For example : the translation which we find here of the Greek disjunctive by " or " instead of " and," as in our version, in 1 Cor. xi. 27, is evidently correct : " Whoever shall eat this bread and (or) drink this cup of the Lord unworthily, shall be guilty of the body and blood of the Lord." "True, some good manuscripts read ' and ' (*και*)," says Olshausen, "but without doubt ' or ' (*η*) is preferable as the more usual form."

Matt. x. 16, is better rendered by the Rheimish translators, " simple as doves," rather than " harmless as doves," as in our version, which however has simple in the margin, according to Wiclif. There can be no doubt but they have adopted a better translation of Matt. xiii. 25, than our own : " But while men were asleep his enemy came and oversowed cockle among the wheat." The manuscripts differ, it is true, but the preponderance is in favor of *επεσπειρεν*, over-sowed, rather than *σπειρεν*, sowed." See Alford's Gr. Test., *in loco*.

So again the rendering of Mark vi. 20, is preferable to our own : "Herod feared John, and kept him," that is, from the malice of Herodias who was seeking occasion to kill him. The margin of our version has " kept him, or saved him." Either of these would have been preferable in the text to " observed him."

The rendering of James i. 26, " If any man think himself to be religious," is far better than ours : " If any man seem to be"; the reference being to the man's own estimate of himself, and not at all to the judgment of others.

But while the translation of here and there a word is preferable to our own, as would very naturally occur, it will stand no comparison with it, as a whole, in purity of diction, and freedom from grave doctrinal errors.

One of the first things that arrests our attention in opening the Catholic Bible is the addition of the following books and parts of books, that are not found in our own : Tobias, Judith, Ecclesiasticus, Wisdom, Baruch, First and Second Maccabees, six and a half chapters added to Esther, and two and a half added to the book of Daniel. They have been termed Apocryphal, or The Apocrypha—hidden, secreted, mysterious, because, says Augustine : "Their original is obscure, they are destitute of proper testimonials, their authors being unknown, and their characters either heretical or suspected." Here, however, they are ranked among the canonical books, and esteemed of equal authority. But the question will be asked, What is the evidence that they are not inspired books? We answer :

1. Their writers did not claim to be inspired. The first and second Maccabees are regarded as the most important of these added books, being valuable, especially the first, as ancient history, having been "written with great accuracy and fidelity." And yet their inspiration is distinctly disclaimed. In the first book, it is said, that at the time it was written, there was no prophet in Israel. "They laid up the stones in the mountain of the temple till there should come a prophet, and give answer concerning them." iv. 46. And again it is said : "There was made great tribulation in Israel, such as was not since the day that there was no prophet seen in Israel." ix. 27.

At the close of the second book we read : "If I have done well, and as it becometh the history, it is what I desired. But if not so perfectly, it must be pardoned me." xv. 39. This is not the language of one claiming to be inspired. It is not after the manner of the writers of the inspired books. Valuable ancient history these books may be, but they are not to be regarded as Scripture.

2. The Apocryphal books never constituted a part of the Hebrew Bible. They were written after the age of Malachi, and when there is no reason to suppose there was any prophet in Israel. The Jews never acknowledged them to be inspired books, though some portions contained accredited history, and others, as "The Book of Wisdom," and "Ecclesiasticus" eminently wise and sententious proverbs.

3. The writers of the New Testament never quoted the Apocrypha. This must be regarded as very significant. They were under the spirit of inspiration. They were continually quoting the Old Testament as contained in the Hebrew Scriptures ; more than five hundred instances might be cited, but they made no account of these Apocryphal books. This entire neglect, by the inspiring Spirit, can be regarded in no other light than as a witness against their inspiration.

4. There is the clearest historic evidence that the Old Testament Scriptures, as read, quoted and commended by Christ and the Apostles, did not contain the Apocrypha. When Christ said to his hearers, "Search the Scriptures," he alluded to a definite book, or collection of writings, which could be referred to with as much precision as the Scriptures of the present day.

The term had a definite meaning, embracing so much, no more. When he met his disciples after his resurrection, he said to them, "All things must be fulfilled which were written in the law of Moses, and in the Prophets, and in the Psalms concerning me." He comprised the entire collection of the sacred writings in the three-fold division, "Law of Moses," "Prophets," and "Psalms."

Luke casually referred to the same classification. Speaking of the discourse of Christ to the two disciples on the way to Emmaus, he says: "Beginning at Moses, and all the Prophets, he expounded unto them in all the Scriptures the things concerning himself." Here the writings of Moses and the Prophets, and certain other portions are referred to, as constituting "all the Scriptures." Now "the Law," or "Moses," comprised the Pentateuch, the first five books which Moses wrote; "The Prophets" embraced the prophetical and remaining historical portions which were written by them; and "the Psalms" was an abbreviated expression for the poetical books. Was the Apocrypha included in these three divisions, or did it originate after the Old Testament canon was complete?

Ecclesiasticus, one of the Apocryphal books, was written about one hundred and eighty years before Christ, by one Jesus, the son of Sirach, of Jerusalem. It was written in Hebrew, and translated by his grandson into Greek about half a century later. In his preface to his translation the grandson of Sirach says: "My grandfather, Jesus, after he had given himself to a diligent reading of the Law and the Prophets, and the other books of the Fathers, had a mind to write something himself." Here, it will be seen, he refers to the Scriptures as they were known in his day, and which his grandfather had studied, in almost the same language as Christ and Luke, marking accurately the same threefold division of the books, "The Law, the Prophets, and the other books of the Fathers." Three times is this classification of the sacred books referred to in his preface, though occupying less than half a page. But his grandfather's book, Ecclesiasticus, was not contained in either of these departments, since he did not write it until "after he had given himself to a diligent reading of these."

It is equally evident that the first edition of the Septuagint could not have contained it.   For that translation of the old Hebrew Scriptures into Greek was made, as we have seen, about two hundred and eighty five years before Christ, or one hundred years before the son of Sirach wrote, and one hundred and fifty years before his work was translated into Greek.

Perhaps we may find something in the book itself which will give us the opinion of the son of Sirach concerning the Scriptures as he studied them.

Referring to Moses he says, (chap. xlv. 6), "He [God] gave him commandments before his face, and a law of life and instruction, that he might teach Jacob his covenant, and Israel his judgments."   Here is an obvious reference to the first of the three divisions of the sacred book, the Law of Moses. Referring to others of the ancients he says, (chap. xliv. 3), "They gave counsel by their understanding in prophecies," which include the second division.   Eulogizing others, he remarks, (chap. xliv. 5), "They sought out the melody of music, they composed poems in writings."   Here is a reference no less obvious to the Psalms, and other poetical portions of the Scriptures.   The son of Sirach was familiar with the classification of the books of the Old Testament.   It was the same as in the age of Christ and his Apostles.   The canon had been completed in his day more than two hundred years, or since the days of Malachi.   Neither he nor his grandson claimed that *his* writings ought to have a place there.

Josephus, who was born only a few years after the crucifixion of Christ, and who was the most reliable historian of that age, refers to the same threefold division of the books of the Scriptures, and marks accurately the time when the Old Testament canon was regarded as complete.   "This period," [comprised in the five books of Moses] "lacks but little of three thousand years.   From the death of Moses until the reign of Artaxerxes, the prophets have described the things which were done during the age of each one respectively, in thirteen books. The remaining four contain hymns to God, and rules of life for men."

Having made this reference to Moses, the Prophets, and the Psalms, he adds: "From the time of Artaxerxes, moreover, until our present period, all occurrences have been written down, but they are not regarded as entitled to like credit with those which precede them, because there was no certain succession of prophets."

Here seems to be a distinct reference to the books called the Apocrypha, but in his age, which was the age of the Apostles, they were not regarded as inspired.   There had been no accredited prophet from the time of Artaxerxes, whose reign extended from four hundred and sixty four to four hundred and twenty four years before Christ.   This was about the age of the prophet Malachi.

Advancing now one step further, we come to distinct catalogues of the books of the Bible.   In a letter of Mileto, a bishop of Sardis, to his brother, about A. D. 170, he says: "Making a journey into the East, I have arrived at the place where these writings were proclaimed and translated.   I have learned accurately the books of the Old Testament, which I here arrange and transmit to you."   Then follow the names of all the books as they are found in the Hebrew Scriptures, and in our own version, with the exception of Nehemiah and Esther.   Not one of the Apocryphal books is included.   Besides, there is presumptive evidence, in the order of the books as given in his list, and in the classification of the books of Samuel as I and II Kings, that he drew up his catalogue from the Septuagint version rather than from the Hebrew.   At any rate, the evidence is clear, that down to the close of the second century, the church at Jerusalem and vicinity accepted no one of the books as authentic that is contained in the Apocrypha. The earliest editions of the Septuagint, those used by Christ and his Apostles, did not contain them.   They were not a part of "the Scriptures," which Christ commanded his hearers to "search," and for "searching which daily," Luke commended the Bereans.

A question then arises, and it is an interesting one in this connection, When were the Apocryphal books introduced into the canon, and for what purpose?   Light will be thrown upon this question by the following facts.

Origin, writing in the third century, mentions the first Book of Maccabees, but "expressly separates it from the canonical books."   Hilary, a cotemporary, says, at the close of a catalogue of the books, "to some it seems good to add Tobit and Judith." The question respecting the introduction of other books was beginning to be discussed. This was in the third century.

Athanasius, who wrote near the beginning of the fourth century, expresses the "fear that the simple may wander away from their simplicity and purity, by reason of the craftiness of certain men, and finally may begin to take to themselves the books called Apocryphal, being deceived by their likeness to the true books."

Speaking of books which are "not canonical," he mentions, "The Wisdom of Solomon, The Wisdom of Sirach [Ecclesiasticus], Esther, Judith, and Tobit." For some unknown reason, Esther, though found in the Hebrew Scriptures, was here spoken of as "not canonical." Mileto, as we have seen, also omitted it in the former century from his list.

About the middle of this century, Cyril of Jerusalem included Baruch in his catalogue, and the council of Laodicea decreed that it "ought to be read." Epiphanius speaks of the Wisdom of Sirach and the Wisdom of Solomon as "doubtful," and of certain other books as "Apocryphal."

Later in the century, we find Jerome and Rufinus opposing the introduction of these Apocryphal books. This of itself is sufficient evidence that the early editions of the Vulgate, which took shape under the pen of Jerome, did not contain these books. He would not have introduced books into the canon while openly opposing their introduction. But in the last decade of this century, two provincial councils, the one at Hippo, and the other at Carthage, declared The Wisdom of Solomon, Ecclesiasticus, Tobit, Judith, and First and Second Maccabees to be canonical.

There is another source of evidence. During this century the Armenians were converted to Christianity. And when, early in the following century, 411, the Scriptures were translated into their tongue from the Septuagint version, the Apocrypha was not included. As late as the commencement of the fifth century, therefore, though certain writers and certain provincial councils had declared in favor of these books, the most authentic editions of the Septuagint did not contain them. The Armenian church has never considered them to be canonical.

Such, in brief, is the nature of the evidence that proves conclusively that it was not until about the commencement of the fifth century that the Apocryphal books were introduced into the sacred canon. Christ and his Apostles, and the united church of the first and second centuries rejected them. In the third they began to take rank as important ecclesiastical but uninspired books. In the fourth they were spoken of by individuals and councils as worthy to be ranked among the inspired books. In the fifth, and later, they were foisted into the sacred text. From the Septuagint, or Greek version, as thus augmented by the addition of seven entire books, and several chapters added to two others, the Vulgate was translated; and this, as we have seen, was made the basis of the Douay or Catholic translation in the sixteenth century.

Such being the origin of the Apocryphal books, and the circumstances of their introduction to the canon, we are compelled to regard them as without authority, uninspired, and uncanonical, and therefore as necessarily vitiating any version of which they form a part.

It is time to direct our attention to the text of this Douay version, in order to point out some of its prominent defects.

1. It is corrupted by the characteristics of the Apocrypha. Passing by the uncanonical character of these books, there are many passages in them especially objectionable. But these have always given them importance in the eyes of Romanists, because justifying doctrines and customs which by the Protestant church are deemed heretical.

They abound in extravagant stories, and marvellous events, which favor the tendency in the Papal church to multiply signs and wonders, and miracles, those characteristics of the "man of sin" as described by the Apostle Paul. For example: The History of Bel and the Dragon; Habbaccuc's journey through the air to Babylon; the miraculous movement of the tabernacle and ark, as it followed Jeremiah into the wilderness; the assassination of Holofernes by the hand of Judith, and the lascivious stories of Tobias and Susanna.

They favor the doctrine of justification by works, without

faith in Christ.   Thus we read in Ecclesiasticus xxxv. 3 : " To depart from injustice is to offer a propitiatory sacrifice for injustices, and a begging of pardon for sins."   And in Tobias xii. 8, 9, "Prayer is good with fasting and alms, more than to lay up treasures of gold.   For alms delivereth from death, and the same is that which purgeth away sins, and maketh to find mercy, and life everlasting."

By such passages the doctrine of justification " by grace through faith " is discarded, and penances, alms and prayers are set forth as the procuring cause of everlasting life.

Prayers for the dead also are commended in 2 Mac. xii. 42–46, where it is said that Judas Maccabeus " sent twelve thousand drachms of silver to Jerusalem for sacrifice to be offered for the sins of the dead," who had fallen in battle. And it is added : "It is therefore a wholesome and holy thought to pray for the dead, that they may be loosed from their sins."

This passage is accompanied, in the version which was authorized by Archbishop Hughes to be used by the Catholics in this country, by the following note : " Here is an evident and undeniable proof of the practice of praying for the dead under the old law, which was then strictly observed by the Jews, and consequently could not be introduced at that time by Judas, their chief and high priest, if it had not been always their custom."   A passage so important as this, for a church that derives an immense revenue from its masses for the dead, could not fail to be accounted important.   It is easy to see one reason, at least, why the book that contains it was introduced into the catalogue of inspired writings.

But turning from the Apocrypha to the characteristics of this version as affected by the uncritical labors of the translators, we shall find many things that mar it sadly, and render it an imperfect exponent of the mind and will of God.   Among these we may mention,

2. The translation is harsh and inelegant, abounding in obsolete and untranslated words. It bears no comparison, in these respects, with King James' version, as any one can see by turning to any chapter and placing them side by side.   This is especially true of the New Testament.   These characteristics were well described by Brownson when he said : " In literary merit it

can in no respect compare with the Protestant version; compared with that it is weak, tasteless and inharmonious." They led Trench to say that, " The authors of the Rheimish version seem to have put off their loyalty to the English language with their loyalty to the English crown."

Selecting a few passages almost at random, we read, " If thy right hand scandalize thee." Matt. v. 30. " Take heed that ye do not your justice before men to be seen by them." Matt. vi. 1. " And when you are praying speak not much, as the heathens." Matt. vi. 7. " If thine eye be single thy whole body shall be lightsome. But if thine eye be evil thy whole body shall be darksome." Matt. vi. 22, 23. "And on the first day of the azymes the disciples came to Jesus saying: Where wilt thou that we prepare for thee to eat the pasch?" Matt. xxvi. 17. The word for passover in the Old Testament in this version is phase. Thus in the passage describing its institution, Ex. xii. 11: "It is the phase (that is the passage) of the Lord." In the Old Testament it is uniformly translated phase, in the New, pasch.

" Purge out the old leaven, that you may be a new paste, as you are unleavened." 1 Cor. v. 11. " For Christ our pasch is sacrificed." 1 Cor. v. 7. "And it came to pass when the the days of his assumption were accomplished." Luke ix. 51. " The fruit of the spirit is longaminity." Gal. v. 22. " Holocausts for sin did not please thee." Heb. x. 6. " The chalice of benediction." 1 Cor. x. 16. "But the Paraclete, the Holy Ghost." Jno. xiv. 26. " And when the evening was now come, because it was the parasceve, that is, the day before the Sabbath." Mark xv. 42. " He who soweth sparingly shall also reap sparingly; and he who soweth in blessings, shall also reap of blessings." 2 Cor. ix. 6. " Abraham believed God, and it was reputed to him unto justice." Rom. iv. 3. " You are made void of Christ, you who are justified in the law; you are fallen from grace. For we in spirit, by faith, wait for the hope of justice." Gal. v. 4, 5. " You are fellow citizens with the saints and the domestics of God." Eph. ii. 19. "Of whom all paternity in heaven and earth is named." Eph. iii. 15. " And that every tongue should confess that the Lord Jesus Christ is in the glory of the Father."

Phil. ii. 11. "Who shall suffer eternal punishment in destruction from the face of the Lord." 2 Thess. i. 9. "Christ was offered once to exhaust the sins of many." Heb. ix. 28. "We are not the children of withdrawing unto perdition." Heb. x. 39. "And they sung as it were a new canticle before the throne. And no man could say the canticle," see Rev. xiv. 3. "He that hurteth let him hurt still, and he that is filthy, let him be filthy still." Rev. xxii. 11.

Of such weak and imperfect translations this version is full. They occur on every page, confirming the judgment of Brownson respecting the translation : "They were learned men, but had to a great extent lost the genius and idioms of their own language, and were evidently more familiar with Latin and French than with their mother tongue." But why need they have left so many words untranslated, words which express nothing to the English ear? A very large number of passages are darkened by this neglect, if not rendered entirely unintelligible to the common mind.

But the late editions of the Douay, (from one of which, approbated by John Hughes, Bishop of New York, 1844, these examples have been taken,) give us no correct conception of the imperfection of the Rheimish New Testament as it came from the hands of the first translators. The Papal church has published no edition for about two hundred and fifty years which retains their translation entire.

As a specimen of the imperfect manner in which they performed their work, and of the changes that have crept into every chapter, and almost every verse since the work came from their hands, let us place side by side several passages from the text of the Rheimish doctors, and the modern edition approbated by Bishop Hughes.

EDITION OF 1582.	EDITION OF 1844.
Mk. v. 22. "And there cometh one of the archsynagogues, named Jairus.	"And there cometh one of the rulers of the synagogue named Jairus."
Mk. v. 40–42. "And they derided him. But he having put forth all, taketh the father and mother of	"And they laughed him to scorn. But he having put them all out, taketh the father and mother of the

the wench, [Gr. παιδίον called daughter v. 23] and them that were with him, and they go in where the wench was lying. And holding the wench's hand, he saith to her. Talitha cumi, which is being interpreted, Wench, I say to thee, arise. And forthwith the wench rose up and walked."

Ac. ix. 20, 21. "And incontinent entering into the synagogues, he preached Jesus, that this is the Son of God. And all that heard were astonished, and said, Is not this he that expugned in Jerusalem, those that invocated this name?"

1 Cor. v. 6–8. "Know you not that a little leaven corrupteth the whole paste? Purge the old leaven that you may be a new paste as you are azymes. For our pasch, Christ is immolated. Therefore let us feast, not in the old leaven, nor in the leaven of malice and wickedness, but in the azymes of sincerity and verity."

1 Cor. xv. 54. "This corruptible must do on incorruption, and this mortal do on immortality."

Eph. iii. 11. "According to the prefinition of worlds, which he made in Christ Jesus our Lord."

Eph. iv. 30. "And contristate not the holy Spirit of God: in which you are signed unto the day of redemption."

1 Tim. vi. 20. O Timothy, keep the depositum, avoiding the profane novelties of voices, and oppositions of falsely called knowledge."

2 Tim. i. 12, 14. "I am sure that he is able to keep my depositum unto that day. Keep the good depositum by the Holy Ghost, which dwelleth in us."

damsel and them that were with him, and entereth in where the damsel was lying. And taking the damsel by the hand, he saith to her: Talitha-cumi, which is, being interpreted; damsel, I say to thee arise. And immediately the damsel rose up and walked."

"And immediately he preached Jesus in the synagogues, that he is the son of God. And all that heard him were astonished, and said: Is not this he who persecuted in Jerusalem those that called on this name?"

"Know ye not that a little leaven corrupteth the whole lump. Purge out the old leaven, that you may be a new paste, as you are unleavened. For Christ our pasch is sacrificed. Therefore let us feast, not with the old leaven, nor with the leaven of malice and wickedness. but with the unleavened bread of sincerity and truth."

"This corruptible must put on incorruption; and this mortal must put on immortality."

"According to the eternal purpose. which he made in Christ Jesus our Lord."

"And grieve not the holy Spirit of God; whereby you are sealed unto the day of redemption."

"O Timothy, keep that which is committed to thy trust, avoiding the profane novelties of words, and oppositions of knowledge falsely so called."

"I am certain he is able to keep that which I have committed unto him against that day. Keep the good thing committed to thy trust by the Holy Ghost, who dwelleth in us."

Heb. ix. 3. "But after the second vail, the tabernacle, which is called sanctum sanctorum."	"And after the second vail, the tabernacle, which is called the Holy of Holies."
1 Pet. ii. 5. "Be ye also yourselves superedified as it were living stones, spiritual houses, a holy priesthood, to offer spiritual hosts."	"Be you also as living stones built up, a spiritual house, a holy priesthood, to offer up spiritual sacrifices."
Rev. i. 10. "I was in the spirit on the Dominical day."	"I was in the spirit on the Lord's day."

These passages are sufficient to show the changes that have been made in the Rheimish Testament since it came from the hand of its translators. The most careless reading will show any one that they are improvements upon the old translation, and in almost all instances the changes are approximations to the version of King James. And it would not be too much to say, probably, respecting the number of the changes, that they outnumber the verses of the whole New Testament. The felt necessity for these changes of words, construction and punctuation shows in a clear light the imperfection of the work, as it came from the hands of the " learned men " at Rheims.

But what becomes, in view of these changes, of the Papal argument in favor of their version, that it is fixed and unchangable, while the versions of the Protestants are many and contradictory? And who will tell us by what authority these changes, that have been going steadily on for the last two hundred and fifty years, have been made? Has any council been called to act upon these revisions, sanction, and give them, *ex cathedra*, the seal of inspiration? Has any Pope approved them, and authorized their publication and distribution in their present form among the subjects of his holiness? If not, how does any Catholic know that he possesses the inspired word of God? The version which he holds in his hand differs very materially from the Rheimish, which it pretends to be on its title page. And the changes have brought it into nearer and nearer proximity to the Protestant version, which he esteems so lightly. Manifestly there was need enough for all these changes ; and it is equally manifest that there is need of still further changes, to make it conform to the earliest manuscripts extant, the foundations of all our knowledge of divine things.

3. The translators have not accurately indicated the words they introduce which had no corresponding word in the original text.

Any translation from one tongue into another, will require the addition of some elements not found in the former, to make it conform to the genius of the latter. These the translators of the Protestant version have scrupulously preserved in italics. It is easy for the reader to see in every sentence what was added to make a smooth English rendering, and what was contained in the inspired originals. If any one thinks the translators erred, and have obscured the sense, he is at liberty to reject these italicised words, or to introduce others to make the sentence perfect, according to his judgment of the sense. As our version was translated directly from the original tongues, there is no possibility of being led far astray from the mind of God. On the other hand, the Douay version of the Old Testament being three removes from the original Hebrew, and the Rheimish version of the New being two removes from the original Greek, the translators, by neglecting very generally to mark the added words, have deprived the common reader of the means of knowing precisely what elements were in the Hebrew and Greek, and what were added in the process of the several translations.

4. A fourth objection to this version is, imperfect translations of the original Hebrew and Greek.

Whether the errors complained of first existed in the Septuagint or Vulgate, or were introduced by the Douay and Rheimish translators, it makes no difference. It was the business of these latter to have corrected the errors of the former by reference to the original manuscripts.

In Isaiah liii. 4, we read in the Douay :

"Surely he hath borne our infirmities and carried our sorrows. And we thought him as it were a leper, as one struck by God and afflicted." The word here rendered " a leper,"is a participle, not a noun, in the original, and translated by Gesenius " smitten." No rendering could be more literal, or more in accordance with the facts. We have no evidence that Christ was supposed to have the leprosy. But the Jews did suppose that his sufferings and death were the result of ambi-

tious and blasphemous pretentions. That God in his providence
had brought him to justice, and that he was literally " smitten,
stricken of God."

This error reveals in a very clear light the impossibility of
securing a reliable translation from any version that has come
through several dialects. The Hebrew of this word is נָגַע
"smitten." The LXX has εἶναι ἐν πόνῳ, "to be in distress," or
"affliction." And the Vulgate *quasi leprosum,* "as leprous."

The error then lay back of the Douay translators. But this
can not make their translation either correct or authoritative.

The ninth verse of the same chapter Alexander has termed
"a curiosity": "He made his grave with the wicked, and with
the rich in his death," so it is rendered in the authorized version, referring to his crucifixion between two thieves, and
burial in a rich man's tomb. The Douay, following the LXX
and the Vulgate, renders it: "He shall give the ungodly for
his burial, and the rich for his death ;" a rendering equally removed from the original prophecy, and the facts of Christ's
death and burial. Indeed it is difficult to extract from it any
sense whatever.

Little better is the rendering of Jer. xi. 19, which in the authorized version is : "Let us destroy the tree with the fruit
thereof." It is a figurative expression, denoting complete destruction. The Douay version renders it, "Let us put wood on
his bread." Thomas Ward in his "Errata" quotes St. Hierom
as interpreting it, "the cross upon the body of our Saviour."
But no idea can be more fanciful. The LXX mistook the
meaning of the verb שָׁחַת, to destroy, to ruin, and translated
it by ἐμβάλλω. The Vulgate adopted *mitto,* and thus the idea
of destruction was lost, which the connection imperatively required, as the reader of the passage will see.

The words of Ezekiel, vii. 17, "All knees shall be weak as
water," which is a figure of great force, as applied to a terror-
stricken people, is rendered by the senseless phrase, " all knees
shall run with water."

Take the first verse of the first Psalm. " Blessed is the man
who hath not walked in the counsel of the ungodly, nor stood
in the way of sinners, nor sat in the chair of pestilence." What
nonsense is made of this last clause ! What a complete failure

to preserve the beautiful climax of the original; " Walking in the counsel of the ungodly," implying casual intercourse; then " standing in the way of sinners," implying delight in the company of the openly wicked, and stopping to enjoy it; and finally "sitting in the seat of scorners," as companions.   The Hebrew לֵצִים scoffers or scorners, is the plural participle from the verb לוץ, "to stammer, speak in a foreign tongue, to deride, mock. Part. לֵץ, a mocker, scoffer." (Gesenius' Lex.)   The LXX mistook the sense and rendered ἐπὶ καθέδρᾳ λοιμῶν, "in the seat of the plague."   The Vulgate failed to correct the error, *in cathedra pestilentiæ;* and the Douay translators were bound by the decrees of the Council of Trent to render it as they did, "in the chair of pestilence."   Such is the history of the error.

The fourth verse of this Psalm is as faulty as the first : "Not so the wicked, not so : but like the dust which the wind driveth from the face of the earth."

The second "not so" is not in the Hebrew.   It first appears in the Greek, was copied into the Vulgate and of course appeared in the Douay.   The same is true of the last clause, "from the face of the earth."   The Hebrew verb means simply "To drive asunder, disperse, scatter."

The word "dust" is a mistranslation.   The Hebrew is מֹץ, "chaff."   This is its only definition.   The Greek translated it by χνοῦς "something scraped from the surface of anything."   And the Vulgate by *pulvis,* whence the Douay "dust."

Take the earnest entreaty of the second Psalm : "Kiss the Son lest he be angry, and ye perish from the way when his wrath is kindled but a little."   Read this a second time and see how congruous are its parts, how appropriate the exhortation to those who had "set themselves against the Lord, and against his Anointed."   There is evidence on the face of it that the translation is spirited and faithful.   Read now the rendering, and mark the punctuation of the Douay.   "Embrace discipline, lest at any time the Lord be angry, and you perish from the just way.   When his wrath shall be kindled in a short time, blessed are all they that trust in him."   What fear is there that any man will "perish from the just way"?   And why is he especially "blessed" who trusts in God after his wrath has been kindled "a short time"?   Every reader must feel that this is an imperfect rendering of the entreaties of God, while the critical scholar will see that it has no warrant in the Hebrew text or punctuation.   It appears in the LXX., was copied into the Vulgate and the English, with no reference, apparently, after the first translation, to the original Hebrew.   No, for the Council of Trent had anathematized all who should go behind the Latin Vulgate.

Let us take a few illustrations from the New Testament. " My Father which gave them me," said Christ of his disciples, "is greater than all."   Such is the rendering of John x. 29, in the authorized version.   It is very difficult to see how a more literal translation of the original : 'Ο πατήρ μου, ὃς δέδωκέ μοι, μείζων πάντων ἐστί, could be given.   And yet the Rheimish translators have this false statement, which can by no possibility be extorted from the Greek, and which stands in no proper connection with the remainder of Christ's discourse : "That which my Father hath given me is greater than all."

Here again we come to the original sin of the version in question, a servile copying of error.   For turning to the Vulgate we find, " Pater meus, quod dedit mihi, majus omnibus est."

How feeble is the rendering of Paul's words in Heb. iv. 16 : "That we might find grace to help in time of need," "Find grace in seasonable aid."

How the meaning of the Greek ἐπιούσιον is obscured by the uncouth word, "supersubstantial," in Matt. vi. 11, " Give us this day our supersubstantial bread."   Donnegan in his Lexicon renders the word "sufficient for sustenance."   Robinson, (Gr. Lex.) says, "While some translate 'bread for sustaining life,' others, adopting a different derivation, translate 'to-morrow's bread, bread for the coming day, e. g., daily bread.' "

The Rheimish translators attempt to justify their rendering by the following note :

" By this bread so called here according to the Latin word and the Greek, we ask not only all necessary sustenance of the body, but much more, all spiritual food, namely, the blessed sacrament itself, which is Christ, the true bread that came down from heaven, and the bread of life to us that eat his body.   And therefore called here supersubstantial ; that is, the bread that passeth and excelleth all creatures."

And yet when the phrase occurs in Luke, xi. 3, they render the same word as in the Protestant version, " Our daily bread."

5. Obvious perversions and falsifications to favor the doctrines of the Catholic church.

It is not pleasant to be compelled to speak of false translations, but there are some instances in which the corrupt doctrines of the Papacy evidently lent their corruptions to this version. Heb. xi. 21, is most grossly perverted to favor the worship of images. It is as follows : " By faith, Jacob dying, blessed every one of the sons of Joseph, and adored the top of his rod." This is accompanied by the following note :

" The Apostle here follows the ancient Greek Bible of the seventy inte.preters, which translates in this manner, Gen. xlvii. 31, and alleges this fact of Jacob, in paying a relative honor and veneration to the top of the rod or sceptre of Joseph, as to a figure of Christ's sceptre and kingdom, as an instance and argument of his faith. But some translators, who are no friends to this relative honor, have corrupted the text by translating it, ' He worshipped, leaning upon the top of his staff,' as if this circumstance of leaning upon his staff were any argument of Jacob's faith, or worthy of being thus particularly taken notice of by the Holy Ghost."

The author of this note has most evidently mistaken the grammatical construction of the verse. The subject of it being Jacob, the concluding phrase, " his rod,' or " staff," most naturally refers to a staff in the hand of Jacob, and not in the hand of Joseph.

But not only is the translation defective, but the note also is incorrect, when it asserts that such is the statement of the Septuagint. Neither the Greek of the Apostle, nor the Septuagint which he followed, no, nor the Hebrew of which it is a translation, says," he adored the top of his rod." In all of them there is the preposition "upon," which the Douay suppresses. It is difficult to see how it could have been ignorantly done. The Greek o· | ·· |· ssage in Hebrews, and of the Septuagint translation of Gen. xlvii. 31, do not differ by a letter. It is as follows : προσεχύνησεν 'Ισραὴλ ἐπὶ τὸ ἄχρον τῆς ῥάβδου αὐτοῦ. The Hebrew has the preposition עַל corresponding with the Greek ἐπὶ. וַיִּשְׁתַּחוּ יִשְׂרָאֵל עַל־רֹאשׁ הַמִּטָּה. There is no warrant then either in the Hebrew, the Septuagint translation, or Paul's quotation of it for the Douay version, or the note appended to it. The fact obviously was, he worshipped God upon the top of his own staff, not a staff in the hand of Joseph.

The word here rendered "adore," or "worship," both in the Hebrew and Greek, implies an act of prostration upon the ground, with the face to the earth ; such was the custom of past ages. This Jacob being unable to do from his great age and infirmity, he bowed himself upon his staff, and worshipped Jehovah. Our version has very properly added in italics the word " leaning." " He worshipped, *leaning* upon the top of his staff." For to worship upon it can mean nothing other than resting or leaning upon it while worshipping, instead of prostrating himself upon the ground.

While on this subject, we must not forget to refer to an imperfect rendering of this passage in Genesis, in both King James' and the Douay versions. In the former it is rendered, " And Israel bowed himself upon the bed's head." In the latter, " Israel adored God, turning to the bed's head."

This defective translation arose, doubtless on this wise. The Hebrew word has two significations : מִטָּה "bed," and מַטֶּה "rod," or "staff," according to two different ways of pointing it. The radical letters are the same, the vowel points are different. The Septuagint translators, making their version, as they did, several centuries before the vowel points were adopted, and before the Hebrew had entirely fallen into disuse as a spoken language, translated the word by ῥάβδου, "a rod, wand, or staff." This rendering the Apostle Paul sanctioned, for he evidently understood the sentence in the light of that meaning. He copied the Septuagint *verbatim et literatim.*

When, however, the Hebrew was no longer spoken, and doubts arose respecting the powers of the radical letters, and the correct manner of pronouncing them, a system of vowel points was invented. " This was completed," says Nordheimer, " about the seventh century of the Christian era." By the authors of this system of points, the word in question was understood to signify "bed," and was pointed accordingly.   This sense of the word reappears in the Vulgate.   *Adoravit Israel Deum, conversus ad lectuli caput;* and this gave form to the Douay.   The same cause decided the translation in King James' version, which, as will be seen, is more literal than the former, " Israel bowed himself upon the bed's head."   Such seems to be the history of the discrepancy between Gen. xlvii. 31, and Heb. xi. 21, which is a quotation of it ; a discrepancy greatly to be regretted, though leading to no such evil conse-quences as the false rendering of the latter text in the Douay.

The question will perhaps be asked, Which is the correct translation of the original word?   Shall we follow the Septua-gint translators, or the authors of the Hebrew vowel points? We must give the preference to the judgment of the Seventy for the following reasons :   They made their translation while the Hebrew was to some extent a spoken language, and before the method of pronunciation was wholly lost.   Their rendering is sanctioned by the Apostle Paul when writing under the guid-ance of the inspiring Spirit.   He had before him at the time of making the quotation both the Hebrew and the Septuagint trans-lation.   He adopted the latter as a correct rendering.   Besides, there is no evidence that Jacob was at that time sick, or upon a bed.   It is said, indeed, in verse 29th, that "the time drew near that Israel must die."   This fact occasioned the transac-tion under consideration.   But in the verse following the one we have been examining, it is said : "After these things one told Joseph : Behold, thy father is sick ;" implying that at the time of the transaction he was not sick.   Furthermore, the Scrip-tures make no other reference to the head of a bed ; nor had the bed in oriental countries, properly speaking, such an ap-pendage.   For these reasons, the rendering of the Septuagint is greatly to be preferred, and the translation of the word in Genesis must be regarded as defective, in both versions.

The tendency, which has been revealed in this passage to favor the worship of sacred things, most evidently corrupted the translation of Ps. xcix. 5 : "Exalt ye the Lord our God, and adore his footstool, for it is holy."   There is here a delib-erate suppression of the Hebrew ל, before footstool, which in the authorized version is appropriately rendered, "at."   "Worship at his footstool." This last translation is sustained by the Greek which renders footstool in the dative case, and not in the accusative, τῷ ὑποποδίῳ τῶν ποδῶν αὐτοῦ. The phrase "worship at his footstool," is evidently a repetition of the thought in the first clause : "Exalt ye the Lord our God," the true object of worship being God, the second clause adding the place where that worship is to be rendered. Robinson in his Lexicon says : "πρός with the dative marks a place or object by the side of which a person or thing is, by, at, near ; as if in answer to the question, where?" Here the πρός in composition, προσκυνεῖτε, seems to have this original force. The LXX also sanctions the authorized version of the last clause, ὅτι ἅγιός ἐστι : "For he is holy." The ἅγιος can not refer to ὑποποδίῳ which is a neuter noun, but to the preceding κύριον τὸν θεόν. The error was first made in the Vulgate which is as follows : *adorate scabellum pedum ejus, quoniam sanctum est.*

Another passage, whose rendering in this version finds no warrant either in the Hebrew or the Septuagint is Ex. xxxiv. 29, the thought being repeated also in verses 30, 35.

"Moses knew not that his face was horned from the conversation of the Lord." The Hebrew of the phrase, "his face was horned," reads as follows : קָרַן עוֹר פָּנָיו. This can admit of only one rendering : "The skin of his face emitted rays," or "shone." This it will be seen is the authorized version. The Greek version is similar : δεδόξασται ἡ ὄψις τοῦ χρώματος τοῦ προσώπου αὐτοῦ. "The appearance of the skin of his countenance was glorified," or "made glorious." Hence Paul, when referring to the fact, says : "The children of Israel could not steadfastly behold the face of Moses for the glory, [δόξα,] of his countenance."

If now we turn to the Vulgate we shall find the source of this defective translation. *Ignorabat quod cornuta esset facies sua,* "He knew not that his face was horned." The Douay has perpetuated this defective rendering, affording another proof of the principle laid down on a preceding page, that any version three removes from the original Hebrew can hardly fail to be burdened with errors.

Ward, in his labored Errata of the Protestant Bible, says :

"The English Protestants, on purpose to abolish the holy sacrifice of the mass, did not only take away the word altar out of the Scrip-

tures, but they also suppressed the name priest, in all their translations, turning it into elder; well knowing that these three, priest
sacrifice and altar, are dependents and consequences one of another;
so that they can not be separated.   If there be an external sacrifice,
there must be an external priesthood to offer it, and an altar to offer
the same upon.   So Christ, himself, being a priest, according to the
order of Melchizedek, had a sacrifice, 'his body,' and an altar,
' his cross,' on which he offered it.   And because he instituted this
sacrifice, to continue in his church forever, in commemoration and
representation of his death, therefore did he ordain his Apostles
priests, at his last supper ; where and when he instituted the holy
order of priesthood or priests, saying, *hoc facite*, ' Do this,' to offer
the self-same sacrifice in a mystical and unbloody manner, until the
world's end."

The force of all this reasoning turns upon this last assumption, that Christ instituted the supper to be a sacrifice, and not
rather to commemorate a sacrifice.   Paul seems to have been
oblivious of any such use of this sacrament, when he said,
Rom. vi. 10, " In that he died, he died unto sin once for all" ;
εφαπαξ, "once for all, once." (Donn. Lex.) So also i n Heb. ix.
25, 26, 28 ; x. 10.   " Nor yet that he should offer himself often," πολλάκις, "many times, frequently." (Donn. Lex.)
" Now once in the end of the world, hath he appeared to put
away sin by the sacrifice of himself.   Christ was once offered
to bear the sins of many.   We are sanctified through the offering of the body of Jesus Christ once for all," εφαπαξ.

On Heb. ix. 25, we find this note in the Catholic Bible, lest
the faithful should be led astray by the assertion, " Nor yet that
he should offer himself often" :

" Christ shall never more offer himself in sacrifice, in that
violent, painful and bloody manner, nor can there be any occasion for it ; since by that one sacrifice upon the cross he has
furnished the full ransom, redemption and remedy for all the
sins of the world."   Very well said !   Why not stop here and
leave the impression just where the Apostle leaves it ?   But
this would not answer.   The note proceeds : " But this hinders
not that he may offer himself daily in the sacred mysteries, in
an unbloody manner, for the daily application of that one sacrifice of redemption to our souls."   This clause conflicts direct-

ly with the former, and with the words and arguments of the epistle.

The Apostle Peter in his first epistle, iii. 18, affirms the same truth, making no reference to frequent sacrifices for sin : " Christ also hath once suffered for sins, the just for the unjust, that he might bring us to God."

Now if there is no sacrifice to be offered under this dispensation, there is no need of a priest, nor should we expect to find a constant reference to a priesthood, as under the old economy.   But the Douay has uniformly rendered the Greek, πρεσβύτερος, "priest."   For example, Ac. xiv. 23 ; xv. 2, and Jas. v. 14.   "They ordained to them priests in every church." " They determined that Paul and Barnabas, and certain others of the other side should go up to the Apostles and priests at Jerusalem."   " Is any sick among you, let him bring in the priests of the church."

Now πρεσβύτερος, a comparative form, from πρέσβυς, which means a man between the ages of fifty two and sixty four, signifies primarily an older person ; in the plural old men, seniors, aged.   Such were called to take part in the management of civil and ecclesiastical affairs.   To them was committed the management and government of individual churches. They were aged men, and because of their ordination were called the elders, or πρεσβύτεροι.   But this term is nowhere applied to the priests of the old dispensation, to Christ as a spiritual high priest, or to Christians who are denominated priests unto God.   Thus, Mat. xii. 5 : " The priests in the temple profane the Sabbath and are blameless."   The reference here is to the Levitical priests, and the term ἱερεύς is used, as also in all other places in the New Testament, where a priest is referred to.   If Christ is spoken of as the great high priest, it is ἀρχιερεύς, as in Heb. iv. 15 ; v. 1.   If again he is referred to simply as a priest, without the prefix "high," the term used is ἱερεύς, as in Heb. v. 6, quoted from Ps. cx. 4, where the Septuagint has the same word.   In like manner where the term is applied to Christians, as in Rev. i. 6 ; v. 10 ; xx. 6 : "Priests unto God and his Father ;" "Unto our God kings and priests ;" "Priests of God and of Christ," the term ἱερεύς is uniformly found.

On what principle of correct interpretation could the Douay translators have proceeded, when they invariably rendered πρεσβύτερος by "priest", making no distinction between this word and ἰερεύς? With the passing away of the Mosaic economy the term priest was dropped, and the officers of the Christian churches are denominated ὃι πρεσβεύτεροι, which can not be translated priests, but elders, as in our authorized version. Christ was the last priest on earth, his body the last atoning sacrifice, his cross the last altar.

We come now to what must be regarded as the worst defect of this version, the rendering of the words μετανοέω and μετάνοια by "penance." In the Romish church penance means "Suffering, labor or pain which a person voluntarily subjects himself to, or which is imposed on him by authority, as a punishment for his faults, or an expression of penitence; as fasting, flaggellation, wearing chains, &c. It is one of the sacraments of the Catholic church." (Webster.)

In Matt. iii. 2, John is represented as exhorting the people, as the burden of his message, to "Do penance, for the kingdom of heaven is at hand." As this is the first instance of the use of the word μετανοέω, it is accompanied by the following note to justify the rendering: "This word, according to the use of the Scriptures, and the holy fathers, does not only signify repentance, and amendment of life, but also punishing past sins by fasting, and such like penitential exercises."

Here is a virtual acknowledgment that "repentance and amendment of life" are the primary meaning of the word. Of course it ought to have governed the translation, unless there was something in the connection that modified its meaning. Besides, the authorities do not justify the rendering of the word do penance, or confirm the truthfulness of the note.

Donnegan's Greek Lexicon says it means "To change one's mind on subsequent reflection; to change one's resolution, to repent or regret, to rue an action." The corresponding noun is defined as "a change of mind or purpose on subsequent reflection or experience; repentance, regret." Robinson's Lexicon of the New Testament gives the same definitions essentially, but refers to some passages where the repentance was attended with "acts of external sorrow, penance;" as "Tyre and Sidon would have repented long ago sitting in saccloth and ashes."

But even here the repentance was an inward spiritual act. The penance is not designated by the word μετανοέω, but by the phrase sitting in "saccloth and ashes."

There is then no sufficient warrant for the translation, "do penance." This is a perversion of the great command, which looks only and entirely to a change in the subjective state of the sinner in respect to his sins, not at all to "acts of external sorrow." The rendering "do penance," turns the mind directly away from the spirit of the command. It leaves the sinner to cling to his sins, and think only of some outward infliction of suffering; leaves him in impenitence, and under the wrath of God still.

This perversion of the most vital doctrine of the Gospel will help us to account for a strange feature of the Romish communion, that with all their religiousness, their conscientious performance of outward rites and ceremonies, they have nevertheless, very little conscience of sin. They can commit the most glaring acts of sin, as profanity, intemperance or Sabbath desecration, and yet feel no compunction, nor prejudice their standing in the church. The Scriptures, as they possess them, and hear them read and explained, deceive them respecting the method of salvation, holding the mind to bodily mortification, rather than godly sorrow. We may hope that by the Spirit's work in the heart, many go further than this, but we have little reason to expect renunciation of sin, when the commands of God respecting it are robbed of all their life, and can be satisfied with external acts of mortification.

It is not necessary to refer to all the passages where this false rendering is found. The following may serve as a specimen:

"I baptize you in water unto penance." "Jesus upbraided the cities wherein were done most of his miracles, because they had not done penance." "The disciples went and preached that men should do penance." "There is joy in heaven over one sinner that doth penance." "If thy brother sin against thee, reprove him, and if he do penance, forgive him." "Knowest thou not that the benignity of God leadeth thee to penance?" "The sorrow that is according to God worketh penance."   " The Lord is not willing that any should perish, but that all should do penance."

How easily from such a version, the conscientious Catholic derives the doctrine that his salvation is sure if he performs the penances regular and occasional, laid upon him by his church ! We can understand, in the light of this perversion of truth, what feelings actuated Luther, as on his knees he slowly and painfully ascended the steps of Pilate's stair-case at Rome. We can understand what are the feelings that actuate every Romanist, as he observes scrupulously the weekly and Lenten fasts appointed by his church. The last passage given above will explain it all. Mere penance will be relied upon to secure his salvation, whatever may be the state of the heart.

By a strange inconsistency, the rendering of the words μετανοέω and μετάνοια in a few instances is correct. " They glorified God, saying, then hath God also to the Gentiles given repentance unto life." Peter exclaims, "Be penitent, therefore, and be converted, that your sins may be blotted out." " Him hath God exalted to give repentance to Israel and remission of sins." Speaking of Jezebel, God says, " I gave her a time that she might do penance, and she will not repent of her fornications."

In the Greek the same verb is found in both these sentences, and they should most obviously have been both translated "repent." Nor is the rendering of the Douay justified by the Latin Vulgate : *ut pœnitentiam ageret; et non vult pœnitere*. The phrase *ut pœnitentiam ageret*, means simply "that she might repent," or "to repent." Ainsworth, in his Lexicon says, " The verb *ago* is often Englished by the verb of the following noun." And among other numerous illustrations, he gives " *agere pœnitentiam*, to repent." So that there is no warrant even in the Vulgate where we have found so many errors, for the translation, " that she might do penance."

To these examples of gross perversions of the Scriptures, to favor the corrupt doctrines and practices of the Romish church, there should be added such translations as are not sustained by the best manuscripts.

In 2d Peter, i. 10, we read in our version : "Wherefore the rather brethren, give diligence to make your calling and elec-

tion sure;" a rendering perfectly literal of the Greek, Διὸ
μᾶλλον ἀδελφοί, σπουδάσατε βεβαίαν ὑμῶν τὴν κλῆσιν καὶ ἐκλογὴν
ποιεῖσθαι.

The Rheimish version following the Vulgate, has the added
phrase "by good works," *per bona opera.* This was not
manufactured by the Rheimish doctors, it was not original with
the Vulgate. The Syriac and a few Greek manuscripts contained it, though the weight of authority was against it. But
it would be natural for a church that depends so much upon
good works for justification, in distinction from justification by
faith, to retain this passage, though the evidence of its genuineness was very slight.

Turning from this addition, we find in Rom. xi. 6, an important omission which subserves a similar purpose. Speaking of
election as a matter of grace, Paul says, "If it be of works,
then it is no more grace, otherwise work is no more work."
This sentence is suppressed in the Romish version, on the authority of three MSS., while the weight of evidence is decidedly
in its favor. The tendency to a righteousness of works that retained the one, would suppress the other.

To these sectarian features of the Papal version of the Scriptures, there should be added a few more of the notes which always accompany this version. The Catholic clergy are always
afraid of the Bible without note and comment. They circulate
no editions of the word of God without accompanying them
with their own interpretations.

In the words of Paul, "There is one God and one me
diator between God and man, the man Christ Jesus;" the note
says; "Christ is the only mediator, who stands in need of no
other to recommend his petitions to the Father. But this is not
against our seeking the prayers and intercessions, as well of the
faithful upon earth, as of the saints and angels in heaven."
Here prayers to saints and angels are distinctly commended,
though directly in the face of the text.

On the words of Paul describing those who "give heed to
doctrines of devils, forbidding to marry, and comanding to abstain from meats," we find the following note : "He speaks of
the Gnostics, the Marcionites, the Encratites, the Manicheans,
and other ancient heretics, who absolutely condemned marriage,

and all kind of meat ; whereas, the church of God, so far from condemning marriage, holds it a holy sacrament, and forbids it to none but such as by vow have chosen the better part ; and prohibits not the use of any meats whatsoever in proper times and seasons, though she does not judge all kinds of diet proper for days of fasting and penance."

But what right, we may ask, has the church to forbid marriage to any, when the Apostle Paul declares that "marriage is honorable in all ;" and when the Apostle Peter himself, whom the Catholic regards as the stone upon which the church is built, had a wife ! What right has it to forbid the use of meats, to make any fasts obligatory, under pains and penalties? The note is directly opposed to the text, and demanded only to save the institutions of the Catholic church. The judgment of Paul in such a case is, " Let God be true, but every man a liar."

It is not necessary to carry this investigation further. We have seen that the remoteness of the Douay version from the original Hebrew and Greek, must of necessity render it imperfect.

That the circumstances under which the translation was made were unfavorable to an elegant or faithful expression of the thoughts of God in our own vernacular is evident.

That it is encumbered with the Apocrypha, of whose inspiration we have no shadow of evidence, is a serious objection.

We have seen that in the progress of the translations from Hebrew to Greek, Greek to Latin, and Latin to English, no discrimination has been made between the words found in the originals, and those added to make the successive versions smooth and intelligible. The reader of the Douay translation has therefore no means of knowing what words have their synonyms in the ancient Hebrew and Greek manuscripts, and what have been brought in, in the process of translation.

We have shown, by a careful study of numerous passages, that the sense has often been lost by the causes enumerated above, and have pointed out the particular translation where the errors originated.

We have moreover found that numerous passages have been corrupted by defective and false translations, apparently to favor the errors of the Romish church, and that it is encumbered with notes for the same object, which are not justified by the text, and which render the version intensely sectarian, as well as an imperfect expression of the mind and will of God.

We will only add, lest we should seem to have conducted this discussion in a censorious spirit, that with all its defects, speaking of it as a whole, the Catholic version should be regarded as the word of God.   It is an expression of it sadly and needlessly imperfect, since better translations have been made into various languages, yet not so imperfect as when it came from the hands of its translators at Douay and at Rheims.   The numerous changes it has undergone are improvements, though in particular passages, its doctrines are still obscured, or perverted to the advocacy of error.   Still, considered as a whole, we should speak of it as the word of God, and should desire its circulation, rather than that individuals and communities have no Bible. Here are the great outlines of history, prophecy, and doctrine. Here the Ten Commandments unmutilated, forbidding the worship of images, though perverted by a foot-note commending images and pictures "even in the house of God, and in the very sanctuary" as "expressly authorized by the word of God."   Still, here is the entire law standing over against these traditions of men.   Rome has expunged the second commandment from her Breviaries and Manuals, making up the number by dividing the tenth.   She has not dared to remove it from its place in the sacred word.   Here is the history of the world for four thousand years, of which we have no other authentic record.   Here are the prophets translated with tolerable accuracy, though filtered through the Greek and Latin tongues. Here are the life and teachings of Christ, in the great outline correct.   Here is the record of his death, his resurrection and ascension to glory.   Here too are the writings of his Apostles, and the glorious Apocalypse shown to the exile of Patmos.

It is to us a matter of interest that not less than forty five editions of the Douay have been published in this country : that recent editions have been so altered as to approximate more nearly to the original Hebrew and Greek ; and that these latter are encumbered with the fewest notes.

The Turk, it is said, will not tread upon a piece of waste paper, without examining it, lest the divine name should be on it.

Let us show respect to the word of God, though in an imperfect translation, and strive to win the admiration even of the Papist, for our own incomparable version.

ARTICLE VII.

SHORT SERMONS.

" Samuel ministered before the Lord, being a child, girded with a linen ephod. Moreover, his mother made him a little coat, and brought it to him from year to year, when she came up with her husband, to offer the yearly sacrifice." 1 *Sam.* ii. 18, 19.

Historical Introduction. We have here a simple, tender and instructive item of family history. (1) Devout parents, Elkanah and Hannah. (2) A consecrated child. (3) Of tender years, yet already in the temple ministering in holy things. (4) He is not forgotten at home, but talked of, prayed for, and often seen, though twenty-five miles away. (5) The annual visit to Shiloh and the sacrifice, with their devout preparation and anticipation. (6) The " little coat"; its material and preparation ; the making; the talk of Elkanah and Hannah over it; every stitch is with prayer. (7) The going up to Shiloh and carrrying it, and the conversation about the boy. (8) Samuel's childish anticipations of the visit and of the " little coat," and the counting of the days till it came. (9) The meeting and rejoicings. (10) The coat presented and examined, and talked over and delighted in. (11) He wears it about the temple, thinking who made it, while the parents watch their child.

So are the parents and the child bound together. So are Samuel's memories of home kept fresh and joyful and sacred.

Topic given by the text : The Need and the Uses of Memorial days and Holidays for children, with Gifts and Pleasures.

I. The Nature and Necessities of a child lay a foundation for these.

1. The necessities of a child for these are as real as those of manhood.

2. The desires of the child for enjoyment are as reasonable as those of manhood.

3. And they are as strong.

II. These natural Necessities of the child for enjoyment should be provided for.

1. Because they are a proper part of human nature, common to the child and adult, and gratified in the latter.

2. If pleasures are not provided for them, children will provide their own. For, nature is stronger than parental authority, or selfishness or indifference. It is better, therefore, to provide and so control them.

3. Their enjoyments should be made childlike, according to their nature, and capacity and desires. We too soon forget our own childhood. Paul remembered his : " When I was a child," etc. It is unnatural, unwise and unkind to try to lift prematurely a child out of childhood ; a child pushed up into " a little man," " a little lady," is a repulsive sight.

The advice of Sir Thomas Browne to adults may be profitably remembered and used by them when dealing with children : "Confound not the distinctions of thy life which nature hath divided ; that is, youth, adolescence, manhood and old age ; nor in these divided periods, wherein thou art in a manner four, conceive thyself but one. Let every division be happy in its proper virtues. . . . . Do as a child but when thou art a child, and ride not a reed at twenty." But we must give the child his hobby-horse, even as we have ours, Bonner-like, a more costly and faster, though perhaps not less foolish " reed."

III. Anniversary Days and Gifts are highly useful in the proper training of a child.

1. Anticipation of them does the child good. How joyfully Samuel anticipated the visit and " little coat " !

Such concentration of joys into set days and occasions makes a cheerful character and sunny life for the child. A year without an anniversary day or gift for a child is a serious thing.

2. The mutual giving of gifts breaks up selfishness, binds a family together, and the children to their home. So Christmas and New Years, birth days, etc., are of immense value in a family.

3. It is wise to connect the gift with occasions : as the first Bible on some birth day, the skates at Christmas, etc. Those gift days become a power over the child. The cost, the time, or the trouble is but little to the parent, but the remembrance by some token is much to Samuel, "being a child." A friend writes us thus :

" D———, Dec. 18, 1865.

" . . . . The children are full of buying Christmas presents. Alice is making a portfolio to be filled with original drawings by herself from Pickwick, for her father. They are really very good and have taken much time. The boys have purchased a China cup and saucer for father. They have likewise had numerous discussions about buying mother's presents. I can guess just what they have all bought me. but of course know nothing, see nothing, and have no idea of what is going on. They have all bought each other gifts, which I have secreted safely."

How much such a family has of love and joy within itself. What attachment to home ; and so their sports and games and toys are kept within the safe circle of home.

Who can tell how much the annual " little coat " had to do in making the pious boy, the noble youth, and the most noble man, Samuel? View this boy when a man, late in life, "old and gray-headed" : " I have walked before you from my childhood unto this day. Whose ox have I taken? Or whose ass have I taken? Or whom have I defrauded? Whom have I oppressed? Or of whose hand have I received any bribe? And I will restore it unto you. And they said : Thou hast not defrauded us, nor oppressed us, neither hast thou taken aught of any man's hand." A good return, such a man, for "a little coat."

REFLECTIONS.

1. Juvenile crime increases, truancy, stubbornness before parents, rowdyism, theft and worthlessness.

2. What is our remedy? Restore the family to its proper place, and functions, as the place of full obedience. of the highest joys, and most tender memories. To this end there must be memorial days when Samuel can put on his " little coat," and Hannah and Elkanah rejoice with him.

" He that sinneth against me wrongeth his own soul."—*Prov.* viii. 36.

THE infinite and eternal Wisdom, the omnipotent Word, who was before the beginning of creation, and by whom the worlds were made, here speaks to men, saying: "He that sinneth against me wrongeth his own soul."

(*a.*) All sin committed by men is against God. Sin is a transgression of his holy law. Our neighbor may suffer wrong at our hands, but he is only the medium through which a blow is aimed at the moral government of the supreme lawgiver. Every true penitent becomes sensible of this, as was David, when in view of the twofold wrong he had committed against one of his subjects. In the deep consciousness of his guilt, he confessed his sin, saying:

"Against thee, thee only, have I sinned, and done this evil in thy sight." Uriah was atrociously wronged, and finally slain. David was the guilty man. The sin was against God.

(*b.*) Although all sin committed by men is aimed directly or indirectly against God, there is a vast force in the recoil thereof, which comes back upon the sinner. Sin is directed against God from human wills and arms of flesh, and is turned back upon the sinner in conscious guilt and unending penalties; so the transgressor can not contend unharmed with an omnipotent arm and the force of divine justice.

(*c.*) In sinning against God the sinner himself is the greatest sufferer. God is not essentially injured by any thing which men can do, however great their sins may be, but the sinner wrongs himself. This idea of self-inflicted wrong is a truly startling one. It would seem that self-interest ought to ensure us against such an outrage inflicted on ourselves. We do not act thus in our temporal affairs. We may cheat and defraud our fellow-men, but generally keep a sharp lookout that no harm comes to ourselves. Surely there is an unfathomable depth of depravity in the human heart.

(*d.*) If men by sinning against God should injure themselves in health, property, or reputation, and deprive themselves of happiness in this life merely, as they often do when under the power of sensual vices, as if the recoil of sin were a mere temporal matter, then men might venture to risk the consequences; but in sinning, the soul is wronged, ruined for time and eternity. It is a radical, everlasting wrong.

How blind to their own eternal welfare, and how infatuated do men become when acting under the power of depraved natures.

Beware of the self-inflicted wrong of sinning against God.

ARTICLE VIII.

LITERARY NOTICES.

1.—*Homiletics and Pastoral Theology.* By WILLIAM G. T. SHEDD, D. D., Baldwin Professor in Union Theological Seminary, New York City. New York: Charles Scribner & Co. 1867.

WE entertain a very high opinion of Professor Shedd as an author. Whatever he sends forth is scholarly, elegant, rich in thought and illustration, and fitted to subserve high ends in the church and in the republic of letters. The present volume answers fully this description, in every point. We doubt if any one of his works surpasses it in value. It discusses topics of vital importance always, and of special interest at the present time, when the question is being deeply and sorrowfully pondered by good and thoughtful men in our own country and in England : How shall the pulpit regain the power with the masses which it has lost to a fearful extent, and is losing more and more every day? This volume of Professor Shedd is an important contribution to the solution of the question. Every young minister and every theological student should obtain it without delay. That he will read it with deep interest, from the beginning to the end, is, we think, as certain as that he has any adequate idea of the greatness and difficulty of his work.

The part of the volume devoted to Homiletics comprises twelve chapters. The first, on the "Relation of sacred eloquence to Ritual Exegesis," is a masterly argument for the exegetical study of the Bible as lying at the foundation of all true and lofty pulpit oratory. "The duty and function of the theologian is most certainly that of an interpreter, and that alone." This point he beautifully illustrates by reference to natural science, and shows that the great law of investigation is in both cases precisely the same. "The attitude, therefore, of the human mind toward revelation should be precisely the same as toward nature. The naturalist does not attempt to mould the mountains to his patterns ; and the theologian must not strive to prefigure the Scriptures to his own private opinions." "The author insists mainly on two "oratorical influences," as proceeding from a thorough exegetical acquaintance with the Scriptures, which are, *originality* and *authority.* How the quality of originality has been exhibited in the men who have been lifelong and humble students of the inspired Word, imparting a mighty power to their preaching, he shows by reference to the great pulpit orators of the sixteenth and seventeenth centuries : Hooker, Howe, Taylor, South, Barrow, Bates, in striking contrast with the "smooth commonplaces" of Alison and Blair in the century following, making clear to a demonstration his point that the Christian Scriptures "are the great and transcendent source of originality and power for the human intellect." Having treated the other point with equal force and beauty of argument and illustration, he concludes : "He, then, whose public discourse is pervaded with the spirit of revelation, and who speaks as the oracles of God, will be eloquent in the highest style."

In discussing the nature of Homiletics, the Professor describes a sermon as the most difficult of orations, because intended to influence the whole nature of man ; and the difficulty is greater now, he affirms, than fifty years ago, because men are more vivid in their thinking, and impatient of prolixity.

The chapter on style is of exceeding value, and is, in itself, a fine illustration of the leading qualities, which he indicates ; that it be intelligible, "not only clear like the light, but round like the sun."

We would like to present Professor Shedd's rules for sermonizing, both general and special ; but our limits forbid. On "Species of sermons," he clears away a large amount of rubbish which has, for many years past, caused no little embarrassment to young preachers who have tried to go by rule. He finds only three, Topical, Textual, Expository. Passing the chapters on the choice of a text, and the plan of a sermon, we come to a topic which is exciting more than usual attention at the present day, Extemporaneous Preaching. This is treated with much breadth and with masterly skill, and for every young preacher certainly, the chapter is worth many times the price of the volume.

In treating "The Matter and Manner of Preaching," the author insists that the constant aim should be to be evangelical, and that the preacher should be willing to leave many books unread that he may be thoroughly acquainted with the Bible. In the chapter on Preacher and Hearer, are some striking and valuable thoughts on the duty of auditors to the preacher. "Eloquence, in its highest forms and efforts," he says, "is a joint product of two factors : of an eloquent speaker, and an eloquent hearer."

Under Liturgical Cultivation, are included reading of the Scriptures, selection of hymns, and prayer.

The concluding one-fourth of the volume is devoted to Pastoral Theology, and is divided into six chapters on the following topics : Definition of Pastoral Theology ; Religious Habits of the Clergyman ; Intellectual Character and Habits of the Clergyman ; Social and Professional Character of the Clergyman ; Pastoral Visiting ; Catechising.

Our readers, many of them, will have perceived that these essays are not new. Most of them have appeared in other forms. In a brief "Prefatory Note," Prof. Shedd says :

"Most of the materials of this treatise were originally composed in the form of lectures, in the years 1852 and 1853, when the author held the Professorship of Sacred Rhetoric and Pastoral Theology in Auburn Theological Seminary. Upon entering on other lines of study and instruction, they were thrown aside. Several of them within the past two years have appeared in the *American Theological*

Review, and the interest which they seemed to awaken, has led to the revision of the whole series, and to their combination (with two or three other essays upon kindred topics), into the form of a book. Although constructed in this manner, the author believes that one 'increasing purpose' runs through the volume, and hopes that it may serve to promote, what is now the great need of the church, a masculine and vigorous rhetoric, wedded with an earnest and active pastoral zeal."

2.— *The Household of Sir Thomas More.*   By the author of "Mary Powell."   New edition, with an appendix.   New York: M. W. Dodd.   1867.

ANOTHER charming book in the new and happy vein of the writer. We hardly see the pleasant device of the modern antique, so well is the ancient dust made to order and laid on.   It is not so easy to gain so intimate and accurate a view of the every day life and times of Sir Thomas in any other way, as in this little volume.   The leading facts in his great life are woven in most naturally, and you lay down the book feeling that you have been spending a few days yourself at Chelsea.   The simple narration throws, if it were possible, a deeper shade over the dark name of Henry VIII.   The appendix is a happy and profitable afterthought in this edition.

3.— *Wool-Gathering.*   By GAIL HAMILTON.   Author of etc., etc. Boston : Ticknor & Fields.   1867.

A CHATTY, rollicking, capering, episodical, scathing, self-satisfied, readable, bewitching book.   Nothing in it that you have not seen, felt and talked of, if you have been on the cars to Albany, Buffalo, and Chicago, on the steamer of any Western river, and on a prairie and a Western farm, and an old Virginia plantation.   But Miss Gail tells it all so easily and prettily, that you delight to have it said over again, and specially delight to have her do it.   You wonder that any one should take the labor and pains to put so many little, way-side, every-day, and most common-place items on paper and type, and a counter, but you are glad that she has done it, particularly when you feel that in doing it no domestic duties were neglected. The book is a delightful trifle, and reminds us of those exquisite paintings of a hen and chickens.   Everybody is familiar with the scene, but very few can paint it.

We presume the authoress went to Minnesota alone, so the book impresses us ; nor does the journey indicate the lack of a cicerone. She is sufficient ; indeed our compassion rather is stirred a little for some of the barbaric officials on the road.   This easy pen has a facile aptness in expressing feelings as well as views. Witness the parting benison when our gentle authoress takes her tiny foot off the steamer.

"Good bye, Damsel. May you sink a thousand fathoms deep, or ever I set foot on your horrid deck again! May forty snags crush your timbers, and drag you down into the turbid depths! May you blow up with kerosene when no passengers are on board!—as to officers and crew I make no stipulations. May you run aground and stick fast, and snap every pole that you try to push off with! May you be overthrown by wild winds on the eastern shores of Lake Pepin, and never heard of more! May every raft butt you, and every big steamer run you down, and every little steamer outstrip you! May water drown you, and fire burn you, and your sky rain thick disasters, till you cease to be a pestilent speck on the bosom of the River of Greatness." p. 74. There! Who says women ought not to vote, make speeches and laws, and be chairmen of Congressional Committees on railroads, steam navigation, and natural comforts generally.

We have enjoyed this book, and the more so because it is not anonymous.

4.—*Expository Lectures on the Epistle to the Ephesians.* By the Rev. ROBERT MCGHEE, A. M., M. R. I. A., etc., Dublin. New York: Robert Carter & Brothers. 1867.

WE regard this course of Fifty Two Lectures as an admirable specimen of expository preaching. It is historical, biographical, geographical, exegetical, argumentative and practical. There is a good use of biblical scholarship, without any peculiar show of it. The lectures are totally free from philological and extremely critical exposition, so common and legitimate in the professional commentator. While Mr. McGhee follows closely the text, he enriches his discourses by an inflowing from the other Scriptures, so making them more like topical discussions. The personal and direct uses, to which he puts the truths of the Epistle, give life and earnestness to the expositions. Here he has escaped the evil of dulness, the common bane of expository preaching, and given us reading for devotion as well as instruction. It is true the Lectures assume a large measure of intelligence on religious truth in his audience. This the preacher can always assume, if he will stick fast to the revealed religion of the Gospel or Epistles, and let philosophies, metaphysics, and school-isms alone.

We can not but think it would be better for the American pulpits

—

and audiences if ministers would substitute more of this kind of preaching, so common in Great Britain and on the Continent, for our classic essays, falsely called finished sermons.

5.—*Lectures on Christian Theology.* By ENOCH POND, D. D., Professor in the Theological Seminary, Bangor. Congregational Board of Publication. 1867.

THIS is a new edition with a full index. The work itself has been already favorably noticed in these columns. We can only add that the index increases the value of the treatise, stating also our satisfaction at learning that the venerable Professor has prepared a question book to accompany it, more especially for the use of Bible classes. Let him also make a smaller treatise for the same use.

6.—*The Theology of the Greek Poets.* By Rev. W. S. TYLER, Williston Professor of Greek in Amherst College. Boston : Draper & Halliday. 1867.

THE several chapters of this learned and solid book have already appeared in the *Biblical Repository and Bibliotheca Sacra*, and the *Theological Review*, and have probably been read by most of our clerical subscribers. They will be glad to have them in this single volume, and will be justly grateful for the literary, scholarly and Christian labor of the author.

7.—*First Historical Transformations of Christianity.* From the French of Athanase Coquerel, the Younger. By E. P. EVANS, Ph. D., Prof., etc., Ann Arbor, Michigan. Boston : Wm. V. Spencer. 1867.

WE think the University of Michigan might find better employment for its Professor than the translation of this volume and others, in advocacy of rationalism, which have lately come from his pen. Athanase Coquerel, Jr., is a leader in the advanced or infidel wing of Unitarianism. This book treats of religion as a development, taking on new modifications with the progress of the ages. Its author discusses successively the Christianity of Jesus Christ, Judaical Christianity, Hellenistic Christianity, The Christianity of St. Paul, St. Peter, St. John, Roman Christianity, The Christianity of the First Fathers, and the First Heretics. A specious book.

8.—*Chemistry of the Farm and the Sea. With other Familiar Essays.* By J. R. NICHOLS, M. D., Editor of the Boston Journal of Chemistry, etc., etc.

NINE Essays, eminently practical, and thoroughly scientific, written in a language for the common reader. "Chemistry of the Sea," "of the Farm," "of a Bowl of Milk," "of the Dwelling," "of a Kernel of Corn," "of the Sun," on "Obscure Sources of Disease," "Local Decomposition in Lead Aqueduct Pipes," and on "Bread and Bread-making." There is a rare amount of common sense and uncommon information in these papers, and they happily illustrate the fact, that what is useful in science can be made clear to the popular mind by a man who understands his subject. It is the imperfect master who speaks obscurely in practical science.

9.—*Jaques Bonneval, or the Days of the Dragonnades.* By the author of "Mary Powell," etc. New York: M. W. Dodd. 1867.

This story opens in the year 1685, made forever memorable and horrid in the bloody calendar of Rome Papal, by the revocation of the Edict of Nantz. In the graceful and natural style of this fascinating writer, we are passed through one of those terrible scenes of Roman Catholic persecution, that so stain and blot the history of Christendom. He who begins the book will finish it, and he will never forget it. We hope we are a little nearer the millennium than the times here so graphically and truthfully portrayed.

10.—*Sermons by the late Alexander McClelland, D. D.* New York: Robert Carter & Brothers. 1867.

These seventeen sermons will recall a good man to the memory of many, and they will love to read and own what they were once delighted to hear from his lips.

The style is simple, the doctrines evangelical, and the connecting thoughts mighty. The discourses have just the least possible of that flippancy which gains for the pulpit a noisy and short popularity.

11.—*The Bulls and the Jonathans; comprising John Bull and Brother Jonathan, and John Bull in America.* By James K. Paulding. New York: Charles Scribner & Co.

This volume of satire grew out of the disturbed relations between the United States and Great Britain, that culminated in the war of of 1812. It is full of uncomfortable facts, keenly set in chapters, and scathingly and jocularly turned back on our step-mother, Britannia. The key to the music of the book is struck in the first sentence: "John Bull was a choleric old fellow, who held a good manor in the middle of a great mill-pond."

It is lively reading, and the reprint reads the more oddly, after half a century, when Jonathan has become a little taller than John.

12.—*Kathrina ; Her Life and Mine, in a Poem.*   By J. G. HOLLAND,
author of "Bitter Sweet."   New York : Charles Scribner & Co.
1867.

THIS new Poem of Dr. Holland, though in dramatic power and
varied interest it may not be equal to " Bitter Sweet," is yet a very
beautiful production.   To some passages we take exceptions.   For
example, to the mulierolatry of the following on the 8th page :

> " If God be in the sky and sea,
>   And live in light and ride the storm,
> Then God is God, although He be
>   Enshrined within a woman's form :
> And claims glad reverence from me.
>
> " So as I worship Him in Christ,
>   And in the forms of earth and air,
> I worship Him imparadised,
>   And throned within her bosom fair
> Whom vanity hath not enticed."

The author must have confused ideas as to how God is in Christ.
He seems to be a pantheist.   A little more exactness of statement
might be expected even in a poem, from an author who has ven-
tured to discuss such a subject as The Origin of Evil in " Bitter
Sweet."   From another passage, later in the volume, it seems that
Kathrina once attempted to teach the author better theology.

Here is one of the finest passages in the volume.   It depicts a
very common, but very impressive scene.

> " It was Communion Day.
> The simple table underneath the desk
> Was draped with linen, on whose snow was spread
> The feast of love—the vases filled with wine,
> The separated bread and circling cups.
> The venerable pastor had come down
> From his high pulpit, and assumed the seat
> Of presidence, and, with benignant eyes,
> Sat smiling on his flock.   The deacons all
> Rose from their pews—four old brown-handed men,
> With frosty hair—and took the ancient chairs
> That flanked the table.   All the house was still
> Save here and there the rustle of a silk
> Or folding of a fan ; and over all
> Presided the dove of peace.   I had no part
> In the fair spectacle, but I could feel
> That it was beautiful and sweet as heaven."

It is rather hard, however, to believe that "Paul" was really drawn
into that church in Hadley by the charm of Kathrina's voice.   But,

seeing he was a poet and a singer too, perhaps he was. We give him the benefit of the doubt.

We believe in Dr. Holland. He is true to his moral instincts and noble in his aims; but in theology he makes out about as well as Henry Ward Beecher, once his pastor, to whom he dedicates his "Titcomb Letters." To our mind, such a writer outweighs a hundred-fold such men as make ridicule of serious things the grand aim of their literary efforts, though he does make an occasional slip in theology.

ARTICLE IX.

THE ROUND TABLE.

A NEW LAW. "That is a bad religion which makes us hate the religion of other people." So says *The Advance.* The author appears to be that "mother of invention" whose sententious wisdom is so often required to fill out a newspaper column, and who sometimes speaks aphoristically without due reflection. Maxims are mighty things, chapters condensed into few words, or else brief statements latent with possible chapters. They are quickly read, and their terseness and point cause them to stick in the memory. They are often adopted as articles of faith, and rules of action. They are "aids to reflection" not only, but aids to wit and speech and influence. Hence the importance of their moral quality. If true, they are universally applicable, and potent for good. If totally false, they are never applicable; but though often applied, their potency for evil is limited by their palpable falseness. If half true, they are applicable only within certain limitations; but since the true in their mixed quality is but the sugar coating of the false, they are apt to gain a currency for truth, and a power for harm, otherwise impossible.

The maxim above quoted has a very charitable sound. There is a show of brotherly love in the echo. It seems to be the utterance of a heart ready to take into its friendship and fellowship the advocates and devotees of every religion, except those who "hate the religion of other people." But here is a dilemma. For dame Necessity evidently deems her own religion good, and condemns as bad the religion of all who hate it; while, according to her maxim, her own religion is bad because it makes her hate theirs. If no religion is good which makes us hate a bad one, then the bad is lovely and the lovely is not good. The distinction between a good and a bad religion is thus annihilated, and Christianity is reduced to a level with every form of the religion of antichrist. The charitableness of the maxim is a little too far advanced.

Within certain limitations the saying is true enough. There are many religions that make men hate the religion of others. There is but one true religion, and that is Christianity; and against this all false religions are essentially in league. Judaism, Mohammedanism, Romanism, Unitarianism, Universalism, Mormonism; these, beyond question, make their respective adherents hate evangelical religion, and are therefore bad. Indeed every false religion is apt to hate every other false religion as well as the true one. If there be any two false religions between which there is not mutual hatred, it is because their respective adherents fail to discern any radical difference between them, and differ only by accident of position or of taste. Possibly Unitarianism and Universalism are examples of such mutual toleration.

Beyond these and similar limitations, however, the saying is false. Christianity in all its essentials differs from all false religions in being supernatural and divine. Between two Christians as such there can be no radical difference, because they all accept "Jesus Christ and him crucified," as the only ground of human salvation. Therefore, though they may be known by different names, according to their preferences in things left to human judgment and taste, no denomination of Christians can hate another. But Christianity, under all its denominational names, is opposed to every false religion and teaches us to hate every religion as false which does not rest on Jesus Christ as the Godman, delivered for our offences, and raised again for our justification. "If there come any unto you, and bring not this doctrine, receive him not into your house, neither bid him God speed; for he that biddeth him God speed, is partaker of his evil deeds." According to John, then, not to hate antichrist is to fellowship him and bid him God speed. And Jesus Christ, who spake by John in exile, declared that he hated the doctrine of the Nicolaitans, and commended the church of Ephesus for hating it. The Psalmist wrote, "Through thy precepts I get understanding: therefore I hate every false way." Christians are not worthy the name who do not thus sympathise with Christ, and with all true members of his church in hating every false religion. Christianity, because it is the true and the only good religion, makes us hate every other so-called religion as false and bad. The good and true religion makes good men, while a bad religion makes those who espouse it worse than they were before. That is not Christian charity which does not hate a false religion; a false religion is bad because sinful, and therefore

God and good men hate it.   Christianity teaches us to love our neighbors as ourselves, but it does not teach us to love their false religions.   As God hates sin and loves the sinner with such compassion as to offer him salvation by grace, so Christians should hate all false religions, but pity and pray for, and labor to save the victims of them.

The maxim belongs to the category of the half-true.   It is just as true and just as false as if it read, " That is a bad religion which does not make us hate the religion of other people ;" or as if it read, " That is a good religion which makes us hate the religion of other people."   Neither is wholly true, or wholly false ; but either, if adopted, would have a pernicious influence.   It is a positive injury to the deluded to treat their delusions as not to be hated.   It is the glory of Christianity that it will neither tolerate nor be charitable towards antichrist, while in forbearance, meekness and love, it endeavors to reclaim the victims of antichrist.

Popish Pretentions not Abated.   There certainly has been an improvement in some of the fashions of papal Rome since the days when Montaigue found the pope and cardinals drinking the sacramental wine from the chalice, with " an instrument " contrived " to provide against poison"; and saw at the mass " the pope, the cardinals, and other prelates . . . . seated during nearly the whole mass, with their caps on, talking and chatting together."   The civilization of the Vatican is better than then ; but its Christianity, not a whit.

Indeed, we are almost inclined to withdraw the concession just made, as to any essential improvement in the civilization of the papacy, when we find the same intolerant bigotry ruling its counsels as in the sixteenth century.   What sort of a thing is a civilized spirit of persecution which can to-day defend the Roman Inquisition as a justifiable religious and civic institution?   But this is done unblushingly by popish apologists.   The late affair of the interdict of Protestant worship at Rome has brought out several staunch maintainers of the duty of the pontiff of that city thus to resist such a movement of the " gigantic rebellion against the church of God," as Protestantism is called.   " Why," asks one of those champions of antichrist, himself the son of an American Episcopal bishop, "why should a congregation, rebellious in a religious point of view, be allowed within the walls of Rome ?" that one spot on earth, " where error," says this pervert, " has never been permitted to have a foothold" !   Rome "claims the earth for an inheritance," adds our pamphleteer, into which "Protestantism is everywhere the intruder." Of course, this intruder is to be whipped out of the earth, wherever it appears, if the old toothless giant has force enough at command to do it. It may be done at Rome, perhaps; but hardly in this region quite yet. Wherever it is possible, Rome claims such hunting-grounds for her inquisitorial hounds as arrogantly as ever, only these must not bark too loudly. To deny this is to charge her with what she would resent as an unpardonable insult—a repudiation of her once avowed policy. For is not the Roman church infallible? And can the infallible ever contradict itself? Rome must be a persecuting hierarchy so long as she is Rome ecclesiastically, whether that Rome be in Italy or in America. If her sword is here sheathed, it is simply and only because the attempt to draw it would endanger her own head: and this she is not ready yet to offer upon the altar of martyrdom.

In our opinion, these things are pretty generally understood by our people. We do not believe that much faith is put in papal pretences to love of popular liberty among us, except such liberty as now and then breaks out in a rough and tumble riot in New York and elsewhere, in the interests of this mediæval concentration of ignorance and superstition. But too much faith is put in the supposed impossibility of Rome's ever becoming really dangerous to our national welfare. She knows this, and plays upon our credulity with great skill. We have sometimes almost wished that she would forget herself, and adventure some genuine piece of ultramontane churchcraft upon us, if sooner too self-confident and secure lovers of liberty might get a galvanic shock which should show them, once for all, what a thorough foe of freedom we are sheltering in our bosom. The history of our war, which some thought would disprove these perils, or remove them, has really done nothing in that direction, whatever exceptional instances of a true loyalty to free institutions may be on record. The sympathy of the priesthood, from His Holiness down, with the rebellion, is the proper and the certain gauge of that matter. Rome, in this country, is what and where she always has been, and always must be, till her race is run, and "Babylon is fallen!" is written over her utter desolation. But before that comes, she expects to add the negro vote to the Irish and by this union of races at the ballot-box in her behalf, to replace for a long term of power on this continent, the loss of the pope's temporal dominion abroad. Said a Jesuit, the other day, to a friend of ours: "The ballot here will more than compensate us, in a few years, for our losses at Rome."

ACADEMIC HONORS. Since our last issue, two more of our editorial corps have been put upon the retired list and garnered into the class of most reverend D. D.'s. A strange fatality attends the publicity which an editorial position imposes ; and so fast has the number of our untitled ones decreased within the two years past, that we are compelled to adopt the language of Job's servants, fresh from the scenes of his accumulated catastrophies : "And we alone are escaped to tell thee !" Should the same fatality continue, thus removing from the remaining editors all motive to exertion, we suppose the *Review* must cease to be. *Quod avertant dii !*

ECCE HOMO.

Tell me where I can behold Him,
  Him, the God in human form ;
Can my arms of love enfold Him,
  Will he hear my accents warm ?

Lo the Man ! on cross uplifted,
  Lo the Man ! with thorn-set crown ;
Side with cruel spear-thrust rifted,
  Head in anguish hanging down :

Hands outstretched, with nails thrust through them,
  Breathing forth his human life ;
Hark, what accents ! listen to them,
  Catch his agony and strife.

It is finished ! this oblation
  That the prophets had foretold ;
It is finished ! this creation
  Of the new man from the old.

Here I see earth's greatest wonder,
  Here I see Time's ripest fruit ;
God in man, man's burdens under,
  God in man, to man makes suit.

Ecce Homo ! O ye nations,
  See His cross uplifted high ;
'Neath its shadow take your stations,
  Look to Him and never die !

BAPTISMS PECULIAR, IF BY IMMERSION. Mr. Dale, in his Classic Baptism, noticed by us in the July Number of the *Review*, gives some very singular cases of "immersion," as the Greeks used the word baptize. We quote a few of them from the forty or fifty authors, whom he cites.

—

Baptizes, [βαπτίζει] the breathing of the intellect.   *Achilles Tat.* iv, 10.

The soul being baptized [βε,βαπτισμένην] very much by the body. *Alex. Aphrod.* i, 38.

Many inclosed by the river perish, being baptized. *Diod. Sic.* i, 86.

Dip, βάπτω, that word of stumbling over which our Baptist brethren fall into deep water, means to put an object into a fluid, (when a fluid is implied,) for a very brief time. Brief continuance in the fluid is one of its strong and radically distinctive marks, as different from βαπτίζω. Its continuance is momentary. But βαπτίζω means continuance without limitation. The classic import of βαπτίζω makes no provision for taking its subject out of the water, when water is the element that is made to surround it. Very many cases, like the last quoted, show this. So but for borrowing the meaning of βάπτω, dip, a word foreign to baptism, the immersionists would leave all their subjects in the water. Their theory is built on βάπτω, which, unfortunately for them, is not the scriptural word.

Carrying down many, baptized them. [εβάπτιζε] [drowned them.] *Diod. Sic.* xvi, 80.

Baptizing killed him. *Æsop, Ape and Dolphn.*

One saved in the voyage, whom it were better to baptize, [drown.] *Themistius, Orat.* iv.

Baptized by the passion, [βαπτιζόμενος ὑπὸ τῆς ἐπιθυμίας] the noble man attempted to resist. *Chariton Aphrod.* ii, 4.

But Dionysius was baptized as to his soul. *Do.* iii, 2.

To be baptized by such a multitude of evils. *Achilles Tatius.*

Baptized by anger. [τῷ θυμῷ] *Do.*

Misfortunes befalling baptize us, [βαπτίζουσαι ἡμᾶς.] *Do.*

They do not baptize the people by taxes. *Diod. Sicul.* i, 73.

Baptized by the calamity. *Heliodorus Æth.* ii, 8.

The events still baptized you. *Do.* v, 16.

Grief baptizing the soul and darkening the judgment. *Libanius Emp. Jul.* 148.

Baptized either by diseases or by arts of the wizards. *Plotinus Enn.* 1. 4. 9.

We, baptized by the affairs of life. *Plutarch, Soc.*

Baptized by debts of fifty millions. *Plutarch, Galba.* xxi.

Baptized by unmixed wine. *Athenæus, Phil. Banq.* v, 64.

Having baptized Alexander by much wine. *Conon ; Narrat.,* L.

Baptizing out of great jars of wine, drank to one another. *Plutarch, Alex,* lvii.

Crippled and baptized by yesterday's debauch. *Plutarch, Water and Land Anim.,* xxiii.

This allusion to wine, and others to opiates and poisons, as the element for "baptisms," as also those "baptisms" by anger, grief, evils, etc., shows us the "mode," if baptism can be said to have any mode. Certainly the subject could not have been "immersed" in the various elements here mentioned. Baptism is simply a thorough change of the condition or state of the subject. Therefore a drop of poison, an event, a bottle of wine, the river Jordan or a teaspoonful of it, a burst of passion, a debauch, a sluggish body, a misfortune, heavy tax-bills, a fever, or the common affairs of life, may baptize one. Anything can do it that thoroughly changes the character, state or condition of the person, be it a tide of evils or one of them, the Atlantic Ocean or a drop of it.

WANT OF ROOM compels us to hold over to our next Number many Book Notices prepared ; and several books were received too late for examination.

INDEX.

CPSIA information can be obtained
at www.ICGtesting.com
Printed in the USA
BVHW082201110819
555624BV00019B/2833/P

9 781318 705382